REGISTRATION CODE

2BUF-04RI-0Z9K-IJ4C-34V3

D0080615

American Voices

CULTURE AND
COMMUNITY

American Voices

CULTURE AND COMMUNITY

SIXTH EDITION

Dolores laGuardia
Santa Clara University

Hans P. Guth
Santa Clara University

Boston   Burr Ridge, IL   Dubuque, IA   Madison, WI   New York   San Francisco   St. Louis
Bangkok   Bogotá   Caracas   Kuala Lumpur   Lisbon   London   Madrid   Mexico City
Milan   Montreal   New Delhi   Santiago   Seoul   Singapore   Sydney   Taipei   Toronto

Higher Education

AMERICAN VOICES: CULTURE AND COMMUNITY
Published by McGraw-Hill, a business unit of The McGraw-Hill Companies, Inc., 1221 Avenue of the Americas, New York, NY, 10020. Copyright © 2006, 2003, 2000, 1998, 1996, 1993 by The McGraw-Hill Companies, Inc. All rights reserved. No part of this publication may be reproduced or distributed in any form or by any means, or stored in a database or retrieval system, without the prior written consent of The McGraw-Hill Companies, Inc., including, but not limited to, in any network or other electronic storage or transmission, or broadcast for distance learning.
Some ancillaries, including electronic and print components, may not be available to customers outside the United States.

This book is printed on acid-free paper.

1 2 3 4 5 6 7 8 9 0 DOC/DOC 0 9 8 7 6 5

ISBN 0-07-298264-0
Editor in Chief: *Emily Barrosse*
Publisher: *Lisa Moore*
Sponsoring Editor: *Christopher Bennem*
Developmental Editor II: *Bennett Morrison*
Marketing Manager: *Lori DeShazo*
Managing Editor: *Jean Dal Porto*
Project Manager: *Catherine R. Iammartino*
Art Director: *Jeanne Schreiber*
Lead Designer: *Gino Cieslik*
Cover Designer: *Kristin Hull*
Photo Researcher: *Jennifer Blankenship*
Art Editor: *Emma C. Ghiselli*
Cover Credit: *Digital Image © The Museum of Modern Art/Licensed by SCALA/Art Resource, NY*
Senior Media Producer: *Todd Vaccaro*
Lead Media Project Manager: *Marc Mattson*
Associate Production Supervisor: *Jason I. Huls*
Permissions Editor: *Marty Granahan*
Composition: *11/12 Bembo by G&S Typesetters*
Printing: *Black, 45 # New Era Matte, R.R. Donnelley and Sons, Inc./Crawfordsville, IN.*
Credits: The credits section for this book begins on page 787 and is considered an extension of the copyright page.

Library of Congress Cataloging-in-Publication Data
LaGuardia, Dolores.
    American voices: culture and community / Dolores laGuardia, Hans P. Guth.—6th ed.
    p. cm.
    ISBN 0-07-298264-0 (softcover : alk. paper)
      1. Readers—United States. 2. English language—Rhetoric—Problems, exercises, etc.
  3. Pluralism (Social sciences)—Problems, exercises, etc. 4.   Ethnology—United States—
Problems, exercises, etc. 5. Critical thinking—Problems, exercises, etc. 6.   Ethnic groups—
Problems, exercises, etc. 7. Culture—Problems, exercises, etc. 8. College readers. I. Guth,
Hans Paul, 1926- II. Title.
  PE1127.H5L25 2006
  808'.0427—dc22
                                                                          2005043759

The Internet addresses listed in the text were accurate at the time of publication. The inclusion of a website does not indicate an endorsement by the authors of McGraw-Hill, and McGraw-Hill does not guarantee the accuracy of the information presented at these sites.
www.mhhe.com

CONTENTS IN BRIEF

CONTENTS

STEVEN WIN, "Get Motivated!" *482*
"Anyone with a computer can get rich by spending 10 minutes a day buying and selling stocks online. Seventeen percent is totally doable in any market."

Poem: ROBERT HAYDEN, "Frederick Douglass" *487*
During the Civil Rights era, writers and artists like Robert Hayden rewrote American history by honoring leaders in the struggle against injustice.

FORUM: Exceptional Lives *489*
ANDREW DELBANCO, Book Review: "The Autobiography of Billy Graham" *490*
"They had a camera there, and as you walked by, you could see yourself on the screen. We never thought it would amount to anything, though. It seemed too incredible!" The rest is evangelical history.

LESLIE GORNSTEIN, "The Digital Amazon" *494*
She became the founder of Digital Amazon, a Web consulting firm, and also "the brain behind Amazon City, an online women's community, and one of the driving forces behind the growing women's presence in cyberspace."

DAVE FORD, "Public Interest Lawyer" *496*
"You have to keep moving forward. I guess the point is not to lose heart."

WRITING WORKSHOP 8: *Weighing Your Options* *500*

9 *LANGUAGE: Bond or Barrier?* *510*

Visual Literacy 9:
HEADLINES: Spinning the News *511*

DEBORAH TANNEN, "Talk in the Intimate Relationship: His and Hers" *514*
"Male-female conversation is cross-cultural communication."

BERNICE SANDER, "Men and Women Talking" *525*
"Women's behavioral style—listening, clarifying and providing affirmative verbal and nonverbal feedback such as nodding—encourages others to speak and participate."

AMOJA THREE RIVERS, "Cultural Etiquette: A Guide" *531*
"Cultural etiquette is intended for people of all 'races,' not necessarily just 'white' people, because no one living in Western society is exempt from the influences of racism, racial stereotypes, race and cultural prejudices."

ANDREW BROWNSTEIN, "A Battle over a Name in the Land of the Sioux" *536*
"Onlookers at a homecoming parade performed the Atlanta Braves' 'tomahawk chop' as dancing American Indian children passed on a float, and then yelled at them to 'go back to the reservation.'"

TO THE INSTRUCTOR

American Voices is a textbook for the courses in writing and critical thinking that are the core of a college education. We aim at helping students become alert readers, purposeful and effective writers, and committed thinking participants in the public dialogue.

Generation 1½

We address today's diverse student population—students coming to our classrooms from diverse backgrounds and with a range of preparation and motivation. Many represent today's Generation 1½ (or 1.5), requiring new kinds of validation and confidence-building, habit-building pedagogies. We offer special recognition and encouragement to the growing numbers of students writing American English as a second language and a second culture.

Building the Reading Habit

We aim at helping the instructor turn reluctant readers into motivated purposeful readers, introducing them to the range of informed opinion, careful argument, and authentic personal testimony. Exceptional reading apparatus builds habits of close reading, critical evaluation of sources, and informed reader response.

Empowering Student Writers

Students experience the power of writing rooted in authentic observation, drawing on informal and formal research, targeting the intended audience, structuring promising material, and evolving in response to feedback from instructor and peer review. We stress the continuity between personal and public discourse—moving from the exploration of personal experience to the discussion of public issues that matter in people's lives.

Computer Literacy

We aim at helping students become efficient and responsible users of the full range of Internet and media resources. We early provide guidelines for navigating the Internet and evaluating the flow of electronic information. We have greatly expanded the treatment of computer searches and updated the documentation of electronic sources in the workshop on research-based writing.

Word and Image

Teaching visual literacy is broadening our concern with the full range of media and genres that carry information and ideas in today's world.

Focus on the interaction of word and image promotes critical reading of the rapidly changing images that are an ever-present part of our students' visual environment.

READINGS FOR THE WRITING COURSE

A high-interest reading program engages student readers in today's issues and introduces them to the true range of informed opinion in a democratic society.

Exploring Today's Issues

The readings in this book engage students in the exploration of issues that are shaping their future. Vital themes generating class discussion and committed student writing include the following:

- Generation 1½
- Bilingual and Bicultural Young Americans
- Diversity and Searching for Community
- Class in a Classless Society
- Redefining Gender Roles
- Rethinking Race
- The Search for Role Models
- Gay and Lesbian Rights
- Outsiders: Prisoners, Illegals, and the Disabled
- The Culture of Violence
- Virtual Reality of the Media
- Saving the Environment
- The New Terrorism

Bridging Thematic and Rhetorical Concerns

American Voices suggests a course outline that integrates thematic and rhetorical concerns. The Alternate Rhetorical Table of Contents helps organize a rhetoric-centered course focused on modes and genres. Chapters, reading selections, and writing workshops are self-contained and may be arranged to suit the needs of different classes or programs.

Authorship Representing Today's America

This book makes students share in the true rich diversity of the American experience. Many selections honor diversity while searching for the common center. The range of authorship reflects the multi-faceted richness of today's American culture, including testimonies and discussions by Americans with Hispanic or Latino, African American, Cuban American,

Native American, and Asian American roots. The authors include writers moving on to new perspectives on race, gender, and sexual identity.

A Range of Perspectives

"Forum" sections appear at the end of each chapter. The short focused selections in each forum explore a range of views, probing a key topic from diverse perspectives. Students confront views that play off differing perspectives on such issues as freedom to worship, disparity of wealth, same-sex marriage, the broken-window theory, or censorship in cyberspace. Expanded "Other Voices" sections follow key selections.

STATE-OF-THE-ART PEDAGOGY

American Voices implements class-tested strategies for engaging today's students and developing their potential.

Motivating Student Apparatus

Exceptional apparatus throughout the book is designed to engage students' attention, help turn "reluctant" or sometime readers into alert critical readers, and guide them in moving from reading and surfing the Net to purposeful and effective writing.

- Headnotes for reading selections dramatize issues, provide essential context, or highlight an author's experience and commitment.
- "Thought Starters" focus students' attention and activate what they bring to a selection.
- "Responsive Reader" questions foster close reading. They direct attention to key points, walking the student reader through a structured discussion or argument.
- "Talking, Listening, Writing" questions validate the range of reader response, encouraging students to formulate their own personal reactions and to engage in a dialogue with their classmates.
- "Find-It-on-the-Web" entries guide and encourage students in their use of the full range of Internet resources.

Hands-On Writing Instruction

The expanded completely updated writing workshops following each chapter offer supportive guidance and direction to student writers. Exceptionally accessible and motivating workshops help student writers move from writing from experience, through writing from their reading and Internet surfing as well as oral sources, to structured papers employing major writing/thinking strategies. We stress the informal research that goes into all writing, preparing students to move from informal to formal research and the documented research-based paper.

Validating Student Writing

A rich selection of student models helps instructors validate student writing. A full sampling of search materials, working outlines, and annotated drafts model the the writing process for today's student writers. Especially helpful and accessible guidelines for the current MLA and APA research paper style demystify documentation styles.

NEW TO THE SIXTH EDITION

Responding to extensive thoughtful reviews by instructors from throughout the country, we have built on the strengths of previous editions to give instructors a state-of-the-art composition text addressing the needs of today's students and the challenges of today's changing world.

Word and Image

A strong expanded visual literacy strand helps students become alert critical observers of our visual environment. As chapter-openers, attention-getting, thought-provoking images and displays focus attention on how images carry information, steer reactions, and shape attitudes. Focus on the interaction of word and image makes student see the written word as a vital part of the full range of communication in the age of the knowledge explosion and and the information highway.

New Readings on Current Issues

Belying stereotypes about student apathy or student "resistance," students respond in class discussion, in small groups, and in writing to today's "hot-button" issues:

- testing vs. teaching
- Asian immigration in a multicultural America
- bilingual and bicultural Generation 1½
- football powers or citadels of learning
- gender gap in cyberspace
- same-sex marriage or second-class citizenship
- divided loyalties at the Alamo and the southern border
- the rhetoric of war and probing the causes of terror

Computer Literacy

We have updated and greatly expanded the treatment of computer searches, helping students sift and evaluate the vast range of materials available on the Internet. We have updated the documentation of electronic sources in the workshop on the documented paper. The Find-It-on-the-Web entries guide and encourage students in their use of the full range of Internet resources.

Expanded Writing Workshops

Fully reworked and expanded writing workshops build the confidence of student writers and their command of the resources and strategies of successful writing. Hands-on writing instruction focuses on how effective writing takes shape—stressing the role of trial theses and working outlines, and responding to audience feedback. Sample papers serve as positive writing models with graphic demonstration of instructors' annotation and revision.

RESOURCES FOR TEACHING *AMERICAN VOICES*

Teaching *American Voices*

The instructor's resource manual is available online. It provides additional context and detailed responses to reading apparatus, with a sampling of representative student answers to both reading questions and questions for the new Visual Literacy strand. An Update of the composition bibliography concluding the manual provides a sampling of current discussion of issues facing today's writing programs and writing faculties.

Catalyst 2.0

The Online Learning Center (OLC) at www.mhhe.com/amvoices now provides students with access to Catalyst—McGraw-Hill's premier composition software—where they can find over 3,000 grammar and usage exercises; tips on effective revision strategies, Bibliomaker software that formats source information in one of five documentation styles, including MLA and APA; an online source evaluation tutorial; and much more.

ACKNOWLEDGMENTS

We owe a special debt to the many committed teachers who have shared with us their concerns and enthusiasms in professional meetings and workshops around the country. We have again profited from helpful detailed feedback from professional and dedicated reviewers: Chris Antonsen, Western Kentucky University; Sylviane Baumflek, Kingsborough Community College; Paula Eschliman, Richland College; Clark Draney, Idaho State University; Mallory Dubuclet, Southern Methodist University; David Hopcroft, Quinebaub Valley Community College; Emily Isaacs, Montclair State University; Kate Miller, Whatcom Community College; Ruth Miller, University of Louisville; Elizabeth Rich, Saginaw Valley University; T. Sean Rody, Shoreline Community College; Jill Rossiter, Lewis-Clark University; Pamela Spoto, Shasta College.

Above all, we continue to learn from our students. Often, struggling against odds, they maintain their faith in American education. Their candor, intelligence, and idealism are an inspiration for the uncharted future.

Of the many students who have permitted us to reprint or adapt their writing, we want to thank especially Kevin Janda, Sarah Smialovicz, Amanda Lieu, Ronald Lau, Kellyn Hohnbaum, Alana Okamoto, Patricia Hua, Monica Quinonez, Daniel Katzen, Antonio Valdez, Heidi Choy, Victoria Sies, Karen Henderson, Nathan Holste, Keith Thompson, Harjeet Sekhan, Alisa Garni, Gayle Tan, Lisa Tankersley, Nicole Hancock, and Warren Wong.

Dolores laGuardia
Hans P. Guth

TO THE STUDENT

Written communication is a central medium of communication and human interaction in today's world. Whether scripted for an oral presentation, reaching us in printed form, or transmitted in an electronic format, the written word is the basic medium for shaping and sharing information and ideas.

- In the world of education, the written word is a chief tool for those who gather and share knowledge, who exchange informed opinion, or who organize and disseminate research.
- In the workplace, written communication is the medium for much of the world's work—in the corporate environment, in the world of advertising and promotion, and in countless uses in planning, reporting, and evaluation.
- In interpersonal communication, we use writing as well as voice contact to communicate with others—to share our views and concerns, to promote our private and public agendas.
- In the give-and-take of the political process, alert readers and effective writers participate effectively in the public dialogue. They make their voices heard in local grassroots politics or on the larger stage of public discourse.
- In the world of electronic communication, the computer has shortened the distance between the way we talk and the way we write. It has made writing more informal and natural but also more everpresent and widespread. It makes possible instant feedback from peers, editors, and reviewers.
- Increasingly readers and writers are alert to to the power of images to inform and persuade and to the interaction of word and image in much of our visual environment.

This textbook is designed to help you become a more confident and effective reader, writer, and user of the Internet. Effective readers and writers put their ideas and feelings into words. They know how to access information and put it to their own uses. They know how to evaluate and organize input from a range of sources. They use language to organize their own thinking. In targeting an intended audience, they know how to lay out information and ideas to make them accessible and persuasive. They share data, observations, and ideas and update or revise in response to queries and feedback from a range of sources.

This book will give you many opportunities to practice and improve your communication skills. It will give you many opportunies to read, write, and think about today's challenges and today's issues. The authors reprinted in this book are writing about subjects that matter to them and that concern us all. This book gives you many opportunities to join in the dialogue—to join in the conversation. Here are some key questions writers explore in this book:

DIVERSITY AND COMMUNITY

What does it mean to be an American? What are we today as a people? How do we honor diversity while searching for community? What common future is emerging from the meeting of cultures in a multicultural society? How do Americans from different ethnic and cultural backgrounds today define their identity and shape their destiny?

RETHINKING GENDER ROLES

In the world of work or in professional life, what barriers have women overcome, and which are still facing them? How is the self-image of young males today different from that of their fathers? How far has society moved toward accepting people with a different sexual orientation or an alternative lifestyle?

BEYOND RACISM

Are we moving toward a color-blind society? What progress has the country made in the area of race relations? Why do some observers paint a positive and others a negative picture of the opportunities and status of African Americans, Latino Americans, or recent immigrant populations? Are we moving towards a new kind of American mosaic or toward separatism or de facto segregation?

CLASS IN A CLASSLESS SOCIETY

What invisible walls divide people from different layers of society? What jobs and educational opportunities are open to Americans from different social classes—to people with different family background or social status? How much human solidarity will bond a society where huge disparities of income and privilege divide the rich and the poor? Will tomorrow's American be a status society ranging from a small upper level of the super rich to an underground economy of illegals?

VIRTUAL REALITY OF THE MEDIA

How much is our world shaped by the media? Do the media give us news, or do they give us someone's spin on the news? Who decides what we should know and believe? How does television and movie entertainment shape our perceptions of other people and other nations? Do the media make us more tolerant or less tolerant of violence in a violent world?

PROTECTING THE ENVIRONMENT

Is it our responsibility to "save the planet"? Can we protect the remaining forests and the endangered wildlife? Will the wild salmon and the big birds follow the dodo and the passenger pigeon into oblivion? Will we heed warnings asking us to keep the air and the rivers from being polluted, natural resources from being depleted, and the oceans from being fished out?

THE UNCERTAIN FUTURE

What future awaits the next generation? In the global economy, what will replace outsourced or offshored jobs? Who will pay for child care, health care, elder care? In the war against terror, who is the enemy?

Working with this book will give you a chance to study and reexamine your roots and your assumptions. It will give you a chance to explain to yourself and to others who you are and what kind of world you want to live in. It will help you make your voice heard when defending your interests or when working for a good cause. It will help you learn how to get others to listen as you work for change or defend tradition. Let this book help you build up your confidence and your effectiveness as a reader, writer, and viewer.

Dolores laGuardia
Hans P. Guth

ALTERNATIVE RHETORICAL TABLE OF CONTENTS: MODES AND GENRES

WRITING WORKSHOPS

ABOUT THE EDITORS

Dolores laGuardia is a writing teacher with a loyal following among students. She is currently the Co-director of the Santa Clara University Professional Communication Program. At the University of San Francisco, she developed a course sequence titled "American Voices: Ourselves and Each Other," focused on African Americans, Asian Americans, Latinos, Native Americans, religious minorities, and alternative lifestyles. She served as the writing specialist for a large Federal grant designed to improve writing instruction at the community college level and does curriculum work for a number of Bay Areas institutions. She has TESOL certification and has extensive experience working with students using English as a second language. She has conducted workshops on computer education for the Russian Ministry of Education. laGuardia has participated in a number of mentoring programs and is a diversity management consultant for Bay Area universities and senior communities.

Hans P. Guth has worked with writing teachers in most of the fifty states. He has served on national committees and commissions, and he has spoken at many national and regional professional meetings on revitalizing composition programs, validating student writing, and improving the professional status of writing faculties. He has authored many widely used and influential composition texts. He was co-director and program chair of the annual Young Rhetoricians' Conference in Monterey from 1984 to 1994, and he has participated in institutes or has organized workshops at institutions including University of Illinois, Stanford, Oxford, and Heidelberg University. Being himself an immigrant speaking and writing English as a second language, Guth has called for fresh approaches to honoring and teaching the growing, increasingly diverse Generation 1½ and ESL populations in our composition classrooms.

PREVIEW
Word and Image

Word and image often join to send the message in today's world.

WORD AND IMAGE

When you look at the image at the beginning of this preview chapter, what do you see? How do you respond?

The visual on the opening page brings together visual elements of the kind that are a familiar part of our visual environment—where often words and images work together. The page is a *collage*—a combination of visual elements brought together to create an overall effect. It combines in a single layout visual elements from promotional ads and posters that are part of the constant stream of messages competing for our attention. The images clustering around the message "Vote!" are from a mail promotion sent out by the *New York Times* before a presidential election. The "Immigrant Freedom" sign was photographed for the Associated Press by a Latino photographer in October 2003.

YOUR TURN:

Your instructor may ask you to write a viewer response. What do you see? What associations or attitudes does the visual bring into play? What is familiar, and what is different? How do words and images work together here? What does the combined visual tell you about the society in which we live? How do you respond?

PREVIEW

Reading, Writing, Thinking, Viewing

You all know the basic tools as well as I do—write, phone, fax, e-mail, march, sing, make up funny and poignant signs.
—MOLLY IVINS, NATIONALLY SYNDICATED TEXAS COLUMNIST

Using language effectively is an essential qualification in to-day's world.

In today's information society, communication—printed, electronic, spoken, or visual—is the central medium of interaction and tool of the world's work. Written communication is a survival skill in school and in the workplace. It is a powerful tool in the worlds of politics and law and in the give-and-take of public opinion. We live in a world where billions of words flow through the entire range of media every day to do the world's work, shape people's opinions, and guide people's actions.

This book is designed to help you become a better reader, a more confident writer, and a more resourceful user of the Internet. It will help you process information and ideas. Work with reading and writing strategies will help you share information and ideas with your intended audience. It will help prepare you to join in the public dialogue and make your voice heard. Studying the close interaction of word and image will help you sift and evaluate the images that are a major dimension of communication in our modern world.

These are goals this book is designed to help you achieve:

■ *Become a more alert reader.* Is it true that a new generation grew up on sound bites and has a short attention span? To be successful in school and in the workplace in today's world, you learn to pay close attention. Though you may skim material to see if it will prove relevant or useful, you develop the habit of close, attentive reading: You make it a habit to highlight key points in an important printout. You sift and evaluate supporting evidence and credible testimony. You learn where to find and evaluate reliable data and statistics. When you write, you draw on your reading for input, which may range from hard data, firsthand witnessing, and informed opinion to insider's testimony or the research findings of experts.

■ *Become a more effective writer.* How good are you at bringing an issue or a task into focus? How resourceful are you when working up promising material on a current topic? How well do you size up a target audience? How articulate are you when it comes to putting your ideas into words?

How good are you at joining an ongoing discussion and making your voice heard?

As you become a more effective and more confident writer, you learn to draw on a full range of sources—from your own personal experience and observation, through reputable news sources and editorial opinion, to research based or scholarly material. For instance, writing about trends in the job market, you know where to turn for data from trend watchers and experts. You know where to look for testimony from people who have undergone downsizing, outsourcing, or restructuring. When you join in the public dialogue, you become better at defusing hot-button topics, finding common ground, and presenting an informed opinion that people of good will should be willing to consider.

- *Organize your thinking*. The computer has shortened the distance between how we think and how we write. Writing on the computer, you see your thinking take shape on the screen in front of you. How good are you at sizing up an issue, checking out relevant facts, and bringing together rough notes? How good are you at making sense of them, pushing toward a thesis or overarching central idea? How good are you at thinking critically—going beyond hearsay or "what everybody says"? Are you prepared to "listen to the other side"—weighing alternative views? Are you good at identifying the strong points and the weak links in an argument?

- *Make full use of Internet resources*. How computer-literate are you? As a writer and researcher today, you have instant access to a vast range of background knowledge, up-to-date data, informed opinion or commentary, and research information from experts or established authorities. You develop your own techniques for navigating the Internet, choosing the most productive search engines, and evaluating promising material. You come to know key websites and tap into databases most relevant to your field of interest or to a current assignment.

- *Interpret and evaluate the flood of images that are part of our world*. Literacy long meant mainly effective use of the written word. Today it includes both computer literacy and visual literacy. In much of today's world of communication, word and image work together. Striking images and visual outlays attract and hold our attention. They bring ideas or slogans to life. Then the written word will often spell out or drive home the message. Political campaigns and corporate promotions use and abuse powerful symbols like the Statue of Liberty and the flag.

BECOMING A BETTER READER

Alert readers actively process information and ideas and put them to good use.

The habit of alert reading makes you a better informed student, jobholder, and member of the community. It prepares you to deal with public issues and with areas of special concern to you in your professional and personal life. As a good reader, you know where to turn for data and informed opinion for your own writing.

How well do you read? As an active reader, you retrace the writer's steps. You follow the writer's train of thought. The writer's ideas come to life as you take in, interpret, and respond to what the writer is intending for the audience.

- *Look early for a hint or preview of the writer's purpose.* What is the agenda here? Who is the target audience? What is the writer trying to accomplish?
- *Look for key ideas or main points.* What claims or central claim is the writer promoting? What findings or conclusions is the writer defending?
- *Read for clues to the writer's program or plan.* What stages in an intellectual journey or steps in an argument will you be expected to follow?
- *Check how the writer supports key points.* What are key examples? What are telling or revealing details? What does the writer offer as supporting evidence or testimony?
- *Track how the writer handles opposing views.* How one-sided or how balanced is the writing? How does the writer handle possible objections or opposing arguments?

The following passage is from an article published toward the beginning of the new century. Like much writing published at the turn toward the new millennium, the article asked: "Where are we now?" Throughout the article, the author returns to his central **thesis**—his overarching point or central message: The end of legal segregation and of overt institutional discrimination had brought major advances. However, it had also left basic social problems unresolved. Here is how you might track the ideas in the passage and make mental or written notes:

Beyond Color-Blindness

THESIS: The dismantling of legal segregation in the sixties created almost as many problems within the African-American community as it resolved. . . .
————>>>>>>>>>>>>>>

(Here is the first of several statements of the author's central claim or thesis: Pundits and politicians claim that the end of official racism is moving us toward a "color-blind" society. However, most African Americans live in communities where severe new problems were created.)

With the rapid expansion and assimilation of the black middle class into white suburban culture, and the simultaneous economic meltdown of central cities, the traditional institutions of black civil society were profoundly shaken. . . .———>>>>>>>>>>>>>>>

(The legacy of the civil–rights movement has been double-edged: A new middle class of successful African Americans was created, but they moved out of the inner cities. At the same time, the cities were losing the local businesses and industry that had been their economic base.)

State-supported historically black colleges and universities, which had been created to preserve racial segregation in higher education, are being either dismantled or pressured to integrate. . . .———>>>>>>>>>>>>>>

(Traditionally black colleges were originally created to keep African Americans out of white institutions, but they did provide moral support and role models for black students. They are now endangered in the name of integration. . . .)

The black-owned newspapers and journals that were filled with lively political discourse several decades ago have been largely replaced by cable television and mainstream publications. . . .———>>>>>>>>>>>>>>

(A lively local press used to give voice to the concerns of the African American community, but now everyone gets the same homogenized material as the rest of society.)

Many black elected officials want not to be designated a "black candidate" but rather to be a representative of all groups. . . .———>>>>>>>>>>>>>>>

(To be elected, African American candidates have to speak for whites and also minorities other than blacks—so they cannot really be strong voices for the concerns of the black community.)

—from Manning Marable, "Beyond Color-Blindness," *Nation*

Guidelines for Readers

As an alert reader, keep questions like the following in mind:

1 **What is the key issue?** What is the key question, and how is it brought into focus? How did the author dramatize the issue—bring the topic to life?

2 **Who is the intended audience?** Who would care? Who would have (or who would lack) the necessary background?

3 **Is there a thesis?** Is there an early statement or hint of the author's answer to the central question? Where is the author's message stated most directly or most eloquently? How carefully or how aggressively does the writer state the main point?

4 **Does the argument hinge on a key term?** Does much depend on what we mean by a term like *parity, assimilation, self-esteem, the poverty*

Guidelines for Readers (continued)

line, or *affirmative action*? Where and how is it defined? Are there key examples or test cases that clarify the term?

5   **What is the plan?** Is there an early hint of an overall plan or organizing strategy? For instance, is an article going to contrast the then and now? Is it going to start with first impressions and then take a closer look? Is the writer going to look first at arguments on one side and then at arguments on the other?

6   **What backup is there?** What examples or evidence does the author use to support a general point? Which are most striking or convincing? Where does the writer turn for personal witnessing, facts or hard data, expert testimony, inside information?

7   **How single-minded or how balanced is the argument?** Does the author recognize possible objections or counterarguments? Are they brushed off or are they taken seriously?

8   **Does the author conclude on a strong note?** Does the conclusion merely summarize points already clear, or does it go a step beyond what the author said before? For instance, is there a clinching final example or an effective punchline? Does the author relate his argument to the larger picture or a plea for action?

9   **How reliable or credible are the writer's sources?** How much was fact or hard data, and how much was one person's opinion? When the author cites authorities and insiders, do I accept them as authoritative sources?

10 **What is my personal response?** Where do I stand on this issue? What assumptions do I bring to this topic, and which seem to be shared by the writer? How does my own experience compare with that of the author?

TESTING YOUR READING SKILLS How well do you read? Use the following shortened essay by a well-known Boston columnist to test your capacity for close, responsive reading. The questions that precede the text will walk you through the essay. They will ask you to pinpoint the ideas and the features that give the essay shape and direction. How well do you follow the author's trend of thought? How quick are you to take in key points and key examples?

Answer the following questions as you work your way through the essay:

- What does the *title* make you expect?
- What is the common pattern in the examples Goodman uses for her *introduction*? What word provides the common thread? (What meanings or associations does it have for you?)
- How does the introduction lead up to the central idea or *thesis*? How does the thesis serve as a preview of the basic contrast that shapes much of the essay?
- What kind of *support* does Goodman offer to clarify and develop the basic contrast? How does she use material from personal experience or observation? How does she go beyond it?
- Where does Goodman offer a *concession*—anticipating possible objections, admitting that there are exceptions to her claims?
- What does the *conclusion* add to the essay? Does it merely summarize, or does it go beyond what the author has already said? (How does the last sentence circle back to the title of the essay?)
- Can you relate Goodman's points in any way to your personal experience or observation? (Can you make a *personal connection*?)
- Do you agree with the author wholeheartedly, or do you want to take issue with any of her points? What would you say if you were asked to respond to her or talk back?

WE ARE WHAT WE DO

Ellen Goodman

I have a friend who is a member of the medical community. It does not say that, of course, on the stationery that bears her home address. This membership comes from her hospital work. I have another friend who is a member of the computer community. This is a fairly new subdivision of our economy, and yet he finds his sense of place in it. Other friends and acquaintances of mine are members of the academic community, or the business community, or the journalistic community. Though you cannot find these on any map, we know where we belong.

None of us, mind you, was born into these communities. Nor did we move into them, U–Hauling our possessions along with us. None has papers to prove we are card–carrying members of one such group or another. Yet it seems that more and more of us are identified by work these days, rather than by street.

In the past, most Americans lived in neighborhoods. We were members of precincts or parishes or school districts. My dictionary still defines community first of all in geographic terms, as "a body of people who live in one place." But today fewer of us do our living in that one place; more of us just use it for sleeping. Now we call our towns "bedroom suburbs," and many of us, without small children as icebreakers, would have trouble naming all the people on our street.

It's not that we are more isolated today. It's that many of us have transferred a chunk of our friendships, a major portion of our every day social lives, from home to office. As more of our neighbors work away from home, the work place becomes our neighborhood. . . . We may be strangers at the supermarket that replaced the corner grocer, but we are known at the coffee shop in the lobby. We share with each other a cast of characters from the boss in the corner office to the crazy lady in Shipping, to the lovers in Marketing.

It's not surprising that when researchers ask Americans what they like best about work, they say it is "the shmooze (chatter) factor." When they ask young mothers at home what they miss most about work, it is the people. Not all the neighborhoods are empty, nor is every work place a friendly playground. Most of us have had mixed experiences in these environments. Yet as one woman told me recently, she knows more about the people she passes on the way to her desk than on her way around the block. . . .

It's not unlike the experience of our immigrant grandparents. Many who came to this country still identified themselves as members of the Italian community, the Irish community, the Polish community. They sought out and assumed connections with people from the old country. Many of us have updated that experience. We have replaced ethnic identity with professional identity, the way we replaced neighborhoods with the work place.

I don't think that there is anything massively disruptive about this shifting sense of community. The continuing search for connection and shared enterprise is very human. But I do feel uncomfortable with our shifting identity. The balance has tipped and we seem increasingly dependent on work for our sense of self. If our offices are our new neighborhoods, if our professional titles are our new ethnic tags, then how do we separate ourselves from our jobs? Self-worth isn't just something to measure in the marketplace. But in these new communities, it becomes harder and harder to tell who we are without saying what we do.

FROM READING TO WRITING Good readers make a receptive audience. They take in what an author has to say. At the same time, good readers make what they read their own. They interact with what they read. They do not accept everything the writer says at face value.

Often, your reading will trigger your writing. You may write to express your strong agreement with or support for the author's position. You may write to clarify something that the writer obscured or glossed over. You may feel the need to correct a stereotype or a misrepresentation. You may want to pay tribute to someone the writer ignored. Whether you agree or not, a strong reading selection will make you think. It will stimulate you to think the matter through.

BECOMING A BETTER WRITER

Experienced writers focus on their task, gather and organize their material, and profit from feedback and opportunities for revision.

Writing worth reading goes through a process. You go through phases or overlapping, intermeshing stages:

- focusing on a topic or a task
- sizing up your audience
- gathering and sifting promising material
- developing your organizing strategy
- shaping a rough draft
- revising in response to feedback and review
- final editing for standard English and questionable language

These phases intermesh. For instance, you may rearrange major sections of a draft while still searching for further supporting material. Also, the process does not move in a straight line: For the experienced writer, promising leads that do not work out and last-minute adjustments are part of the day's work.

Triggering

Write with a purpose.

What makes writers write? What triggers writing—what brings it on? Writers write because they have something to say to other people. Here are motives that may trigger your writing:

- *Writers respond to a practical need.* You write a résumé because you need a job. Your neighbors write to a planning commission to head off a decision that would hurt. You write a letter to the editor of a major newspaper to help mobilize opposition to changing qualifications for student loans.

- *Writers write to explain.* After investigating a problem or a difficult task, they share their findings with a larger audience. They may write about the problems caused by spamming or electronic junk mail. They may try to explain why youngsters join youth gangs in local schools and what educators and community leaders are doing to reverse the trend.

- *Writers help guide the readers' choices.* Should the readers rent, lease, or buy? Should they opt for a public or a private school? Should they support pro-development, "pro-growth" candidates or anti-development, "save-our-community" candidates? Should readers support initiatives to bring back the wolves, or should they support a backlash aimed at protecting livestock and people?

- *Writers write to set the record straight.* You may be reading about how Southern whites supposedly feel about African Americans, or about how American males of your generation allegedly feel about women. You may find yourself saying: "That's not the way it is! I know something about this from firsthand experience!"

- *Writers write to pay tribute or to plead for support for a cause.* You may be asking your readers to honor a group of people whose contribution often goes unrecognized. You may be urging your readers to support an organization and/or initiative that you know well and in whose goals you believe.

- *Writers write to air grievances.* They appeal to their readers' sense of fairness. They may be registering their solidarity with people trying to make ends meet by working two jobs on minimum wage, trying to keep their children healthy without health insurance and with restricted access to overburdened public health facilities.

Gathering

Build up a rich fund of promising material.

To write a convincing paper, you have to work up the subject. You may start by calling up from the memory bank of past experience the events, buzzwords, and arguments that cluster around your topic. You read up on the issue, taking detailed reading notes. You discuss it with friends and roommates, or you interview people who might have the inside story.

Do you ever suffer from "writer's block"? Here are **prewriting** techniques that can help you work up promising material for a paper:

BRAINSTORMING **Brainstorming** and other preliminary exploring or mapping techniques roam freely over a topic. Brainstorming dredges up any memories, images, events, or associations that might prove useful. Exploring the ideas related to the word *macho*, for instance, you jot down anything that the word brings to mind. You write quickly and freely, allowing one idea to lead to another. There will be time later to sort out these preliminary jottings—to see how they add up, to see what goes with what.

The following brainstorming exercise has already brought together much promising material. What major points for a paper are beginning to come into focus?

BRAINSTORMING

The Weaknesses of Macho

Macho: Big, muscular, unfeeling, rough—harsh, moves to kill. (Sylvester Stallone: I hated what he promoted.) Negative impression. Hard craggy faces with mean eyes that bore holes in you.

Men who have to prove themselves through acts of violence. The man who is disconnected from his feelings, insensitive to women's needs—cannot express himself in a feeling manner.

The word seems to have negative connotations for me because I have worked part-time in a bar. I was forever seeing these perfectly tanned types who come on to a woman. When I was a child, macho had meant a strong male type who would take care of me—paternal, warmth in eyes. John Wayne: gruff, yet you felt secure knowing someone like this was around.

Crude, huge—the body, not the heart—tendency to violence always seems close to the surface. Looks are very important. Craggy face. Bloodshed excites them. Arnold Schwarzenegger muscles, gross.

Tend to dominate in relationships—desire for control. "Me Tarzan—you Jane."

DISCOVERY FRAMES Use sets of questions that can guide you in exploring a topic. Suppose you are working on updating the definition of feminism. Is there a "second wave" or "third wave" of the women's movement? What does the term mean to someone of your generation? The following **discovery frame** provides a model that you can adapt—change or expand—for other current topics. What materials could you fill in under the tentative headings?

DISCOVERY FRAME

What Is Post-Feminism?

PERSONAL CONNECTION   What role have feminist concerns or women's rights played in your own experience? Where have you encountered ideas associated with the women's movement?

HISTORICAL BACKGROUND   What do you know about the history of women's rights? What have been outstanding leaders, role models, and key events? (What do you know about Sojourner Truth, Elizabeth Cady Stanton, or Margaret Mead?)

RELATED TERMS   How is the term *feminism* related to similar terms— *emancipation, women's liberation, the suffragist movement, the women's movement?*

MEDIA COVERAGE   What is current media coverage of successful or admirable women or role models? What images of women are projected in the news, in movies, in advertising? Do earlier stereotypes survive? Are there positive images of "strong women" or "independent women"?

COUNTER TRENDS   Has there been a backlash against the women's movement? Do young women today shy away from the feminist label? Do they take the gains of the women's movement for granted?

LOOKING AHEAD   What does the future hold? Is the wage differential between men and women shrinking or holding steady? Are women in politics and in management overcoming the "glass ceiling"? Are more working class women joining the movement?

COMPUTER FILES   Experienced writers are often compulsive note takers. For a current or future writing project, they build up a computer file of potentially useful material. Here are sample entries from a student's computer file. The student writer was investigating efforts to curb hate speech or offensive language, with special attention to the issue of hate speech on the Internet.

HATE SPEECH 1

Beth McMurtrie, "The War of Words," *Chronicle of Higher Education* 23 May 2003 (Vol. 49 Issue 37, pages A31–32)

In the 1990s, colleges adopted hate-speech codes that threatened to penalize students if they used racial slurs or other offensive comments on their campuses. The codes were a response to "what some educators saw as an alarming increase in racist incidents." However, vocal critics attacked the codes as "political correctness," and state and federal courts struck down several of the codes for violating students' First Amendment rights.

HATE SPEECH 2

Patrik Jonsson, "Racial Harassment Rises in a Ruder America," *Christian Science Monitor* 26 Dec 2000 (Vol. 93 Issue 22, page 3)

In spite of the "political correctness" campaign, employees at companies ranging from an Atlanta aerospace firm to a Florida citrus company were complaining about racial epithets and verbal abuse ("Go back to Africa"). Minorities in record numbers were filing suit against their employers, complaining of harassment at work. Jonsson quotes Gail Wolfe, a workplace psychologist in Chicago, as saying, "If you complain, at the very best you're going to lose your job . . . the burden is still really on the employee," and in most cases they would rather put up with the harassment.

HATE SPEECH 3

Laura Leets, "Should All Speech Be Free?" *Quill* May 2001 (Vol. 89 Issue 4. D38–39)

"Even though prevailing First Amendment dogma maintains that speech may not be penalized merely because its content is racist, sexist or basically abhorrent, Internet law is a dynamic area and as such is not completely integrated into our regulatory and legal system." As a result, many questions remain about how traditional laws should apply to this new and unique medium. Unlike users of the older media, those on the Internet have the power to reach a mass audience, but at the same time the audience must be more active in seeking information.

"It is unclear whether content-based restrictions found in other technological media may be permissible for the Internet."

Shaping

Sort out your material and work out a clear plan.

How do you turn a rich collection of material into a coherent paper? Successful writers employ or adapt basic organizing strategies.

■ *Bring your central issue into focus.* A focused paper does not roam over several topics, giving opinions about this and that. Instead, it zeroes in on an issue or a limited area and does it justice. Early in a paper, raise the issue. What is this all about? Dramatize the issue by a key example or by a key quotation that brings the issue to life.

> STARTER QUOTE: While teenage girls are enrolling in science classes in record numbers, a new study claims that "an alarming new gap" between the genders is taking shape in the computer classes that lead to the highest-paying jobs.

> STARTER STATISTICS: In California alone, an estimated two million illegal aliens live, working in the underground economy with many of them raising families.

■ *Push toward a thesis.* What is your paper as a whole going to say? What is it going to prove? After exploring the topic, after reading and talking about the issue, you move toward a summing up. What is going to be your main point? What is going to be your **thesis**—your central idea, your unifying message? In the early stages of your paper, your thesis will be a **trial thesis** or a working thesis. You stake out a claim or make an assertion. You adjust it as necessary as you look at further examples, evidence, statistics, or expert testimony.

> THESIS: Although opponents claim that many affirmative action students drop out, those who graduate often have successful professional careers and serve as role models for other minority students.

Try summing up the central message of your paper in a sentence that will serve as your **thesis statement** early in you paper. Use the next few sentences to spell out the full meaning of what you claim or assert:

> THESIS: Retraining programs for the unemployed may train them for jobs that also no longer exist. The educational system may be preparing people for jobs that have already been automated, taken by robots, or shipped overseas.

> THESIS: Downsizing and outsourcing have caused a general a decline in employee loyalty. Employees who see their coworkers depart no longer feel that the company can be trusted to take care of long-time loyal workers.

■ *Work out a clear overall plan.* How are you going to lay out your material? What is your program? In an early stage of a writing project, start jotting down a scratch outline, with just a few tentative points. Develop it into a **working outline.** A working outline helps you visualize your tentative plan—a plan that is subject to revision.

If you are to take your readers with you, they need to feel that you have a planned itinerary. Your readers need to know where you are headed—and they appreciate early signals of what lies ahead. Where are you taking them? Often an effective thesis statement provides a preview of the overall plan. A **preview thesis** or program thesis creates expectations that the paper then satisfies.

Study the following frequently used organizing strategies that alone or in combination can help you structure your paper.

TIMELINE PLAN

A successful paper often follows a **timeline,** with major stages of development presented in chronological order. The following might be an early version of a student's working outline for a paper questioning progress toward the "color-blind" society of the future. The preview thesis already sets up three major stages or waystations in an ongoing process. The reader will expect that a major section of the paper will be devoted to each of the three stages the thesis sketches out:

The Long Road

THESIS: Race relations in this country have moved from legalized segregation, through the legal outlawing of discrimination, to the struggle to change "hearts and minds" about race.

1 injustices of the past
- movies like *Beloved* and *Amistad* dramatize the evils of slavery
- the *Rosewood* movie chronicled the destruction of a black community

2 continued de facto segregation
- inner-city schools are more segregated than ever
- courts have retreated from busing and forced integration

3 lack of minority role models
- lack of minority teachers
- scarcity of minority doctors and lawyers
- growing but still limited hiring of minorities for police work

KEY POINTS PLAN

A successful paper often identifies several key points in an argument or several important reasons for change. It arranges them in the order that will best build a case. For example, citizens groups and elected officials in communities around the country have in recent years become concerned about large chains and megacorporations driving out small local business. The large chains may be accused of depressing wages and lowering the living standard of workers and their families. The following sample plan will make sure that the writer will focus on and follow up one key point at a time:

Walmartization: A High Price to Pay

THESIS: The billion-dollar Walmart retail organization had to launch a million-dollar public relations campaign to refute charges that it was harming communities and workers.

1 PROTECTING THE COMMUNITY A grown community has a web of small businesses run by people who know and trust their customers and vice versa. They pay local taxes and support local schools and law enforcement. Huge chains that run out local business are run by anonymous impersonal out-of-state forces with no roots or loyalties in the community.

2 PROTECTING EARNING POWER Although the corporation may claim it pays "competitive" wages, the income of many temporaries and part-time employees is close to or below government poverty guidelines.

3 PROTECTING HEALTH CARE Critics of corporate policies claim that many employees with no or inadequate health benefits have to turn to already overburdened public health facilities at an added cost to the taxpayer, thus forcing the taxpayer to subsidize the corporation.

4 PROTECTING WORKERS' RIGHTS TO ORGANIZE As isolated individuals, workers are powerless when facing the vast financial and legal resources of a megacorporation. The corporation may actively discourage or undercut labor union representation, banning organizing activities and harassing or firing employees suspected of participating in union activities. The corporation is strongest in nonunion states or territories.

5 PROTECTING WOMEN'S PROGRESS TOWARD EQUALITY Critical articles and lawsuits claim that earnings of female employees are consistently lower than those of males. Lawsuits allege that women managers hit a "glass ceiling."

PRO-AND-CON PLAN

A successful paper often asks readers to listen to both sides. What are the arguments on one side of a contested issue? What are the arguments on the other side? Can you do both sides justice—without brushing off or ridiculing one side or the other? In a best-case scenario, can you make readers see that there might be common ground or a meeting of minds? On a serious issue, readers may actually be prepared to listen to *more* than two sides. They may be ready to examine in turn several points of view. If you weigh arguments from different points of view, will your readers be ready to support a balanced or responsible conclusion?

Unlicensed Drivers: Getting to Work

THESIS: Torn between those who oppose legal recognition of illegal workers and those who know their need for transportation, some states are experimenting with driving certificates that are not full licenses or legal IDs.

ARGUMENTS AGAINST DRIVER'S LICENSES FOR ILLEGALS

1 Issuing driver's licenses to illegal immigrants rewards law breakers.

2 Driver's licenses serve as a national ID that can be used in applying for benefits.

ARGUMENTS FOR DRIVER'S LICENSES FOR ILLEGALS

1 Unlicensed drivers pass no tests and may be a menace on the road.

2 Unlicensed drivers cannot get insurance.

3 If we employ illegals, we should enable them to get to work, to get their children to school, and to get their families to hospitals.

FINDING A COMPROMISE SOLUTION

Some states have experimented with issuing driver's certificates (not regular licenses) for purposes of registration, testing, and securing insurance.

- *Feed in your supporting material as you write your draft.* Follow up or follow through as you reach each point or subsection in your working out-line. Remember that any point worth making is worth backing up. Support the points you make with key examples, authoritative data, or relevant evidence. Bring in material from interviews and weave in quotable quotations. Bring in insider's insights or expert perspectives.

As you move from section to section or from waystation to waystation in your draft, give some thought to providing the thought links or **transitions** that will make your readers see the connections and take them along. Signal turning points—as you move from then to now, or from pro to con.

Revising

Build on your strengths and shore up weaknesses as you respond to instructor's feedback or peer review.

Whenever possible, allow some time before you go back to an early draft. When you come back to the paper, you may see missing links, apparent detours or digressions, or awkward backtrackings. You may feel the need to scale back exaggerated claims or tone down personal attacks.

INSTRUCTOR FEEDBACK   Each paper has its own strengths and weaknesses. Even so, teachers, reviewers, and editors often return to familiar advice. Points like the following often recur in instructor feedback or guidelines for revision:

- *Sharpen your focus.* What is the basic problem, and what are the possible answers? What is the striking contrast you want your readers to think about? Or what is the contradiction that your paper will try to resolve? For example, do you agree that the writer's central concern comes clearly into focus in the following introduction?

Turning Out the Vote

In my part of New Mexico, only 35 per cent of the voters came to the polls in a recent election. In my hometown in Texas, the turnout in a recent primary election was dismal. This may be the only community where total turnout in municipal elections dips into the single digits. I read about a campus where registrars canceled plans for an on-campus voting booth because only 236 students of a 5000 student body registered. When I drove through the town of Las Cruces, there were more customers lined up at the Megaplex to see a movie than I have seen recently at polling booths. Maybe we should offer popcorn and a Mel Gibson movie to citizens who will turn out to vote.

- *Review your organizing strategy.* For example, should you go more consistently from the simple to the difficult? When you deal with a controversial or currently debated subject, should you look first for areas of agreement and put your readers in an assenting mood? Should you lead up better to the parts of your paper that are challenging or controversial? In a paper questioning a decision or new theory, should you take more time to explain what it is and what made its supporters promote it before you show what is wrong with it?

▪ *Build up your examples.* In the first-draft stage, student writing often stays on a very general level. Try to bring a general point to life by presenting a striking, dramatic example. How do your reactions differ for the before-and-after versions of the following passage?

GENERAL: In patriarchal societies, men are in a position of power where women are often powerless to confront an accuser. It is ironic that rape, a crime that often enables women to identify their attackers, at the same time often leaves them in a position that forces them to keep silent and not seek remedy. Many women keep their secret to themselves, afraid that they will not be believed.

REVISED: It is ironic that rape, a crime that often enables women to identify the attacker, often leaves them in a position that forces them to keep silent and not seek remedy. About five years ago, one of my best friends and I were pulling into a gas station; standing at another pump was a medium built, thirtyish middle-class male. "Back up and get out of here. That man raped me," my friend blurted out. I was outraged. I wanted to stop the car, get out, confront him, get his name into the paper, let everyone know. But all she wanted to do was hide, leave, deny, fade away, let go. She said that almost no one else supported her. She was raped by an acquaintance; the gas station customer was a classmate. The police had discouraged her from pressing charges. The circumstances made a conviction too precarious to attempt.

▪ *Add striking supporting quotations.* Quote insiders or bring in expert testimony. Issues come to life when we hear the authentic voices of the people involved.

DIRECT QUOTATION: As a men's coach, Dorrance says, he used a lot of negative techniques, yelling at and bullying his athletes, waging a constant battle of egos with his players. "You basically have to drive men, but you can lead women," he writes. "And, in my opinion, the way you coach women is a more civilized mode of leadership."
—Ruth Conniff, "The Joy of Women's Sports," *Nation*

▪ *Leave your readers with a strong final impression.* Try using a **clincher quote.** Or leave your readers with positive suggestions for action. Try to give readers a punchline they can remember.

CONCLUSION: People in the black community are tired of theories, studies, and calls for dialog. Instead, they look for "real steps" that can be supported on the community level. They pressure school boards and city leaders to expand Headstart programs to give their children a better start. They start letter writing campaigns to provide bad publicity for corporations that shut down neighborhood stores or branch offices of banks. They badger neighbors to register to vote. They no longer believe in a "magic bullet" or a quick fix.

PEER REVIEW *Peer reviews make both writer and reader more audience-conscious.* Peer reviews may range from informal sharing of drafts to a detailed evaluation of a paper by one or more readers. Peer reviewers make writers more audience-conscious by helping them see their writing through the reader's eye. At the same time, you as the reviewer begin to look at your own writing more critically. You learn to anticipate readers' reactions. You become more aware of questions they might ask, backup they might need, or objections they might raise.

The following might be instructions for peer review of a paper you wrote dealing with a current issue:

Peer Review of Current Issues Paper

author_____   reviewer_____

INSTRUCTIONS: Show you are a careful responsive reader. Read the whole paper before you answer the peer review questions. Do not write on the student's paper. If you wish, take preliminary notes on a separate sheet. Write your answers legibly!

1 BEGINNINGS—How does the paper start? Is the title informative and inviting? Does the introduction bring the topic into focus? Does it bring the topic to life or dramatize the issue?

2 THESIS—Does the paper have a clear or strong thesis? How would you restate it in our own words? Does it serve as a preview, setting up a program or pattern for the paper to follow?

3 ORGANIZATION—What is the organizing strategy or overall plan? Are there major stages or subdivisions? What are they? How or in what order are they followed up?

4 SUPPORT—How does the writer support specific points? What supporting material did the writer use to back up claims or generalizations? How well are sources identified? Which supporting material was strongest? Did any seem weak?

5 CONCLUSION—How does the writer end the paper? Does the conclusion add anything to the paper? Does it conclude the paper on a strong note? Does it give you something to remember—a striking final example, a punchline, a clincher quotation, or a positive recommendation?

6 READER RESPONSE—Are you a good audience for this paper? Did you learn something from it? Did it change your mind? Did you at any point strongly agree or disagree?

Editing

Edit to make sure your text meets standards of educated written English.

Written English is generally more carefully worked out and reworked than casual everyday speech. When you write for a college-level audience, you need to honor the conventions of educated written English. You need to meet accepted standards of clear, effective, and appropriate use of the written word.

- *Edit to meet the standards of educated readers.* Final editing is your chance to take care of misspellings, missing or confusing punctuation, awkward sentences, and misused or blurry words.

- *Edit for inappropriate language.* In final editing, you may have to look for wording that is too chummy or disrespectful for a serious audience. However, you may also have to edit for wording that will seem too stilted or impersonal for a concerned reader. You may have to improve the wording of passages that will be offensive to groups sensitive to slights. Edit for any intentionally or thoughtlessly racist, sexist, or otherwise condescending or demeaning language.

- *Proofread.* Remember that text on a computer screen looks deceptively finished. Professionals recommend that you proofread twice, checking your text line by line—first onscreen and then again as hard copy.

A CHECKLIST FOR FINAL EDITING

The following are high-priority items for final editing:

1   *Check for familiar spelling demons.* Make sure you have not misspelled the "unforgivables": *receive, definite, believe, similar, separate, used to, a lot* (two words). Let your spellcheck catch common problem words: *accommodate, government, predominant, environment, occurred.* Watch for confusing pairs: *accept* (take in) but *except* (take out); *affect* (change in part) but *effect* (the whole result).

2   *Avoid the* it's *trap.* Save yourself grief by changing any *it's* to *it is*—if *it is* what you mean. Otherwise use *its*—a **possessive** showing where something belongs: the band and *its* vocalist.

3   *Check for apostrophes with possessives.* What belongs with what? Distinguish between singular (one *person's* problems) and plural (both my *parents'* attitude).

4   *Hook up sentence fragments.* Look for sentence fragments that should be linked to a preceding sentence from which they have been split off (*To fight disease. Living in the city. Which proved untrue.*)

A Checklist for Final Editing (continued)

Chimpanzees were bred for experiments **to fight disease.**

Her campaign was derailed by last-minute charges, **which proved untrue.**

5   *Use the semicolon between two closely related statements.* Use the semi-colon instead of a comma when there is no other link between the two points.

SEMICOLON: Speed kills; caution saves lives.

6   *Use a comma with and or but; use the semicolon with* however *and* therefore. Use the comma when two statements are joined by *and, but, for, so, yet, or, nor* (coordinators, or coordinating conjunctions). Use the semicolon when two statements are joined by *however, therefore, nevertheless, besides, moreover* (adverbial connectives, or conjunctive adverbs). Note the optional commas with adverbial connectives.

COMMA: Violent crimes have decreased, **but** juvenile crime has gone up.

SEMICOLON: Inflation has slowed down; **however** tuition is going up.
                    Inflation has slowed down; tuition **however** is going up.
                    Inflation has slowed down; tuition is going up **however**.

ADDED COMMA: Inflation has slowed down; **however**, tuition is going up.
                    Inflation has slowed down; tuition, **however**, is going up.

7   *Make a verb agree with its true subject.* Use matching forms for singular (one of a kind) and plural (several). Do not be misled by a wedge that comes between the subject and its verb.

SINGULAR: The **genetic makeup** of chimpanzees **is** 97 percent identical with ours. (not *are*)

PLURAL: Researchers claim there **are genes** predisposing us to diseases. (not *is*)

8   *Deal with the pronoun dilemma.* "Every student turned in **his** exam" used to be grammatically correct. "Every student turned in **his or her** exam" avoids sexist implications. "All of the students turned in **their** exams" changes the whole sentence to plural forms and is gender–neutral. The change to the plural is often the best or least awkward solution.

9   *Use correct forms for pronouns and adverbs.* Use the right forms (**case** forms) for personal pronouns. Use the subject form to tell us who: *I, he, she, we, they.* Use the object forms to tell us at whom an action aims or for whom it is intended (*me, him, her, us, them*).

SUBJECT FORM:	**My classmates and I** did volunteer work.
	She and her mother never got along.
OBJECT FORM:	The manager never liked **my coworkers and me**.
	The news came as a surprise for **her and her mother**.

When you have a choice, use the distinctive adverb form to tell us how (*badly, rapidly, immediately*). Use the adverb *well* to tell readers how.

| ADVERB FORM: | The city had changed **considerably**. (not *considerable*) |
| | Her family spoke English **really well**. (not *real good*) |

10 *Deal with dangling modifiers.* They are left dangling because they point to something that is missing from the sentence:

DANGLING:	*Losing a job*, feelings of self-doubt are natural.
	(*who* lost the job?)
EDITED:	**Losing a job, we** naturally experience self-doubt.

WRITING AND THINKING

Review and strengthen the thinking that goes into your writing.

The computer has shortened the distance between the way we think and the way we write. Much writing at the computer is the electronic equivalent of thinking out loud. We may start with unsorted notes recording tentative ideas and promising material. We sift and test these, putting some aside and following up others. We notice possible connections and follow up key questions that begin to emerge. A tentative overall scheme begins to take shape.

Study sample outlines charting the thinking that gives shape and direction to a well-planned paper.

PROBLEM-SOLVING STRATEGIES *Study thinking strategies you see at work when people search for a solution to problem.* The following sample outline charts a problem-solving strategy that often produces good results. The writer examines and evaluates different solutions in order to find the right one. In this instance, the problem was how to dispose of the mountains of garbage generated in huge metropolitan districts.

PROBLEM–SOLVING PAPER

The Throwaway Society

PROBLEM: **How will our wasteful throwaway society solve its waste disposal problem?**

OPTION 1: We could continue to look for close-by landfill sites, although open space is becoming rare and neighboring communities fight against the garbage dump stench and the congestion from garbage-truck traffic.

OPTION 2: We could build huge modern incinerator plants, although equipment to reduce air pollution or emission of greenhouse gases might prove prohibitively expensive.

OPTION 3: Depending on geographic location, we could load the garbage on trains and ship it into the desert or load it on barges and sink it to the ocean floor, although environmentalists as well as people living near the desert or the coast might organize opposition.

OPTION 4: We could greatly step up promotion and facilities for recycling efforts, although statistics on the percentage of waste actually recycled have been discouraging.

A study group, a planning commission, or legislative body may weigh these options. They may start to put aside those that for one reason or another seem wrong. Various alternatives might prove too expensive or too unpopular. They might be too experimental, or they may have been tried before and failed. By a **process of elimination,** the group may arrive at the option that would address the problem, at least for a time.

REACHING GENERAL CONCLUSIONS   *Much productive thinking goes from the specific to the general.* This generalizing, or **inductive,** model is a discovery mode. It starts from careful observation or data gathering and looks for the common pattern. It finds the the connecting thread. The generalizing or inductive model puts input first: We *earn* the right to have an opinion. Before we generalize, we take a close look at our experience or observation and at data and informed opinion from credible sources.

Trend watchers present generalizations after tracking similar or related examples or incidents. A typical paper will present the general conclusion first and then present the detailed examples that led to it:

TREND-WATCHING PAPER.

A Tale of Three Cities

THESIS: **We treat the homeless not as fellow human beings but as an embarrassment; we hide them for appearances' sake.**

Incident 1: One of the major parties holds its national convention in a big city. The city authorities busily clean up the litter. They pick up the homeless and put them in shelters.

Incident 2: The other major party holds its convention in a big city. The city authorities spruce up the city. Filth is picked up; beggars and homeless people are made to move on or are moved to temporary shelters.

Incident 3: An important foreign visitor—the Pope, the Queen of England—arrives. The city authorities spruce up the city; they make beggars and the homeless less visible, as above.

To make a paper presenting and defending a generalization convincing, remember some basic guidelines:

- *Present representative examples.* Make sure your supporting examples are not isolated examples or exceptions
- *Stay away from made-up examples.* Rely on real-life examples or material from credible sources. "Hypothetical" made-up examples can be tailored to support claims that are really foregone conclusions—conclusions already reached before any research or investigation.
- *Be prepared to adjust a trial thesis.* Revise tentative generalizations as the evidence accumulates.

WEIGHING PRO AND CON *Reach a balanced conclusion after weighing both sides or several alternatives.* Much thinking does not proceed in straight line from evidence to conclusion. We may first lean one way, and then after looking at further evidence or listening to convincing arguments we may incline to the other side. The play of **pro and con** makes us explore both sides of an issue. To arrive at a balanced conclusion, we line up arguments in favor and arguments against. We can then weigh their merits. Often a convincing piece of writing moves from point to counterpoint and from there to a reasonable conclusion. The play of pro and con allows us to weigh the evidence and balance conflicting claims. It is a safeguard against narrow, one-sided views; it keeps us from leaping to conclusions.

The classic scheme for a pro and con argument is *thesis* (first major point)—*antithesis* (counterpoint)—*synthesis* (a balanced view taking both sides into account).

The following might be a student writer's notes for a pro and con topic: Should bikers have to wear helmets? Should motorcycle riders be required to wear safety helmets?

```
┌─────────────────────────┐
│ PRO AND CON PAPER        │
└─────────────────────────┘
```

Fasten Your Helmet

CON—arguments against helmets
freedom of the open road (sense of liberation, free spirits)
exhilaration of exposure to the elements vs. isolation
cost and inconvenience in dragging/storing the clumsy helmets
principle of choice vs. state interference ——>>>>>>>>>>>>>

PRO—arguments in favor of helmets
severe injuries (often more severe than in car accidents)
strain on hospitals and rehabilitation services
horrendous cost to community
trauma to the other motorist (implicated in the death or maiming of another human being) ————>>>>>>>>>>>>>

BALANCED CONCLUSION: New high-tech helmets can protect the biker and
the public and be less confining.

Even a pro and con paper will often present the balanced conclusion
early as the thesis and then take the reader through the weighing of the two
sides that led up to it. The pro and con approach is especially appropriate
when an issue has been the subject of heated discussion: driver's licenses for
illegal immigrants, censorship of the Internet. The commitment to listen to
the other side can counteract our tendency to raise our voices and shout
people down.

ARGUING FROM PRINCIPLE *Apply basic principles or shared values to
current test cases.* Much argument does not start from a patient gathering of
the facts. It starts from what we already know, or think we know. The **deductive** model starts with a general principle and applies it to a specific situation. (This model reverses the itinerary of the inductive model.) You can
model such arguments as follows:

IF: Federal guidelines bar colleges from discriminating against stu-
          dents on the basis of gender.

AND IF: The local women's college still bars male students.

THEN: The college is in violation of federal guidelines.

When we argue from principle, we start from basic assumptions and
apply them to specific cases. Writers who argue from principle appeal to
shared values. Much depends on the reader's accepting the basic assumptions, or **premises.** For instance, on the topic of capital punishment, would
you accept premises like the following?

ARGUING FROM PRINCIPLE

Premise 1: The poor must have the equal protection of the law (but
           they cannot afford the best, expensive legal help and there-
           fore are much more likely to receive the death penalty than
           the rich).

Premise 2: Minorities deserve equal treatment before the law (but the
           death penalty is applied to them much more often than to
           whites).

Premise 3: People innocently convicted must have a chance to be rehabilitated (but the mistake cannot be rectified if the people
have been executed).

You can chart an argument based on these premises according to the
"IF–AND IF–THEN" formula:

IF: Justice requires the justice system to be willing to correct its
          mistakes—to reverse judicial error.

AND IF: Capital punishment makes the reversal of a wrongful verdict
          impossible.

THEN: Capital punishment is inherently unjust.

WRITING AND THE COMPUTER

**Make full use of the opportunities and resources available to-
day to the computer-literate writer.**
The way we write and think is changing rapidly as we do more of our
reading, research, and writing on the computer.

USING ELECTRONIC SOURCES   In the age of the information
highway and the knowledge explosion, background and follow-up on any
major issue are at your finger tips. A few keystrokes will call up on your computer screen information about progress toward a cure for Alzheimer's or
about Thomas Jefferson's relationship with Sally Hemings, one of his slaves.

- You can keep current on issues like offshoring or gasoline prices by
  reading major newspapers online—from the *New York Times* and
  Washington Post to the *Los Angeles Times* and *USA Today*.

- You can check the current status of gun control legislation by going to the **websites** of pro-gun and anti-gun organizations.

- You can call up detailed historical background on the abolitionist
  movement from an encyclopedia like *Encarta* online or on CD-
  ROM, following links to major figures and events in the antislavery
  movement.

KNOWING SEARCH TECHNIQUES   Starting a Web search on a
current issue will often set off an avalanche of related articles and other material. Most users of the net have selected their own favorite **search engine,** such as the now widely trusted Google or the competing Yahoo.
They develop their own search techniques. For instance, is it true that AIDS
education has been a failure, with many teenagers practicing unprotected
sex? A large unrestricted key word like AIDS is likely to call up several
thousand unsorted listings. You will need to start with something more narrowly focused or more selective, like (AIDS EDUCATION) or (AIDS and
EDUCATION). People writing on this topic will not all use this exact
term, so you ask yourself: "How else would people talk about this topic?"
You may try SAFE SEX EDUCATION or TEENAGERS AND AIDS or
UNPROTECTED SEX.

Different search engines provide varying instructions to assist you in finding and sifting promising sources. For instance, to have the computer search not only for titles and descriptions with the exact word *education* but also with related words like *educating*, you may be typing only the root of your key word, followed by an asterisk. If you type *educat**, the computer will search for all versions of the word with different endings, such as *educate, education*, and *educational*.

Special-interest **databases** for areas like literature, psychology, biology, or education will guide you to exceptionally full and up-to-date sources in a field of study or area of research. For instance, the indexes or directories provided by Yahoo! (dir.yahoo.com) for the arts and humanities will include a guide to authors. These may be arranged by kinds or genres of literature or alternatively by time periods. Categories of special interest to you for a writing project may include <u>Author Interviews, Native American, Nature Writers,</u> or <u>Southern (U.S.)</u>

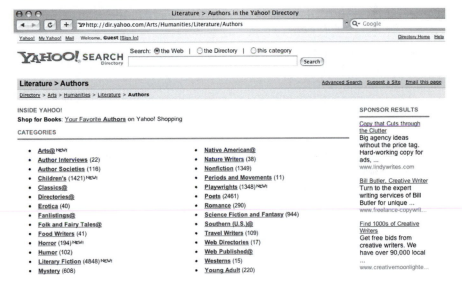

Reproduced with permission of Yahoo! Inc. Copyright © 2000 by Yahoo! Inc. YAHOO! and Yahoo! logo are trademarks of Yahoo! Inc.

THE RANGE OF SOURCES In your search for promising material for a paper on a current issue, you will be able to draw on a whole range of sources. These may include national news sources, publications for the general reader, publications aimed at a more specialized target audience, websites promoting organizations or institutions, and public interest sources.

The following source list was compiled by a group of students. It records promising sources for exploring a "hot-button" issue in communities across the nation: Should communities encourage or slow down the expansion of the nation's "largest retailer"? Most of these entries give two dates. First is the **posting date**—the date the material was first published or posted. Second is the **access date,** the date a student accessed the material. The Internet address (or URL) appears in angled brackets, It enables your reader to go to the original source if it is still a live link.

ELECTRONIC SOURCES

(National news sources)

McKinley, James, "Town Welcomes Wal-Mart, Officially Anyway." *New York Times.* 28 Sept. 2004. 17 Oct. 2004.
    <http:/www.iht.com/articles/540887.html.>

"Illegal Workers Sue Wal-Mart." CNN. 10 Sept. 2004. 17 Oct. 2004.
    <http:/www..cnn.com/2003/BUSINESS/11/10/walmart.suit/index.html>.

(Corporate public relations)

Wal-Mart Foundation. Fall 2004. 17 Oct. 2004.
    <http://www.walmartfoundation.org>

(Pro-business sources)

Zellner, Wendy, "Analyzing the 'Sins' of Wal-Mart". *BusinessWeek.* 15 Apr. 2004. 17 Oct. 2004.
    <http://www.laane.or/pressroom/stories/walmart/040415BizWeek.html>

"Wal-Mart makes direct appeal to Californians." *The Retail Bulletin.* 25 Sept. 2004. 18 Oct. 2004.
    <http://www.theretailbulletin.com/index.php?pae=5&cat=news&id=4838>

(Public interest sources)

Rowell, Andy. "Wal-Mart Brings Inequality and Low Prices to the World." Project Censored. Sonoma State University. Oct. 2004. 17 Oct. 2004.
    <http://www,projectcensored.org/publications/2005/25.html>

"Store Wars: When Wal-Mart Comes to Town." Public Broadcasting Service. 29 Sept. 2004. 17 Oct. 2004.
    <http://www.pbs .or/itvs/storewars/storv.html>.

Steil, Mark. "Wal-Mart Worries Replay the Past." Minnesota Public Radio. 28 Sept. 2004. 17 Oct. 2004.
    <http://news.minnesota.publicradio.org/features/2004/09/28_steilm_retailstruggle/>

EVALUATING YOUR SOURCES How do you evaluate the results of your search? When materials are first published elsewhere and then put on the Net, the Internet serves as an electronic library—an instant access library. You can often retrieve and check the original print publication. (If necessary, you can go back to sources more complete or more carefully checked and verified.) However, increasingly much material is published only on the Net. The Net then serves as a worldwide **electronic publisher**—without the editors, critics, and reviewers that have traditionally sifted and channeled print materials. As in other areas, the computer increasingly allows you to bypass the middleman—the mediator or facilitator.

Since much material on the Net is unedited and unsorted, you will often have to use your own judgment about what you have found. Your instructor or your handbook is likely to give you advice like the following:

Evaluating Electronic Sources

When you draw on electronic sources, keep the following questions in mind:

1   AUTHORSHIP *Who wrote or assembled the material?* Is the author clearly identified? Or is the material anonymous or quasi-anonymous, like much material floating around the Net?

2   CREDENTIALS *How credible are the sources?* Is there any indication of the credentials of the authors? Where do they work or write? What is their academic or professional status? Are they recognized authorities or experts in their field?

3   AUTHENTICITY *Who put this material on the Net?* Was it copied, re-cycled, or pirated from somewhere? Can you trace it to the original source? Is there any indication of copyright? Who has the rights to this material?

4   BIAS *How objective or reliable does the material seem?* Are opinions carefully presented and supported by credible evidence or data? Does the material seem slanted or one-sided? Does the material read like corporate public relations or partisan campaign rhetoric?

5   COMPLETENESS *How reliable and complete is the current version?* Has it been excerpted, and by whom? Has it been adapted or updated, and by whom? Is anyone responsible for accuracy and completeness of the current version? Can you trace a more complete original version?

6   PERMANENCE *How long will this material be accessible?* Will other people be able to retrieve and verify it at a later date?

WRITING ON THE COMPUTER While the computer has changed the way we read and do research, it is also changing the way we write:

- *Writing has become more natural.* It has moved closer to talking, with writer's block being for many writers a thing of the past. Writing on the computer screen, you can easily change, expand, or shorten your material. You can build up a computer file by pasting in material or transferring files. You can electronically scan texts you want to quote in a paper.

- *Revision has become a more natural part of writing.* You can easily adjust a text to accommodate new information and second thoughts. You are less likely today to think of a piece of writing as finished and done with. You are are more likely to use opportunities for ongoing revision and for adapting material to different uses.

- *Writing has become more interactive.* Writers today are prepared for the instant reply. Participating in an e-mail exchange or electronic conversation is likely to make you more audience-conscious. You become more aware of your readers and what is going on in their minds.

At the same time, media watchers warn of the possible downside of electronic reading and writing. Are we beginning to rely too much on sound bites? Do we accept bit facts and "off-the-top-of-your-head" opinions at face value? A general effect of publication on the Web has been to reduce print content. We are getting used to glossy bits of news and gossip in the opening pages of news magazines. Instructions for creating **websites** encourage the authors to cut back on plain prose. They show how to concentrate on attractive layouts and liven up the page with graphics. Will a new generation suffer from a short attention span?

VISUAL LITERACY: WORD AND IMAGE

In today's world of rapid worldwide communication, word and image often go together, working hand in hand.

We live in a world where a multitude of messages and rapidly changing images call for our attention. Do you rely mostly on what you read? Do you go mostly by what you see? Do you go mostly by what you hear? Americans today spend much time in the virtual reality of images flashing by on the large and the small screen. Visual messages, often working together with verbal messages, add a major dimension to the world's work. In the million-dollar advertising pages of glossy magazines, images of glitz and glamor reenforce or underline printed text. Along major highways, billboards selling cars, fast food, and banking services call out to drivers: "Look at me!" Hand-lettered signs saying "Cherries" or "Corn" may still invite motorists to stop along a country road.

Are you a passive consumer of images? Or do you select—choosing which to attend to and which to bypass? Do you evaluate what you see? Observers tracking and evaluating the visual component of our world encourage us to ask ourselves questions like the following:

- **What does a photographer or a graphic artist want us to see?** The decision to take a picture is already an act of editorial judgment. It is similar to the decision of an editor to put a story on the front page or bury it later in the paper or magazine. The decision to provide a graph on rising or dropping income levels or unemployment focuses our attention and suggests to us what is important.

- **How does the image shape and frame what it shows?** Like the written word, the language of images does not just hold up an impartial mirror to reality. The camera shapes and selects. It highlights or plays down. It leaves some elements out of the frame altogether. It may select images that reassure us and make us feel good—like a parent in a war zone e-mailing a message to loved ones at home. Or it may select images that grieve or anger us, like flag-draped coffins unloaded from a military cargo plane.

- **What strategies help the image convey its message?** For instance, does it use contrast to expose the contradiction between flattering surface appearances and unwelcome facts? The right camera angle can juxtapose conflicting elements. In a famous depression era photograph, a huge billboard showed an affluent family in a new car complete with a smiling little boy and the cute family dog: "Highest Standard of Living in the World!" Going past the billboard was a long breadline in single file of shabbily dressed Americans waiting for their turn to be given a handout, supplies, or soup.

- **Who is the target audience?** Who is expected to buy the product or support the cause? Glossy ads for luxury automobiles may tell us more about the intended audience than about the cars. Pictures of children in areas of Africa devastated by famine or flooded villages in Bangladesh may assume an audience responding to humanitarian appeals.

- **What helps a powerful image leave a lasting impression?** Viewers and readers are flooded with images that often "speak for themselves." Some have a powerful impact even without the caption or supporting text, like a shot of a giant condor again floating with its huge wingspread over the sun-scorched California hills.

However, in today's world, word and image often work together. They set up an effective one-two, maximizing their combined impact on the reader-viewer. Visual material often works in tandem with printed text—reinforcing each other. It often shows the result of two forces working together so that their combined effect is more than that of the two forces simply added together.

A Viewer's Guide

FAQs for Viewers and Readers

Here are FAQs (Frequently Asked Questions) that you may ask yourself when receiving, decoding, interpreting, or evaluating images. Some may be visual messages only. Others may be text-image messages with a substantial visual component:

1 FOCUS What images get your *attention*? When do you stop to watch and listen? Many viewers avoid intruding or unwanted messages: They mute the sound of commercial or political messages. Others try to fast

forward promotional material on videos or DVD. Can you describe two or three recent visuals—ads, commercials, public service announcements—that caught your eye? What does it take to make visual images attention-getting for you?

2 PURPOSE What is the *purpose*? What function does it serve? What is the image supposed to accomplish? For instance,

 • Does it try to sell you something?

 • Does it ask for your vote?

 • Does it ask you to change your mind about an issue?

 • Does it alert you to a problem that needs attention in your community?

 • Does it try to improve the public image of of a corporation or a candidate?

3 AUDIENCE Who is the intended *audience*? Which of the following descriptions of images might make you say: "This message is for me"?

 • cheerful young people by a mountain stream ready to light a cigarette or drink ice-cold beer

 • emaciated slum child who would profit from your donation

 • powerful truck driving through rugged terrain

 • financial service touting ways to consolidate credit card debt

 • promotion of a new album by a favorite singer

4 STRATEGIES What *appeals* are used to influence or sway the viewer-reader? For example, does the image or the image-word combination appeal to emotions? Does it stir up fear or resentment? Does it appeal to sympathy or compassion? Does it respond to the viewer's need for hopeful or inspirational messages? Does it use facts-and-figures evidence or statistics that seem relevant or legitimate?

5 TONE What is the *tone*? For instance, is the message low key? Does text that is part of a visual use a confidential tone? Is it "nuanced"—carefully qualified or hedged? Or does it come on as brash or aggressive? Is its tone friendly or even chummy?

6 EVALUATION How would you *rate* or judge a visual or a text-and-image message? For instance, would you rate the image or the image-word combination as fresh and imaginative? Or is it predictable and trite, relying on overused elements or methods? Does it respect the viewer's intelligence? Was it created by people that you might respect or trust? Do you think it is effective—achieving its goals?

YOUR TURN: THE CAMERA EYE

Photography became a powerful medium for capturing, recording, and interpreting reality. In the flow of images you encounter every day, would you stop to take in the photographs on the following pages? Why or why not?

Prepare your responses to the "Reading the Image" questions that follow each photograph. Prepare to share your responses with your class or a group.

VISUAL LITERACY 1
THE ELOQUENT IMAGE: Alternative Energy

Often a striking, attention-getting image alone tells a story.
When is a picture worth many words? The image may bring an important question into focus. It may dramatize and highlight what it shows. It is likely not to be not cluttered, not making us look this way and that way. It will often seem to be all of one piece, calling out to us: "Here, take this in. Take a good look. Think about it." The photographer focusing our attention on the wind power installation was struck by the eye-catching sight of the sleek modern towers generating energy on wind-swept hills. Advocates of alternative energy promote renewable natural resources that are not destructive to the environment. At the same time, resources like wind power or solar power become a test of human ingenuity and engineering skills. Do you think this image effectively conveys this message?

Reading the Image

1 What makes this an *attention-getting* picture? In this image of an alternative energy installation, what do you see? At first glance, what does the image say to you? Does it raise questions in your mind? Would you give it a second look?

2 How does this photograph *direct* your attention? The **foreground** is the area closest to the viewer. In this picture it is dominated by the sleek poles and the compact modernistic generators they hold up to capture the wind. Are you surprised there are so many of them, clustered together? Does generating energy from wind power here seem an experimental, isolated undertaking? Why or why not?

3 Does the *setting* matter? To judge from the **background** or more distant part of the image, where are we? When you think of industry, do you expect to see smokestacks or rust-belt factories? Is it part of the message of this picture that we seem to be out in the country, not near human habitation? Does it matter?

4 Does the world of industry have to be ugly? In the practical world of energy resources, do *aesthetics* matter—the way our world satisfies our need for shape, pattern, harmony, or color? Critics of the new industrial age long expected the world of modern progress to offend the eye and the ear. Asphalt was paving over fields and streams; workers saw slag heaps instead of rolling hills. Would you call this picture beautiful? Why or why not?

5 Should this image be more *explicit*—spelling out the implied message, maybe with the help of a caption or signs that are part of the site? Or does it speak for itself?

VISUAL LITERACY 2
LANGUAGE OF SIGNS: Janitors on Strike

Signs, placards, and posters play a large role in community initiatives and political campaigns.

Placards, posters, and banners often sum up an agenda that unites large numbers of people sharing the same grievance or aim. Those bearing the placards have boiled down their message to the essential point or points. They need to project a brief message in large letters that can be read from a distance. In the past, images of strikers or of protests about workplace issues have often showed working class Americans participating in well-organized labor union activities protecting the wage gains or pension rights of factory workers or truck drivers, for instance. In recent years, reports on protests and strikes have begun to show images of what for many Americans is still a largely invisible underground economy of the lowest paid, such as maids and dishwashers at posh hotels, or janitors at corporate offices and universities.

Reading the Image

1   How would you sum up in one sentence the *message* conveyed by the signs carried by the strikers?

2   How much *information* does this image give you about the people and their situation? Are you surprised the strikers are janitors? Why or why not? What story do the signs tell? The signs are bilingual. What does that tell you about the workers and their work?

3   Do the media perpetuate *stereotypes* about strikers or protesters? Do they portray protesters as troublemakers who might turn violent and get out of control? How are these protesters different? Do they seem disorganized or organized? Do you see evidence of a substantial organizing effort? Are there any hints of possible trouble or violence?

4   Are you a good *audience* for appeals like the ones shown in this image? When you hear there might be a protest, demonstration, or riot, do you tend to stay away? What kind of protest meeting might you attend?

5   Do you think the kind of activity pictured here has an effect on *public opinion*? Do activists or reformers going out into the street get a hearing in your community or in the larger society?

6   Social critics claim that as a society we are becoming jaded or hard-nosed about appeals for help from the *down and out*. How much attention do you pay to hand-lettered signs asking for help? Do you pass on without paying attention when you see a message lettered on a piece of cardboard saying the person is hungry, unemployed, or living as a homeless veteran?

VISUAL LITERACY 3
NONVERBAL LANGUAGE: Lost Generation

Much language is nonverbal; it communicates without words.

Nonverbal communication talks to the eye rather than the ear. The beginnings of human language may have been partly meaningful sounds. However, much early human communication may also have been body language—threatening postures, friendly gestures. Still today our changing facial expressions signal what we think and feel. We still use gestures to express a whole range of attitudes and emotions. These may include surprise, disbelief, disgust, pleasure, rejection, fear, or awe. We still send a message by the way we stand proudly or defiantly—or by the way we cower in fear or submission. How much attention do you pay to the language of gestures? How well do you read nonverbal language?

This picture was taken at a time when psychologists, social scientists, and educators were probing the motives and loyalties of growing and increasingly violent youth gangs. Does this picture help you hear the language of the "unheard"?

Reading the Image

1   What *message* does this picture convey to you? The young people in the picture use the same gesture or hand signal. What do you think this hand signal means? What does it tell you about the people in the picture?

2   Sometimes an image is arranged in such a way that a central figure or object is highlighted or stands out. What is *highlighted* in this picture? What statement is the young woman making who is holding what looks like a gun?

3   How did the people in this picture *pose* for the camera? Sometimes the photographer poses the subjects for the desired effect. However, often also the subjects tell us something about themselves by the poses they have assumed for the camera. What does their grouping and arrangement in this picture convey to you or tell you?

4   How much of the message or emotional impact of this image derives from the *setting*? Where does the picture take us? The graffiti on the walls are not legible. What are they like? Do they tell you anything about the setting or the people?

5   What is your *viewer response* to this picture? Are you shocked? Are you puzzled? Are you offended? Do you feel you recognize or relate to the people shown? Do you feel you are learning something by looking at this image?

6 What do you think was the photographer's *intention*? Some photographers pride themselves on giving us an impartial, unretouched record of reality. Others are people with a mission or an agenda. Why do you think the photographer brought this image to viewers' attention?

Starting a Journal

To make writing a natural everyday activity, start a writing journal or writer's log.

How do you make writing a habit? No one becomes a good violinist or an outstanding volleyball player by practicing reluctantly and only off and on. What will help make writing a natural, familiar activity for you? How will it become for you a medium of keeping a record, of thinking through what matters, of informing your readers, and of making your voice heard?

Write in your journal maybe twice a week. Your entries may range from half a single-spaced page to a page or more.

TOPICS FOR JOURNAL WRITING   Use your journal for a running commentary on what you observe, view, and read. Your first entries might be about yourself. You may talk about your family background, your happy or unhappy memories of school, or your major interests. Gradually, you will be branching out. Here are suggestions for sample entries:

- *Write about an incident that made you think.* What happened? Why did it shake you up or change your mind about something?
- *Write about a person who has mattered to you.* What people do you relate to, and why are others a problem for you?
- *React to news stories that made you angry or glad.* Why are some news reports close to home for you?
- *Record conversations that touched a nerve.* Do you keep quiet when people say things you find objectionable? Or do you talk back?
- *Write about a visit to the theater or to a museum.* Write about a spectacular student performance of an ancient Greek play or a traveling exhibit honoring *Americanos*—Latino Americans.

SHARING AND FUTURE USE   In your journal, you will be writing spontaneously and informally. Your instructor may ask to read all or a sampling of it—but mainly as an interested reader, with only informal comments. You may share entries with your classmates. You will be able to be more candid or unguarded than in formal papers. You will be able to put down first impressions as well as second thoughts. You can explore puzzling questions as well as tentative answers.

In addition to giving you practice in putting your thoughts and feelings into words, your journal will serve you as a source of material for more structured papers. Often an entry will give you a headstart: It may already contain the germ of an idea for a paper. For instance, in developing a paper about an important incident or event, you might use what you already have but look for related similar incidents that become part of a pattern. You can fill in background for something that happened, tell your reader more about the people involved, or bring the story up to date.

Writing the Personal Résumé

Use the first few entries of your journal for a personal résumé.
Writing a personal résumé will give you a chance to take stock of your personal resources. What background do you bring to your writing class? What experiences will you be able to draw on in your writing? What will give classmates and your instructor a sense of who you are? Write entries under headings like the following:

- ROOTS—family background, ethnic or racial identity, the meeting of cultures;
- SCHOOLING—teachers and classmates, goals and obstacles, successes and failures;
- FLASHLIGHT MEMORIES—vividly remembered incidents that have a special meaning for you;
- WORK—part-time jobs, experiences as counselor or mentor, initiation to the workplace;
- PERSONAL ISSUES—personal goals and commitments, causes you support, problems in your life.

Study the following sample journal entries. What might each writer do to expand the entry into a fully developed paper?

ROOTS Most people my age do not realize how hard it was for the older generation to make a new start in a new country. When my grandfather immigrated to the U.S. from China, he had to buy fake identification papers that said he was younger than he actually was. According to my grandfather, a person under the age of 20 could leave the country, but people over 20 had to serve in the Chinese army and were not allowed to leave. My grandfather was 20 and had to buy fake identification papers saying he was only 18. These papers also changed his name from Cheg to Liu, so they not only changed his age but also gave him a new identity. I guess one could say that he was an illegal immigrant. This was taking a big risk for him because he could have been caught, but he thought it was worth it, just to come to America.

WORK   When I entered high school, I was a shy, insecure person. It was not hard for me to make friends, but it was difficult for me to feel accepted. I usually camouflaged my real feelings with a fake smile. What helped me to shed the layers of self-doubt was working at the Living Tree Coffeehouse. I spent a year serving mochas and lattes, meeting people, and basically having a great time. The atmosphere was warm and cozy, with antique furniture and velvet couches. People came there not only to socialize but also to listen to good music or study for midterms. There was a real sense of community without everyone only trying to get ahead of everyone else. About the same time, I ran for the Associated Student Body Council, and serving on the council helped me overcome my insecurities. I learned that it is perfectly fine to express my feelings or express dislike toward someone else's ideas.

PERSONAL ISSUES   As a woman, terms that offend me include *babe* and *baby*. Women are not infants, and when they are called these names, the implication is that women are childish, immature, and unable to take care of themselves. *Chick* and *fox*: women are not feathered or furry animals. If these terms are used to "compliment a female's appearance," why not compliment her intelligence? her sense of humor? her ability in sports? Granted, words are "just words." However, they are often a fairly accurate indicator of how a person might act. Unfortunately, I was able to see the connection between words and feelings at first hand. I had grown close to my cousin Ben, who was funny and pleasant to be around. I was working in his father's store, and one day when I asked a customer if I could help him, the customer said: "I don't want no woman waiting on me!" As I stood there agape, my uncle helped him and laughed at the "joke." That night I received a phone call from Ben. He told me that I really ought to toughen up if I wanted to make it in the business world.

1

INITIATION
Growing Up American

VISUAL LITERACY 1
CANDID PHOTOGRAPHY: Rainy Day

Photographers love to catch people in candid, unposed moments. When people move naturally, we hope to catch a glimpse of their true selves. We like to believe that a candid shot will reveal some of their true personality— different from the smiles of family pictures or the solemn poses of group portraits. This "Rainy Day" image by a student photographer appeared in a campus publication in 2003 in a Spring/Summer issue. At the time, newspapers carried many reports of problems, traumas, and violence involving young people. Does the photographer succeed in counteracting media images of troubled youth?

Reading the Image

1   Often the first step for a photographer is to bring the subject into *focus*. The two people in this photograph fill most of the frame. Does anything else in the picture matter? Who are these two? Why are they happy? What kind of people are they? Can you tell anything from the way they are dressed and from their umbrellas? Can you construct a brief scenario of what might have led up to this snapshot?

2   Professional photographers carefully plot or chart the *composition* of a picture. They give careful thought to how the parts of an image are positioned in relation to each other. How do the key elements of this image work together? What kind of bonding between these two does the image suggest by the way they are turned to each other, look at each other, and are laughing together?

3   Are you a good *audience* for this photographic artist? How do you feel about what you see in this picture? Does it make you feel happy? Do you identify with the people, or do you feel these are not your kind of people?

4   Do you think you make a good *subject* for a photographer? Why or why not? Do you like to be photographed? Or are you camera-shy? If a photographer were to catch you at your best, what would you want the situation or the pose to be?

1

INITIATION

Growing Up American

"One writes out of one thing only—one's own experience. Everything depends on how relentlessly, one forces from this experience the last drop, sweet or bitter, it can possibly give."

—JAMES BALDWIN

Much powerful and effective writing is anchored in the writer's own firsthand experience. We all have a story to tell that reveals who we are and how we became who we are. When we trust the listener or reader enough, we may tell that story. Many such stories are stories of growing up, of initiation. We move from an earlier stage to a new stage that requires us to learn. We face a challenge that may seem new and overwhelming to us. However, we may discover later that many others before us had to face it in their own way. We find ourselves reliving an archetypal experience—reliving a pattern that has been played out by many earlier generations.

One such archetypal experience is the move from a protected childhood to an adult world. We begin to face new problems and responsibilities. We may slowly discover that a person we trusted has serious flaws. We may be outgrowing an institution or ideas that at one time seemed to serve all our intellectual or spiritual needs. We discover what it means to make our own decisions and make our own choices and mistakes.

For many young Americans, an archetypal experience of growing up has meant moving from one environment to another—from country to city, or from the Old Country ways of immigrant parents to the American world of school and profession. Often that move is a time of confusion, with people trying to find their bearings. It is a time of breaking away and searching for a new identity. People may find their loyalties divided between different ways of life and often different languages. They may be trying to bridge different cultures—"straddling two cultures," as Caroline Hwang says in one of the selections in this chapter. Sometimes the initiation or awakening centers on the rediscovery of a culture or a language that was part of the family's past—but that was left behind in the attempt to assimilate, to become part of the mainstream of American life.

Many of the selections in this chapter tell the story of such a journey in quest of the writer's identity.

LAKOTA WOMAN

Mary Crow Dog

"You can't live forever off the deeds of Sitting Bull and Crazy Horse. You can't wear their eagle feathers, freeload off their legends. You have to make your own legends now."

The following account was first published in 1990, at a time when writers, artists, and textbook authors were rewriting American history to correct movie stereotypes about Native Americans and to tell the story of a defeated nation.

Lakota Woman (written with Richard Erdoes) is the story of Mary Crow Dog, who grew up on a reservation in South Dakota in a one-room cabin, without a father in the house and without running water or electricity. Her publisher said about her, "Rebelling against the aimless drinking, punishing missionary school, narrow strictures for women, and violence and hopelessness of reservation life, she joined the new movement of tribal pride sweeping Native American communities in the sixties and seventies and eventually married Leonard Crow Dog, the movement's chief medicine man, who revived the outlawed Ghost Dance."

William Kunstler called the book the "moving story of a Native American woman who fought her way out of bitterness and despair to find the righteous ways of her ancestors." When she was a child on the reservation, Mary Crow Dog says, "Indian religion was forbidden. Children were punished for praying Indian, men were jailed for taking a sweat bath. Our sacred pipes were broken, our medicine bundles burned or given to museums." For a time, before she set out in search of the native traditions of her people, she conformed to the image of the Christian convert. She remembers being confirmed in a white dress, with veil and candle—"white outside and red inside, the opposite of an apple." What in her story fits in with what you know about the indigenous peoples of North America? What changes your mind about the experience of Native Americans?

Thought Starters: What shaped your early impressions of Native Americans? Have recent readings, movies, or television shows changed the way you think about them?

It is not the big, dramatic things so much that get us down, but just being Indian, trying to hang on to our way of life, language, and values while being surrounded by an alien, more powerful culture. It is being an iyeska, a half-blood, being looked down upon by whites and full-bloods alike. It is being a backwoods girl living in a city, having to rip off stores in order to survive. Most of all it is being a woman. Among Plains tribes, some men think that all a woman is good for is to crawl into the sack with them and mind the children. It compensates for what white society has done to them. They were famous warriors and hunters once, but the buffalo is gone and there is not much rep in putting a can of spam or an occasional rabbit on the table.

As for being warriors, the only way some men can count coup nowa-   *1* days is knocking out another skin's teeth during a barroom fight. In the old days a man made a name for himself by being generous and wise, but now he has nothing to be generous with, no jobs, no money; and as far as our traditional wisdom is concerned, our men are being told by the white missionaries, teachers, and employers that it is merely savage superstition they should get rid of if they want to make it in this world. Men are forced to live away from their children, so that the family can get ADC—Aid to Dependent Children. So some warriors come home drunk and beat up their old ladies in order to work off their frustration. I know where they are coming from. I feel sorry for them, but I feel even sorrier for their women.

To start from the beginning, I am a Sioux from the Rosebud Reservation in South Dakota. I belong to the "Burned Thigh," the Brule Tribe, the Sicangu in our language. Long ago, so the legend goes, a small band of Sioux was surrounded by enemies who set fire to their tipis and the grass around them. They fought their way out of the trap but got their legs burned and in this way acquired their name. The Brules are part of the Seven Sacred Campfires, the seven tribes of the Western Sioux known collectively as Lakota. The Eastern Sioux are called Dakota. The difference between them is their language. It is the same except that where we Lakota pronounce an *L*, the Dakota pronounce a *D*. They cannot pronounce an *L* at all. In our tribe we have this joke: "What is a flat tire in Dakota?" Answer: "A b*d*owout."

The Brule, like all Sioux, were a horse people, fierce riders and raiders, great warriors. Between 1870 and 1880 all Sioux were driven into reservations, fenced in and forced to give up everything that had given meaning to their life—their horses, their hunting, their arms, everything. But under the long snows of despair the little spark of our ancient beliefs and pride kept glowing, just barely sometimes, waiting for a warm wind to blow that spark into a flame again.

My family was settled on the reservation in a small place called He-   *5* Dog, after a famous chief. There are still some He-Dogs living. One, an old lady I knew, lived to be over a hundred years old. Nobody knew when she had been born. She herself had no idea, except that when she came into the world there was no census yet, and Indians had not yet been given Christian first names. Her name was just He-Dog, nothing else. She always told me, "You should have seen me eighty years ago when I was pretty." I have never forgotten her face—nothing but deep cracks and gullies, but beautiful in its own way. At any rate very impressive.

On the Indian side my family was related to the Brave Birds and Fool Bulls. Old Grandpa Fool Bull was the last man to make flutes and play them, the old-style flutes in the shape of a bird's head which had the elk power, the power to lure a young girl into a man's blanket. Fool Bull lived a whole long century, dying in 1976, whittling his flutes almost until his last day. He took me to my first peyote meeting while I was still a kid.

He still remembered the first Wounded Knee, the massacre. He was a young boy at that time, traveling with his father, a well-known medicine man. They had gone to a place near Wounded Knee to take part in a Ghost Dance. They had on their painted ghost shirts which were supposed to make them bulletproof. When they got near Pine Ridge they were stopped by white soldiers, some of them from the Seventh Cavalry, George Custer's old regiment, who were hoping to kill themselves some Indians. The Fool Bull band had to give up their few old muzzle-loaders, bows, arrows, and even knives. They had to put up their tipis in a tight circle, all bunched up, with the wagons on the outside and the soldiers surrounding their camp, watching them closely. It was cold, so cold that the trees were crackling with a loud noise as the frost was splitting their trunks. The people made a fire the following morning to warm themselves and make some coffee and then they noticed a sound beyond the crackling of the trees: rifle fire, salvos making a noise like the ripping apart of a giant blanket; the boom of cannon and the rattling of quick-firing Hotchkiss guns. Fool Bull remembered the grown-ups bursting into tears, the women keening: "They are killing our people, they are butchering them!" It was only two miles or so from where Grandfather Fool Bull stood that almost three hundred Sioux men, women, and children were slaughtered. Later grandpa saw the bodies of the slain, all frozen in ghostly attitudes, thrown into a ditch like dogs. And he saw a tiny baby sucking at his dead mother's breast.

I wish I could tell about the big deeds of some ancestors of mine who fought at the Little Big Horn, or the Rosebud, counting coup during the Grattan or Fetterman battle, but little is known of my family's history before 1880. I hope some of my great-grandfathers counted coup on Custer's men, I like to imagine it, but I just do not know. Our Rosebud people did not play a big part in the battles against generals Crook or Custer. This was due to the policy of Spotted Tail, the all-powerful chief at the time. Spotted Tail had earned his eagle feathers as a warrior, but had been taken East as a prisoner and put in jail. Coming back years later, he said that he had seen the cities of the whites and that a single one of them contained more people than could be found in all the Plains tribes put together, and that every one of the wasičuns' factories could turn out more rifles and bullets in one day than were owned by all the Indians in the country. It was useless, he said, to try to resist the wasičuns. During the critical year of 1876 he had his Indian police keep most of the young men on the reservation, preventing them from joining Sitting Bull, Gall, and Crazy Horse. Some of the young bucks, a few Brave Birds among them, managed to sneak out trying to get to Montana, but nothing much is known. After having been forced into reservations, it was not thought wise to recall such things. It might mean no rations, or worse. For the same reason many in my family turned Christian, letting themselves be "whitemanized." It took many years to reverse this process.

My sister Barbara, who is four years older than me, says she remembers the day when I was born. It was late at night and raining hard amid thunder and lightning. We had no electricity then, just the old-style kerosene lamps with the big reflectors. No bathroom, no tap water, no car. Only a few white teachers had cars. There was one phone in He-Dog, at the trading post. This was not so very long ago, come to think of it. Like most Sioux at that time my mother was supposed to give birth at home, I think, but something went wrong, I was pointing the wrong way, feet first or stuck sideways. My mother was in great pain, laboring for hours, until finally somebody ran to the trading post and called the ambulance. They took her—us—to Rosebud, but the hospital there was not yet equipped to handle a complicated birth, I don't think they had surgery then, so they had to drive mother all the way to Pine Ridge, some ninety miles distant, because there the tribal hospital was bigger. So it happened that I was born among Crazy Horse's people. After my sister Sandra was born the doctors there performed a hysterectomy on my mother, in fact sterilizing her without her permission, which was common at the time, and up to just a few years ago, so that it is hardly worth mentioning. In the opinion of some people, the fewer Indians there are, the better. As Colonel Chivington said to his soldiers: "Kill 'em all, big and small, nits make lice!"

I don't know whether I am a louse under the white man's skin. I hope **10** I am. At any rate I survived the long hours of my mother's labor, the stormy drive to Pine Ridge, and the neglect of the doctors. I am an iyeska, a breed, that's what the white kids used to call me. When I grew bigger they stopped calling me that, because it would get them a bloody nose. I am a small woman, not much over five feet tall, but I can hold my own in a fight, and in a free-for-all with honkies I can become rather ornery and do real damage. I have white blood in me. Often I have wished to be able to purge it out of me. As a young girl I used to look at myself in the mirror, trying to find a clue as to who and what I was. My face is very Indian, and so are my eyes and my hair, but my skin is very light. Always I waited for the summer, for the prairie sun, the Badlands sun, to tan me and make me into a real skin.

The Crow Dogs, the members of my husband's family, have no such problems of identity. They don't need the sun to tan them, they are full-bloods—the Sioux of the Sioux. Some Crow Dog men have faces which make the portrait on the buffalo Indian nickel look like a washed-out white man. They have no shortage of legends. Every Crow Dog seems to be a legend in himself, including the women. They became outcasts in their stronghold at Grass Mountain rather than being whitemanized. They could not be tamed, made to wear a necktie or go to a Christian church. All during the long years when practicing Indian beliefs was forbidden and could be punished with jail, they went right on having their ceremonies, their sweat baths and sacred dances. Whenever a Crow Dog got together with some relatives, such as those equally untamed, unregenerated Iron Shells, Good Lances, Two Strikes, Picket Pins, or Hollow Horn Bears, then you could hear the sound of the can gleska, the drum, telling all the world that a Sioux ceremony was in the making. It took courage and suffering to keep the flame alive, the little spark under the snow.

The first Crow Dog was a well-known chief. On his shield was the design of two circles and two arrowheads for wounds received in battle—two white man's bullets and two Pawnee arrow points. When this first Crow Dog was lying wounded in the snow, a coyote came to warm him and a crow flew ahead of him to show him the way home. His name should be Crow Coyote, but the white interpreter misunderstood it and so they became Crow Dogs. This Crow Dog of old became famous for killing a rival chief, the result of a feud over tribal politics, then driving voluntarily over a hundred miles to get himself hanged at Deadwood, his wife sitting beside him in his buggy; famous also for finding on his arrival that the Supreme Court had ordered him to be freed because the federal government had no jurisdiction over Indian reservations and also because it was no crime for one Indian to kill another. Later, Crow Dog became a leader of the Ghost Dancers, holding out for months in the frozen caves and ravines of the Badlands. So, if my own family lacks history, that of my husband more than makes up for it.

Our land itself is a legend, especially the area around Grass Mountain where I am living now. The fight for our land is at the core of our existence, as it has been for the last two hundred years. Once the land is gone, then we are gone too. The Sioux used to keep winter counts, picture writings on buffalo skin, which told our people's story from year to year. Well, the whole country is one vast winter count. You can't walk a mile without coming to some family's sacred vision hill, to an ancient Sun Dance circle, an old battleground, a place where something worth remembering happened. Mostly a death, a proud death or a drunken death. We are a great people for dying. "It's a good day to die!" that's our old battle cry. But the land with its tar paper shacks and outdoor privies, not one of them straight, but all leaning this way or that way, is also a land to live on, a land for good times and telling jokes and talking of great deeds done in the past. But you can't live forever off the deeds of Sitting Bull or Crazy Horse. You can't wear their eagle feathers, freeload off their legends. You have to make your own legends now. It isn't easy.

The Responsive Reader

1 Mary Crow Dog says, "As a young girl I used to look at myself in the mirror, trying to find a clue as to who and what I was." Who is she? What are key elements in her sense of self?

2 What is her attitude toward Native American men? How does she describe and explain their behavior? How does she contrast their past and their present?

3 What do you learn here about the buried or half-forgotten past that, the author says, was for many years "not thought wise to recall"? What is the author's relation to "our people's story"? What do you learn about customs, traditions, beliefs?

Talking, Listening, Writing

4 Some writers speak for themselves as individuals; others give voice to the experience of many. They speak for a group, for a region, or for a generation. Would you consider Mary Crow Dog an effective and representative spokesperson for Native Americans? Why or why not?

5 Do you think white Americans today should feel guilty about the treatment of Native Americans now and in the past? Why or why not?

6 Are you in favor of people like Mary Crow Dog restoring the forgotten or formerly banned culture and religion of their group?

7 Mary Crow Dog says, "You have to make your own legends now. It isn't easy." What does she mean?

Collaborative Projects

8 How much do you know about the American Indian Movement or other organizations dedicated to recovering the cultural heritage of a group in American society? Are there comparable organizations for Spanish-speaking Americans (Chicanos, Latinos), for blacks or African Americans, or for Asian Americans? Pool your knowledge or relevant background with that of other students in your class.

INTERPRETER OF THE SECOND GENERATION

Sandip Roy-Chowdhury

"When I went to Calcutta, my relatives would think of me so much as American. A foreigner. In America it's always, you are from India. When did you come here?"

In many areas, immigrants from India or Pakistan have become a highly visible and prospering minority community. They profit from English having been a semi-official second language in their home countries, which were long under British rule or influence. An educational system there has often prepared them or their children well for today's world, where science and math education are at a premium. Jhumpha Lahiri is a Pulitzer-Prize winning novelist born in London, where her parents had moved from India. Then very soon her parents moved to the United States.

The interviewer who recorded Lahiri's responses to the following questions is an editor for India Currents, *an English-language magazine of news and comment for immigrants from India and their families. A more extended version of this interview was first published in* India Currents *for November 2003. After a brief biographical introduction, the interviewer recorded the novelist's thoughts about her writing and her life, calling her "very much the second generation writer."*

Much in Lahiri's fiction draws on her own experience as a wanderer between two worlds. Like Lahiri, Gogol, who is the protagonist or central figure of her book The Namesake *is born to parents from India and grows up in the United States. How does Lahiri define her identity "between the cracks of two cultures"?*

Thought Starters: Do you know people who have maintained "dual citizenship" in two different national or cultural traditions?

When were you aware that that was something different about your parents?
From a very early age. In school my friends would say their parents met in college or at a high school dance. And I was always aware my parents had married in a very different way. And when people asked me: "Oh, did your parents have an arranged marriage?" in a very bewildered and mildly horrified tone of voice, I was aware it was regarded as a sort of barbaric, unthinkable concept.

There are still people who feel, oh my God, it's such an exotic old-fashioned sort of idea and it's hard to explain that it's very much a living, thriving tradition. It's a way of being married as opposed to the romantic falling in love way that also exists in India.

At the same time, these were my parents and it seemed so normal and I knew so many people whom I was close to and loved who had gotten married this way. So I felt both very protective and defensive of my parents and their tradition and also sort of worried that this might happen to me and that might not be something I wanted.

When your parents moved to Cambridge, MA and then to Rhode Island in the late '60s, what was the community like?

From the stories I hear, it's similar to the world I depict in the novel. My mother was always wandering around the streets of Harvard in Central Square pushing me in my stroller and every time she would see someone who looked Bengali there was this instant "who are you, where are you from, let's be friends." They sort of gathered a community that way literally from spotting each other on the streets. There were enough Bengalis to have a growing circle of friends over the years and my parents are still tied to many of those people, which I think is really remarkable.

But in the book, Gogol, as he grows older, is annoyed by the constant weekend parties with other Bengalis. He describes how his 14th birthday is just an excuse for his parents to have friends from three states visit and cook food, make sandesh out of ricotta cheese and play cards and chat while the bored kids watch television.

It's true I was always of two minds. On one hand I found these get-togethers tedious and monotonous and not what I would choose to do with my weekends every weekend. It was very clear it was very much about the parents and their need to really relax on the weekends. When you are a foreigner and still getting used to the culture, you are walking a fine line. The parties on the weekend allowed them to forget all that and just speak in Bengali and eat food and celebrate in a way that they weren't allowed to on a daily basis.

Once my parents moved to Rhode Island they were still crossing state borders to attend these parties—it was a huge priority in their lives, especially for my mother who was more isolated since she didn't work for a long time.

At one point Gogol goes home and his father starts talking to Manhattanites about how you have to be careful where you park in their quiet suburban towns and Gogol is irritated by his parents' "perpetual fear of disaster." For me that was a telling moment of how immigrants, no matter how long they live here, never quite feel safe.

Yes, absolutely. I have observed that with my parents. Here is one of the things that tipped me off early. None of my friends' parents locked their doors. We grew up in a safe town, a sleepy neighborhood, and I'd go to my friends' homes and their front doors were open and back doors were open. My parents were always locking the door, locking the garage, closing the windows, locking the windows every night, and I think it's just a sense of not feeling on firm ground. And you want to feel protected somehow.

Why have you said you inherited a sense of exile from your parents?

I think that I never feel fully part of the world I was brought up in. My parents were always very resistant in many ways to living in America and missed India so much and had a lot of misgivings about their lives here. It was hard for me to think of myself as fully American. I thought it would be very much a betrayal of my parents and what they believed and who they are. My parents feel less foreign now than they did 30 years ago but they still feel like outsiders.

How then did you feel when you experienced your parents on trips to India? How were they transformed? Gogol is amazed as his mother roams around Kolkata with ease, shopping at New Market, going to films with her friends.

My parents turned into different people. It was like those weekend parties, but even more. It was truly a transformation. They were so much more relaxed, so much more at ease and I felt there was happiness that they were deprived of in their normal lives and that they could finally connect to. When I think of it now and I try to imagine what it would be like to see my parents and my sister once every two or three years, I am amazed at what my parents dealt with.

When I was growing up, the separation felt so great, so insurmountable. There was no e-mail. Phone lines were dreadful and so expensive, and every call from India was bad news. The world seemed so much more vast and so much more difficult to navigate.

But does that put a weird pressure on people like you, the second generation, to see your parents so palpably happy in India and realizing that in some ways they gave up this happiness for a better life for you?

This was one of the things that really separated me from my parents. I could try to sympathize, empathize the best that I could, but the fact of the matter is that my connection to India will never be what my parents' is. I always feel I both belong and don't belong there. But the older I've gotten the more I realize I do belong more to America than India just because I have spent so much more of my life here.

But I have often wondered why did my parents really come here. So many of these Bengali immigrants don't really come to America for a life and death situation. Most of them have not escaped excruciating war, poverty, or political persecution that many other immigrants have experienced. Not to say their experiences were not painful, but my parents were so ambivalent and so guilt-ridden about coming here. That's because they came essentially for opportunity and a better life. But my parents could easily have stayed in Kolkata and raised a family and had a nice home. Coming to America was a choice to have a better life for themselves and their children, thereby sacrificing connections to their families.

But though you now feel more American than Indian, are you surprised that the first stories you wrote were set in India? I read you wrote your first novel when you were seven. Was that set in India?

(Laughs) I called them novels but they weren't very long. They were just stories about girls having various adventures in boarding schools. Some of them were with supernatural powers.

The first stories I wrote from *Interpreter of Maladies* were set in India. But before that I wrote many other stories I was not happy with. Maybe it was the distance that allowed me to write about India. Often, for a writer the hardest things to write about are the things that are closest because you have to be objective. It's a greater challenge for me to tell a story like the one in *The Namesake*.

Your work is so tied to ethnicity and roots. Yet your husband is Guatemalan-born of Greek heritage. What do you think of roots and knowing where you come from when you look at your son?

I have never felt a strong affiliation with any nation or ethnic group. I always felt between the cracks of two cultures. So much of it was about where I was and who was viewing me. When I went to Calcutta my relatives would think of me so much as American. A foreigner. In America it's always, you are Indian, when did you come here.

I hope for my son that it will be something he may be confused about for a time but that he will accept it and just understand that this is what can happen and it's neither a good thing nor a bad thing to be a little mixed up.

But you have held on to your roots. Though you never grew up in Kolkata, you have retained your mother tongue—Bengali.

I don't know, but it must be hardwired. When I first saw my son I didn't say: "How cute!" It just came out in Bengali. That's the language of tenderness for me.

The Responsive Reader

1 Lahiri is an alert observer of *changing trends* in ethnic communities. Previous generations of immigrants often stayed for a time "with their own kind" in ethnic neighborhoods before they began to move on to blend into the larger society. To judge from this article and your own observation, is the trend for staying in an ethnic neighborhood with strong ties to the past stronger with recent waves of immigration?

2 Lahiri understands the *psychology* of being an outsider. According to Lahiri, after thirty years in this country some Americans still feel or behave in some ways like foreigners. Is being a foreigner in part a state of mind?

3 How strong was the *presence of the past*? Lahiri observed that on return trips to India her parents turned into different people. How and why? How did their behavior and their attitudes change? Would you describe what moves them as nostalgia, or is it more than that?

4 Lahiri testifies to the *divided loyalties* of a second generation. She says she "was always of two minds" when finding herself at the crossroads of the two cultures. Where or how did or does she still feel the strong pull of

her parents' culture? What are features that make her different from her parents' generation? For you, what makes her truly "second generation"?

Talking, Listening, Writing

5 Millions of foreigners have become Americans. Do you think there is a crossover point when someone from a foreign country ceases to be a foreigner? Where would you mark the line? What revealing signs would you look for?

6 When does an original first language become a second language? Language is a large part of national identity and of our own personal identity. Lahiri and her parents speak Bengali, one of the major national languages of India, as their first language. Do you think there is a crossover point when for a foreign-born or foreign-descended American American English ceases to be a second language? Where would you mark the line?

BORN AMONG THE BORN AGAIN

Garrison Keillor

"In a town where everyone was either Lutheran or Catholic, we were neither one. We were Sanctified Brethren, a sect so tiny that nobody but us and God knew about it."

The following selection, although first published in a 1985 collection of his bittersweet tales and reminiscences, is part of Keillor's long-lasting and ongoing love affair with his heartland audience and others suffering from nostalgia for a more innocent small-town America.

Garrison Keillor became legendary in the Midwest as the host of A Prairie Home Companion, *a live radio show originating in St. Paul, Minnesota, and giving audiences a nostalgic mix of old-style storytelling, savvy appeals to local pride, the sentimental songs of barbershop quintets and crooners, and homespun humor delighting in the quirks and foibles of family and neighbors. Keillor is a master at creating a nostalgic vision of a small-town American past removed from the upheavals and paranoias of the twentieth century. He collected many of the stories he told on his show in* Lake Wobegon Days *(1985), explaining that many were "true stories from my childhood, dressed . . . up as fiction." He said in an interview in* Time *that he looked to the stories he heard in his family as a child "as giving a person some sense of place," reassuring us "that we were not just chips floating on the waves, that in some way we were meant to be here, and had a history. That we had standing."*

In recent years, Keillor has taken his show on the road, showing an uncanny knack for relating to the local subculture—its history, its folk music, its in-jokes—in places as far apart as San Jose, California, and Fairbanks, Alaska, or New York City, New York. In the selection that follows, Keillor replays a classic story of growing up: A youngster growing up in a family with strong religious views (or other strong beliefs) starts to rebel against having to be "different" from his peers. How much in this story shows Keillor's homespun sense of humor? How much is serious or thought-provoking?

Thought Starters: What has shaped your impressions of small-town or back-country American life? Do you share the nostalgia for a simpler small-town life?

. . . In a town where everyone was either Lutheran or Catholic, we were neither one. We were Sanctified Brethren, a sect so tiny that nobody but us and God knew about it, so when kids asked what I was, I just said Protestant. It was too much to explain, like having six toes. You would rather keep your shoes on. *1*

Grandpa Cotten was once tempted toward Lutheranism by a preacher who gave a rousing sermon on grace that Grandpa heard as a young man while taking Aunt Esther's dog home who had chased a Model T across town. He sat down on the church steps and listened to the voice boom out the open windows until he made up his mind to go in and unite with the truth, but he took one look from the vestibule and left. "He was dressed up like the Pope of Rome," said Grandpa, "and the altar and paintings and the gold candlesticks—my gosh, it was just a big show. And he was reading the whole darn thing off a page, like an actor."

Jesus said, "Where two or three are gathered together in my name, there am I in the midst of them," and the Brethren believed that was enough. We met in Uncle Al and Aunt Flo's bare living room, with plain folding chairs arranged facing in toward the middle. No clergyman in a black smock. No organ or piano, for that would make one person too prominent. No upholstery—it would lead to complacence. No picture of Jesus—He was in our Hearts. The faithful sat down at the appointed hour and waited for the Spirit to move one of them to speak or to pray or to give out a hymn from our Little Flock hymnal. No musical notation, for music must come from the heart and not off a page. We sang the texts to a tune that fit the meter, of the many tunes we all knew. The idea of reading a prayer was sacrilege to us—"If a man can't remember what he wants to say to God, let him sit down and think a little harder," Grandpa said.

"There's the Lord's Prayer," said Aunt Esther meekly. We were sitting on the porch after Sunday dinner. Esther and Harvey were visiting from Minneapolis and had attended Lake Wobegon Lutheran, she having turned Lutheran when she married him, a subject that was never brought up in our family.

"You call that prayer? Sitting and reciting like a bunch of school-children?"

Harvey cleared his throat and turned to me and smiled, "Speaking of school, how are you doing?" he asked.

There was a lovely silence in the Brethren assembled on Sunday morning as we waited for the Spirit. Either the Spirit was moving someone to speak who was taking his sweet time or else the Spirit was playing a wonderful joke on us and letting us sit, or perhaps silence was the point of it. We sat listening to rain on the roof, distant traffic, a radio playing from across the street, kids whizzing by on bikes, dogs barking, as we waited for the Spirit to inspire us. It was like sitting on the porch with your family, when nobody feels that they have to make talk. So quiet in church. Minutes drifted by in silence that was sweet to us. The old Regulator clock ticked, the rain stopped, and the room changed light as the sun broke through—shafts of brilliant sun through the windows and motes of dust falling through it—the smell of clean clothes and floor wax and wine and the fresh bread of Aunt Flo, which was Christ's body given for us. Jesus in our midst, who loved us. So peaceful; and we loved each other, too. I thought perhaps the Spirit was leading me to say that, but I was just a boy, and children were supposed to keep still.

And my affections were not pure. They were tainted with a sneaking admiration of Catholics—Catholic Christmas, Easter, the Living Rosary, and the Blessing of the Animals, all magnificent. Everything we did was plain, but they were regal—especially the Feast Day of Saint Francis, which they did right out in the open, a feast for the eyes. Cows, horses, some pets, right on the church lawn. The turmoil, animals bellowing and barking and clucking and a cat scheming how to escape and suddenly leaping out of the girl's arms who was holding on tight, the cat dashing through the crowd, dogs straining at the leash, and the ocarina band of third graders playing a song, and the great calm of the sisters, and the flags, and the Knights of Columbus decked out in their handsome black suits—the whole thing was gorgeous. I stared at it until my eyes almost fell out, and then I wished it would go on much longer.

"Christians," my Uncle Al used to say, "do not go in for show," referring to the Catholics. We were sanctified by the blood of the Lord; therefore we were saints, like Saint Francis, but we didn't go in for feasts or ceremonies, involving animals or not. We went in for sitting, all nineteen of us, in Uncle Al and Aunt Flo's living room on Sunday morning and having a plain meeting and singing hymns in our poor thin voices, while not far away the Catholics were whooping it up. I wasn't allowed inside Our Lady, of course, but if the Blessing of the Animals on the Feast Day of Saint Francis was any indication, Lord, I didn't know but what they had elephants in there and acrobats. I sat in our little group and envied them for the splendor and gorgeousness, as we tried to sing without even so much as a harmonica to give us the pitch. Hymns, Uncle Al said, didn't have to be sung perfect, because God looks on the heart, and if you are In The Spirit, then all praise is good.

The Brethren, also known as The Saints Gathered in the Name of   10
Christ Jesus, who met in the living room were all related to each other and raised in the Faith from infancy except Brother Mel, who was rescued from a life of drunkenness, saved as a brand from the burning, a drowning sailor, a sheep on the hillside, whose immense red nose testified to his previous condition. I envied his amazing story of how he came to be with us. Born to godly parents, Mel left home at fifteen and joined the Navy. He sailed to distant lands in a submarine and had exciting experiences while traveling the downward path, which led him finally to the Union Gospel Mission in Minneapolis, where he heard God's voice "as clear as my voice speaking to you." He was twenty-six, he slept under bridges and in abandoned buildings, he drank two quarts of white muscatel every day, and then God told him that he must be born again, and so he was, and became the new Mel, except for his nose.

Except for his nose, Mel Burgess looked like any forty-year-old Brethren man: sober, preferring dark suits, soft-spoken, tending toward girth. His nose was what made you look twice: battered, swollen, very red with tiny purplish lines, it looked ancient and dead on his otherwise fairly handsome face, the souvenir of what he had been saved from, the "Before" of his "Before . . . and After" advertisement for being born again.

For me, there was nothing before. I was born among the born-again. This living room so hushed, the Brethren in their customary places on folding chairs (the comfortable ones were put away on Sunday morning) around the end table draped with a white cloth and the glass of wine and loaf of bread (unsliced), was as familiar to me as my mother and father, before whom there was nobody. I had always been here.

. . . So one Sunday our family traipsed over to a restaurant . . . that a friend of Dad's had recommended, Phil's House of Good Food. The waitress pushed two tables together and we sat down and studied the menu. My mother blanched at the prices. A chicken dinner went for $2.50, the roast beef for $3.75. "It's a nice place," Dad said, multiplying the five of us times $2.50. "I'm not so hungry, I guess," he said. "Maybe I'll just have soup." We weren't restaurantgoers—"Why pay good money for food you could make better at home?" was Mother's philosophy—so we weren't at all sure about restaurant customs. For example, could a person who had been seated in a restaurant simply get up and walk out? Would it be proper? Would it be *legal*?

The waitress came and stood by Dad. "Can I get you something from the bar?" she said. Dad blushed a deep red. The question seemed to imply that he looked like a drinker.

"No," he whispered, as if she had offered to take off her clothes and   *15* dance on the table.

Then another waitress brought a tray of glasses to a table of four couples next to us. "Martini," she said, setting the drink down, "whiskey sour, whiskey sour, Manhattan, whiskey sour, gin and tonic, martini, whiskey sour."

"Ma'am? Something from the bar?" Mother looked at her in disbelief.

Suddenly the room changed for us. Our waitress looked hardened, rough, cheap; across the room a woman laughed obscenely, "Haw, haw, haw"; the man with her lit a cigarette and blew a cloud of smoke; a swearword drifted out from the kitchen like a whiff of urine; even the soft lighting seemed suggestive, diabolical. To be seen in such a place on the Lord's Day—*what had we done?*

My mother rose from her chair.

"We can't stay. I'm sorry," Dad told the waitress. We all got up and   *20* put on our coats. Everyone in the restaurant had a good long look at us. A bald little man in a filthy white shirt emerged from the kitchen, wiping his hands. "Folks? Something wrong?" he said.

"We're in the wrong place," Mother told him. Mother always told the truth, or something close to it.

"This is *humiliating*," I said out on the sidewalk. "I feel like a *leper* or something. Why do we always have to make such a big production out of everything? Why can't we be like regular people?"

She put her hand on my shoulder. "Be not conformed to this world," she said. I knew the rest by heart ". . . but be ye transformed by the renewing of your mind, that ye may prove what is that good and acceptable and perfect will of God."

"Where we gonna eat?" Phyllis asked.

"We'll find someplace reasonable," said Mother, and we walked six 25
blocks across the river and found a lunch counter and ate sloppy joes (called Maid-Rites) for fifteen cents apiece. They did not agree with us, and we were aware of them all afternoon through prayer meeting and Young People's.

The Responsive Reader

1 How does Keillor take you into the Brethren's world of attitudes and beliefs? What would you stress in trying to initiate an unsympathetic listener into their lifestyle, their way of thinking and feeling? (What role does Brother Mel play in this story? What does he contribute to your understanding of the family's religion?)

2 For the author, what was the appeal of the strange and different Catholic tradition?

3 The story leads up to a high point—to a climactic incident that dramatizes the boy's feelings about his background, about his family. What *are* the boy's feelings? Where do you first become aware of them? Do you sympathize with him?

Talking, Listening, Writing

4 Religion often seems a taboo subject in our society. Why? Courts ban displays of the Christmas scene on public property as well as prayers in public schools or at commencement ceremonies. Why? Where do you stand?

5 Have you ever felt the urge to speak up on behalf of a group considered different or alien or undesirable in our society? Speak or write in defense of the group.

6 Has the awareness of being "different" played a role in your life or in the life of someone you know well? (Or have you ever worried about being too much the *same* as everyone else?)

Collaborative Projects

7 Is there a "religious revival" among the young? What kind of religious ideas or religious affiliations appeal to young people today? Help organize an informal poll of your classmates that would shed light on these questions.

GROWING UP HIPPIE

Adriana Barton

"Growing up in my family was a trip."

A generation of Americans grew up as children of the counterculture. How did the experience shape their outlook and their lives?

The cultural revolution of the hippies or "flower children" had its roots in the movement of protest against the war in Vietnam. Early dropouts from the mainstream culture had seen friends shipped backed in boxes from a war they did not believe in or support. The antiwar rebellion merged with an alienation from the consumerism of a materialistic society and the dead conformity of suburbia. On campuses and at Grateful Dead concerts, tie-dyed shirts, sandals, long hair, and pony tails for males became a common sight. Some joined communes or were part of homegrown back-to-the-land movement to grow simple food without toxic additives. They explored their affinity with indigenous cultures closer to nature and to natural ways living and of raising children.

Although much ridiculed in the mainstream media, the hippie movement acquired a large following among American youth. Its heroes were legendary musical performers from Joan Baez and Jimmy Hendrix to Janis Joplin or John Lennon and Yoko Ono. These became icons of American popular culture and eventually of the youth culture of the world.

Slowly the early phase of youth festivals and psychedelic happenings faded into the dead-end realities of alienated lives. Major figures overdosed and disappeared from the scene. A conservative backlash produced the war on drugs that sent tens of thousands for much of their lives to overcrowded jails. However, writers like Ariana Barton see a lasting legacy of the youth movement in society's openness to less uptight, less emotionally starved alternative lifestyles or the search for more people-friendly urban environments. Barton is a journalist based in Vancouver in British Columbia who covers art, architecture, and changing cultures. She says she has jammed with musicians in Brazil and Cuba, and she traveled in the Islamic Arab world after 9/11. Her testimony was first printed in the Canadian magazine Elm Street *for April 2003 and reprinted in the* Utne Reader.

Thought Starters: Some youngsters adopt the values and conform to the lifestyle of their parents. Others go through a stage of adolescent rebellion when they reject much of their parents' world. Which do you think was more typical of your generation?

My mother and her friends considered themselves artists, not hippies. But to everyone else they were flower children. Maybe it was the Mexican and Indian peasant clothes they wore—even on formal occasions like wed-dings—or their childlike belief in the magical powers of plant foods: gold-enseal for flu and pickled plums for sore throats. My mom even tried to cure my vision problems with eye exercises ("place your palms on closed lids and visualize spirals"), until a teacher persuaded her that it was time to get me glasses.

The counterculture was a strange world to be born into. Or, more specifically, to fall into—in the arms of my yogi/mathematician father, who delivered me without benefit of medical training. (I was the second of my mother's four home births.) Like many hippies, my father had led a no-madic existence. In 1965 and 1966, he was featured in a series of *Toronto Star* articles documenting his spiritual journey overland to India in a vintage Cadillac and describing his goal to found what the newspaper called an "ashran." Sadly, he died of cancer when I was a year old.

After his death, my 26-year-old mother bundled up my older sister and me and hit the road. We shared a ride from Toronto to Vancouver, where we spent a winter near Kitsilano's hippie haven, now yuppified West Fourth Avenue. Then she piled us into an old truck rigged with a camper and headed for Mexico. En route, she and her new boyfriend, a dropout from Berkeley, held "spontaneous music workshops" for patients with mental disabilities.

In the villages of Chiapas, Mom went native. She ground corn by hand to make tortillas and embroidered her own designs on blouses, much to the amusement of the Mayan women. She and her boyfriend held jam sessions with Mayan musicians, a radical activity for gringos back then. "What we were doing was revolutionary," she recalled recently. "We were part of the revolution!" One of her boyfriend's goals was to set up a Mayan-run radio station. He succeeded after we left him there when I was 3.

Mom returned to Ottawa to live with my future stepfather, Russell. He was one of the men behind the Wasteland, a coffeehouse that drew counterculture heroes like Bruce Cockburn and John and Yoko. Drugs were surely in the background of this scene, but my strangely puritanical parents avoided them. They didn't live in a commune, indulge in group sex, or drop LSD. The only hydroponic thing in our household was the com-mercial alfalfa sprout farm in our basement—15 bathtubs full of seeds that I watered in return for an allowance.

My assumptions about life, from relationships to morality, were shaped by these people, who quoted Zen Buddhism and traded tips on building yurts—those circular Mongolian tents that were a hippie obses-sion. Though less notorious than their Haight-Ashbury counterparts, my mother's crowd also represented an iconoclastic and influential radical ethos. They were spiritual seekers, committed to personal and social trans-formation and abstemious to the point of asceticism. Their life choices were part of a continuing social experiment, from earnest meditation practices to a willingness to go on welfare rather than compromise their values. As their own purse-lipped parents would say, "That's all fine and good for them, but what about the children?" Nobody knew how offspring of the Age of Aquarius would turn out. Well, I do.

From childhood embarrassment to adolescent conformism, it was hard not to rebel against my parents' free-wheeling ways. A week before starting first grade, I begged my parents to buy me a lunch-box: a spanking new plastic one with a picture of Sesame Street or Barbie, the kind every other child in school would bring. For days I lobbied, emphasizing that it came with a Thermos, but my mom and stepfather couldn't understand why I wanted such a tacky, commercial thing. On the morning of the big day, they presented me with a plain cardboard box with a thick wire for a handle. Inside was a jar of milk, an apple, and a whole-wheat sandwich. Pleased with their ingenuity, my parents beamed. I was crestfallen. At noon hour I sat in a corner, trying to avoid the stares and snickers.

Desperate to be normal, I rarely invited kids over. They would see the outboard motor stored in plain view in our dining room.

Like many adult children of hippies, by the time I hit university I had turned to therapy to try to make sense of my family and to adapt to main-stream society. My current therapist is an expert on perfectionism. He be-lieves people develop this trait as children in the attempt to create order out of a chaotic environment. For me, this took the form of a boot-camp ap-proach to life: As a 12-year-old, I kept color-coded logs of when I exer-cised, what I ate, and how much I practiced my cello, down to the minute.

In high school, I would turn down dates because boys might interfere with my regimen as a classical musician-in-training. By 16, I earned a mu-sic scholarship to a prestigious American university. At 22, I had already performed with an orchestra at Carnegie Hall. But raised to value creativ-ity and originality above all, I was devastated when it dawned on me that I had never played for pleasure or made my own music. So I dropped the cello entirely. This may seem like a waste, but for 17 years the rigid, high-performance world of classical music had provided a refuge of structure and consistency so lacking at home.

One had only to see my bedroom in high school to get the picture: It was as orderly as that of a Victorian spinster, a beacon of neatness amid the piles of paper strewn about every surface of the dining room, the mess of my Mom's in-home painting studio, and the crumbs ground into the threadbare antique Chinese carpet my grandmother had left us. My com-pulsive tidiness was a form of rebellion, a goad to a disorganized mother who had fought hard to escape the oppressive spotlessness and formality of her own privileged childhood. The intergenerational pattern continues.

Every stick of furniture in my parents' house was secondhand, long before recycling became hip; so were my decidedly unfashionable clothes, mostly from Salvation Army thrift stores. To this day, my mother is more likely to invest in pottery and paintings than something as banal as a new couch. Buying furniture seems so suburban.

I recently bought a mattress, one with coils and a box spring—something no one in my family has ever owned. Before it was delivered, I was plagued with unease. Money wasn't the issue; as a magazine editor I can afford it. Rather, a vague sense of imprinted guilt crept in, accompanied by images of distended coils rusting in a landfill. What if everyone on the planet had a mattress like this? Where would all the mattresses go when people had finished with them?

As I grew up, food was imbued with powers of good and evil. Sugar was excessively yin and naturally verboten, but seemingly innocent foods were equally suspect. Potatoes, along with tomatoes, peppers, and eggplant, were found to be in the same family as deadly nightshade and therefore viewed as toxic.

Sugar became my drug of choice. Today I can mainline up to three packs a day of Werther's Originals, those diabolical butterscotch candies. I swear off them for months at a time but, like a woman obsessed, I inevitably fall off the wagon. Last night I enjoyed a dinner of brown rice, tofu, and salad—followed by a bag of licorice and jujubes.

Living with hippie parents wasn't all bad. Despite our modest means, I grew up in an exceptionally rich cultural environment. My mother painted exuberantly and my community-minded stepfather funded multicultural arts groups as a bureaucrat and taught fiction writing. I was surrounded by sculptors, poets, musicians, and intellectuals. My accomplishments as musician, writer, adventurer, and friend are directly related to the values I grew up with.

At least one study bears this out. In the early 1990s, after many hippies' kids had graduated from high school, Thomas Weisner, an anthropologist at the University of California, Los Angeles, reported that "a strong parental commitment to one's family lifestyle can contribute positively to children's school achievement." This was certainly true for my older sister and me, who were placed in enriched and gifted classes in grade school.

Being a hippie kid was cool in some ways. While classmates zoned in front of the idiot box (mostly off-limits to me), I spent my free time crocheting Rasta-style hats, playing make-believe, and pounding clay. By 13, I was sewing my own clothes and working my way through my parents' boxes of books, from *Siddhartha* to *The Joy of Sex*. And whatever my siblings and I might say today about the care we got from that free-spirited generation, we always knew we were loved.

It helps to remember that my mother was widowed with two kids when she was barely an adult herself. She has long since finished growing up. Today, she is a confident woman whose paintings are shown in prominent galleries and purchased for major art collections. I now turn to her with creative dilemmas, as well as issues ranging from office politics to my sex life. My mother and my stepfather have each come to resemble the parent I craved and now aspire to be: warm, attentive, inspiring, and actively engaged in the outside world.

The Responsive Reader

1   What features of the counterculture did the author's life with her parents illustrate? Which seem familiar? Which seem striking or unexpected? What would you include in a *capsule portrait* of the author's mother as a child of the "Age of Aquarius"?

2   What were major *waystations* in her mother's "nomadic" life? What was the lure or attraction of each?

3   Adolescents may go through a phase when they rebel against the world of their parents and the roles they are expected to play. They sometimes *compensate* by going to an opposite extreme. How does Barton's story follow this pattern? What are key examples?

4   On the other side of the ledger, what does the author value in her childhood experience? What does she value most? What had the most lasting influence on her adult life

5   What *allusions* to the era of the counterculture do you recognize? For which can classmates offer help? Which do you have to track or look up? (Can you explain *Age of Aquarius, Haight Ashbury, Zen, jam sessions?*)

Talking, Listening, Writing

6   As a whole, does this account confirm or challenge familiar stereotypes?

7   Do you think the world of artists and musicians is basically a different world from that of people in the business world?

8   Have you or people you know well ever been "desperate to be normal"? Have you ever tried hard to "blend in"?

9   Spiritual descendants of the counterculture flock to events like the million-souls Love Parade in Berlin. They find time to teach pro bono in the jails or befriend the homeless or the poor. Have you encountered or observed survivals of the commitments or alternative lifestyles of the counterculture?

MERICANS

Sandra Cisneros

Young Americans encounter tradition-bound Old Country relatives and culture tourists from the more recent past.

After the publication of her recent Caramelo, *Sandra Cisneros was invited as an outstanding Mexican American author to the 2004 Festival American in France. When an interviewer asked her if the American dream was still alive, she said that her own American dream had been to have her own house and time to write. However, when her father had immigrated from Mexico, his dream had been to buy the biggest and best television set possible. Today, Cisneros said, the immigrants hope to find at least a job, any job, paying enough so that their families don't starve to death.*

Like the young travelers in the following short story, millions of young Americans come from a Spanish-speaking background. Their families may have had ties with the culture of Mexico or Puerto Rico or Cuba. They may have grown up speaking or hearing Spanish and learned English as a second language. Sandra Cisneros was born of a Mexican father and a Mexican American mother in Chicago. She became one of the country's best-known Chicana—*short for* Mexicana—*authors. For her many readers, the stories in her collection* The House on Mango Street *bring to life the Spanish-speaking neighborhoods that are enclaves in many American cities. The following story is from a later collection,* Woman Hollering Creek *(1991). The story focuses on Mexican American children visiting their grandmother in Mexico. How American are they? How Mexican are they? La Virgen de Guadalupe is the Virgin Mary of Guadalupe, at whose church the grandmother prays. The PRI is the traditional Mexican ruling party, often criticized by progressives for having abandoned the original ideals of the Mexican revolution.*

Thought Starters: What do you know about Hispanic or Latino Americans from sources other than TV or movies? Does your community have a barrio? Does it have Spanish-language stations or publications?

We're waiting for the awful grandmother who is inside dropping pesos into *la ofrenda* box before the altar to La Divina Providencia. Lighting votive candles and genuflecting. Blessing herself and kissing her thumb. Running a crystal rosary between her fingers. Mumbling, mumbling, mumbling.

There are so many prayers and promises and thanks-be-to-God to be given in the name of the husband and the sons and the only daughter who never attend mass. It doesn't matter. Like La Virgen de Guadalupe, the aw-

1

ful grandmother intercedes on their behalf. For the grandfather who hasn't believed in anything since the first PRI elections. For my father, El Periquín, so skinny he needs his sleep. For Auntie Light-skin, who only a few hours before was breakfasting on brain and goat tacos after dancing all night in the pink zone. For Uncle Fat-face, the blackest of the black sheep—*Always remember your Uncle Fat-face in your prayers.* And Uncle Baby—*You go for me, Mamá— God listens to you.*

The awful grandmother has been gone a long time. She disappeared behind the heavy leather outer curtain and the dusty velvet inner. We must stay near the church entrance. We must not wander over to the balloon and punch-ball vendors. We cannot spend our allowance on fried cookies or Familia Burrón comic books or those clear cone-shaped suckers that make everything look like a rainbow when you look through them. We cannot run off and have our picture taken on the wooden ponies. We must not climb the steps up the hill behind the church and chase each other through the cemetery. We have promised to stay right where the awful grandmother left us until she returns.

There are those walking to church on their knees. Some with fat rags tied around their legs and others with pillows, one to kneel on, and one to flop ahead. There are women with black shawls crossing and uncrossing themselves. There are armies of penitents carrying banners and flowered arches while musicians play tinny trumpets and tinny drums.

La Virgen de Guadalupe is waiting inside behind a plate of thick glass. 5 There's also a gold crucifix bent crooked as a mesquite tree when someone once threw a bomb. La Virgen de Guadalupe on the main altar because she's a big miracle, the crooked crucifix on a side altar because that's a little miracle.

But we're outside in the sun. My big brother Junior hunkered against the wall with his eyes shut. My little brother Keeks running around in circles.

Maybe and most probably my little brother is imagining he's a flying feather dancer, like the ones we saw swinging high up from a pole on the Virgin's birthday. I want to be a flying feather dancer too, but when he circles past me he shouts, "I'm a B-Fifty-two bomber, you're a German," and shoots me with an invisible machine gun. I'd rather play flying feather dancers, but if I tell my brother this, he might not play with me at all.

"*Girl.* We can't play with a *girl.*" Girl. It's my brothers' favorite insult now instead of "sissy." "You *girl*," they yell at each other. "You throw that ball like a *girl.*"

I've already made up my mind to be a German when Keeks swoops past again, this time yelling "I'm Flash Gordon. You're Ming the Merciless and the Mud People." I don't mind being Ming the Merciless, but I don't like being the Mud People. Something wants to come out of the corners of my eyes, but I don't let it. Crying is what *girls* do.

I leave Keeks running around in circles—"I'm the Lone Ranger, 10 you're Tonto." I leave Junior squatting on his ankles and go look for the awful grandmother.

Why do churches smell like the inside of an ear? Like incense and the dark and candles in blue glass? And why does holy water smell of tears? The awful grandmother makes me kneel and fold my hands. The ceiling high and everyone's prayers bumping up there like balloons.

If I stare at the eyes of the saints long enough, they move and wink at me, which makes me a sort of saint too. When I get tired of winking saints, I count the awful grandmother's mustache hairs while she prays for Uncle Old, sick from the worm, and Auntie Cuca, suffering from a life of troubles that left half her face crooked and the other half sad.

There must be a long, long list of relatives who haven't gone to church. The awful grandmother knits the names of the dead and the living into one long prayer fringed with the grandchildren born in that barbaric country with its barbarian ways.

I put my weight on one knee, then the other, and when they both grow fat as a mattress of pins, I slap them each awake. *Micaela, you may wait outside with Alfredito and Enrique.* The awful grandmother says it all in Spanish, which I understand when I'm paying attention. "What?" I say, though it's neither proper nor polite. "What?" which the awful grandmother hears as "¿*Guat?*" But she only gives me a look and shoves me toward the door.

After all that dust and dark, the light from the plaza makes me squinch   15
my eyes like if I just came out of the movies. My brother Keeks is drawing squiggly lines on the concrete with a wedge of glass and the heel of his shoe. My brother Junior squatting against the entrance, talking to a lady and man.

They're not from here. Ladies don't come to church dressed in pants. And everybody knows men aren't supposed to wear shorts.

"¿*Quieres chicle?*" the lady asks in a Spanish too big for her mouth.

"*Gracias.*" The lady gives him a whole handful of gum for free, little cellophane cubes of Chiclets, cinnamon and aqua and the white ones that don't taste like anything but are good for pretend buck teeth.

"*Por favor,*" says the lady. "¿*Un foto?*" pointing to her camera.

"*Sí.*"   20

She's so busy taking Junior's picture, she doesn't notice me and Keeks.

"Hey Michele, Keeks. You guys want gum?"

"But you speak English!"

"Yeah," my brother says, "we're Mericans."

We're Mericans, we're Mericans, and inside the awful grandmother   25
prays.

The Responsive Reader

1 What makes the "awful grandmother" in the story the representative of the Old Country culture and Old Country ways? What do you learn

about her religion—about the church where she worships, about saints and miracles, and about her prayers? Why are there so many "don'ts" in what she tells her grandchildren? Why does she think of Americans as barbarians?

2   Does Cisneros intend the American tourists at the end of the story to be stereotypically American? How does Micaela see them? Is she making fun of them—if so, why? (Does the tourist lady get any credit for having studied Spanish?)

3   Like many young Americans, Micaela and her brothers are somewhere on the spectrum that runs from the Old Country culture to stereotypically all-American ways. Where on the spectrum would you place them? How "Merican" are they? What is revealing about the names they call each other, their play, their fantasy world, their manners?

Talking, Listening, Writing

4   Students with a Hispanic or Latino background point out that part of the traditional culture is the requirement to be respectful toward your elders. Do you think Micaela, the girl telling the story, is too disrespectful or negative about the grandmother? How far has Micaela gone toward being alienated from the traditional culture?

5   Have you ever felt like one of the "in-between" people—unable to identify fully with what was expected of you as a member of a family or group?

FORUM: *Bridging the Cultures*

I identify with Americans, but Americans do not identify with me.

Caroline Hwang

For many young Americans, growing up with diverse cultural influences is as American as pizza. America may no longer be a nation of immigrants, but for many it is still a nation of the children of immigrants. For many others, it has been a nation of working-class families trying to ensure a better education and a better life for their sons and daughters. For still others, it has been a nation where parents try to preserve their traditional values while their offspring feel the pull of the lifestyles of a new generation.

Many American life stories chronicle the move from one world to another. A typical life story may record the mental journey from the world of a traditional immigrant home to the American world of school—with baseball, proms, cheerleaders, dating, junk food, and diet cola. The book *Fifth Chinese Daughter* tells the story of moving on from a home where elders were revered, where boys had many privileges while girls did the chores, and where dating was considered sinful. It tells the story of trying to become part of a new world where girls were told to speak up!—to form their own opinions and make their own decisions.

Does the diversity of the American experience have to lead to a clash of cultures, or can it lead to a meeting of cultures? What is likely to be more common—confrontation or fruitful interaction and change? Is growing up in a diverse society likely to produce a new blend and a rich mix—or a lack of orientation and unresolved issues?

THE GOOD DAUGHTER

Caroline Hwang

"Children of immigrants are living paradoxes. We are the first generation and the last. We are in this country for its opportunities, yet filial duty binds us."

Caroline Hwang published the following candid personal testimony in the glossy newsmagazine Newsweek *in 1998. She was at the time an editor of* Redbook *magazine, a former English major, and an aspiring novelist. Her parents came to this country from Korea, and she is part of the Asian American minority that is becoming increasingly visible in American life. Hwang is one of millions of young Americans who "straddle two cultures"—and who at times feel like foreigners in their own land. Hwang says, "I feel displaced in the only country I know." Like many first-generation Americans, she found she was torn between the need to shape her own life on the one hand and filial duty on the other—the attitude of a dutiful son or daughter trying to please the parents.*

Thought Starters: Can you tell when classmates or newcomers are the children of immigrants? How can you tell? Do you think of them as "all American" or as immigrants?

The moment I walked into the dry-cleaning store, I knew the woman behind the counter was from Korea, like my parents. To show her that we shared a heritage, and possibly get a fellow countryman's discount, I tilted my head forward, in shy imitation of a traditional bow. 1

"Name?" she asked, not noticing my attempted obeisance.

"Hwang," I answered.

"Hwang? Are you Chinese?"

Her question caught me off-guard. I was used to hearing such queries from non-Asians who think Asians all look alike, but never from one of my own people. Of course, the only Koreans I knew were my parents and their friends, people who've never asked me where I came from, since they knew better than I. 5

I ransacked my mind for the Korean words that would tell her who I was. It's always struck me as funny (in a mirthless sort of way) that I can more readily say "I am Korean" in Spanish, German and even Latin than I can in the language of my ancestry. In the end, I told her in English.

The dry-cleaning woman squinted as though trying to see past the glare of my strangeness, repeating my surname under her breath. "Oh, *Fxuang*," she said, doubling over with laughter: "You don't know how to speak your name."

I flinched. Perhaps I was particularly sensitive at the time, having just dropped out of graduate school. I had torn up my map for the future, the one that said not only where I was going but who I was. My sense of identity was already disintegrating.

When I got home, I called my parents to ask why they had never bothered to correct me. "Big deal," my mother said, sounding more flippant than I knew she intended. (Like many people who learn English in a classroom, she uses idioms that don't always fit the occasion.) "So what if you can't pronounce your name? You are American," she said.

Though I didn't challenge her explanation, it left me unsatisfied. The fact is, my cultural identity is hardly that clear-cut.   *10*

My parents immigrated to this country 30 years ago, two years before I was born. They told me often, while I was growing up, that, if I wanted to, I could be president someday, that here my grasp would be as long as my reach.

To ensure that I reaped all the advantages of this country, my parents saw to it that I became fully assimilated. So, like any American of my generation, I whiled away my youth strolling malls and talking on the phone, rhapsodizing over Andrew McCarthy's blue eyes or analyzing the meaning of a certain upperclassman's offer of a ride to the Homecoming football game.

To my parents, I am all American, and the sacrifices they made in leaving Korea—including my mispronounced name—pale in comparison to the opportunities those sacrifices gave me. They do not see that I straddle two cultures, nor that I feel displaced in the only country I know. I identify with Americans, but Americans do not identify with me. I've never known what it's like to belong to a community—neither one at large, nor of an extended family. I know more about Europe than the continent my ancestors unmistakably come from. I sometimes wonder, as I did that day in the dry cleaner's, if I would be a happier person had my parents stayed in Korea.

I first began to consider this thought around the time I decided to go to graduate school. It had been a compromise: my parents wanted me to go to law school; I wanted to skip the starched-collar track and be a writer—the hungrier the better. But after 20-some years of following their wishes and meeting all of their expectations, I couldn't bring myself to disobey or disappoint. A writing career is riskier than law, I remember thinking. If I'm a failure and my life is a washout, then what does that make my parents' lives?

I know that many of my friends had to choose between pleasing their   *15* parents and being true to themselves. But for the children of immigrants, the choice seems more complicated, a happy outcome impossible. By making the biggest move of their lives for me, my parents indentured me to the largest debt imaginable—I owe them the fulfillment of their hopes for me.

It tore me up inside to suppress my dream, but I went to school for a Ph.D. in English literature, thinking I had found the perfect compromise.

I would be able to write at least about books while pursuing a graduate degree. Predictably, it didn't work out. How could I labor for five years in a program I had no passion for? When I finally left school, my parents were disappointed, but since it wasn't what they wanted me to do, they weren't devastated. I, on the other hand, felt I was staring at the bottom of the abyss. I had seen the flaw in my life of halfwayness, in my planned life of compromises.

I hadn't thought about my love life, but I had a vague plan to make concessions there, too. Though they raised me as an American, my parents expect me to marry someone Korean and give them grandchildren who look like them. This didn't seem like such a huge request when I was 14, but now I don't know what I'm going to do. I've never been in love with someone I dated, or dated someone I loved. (Since I can't bring myself even to entertain the thought of marrying the non-Korean men I'm attracted to, I've been dating only those I know I can stay clearheaded about.) And as I near that age when the question of marriage stalks every relationship, I can't help but wonder if my parents' expectations are responsible for the lack of passion in my life.

My parents didn't want their daughter to be Korean, but they don't want her fully American, either. Children of immigrants are living paradoxes. We are the first generation and the last. We are in this country for its opportunities, yet filial duty binds us. When my parents boarded the plane, they knew they were embarking on a rough trip. I don't think they imagined the rocks in the path of their daughter who can't even pronounce her own name.

The Responsive Reader

1   In what ways did Hwang's parents try to have her become "fully assimilated"—and why? In what ways did she grow up "all American"? How did she discover that at the same time they wanted her to be true to her ethnic heritage?

2   What is a paradox? Why does Hwang consider herself a living paradox? What would you include in a composite portrait of her "cultural identity"? Would you call her life a "life of halfwayness"? Why or why not?

Talking, Listening, Writing

3   Do young people from immigrant families have a special problem trying to "choose between pleasing their parents and being true to themselves"? Do you tend to agree a "happy outcome" is impossible? Have you seen evidence to support this view, or have you seen evidence to the contrary? Can something similar be true for everyone—regardless of ethnic roots?

4   Telling the story of the Korean woman who laughed at the way she pronounced her name, Hwang says, "Perhaps I was particularly sensitive at the time." Do you think Hwang is oversensitive about her problems of

identity? Do you think Americans from an immigrant or a minority background tend to be oversensitive about how they are seen by others?

5 Hwang says that she knows more about Europe than about the continent her parents came from. Do you think this is still true of most Americans who came from immigrant backgrounds and received a Eurocentric education? How Eurocentric was your own education?

6 Have you ever tried to get any special favor because of your being part of a group? Have you ever tried to obtain the equivalent of a "fellow countryman's discount"—and with what result?

Collaborative Projects

7 What's in a name? (As a friend or prospective employer, would you have advised Hwang—Fxuang—to change her name to something more American? Why or why not?) Names of media celebrities used to sound like inventions of public relations specialists: Dylan Thomas, Tony Curtis, Marilyn Monroe, John Wayne. (What were their real names?) A reverse trend set in some years ago: Among white ethnics, Judy again became Tschudi, Rusk again became Ruszkiewicz. At the same time, among African Americans, Leroy Jones became Imamu Amiri Baraka, Cassius Clay became Muhammad Ali, and many others followed suit. What additional examples can you track down? What do these name changes tell you about trends in American culture or in "identity politics"?

A DAUGHTER'S STORY

Nguyen Louie

**"I am a Chinese-Korean-American young woman.
Being a feminist is an integral part of who I am, but it
is not all that I am."**

The following mother-daughter story first published in 1996 raises the question: Is there a typical American student? Or is it typically American for everyone to have the right to be his or her own person? What is familiar or predictable about the following life story of a fellow student? Is there anything representative about waystations in her life, about her relationship with her parents, or about her thoughts and feelings while growing up? What, if anything, is different or unexpected about Nguyen's story? In what ways is her story different from yours? Can you relate to some of the things that make it different?

Nguyen Louie wrote this autobiographical essay when she was a student at Brown University. It was first published in Ms. magazine as part of a series of testimonies exploring mother-daughter relationships. In Nguyen's story, her relation to the ethnic history of her parents and to a second culture plays a role—but, as with many other young Americans, it is only part of the story.

Thought Starters: Has the "generation gap" become a cliché, or is it still a live issue for many young Americans during their growing up?

I was born two days before International Women's Day (IWD). As I was growing up, this was always a hectic time of year because my mother was busy going to meetings and organizing programs for the IWD event. I resented the fact that it seemed to take precedence over my birthday. I always wanted a full-fledged birthday party with a dozen friends, junk food, and presents. Instead, I stayed in day care with other children whose mothers were members of the Third World Women's Alliance. On my eleventh birthday I was allowed to be part of the IWD event; I gave a speech in front of 300 people to raise money for a child care center in Angola. My mother coached me and bought me a purple jumpsuit for the occasion. For the first time, I was doing something that might make a difference on the other side of the world. I think I grew more during that five-minute speech than I had during the previous year. That's when I realized why my mother did what she did and why it was important.

My parents were at Berkeley during the sixties. They agitated for the development of ethnic studies, dropped out of school, and protested against the Vietnam war. They were very liberal. They also gave me a lot of freedom to grow on my own. With that flexibility, I didn't feel the need to rebel. I don't really understand the kinds of relationships my girlfriends have with their mothers. Usually their mothers were overprotective, making my friends want to defy them even more. Although my mom and I are not equals, we are best friends. I can talk to her, confide in her, laugh with her, and cry with her.

We weren't always so close. As a young child, I was resentful that she didn't have much time to spend with me. I felt closer to my father; he did things with me. We watched videos, ate potato chips, played board games, and went for walks together. When my dad brought his paperwork home, I would poke around and ask him what he was doing. My parents were probably gone from home the same amount of time, but I blamed my mother more. I guess it was because I thought my mother was supposed to be around.

When I was six, my mother became pregnant with my brother, Lung San. I was lonely and looked forward to having a sibling to play with, but I didn't expect my parents to spend so much time with him and not with me. Again, I blamed my mother. I tried to run away, but made it only to the corner because I wasn't supposed to cross the street. Consequently I was forced to compromise with my parents and accept my new role as a responsible big sister, one who was too mature to have tantrums and run away. By age 12, I preferred to stay home from the conventions my parents went to and take care of my brother.

Looking back, I realize that my mother always made sure we had qual- 5
ity time together. My father and I were content to bum around the house,
but my mother insisted that we go out and do things. We went on excur-
sions to the Berkeley marina, Golden Gate Park, and Chinatown, and we
took family vacations in Santa Cruz and Hawaii. Although it may sound
cheesy, my family is very trusting, loving and closely knit.

I used to feel pressure to be active in my mother's causes. I felt that I
was letting her down if I didn't go to meetings. Being active was the right
thing to do, but it wasn't always what I wanted to do. I wanted to be a "normal" teenager, to go to the movies or bowling with my friends. Often it
seemed like my parents did not have any fun; they were always gone, and
they came home exhausted. I wasn't able to see that their work was interesting or worthwhile. To me, it seemed oppressive. In a lot of ways I am
more conservative than my mom. I often fight change. My mom wants me
to get out there and be more active, and sometimes I just don't think I have
the time or energy for it. I just want to be myself.

When I was 13, my parents sent me to Cuba for a month with an international youth organization. My mother said, "It will open your eyes,
and you'll learn so much." I adamantly did not want to go. My body was
changing and I had started to menstruate, and I was insecure and anxious
about having to deal with guys or compete with girls on this trip. The mere
thought of it terrified me. But my parents were firm; they put me on the
plane, and I went.

My parents were right. It was an eye-opening experience. Delegations
of young people had come to Cuba from all over the world. I learned how
impoverished some other kids were and about the struggles they were going through. When I went home I felt I had a responsibility to do something, to use the information I had gained and become more active. I
started out with good intentions, but my resolve dwindled when I went to
junior high school. There were cliques that required being popular and
looking cute, and I wanted to be myself. I didn't want to change myself to
fit into any clique. I was often lonely and miserable. I hated junior high.

In high school I discovered it was O.K. to be myself. In fact, it was
cool to be an individual. I became secure and comfortable with myself and
made a lot of good friends who accepted me for who I was. When I was a
sophomore I was a founding member of the Asian Awareness Club. When
complaints arose about Asian students getting beaten up and kicked in the
hallways, we organized workshops on interracial relationships and Asian
stereotypes. Part of what I liked about the club was organizing with my
friends and deciding to do it on my own. My parents weren't telling me,
"You are going to this meeting and will learn something from it." I planned
the meetings and the different issues we discussed.

I decided to go to Brown because of its academic diversity and the fact 10
that it offered the flexibility of creating your own major. Also, being at

home with my parents was too comfortable; I needed to get out on my own and be more independent. Breaking away from my parents was the hardest thing for me to do. But my parents made the transition easier by flying out with me to the East Coast and giving me lots of support.

When I got to Brown, I went through a difficult time. I had never been so aware of my socioeconomic background, but at Brown it seems that the majority of the students have been through private East Coast preparatory schools, and I felt they had the upper hand. I also found it strange to meet so many students whose primary goal is to make money. Many students aspire to be doctors not because they want to help people, but in order to have extravagant lifestyles. I was disheartened by this attitude. The first semester was a struggle for me. My parents stressed that although grades are important, they are not matters of life and death. They just said, "Do the best you can." I still feel the need to work, but the pressure is coming from within myself.

I am a feminist by my own interpretation: I believe that men and women are equal physically and intellectually; therefore, they are entitled to equal rights, treatment, and respect. I take this for granted, and I immediately assume people are wrong for thinking otherwise. It's almost instinctive. Yet I would never introduce myself as a feminist; I am a Chinese–Korean–American young woman. Being a feminist is an integral part of who I am, but it is not all that I am.

I can't see myself being as much of an activist as my mother, but activism is definitely a part of me. It's in my blood. I'm not sure whether that's a blessing or a curse. I plan to tap into the activism on campus, but I don't want to devote my life to it. I prefer to deal with things on a personal level. What I want from life is to achieve my maximum potential, to be happy, and to be comfortable. I want to find a balance.

The Responsive Reader

1   What do you learn about the mother's involvement as an organizer or activist? What is the author's attitude toward her mother? How did it develop or change during her growing up? (Does the author consider herself an an "activist"?)

2   Has the term *liberal* become a dirty word in our society? In what sense were Louie's parents "liberals"? What do you learn here about traditional liberal causes? Why would ethnic studies be one of them?

3   Phrases like "sibling rivalry," "quality time," and "the desire to be normal" are familiar to students of pop psychology and of talk shows focusing on personal concerns. Are these phrases just buzzwords? What role did they play in Louie's growing up?

4   "Educational experiences" that people might mention in a vita might include travel and contrasting experiences at different stages of their schooling. What was eye-opening about the author's trip to Cuba? What

made the difference between her junior high and her high school experience?

5 How did the author become aware of the role of race or ethnicity? What shaped her attitude toward or interest in "diversity"? How did she become aware of the role of class in American society?

6 Louie says, "I am a feminist by my own interpretation." What *is* her own version of feminism? How does it compare with yours or with your definition of the term?

Talking, Listening, Writing

7 Do you think Nguyen Louie could be called a typical or representative young American? Why or why not? Do you think she has had a privileged or sheltered experience while growing up? Do you think she has allowed herself to be steered too much by her parents?

8 Was there a waystation or a turning point in your growing up when you discovered the role of poverty, of race, of class, or of gender in our society?

9 Is there activism on your campus? What form does it take? Who gets involved? Do you?

CULTURE AS A TWO-WAY STREET

Kevin Janda

"As we are moving further away from the original immigrants we are moving further from our roots, but we can never lose our past."

The author of the following student essay represents a new Generation 1 1/2 that does not fit traditional labels and classifications. Its members do not easily fit traditional descriptions of "second-generation" Americans. Although many are children of immigrants, they move easily in the American society and culture while maintaining close ties with the traditional culture. Many are close to being fully bilingual and bicultural. They have adopted many features of the American youth culture; however, they also read publications like India Currents, *whose editors challenge the "bad rap" immigrants have gotten after the September 11 attacks. They remind us that "immigrants have always formed the bedrock of American economy and culture. They do much of the research in our universities, provide health care in remote areas, build our homes, harvest our crops, and drive technical innovation."*

Kevin wrote this essay during a winter term in early 2004. Traditionalists in his home country were worrying about the "Americanization" of much of their culture, and conservatives in America saw a threat to traditional American values from a new wave of immigration.

Thought Starters: Do you know friends or fellow students who switch easily while talking from one language to the other? Do you feel left out when that happens?

It is October in California, and my father's flight has just come in. My grandparents and my father get off the plane and take their first steps on American soil with only a combined seven dollars in their pockets, five of which my grandfather decides to spend on beers. They are greeted by relatives and immediately begin to work in the fields of Yuba City. My parents had no previous exposure to any culture other than their own. As we, the children, mature we are exposed to the culture, but as the generations progress we are slowly losing our original culture.

As my parents came to America, they were not assimilated at all. They had grown up in India and had no exposure to any other culture. When they came to America they were surprised at the way things were conducted. When I asked my mom she stated, "In India women were not allowed to socialize with anyone else, and spent most of their time in the kitchen. Here in America things were totally different." As they became more settled in America, they began to adopt some American ways, but still remained very close to their original culture and language. This love for the culture was then instilled in us.

As I grew up, I was taught my native language first, and English came second. I was very much in touch with my culture and not so much with the American culture. All I listened to was music from India, and it was not until high school that I got into American music. Also I did not watch many American movies as a kid; I stuck mostly to Indian movies. I was very in touch with my culture, but as my younger brother grew up he drifted away. My brother had the influence of me and my other cousins, and we would always talk to him in English so he cannot speak Punjabi very well. He can only speak enough to get by with a light conversation. Also he has no interest in the Indian movies we watch; the only thing he really enjoys is the Indian music. Since I was the first kid I was closer to my parents and grandparents, but my brother grew up with us and was less in touch with the original culture.

As I wake up on the weekend mornings I turn on the television, and begin to watch the Indian programs. In recent days I noticed that things have really changed since the early days. I remember when the actresses were dressed in traditional Indian clothing and would dance to a traditional beat, but nowadays as I watch all the actresses are wearing barely anything and they are bouncing to an upbeat Americanized tune. Now I am not complaining at all, but when we watch these kinds of shows with our grandparents the atmosphere can become uncomfortable. My grandmother always states "Dhecko aakkal kee kuriye kidhan dhiya kapra poundhia," which translates into "Look at what these girls are wearing; do they have any self-respect?" Many of the Indian movies and people are becoming more westernized. The themes are no longer focusing on traditional love stories between Indians, but now are focusing on interracial marriages. They are still using the traditional language, but they are mixing the cultures and techniques.

Most generations are approaching a crossroads when it comes to cultures. They are not really sure which one they really belong to. Pulitzer Prize winner Jhumpa Lahiri stated that she "never felt a strong affiliation with any nation or ethnic group. I always felt between the cracks of the two cultures." And as the questions of marriage and the future rise we are even more confused. In the Indian culture, the marriages were arranged, and love marriages were very rare. In my early years of high school whenever we studied India and its culture, my fellow students would always ask me if I was willing to undergo an arranged marriage. Since my parents have been here for a while now, they have become accustomed to some of the ways and are not forcing anything on me, but more and more people in India and America are opting for love marriages.

As we are moving further away from the original immigrants we are moving further from our roots, but we can never lose our past. "American Desi" is a great movie about a college freshman who can't wait to get away from his Indian culture. He goes to college and tries to escape his culture, but realizes that it is not that bad and begins to like it. As I and my generation grow up I personally do not think I will be able to instill the same Indian values in my children, as were instilled in me. Because I was born in America I am not as in touch with my culture as my parents, and though I would like to teach my children the same cultural facts I learned, I don't think it would be possible.

The Responsive Reader

1 In this account, what seems representative of the *immigrant experience*? Many of the stories of new arrivals in America are similar, and yet at the same time they are different or unique. In this student's account of his parents' new start in America, what seems typical of the experience of new arrivals? What seems different? What for you was surprising or unexpected?

2 Much writing about today's multicultural America focuses on the meeting of cultures or the clash of civilizations. What are the major *points of comparison* in this paper? In what areas of life does the difference between the two cultures show? Where does it show most vividly or most strongly?

3 What *stages of assimilation* or phases of acculturation does this student writer track? (We usually compare first-generation and second-

generation immigrants. However, in this paper, there is already a difference between the older and the younger brother. How would you sum
up the difference?) Can you suggest a label for the different stages of
assimilation?

Talking, Listening, Writing

4   Clothes often "make a statement." Contrasts between traditional dress
and modern American dress are often an outward sign of different cultural traditions. The student writer stresses the difference but does not
give us much lively visual detail. What questions would you ask the
writer about traditional dress for men and women?

ON BEING WHITE

Mara Joseph

**"I agree with those who say that people should never
be judged based on the color of their skin—so why are
these same people often the first to judge me for the
color of mine?"**

*For decades, the national dialogue about race highlighted demands from un-
derprivileged groups aspiring to their place in the sun. Affirmative action programs took aim at compensating for the results of poverty, residential segregation, underfunded schools, and discrimination in employment. As affirmative
action programs slowly made Americans from minority backgrounds more visible in government employment, higher education, and management jobs, a
backlash developed amid charges of reverse discimination. Whites passed over
for college admission, hiring, or promotion began to make their grievances heard.
When she wrote the following short essay in 2001, Mara Joseph was a cultural
anthropology major at the University of California at Davis. She is on the defensive concerning challenges to the status of her privileged class, and she objects
to the politicizing of classes that should be devoted to impartial scholarship.*

Thought Starters: What was your first experience with prejudice—
either as a person experiencing prejudice or as someone realizing that you
were prejudiced against others? Did the experience make a lasting impression on you? Why or why not?

I admit it freely. I am a privileged individual. I grew up in a wealthy   *1*
area outside of Los Angeles, went to a very good public high school and
have had all the things I could possibly need or want provided for me by
two loving parents.

Until one day last month, I have never felt like I was being discriminated against. That day, while sitting in an anthropology lecture about race, class and gender, I started to feel as though the color of my skin (a rather blinding white at this time of year) was putting me in an unfair position.

And recently, I discovered that I am not the only person to feel this way either.

Just the other day, a friend told me about the cultural English class he had taken, in which he was the only white person. The main assignment in the class? Write about your experience as an immigrant to America who does not speak English.

Needless to say, my blue-eyed and blond friend, who is probably a   5
fifth- or sixth-generation American, didn't do very well in the class.

Another friend had a similar experience in her Asian American studies class, in which she was expected to write about her life as an Asian American (clearly a bit difficult for a person of European descent).

Once again, she did poorly in the class, and so did the few other white people in it.

On a similar note, David Horowitz's article decrying reparations was published recently in my college newspaper, although it was quickly revealed as an oversight by the editor who extended sincere apologies for the mistake.

I never saw the article, but I know the general idea behind reparations: Payment should be given to African Americans to compensate for the atrocities their ancestors endured as slaves.

Of course, I agree that slavery was a horrible tragedy and a scar on our   10
country's history, as it is among many other countries involved in the slave trade during previous centuries. But I don't see how I am in any way responsible for it.

In fact, I don't see how my ancestors are either, because, like many other Americans, I am descended from recent immigrants.

Just years before the civil rights movement began in this country, my relatives were busy dealing with their own problems—namely Hitler and Nazi Germany (they were Austrian Jews).

Even if my relatives were among early British colonizers in this country and owners of slaves, I would hope to not be held responsible for their ignorance and injustice. To punish someone for actions they didn't commit is as unjust as punishing someone for the color of their skin.

But instead of learning from the past and moving on, it seems that many people would rather dwell and seek revenge. Instead of using college courses to teach students what the immigrant or racial experience is like, the classes catered to members of that particular culture.

Because so many of the other comments I have made in my afore-   15
mentioned anthropology class have been shot down or ignored, I am writing this in hopes of reminding others that we are all immigrants in the United States (with the notable exception of Native Americans), and we all have our own unique stories and valid opinions to share.

I agree with those who say that people should never be judged based on the color of their skin—so why are these same people often the first to judge me for the color of mine?

The Responsive Reader

1   What is provocative or attention-getting about Joseph's title? How do you react to it?

2   What mental picture do you form of the writer after reading her first two paragraphs? Do you tend to identify or sympathize with her, or do you find yourself prejudiced against her? Do you think that from the start her essay will divide her audience along racial lines?

3   Do you agree that today's generation of young white Americans should not feel "in any way responsible" for the atrocities of slavery and the slave trade? Do you agree with her that reparations for the harm done by slavery would punish people "for actions they didn't commit"?

4   What charges does the writer make concerning political and racial bias in her classes? How convincing are her examples?

5   What is Joseph's point in saying that "we are all immigrants"? Do you think it is an important point of valid argument in discussions of inequalities in our society?

6   How do you think Joseph would want us to "learn from the past and move on"?

Talking, Listening, Writing

7   Joseph says that some college courses are catering to students of particular backgrounds rather than "using college courses to teach students what the immigrant or racial experience is like." Have you observed a political or ideological slant in any of your own classes? In what classes is slanting toward one or the other end of the political spectrum likely to be an issue? How do you or your fellow students cope with it?

8   Do you ever feel singled out because of the way you look or because of other features that might identify you as a member of an ethnic or religious group? What reactions do you face from people who are from different racial, ethnic, or religious backgrounds? Why do you think they react as they do? How do you respond? How would you like them to react to you?

9   Are aggrieved whites in general or especially angry white males a factor in your classes or on your campus? What role do they play? How do you relate to them?

10   Should colleges limit enrollment in ethnic studies classes or similar courses specifically to members of the racial or ethnic groups that are the focus of a course?

Drawing on Your Experience

The Writing Process

1 **Drawing on Your Experience**
2 From Reading to Writing
3 Exploring Internet and Nonprint Sources
4 Pushing Toward a Thesis
5 Organizing Your Writing
6 Feedback and Revision

Draw on personal experience and firsthand observation.

Much strong writing is rooted in firsthand experience. The life story of the poet Maya Angelou—born in the segregated Old South, overcoming the obstacles in her path, becoming a widely admired performer—made her a role model for a younger generation. The story of Richard Rodriguez—finding himself the only Mexican kid in an all-white classroom and knowing only a few words of English—has had a special meaning for readers charting their passage from an immigrant past to an American future. The story of Americans from an immigrant or working class background who have overcome poverty or prejudice to claim their place in the sun is a favorite of readers believing in the American Dream.

Writing that draws on personal experience has special strengths:

- *Writing about your personal experience, you write about what you know best.* No one is more of an expert than you on what matters to you as a person. You are the authority on where and how you grew up. Nobody knows better than you what home or family meant to you. No one else has the inside story on what helped and hindered you in school or on the job.

- *Writing from experience sets up a special relation of trust between you and your reader.* As the writer, you show that you trust your readers

86

enough to share with them your personal thoughts and feelings. When you take stock honestly of your own experience, you trust that readers will be able to relate—to see the connection with what matters in their own lives.

- *Drawing on personal experience gives a special authority to the discussion of larger issues.* Reading about gender roles or the immigrant experience, we like to think that the writer knows the subject at first hand. Reading about affirmative action, we want to know if the author can say: "I was there"—as a target, a beneficiary, a witness, or a caring observer. We want to see what theories or statistics mean to the lives of people the author has known or observed.

Triggering

Write about experiences that had a special meaning for you.
Millions of readers buy the books of authors who wanted to tell their life stories or set the record straight. Papers based on personal experience often seem more real and better motivated than other kinds. Here are some reasons for you to do this kind of writing:

- *Writers want to share what they have experienced.* Have you ever felt uprooted from friends or from familiar surroundings? Have you ever had to leave bad company behind? Have you ever felt like an outsider in your school or your neighborhood? Have you gone through the breakup of a family—or been part of building a new family or finding a new home? Tell your story. Writing about a family issue, serious illness, or living with disability helps writers cope.

- *Writers sort things out in their own minds.* Have you experienced conflicting advice from an older generation or from two sides of the family? Have you been divided between what your friends expected and what was expected of you in school? Writing gives you a chance to go back over what happened and try to understand.

- *People feel the need to pay tribute.* They experience pleasure in sharing what is good—discovering the rewards of tutoring or being a mentor, for instance. They pay tribute to someone who served as a role model or helped them in time of need. They try to show what real difference someone made in their lives.

- *People feel the need to state a grievance.* When people have been wronged, they may feel the need to go on record. Have you witnessed a wrongful arrest? Have you seen people denied benefits that were rightfully theirs? When you have witnessed an incident of neighborhood crime, police harassment, or official delay, you may feel the need to make your voice heard. When you hear a speaker criticize welfare mothers or young people in trouble you may want to testify in their behalf.

Gathering

Work up a rich fund of material from firsthand experience and observation.

What will make a paper about your personal experience become real for your reader? What sights, sounds, or emotions do you remember? What really happened? What do you remember about the people? What did they look like, and how did they talk? What were your honest feelings?

Journal entries recording personal experiences or "Notes to Myself" in a log or diary are a basic resource for many writers. The following are preliminary notes for a paper about the writer's first experience in the world of work. For you, do they have the ring of authentic personal testimony?

Berry-Picking Time

The summer before the sixth grade, my mother decided it was time to send me out into the berry fields. I hated it. I made barely any money for the time I was out there. My back ached from bending and picking strawberries, and my hands were forever purple. All my friends were frolicking in the sun while I was stuck in the fields. However, after a few summers of picking, the owners moved me up to the supervising/truck working position. I now got paid by the hour and achieved a status my older brothers had never achieved. This past summer was probably the last summer I will ever work in the fields. I came to love associating with the pickers. The migrant workers are some of the best people I know. Because of working outside, I got a great tan. I know how to drive tractors or tie down trucks, and I was the only girl at my position. However, the time had come to move on. Berry picking was a great experience, but there are other places out there for me too.

The following are notes for a student's paper on the struggle to live up to the stereotype of the "ideal woman." Note her use of real-life material. She says, "no matter how skinny we became, we never thought we were thin or perfect enough."

Skin and Bones

When I was fifteen, two of my girlfriends taught me to throw up. We thought we were terribly clever; we could gorge with impunity and not gain weight. It was a lark and a clever act of rebellion against the constant dieting we subjected ourselves to and that our girlfriends, mothers, or older sisters continued to endure. For my friend, bingeing and purging was her solution to being thin and not having to diet. To her, it was her rebellion against a system that required women to look skinny and starved. She and her friends would eat vast quantities of food: an entire roast chicken; leftover pasta with salmon in heavy cream sauce; salad with walnuts, Roquefort cheese, and homemade croutons; key lime and apple pies; and peach cobbler with ice cream. By bingeing and purging, she was able to appear "fragile, helpless, and weak—all the qualities so admired in females." Trying to stop, my friend went to therapists, doctors, meetings, and Overeaters Anonymous. A woman running one meeting asked, "Would you be willing to stop if it meant gaining ten pounds?" No one in the group could say yes.

EDITOR'S TIP: *Make your experiences and feelings real for your reader.* Make incidents and situations concrete—share what you took in through your senses of sight and hearing and sometimes also of taste, smell, or touch. Help your readers see, hear, and feel what you saw, heard, and felt. Re-create the people, the places, or the events, so that words will not just remain words. Practice writing snapshot sentences using concrete detail like the following:

A timid-looking student sat alone twirling spaghetti around a fork while those in the clique whispered and joked together over their lunches.

In the coffeehouse, I worked surrounded by the **smells of espresso, chocolate, and pastries; the hissing sound of the espresso machine; and the soft playing of mood music by a guitar.**

SHAPING—**Make your memories add up to a story with a point.**

Unsorted experience tends to be miscellaneous. One thing happens after another. To turn your memories into a structured paper, you focus on something that really mattered to you. An effective paper brings a key issue or concern into focus. It may highlight a major strand in your life, leaving much else aside. Try to avoid writing a paper that falls into the "and-then" pattern: This happened, and then this happened, and then this happened.

Here are organizing strategies that can give shape and direction to your paper:

• *Push toward a thesis.* In a successful paper about personal experience, different incidents have added up. They have become part of a pattern. The author has pushed toward a **thesis,** or unifying central idea. The following passage by a student of Japanese descent sums up his strong personal feelings about his "Mixed like Me" heritage. This paragraph could be the key passage of a paper about the experiences that helped make the question of identity a major issue in the student writer's mind:

Who Am I?

"What are you?" I was long at a loss for words as to how to answer this question. Should I answer, Japanese? American? Japanese American? I did not consider myself fully Japanese, since I had not been brought up with the language and the strict traditional culture. I was not an ordinary American because of obvious visible differences. **Trying to answer this question often left me in an awkward position and sometimes led me to regret my existence.**

■ *Focus on the key issue in a series of events.* The same question or the same issue may have come up more than once till it finally became a problem or a challenge. Maybe you will tell the story of your attempt—successful or not—to become part of a new family after the parents' separation. Your paper might in turn answer questions like the following:

- What kind of welcome did you expect?
- What events made you think there might be a problem?
- What were some revealing things that were said?
- What efforts did you make to be accepted?
- Did things lead up to a confrontation or a serious break?
- Was there a reconciliation or at least a truce?
- Looking back, would you do anything differently given a second chance?

■ *Organize a paper about growing up by tracing major stages.* You may structure your paper by marking off major stages or phases. Or you may use a **then-and-now** pattern. Questions like the following can set up the program for your paper:

Playing the Role

THESIS: Like several of my friends, I went from living up to the expectations of others to setting goals for myself.
Questions:

What were the gender roles when you grew up?

When did you first face up to questions or change your thinking?

Did you go through a phase of rebellion or confusion?

Are you now "comfortable" in your role?

What are you going to tell the next generation?

A variation of such a timeline pattern may lead up to a **turning point** in the writer's experience. Your paper may lead up to and then follow up a crucial turn in the road toward becoming your own person. A happy childhood may have ended when the family left your native country. After you at first did poorly in school, discovering your talent in music or your athletic ability may have changed your attitude and the future course of events.

One of the Crowd

THESIS: I did not find that the new country welcomes the stranger "with open arms."
- The happy childhood home became a thing of the past.
- In a strange new country it was hard to do well in school.

- I tried hard to lose my accent and "blend in."
- The older people in the family did not always help, saying I was becoming "whitewashed."
- The turning point came when I discovered my talent for music.
- A teacher sponsored me, and fellow musicians encouraged me.
- I was very slowly becoming "one of the crowd."

■ *Track the pull of divided loyalties.* You may trace the conflict of two strong influences in your growing up. Perhaps your allegiance was divided between two parents who were different in their personalities and commitments. Perhaps one was very literal-minded and organized, whereas the other was very imaginative and artistic. Or perhaps you experienced a strong pull between the traditional culture of the home and the peer culture of the neighborhood or school. Like several of the authors reprinted in this book, you may have been "a traveler between two worlds."

Revising

Revising your paper, look at your own writing with the reader's eye.

Allow time for revision. Check an early draft to see what needs work:

■ *Move in for the closer look.* Build up concrete detail. Add lifelike detail to make your readers visualize the setting. Add physical details, revealing gestures, or favorite sayings to make us see and hear a favorite uncle or cranky neighbor. Act out key events in more striking detail.

■ *Reconsider when you may have fallen back on clichés.* Ready-made phrases are handy: "breakdown in communication," "the fear of commitment," "the dysfunctional family." Try to make sure that when you use these phrases they do not sound second-hand. Aim at your own way of saying what you feel—which may be different from what others have felt before you.

■ *Check for hasty generalizations.* Try not to overgeneralize. Are you reading too much into a single incident? A key incident may dramatize a pattern—but it may also have resulted from an unusual combination of circumstances. A teacher or police officer who is usually helpful may have had a bad day. A heart-warming generous gesture may have been a once-in-a-lifetime event. A foreign student whom you considered a typical representative of his country may turn out to be very different from his own closest friends.

■ *Try not to sound one-sided or self-righteous.* Readers get wary when everything that went wrong in a situation was someone else's fault.

EDITOR'S TIP: Do you sometimes try to make everything sound zany or funny? A sense of humor is a special gift, but readers tire of a strained facetious tone. A good tone to aim at may be to be basically serious with an occasional lighter touch.

A Paper for Peer Review

Do you agree that the following personal experience paper is a strong paper? What is the connecting thread or unifying idea? What are striking details that a reader might remember? What suggestions would you make for revision? Where do you think the writer might need to work in more real-life examples or striking details?

Life on the East Side

I grew up on the east side of my town. Until I moved into the college dorms, the east side was the only environment I really knew. **I suppose you would call it a rough neighborhood.** There are no white picket fences, nor do children roam the neighborhood freely. In my neighborhood and in my old high school, drugs and gangs are serious problems. There are few traditional families left. Most kids do not come home from school to parents waiting with milk and cookies but to babysitters or empty houses. While students in other parts of town go to band practice or hang out at the mall with their friends, kids on the east side hang out with their fellow gang members spraypainting the local park.————>>>>>>>>>>>>>>

(The introduction creates the **setting,** developing the contrast with more comfortable traditional neighborhoods.)

Life on the east side gives one a different perspective. It has taught me realities that I might not otherwise have learned. **Basically, living in an environment such as this limits a person's freedom.** Growing up, I was denied the luxuries that people from "better" neighborhoods take for granted. In my neighborhood, my friends could not go to the local bowling alley, mall, or miniature golf course without running into gang members. There aren't many places to go for someone without a driver's license because the local hangouts just aren't safe. Driving was especially important to my friends and me because it meant we were not limited to places near our homes and could go to places where we felt more secure. It is said that fear of violence prevents parents from letting their children go to the local rollerskating rink, but on the east side this is just a reality one accepts.

(After the **thesis** setting up a general perspective, this paragraph focuses on the **people** and the way life in a low-income neighborhood limits their freedom.)————>>>>>>>>>>>>>

My family is typical of the east side in that we never had much money. It hasn't been easy coming from a family that lives from paycheck to paycheck. There is always a sense of tension in the house that comes from the uncertainty of not knowing if there is going to be enough money to pay the bills or where the money for unexpected expenses like car repairs will come from. It is hard to watch my parents struggle. Neither of my parents attended college, and they thus had limited options for work. My dad works long hours at a job he doesn't like and consequently usually comes home overtired and in a bad mood. My sister and I have had all our physical and emotional needs met, however. My parents always found the money for things like braces for our teeth, prom dresses, and class trips. Obviously, I have never had a brand new car or taken a trip to Europe, but I have never felt deprived either. ————>>>>>>>>>>>>

(This paragraph focuses on the economic realities that defined the family's **social status.**)

I do not live in the worst part of town. In high school, I had friends who hated walking down the street to their own houses because they were afraid. At least I can walk through my own neighborhood during the day and feel fairly secure. That I consider a luxury. I have learned not to take anything for granted. I believe people spend too much time obsessed with what they don't have. My house is tiny, and all four of us have to share one bathroom. This used to be a problem for me, and I was jealous of friends who lived in large houses with their own bathrooms. Then I volunteered for work in homeless shelters. Now I am thankful that I have a house.————>>>>>>>>>>>>

(This paragraph conveys the writer's basic **positive attitude** in spite of problems and hardships.)

I learned much during my four years at my east side high school, and much of this learning occurred outside the classroom. With more than four thousand students, the school is a model of cultural and economic diversity. I was lucky to have friends from many different backgrounds. I am comfortable with all races and religions. The school has its problems, but it also has many strengths that outsiders overlook. ————>>>>>>>>>>>>

(This paragraph makes a strong statement about the value of diversity and learning to relate to Americans from a range of backgrounds.)

Being in college I get to live out a dream, but the new environment also presents me with new obstacles. While I am not ashamed of my past, I still feel as though I have to prove that I belong here. I have made friends and am treated no differently than anyone else. Yet coming from a school with a bad reputation I feel I have to do everything twice as well as other people. I know that no person is inferior to another person, but there is still a small part of me that can't help feeling tainted by negative images of the east side. However, there are few things I would change about my past. My environment has had much to do with who I am today.

(The conclusion takes the **next step** toward the promise and challenges of the future.)

YOUR TURN:

1 Did this paper change your ideas about what life is like in the low-income or poor sections of town? Why or why not?

2 What is the writer's strategy for looking at the negative and the positive sides of his experience? Do you think the overall order of points works well? Why or why not?

3 Are there parts of the paper where you want the author to tell you more or to take a closer look? For instance, would you ask the student writer to bring in some real-life examples of friends from different backgrounds?

4 Do you make a good audience for this paper? Would the reader need firsthand experience with life away from affluent neightbor-hoods to respond well to this paper? Why or why not?

Writing Options 1: Experience-Based Papers

1 Are you a follower or a rebel? Have you rebelled against a tradition or approved way of thinking? Have you ever returned to a tradition that you had left behind? What led to your change of heart? Was there a turning point? What was the outcome?

2 Have you experienced divided loyalties? Have you ever been torn between competing influences on your life or your thinking? How did you sort them out?

3 What does it mean to become an American? Has the immigrant experience played a role in your upbringing or later life? What has been your observation of the challenges of assimilation or acculturation? Are there major stages in the process?

4 What has been your experience with discrimination or prejudice? Have you encountered special obstacles—or special opportunities—because of who or what you are? (Or, what is your experience with favoritism or having the "inside track"?)

5 Have you felt defensive about your identity? Have you ever felt embarassed about your background? Do you feel uncomfortable when people pry into where you came from or what you are? Why or why not? How do you cope?

6 In your growing up, have you encountered a challenge to your sense of self-worth? Has a problem in your family or personal life affected your outlook or helped shaped your personality?

7 Where or how did you become aware of race or national origin? Where did you become aware of the role of race or ethnicity? What difference has race or ethnicity made in your life or in the lives of people you know well?

8 Have you ever discovered a new lifestyle? Or have you ever rediscovered a cultural identity? What difference has it made in your life?

9   Have you changed your mind on a major issue? Have you ever had a change of heart on a subject like marriage, having children, or divorce?

10 Do you believe in the work ethic? What has been your initiation into the world of work? What jobs—good or bad—made an impression on you?

2

SCHOOL
Learners and Institutions

U.S. Schools: Underperforming

LOSING OUR EDGE?

Budget cuts: The more things change . . .

Getting Girls to the Lab Bench

To remain competitive, the U.S. must close the gender gap in science

Reading, Blogging, and 'Rithmetic?

What Is a Web Log?

44.5 percent of all college faculty employed part-time

SILENCING SPEECH ON CAMPUS

VISUAL LITERACY 2
HEADLINES: EDUCATION IN THE NEWS

IN TODAY'S AMERICA, IS MEDIA COVERAGE
OF EDUCATION MOSTLY BAD NEWS?

Headlines—and especially front-page headlines—are what first catches the newspaper reader's eye. Vendors used to shout "Extra! Extra!" and repeat the latest headlines to attract buyers of the day's news. Today the wording and placing of headlines serve to play up or downplay current developments—and also to steer the reactions of readers. The following headlines were gathered from sources ranging from a national business weekly and a big-city newspaper to a professional journal for educators. These beckoning headlines appeared at a time when questions about "failing schools" or the "crisis in education" were dominating education coverage.

Reading the Image

1 Which of these headlines would catch your eye? Which of the articles they head would you want to read? Which article would you read first, and why? What would your answer to these questions tell journalists about the *target audience* you are likely to represent?

2 Do the headlines seem *one-sided*—seeming to promise all bad news? Why, or why not? Writers of headlines are sometimes accused of making them "sensational" or "alarmist." Do you think such charges could be brought against any of these examples?

3 Journalists have traditionally prided themselves on maintaining the distinction between news reporting and *editorial* commentary. Do these headlines tend to make you expect objective news reporting, or do they seem to have an editorial slant? If there is an editorial slant, what is it?

4 In current discussion about the schools, do you think of yourself as a passive spectator or an active *participant*? Do you turn out for meetings or protest actions calling attention to the needs of today's embattled schools? What poster or other visual art would you or your group produce to call attention to the needs of your school or the schools in your community?

2

SCHOOL

Learners and Institutions

"If you don't do well in school, you can't get a job."
—VICE-PRESIDENT OF A HIGH-TECH COMPANY

Education is much in the news. The widespread perception is that the nation's schools are failing. Employers complain about job applicants lacking basic skills. In the high-tech sector, employers bring in employees from India and Pakistan with the necessary grounding in math and computer science. There is much talk about education reform, much of it centered on increased standardized testing.

Here is a sampling of news items on the currents and crosscurrents that impinge on the successes and failures of the nation's schools.

A new federal initiative mandates testing every year, with financial rewards and penalties for high-performance and underperforming schools.

"High-stakes" testing will deny many unqualified students a high school diploma.

A teacher says that support personnel and teacher's assistants disappeared, but "every social problem in our society walks through the schoolroom door."

The poorest schools with the most urgent student needs have the highest proportion of underqualified or uncredentialed teachers.

A parent sues a school district for $1.8 million because the son was cut from the varsity team, thus damaging his chances to go on to a career as a highly paid professional athlete.

A student who was told he could not enter a classroom to say good-bye to a girl returns with a gun and kills the teacher, shooting him point-blank in the face.

College football coaches earn million-dollar salaries.

The following reading selections feature testimonies from teachers and students, whose voices are often not heard in the clamor over educational reform. Writing in a professional journal for educators, a teacher reported that in the planning of a major statewide new testing program the input from teachers had been "minuscule."

GOING TO SCHOOL IN EAST L.A.

Mike Rose

Mike Rose is a university teacher whose reports from the front lines of our educational system have inspired other teachers and students. Himself the son of poor Italian immigrants, Rose has devoted his career to helping students from minority or low-income backgrounds succeed in our system of education. He believes in the untapped potential—the native intelligence and ability to learn of students shortchanged by traditional educational assumptions and procedures. Rose first reached a wide audience with his Lives on the Boundary *(1989). He wrote this book to explore how his own early experiences were "reflected in other working-class lives I have encountered: the isolation of neighborhoods, information poverty, the limited means of protecting children from family disaster" and also "the resilience of imagination, the intellectual curiosity and literate enticements that remain hidden from the schools, the feeling of scholastic inadequacy, the dislocations that come from crossing educational boundaries." The following selection is from* Possible Lives; *the book Mike Rose published as a sequel or companion volume to* Lives on the Boundary *in 1995.*

Thought Starters: Mike Rose has been fascinated by the way American education helps define and perpetuate the class structure of this country. Did you go to school, or are you going to school, mostly with students of your own class or social level? Or did or do you study and associate with students from a cross section of American society?

It was early in the morning, the sky beginning to lighten, when Carlos Jiménez and I passed East Los Angeles Community College on our way to Garfield High School, close to the eastern boundary of East Los Angeles. The sun was coming up, breaking through the clouds, light gray and pearl, shining on beige stucco houses, small Spanish arches. Carlos's mother had taught at Garfield, and he's taught there for eleven years. The school was built in 1925, originally serving a predominantly Anglo and immigrant Jewish, Armenian, and Japanese population, but since World War II the surrounding community has become more Mexican in character and has been relatively stable; it is not uncommon for families to remain in the area for two generations, unusual in highly mobile Los Angeles. As the demographers would put it, it is a blue-collar community with a low transiency rate. One indicator of this residential stability is that Garfield, whose constituency is overwhelmingly Latino, needs to provide English-as-a-second-language instruction for only about 15 percent of its student body. Many schools outside of East LA have a higher Latino immigrant population.

Garfield High School was the location for the movie *Stand and Deliver*, the tribute to calculus teacher Jaime Escalante, but though Carlos respected Escalante's work (Escalante is no longer there), he bristled at the film's portrayal of the school as a place that did not believe in the potential of its students. There was a time when the school was in terrible shape, had one of the highest drop-out rates in the city, but student and community activism in the late 1960s contributed to change in general conditions. And during the mid-seventies, before Escalante's tenure, a core of dedicated teachers (John Bennett, Dennis Campagna, Tom Woessner) began building a rigorous advanced placement program, made up of courses, like those depicted in *Stand and Deliver*, which prepare students for tests that secure college credit. For some time, John Bennett has been preparing successful teams for the city's Academic Decathlon competition. "It's a decent school, and the kids are so damned nice," Carlos said en route. "There are the problems that come with poverty—kids are absent, some run away from home, and there is some gang activity—but by and large we don't have too many problems. Some LA schools have it a lot harder." One thing going for Garfield is that it is connected to its community. The annual football game with crosstown rival Roosevelt (another famous East LA school, but farther west, closer to the LA River and the downtown Civic Center) draws twenty-five thousand people. As one young local explained to me, "You look at the band and the parade—you can see that Garfield is real together. The people there are united."

Carlos would get to Garfield about seven—the time we arrived—and that would give him an hour to arrange his day. He taught U.S. history, two sections of advanced placement history, a course in Mexican-American history, and he coached field events and sprints for the track team. Because there had been so few materials available, he wrote the book he uses for the Mexican-American history course, sitting at his kitchen table, a pile of library books before him, typing units on Cortés or the Mexican Revolution or the Zoot Suit Riots onto duplicating stencils and distributing them to this class the next day. The materials have been revised and published as a textbook. His interest in athletics went back to his own career as a high school and college sprinter and triple-jumper, and he has developed his coaching skills in a series of sports clinics. He was a methodical teacher, relying on detailed notes, working from an outline of events displayed via an overhead projector, giving frequent quizzes, and assigning lots of writing. He would leave school about five, except on those days when there was a track meet; then it would be closer to seven-thirty or eight.

Along the entire south wall of Carlos's classroom was a series of pictures and texts that represented the sweep of Mexican and Mexican-American history: from a drawing of three Aztec warriors looking at an eagle with a snake in its beak to Hernán Cortés to Miguel Hildalgo and the Grito de Dolores, calling for "freedom and justice for the common man." Then came a picture-list of the Mexican presidents, drawings of Benito Juaréz and Emiliano Zapata, a poster for Luis Valdez's *Zoot Suit*, another poster of Cesar Chávez, the cover from Richard Vasquez's novel *Chicano*, a photograph of one of the murals that decorate the walls in East LA—a strong female figure in the style of Diego Rivera harvesting the fields: brown, orange, gold, and blue. At the very end of the pictorial time line was a poster for the Garfield-Roosevelt football game, the two team captains shaking hands, "a winning tradition."

Following Carlos through his day, I got to hear lectures on the Texas   5
Revolt and the short-lived Lone Star Republic, on the Spanish-American War and the debates within the United States between the Internationalists and the Anti-Imperialism League, on the major battles of World War II—Guadalcanal, Anzio, Iwo Jima—watching an old film, watching the faces of the students as the camera focused on the young faces of dead soldiers, listening to a girl beside me, her hand to her mouth, whisper "No." I sat through homeroom ("Good morning, Bulldogs . . ." the public address system blared) and a conference period during which Carlos dealt with a boy who had been kicked out of his house. I sat in as Carlos and another advanced placement teacher brought their classes together for an academic decathlon-style competition. I watched Carlos coach his pole vaulters. And through the day, I got to talk with his students. Here are [. . .] interviews with Ana Gaytan—a junior who was in Carlos's homeroom, had elected one of his sections of advanced placement history, and ran the two-mile for the track team—and Eddie Torres, a senior in Carlos's Mexican-American history class who was in the process of sending out applications for college.

Ana was about five foot two, slim, stood with her back straight, held her books to her chest. She talked about the way Carlos's room made her feel: "comfortable" and "at home." "Spanish was the first language I spoke and wrote," she explained, "and it feels good to see it reflected here. Sometimes during homeroom I'll turn around and just start reading the things on the wall—you know, about the Aztecs or about Father Hidalgo—and it makes me want to know more about it." Eddie—hint of a mustache, neat in T-shirt and jeans, opening a big binder he carried instead of a book bag—explained further as he looked for his homework. "If you grow up in East LA, all you hear are negative things. The movies, negative. The news, negative. The newspapers, negative. But, you know, this room is something *positive*. As you walk around the room, you say, 'Hey, we're somebody!' So that's why I took the Mexican-American history course. I wanted to know who we are."

Ana was interested in working with children—she volunteered at a nearby center for handicapped children—and hoped someday to be a pediatrician. Her days were very full, helping at home, attending a church group, school, homework, track practice. Her father was a lithographer and was going to night school to improve his English, but the family always tried to have dinner together. After dinner, she would clean up, then take a shower to jolt herself awake for her homework. When we spoke, she had just finished a paper for her English class on the emptiness of the character Daisy in *The Great Gatsby.* "Over the years," she said, "you just learn to set a schedule for yourself."

Eddie had more recently found his way. "Many of my friends have dropped out." He shrugged. "The hope, the self-esteem, was not there." He used to take general courses, and according to Carlos, his writing was not up to par. But he got tired of the "worksheets and busy work" and wanted classes where "you could give your own opinion—discuss and debate"—courses that "would help me in the future." He wanted to go away to college, to see new things. "Sometimes we Mexicans stay too tied to the family, but I think we need to gain new experience also." So he elected Carlos's Mexican-American history and advanced placement courses in history and Spanish. "I wanted to feel the pressure of the tough courses," he explained. "I wanted to know what that was like."

The Responsive Reader

1   Many people spend a large part of their lives in a school setting. Rose starts with a brief description of the school that is the setting for the students in his account. What would you include in your own capsule portrait of the school? What features or details seem most important as "indicators" of what the school is like? Is anything different from what you might have expected?

2   Do the students in Rose's account become real to you? What kind of people are they? Do you think of them as strangers, or do you come to know and like or dislike them? What are you likely to remember about them?

3   Richard Rodriguez, author of *Hunger of Memory,* once said that Mexican American students used to learn more about the wars of distant British warlords than about the work of their own parents and grandparents in the fields. In recent years, schools have started to honor the history of students from diverse backgrounds. What role does the concern with Mexican American history play in this account?

4   Rose has long promoted and paid tribute to the work of dedicated teachers working against odds. What role do such teachers play in this account? What motivates them? What are their methods and attitudes? What obstacles do they encounter, and how do they deal with them?

5   Rose stresses the vital connection between the school and the community as a key to the success of a school. How does he show this connection in this account?

Talking, Listening, Writing

6 In Rose's piece, Carlos Jiménez creates his own textbook to teach Mexican American history. Have you observed similar initiatives to put students in touch with their roots or their heritage? Supporters say that such initiatives promote self-esteem and help students overcome negative attitudes toward school. Critics claim that such initiatives may prove divisive, with other students feeling left out. What is your own estimate of the challenges and results?

7 What would you tell interested outsiders about your high school or college? What would you include beyond dry facts to give them a sense of what it is like to go to school there? What would you say about facilities, atmosphere, teachers, students, or community support?

Collaborative Projects

8 Carlos Jiménez decorated his classroom wall with "a series of pictures and texts that represented the sweep of Mexican and Mexican-American history." Suppose you were working on a class project to create an introduction to an ethnic, racial, or religious group to which you belong or in which you have a special interest. What would you include? What themes or key ideas would you stress? What assumptions or stereotypes that readers and viewers might bring to your project would you try to address?

MY DAUGHTER, CHILD #008458743

Jeff Zorn

Jeff Zorn teaches at Santa Clara University, a Jesuit university with high academic standards and an increasingly diverse often bicultural student population. He published his article criticizing the growing emphasis on testing in the nation's schools in the winter of 1999–2000, at a time when the movement to reform education by more and earlier testing was gathering momentum.

The media were sounding the alarm about "failing schools." Many teachers believed that it was the media and the parents who were failing teachers and students. Teachers and librarians were being laid off. Library hours were being cut back. Counseling staffs and other support personnel had been severely reduced. Art and music programs had been discontinued. In one school district, when art, music, library offerings, and athletics programs were being terminated, concerned parents drummed up donations to save the athletics program.

At the same time, the testing industry flourished. Raising test scores became a survival skill for teachers and administrators. After a major testing program was imposed in one flagship state, a teachers' organization testified that the actual input from teachers had been "minuscule." In 2004, a major testing industry organization admitted it had mistakenly rated thousands of aspiring new teachers as unqualified, denying them a chance for full-time employment and forcing them to take part-time employment at near-poverty-level wages. The organization offered to reimburse them for the fees they had charged for the faulty test.

Thought Starters: What is your history as a test taker? Have you done well on tests? Why or why not? Do you do well on some kinds of tests but not on others? What role have tests played in your progress through the school system?

After a two-month delay, California parents, educators, and newspapers finally got the results of last spring's STAR (Standardized Testing and Reporting). Probably no group was more deeply affected than the parents of the youngest students tested, the second graders.

My own daughter, Sarah Jane, heretofore a winsome if silly denizen of my household, was suddenly redefined as "Child #008458743." Her school, a Chinese Language Immersion School, became School #6113245.

Sarah Jane's permanent record now shows where she stands, on a percentile basis, among American children on particular subskills of language and mathematics. A more educationally worthless and civically damaging conception of children like Sarah Jane cannot be imagined.

STAR features Harcourt-Brace's Stanford 9 test, administered this year to over 4.5 million California public school students in grades two through 11. Sarah Jane's Stanford 9 scores told nothing useful about her intellectual development, either to me or to her teachers down at School #6113245. Anchored only to scores of other kids her age, they do not point to the mastery of any assigned curriculum materials, nor to the development of any particular habits of mind. They are merely invidious comparisons between my daughter and her age-mates, and they say nothing about Sarah as a learner.

School #6113245 is the Alice Fong Yu Chinese Language Immersion School. Sarah's teachers have spoken to her and her classmates in Cantonese since kindergarten. The English-language component of the curriculum has gone up from 10% to 20% of the day's activities, but Chinese language defines the school's purpose. Nothing in STAR speaks to what Alice Fong Yu has meant to Sarah—in terms of her language development, her sense of cultural difference, her sense of fitting in as a minority, her ability to look at problems from different vantage points, even her frustrations with writing complex characters in proper stroke order. STAR scores are fully reductive of all such long-term educative experiences.

And some details in STAR are ludicrous. Under "Word Study Skill," Child #008458743 answered 16 of 18 questions correctly on "Phonetic Analysis—Consonants" but only 9 of 18 questions correctly on "Phonetic Analysis—Vowels." In real life, trust me, Sarah has command of both vowels and consonants. Had she gotten as few "Consonants" questions right as she got "Vowels" questions, her overall score as a reader would have gone down into the next quartile, a negative mark not only for herself but for her school. Had she gotten as many "Vowels" questions right as she got "Consonants" questions, she would appear a truly outstanding reader and the Alice Fong Yu school that much more an outstanding inspirer of reading.

Why the discrepancy in her vowels and consonants scores? Who knows, maybe she was tired, or just tired of being tested, or the questions were phrased differently, or she'd been taught the material differently. The salient point is the scores reflected nothing important about Sarah but only her ad hoc response to a particular test-taking situation.

However inexact, however gratuitous educationally, STAR scores have great importance in a competitive society ever less squeamish about distributing its bounties unequally. Based on these and similar scores, children will be tracked high or low, accelerated or remediated through school, win more or less impressive credentials, and land accordingly in our social hierarchy.

I resent every minute of the month (yes, an entire month) that the Alice Fong Yu school was forced to spend on preparing children for STAR and then actually administering the test. I feel a sense of uncleanliness in involving her in a travesty of pseudo-scientific measurement and covert engineering.

The Responsive Reader

1   What is the purpose or the message of Zorn's *title*? If you saw it in a listing of articles about testing, would you be likely to check the article out? Is there anything wrong with a child and also her school being given a number?

2   What *factual information* about tests and testing can readers derive from this selection? What do you learn about the test the daughter took and about tests and and testing programs more generally?

3   Standardized tests are built on the claim that millions of young people can be measured and classified by objective measurements. How would you sum up Zorn's basic objection to this premise? What sentence (or sentences) in his statement can serve as his *thesis*?

4   Critics of the current testing emphasis often ask readers to look at one or more test items as a *test case*. Why is Zorn especially angry about the vowels–and–consonants test items? What to Zorn would make such an item "pseudo-scientific"? What makes the tests he describes "reductive"? (What is a "travesty"?)

5   Why is Zorn particularly concerned about testing and ranking students at a very young age? As a parent, would you also be particularly concerned?

Talking, Listening, Writing

6   Testing is a major means of *educational tracking* and screening. In countries like Britain, France, Germany, and Japan, testing at a young age has long tracked students into educational programs that determine their future place in the class structure of the country. Is increased emphasis on testing serving as a similar mechanism in this country? Have you seen evidence that tests can determine a student's future in the "social hierarchy"?

7   Do you think education can develop the *habits of mind* that Zorn says are missing from the tests he attacks? Do you think there are ways to measure a student's "sense of cultural differences"—an ability to understand and appreciate other cultural values or traditions? Are there ways to judge her sense of "fitting in as a cultural minority"—her self-image as a member of a minority? Can schools or teachers track "ability to look at problems from different vantage points"—open-mindedness or critical ability to think about different ways of solving a problem?

Collaborative Projects

8   Working alone or with a group, you may want to develop a *questionnaire* or other measurement instrument designed to rank fellow students on one of the educational achievements or teaching goals Zorn mentions. How objective can you make your instrument? How revealing or instructive are your results?

BAD AS THEY WANNA BE

Thad Williamson

For many students, intercollegiate athletics is a cornerstone of their college experience. Like the author of the following article, they remain lifelong fans of their college teams. He has said, "the team you root for inevitably becomes part of your identity." He says that in his part of the country a passion for college basketball is a tie that binds major schools that play in the "Triangle." The University of North Carolina (the Tar Heels) is a leading public university. North Carolina State has historically been focused on agriculture and engineering. Duke University is a highly ranked nationally known private university. As a devoted follower of Atlantic Coast basketball, Williamson wrote a column for an independent magazine and website devoted to UNC sports. He watched many games an an operator of an old manual scoreboard.

Williamson, who called himself "a thoughtful fan of college sports," criticized trends in collegiate athletics that work against the educational mission of the host institutions. He published the following article in the independent weekly The Nation *in 1998. Today, faculty groups or faculty voices continue to question the funding and educational benefits of big-time collegiate spectator sports.*

Thought Starters: Do you know students, or do you know about students, who were granted scholarships to go to college? What kind of scholarships were they? Were any or most of them athletic scholarships? How did the students obtain them or qualify for them?

The appeal of college athletics has long rested on their "amateur" status, the notion that the kids play mostly for the love of the game, without the pressures and influences that suffuse professional sports. These days, however, it's increasingly clear that big-time college athletics—in particular, men's basketball and football—are as wrapped in commercial values as the pros, and the system is rapidly spinning out of control.

In college arenas the best seats are now routinely reserved not for students and die-hard fans but for big-money boosters and private donors to the universities. The arenas themselves are being turned into prime advertising venues: Georgia Tech's revamped Alexander Memorial Coliseum, for example, goes so far as to place the McDonald's trademark "M" on the floor. Meanwhile, the NCAA's lucrative television contracts—an eight-year, $1.7 billion deal with CBS for broadcast rights to the Men's Division I basketball tournament and similar deals in football—are changing the fabric of the game, as top competition is slotted for prime-time viewing hours and games are steadily lengthened by TV timeouts.

Even the school I cover, North Carolina, which to this day bans all corporate advertising inside arenas, has largely succumbed to the trend. In the eighties UNC used some $34 million in private funds to build a 21,500-seat basketball arena, in the process setting a precedent of entitlement for major boosters. Not only did they win rights to the best seats in the arena, they are also allowed to pass on those seats to their progeny. More recently, university officials convinced the state highway board to authorize $1.2 million for a special road to allow top-dollar Tar Heels donors a convenient exit from home games.

There's more. Last summer the university signed a five-year, $11 million contract to use Nike-provided gear in all practices (for all sports) and to wear the familiar swoosh. No faculty members or students were directly involved in the negotiations, and no serious questions were raised about Nike's notorious labor practices abroad. Subsequently, concerned UNC students and faculty generated considerable public debate about the deal, but UNC plans to remain on the take.

Indeed, shoe companies like Adidas and Nike are now prime players in the college game. Most major Division I football and basketball coaches receive lucrative payments from the companies in exchange for outfitting their teams with the appropriate logo—and in some cases, such as the University of California, Berkeley, for encouraging their players to buy additional Nike gear. The sneaker sellers also operate most of the major summer camps for elite high school athletes, where schoolboy stars show their wares to college coaches (many of whom are themselves on Nike's or Reebok's payroll) in hopes of landing a top-flight scholarship. While the hottest prospects are showered with expenses-paid travel and free athletic gear, the companies develop relationships with future stars that might culminate in endorsement contracts.

Nowhere are the priorities of the new corporate order of college sports clearer than in the treatment of athletes—though you'd never know it from the popular image of those athletes as coddled superstars. In *He Got Game*, Spike Lee depicts the campus as a pleasure dome for young men treated to unlimited cars, women and material perks for four blissfully hedonistic years.

The truth is often far less alluring. "It's not as glamorous as people think," cautions Sheray Gaffney, a former reserve fullback for the football powerhouse Florida State Seminoles. "If you're in the program, it's not glamorous at all."

One reason for this is the so-called grant-in-aid system that characterizes all athletic scholarships in the NCAA. Originally established in 1956, grant-in-aid was intended to level the playing field by providing a fixed set of benefits to college athletes. Schools were allowed to offer scholarships of one to four years and were bound to honor them even if the athlete quit the team altogether. In 1973, however, the NCAA abruptly shifted course and mandated that the grants be limited to a one-year, annually renewable grant. The purpose of this change was to enable schools—in actuality, coaches—to keep tabs on each player's performance from year to year, and to cut off the scholarships of those whom the coach considered dispensable.

"Colleges changed the rule so they could run off the athletes who weren't good enough," explains Walter Byers, who oversaw the growth of college athletics while serving as NCAA executive director from 1951 to 1987. Back in the fifties Byers coined the term "student-athlete," a romantic idea that the NCAA continues to use in its promotional literature. These days, he is one of the NCAA's leading critics. "Once the colleges gave coaches the power to control those grants," he says, "that was a perversion that permanently changed the way things were done. It used to be that at least athletes could get an education if they couldn't play for the team."

Indeed, under the new system athletes do as the coaches say or risk being kicked out. Coach Rick Majerus of Utah, whose team reached the NCAA basketball finals this year, recently "released" Jordie McTavish saying he just wasn't good enough. A year ago, Coach Bobby Cremins of Georgia Tech asked freshman point guard Kevin Morris to leave for the same reason. More often than direct dismissals, coaches pressure players to leave on their own. Indiana's Bobby Knight, seeking to clean house after a disappointing 1996–97 season, drove starting point guard Neil Reed out of town with one year of eligibility remaining. Reed left, but not before accusing Knight of physical and emotional abuse.

Given the pressures to stay in the good graces of coaches—players know that missing even one session in the weight room risks incurring the coach's wrath—it's no wonder that graduation rates for Division I football and basketball players in the NCAA hover at roughly 50 percent, a figure that exaggerates the amount of learning that actually takes place. Instead of promoting a balance between sports and academics, the system forces athletes to pour every ounce of energy into the game, with little recognition that the vast majority of players are in a vocational dead end. A sad rite of passage for most college athletes is the existential realization that they will never make it to the pros. "What was astonishing was the number of scars that [the program] left on athletes that came to the surface behind closed doors," recalls Gaffney. "It was painful to see athletes crying in distress because they see their dreams slowly fading away. All of a sudden at age 20, 21, they are required to make a complete transition."

True, college sports still represent a way out for poor or working-class athletes. Some, with the help of coaches like Dean Smith, find jobs in coaching, pro leagues overseas or business. Others succeed in getting an education. But the inequities are glaring. While generating an enormous revenue stream for their universities through ticket sales, merchandising, advertising and TV deals, athletes are forbidden from sharing in any of the gains. "When these commercial activities came along," notes Byers, "the overseers and supervisors made sure that the benefits went to them, not the athletes." College coaches routinely earn six-figure salaries, sign endorsement deals with corporations and jump from school to school for more lucrative contracts. The athletes, meanwhile, are the focus of scandal and media outrage if they so much as accept money for an extra trip home. Under the grant-in-aid rule, athletes may not use their talent or name recognition to earn money while in school except under tightly defined conditions.

In Byers's view, the "gobs of money" now flowing to the universities makes a return to the amateur ideal impossible. What is possible, he believes, is scrapping the current grant-in-aid system, which leads not only to the rampant exploitation of athletes but, he argues, violates antitrust laws because colleges essentially operate as a cartel, setting a national limit on what a whole class of students can earn. He would require athletes to apply for financial aid like any other student but would remove all restrictions on how they could earn money while in college.

Rick Telander, a *Sports Illustrated* writer and author of *The Hundred Yard Lie*, an exposé of college football, proposes a more radical solution: namely, severing big-time college football programs from the schools that lend them their name. In Telander's view, an NFL-subsidized "age-group professional league" could be established in which universities would own and operate teams, using university facilities and traditional school colors. Players need not be students but would earn a year of tuition for each year played, redeemable at any time, during or after their playing careers. College basketball would also benefit from the creation of an NBA-backed age-group league. Such leagues could offer gifted players with no interest in academics a credible alternative to college, and a second chance to earn an education should their professional dreams fade.

Of course, given the entrenched institutional support for the status quo, none of this can happen without a sustained demand from the public, including students, coaches not yet corrupted, and athletes themselves. In the meantime, students and faculty can make their voices heard by continuing—and expanding—their campaigns challenging the corporate sponsorship of university athletic departments. Over the past year campus activists at Duke and other universities have successfully pushed administrators to adopt rules requiring that all campus sweatshirts and athletic gear be produced in compliance with labor and human rights standards. These same activists should insist that corporate advertising be banned from all arenas; that universities cap athletic budgets for football and basketball and put an end to the "arms race" for bigger facilities and more amenities; and that the influence of big-money donors be limited so that students and fans can continue to attend athletic events at reasonable prices. Activists might also find unexpected common ground with coaches and fans concerned about how the integrity of the game has been subordinated to television, or how corporations are colonizing and poisoning the high school recruiting scene.

Speaking for myself, probably only death will cure my love affair with North Carolina basketball, and no doubt there are millions of people who feel the same way about their own teams. But loving the game need not mean having a romantic view of how college sports are organized. College sports are far too visible an arena in American society to be simply thrown to the wolves. Ultimately, the only productive route forward is to insist that those who love the game also fight to change it.

The Responsive Reader

1 Who are the big-time *supporters* of college sports? Williamson used much of his article to put the spotlight on the role of wealthy alumni and influential corporate sponsors in college sports. What are striking facts or claims in this article about arrangements, major deals, and perks or rewards? (Do they seem surprising or unusual to you?)

2 What is the *academic record* of college athletes? Are college athletes in big-time programs getting an education? There has been much publicity about eligibility rules and graduation rates. How many college athletes are bona-fide college students who complete a major and graduate?

3 What changes does Williamson report in the conditions under which *athletic scholarships* were granted? Do you think a college should be allowed to cancel an athletic scholarship when a team or coach no longer wants the scholarship athlete?

4 Is it true that college athletes are *exploited*? Although players are lionized or admired, do they in basic ways get an unfair deal? How and why? What examples or evidence does Williamson cite?

Talking, Listening Writing

5 Public figures and public employees are often investigated for conflicts of interest. Do you think coaches who are college or university employees should at the same time be on the payrolls of private sponsors?

6 The quarterback of a championship football team was asked by sportswriters how he reconciled the bone-crushing violence on the football field with his religious beliefs. He said, "Football is not violent. When a kid puts a gun up to another guy's head and blows it off, that's violence. . . . We don't go out to kill each other. We go out to win." Do you think that was a good answer? Why or why not?

OTHER VOICES

The Bottom Line of College Sports

Do big-time college sports support their institutions? Or do they syphon funds that should go to educational programs?

- According to a 2004 cover story in *USA Today* developed as a joint venture with the *Des Moines Register*, about 60 percent of Division I schools rely on student fees to help the athletic department, with fees ranging from $50 to $1,000 a year. The University of Louisville had hired a big-name men's basketball coach with a six-year $12.4 million contract, "hoping he would restore the men's basketball team to its former glory." It also still had to pay $2.5 million to the former coach. The university agreed to support the athletic department. The average head football coach's base salary was $388,600.

- The athletics director at a Midwestern school whose team won the football national championship in a recent year called his overall sports program a "mammoth" program budgeted at over $80 million a year. During a five-year period when undergraduate teaching was increasingly handed over to part-time temporary faculty, salaries, wages, and benefits for his university's athletic personnel had gone up more than 50 percent.

Working alone or with a group, research the finances of college sports locally or nationally. For instance, you may want to concentrate on one major institution as a test case. Or you may want to focus on one major sport, such as football or basketball.

A DAY IN THE LIFE OF A LAB RAT

Shaughnessy Bishop-Stall

**"I am here because my money ran out before my
school term, my lease, and my need for food."**

*A major part of the reality of student life is the struggle of working students to raise
enough money to pay the rent and steadily rising tuition. Shaughnessy Bishop-
Stall tells the story of a student who signed up as a human guinea pig for the
booming pharmaceutical industry. He takes us to a dimension of student life not
often recognized in the sports media buildup to the Big Game or the Final Four or
in the commencement speeches by visiting dignitaries.*

*How do students who do not have wealthy parents or athletic scholarships
work their way through school? How do they deal with rising tuition fees and
encumbering student loans? The author reminds readers of the large and often
unreported subculture of working students: They serve at tables or do the dishes
at patrons' dinners for affluent alumni. They work late hours in restaurants or
cheap bars and then appear after a few hours of sleep for 8:30 classes. They sign
up like the author of the following account for jobs they cannot afford to refuse.
The following account was first published in* Saturday Night *for September 1999.
Like other testimonies later reprinted in the* Utne Reader, *it is more candid and
personal than much that is published in the mainstream media.*

Thought Starters: Do you know people who work part-time or full-time
jobs to enable them to stay in school? Have you ever given blood to raise
badly needed cash? What is the worst thing you have had to do for money?

It is 6:35 Friday morning and I'm watching cartoons with 31 other
men. Some of them are still in their underwear, alternately gazing up at the
television and down at their bare feet, muttering, "Coffee, coffee. . . ."
Others have already showered and combed their hair and are now sitting up
straight, with their backs to the television, watching the clock across the
room as if it were a descending deity. The rest of us are bunched over, glaring at *Muppet Babies* through half-closed eyes. I look down at the piece of
paper in my hands. My gaze rests on the third line:

3. I wake up fresh and rested most mornings.

A voice crackles over the loudspeaker. "Number One—Rupert.
Lab." This is the first thing the voice has said since it told us to wake up,
to get out of bed, to sit in these chairs. And now everyone glances over at

Rupert as he stands and makes his way past the pool table, past the Super Nintendo station, past the dining tables, across the gray room lit by fluorescent bulbs.

> *9. My daily life is full of things that keep me interested.*
> *10. I am afraid of losing my mind.*

It's 6:42. None of us has had much sleep, and now the door to the sleeping room is locked. We won't be given any food until noon. I decide not to look at the clock anymore. Without it, however, it could be any time of day; heavy venetian blinds close out the world. The only way out is a door on the far side of the room. But if anyone tries to open it a siren will sound.

"Number Five—Jesus. Lab." Jesus is a big smiley guy from Colombia who punches me in the arm when I beat him at pool and lifts me off the ground in a bear hug when I lose. The voice over the loudspeaker does not pronounce his name with the Latin accent, *Hey-Zeus*, or even with the French one: *Jay-Zoo*. Here he is just plain "Jesus."

Jesus mutters something in Spanish as he pushes himself out of his chair.

"What did he say?" asks Number Four, sitting down.

"Think of the money," I say.

Number Four nods. It has become a sort of materialistic mantra around here—"Think of the money." This is not, after all, a jail, nor rehab, nor some Orwellian summer camp. This is Phoenix International Life Sciences Inc.—the Rolls Royce of clinical testing. And we're all in it for the money.

If you want to make some cash as a human lab rat, this is the place to be. According to the company's prospectus, it is "the world's fifth-largest contract research organization serving the pharmaceutical, generic drug, and biotechnology industries." With net revenues of $171 million in 1998, Phoenix pays top dollar to healthy males for the right to test drugs on their bodies. And although it now has clinics across the United States and Europe, Phoenix is wisely based in Montreal, a city overflowing with poor young men.

"Number Six—Sauganee. Lab." This is actually as close as they've come to my name so far.

I am here because my money ran out before my school term, my lease, and my need for food. And although I've had no trouble finding work in cities all over the world, from Veracruz to Venice, Montreal is different, especially if your French is about on a par with Andrew Dice Clay's. So, after a long desperate job search (which included applying for such positions as "promotional swordfighter" and "Jewish homeworker"), I finally decided to answer a long-running ad in *HOUR* magazine for "participants in a study," promising "compensatory indemnity of up to $1,000."

I signed myself up for the first available study and had only to pass the medical exam and screening process. Phoenix took samples of my blood and urine, measured my height and weight and EKG levels, asked a bunch of questions, then sent me home. I felt pretty confident. After all, I was young and resilient—a perfect specimen.

The next morning I got a phone call: "Unfortunately, Mr. Shaugauness, your liver enzymes are above the acceptable level."

"What does that mean?" I asked.

"It means," my girlfriend told me later, "that drinking like Bukowski since the age of 15 does not a good guinea pig make."

The next day, she came home from the library with information on the ultimate liver-cleansing diet.

"No drinking," she said.

"Yeah, I should get up early tomorrow anyway," I said.

"No. No drinking for at least a month. And no coffee. No drugs. No smoking."

"Uh . . ."

"No meat. No fried food. No processed food."

"But . . ."

"By the time we're finished you'll have the liver of a 6-year-old girl." I'm looking down at the paper in my hands, my pencil hovering in the air. There are still four hours until lunch, and no more blood draws or EKGs until afternoon. And so I've decided to work some more on this questionnaire.

> 90. *If I were an artist, I would like to draw flowers.*
> 91. *I have never vomited blood or coughed up blood.*

It turns out that Montreal is a mecca of clinical testing, and during my liver-cleansing month I was able to secure a couple of less lucrative studies. One of them includes this list of 400 statements to which I must respond either yes or no. So far, very few of them have proved easily answerable.

> 95. *The top of my head sometimes feels tender.*
> 96. *I like to go to parties and other affairs where there is lots of loud fun.*

It is 8:53 A.M. and in my hand I'm holding four pink pills that may or may not contain calcitriol, a synthetic vitamin D analogue used as a calcium supplement. The drawl of *Fried Green Tomatoes* echoes behind the staccato click of pool balls and the incessant *beboop-boop* of Super Mario Bros. I swallow the pills and gulp down a glass of water.

"Open your mouth, please," says the nurse. I open my mouth. She looks in, prying back my cheeks with a tongue depressor. "Lift up your tongue." I lift my tongue. She looks under it. "Please open your hands."

"Excuse me?"

"Your hands. Please open them and show me the palms." I imagine Jesus coming in after me and slowly, coyly, revealing his stigmata.

Then I realize what she's looking for. After all I've been through, a month of shakes and cold sweats, nic-fits and caffeine withdrawal, and endless brown rice and vegetables, with not even a beer to wash them down, Phoenix thinks there's a chance I would palm their little pink pills. What for? To save them for later? To sell them to some milk junkie? But I do not protest. I show her my palms.

190. At times I feel like smashing things.
191. Someone has control over my mind.

It is 9:14 P.M. We have had lunch and dinner and have just finished our evening snacks. We have had 16 different needles pushed into our veins. Our arms are swelling and bruised and one person has fainted and one has vomited and three seem to have disappeared. I have responded yes or no to 244 inane statements. Besides *Fried Green Tomatoes*, we have watched *Nell* and *Spaceballs* and *ConAir*, and *Dances with Wolves* and now, as they are attaching the electrodes to me for the last of the day's 15 EKGs, I can hear the TV blaring the fourth movement of Beethoven's Ninth Symphony.

An urgent voice blasts over the loudspeaker: "Number 5—Jesus—to the kitchen to finish his milk. Jesus did not finish his milk."

"¡No me gusta leche, por nada!"

"What is Jesus saying?"

"He's saying he doesn't like milk. That's all. He just doesn't like it. And please don't shave my chest."

The electrodes are attached to my nipples, my stomach, my shins. I'm staring up at the ceiling, listening to a room full of mumbling men and Beethoven and Jesus and an impatient nurse. There are four more days of this, 24 more blood draws, 18 more EKGs, countless more movies, urine samples, pills, glasses of milk. I tell myself to think of the money.

Instead, I think of a real job—one where you dig the earth, or lift big boxes, or cook food, or save people from drowning. I think of the men in the other room. Benoit is an actor and a security guard, but he can't make enough to feed his kids. Enrique was a lawyer in Mexico and has applied to every Mexican restaurant in the city. As companies like Phoenix expand, I can see men in cities all over the world moving into clinics, closing the blinds, turning on the TV, sipping their milk.

I tell myself this isn't it, this isn't all. I'm still young; I can still be whatever I want to be. I just need some money right now. I just have to pay the rent, curb my student loans. That's all.

I think of the setting sun, of waterfalls and road trips, of open-air concerts and the desert and stars and swimming in the ocean. Then I think of the money.

The Responsive Reader

1   What do you learn about the *author*? What would you include in a brief vita? What would you include in a psychological profile?

2 What basic *facts* do you gather about the company conducting the testing? Who are they? What are their goals? What is their basic MO or operating procedure? In the description they give or their work, what is informative, and what sounds like corporate promotion or PR?

3 What is the author's prevailing *attitude* toward the assignment? What made the assignment alienating for the author? Do you think the project as a whole or some of the procedures are demeaning or dehumanizing?

4 What kind of cultural literacy does the author expect in his *audience*?

   ▪ For instance, why does he call an often repeated saying a "mantra"?

   ▪ How would an "Orwellian" experience be at the opposite scale of expectations from a "Rolls Royce" experience?

   ▪ Why would someone like the author be amused by the company's calling itself the "Phoenix International Life Sciences" corporation?

   ▪ What is weird about the human guinea pigs hearing the fourth movement with the "Ode to Joy" from Beethoven's Ninth Symphony from the TV in the lab?

5 What is your *response* as a reader? Can you identify with the author? Why or why not? Do you think he is being oversensitive? Do you think he is representative or unrepresentative of today's student population?

Talking, Listening, Writing

6 How do you or how do students you know well cope with the rising cost of a college education? What is your or their experience with student loans, grants, scholarships, or other sources of financial support? What is your or their experience with low-end or marginal jobs helping students stay in school?

7 Toward the end of the article, Bishop-Stall thinks about what a "real job" should be like. What is his idea of a real job? What is yours?

8 The author intersperses his day's log with sample questions from his reading of a psychological aptitude test of the kind widely used by personnel departments of prospective employers. To judge from the fragmentary sampling included here, what are they checking for? What are they trying to weed out? Who would be the ideal employee? What advice would you give to a test taker? (On some of these, how would you know which is the right answer?)

FIND IT ON THE WEB

Animal rights activists have vigorously attacked uses and abuses of animals in research. Can you find recent discussions of the use of human subjects in research? Are there ethical standards, widely known guidelines, or discussions of test cases?

MARKETERS ARE STORMING THE SCHOOLHOUSE

Michael J. Sandel

"Corporations consider young kids and teenagers as consumers in training."

—STUDENT READER

In recent years, aggressive advertisers have moved into new areas in the search for ways to get commercial messages to the consumer. Fans shrug when sports arenas with time-honored names like Candlestick Park or Texas Stadium turn into 3-Com Park or Coca-Cola Arena. College athletes are becoming used to being walking advertisements, carrying a corporate logo on their uniforms and running shoes. School districts sign exclusive contracts with manufacturers of soft drinks to supplement tight budgets. Are critics of the growing "commercialization of schools" waging a losing battle? Michael J. Sandel wrote the following article for the "Hard Questions" column of the New Republic, *a journal of commentary and informed opinion offering readers a range of views.*

Sandel published this article in 1997, at an early stage of marketers' campaigns to sell and promote their products in schools and have corporate promotional materials used as instructional materials by students. (Candlestick Park was recently renamed Monster Park, adopting the name of a new corporate sponsor.)

Thought Starters: Americans are used to being surrounded by advertising. Keep a log of the commercial messages you encounter during a single day. Which of them did you really notice? Which of them might have an impact on your behavior as a consumer?

When the Boston Red Sox installed a display of giant Coke bottles above the left field wall, local sportswriters protested that such tacky commercialism tainted the sanctity of Fenway Park. But ballparks have long been littered with billboards and ads. Today, teams even sell corporations the right to name the stadium: the Colorado Rockies, for example, play in Coors Field. However distasteful, such commercialism does not seem to corrupt the game or diminish the play.

The same cannot be said of the newest commercial frontier—the public schools. The corporate invasion of the classroom threatens to turn schools into havens for hucksterism. Eager to cash in on a captive audience of consumers-in-training, companies have flooded teachers with free videos, posters and "learning kits" designed to sanitize corporate images and

1

emblazon brand names in the minds of children. Students can now learn about nutrition from curricular materials supplied by Hershey's Chocolate or McDonald's, or study the effects of the Alaska oil spill in a video made by Exxon. According to *Giving Kids the Business*, by Alex Molnar, a Monsanto video teaches the merits of bovine growth hormone in milk production, while Proctor & Gamble's environmental curriculum teaches that disposable diapers are good for the earth.

Not all corporate-sponsored educational freebies promote ideological agendas; some simply plug the brand name. A few years ago, the Campbell Soup Company offered a science kit that showed students how to prove that Campbell's Prego spaghetti sauce is thicker than Ragu. General Mills distributed science kits containing free samples of its Gusher fruit snacks, with soft centers that "gush" when bitten. The teacher's guide suggested that students bite into the Gushers and compare the effect to geothermal eruptions. A Tootsie Roll kit on counting and writing recommends that, for homework, children interview family members about their memories of Tootsie Rolls.

While some marketers seek to insinuate brand names into the curriculum, others take a more direct approach: buying advertisements in schools. When the Seattle School Board faced a budget crisis last fall, it voted to solicit corporate advertising. School officials hoped to raise $1 million a year with sponsorships like "the cheerleaders, brought to you by Reebok" and "the McDonald's gym." Protests from parents and teachers forced the Seattle schools to suspend the policy this year, but such marketing is a growing presence in schools across the country.

Corporate logos now clamor for student attention from school buses to book covers. In Colorado Springs, advertisements for Mountain Dew adorn school hallways, and ads for Burger King decorate the sides of school buses. A Massachusetts firm distributes free book covers hawking Nike, Gatorade and Calvin Klein to almost 25 million students nationwide. A Minnesota broadcasting company pipes music into school corridors and cafeterias in fifteen states, with twelve minutes of commercials every hour. Forty percent of the ad revenue goes to the schools.

The most egregious example of the commercialization in schools is Channel One, a twelve-minute television news program seen by 8 million students in 12,000 schools. Introduced in 1990 by Whittle Communications, Channel One offers schools a television set for each classroom, two VCRs and a satellite link in exchange for an agreement to show the program every day, including the two minutes of commercials it contains. Since Channel One reaches over 40 percent of the nation's teenagers, it is able to charge advertisers a hefty $200,000 per thirty-second spot. In its pitch to advertisers, the company promises access to the largest teen audience in history in a setting free of "the usual distractions of telephones, stereos, remote controls, etc." The Whittle program shattered the taboo against outright advertising in the classroom. Despite controversy in many states, only New York has banned Channel One from its schools.

Unlike the case of baseball, the rampant commercialization of schools is corrupting in two ways. First, most corporate-sponsored learning supplements are ridden with bias, distortion and superficial fare. A recent study by Consumers Union found that nearly 80 percent of classroom freebies are slanted toward the sponsor's product. An independent study of Channel One released earlier this year found that its news programs contributed little to students' grasp of public affairs. Only 20 percent of its airtime covers current political, economic or cultural events. The rest is devoted to advertising, sports, weather and natural disasters.

But, even if corporate sponsors supplied objective teaching tools of impeccable quality, commercial advertising would still be a pernicious presence in the classroom because it undermines the purposes for which schools exist. Advertising encourages people to want things and to satisfy their desires: education encourages people to reflect on their desires, to restrain or to elevate them. The purpose of advertising is to recruit consumers; the purpose of public schools is to cultivate citizens.

It is not easy to teach students to be citizens, capable of thinking critically about the world around them, when so much of childhood consists of basic training for a commercial society. At a time when children come to school as walking billboards of logos and labels and licensed apparel, it is all the more difficult—and all the more important—for schools to create some distance from a popular culture drenched in consumerism.

But advertising abhors distance. It blurs the boundaries between   10
places, and makes every setting a site for selling. "Discover your own river of revenue at the schoolhouse gates!" proclaims the brochure for the 4th Annual Kid Power Marketing Conference, held last May in New Orleans. "Whether it's first-graders learning to read or teenagers shopping for their first car, we can guarantee an introduction of your product and your company to these students in the traditional setting of the classroom!" Marketers are storming the schoolhouse gates for the same reason that Willie Sutton robbed banks—because that's where the money is. Counting the amount they spend and the amount they influence their parents to spend, 6- to 19-year-old consumers now account for $485 billion in spending per year.

The growing financial clout of kids is itself a lamentable symptom of parents abdicating their role as mediators between children and the market. Meanwhile, faced with property tax caps, budget cuts and rising enrollments, cash-strapped schools are more vulnerable to the siren song of corporate sponsors. Rather than raise the public funds we need to pay the full cost of educating our schoolchildren, we choose instead to sell their time and rent their minds to Burger King and Mountain Dew.

The Responsive Reader

1 What is the "bottom line" underlying the controversy? How does Sandel size up the buying power of young Americans and the corporate respect for it?

2 What is Sandel's analysis of "news programs" distributed by corporate sponsors. What are his objections? How justified or well-founded do they seem to you?

3 Sandel and other critics of corporate dealings with the schools claim that gifts of equipment or products to the schools are often not really public-spirited and beneficial to learning and students' growth. They are "free-bies"—offered with ulterior motives. What are Sandel's examples, and how convincing are they?

4 A major public relations strategy of corporate advertisers is the effort to co-opt the concerns of public-spirited citizens—for instance, to stress the environmental or health benefits of corporate products or practices. What are Sandel's examples? Why does he find them objectionable?

5 Sandel employs the traditional strategy of satire—holding up the most outlandish examples of a trend or phenomenon to ridicule. What to you are the most ridiculous or outlandish examples Sandel cites?

Talking, Listening, Writing

6 Have you, or has someone you know well, been exposed to advertising in the classroom or on campus? What form did it take? What was your or the other person's reaction? Was the advertising effective? Was it objectionable?

7 Do you agree with Sandel's basic assumption that there is an essential difference between advertising to adults and the commercial exploitation of the young? Why or why not?

8 How would you define *consumerism*? What are its key features? How essential is it to the functioning of American society or the American way of life?

9 Developments like those criticized by Sandel in this essay often precipitate vigorous debate in the concerned communities. Would you get involved? Choose from one of the following letter-writing assignments or take on another similar writing task:

- Write a letter or e-mail as a corporate public relations person to respond to Sandel's argument.

- Write a letter or e-mail from a school administrator to concerned parents.

- Write a letter or e-mail from a college athlete objecting to or defending the use of a corporate logo on athletic uniforms and equipment.

- Write a letter or e-mail to the editor of *New Republic* to accuse its columnist of being anti-business or to defend him against the charge.

ELECTRONIC COMMUNICATION MAY AID SOCIAL INTERACTION

Stanford Report

"The computers became a tool for building, rather than destroying, social relations."

The following report from a campus newsletter was first disseminated by the Stanford University News Service in April of 1998. It addressed an issue that was to be the subject of much discussion: Is the computer revolution going to kill genuine face-to-face human interaction, making us instead spend hours looking at faceless messages on a small screen?

Supporters of the computer revolution aim at providing computer access for every student. Enthusiastic advocates made computer literacy the fast lane to the age of the information highway and the knowledge explosion. The "information resources specialist" featured in the following report was an early leader in the movement to help teachers and students become computer literate and make full use of the resources of the Internet. At the same time, promoters of the cyberspace revolution heard from critical observers and cyberskeptics warning against inflated expectations and negative side effects.

Thought Starters: When did you first start to become computer literate? Who or what initiated you? What early obstacles or problems did you encounter? How would you rate your computer literacy now?

Consider Zachary,★ made to order for isolation by computer. A self–described loner, he asked for a single room when he arrived as a freshman in 1995. His room, like most at Stanford, was wired directly to the university's computer network. Critics of this "plug-per-pillow" arrangement said it would lead students to hide in their electronic caves, avoiding face-to-face interaction, not to mention ruining the chance to develop the proper wrist action for Frisbee. Zachary was poised to be their poster boy.

His dorm, Rinconada House in Wilbur Hall, was the first college dorm in the world with its own web page and one of the first to use "list-serv" software that permitted all 96 residents to send and read e-mail messages circulated to the entire group. Zachary soon plugged in to these on-line discussions and became one of the list's most frequent correspondents.

Isolation city? Au contraire. At meals, other students sought him out to comment about his online musings. People dropped by his room to talk.

1

★All student names are pseudonyms.

Over the year, resident fellows Rich and Roni Holeton watched Zachary gradually become gregarious and adopt his dormmates as extended family. "Without his e-mail postings, this might never have happened," Rich Holeton says. "We might never have learned what a thoughtful guy he is."

Holeton (A.B. '75) found a number of surprises that jolt conventional wisdom about computer communication in research he conducted of Rinconada's e-mail discussions for the 1995–96 academic year. Instead of being an "either-or" situation, where time spent on computers takes away from time spent with others, e-mail extended and added to personal conversations, drawing in new members of the community, he found.

"The computers became a tool for building, rather than destroying, social relations," he said.

Residents used the e-mail discussion list, along with meetings, hallway conversations, phone calls and notices posted on the walls, to organize and publicize events, find lost keys, trade jokes and call out players for that quick game of Frisbee. They used this computer grapevine, along with conversations and dorm meetings, to hammer out community issues like how much noise is too much during study hours. They added e-mail to the traditional bull session when they wanted to talk about social and political issues ranging from a grape boycott to date rape. When a dormmate died suddenly, the e-mail list was one of the ways they shared their grief.

Several studies have been made of computer-mediated communication in virtual communities linked by work or common interest, but Holeton said to his knowledge, Rinconada is the first real community to be studied—the first place where e-mail list correspondents live together and see each other day and night.

He analyzed all the messages posted to the Rinconada list for a year, and compared his findings with the results of a survey in which the students rated the usefulness of e-mail as a form of communication.

Except as a means of discussing academics, e-mail was considered by the students to be as useful or more useful than other means of dorm communication. (Holeton's study results—including data, analyses and samples of online discussions on topics from free speech to planning a dorm dance—can be viewed at http://www-leland.stanford.edu/-holeton/ wired-pages/wired-main.html.) *10*

Holeton is an information resources specialist, teaching language and literature professors new ways to use electronic media in the classroom. He spent 10 years as a Stanford writing instructor; his third anthology for writing classes, *Composing Cyberspace*, has just been published. In his writing classes, he used computer discussion groups as a way to expand the usual classroom dynamic, where a few gregarious people usually dominate the conversation. He found that online, he could get everyone involved.

Students in a dorm are not subject to a teacher's prodding, however. As he expected, Holeton found that a small core of a dozen students dominated Rinconada's e-mail discussions. But even shy students who seldom posted messages were using the list to keep themselves cued in to the community.

"Most students rated themselves as occasional writers but frequent readers of the list," Holeton says. Those so-called lurkers used the list mostly for housekeeping purposes, that is, to find out about events or ask if anyone had seen a chemistry book left in the lounge. But in dialogues about social and political issues, some of the most thoughtful commentary came from lurkers who clearly felt comfortable jumping into a conversation that they had been following in silence.

Holeton says one thing his study couldn't find out was whether shy students used e-mail to avoid face-to-face conversations. His personal observations showed that for some, like Zachary, e-mail was an icebreaker that helped open up personal contact.

Men traditionally dominate discussions in dorm meetings as well as in the classroom, and Holeton says he was troubled to find that the same dynamic continues online. One woman, Hillary, posted more messages to the list than anyone else, but she and Bertha were the only two in the core group who participated often. Men also dominated the discussions that Holeton labeled "critical dialogue," the sort of social and political debate that an academic setting is designed to promote; women joined in more often in discussions about the dorm community. "Men may participate more because they are more comfortable with the traditional combative debate style of critical dialogue," Holeton says.

15

When he looked more closely, however, he found some of the most interesting debates were initiated and joined by women. One thread of conversation that went on for several months began when Mona passed on a letter from another college, a cautionary tale about date rape. A thoughtful debate continued among several men about responsibility for consent in sex and for violence against women. Betty was the one to add, "It's fine to analyze all the little points of the law and of ethics on a theoretical level, but it seems to me that the real issue here is . . . about respect and communication."

The particularity of the Rinconada online study is that the participants see each other every day at dinner or in the dormitory hall. Instead of igniting "flame wars" that sometimes turn computer discussion groups into a mess of personal insults, Rinconadans composed thoughtful, reasonable disagreements, often with a phrase like, "I attack your arguments, but not your character."

Says Holeton, "They were a special community, and they knew it. Their intellectual exchange on the e-mail list was enhanced by their feelings for each other, and their friendships and group feeling were enhanced by their written exchanges. At their best, they modeled an intellectual community in a new, fuller sense."

The Responsive Reader

1 What are the criticisms or negative expectations that this report sets out to defuse or counteract? How does Zachary, poised to be "poster boy" for negative criticism, become the hero of this account?

2 What are the findings of the various studies this report cites? What did they show about "computer-mediated communication" and "virtual communities"? How solid or authoritative do these studies seem to you? According to the researchers, what questions did they leave unanswered?

3 What light did Holeton's studies shed on the gender gap in the world of computers? What gave males the edge in online discussion? Have you made similar or different observations?

4 Do you think that Rinconada House is a special case, or can computers enhance social interaction in other, less enclosed, settings? Why or why not?

Talking, Listening, Writing

5 Have you ever thought that you might be interacting with the computer at the expense of interacting with real people? Are you a member of any e-mail groups or listservs? How much do you feel a part of those "communities"? How well do you know the other respondents and lurkers?

6 Luddites are critics of the worship of technology in modern society. They think that we were better off when we walked to work, ate home-grown food, and found inspiration not in movie multiplexes but in the great outdoors. Have you seen evidence of the attitude of cyberskeptics who feel that the promise or benefits of the computer revolution have been overrated? Do you personally see computers as "a tool for building . . . social relations" or as an obstacle to normal social interaction?

Collaborative Projects

7 Working with a group, conduct an informal survey to explore a question like the following: Is there a gender gap in computer literacy and utilization of the Internet? (Is it true that women students spend relatively less time at the computer and rely less on electronic sources than males? Is gender a factor in decisions to participate or not to participate in online discussions?) How does social background or economic status affect students' access to computers and electronic resources? (How significant is the disparity in the availability and utilization of resources?)

FIND IT ON THE WEB

Pioneering educators who have kept teachers and students up-to-date on developments in computer use and Internet resources include Richard Holeton, Cynthia Selfe, and Christine Hult. Institutions that have played leading roles in supporting research and programs include Michigan Technological University and Colorado State. Check these or similar sources for recent publications on current challenges and issues.

The following are sample titles from one student's search:

Dawson, Jerry. "The Future of Educational Technology." 15 Jan. 2003. <http://horizon.unc.edu/projects/monograph/CD/Instructional_Technology/Dawson.asp>

Holeton, Richard. "The Semi-Virtual Composition Classroom: A Model for Techno-Amphibians." 14 Jan. 2003. <http://horizon.unc.edu/projects/monograph/CD/Language_Music/Holeton.asp>

Pacheco, Maria. "Use of Computers and Computer Networks in the Physical Chemistry Laboratory and Lecture." 15 Jan 2003. <http://horizon.unc.edu/projects/monograph/CD/Science_Mathematics/Pacheco.asp>

INDIAN BOARDING SCHOOL: THE RUNAWAYS

Louise Erdrich

"Home's the place we head for in our sleep." Young runaways are returned to forced schooling separating them from their homes and culture.

Erdrich's poem was first published in a collection of her poems in 1984, at a time when Native American authors were reaching a large audience with writing honoring the history and traditions of a "defeated nation." Her poetry and fiction made many readers rethink failed policies of assimilation.

Of Chippewa and German-American descent, Erdrich grew up in North Dakota and later went to live in New Hampshire. Her best-selling novel, Love Medicine *(1984), won the National Book Critics Circle Award; among her other books are* The Beet Queen *(1986),* Tracks *(1988), and* The Bingo Palace *(1994). Her poem is a vivid expression of rebellion against schooling that becomes forced conversion to a different way of life.*

Thought Starters: What are your thoughts about "Americanizing" cultural minorities?

Home's the place we head for in our sleep.   *1*
Boxcars stumbling north in dreams
don't wait for us. We catch them on the run.
The rails, old lacerations that we love,
shoot parallel across the face and break   *5*
just under Turtle Mountains. Riding scars
you can't get lost. Home is the place they cross.

The lame guard strikes a match and makes the dark
less tolerant. We watch through cracks in boards
as the land starts rolling, rolling till it hurts   *10*
to be here, cold in regulation clothes.
We know the sheriff's waiting at midrun
to take us back. His car is dumb and warm.
The highway doesn't rock, it only hums
like a wing of long insults. The worn-down welts   *15*
of ancient punishments lead back and forth.

All runaways wear dresses, long green ones,
the color you would think shame was. We scrub
the sidewalks down because it's shameful work.
Our brushes cut the stone in watered arcs   *20*
and in the soak frail outlines shiver clear
a moment, things us kids pressed on the dark
face before it hardened, pale, remembering
delicate old injuries, the spines of names and leaves.

The Responsive Reader

1   What were the runaways running away from? What do you learn about their past history? What do you learn about the system against which they are rebelling? What is in store for them?
2   Much of what we observe in this poem has symbolic meanings and overtones. What vivid details in the runaways' surroundings mirror their thoughts and feelings?
3   One editor said that "the language of hurt and injury pervades this poem." What examples can you find? What role does each play in the poem?

Talking, Listening, Writing

4   Does the intense sense of grievance in this poem take you by surprise?
5   In your own experience, has schooling been a means of liberation, widening perspectives and extending opportunities? Or has it been an instrument of oppression—aiming at forced changes in attitudes, narrowing your outlook, or trying to make you over into something you did not want to be?
6   Is there something to be said in defense of policies of enforced Americanization?

Collaborative Projects

7   In the school district(s) in which you live, what is the policy regarding cultural diversity? If you can, talk to teachers or administrators in a position to know.

FORUM: *Free to Worship*

Many immigrants came to this country in search of religious freedom. They ranged from Puritans who had been persecuted as dissenters in England to Jews who had been the victims of pogroms in czarist Russia. The separation of church and state, enshrined in the American Constitution, promised freedom of worship and liberty of conscience. America would not have an established religion that would become a center of power and privilege and whose adherents would exclude outsiders from public office or a university education.

Although the religious beliefs and practices of Native Americans were suppressed, America presented a spectrum of beliefs and rituals astonishing by Old World standards. In New England, where Puritans had at first persecuted backsliders and killed fellow citizens as witches, Quakers and Unitarians became part of the social mix. Mormons became an influential and prosperous minority after the initial years of persecution. Americans in the heavily Baptist South gradually overcame traditional prejudices against Catholics. In the Midwest, a rainbow of denominations and sects built their own chapels and preached and worshipped as the spirit moved them. Recent times saw the establishment of Buddhist congregations and a new American form of Islam.

Today, many observers see in our society a movement toward a new spirituality. People are looking for spiritual significance in their lives, drawing on a wide range of sources. They are looking for an antidote to fashionable cynicism, for an answer to pessimism or despair. At the same time, powerful forces are pushing the nation toward a common center of religious belief. Is this country a "Christian nation"? Are there religious beliefs that we should all share?

MY 60-SECOND PROTEST FROM THE HALLWAY

Emily Lesk

"I understand how she felt because I wouldn't want to be pressured into prayers other than my own and especially at school."

—STUDENT READER

American tradition and folklore have long honored the maverick—the non-conformist who marches "to a different drummer." Many Americans came to this country in search of freedom of religion as refugees from societies where religious conformity was required. The founders broke with tradition by refusing to establish a state religion and by keeping church and state separate. Americans have long prided themselves on freedom of choice in matters of religious thought and observance. At the same time, pressures toward religious conformity developed in the new nation. The high school senior who wrote the following prize-winning essay for a Newsweek *student contest in 2001 resisted what she felt was interference in her right to make her own decisions in matters of worship and belief.*

Thought Starters: What has been your experience with religious instruction or religious observance in a school setting? What has been your contact with students from religious backgrounds different from yours? Has difference of religious outlook or of attitudes toward religion ever been an issue for you?

It's 8:32 A.M. School began two minutes ago. My bulging book bag is inside my first-period classroom saving my favorite seat. I am standing in the near-empty hallway, leaning against a locker right outside the classroom. I should be in class, yet my teacher has never objected to my minute-long absence, which has become a daily routine. I trace around the edges of the floor tiles with the toe of my running shoe, pausing several times to glance up at the second hand of the standard-issue clock mounted across the hall.

Although I have casually checked this clock countless times during my high-school career, this year looking at it has made me think about how significant 60 seconds can be. Last spring, the Commonwealth of Virginia passed a law that requires every public school in the state to set aside one minute at the beginning of each day during which students must remain seated while they "meditate, pray, or engage in any other silent activity." Every morning, at around 8:31, a resonant voice echoes over the school intercom, "Please rise for the Pledge of Allegiance." I stand up straight and salute the flag. After the pledge the voice commands me to "pause for a minute of silence." I push my chair under my desk and stride out of the classroom.

My objection to Virginia's Minute of Silence law is very simple. I see the policy as an attempt to bring organized prayer into the public schools, thus violating the United States Constitution. Last June at a statewide student-government convention, I spoke with state lawmakers, who confirmed my suspicion that the minute of silence is religiously motivated. One delegate proudly told me that she supported the law because reciting the Lord's Prayer had been a part of her own public-school education.

I agree with the law's strongest critics, who argue that it promotes religious discrimination because many faiths do not pray in the seated position mandated by the legislation. How would a Muslim third grader react to those students (and maybe a teacher) who might fold their hands and bow their heads to pray? Would she feel pressured to join in just to avoid criticism?

My opposition to this law is ironic because I consider myself religious and patriotic. I recite the Pledge of Allegiance daily (including the "one nation under God" part, which to me has historical, not religious, implications). As a Reform Jew, I get peace and self-assurance from religious worship and meditation, both at my synagogue and in my home. But my religious education also taught me the importance of standing up against discrimination and persecution.

In a school of 1,600 students, fewer than two dozen have joined me in protest. I usually walk out of class with one or two kids, sometimes none. Most days, when I glance back into the classroom, I see several students praying, heads bowed or eyes closed, while others do homework or daydream. Although I have not encountered any outright opposition, I often overhear classmates making sarcastic comments or dismissing the protest as futile. When I see that so many of my peers and teachers find no reason to question something I feel so strongly about, I wonder if my objection is justified. What do my 30 extra daily paces accomplish?

In contemplating that question, I've come to realize that taking a stand is about knowing why I believe what I do and refusing to give in despite the lack of support. My decision to protest was largely personal. Though I stayed in class the first morning the law was implemented—because I was caught off guard and because I was curious to see how others would respond—sitting there felt like a betrayal of my values. I also felt an obligation to act on behalf of the students all over Virginia who found their own beliefs violated but don't attend schools that allow them to express their opinions.

Deep down, I know this issue will be decided in a courtroom, not in my corridor. On May 8, the Fourth U.S. Circuit Court of Appeals heard oral arguments from ACLU lawyers representing seven families who are challenging the law, and will probably reach a decision over the summer. But for now I'll walk out of class each day to show my school community that an easy alternative to complacency does exist. This year I will have spent approximately three hours standing in the hallway in protest, watching the second hand make its 360-degree journey. As a senior about to graduate, I've thought a lot about the impact I've had on my school. I hope that my protest inspired other kids to use the time to think, not about a beckoning test, but about their views—even if those views differ from my own.

The Responsive Reader

1 Many discussions of the school prayer issue move on the level of constitutional principle and legal precedent. What details in Lesk's opening paragraphs help her take the reader to the actual everyday world of school? Have you been a clock watcher? How does Lesk use the time ticking off on the clock to make both the setting and the issue real for her readers?

2 How does Lesk support her suspicion that the new state law mandating the minute of silence was "religiously motivated"? Do you think her suspicion is justified? Do you think the new policy was an attempt to "bring organized prayer into the public schools"?

3 According to Lesk, how or why do the instructions for the minute of silence cause a problem for students of other faiths, like the Muslim third-grader she mentions? What is Lesk's own religious orientation or commitment? How does she use it to explain her taking a stand on the school prayer issue?

4 Lesk describes in some detail the thoughts and feelings before and after her decision. Do you understand how she felt? What were the reactions of other students? Do you think the reactions would have been similar at a school you attended or know well? Would you have been one of the students "dismissing the protest as futile"?

Talking, Listening, Writing

5 Are you surprised that Lesk has no problem with the Pledge of Allegiance? Why or why not? Do you think there is a difference between requiring students to salute the flag or recite the Pledge of Allegiance and requiring them to participate in a moment of meditation or prayer? What is the difference? Or how are they similar or the same?

6 Many people are reluctant to take a stand—to "make waves" or become identified as troublemakers or malcontents. How serious would a problem have to be before you joined in a formal protest? What policy or situation would you be willing to protest?

7 Lesk says that she hopes her example will inspire other students to think about their views and to exercise their right to express their opinions. After thinking about what you believe and what you are willing to stand

up for, what would you include in a "This I Believe" statement presenting your views to others? What stance would you adopt toward others with different views?

8   Can religious issues be avoided in school? Where or how have you encountered them? How did people deal with them?

Collaborative Projects

9   How diverse or how homogeneous is the religious background of students at your school or a school you know well? Working with a group, conduct an informal survey or interviews to find out where your fellow students stand in matters of religious outlook or spiritual commitment. Do students identify with different denominations, and do these differ in outlook? Do Mormons, Jews, Muslims, Buddhists, or Hindus feel they are generally accepted, or do they think they stand out because of their religious affiliation? How do students with no specific religious allegiance identify themselves?

PRAYER ISN'T ALWAYS ALLOWED

Loretta Johnson

"Which school was right? To me, it's the one that allowed references to God during the graduation ceremonies."

Much has been written about the role of the religious revival in recent American politics. Americans with strong religious convictions have become increasingly politically active, organizing support for candidates invoking traditional religious values in situations ranging from school board elections to statewide or national contests. A test issue often is the candidate's stand for or against school prayer. Opponents say that the Constitution forbids making students in public schools join in prayers or other religious observances that do not represent their parents' religious convictions or their own. Advocates of school prayer claim that the founders never intended this nation to be a godless society. The following article was written by the religion editor of the local newspaper in Minot, a farming town in North Dakota, close to the Canadian border. It was first published in the Minot Daily News *in November of 1998.*

Thought Starters: For many Americans, religion is a private matter and a matter of individual choice. Where do you encounter religion in the public sphere? Where have you seen it play a role in American politics?

I love to travel. And my family and friends know that. They also know *1* that when I travel, it's often by car and never alone. There are always four of us in the car: me, myself, God and I.

I am at the wheel; God is in the passenger seat to my right; me and myself are relegated to the rear seat.

In June, I traveled to Oroville, Calif., a small town about an hour and a half north of Sacramento, to attend a friend's graduation from high school. An incident occurred there that still bothers me.

The graduation ceremony of Las Plumas High School took place June 4 at Harrison Stadium. It included an invocation, speeches by the valedictorian and the salutatorian and a benediction.

The invocation began, "Dear Heavenly Father. . . . We thank you for *5* all our family and teachers and for all those who have an impact on our lives" and ended, "We ask this in the name of Jesus Christ. Amen."

Attention getter

A certain part of the valedictorian's address definitely got my attention. It was, "One person cannot dictate what another should be, but one cabinet (body) can have a positive influence on the lives of another by supporting and accepting his progressive character. The people around you should not be the mold for your character. You must be what you want to be."

During the benediction, the graduating senior said, "Tonight we thank you for the many accomplishments we have made. We thank you for the preparation we have been given for the future."

He closed with, "Thank you for sending your Son, Jesus Christ, as the living example to set the standard by which we may live our lives to further succeed. Thank you most of all for sacrificing him onto death on a cross that we may have eternal life by believing in him. I ask you for your blessing on each graduate here as we take this critical step forward in our lives, and I pray he will continually inspire us as we continue on in life, in Jesus' precious and holy name. Amen."

After the Las Plumas graduation ceremony, many of the attendees gathered on the field for congratulatory hugs and handshakes.

Different ceremony

The following evening, Oroville High School, another public school *10* in the same school district, conducted its graduation ceremonies in the same stadium. But things were much different.

The invocation was skipped over. The first co-valedictorian spoke. But, when the second co-valedictorian, Chris Niemeyer, approached the podium, he and the principal exchanged words. Niemeyer was asked to leave the stage.

Some people in the stands shouted, "We want Chris," and stomped their feet. Others held small signs supporting the students in their right to free speech.

Niemeyer left the stage with tears streaming down his face. He paused at the end of the walkway where two of his classmates joined him in a hug. Soon the entire class joined the group in a purple mass of graduation robes, arms and square caps.

Oroville High School Principal Larry Payne called for order about a half dozen times and then finally announced, "If we cannot have proper decorum we will cancel the ceremony." Order then resumed. Two students then sang, "It's All Over Now, Baby Blue." At the end of the song one of the students grabbed the principal's microphone and said, "God bless."

Niemeyer was not allowed to give his address, and a classmate was not allowed to deliver the invocation because they included references to God and Jesus.

Payne had reviewed the talks and rejected them because of their strong religious content. U.S. District Court Judge Lawrence Karlton rejected an emergency, last-ditch plea by the two students asking for the right to make religious references in their addresses.

After Oroville High graduation ceremony, many of the students, their parents and friends gathered for a prayer rally off the field.

The *Enterprise-Record*, a newspaper published in Chico, Calif., which is near Oroville, published the text of the talks in its June 6 edition.

Yes, there were references to God and Jesus in the invocation and valedictory address for the Oroville High graduation.

The invocation began, "Dear Heavenly Father, we humbly come be- *20* fore you this evening to thank you for all that we have accomplished through you. Father God, these last four years have not been easy for us, but we know that you were there with us the whole time, and we thank you for that."

It closed with, "We ask these things in the precious holy name of Jesus Christ. Amen."

Key to success

The co-valedictorian extended his gratitude to the high school staff for the great learning experience he had had. He then went on to say, "Along with the great instruction, I have also been introduced to ideas and philosophies that have not corresponded with my own personal beliefs. I now have the opportunity to speak from my heart and share what I know is the key to success."

He went on to say, "I believe that God has a plan for each of our lives—a plan to prosper us and give us a hope for the future. As individuals, we have a choice of whether to choose his perfect will in our lives or our own futile plans."

Both schools are public and yet the graduation ceremonies were dramatically different. Is there a happy medium possible?

Times certainly have changed. Included in the 10 original amend- *25* ments of the Bill of Rights of the Constitution of the United States, Article

I states: "*Congress shall make no law respecting an establishment of religion, or prohibiting the free exercise thereof; or abridging the freedom of speech, or of the press, or the right of the people peaceably to assemble, and to petition the Government for a redress of grievances.*"

The Supreme Court ruled in a 6-1 decision June 25, 1962, that the recitation of an official prayer in the public schools of New York State was unconstitutional.

And, on June 4, the same day as the Las Plumas graduation, the House failed to ratify a constitutional amendment that would have returned official prayer to public schools and permitted the government to fund religious schools and organizations.

I'm certain the issue of prayer or no prayer in schools will continue as will the issue of guns, knives and drugs in schools.

But, for today, I'm thankful I have the right to exercise my beliefs and not be discouraged by others in what I say, write or do.

Looking back

Back in the '60s, I graduated from a small high school in the Minot *30* area, and to the best of my recollection, all the graduating seniors were present for baccalaureate the Sunday before the actual graduation ceremony. So were their parents. There was no shame in being there.

Prayer was a part of my growing up. I attended church and said evening prayers with my family. Prayer is still a part of my life and has been a mainstay through good times and bad.

Which school was right?

To me, it's the one that allowed the references to God during the graduation ceremonies. So, just as I take God on my journeys, may the graduating seniors have God with them as they start their journeys down a new path.

I'd rather have freedom of prayer in school than the weapons that are being brought there for purposes other than guidance, direction and protection.

Praise be to God. When we hit a deer on the return trip, I used my *35* freedom of speech and said, "Thank God we aren't hurt."

The Responsive Reader

1 What is the issue that was dramatized for Johnson by her trip to California? What were the key differences between the two situations she describes?

2 Johnson repeatedly speaks for "the students"—students who share her views. What would you include in a composite portrait of them? To judge from your own high school experience, how many students share their views?

Talking, Listening, Writing

3 The American Civil Liberties Union (ACLU) has often carried the torch in lawsuits accusing public officials of breaching the wall separating church and state. One ACLU advertising campaign used the headline "Whose Prayer?" If the courts approved a form of prayer in public schools, who would choose the prayer? What kind of prayer with what kind of wording would be acceptable?

4 After the religious wars devastating Europe in the seventeenth century, the British writer Jonathan Swift (author of *Gulliver's Travels*) said: "We have just enough religion to hate but not to love one another." Do you think this charge would be fair or unfair if leveled at Johnson?

5 In 2004, the French government enacted a law banning overt religious symbols in the country's public schools. The law was aimed especially at the headscarf worn by many young Muslim women, but it also banned "large crucifixes" and the Jewish yarmulke. If you had been a member of the French parliament, would you have voted for or against the law? How would you defend your vote?

MY ONLINE SYNAGOGUE

Niles Elliot Goldstein

"Contemporary faith stands at the cutting edge of technology."

—STUDENT READER

The following article was first published in Newsweek *in 1998. Mainstream publications were acknowledging a trend toward their readers looking for spiritual meaning in their lives without necessarily committing to the doctrines and rituals of a specific religious tradition.*

Goldstein and his cybersynagogue give new meaning to the idea of "old wine in new bottles." He developed his style of online Judaism after serving as the rabbi of conventional congregations. He shares the view that many Americans are "nonobservant" or only nominally members of an organized religion. However, they are nevertheless looking for something "that will enrich their lives and root them in a spiritual community." Like many Americans, Goldstein thinks of himself as "ecumenical"—willing to reach out beyond the traditional "boundaries and parameters" that divide one religious group from another. How viable does his new kind of "virtual religious community" seem? Do you think it has a future?

Thought Starters: Where and when do you see religion playing a role in American life? Where do you encounter it?

I am the rabbi of a cybersynagogue. In many ways what I do on the *1* Internet is starkly different from the work I did when I was a pulpit rabbi. For one thing, this congregation is open 24 hours a day. If anyone has a pressing concern or question, all he has to do is leave it on "Ask the Rabbi" (forums.msn.com/Religion), and he'll get a response from me long before most of my colleagues would even receive the message. While you can't perform a bris or conduct a funeral over the Internet, for many people that lack of focus on ritual is itself an enticement. Those turned off by organized religion but open to spiritual issues often find themselves drawn to our section of cyberspace. And because there is no control over who joins our community, not all of our members are Jews. As Abraham welcomed the three strangers into his tent, I welcome our visitors (even the occasional evangelist who tries to convert me) as honored guests. We're as ecumenical as a religious entity can be.

In other ways my work is surprisingly similar to that of a conventional cleric. My "lectern" may be made of wires instead of wood, but I still use it to preach my sermons. I might not teach adult-education classes to congregants while they're seated around a table, but I talk about the Jewish tradition with Internet users every day (and intermittently conduct live discussions on various topics in our Judaism chat room, also at the address above). I may not have an actual office for private counseling or confidential conversation, but I do have an e-mail address for those situations where discretion or personal, one-on-one communication is required. I've led some people through the mourning process and helped others trace their religious genealogies. And though I didn't do the matchmaking at a congregational picnic, three of our married assistants met their spouses online.

When I began serving the Judaism Community a couple of years ago—only one of many faith communities on the Internet, including Christianity, Islam, Buddhism, even paganism—I asked the subscribers what kind of a rabbi they were looking for. Asking a question like this in a conventional congregation would have been difficult, if not impossible. There are so many factors that go into the relationship between spiritual leaders and their congregations—managerial, financial and psychological, to name just a few—that even minor issues can get complicated. Touching a subject as large as the role of a rabbi in a particular religious community is a recipe for conflict.

At one of my former "real" synagogues, when a particularly wealthy member thought his opinion wasn't carrying the weight it deserved, he threatened to leave the temple. Another member who hated public speaking refused, despite my urging, to make known her view on a controversial issue at an important meeting. But in a virtual congregation, where distinctions between congregants don't exist and where boundaries between clergy and laity are more relaxed and less intimidating, I received a great deal of feedback and have been able to adjust my rabbinate accordingly.

With no building to maintain or budget to balance, our cybersynagogue allows democracy to flourish. No congregant can withdraw his support for the capital campaign. No clique can monopolize power. No rabbi can dictate policy.

Like many Americans, most of the users I encounter in the newsgroup   *5* have problems with religious practice. They are often nonobservant and find little meaning in ancient rituals or indecipherable liturgies. But just the fact that they are in the newsgroup is spiritually significant. They, like many of the rest of us in American society, are yearning for something more, something that will enrich their lives and root them in a spiritual community. Historically, religion has been defined by boundaries and parameters, distinctions in beliefs, holy books, practices, calendars. The Internet has no boundaries. I once asked our users what they thought about the notion of creating new rituals, ones that speak more to our own experiences. One woman suggested a liturgy to mark menopause. A father wanted to construct a ceremony for sending his daughter off to college. A teenager argued for a new blessing to be recited at the time of a boy's first wet dream. I didn't like all the ideas, but I loved the free, uncensored exchange of views, an exchange that would have been extremely difficult outside the Internet.

Yet on the Internet, a single individual can cause great damage. With few control mechanisms, anybody can say almost anything to anyone. One of our Jewish participants has been so intolerant, disrespectful and offensive toward those of other faiths—as well as toward fellow Jews—that I have tried to have him banned from the newsgroup. I have not succeeded. He has continued to insult and alienate our members and has interfered with my ability to properly do my job. Flesh-and-blood members of a real congregation would not tolerate this situation. Free speech is and should be a cherished American value, but when it is abused (as it sometimes is on the Internet) it can be destructive to a community.

In an age when religion has been deconstructed and decentralized, few media reach as many potential "congregants" as the Internet. We never have to look for extra chairs to accommodate overflow crowds. Millions of believers can join us from anywhere in the world. The anonymity that a virtual religious community confers encourages people to speak more candidly. But in the absence of face-to-face encounters, relationships between members of our community will always be limited. Nothing will ever be able to replace the embrace of another human being or the feeling of families at prayer. Contact is not communication. We may all be created in the image of God, but only the shadows of those images will be visible online. The Internet is a mixed blessing. It draws people together at the same time that it distances them. It expands the horizons of religion while collapsing its moorings and traditions. Contemporary faith stands at the cutting edge of technology. It may have also reached its final frontier.

The Responsive Reader

1 In practical terms, how does Goldstein's "online synagogue" operate? How does it use the opportunities of cyberspace? How close does it bring religion to "the cutting edge of technology"?

2 When Goldstein ceased being a "pulpit rabbi," what happened to the conventional duties of a rabbi or other leader of a congregation? How are his current functions similar; how are they different?

3 How does Goldstein support his claim that his cyberspace synagogue is more open and democratic than much conventional religion?

4 Is Goldstein candid about the drawbacks and abuses of his kind of cyberspace religion? Does he show it to be a "mixed blessing"? Where or how?

Talking, Listening, Writing

5 Are you one of those who find little meaning "in ancient rituals or in-decipherable liturgies"? Or would you defend ritual and religious observance as an essential part of religion?

6 Do you think that Goldstein succeeds in bringing religion closer to the actual thoughts and feelings of people today—closer to our everyday experience? (Do you think some of the topics or suggestions he mentions are too irreverent or too vulgar?)

From Reading to Writing

The Writing Process
1   Drawing on Your Experience
2   From Reading to Writing
3   Exploring Internet and Nonprint Sources
4   Pushing Toward a Thesis
5   Organizing Your Writing
6   Feedback and Revision

Respond to what you read and put what is valuable to good use.
Are you a good a reader? Reading is an interaction between writer and reader. As you read, your mind does not merely download the text the way a computer would. As an active reader, you process the text: You decide whether to skim it or to study it in depth. You look for clues to the author's intention—what is this all about? You evaluate what the author presents in support of key ideas or claims.

Here are questions that may go through your mind:

- Is what you are reading important enough? If it is, you may start paying serious attention.
- Can you tell why the writer wrote this passage or this piece? Early you mentally highlight clues to the writer's purpose or intention.
- Can you tell how the author would answer if you asked: "Where are we going with this?" You note signals that show the writer's plan.
- Does what the author wrote make sense to you? You interpret what the writer is saying, and you relate it to what you already know.
- Will your reading be useful to you in future writing or research projects?

What motivates readers? What keeps them reading?
At a practical level, you welcome useful information, needed explanations, or good advice. On current issues, you may early start reading with

a receptive mindset, agreeing with what the writer says. Or you may find yourself disagreeing or finding fault. As a writer, you start filing away in informal written notes or in computer files material for future use. You develop a backlog of material that will help you clarify your own thinking and develop and support your own thoughts.

GUIDELINES FOR READERS

Becoming an Active Reader

What do you look for when you start reading? Experienced readers recommend that you look for answers to the following questions:

PURPOSE **What made the writer write?** Look for clues to the writer's agenda: What is the writer setting out to do? What is the writer trying to accomplish? For instance, is the writer's aim to provide information, explain a problem, correct misunderstandings, or promote a cause?

AUDIENCE **What is the writer's intended audience?** Is the writer addressing mainly readers ready to agree—"preaching to the choir"? Or is the writer challenging readers who may hold opposing views? Do you make a good audience for this writer? Why or why not?

FOCUS **What key question or questions is the writer raising?** What key points are beginning to stand out? Does the introduction seem to lead up to a thesis or governing idea that the writing as a whole will support or drive home?

ORGANIZATION **What overall plan is beginning to emerge?** Where does the writing seem to be headed? Do you expect the writer to track major stages in a development? Is the writer going to compare and contrast major alternatives? Or do you expect the writer to take you through major steps in an argument?

SUPPORT **How does the writer back up key ideas?** What key examples support major points? What supporting evidence does the writer bring in? How detailed or carefully presented is it? Does it seem balanced, or is it heavily weighted toward one side?

SOURCES **What were the writer's sources?** Where did the writer turn for data or informed opinion? How credible are they? Are any of the sources experts or insiders? Do any seem biased? Has the author tried to look at opposing arguments or "the other side"?

Reading for Key Ideas

Know when to skim and when to move in for a close reading.
Good writers are likely to be good readers. They look for promising material to draw on in their own work. Working at the computer, they browse, and they frequently track something or look something up. When they take a break from working at the keyboard, they may pick up a magazine or a book. They take notes and collect clippings from newspapers. Working their way through a text, they highlight or underline key ideas. They flag unanswered questions of apparent contradictions.

The following reading sample traces the flow of ideas in an unsigned article in the widely respected conservative British *Economist* newsmagazine. The article appeared when charges of growing anti-American attitudes overseas were widely debated. Disagreements about fighting terror and conflicts about trade policies divided traditional allies on both sides of the Atlantic.

A QUICK FIRST READ   In a first quick reading, you may already circle or highlight key points and puzzling terms or expression. You may start jotting **marginal notes.** You may start writing brief notes or enter queries in the margin. You are finding your bearings. You are looking for clues to the writer's intention and overall plan.

Old America vs. New Europe

(This is strange—isn't it the other way around—Old Europe and New World?)

There are few more enduring assumptions about transatlantic relations than that Europe represents age and America youth. Americans dismiss Europe as an old continent—wonderful place to visit but hardly the anvil of the future. Europeans dismiss America as the embodiment of all the evils of modernity—an adolescent bereft of history and tradition. . . .

(So the writer does know the stereotypes about picturesque old Europe and immature "adolescent" America. How would a country be the "anvil of the future"? An anvil is the metal block on which the smith hammered red-hot iron into a new shape.)

But is the age difference between Europe and the United States really so big? Granted, Europe's history goes back a good deal further than America's. Granted, Europe has chateaux and palaces while America has the Disney castle and McMansions. . . .

(The differences the writer admits are really only superficial? Real castles in France and fake castles in Disneyland—but both are only tourist attractions?)

But the world's first new nation is hardly a recent newcomer. The early settlers arrived in Virginia and Massachusetts when the first Queen Elizabeth was on the throne and England was not yet Britain. Harvard University was founded in 1636. The Declaration of Independence was signed a century before the unifications of Germany and Italy. . . .

(Now we are getting to the point! The Pilgrims came way before the French Revolution. Everyone knows Harvard is old—but that old? When America declared independence, Germany and Italy did not yet exist as nations?)

A CLOSE READING   Study the more detailed **running commentary** that is added in parentheses to the text in the following run-through. It shows a reader charting major points and supporting material during a close reading. Phrases and sentences that the reader is likely to highlight or underline in the text are boldfaced in this version of the text:

Old America vs. New Europe

(The **title** is an attention-getting reversal of a familiar idea: Most readers grew up thinking of Europe as the Old World and America as the New World. Will the article as a whole explain and support this turning upside-down of a widely held belief?)

There are few more enduring assumptions about transatlantic relations than that Europe represents age and America youth. Americans dismiss Europe as an old continent—wonderful place to visit but hardly the anvil of the future. Europeans dismiss America as the embodiment of all the evils of modernity— an adolescent bereft of history and tradition. . . . ———>>>>>>>>>>>>>

(The **introduction** presents the familiar stereotype about the aging, old-fashioned Europe and the dynamic youthful New World. This is the familiar idea that the article as a whole sets out to contradict or refute.)

But is the age difference between Europe and the United States really so big?
- **Granted,** Europe's history goes back a good deal further than America's.
- **Granted,** Europe has chateaux and palaces while America has the Disney castle and McMansions. . . . ———>>>>>>>>>>>>>

(This early paragraph makes a **concession**—it grants or concedes some obvious facts that can be used as examples to support the traditional old Europe and young America idea.)

But the world's first new nation is hardly a recent newcomer.
- The early settlers arrived in Virginia and Massachusetts when the first Queen Elizabeth was on the throne and England was not yet Britain.

- Harvard University was founded in 1636.
- The Declaration of Independence was signed a century before the unifications of Germany and Italy. . . . ———>>>>>>>>>>>>>>

(This key paragraph presents the central **thesis,** supported by a first set of **examples,** giving historical dates.)

Despite its youthful population, America is often more wedded to traditional values.
- American churches are full every Sunday with worshippers dressed in their finery.
- Public events regularly begin with a performance of the national anthem.
- American tabloids do without the naked breasts that bounce all over their European cousins. . . . ———>>>>>>>>>>>>

(This paragraph follows up the thesis by going beyond chronology to a **second major area:** beliefs and values. It presents a second set of supporting examples.)

The American political system is one of the oldest in the world—far older than those upstart regimes in France and Germany.
- America has the world's oldest written constitution (drafted in 1787) and two of the world's oldest political parties (established in 1828 and 1854).
- Americans routinely make monumental decisions such as whether people can carry guns or whether women can have abortions with reference to the designs of a group of 18th-century gentlemen . . . Americans debating current issues from gun control to same-sex marriage invoke the authority of America's 18th-century Constitution. . . .
- Europeans are less happy to dwell on some parts of their history—and not just the obvious world wars. . . . For many east Europeans history seems to have started in 1989. ———>>>>>>>>>>>>

(This section of the article moves to a **third major area** illustrating the writer's thesis: political institutions. It presents a third set of supporting examples.)

Americans tend to avoid some of their past—notably what they did to the American Indians—but they have managed to cast most of their history, including the Civil War, as part of their struggle for freedom.

(Without glossing over the dark side of American history, this strong positive **conclusion** circles back to the beginning. It reinforces the writer's basic claim that the American present is firmly rooted in the past.)

—*The Economist,* February 22, 2003

FROM READING TO WRITING

Draw on your reading as a rich resource.

To dramatize an issue like illegal immigration or children without health insurance, the writer may examine test cases currently in the news. To give meaning to a current buzzword like the *underclass*, a writer may quote a commentator probing the uses and abuses of the term. To support an argument about outsourcing or offshoring, a writer may cite authoritative statistics. For a parting shot or punchline, the writer may conclude with a quotable quotation from a media figure like Ellen Goodman or George Will.

Triggering

Let effective writing provoke a lively response.

Making a piece of writing become a "live link" requires the participation of two people. The writer creates a message that will get and hold the reader's attention and activate a live response. The reader follows the writer's leads, interprets, and reacts.

Writers interact with their reading in a number of ways.

- *Reading often raises an important issue for us.* It often brings issues or questions into focus. An author writing about bringing back the wolves or reviving the draft can bring an important question into focus while leaving us dissatisfied with the proposed answer. We can then set out in search of a better answer.

- *Reading helps us test or firm up tentative ideas.* We may write to show that something that for us was at first only a hunch was confirmed by our reading. A tentative theory was validated by the testimony of experts or insiders. Is it true that a "Clean Air" initiative really loosens restrictions designed to reduce smog or air pollution? When we integrate what we have read, we show that our ideas are more than hearsay or superficial impressions. They have the backing of credible qualified observers.

- *Reading motivates us to respond.* Our reading often triggers a lively response when we want to say: "That is not so" or "That is oversimplified" or "There is another side." We then write to set the record straight. We write to show where we agree with other writers and where we think they go wrong. A proposal to have the Census Bureau abandon racial or ethnic categories will activate vigorous responses from the whole range of the political spectrum.

Gathering

Develop the habit of close reading.

Good writers are not satisfied with reading for "the general idea." They are alert for key points. They take note of important background, and they identify strong supporting evidence. They pull out key quotations for future use. The following are detailed **reading** notes for one major source. The writer was gathering material for a paper asking "Are we moving toward a color-blind society?" Tags already show the material sorted out under subheadings for possible future use.

READING NOTES

Building a File

TOPIC: Are We Moving toward a Color-Blind Society?

Source: David Bernstein, "Mixed Like Me," in *Next: Young American Writers on the Next Generation.*

KEYNOTE: Author describes himself as a "twenty-six year old man, half black and half Jewish." He believes America will look more like him in this century ("Mixed like me").

CAPSULE BIOGRAPHY: Bernstein's parents married in Washington DC, but in close by Maryland miscegenation (mixing of races— marriages between blacks and whites) was still illegal. Author went to a mostly white school but associated with a mixed racial group in jazz clubs. One student called him the N-word but apologized six times.

REJECTING THE STEREOTYPE: "I have not overcome racism or poverty, and people become visibly disappointed when I tell them that my mixed background has not been a cause for distress, or any other difficulty for that matter."

POLITICS: Bernstein founded and edited "a conservative magazine that deals with race relations and culture." At his college, he was elected president of the campus Republicans, who welcomed a black conservative as a minority representative.

POSITIVE OUTLOOK: Among advantages of being mixed, "first is my comfort in moving between worlds of different cultures and colors." He rejects the "conventional wisdom about us mixed-race types, that we are alienated, never feeling comfortable in either culture. . . .I am black. I am Jewish. I am equally comfortable with people who identify themselves as either one or neither one."

KEY QUOTATION: "To me the most defining characteristic of who I am is not my race, ethnicity, religious beliefs, political party, or Tupperware club membership. Rather, I see myself as an individual first, part of the larger 'human family,' with all the suballegiances reduced to ancillary [not really essential] concerns."

Shaping

Make material from your reading part of a well-thought-out plan.
What organizing strategies will help you bring varied promising reading material under control? How will you keep your paper from reading like a collection of miscellaneous notes?

- Are you interpreting or arguing with a single source? A **"Yes, but" pattern** may work well as your overall plan. You first present, explain, and illustrate the author's position. However, you then reach a turning point. You start saying "Yes—but." After being a receptive reader, you then voice doubts and reservations about what you have read.

- Do you prefer to address key ideas **point by point** as your source brings them up? This way you can take your reader through an argument step by step, using transitions like "It is true that" to show agreement and links like "However" to show dissent.

- Are you searching for **common ground** between opposing sides? You may first draw on a source strongly presenting and supporting a prevailing view. Then you may bring in a source presenting a strong challenge to the earlier position. Then you may look for sources reporting on initiatives that might appeal to a cross section of readers.

WORKING OUTLINE: **Our Endangered Forests**

    (first source)   saving forests from clear-cutting

    (second source)   "forest management" to prevent fires

    (third source)   extending protected areas

What does it mean to integrate material from your reading in your own text? When you integrate the material, you feed it into your text as part of a "seamless web." You correlate originally separate items—bringing them together and showing how they are connected.

DRAWING ON ONE SOURCE   In the following passage, the writer has woven in the links and explanations that help readers see the key points. Note the credit tags or source tags that keep reminding the reader of who is being quoted.

Who Pays for College Football?

Years after Title IX mandated equal athletic opportunities for men and women at colleges receiving federal funding, gender parity is still not a reality at many schools. **As Joan Ryan, a columnist for the *San Francisco Chronicle*, explains in her article "Women Athletes Can Sympathize,"** Title IX "did not require a 50-50 split of funding and opportunities. Rather, it said that schools' athletic teams must reflect the gender makeup of the general student body."

However, Ryan cites a *Washington Post* story saying that twenty years later only one of 107 top football schools was in full compliance. In the meantime, women had come to make up more than half of the student population while still accounting for less than a third of all college athletes.

Ryan agrees with other critics that "the biggest myth in college athletics is that football funds the minor sports." Football programs take in large sums of money from ticket sales and television rights, but most don't produce a profit. In fact, "in Division I-A, the big-time football programs, 45 percent lose money." Most other schools just about break even. "In 91 percent of all colleges, football programs do make enough money to pay for themselves, according to an NCAA analysis." **Ryan concludes:**

> By the time a team pays for the equipment, the uniforms, the scholarships, the maintenance of the stadium, practice field and weight room, the dozen or so coaches and trainers, the insurance and the travel and food bills, there is usually not enough money left to buy two clipboards and a water cooler.

DRAWING ON SEVERAL SOURCES   Often you will be bringing together material from several different sources. You can often support a point effectively with quotations from several authorities that all point in the same direction. In papers using material from several sources, you need to guard against presenting undigested chunks of material. In an effective paper, the materials you have brought in will mesh—without the seams showing. Make sure you integrate—you correlate—material from your different sources.

Track the input used by the writer of the following paragraphs:

Defending the Heritage

The political theater of Luis Valdez focuses on the movement by the Chicanos or Mexican Americans of the West and Southwest to preserve and take pride in their traditional cultural identity. **In an article on Valdez' Teatro Campesino, John Harrop and Jorge Huerta see** Valdez' theater as part of "a strong movement to resist anglicization and to retain ethnic tradition." In Valdez' plays, the target of satire or the butt of the joke is often the middle-class Mexican American trying to assimilate and forget the Mexican heritage.

Guillermo Hernandez, in *Chicano Satire*, says that "given the sociocultural conflicts encountered by Mexicans living in the United States, their only viable ethical conduct is to maintain loyalty toward their own group in spite of the overwhelming external pressures to turn against their own." **Hernandez points to** Miss Jimenez, in Valdez' *Los Vendidos*, as the example of "the emerging Mexican American middle class." She works in the governor's office and insists that her Spanish name be given an Anglo pronunciation ("JIM-enez").

In his book, *Necessary Theater,* **Jorge Huerta points to** Mingo in *The Shrunken Head of Pancho Villa* as Valdez' first portrayal of a Mexican American crossing over to the other side. When his father tries to hug him, Mingo offers instead an American handshake, and he pretends to the police coming to the family home that he is not part of the family but only rents a room there.

Revising

Make your readers see how you have used your reading.

Reworking an early draft, you need to look back over how you have worked material from your reading into your own text. How have you introduced and identified quoted material? Provide answers to questions like the following:

- *Who said this and where?* Whenever you can give full names of authors and titles of publications.
- *What makes this author an authority or a reliable source?* What are the quoted author's credentials—affiliation with an institution, official role or position, track record as a researcher or author?
- *What is the point of the quotation?* Why are you using it here, at this place in your paper? What point is it supposed to explain or clarify, or what position is it meant to endorse?

Informative **credit tags** serve as brief lead-ins to a quotation:

SOURCE: **In his article on "Race and Personal Identity in America,"** Glenn C. Loury talks about the "process of becoming free of the need to have my choices validated by 'the brothers.'"

CREDENTIALS: **Ellen Berkowitz, a psychiatrist with the Florida State University program in medical sciences,** summed up the current view when she said, "Mental illnesses are just like any other illness, and for the most part they are treatable."

POINT: Lester C. Thurow, in a review of Greider's *One World, Ready or Not*, **reassured those who fear that the speculative excesses of financial markets will lead to another great collapse:** "Not even spectacular crashes change the economic system appreciably—much less bring it down."

You may need a longer **lead statement** to put an important quotation in the context of a historical situation or a cultural tradition. What should your reader know to appreciate the significance of what is being said?

CONTEXT: **Thomas Jefferson was the lead author of the American Declaration of Independence. He drafted the Virginia Statute for Religious Freedom approved by the Virginia Assembly ten years later.** The document, painted in modern times as an example of mural art on a wall in downtown Richmond, Virginia, stipulates that a citizen "shall not be compelled to frequent or support any religious worship, place, or ministry." All "shall be free to profess, and by argument to maintain, their opinions in matters of religion."

Editing

What questions about format and mechanics do you face when you draw on printed and also oral sources? In editing your paper, make it clear who says what. Clearly identify or set off all material that is coming into your paper from outside sources.

▪ You will often use **direct quotation**—material quoted verbatim, word for word. Copy each quotation exactly. Put all material quoted verbatim in quotation marks. A **colon** may replace the more usual comma before a formal or especially important quotation.

Remember to *close* the quotation with final quotation marks when your direct quotation ends.

DIRECT: Julio Sanchez, a legal scholar specializing in immigration law, says, **"Any coyote in Tijuana can tell you that illegal immigration is inevitable as long as the gap between rich and poor countries continues to grow."**

▪ When you **paraphrase** what someone said, you put someone else's ideas into your own words. Such **indirect quotation** appears in your paper *without* quotation marks:

INDIRECT: According to Julio Sanchez, legal scholar specializing in immigration law, any guide helping Mexicans cross the border would tell us **that illegal immigrants will keep coming as long as the gap between poverty at home and wealth beyond the border continues to grow.**

▪ Use a **block quotation** for a large block of material—four lines or more. Indent a block quotation about an inch or *ten* spaces (no additional indent even if your quote starts at the beginning of a paragraph). *Don't* use quotation marks—the double indenting already signals direct quotation. However, use regular quotation marks for anything quoted *within* the block quotation.

BLOCK QUOTATION:
As one vocal critic of the jargon of Washington insiders has said,
> **In the language of today's spin doctors and practitioners of double-speak, the "bottom line" is that the "window of opportunity" that enabled us to "push the envelope" has developed a "downside" that will "negatively impact" the "parameters" of future growth.**

EDITOR'S TIP   Use block quotations sparingly. Save them for strategic places. For the smooth flow of a paper, rely mainly on shorter quotations and **partial quotation** worked organically into your own text.

PARTIAL QUOTATION: **"Equestrian sports are ideally suited to become a lead-ing women's sport,"** Coach Hiernan claims. Women have an **"intuitive under-standing"** with the animals they train, and they have the patience often lack-ing in male riders, who **"tend to force the issue."**

A Paper for Peer Review

Study the following sample paper. What use does it make of the stu-dent's reading? How well does it identify its sources?

Cultural Tug-of-War

For many young Americans who come from various cultural back-grounds, finding one's cultural identity is a never ending game of tug-of-war. At one end of the rope is loyalty and adherence to one's cultural background, holding onto the culture and the traditions of their ancestors. At the other end, new American ties begin to develop and a different lifestyle of assimila-tion yanks at the rope of their lives. Each side pulls against the other. Does one side need to defeat the other or can they coexist? Can people be integrated in America and still have ties to their previous culture? **Although the battle is often two-sided, the trend today for multicultural Americans is not only towards assimilation but finding a way for both ends of the rope to meet.** ————>>>>>>>>>>>>>>

(The **title** and **introduction** give readers a vivid image of the oppos-ing forces tugging at the second generation. The **thesis** gives readers a pre-view of the student writer's answer to the challenge.)

Many people come from foreign countries to America to give their chil-dren better opportunities, creating a "nation of the children of immigrants." They become the working-class families who want to ensure a better education and a better life for their families. Many parents want their children to assim-ilate, without being held back because of their previous culture. They want a new identity for their children. **In a *Newsweek* article, Caroline Hwang, the daughter of Korean immigrants, said her parents sacrificed to give her the type of life where she could stroll the malls as a youth, talk on the phone, and do the same things young Americans did. Her parents "wanted her grasp to be as long as her reach." They wanted to offer her whatever she needed to be American, but she found that this did not suit her. She felt displaced trying to straddle two cultures while bound by "filial duty." Caroline called herself "a living paradox."**————>>>>>>>>>>>>>

(A mix of paraphrase and direct quotation brings to life a **first source** representing the pressures of assimilation.)

Many Americans like Caroline feel different because of their background, and they struggle to overcome these feelings in order to find their place in

American society. **Arturo Madrid, whose parents came from lands once part of Mexico, said in an article for an educational journal that for him school was where one became an American. His schooling served to socialize him, but in the end it accentuated his otherness. He felt he was an "other" because his background made him different from other Americans. His experience being the "other" made him "invisible" and yet at the same time had him "sticking out like a sore thumb." Although he once struggled with integration he now represents Spanish-speaking Americans of the Southwest and speaks about diversity to associations of higher education.** ———>>>>>>>>>>>>>

(A **second source** highlights the limits of the "melting pot" agenda.)

A different approach, which was more common in the past, takes the opposite side of American culture. Some immigrants view the American culture as so distant and different from their own traditional values that they try to preserve their background and instill in their children the same values. These parents want their children to be proud of their culture instead of trying to assimilate. It is the duty of their children to respect and serve the traditional culture above all, not being a part of the American culture. Finally, some parents find themselves stuck in the middle. **Caroline's parents did not want her to be fully Korean nor fully American.** Like Caroline, many children want not only to satisfy their goals but feel obligated to satisfy their parents' expectations as well as to give back to their parents who have sacrificed so much. ———>>>>>>>>>>>>

(The writer returns briefly to her **first source** for support of the "middle ground.")

Although the struggle is often two-sided, the trend today for multicultural young Americans is not towards total assimilation but finding a way for both ends of the rope to meet. The children of immigrants still feel torn but they seek a middle ground. They want to be American but keep rich ties to their cultural background. Instead of becoming part of the melting pot, they remain as unique ingredients of a tossed salad. **Jorge Mancillas, a Mexican American educator, said in an article in the *Los Angeles Times* that a new generation of Americans are committed to preserving and strengthening a democratic and pluralistic U.S. society but also have a birthright familiarity with their cultural roots. He feels this new generation is a priceless resource with much to contribute.** ———>>>>>>>>>>>>

(A **third source** offers strong support for a future "pluralistic" American society.)

On my campus, the Center for Multicultural Learning brings together students and faculty working to promote a supportive environment for faculty and students of different cultures and of different ethnicities. The center sponsors multicultural clubs that can help students balance their cultural backgrounds with the American lifestyle. Although these young Americans may embrace American traditions, food, and lifestyles, they retain their cultural background—one with different rituals, foods, and customs. For example, Japanese Americans may eat hamburgers and play baseball at school, yet they come home to eat rice and speak to tbeir families in Japanese. The growing trend is towards an allegiance to two cultures. As a result more and more young Americans find themselves participating in a much friendlier game of tug-of-war.

(The writer establishes the connection between her reading and examples from her own firsthand **experience and observation.**)

YOUR TURN:

1 How much use does the writer make of the tug-of-war idea as a central *metaphor* or imaginative comparison? In how many ways does the writer use it to tie the whole paper together? Do you think it works well? (Will everyone know what a tug-of-war is?)

2 How does the writer lead up to her *thesis*? Where in the paper is her thesis echoed or reinforced? Do you think it comes through strongly or clearly?

3 How would you sum up what each *major source* contributes to the paper?

4 What points would you list in a four-point or five-point skeleton *outline* of the paper?

5 Does the *conclusion* do more than repeat the author's main point or points? Does it provide a strong send-off for the paper?

6 Do you make a good *audience* for this paper? Why or why not? Would the reader have to be from a culturally or ethnically diverse background to understand and respond well to this paper?

Writing Options 2: Drawing on Your Reading

1 What makes for a happy childhood? What makes for an unhappy childhood? Draw on the testimony of one or more authors in this book. Possible choices include Garrison Keillor, Susan Miller, Adriana Barton, Caroline Hwang, Nguyen Louie, Kevin Janda, Sandip Roy-Chowdhury, and others.

2 Some people treasure the memories of their school years. Others disliked or hated school. What makes the difference? Look for possible answers in the selections by Mike Rose, Jeff Zorn, Caroline Hwang, or others.

3 Do you see common themes or recurrent topics in readings by or about young Asian Americans? (Are they a "model minority"?) You

may want to read or reread selections by Caroline Hwang, Nguyen Louie, Kevin Janda, Fox Butterfield, Noy Thrupkaew, or others.

4   What makes a maverick or nonconformist? What makes people "nontraditional" students or "unconventional" co-workers? Select testimonies from writing by Adriana Barton, Mara Joseph, Emily Lesk, Shaughnessy Bishop-Stall, or others.

5   Can we honor diversity while at the same time searching for community or the common center? Write a paper in which you study the perspectives on diversity of several writers like Richard Rodriguez, Ana Veciana-Suarez, and Arturo Madrid. Do they represent major contrasting points of view?

6   Do we still consider the traditional marriage a cornerstone of Western civilization? Study the challenges to traditional marriage in one or more selections by authors like Hutchison and Razdan or in one or more key selections from the forum on same-sex marriage.

7   Have fathers lost much of the authority or respect they used to enjoy? The selections by Miller, Barton, and Zorn, and later an article by Robert Bly touch on a father's role in the family or the relationship between father and child. Write about the father's role in one or more of these selections.

8   Are political candidates still claiming to be more "tough on crime" than their opponents? Study selections like those by Glazer or the "Fruitless Punishment" editorial. Or study one or more testimonies from the American prison system.

9   How do you react to current rewriting of American history? For instance, there has been much reexamination and imaginative re-creation of the Native American past. On the role of Native Americans in American history, study one or more selections like Mary Crow Dog's "Lakota Woman" and Harjo's "I Won't Be Celebrating Columbus Day."

10 How far has the country moved beyond a racist past? For many observers here and abroad, race and racism have been the large unresolved trauma of American history. Study the testimony of one or more authors like Zora Neale Hurston, Cynthia Tucker, or David Bernstein.

3

INVENTING AMERICA
Diversity and Community

COMMITTED PHOTOGRAPHY: AMERICANOS

Photographs often serve as a means of advocacy. They can be a powerful means of promoting a cause or supporting a movement. Committed photographers aim at producing a change in people's attitudes and expectations. A traveling exhibition cosponsored by the Smithsonian Center for Latino Studies in 2003 presented an array of photographs of Latino or Hispanic Americans under the heading of "Latino Life in the United States." The exhibit showed "Americanos" from a wide range of backgrounds and occupations. It paid tribute to shared values and a wide range of accomplishments. A central message of the exhibit from the prestigious Smithsonian Institute was that the *Latino* label covers a rich diverse range of people from different racial or ethnic roots, cultural traditions, and walks of life.

Reading the Image

1   The following statement from a photographer contributing to the *Americanos* project sums up her commitment. How would you describe her motivation or *program* in your own words? What for you is the most essential part of her inspiration?

> I am an American of Puerto Rican and Italian descent, and for me, the Puerto Rican Day parade is an important event. Every year it's a wonderful surprise, full of life and action. . . . I choose to focus my camera on my friends, family, people on the street and in studio portraiture to show Latinos in everyday situations in a positive light. I feel that I am letting people see what I see, that Latinos are beautiful, diverse, and intelligent. By revealing our commonality through the daily rituals of home, family, and community, others can see that Latinos are a vital part of America and that we are more than the stereotypes portrayed in most of today's media.

2   What is the best *strategy* for those trying to counteract prejudice or discrimination? Should they ask us to respect differences and honor diversity? Or should they opt for a different strategy: stressing our shared humanity: "We are all alike"? How and how effectively do the two photographs from the *Americanos* exhibit illustrate the second option? Which of the two approaches do you think is today more needed or more effective?

3   Do you make a good *audience* for photographs promoting self-esteem and pride for groups making up the rich diversity of the American experience? Why or why not? Do you prefer instead truth-telling images making viewers face up to the realities of disenfranchisement or discrimination? Why or why not?

4   How do you react to *promotional* images? The covers of college bro-
    chures and corporate public relations pamphlet are often designed to
    create favorable appearances. Have you seen brochures with a rainbow
    of faces of different colors? Can you find some recent examples? Did
    you think they were window-dressing? Did you think they presented
    a worthwhile ideal for the future?

5   Do you think you can be an effective *promoter*? What kind of group
    picture would you help produce or commission to do justice to the
    spirit of your group, your class, or your school?

3

INVENTING AMERICA

Diversity and Community

We are a people in search of a national community.

—Barbara Jordan

I am giving you a version of America, your America, that you may not have chosen to see or may have missed. I used to travel on the train going out to my job in Queens from the Upper West Side. After a certain subway stop, the entire train is filled with nonwhites. And those people are the people I am writing about, saying they have huge interesting lives.

—Bharati Mukherjee

For many years, the unofficial ideology of the United States was that of the melting pot. People came to this country from across the seas and made a new start—with the promise of equal opportunity regardless of class, religion, or ethnic origin. Arriving on these shores, the immigrants would leave old allegiances and old hatreds behind to form a new nation. The American historian Arthur Schlesinger stated a widely held belief when he said in 1959,

> America has been in the best sense of the term a melting pot, every element adding its particular element of strength. The constant infusion of new blood has enriched our cultural life, speeded our material growth, and produced some of our ablest statesmen. Over 17 million immigrants arrived in the single period from the Civil War to World War I . . . the very nationalities which had habitually warred with one another in the Old World have lived together in harmony in the New.

The policy implementing this belief was assimilation—"Americanizing" new immigrants and especially their children. The new Americans would share in a common language and a common culture in "a nation indivisible."

In the years since Schlesinger wrote, the melting pot ideal and the policy of assimilation have come in for much reexamination and revision. The melting-pot theory had not worked or was not working well for large segments of American society. Native Americans lived on isolated reservations. Even after leaving the traditional South, many blacks experienced de facto segregation in inner cities. Many Mexicans and Puerto Ricans lived in Spanish–speaking neighborhoods with strong ties to their own language and culture. A large new Asian immigration transformed parts of the cities into new Chinatowns or Japantowns or Little Saigons.

Increasingly, political leaders and opinion makers called for a recognition of the true diversity of American life and the American tradition. Multiculturalism became the watchword for recognition of different languages and cultural strands existing side by side in a new American mosaic. As in a mosaic, many different particles would fit together in a rich larger pattern, a larger whole. How will tomorrow's Americans think of diversity and community? How much diversity will our society welcome or accommodate? Will Americans of different backgrounds become part of a rich dynamic interaction?

THE MOSAIC VS. THE MYTH

Anna Quindlen

"There is some disagreement over which wordsmith first substituted 'mosaic' for 'melting pot' as a way of describing America, but it is undoubtedly a more apt description."

Anna Quindlen became known as a widely syndicated columnist for the New York Times, *winning a Pulitzer Prize for commentary in 1992. Like other columnists, Quindlen writes about the issues of the day as a shrewd observer who helps her readers make sense of the news. In a media world where much is hype or spin, she helps us become informed readers by furnishing relevant facts and insiders' testimonies and by pointing out revealing contradictions. Like other columnists, Quindlen is a trend watcher who sizes up and explains the changes in awareness and public consciousness that slowly become part of the way we think about the world in which we live. Like other journalists and figures in the public eye, she has come in for her share of hate mail from angry letter writers. She published her second novel,* One True Thing, *in 1994.*

After Quindlen took time out for writing her novels, which were her first love, her byline again appeared with short pointed columns in Newsweek *until she became a syndicated columnist in late 2004. In the following column first published in 1991 in the* New York Times, *Quindlen wrote as an early observer of the gradual shift from the traditional melting-pot ideal of American society to a new outlook more inclusive or more accepting of diversity.*

Thought Starters: How is American society like a melting pot? How is it like a mosaic? How is it like a "tossed salad"? How is it like a quilt? How is it like a _____? (fill in your own favorite metaphor or imaginative comparison)

There is some disagreement over which wordsmith first substituted "mosaic" for "melting pot" as a way of describing America, but it is undoubtedly a more apt description. And it undoubtedly applies in Ms. Miller's third-grade class and elsewhere in the Lower East Side's Public School 20.

The neighborhood where the school is located is to the immigrant experience what Broadway is to actors. Past Blevitzky Bros. Monuments ("at this place since 1914"), past Katz's Delicatessen with its fan mail hung in the window, past the tenement buildings where fire escapes climb graceful as cat burglars, P.S. 20 holds the corner of Essex and Houston.

Its current student body comes from the Dominican Republic, Cambodia, Bangladesh, Puerto Rico, Colombia, mainland China, Vietnam and El Salvador. In Ms. Miller's third-grade class these various faces somehow look the same, upturned and open, as though they were cups waiting for the water to be poured.

There's a spirit in the nation now that's in opposition to these children. It is not interested in your tired, your poor, your huddled masses. In recent days it has been best personified by a candidate for governor and the suggestion in his campaign that there is a kind of authentic American. That authentic American is white and Christian (but not Catholic), ethnic origins lost in the mists of an amorphous past, not visible in accent, appearance or allegiance.

This is not a new idea, this resilient form of xenophobia. "It is but too common a remark of late, that the American character has within a short time been sadly degraded by numerous instances of riot and lawless violence," Samuel F. B. Morse wrote in an 1835 treatise called "Imminent Dangers to the Free Institutions of the United States through Foreign Immigration," decrying such riffraff as Jesuits.

Times are bad, and we blame the newcomers, whether it's 1835 or 1991. Had Morse had his way, half of me would still be in Italy; if some conservatives had their way today, most of the children at P.S. 20 would be, in that ugly phrase, back where they came from. So much for lifting a lamp beside the golden door.

They don't want to learn the language, we complain, as though the old neighborhoods were not full of Poles and Italians who kept to their mother tongue. They don't want to become American, we say, as though there are not plenty of us who believe we lost something when we renounced ethnicity. "Dagos," my mother said the American kids called them, American being those not Italian. "Wops." How quickly we forget as we use prejoratives for the newest newcomers.

Our greatest monument to immigration, the restored Ellis Island, seems to suggest by its display cases that coming to America is a thing nostalgic, something grandparents did. On the Lower East Side it has never been past tense, struggling with English and poverty, sharing apartments with the bathroom in the hall and the bathtub in the kitchen.

They send their children to school with hopes for a miracle, or a job, which is almost the same thing. This past week the School Volunteer Program, which fields almost 6,000 volunteer tutors, sponsored the first citywide Read Aloud: 400 grown-ups reading to thousands of kids in 90 schools. In P.S. 20, as so many have done before, the kids clutched their books like visas.

It is foolish to forget where you come from, which, in the case of the United States, is almost always somewhere else. The true authentic American is a pilgrim with a small "p," armed with little more than the phrase "I wish. . . ." New ones are being minted in Ms. Miller's class, bits of a mosaic far from complete.

The Responsive Reader

1 Do you agree that the term *mosaic* is "a more apt description" for what Quindlen saw on the Lower East Side than *melting pot*? Why or why not?
2 What does Quindlen say about the nature and history of *xenophobia*—the fear of foreigners—in this country? Is hostility toward foreigners or aliens alive in your own community? Do you think it is alive in the media?
3 How does Quindlen forge links between the present wave of immigration and America's past? What is her idea of the "true authentic American"?

Talking, Listening, Writing

4 Do you consider yourself a "true authentic American" in Quindlen's terms? Or are you one of those whose ethnic origins are "lost in the mists of an amorphous"—shapeless, indistinct—past?

Collaborative Projects

5 You may want to work on a family history, with special attention to ethnic or regional origins. Your class may decide to bring these family histories together as a class publication.

YOUR TURN:

1 Have you known people who have totally left the past behind? Have you known people whose "goodbyes had been final"?
2 Immigrants often say that Americans do not fully understand what freedom means because they take their freedoms for granted. What does the word *freedom* mean for a refugee like the author of this passage?
3 Should people bury the past, or should they honor the dead?

OTHER VOICES

To Start All Over Again

Many refugees who found sanctuary in America left everything behind. One refugee from Hitler's Europe said that to "start all over again" was the most American of all American expressions.

The following testimony is from a woman who with her family for a time had been granted grudging protection in neutral Switzerland when Hitler's Germany was starting its campaign of extermination against the Jewish people. Her father had already been on a deportation train headed for the camps. Almost all the members of her father's extended family perished in the Holocaust. As a young student after the war, the author was eager to return to her native Czechoslovakia but decided otherwise after intimidation and "nastiness" from the new Communist regime there gave her a foretaste of what Communist rule was going to be like for the Czech nation.

> Coming to America in the years after the second World War meant leaving the old world behind and starting from scratch as a new person. There was no sense that an integration of events on the two sides of the Atlantic had to occur. Often the goodbyes had been final. There were no expectations that one would see either the people or the conditions of one's pre-American life ever again. The horrors and pain of the abandoned world were simply pushed out of one's ken. I met people in the early fifties who within a couple of years of arriving in America spoke their native language brokenly—and soon not at all. . . .
>
> In America you could change your name, choose your religion, move and live where you wanted. In the Europe of my youth your name was for life, your domicile was registered with the police, your community collected the tax for your religious affiliation, your profession was regulated by endless requirements and licences. To escape who you were in Europe you practically had to engage in fraud. Here you could just do it.
>
> Kitty La Perriere, "The Thread of Time," *Atlantic*

NOTES FROM A CHANGING AMERICA
Richard Rodriguez

"In truth, America exists entire, despite the segmented descriptions offered by our Census Bureau."

Richard Rodriguez grew up as the son of Mexican immigrants and became a successful writer and lecturer and a professor at the University of California. In his widely read and debated Hunger of Memory *(1981), he wrote about the human cost of assimilation and the price that children of immigrants paid for living the American Dream. On his first day of school, he knew only "some fifty stray English words" and was the only Mexican American kid in a class of middle-class Anglo students. He went on to become an English major and studied at colleges including Stanford and Berkeley. In his book, he told the story of the children of immigrants slowly becoming estranged from the world of parents and relatives. Slowly, the familiar, intimate Spanish of his childhood home became distant and awkward for him. Slowly, English, the language of school and public life, became his primary language.*

More recently, Rodriguez has come to see assimilation as more of a two-way street. As immigrants became Americanized, Americans in turn adopted favorite foods from German and Italian immigrants and ways of talking from the Yiddish of immigrant Jews. Today Rodriguez sees the influence of Spanish and the Hispanic or Latino culture everywhere in American life. The following selections, first published in 2000 and 2001, are part of the commentary on diversity issues that Rodriguez is continuing to publish in major national publications.

Thought Starters: Have you seen evidence that the meeting of cultures is a two-way street? Have you seen foods, customs, holidays, or expressions that once seemed new or foreign become part of everyday American life?

I was listening to then Governor Bush speak fluent Spanish to Hispanic voters when it struck me that Spanish is becoming unofficially, but truly, the second language of the United States. Since the mid–19th century, when America became an immigrant country, the unspoken price of admission has been linguistic uniformity. Those of us who are the children of immigrants, who came to this country speaking a language other than English, remember the loosening hold of a grandmother's Swedish, or Yiddish, or Chinese.

Secretary of Education Riley recently proposed dual English–Spanish instruction in American classrooms, but here in California, impatient voters repealed bilingual education. Many, I think, were suspicious of the public role of Spanish in the institution that traditionally has Americanized the immigrant.

Even while bilingual education is prohibited from classrooms in California, Spanish is heard everywhere in the nation. Because of the massive migration of Latin Americans northward, the United States has became the fifth-largest Spanish-speaking country in the world, after Mexico, Spain, Argentina, and Colombia. And today, Los Angeles—this city named in 18th-century Spanish, but laconically renamed by Midwesterners as L.A.—Los Angeles has become a Latin American capital, truly a city named for Nuestra Señora de Los Angeles.

It's the volume of Spanish in America that impresses. Instead of an earlier century's immigrant newspaper, say, on Manhattan's lower East side, today's highest-rated TV and radio stations in Los Angeles and Miami are Spanish-speaking. On Univision, the popular Spanish-language network, there is only español. But the commercials are red, white, and blue: McDonald's and Ford and Colgate-Palmolive.

Univision's audience is primarily working-class and national. Spanish is the language of unskilled, but eager hands, from chicken-plucking southern towns to Alaskan fishing villages from Hartford to Boise.

The genius of America is the way so many foreign phrases and words came into the American tongue, even while the nation assimilated the immigrant. Who can be surprised that so many Spanish words are finding their way into our vocabulary? But vast and the mundane prominence of Spanish today—on public signs, on billboards, on the airwaves—is blurring the linguistic border between the United States and Latin America What's more, this blurring is happening because of the poor. Normally, we expect great social change to happen the other way: To trickle down from on top, or to be mandated from on high.

Spanish is becoming the unofficial second language of America because of dishwashers and gardeners and logically so: If the laborer speaks Spanish, then the contractor needs to learn Spanish. If the housekeeper speaks Spanish, then the upper-middle class children also begin to hear it and know it.

Are we destined to become a bilingual Belgium or a new Quebec?

I predict that the children of today's Latin-American immigrants will come to assume U.S. English as their primary language. But even while they do so, and even while American English remains the language of the world, Americans still come to recognize more and more Spanish: cojones, la vida loca, salsa. Hard to imagine a previous generation of Americans quite so complaisant with political candidates chattering away in Spanish. In times past, we did not expect our presidents or our Texas governors to speak a foreign tongue. We liked it perhaps when Jackie spoke French. But John Kennedy's tag in Berlin—"Ich bin ein Berliner!"—was as much German as we expected him to know.

Now that the nannies and gardeners and maids of Beverly Hills speak Spanish, our movie stars do, too.

Hasta la vista, baby.

As the World Turns

"Of every hue and caste am I," sang Walt Whitman in 19th-century America. Nowadays when we hear America described, it is not usually by the poet, but by statisticians at the Census Bureau. We hear about a segmented America. Millions of Hispanics are distinguished from millions of African Americans; whites from non-whites; Asians from Pacific Islanders.

In truth, America exists entire despite the segmented descriptions offered by our Census Bureau. A far more interesting numerical portrait of America was recently drawn by United Nations' demographers. In a study this spring, the UN predicted that America's population would continue to grow, would grow so markedly that by 2050, America would be the only developed economy within the 20 most populous nations on earth.

The easy explanation for this growth is immigration. So many of the faces one sees in the crowd are from the world's every corner. The new American city, Dallas or Chicago or Boston, resembles the world.

Here in California, the state with the nation's largest immigrant population, whenever anything goes wrong, the easiest explanation proposed by nativists is that California is becoming a third-world country. The commonplace is that third-world despair and high mortality rates create large families, but what we do not understand so well is how optimism creates large families.

Americans who trace their ancestry back to Europe tend to have more children than their European cousins. German Americans in Chicago have more children than their cousins in Munich. And while America keeps growing, Europe is shrinking. More interesting than why and when a country has so many children is why a nation begins to have a negative birth rate. Why is Spain giving birth to fewer children now? And Italy, and Austria? Were it not for immigrants, Europe would be disappearing.

There are, doubtless, some Americans who will look fondly, look greenly toward Europe but our destiny lies in another direction. We find ourselves no longer a green exception, but within the great brown world, and our lessons for survival will come within the experience of density. A few years ago here on Market Street in San Francisco, from a block away you might hear a blaring boom box carried by a teenager—the boom proclaiming his presence. Now kids pass quietly, wearing discreet Sony walkmans invented in Tokyo. Tokyo has become a model for living in San Francisco. The Japanese skill of living within crowded cities, in small spaces, is becoming a California skill after heedless generations of boom.

The most interesting speculation I've heard about America's numerical place in this new world comes from Nicholas Eberstadt, a demographer at the American Enterprise Institute. In a newspaper interview, Eberstadt wonders if there might not be some correlation between America's high fertility rate and our nation's religiosity. After all, the churches of Europe are cold and empty. Cathedrals have become tourist attractions. In Rome, the Pope scolds Europeans for becoming too secular. In Salt Lake City, the Church of Jesus Christ of Latter Day Saints, a church famous for large families, is the fastest-growing religion in the country.

In this new century, the earth's energies, its despair and ambitions and hopes, its hungry children and dreaming poets will belong more to the Southern Hemisphere than the North. Increasingly in the 21st century, the United States will find itself uniquely positioned. As the wealthiest nation on earth we will find ourselves in Davos, in Paris, in Tokyo, sitting with government ministers of prosperous nations of the North, but as a country of great population, we will be linked by common concerns, common solutions, preoccupations, fictions, songs, and linked by common prayers with the vast new cities of the South: Bombay, Lagos, Sao Paolo.

O, brave new world.

The Responsive Reader

1 Rodriguez claims that Spanish is becoming the unofficial second language of America. What *real-life examples* or details support this claim? Have you seen similar evidence of this trend? What countertrend does Rodriguez recognize, and how does he explain it?

2 Mainstream English is often taught as the language of the media and prestige occupations. However, according to Rodriguez, Spanish in this country is still largely the language of the low-wage unskilled worker. So does it seem like a *contradiction* that many Spanish words and expressions are becoming part of mainstream English? How does Rodriguez explain the contradiction?

3 Rodriguez claims that the Census Bureau has created the image of a segmented, divided America. How does the Bureau create or perpetuate this image? Where does Rodriguez see strong *opposing evidence* that America "exists entire"?

4 Nativists champion the rights of native-born Americans and fear that foreign influences will fundamentally change the nature of their country. How does Rodriguez counter the *stereotype* that immigrants will bring with them third-world poverty and negative attitudes?

5 Some agencies and social scientists started to use terms like *European American*, although many European immigrants came to this country because they chose not be European anymore. Rodriguez sees Americans turning away increasingly from European precedents and role models. Where will the country turn instead?

Talking, Listening, Writing

6   Demographics is the study of population patterns and population growth. How does Rodriguez link differences in the role of religion in Europe and in America to patterns of population growth on the two sides of the Atlantic?

7   For many young Americans, pizza, tacos, burritos, food at Thai restaurants, or vegetarian diets similar to those of India have replaced the steak-and-potatoes "real American food" of their elders. What trends have you seen in the eating habits of your generation? Do these trends just affect food, or do they bring with them changes in attitudes or lifestyles?

OTHER VOICES

Puerto Rican Americans

"Much like a quilt intricately interwoven with many beautiful fibers, Latinos are a proud and diverse people woven from indigenous, Spanish European, African, and Asian roots. We are citizens not only of the United States, but of all the Americas."

Edwardjames Olmos, *Americanos: Latino Life in the United States*

Puerto Rico is part of the United States. Spanish-speaking Puerto Ricans are American citizens, and a large migration from the island created a large vibrant Puerto Rican American community in New York City. Lisa Demetriou, the author of the following passage, is a police officer in the New York City Police Department (NYPD). She traces her ancestry on the maternal side to the Taino who were the indigenous Caribbean people the Spaniards first encountered when they reached the Americas. A photographer who describes herself as an "American of Puerto Rican and Italian descent" took Demetriou's picture during a Puerto Rican Day parade.

> Marching with my fellow police officers and with my son in the Puerto Rican Day parade was one of the best times I've ever had. All of my friends came out to watch, everyone was singing "Que Bonita Bandera," and I can't even describe the pride I felt in being part of the NYPD and in being Puerto Rican. My mother was Taino; she descended from an indigenous tribe of Puerto Rico. We grew up with Taino spirituality, music, and food, and I spent every summer until I was 16 in Puerto Rico. But more than anything else, I consider myself "Newyorican." The New York–Puerto Rican culture is unique and very special, and I think it gives me a perspective that makes me a better police officer. I like being someone who can help people, remedy situations, and make a difference in the community.

> Lisa Demetriou, *Americanos* Project

MY LOWLY THATCHED COTTAGE

Ana Veciana-Suarez

**"We all need a place where we belong . . . a place
where we can listen quietly to the stirrings of the heart
and wispers of the soul."**

For millions of Americans, life in this country has been a new beginning. They were immigrants or the children of immigrants. They were refugees from poverty, failed revolutions, or lost wars. They were refugees from religious persecution or political oppression. Many traveled the classic route from being strangers in an alien country to slowly learning to move in a new language and a new environment. They saw their children slowly becoming American- ized—until memories of the Old Country became nostalgic reminiscences to be cherished with old-timers or with young people setting out to rediscover their roots.

Ana Veciana-Suarez is a columnist and novelist who has reached large au- diences with her tales of the odyssey of Cuban Americans who settled in Florida after the Cuban revolution. At first isolated by language and culture, they slowly established a prosperous influential Cuban American society in which Latin and North American influences meet. Veciana-Suarez's husband, David, was Jewish, and their children early lived with the multicultural rich- ness of the American experience. Veciana-Suarez collected many of the columns she wrote for the Miami Herald *in her book* Birthday Parties in Heaven *(2000). Her novel* The Chin Kiss King *(1997) has been praised for its "fierce tenderness, bits of magic up her sleeve, and lusty humor"* (Raleigh News & Observer).

Thought Starters: What do you think of when you hear the word *home*? Is there one place that you will always think of as home, or are there sev- eral places or environments to which you were especially attached?

The Bible's book of Jeremiah traces the fall of Jerusalem, the destruc-　*1* tion of the city and the Temple, and the exile to Babylonia of Judah's king and many of his people. At the end, it precisely tallies the numbers: 3,023 people in the seventh year, 832 in the eighteenth year, 745 in the twenty- third year—in all, 4,600 exiles. You would think that the people of Judah would have gotten the hang of exile by then. After all, their ancestors had wandered in the wilderness for forty years, after they had left Egypt and be- fore homesteading in the Promised Land. Yet, an entire book, Lamenta- tions, is devoted to the aftermath of ruin and exile that followed the de- struction of Jerusalem in 586 B.C.

The old people no longer sit at
the city gate,
and the young people no
longer make music.

Happiness has gone out of our
lives;
grief has taken the place of
our dances.

When the Jewish exiles fled to the Chebar River in Babylonia, and when Moses' Israelites trudged through Moab and Kadesh Barnea, when they crossed the Jordan and camped near the Gulf of Suez, how did they think of home? In what way did they make desert and riverland a familiar, if not welcoming, domicile? Did they carry a potted houseplant from one encampment to the next? Was the carved chair, a family heirloom, given prominent display under the tent? Did they cook food in the same way with the same pots and the same tools? How did they realize they had arrived where they belonged? Was it the certainty of knowing where everything is? The feelings of welcome and repose? Or was it simply arbitrary boundaries drawn from here to there by an alternately loving and wrathful God?

My parents have been exiles for an almost biblical forty years, and though they have not wandered in the physical wilderness like the Israelites, they have known, at least in the beginning, a spiritual wasteland of sorts: the isolation of not belonging, the harshness of the unfamiliar. Their Jerusalem floated one-hundred-and-forty miles from where they live today. It was a paradise of halcyon nights and glorious days, an island where the ocean was bluer, the sand whiter, the palms taller. It never existed, of course. Nostalgia rewrites history. Yet my parents would have given anything over the years to return to Cuba, to live again in Havana's La Vibora neighborhood, in their little tiled house with the wrought-iron, gated porch; to walk the little narrow streets that weren't always clean; and to shop in their little bodegas that weren't always well stocked but where everybody knew their names. (Nineteenth-century American playwright John Howard Payne hit the nail on the head when he wrote in "Home Sweet Home," from the opera *Clari, the Maid of Milan*: "An exile from home splendor dazzles in vain, / Oh give me my lowly thatched cottage again. . . .") Instead of the tiny home in La Vibora, it was *el exilio*—a state of limbo when you are where you don't expect to be—that defined the final years of my parents' youth and all of their middle age. It marked my childhood, too.

We did not celebrate Thanksgiving, the most American of holidays, until my last years in elementary school. I have no early memories of pumpkin pie and sweet potato casseroles, of family gathered around the bounty of a table. Unless it was Christmas Eve. And even then, Christmas was a subdued affair, with none of the overwrought glitz of today. We did not get a Christmas tree until I was in fourth or fifth grade, a fake silver beauty that I watched for hours on end when the revolving colors of a reflector light shone on it. This penury during the holidays, I now believe, had little to do with money but plenty to do with hope—hope that life in these United States would be temporary, hope that next Christmas would be celebrated in Havana, hope that one day they would look back at this period of their lives as something sad but brief, and altogether finished. Celebrating would have been to admit a hopelessness. This is how exile translates into marginality, a living on the sidelines without knowing when to jump into the game.

5

Yet, little by little, first in word then by action, whether they knew it or not, their lives evolved into a search for rootedness. My parents bought a house when they had saved up enough money and explained it this way: Very few people would rent out to foreigners with young children, even if these renters were clean, modestly dressed, well-mannered, and professionals in another country. Eventually they fixed up this house, added a bathroom and bedroom for the in-laws, put up a fence, remodeled the kitchen, planted a mango tree in the back and red ixora bushes in the front. As their children grew older, as their children birthed children in exile, they spoke less of a return to Cuba—"When we go back home . . ."—and more of the horrible possibility that, in their old age, they would be put in a nursing home in much the same way that *los americanos* sent their old folk away. My mother talked about retiring to a condo in Miami Beach; my father spoke of expanding the business.

When did exile become home? After they planted the mango? When the grandchildren were born? Now, as they approach retirement?

I have grown interested in answers as I see David wandering about my house, or collapsing in his old bed in his old house in the grove. No matter what he says, I know he doesn't feel at home in either place. He is where my parents were about twenty years ago—in between, not there but not quite here either.

My family has lived in three different countries and spoken three different languages in the span of three generations. My grandparents, Catalonians on both sides, fled their homeland because of poverty and civil war. Their foods and their language, that rich guttural Catalan I heard in my childhood, eventually melded with the new customs of their new island home. Their children, in turn, later scrambled across the Florida Straits to another exile, also because of political upheaval. What, I sometimes wonder, might be in store for me? As a woman listening to stories of my ancestors' comings and goings, as a Catholic married to a Jew who has never seen his people's Promised Land, the concept of home is important to me. But not only to me—actually to most everybody I know. We all need a place where we belong, a place to return to, where the contours of the bed are well-known and the light switches are just where they're supposed to be: a place where we can listen quietly, comfortably, to the stirrings of the heart and whispers of the soul.

The Responsive Reader

1   Where in the essay does Veciana–Suarez begin to talk about her family's experiences with exile? Why do you think she begins the essay with two paragraphs about exiled peoples in the Bible? How does the introduction prepare you for the rest of the essay?

2   What examples does Veciana–Suarez use to convey her parents' feelings about Cuba and the life of exile? How did these feelings change over time? What caused their feelings to change?

3   The way we celebrate holidays is often a strong indicator of ties or lack of ties with a cultural tradition. What role do holidays play in this selection?

4   Although most of Veciana–Suarez's essay concerns her parents' exile, she concludes by describing other members of her family and by observing that "the concept of home is important" to most people she knows. Why do you think she ends the essay this way? Does the information about her grandparents and her husband contribute to your understanding of her reasons for saying that we "all need a place where we belong"?

5   What experiences have you or others in your family had of leaving a home or a homeland behind? How were those experiences similar to and different from those that Veciana–Suarez describes?

6   Veciana–Suarez's parents explained that they bought a house in the United States because few Americans wanted to rent to foreigners with young children. Do you or people you know think of other people as foreigners? What encounters or experiences does the term bring to mind?

Talking, Listening, Writing

7   In a different part of her book, Veciana–Suarez gives a loving account of how her children were taught to celebrate Passover in the traditional manner, with the appropriate foods, ritual, and prayer. Give an account of this or another cherished ethnic holiday observance that you know well or can research.

8   Is it possible for people to feel that more than one country is home? Have you known people who remained "wanderers between two worlds"?

9   Judging from your experience or observation, do members of ethnic groups or immigrant groups still tend to live in sections of town where they cluster "with their own kind," or do most Americans live in ethnically mixed neighborhoods?

Collaborative Projects

10   Working with a group, use library research and personal interviews to collect first-person accounts by immigrants to the United States from

an area of the world to which you have special ties or in which you have a special interest. Is there a common thread? Are there shared experiences that become part of the collective memory of a group? You may want to share your findings with your classmates as part of a multi-ethnic festival with readings from immigrants' stories.

DIVERSITY AND ITS DISCONTENTS

Arturo Madrid

"My ancestors' presence in what is now the United States antedates Plymouth Rock . . . But I have always known that I was the other, even before I knew the vocabulary or understood the significance of otherness."

The educator whose speech was reprinted in a journal devoted to issues in higher education in May 1988 says that his great-grandparents were already American citizens. His ancestors already lived in this country when the first English-speaking Pilgrims landed in the New World at Plymouth Rock. Why did he feel that many Americans like him are still denied a "voice or visibility or validity in American society"?

Arturo Madrid is a native of New Mexico who studied at the University of New Mexico and at UCLA. His first teaching assignment was at Dartmouth; he later became president of the Thomas Rivera Center at the Claremont Graduate School in California. He represents Spanish-speaking Americans of the Southwest who live in lands that were once part of Mexico and for whom the Anglos, or americanos, *were the "immigrants," or new arrivals.*

The following article is excerpted from a speech he gave at the National Conference of the American Association of Higher Education. He urged his audience of educators to recognize excellence in workers as well as managers, in people who are not glib or superficially sophisticated, and in people regardless of class, gender, race, or national origin. What do you learn from this article about the feeling of being the "other"?

Thought Starters: What does it mean to be "different"? How does it shape a person's outlook and personality?

My name is Arturo Madrid. I am a citizen of the United States, as are   1 my parents and as were my grandparents and my great-grandparents. My ancestors' presence in what is now the United States antedates Plymouth Rock, even without taking into account any American Indian heritage I might have.

I do not, however, fit those mental sets that define America and Americans. My physical appearance, my speech patterns, my name, my profession (a professor of Spanish) create a text that confuses the reader My normal experience is to be asked, "And where are *you* from?" My response depends on my mood. Passive–aggressive, I answer, "From here." Aggressive–passive, I ask, "Do you mean where I am originally from?" But ultimately my answer to those follow-up questions that will ask about origins will be that we have always been from here.

Overcoming my resentment I try to educate, knowing that nine times out of ten my words fall on inattentive ears. I have spent most of my adult life explaining who I am not. I am exotic, but—as Richard Rodriguez of *Hunger of Memory* fame so painfully found out—not exotic enough . . . not Peruvian, or Pakistani, or whatever. I am, however, very clearly the *other*, if only your everyday, garden-variety, domestic *other*. I will share with you another phenomenon that I have been a part of, that of being a missing person, and how I came late to that awareness. But I've always known that I was the *other*, even before I knew the vocabulary or understood the significance of otherness.

I grew up in an isolated and historically marginal part of the United States, a small mountain village in the state of New Mexico, the eldest child of parents native to that region, whose ancestors had always lived there. In those vast and empty spaces people who look like me, speak as I do, and have names like mine predominate. But the *americanos* lived among us: the descendants of those nineteenth-century immigrants who dispossessed us of our lands; missionaries who came to convert us and stayed to live among us; artists who became enchanted with our land and humanscape and went native; refugees from unhealthy climes, crowded spaces, unpleasant circumstances; and, of course, the inhabitants of Los Alamos, whose sociocultural distance from us was accentuated by the fact that they occupied a space removed from and proscribed to us. More importantly, however, they—*losamericanos*—were omnipresent (and almost exclusively so) in newspapers, newsmagazines, books, on radio, in movies, and, ultimately, on television.

Despite the operating myth of the day, school did not erase my otherness. It did try to deny it, and in doing so only accentuated it. To this day what takes place in schools is more socialization than education, but when I was in elementary school—and given where I was—socialization was everything. School was where one became an American, because there was a pervasive and systematic denial by the society that surrounded us that we were Americans. That denial was both explicit and implicit.

Quite beyond saluting the flag and pledging allegiance to it (a very intense and meaningful action, given that the United States was involved in a war and our brothers, cousins, uncles, and fathers were on the frontlines), becoming American was learning English, and its corollary: not speaking Spanish. Until very recently ours was a proscribed language, either *de jure*— by rule, by policy, by law—or *de facto*—by practice, implicitly if not explicitly, through social and political and economic pressure. I do not argue that learning English was not appropriate. On the countrary. Like it or not, and we had no basis to make any judgments on that matter, we were Americans by virtue of having been born Americans and English was the common language of Americans. And there was a myth, a pervasive myth, to the effect that if only we learned to speak English well—and particularly without an accent—we would be welcomed into the American fellowship.

Sam Hayakawa and the official English movement folks notwithstanding, the true text was not our speech, but rather our names and our appearance, for we would always have an accent, however perfect our pronunciation, however excellent our enunciation, however divine our diction. That accent would be heard in our pigmentation, our physiognomy, our names. We were, in short, the *other*.

Being the *other* involves contradictory phenomena. On the one hand being the *other* frequently means being invisible. Ralph Ellison wrote eloquently about that experience in his magisterial novel, *Invisible Man*. On the other hand, being the *other* sometimes involves sticking out like a sore thumb. What is she/he doing here?

For some of us being the *other* is only annoying; for others it is debilitating; for still others it is damning. Many try to flee otherness by taking on protective colorations that provide invisibility, whether of dress or speech or manner or name. Only a fortunate few succeed. For the majority of us otherness is permanently sealed by physical appearance. For the rest, otherness is betrayed by ways of being, speaking, or doing.

The first half of my life I spent downplaying the significance and consequences of otherness. The second half has seen me wrestling to understand its complex and deeply ingrained realities; striving to fathom why otherness denies us a voice or visibility or validity in American society and its institutions; struggling to make otherness familiar, reasonable, even normal to my fellow Americans.

10

I spoke earlier of another phenomenon that I am a part of: that of being a missing person. Growing up in northern New Mexico I had only a slight sense of us being missing persons. *Hispanos*, as we called (and call) ourselves in New Mexico, were very much a part of the fabric of the society, and there were *hispano* professionals everywhere about me: doctors, lawyers, schoolteachers, and administrators. My people owned businesses, ran organizations, and were both appointed and elected public officials.

My awareness of our absence from the larger institutional life of the society became sharper when I went off to college, but even then it was attenuated by the circumstances of history and geography. The demography of Albuquerque still strongly reflected its historical and cultural origins, despite the influx of Midwesterners and Easterners. Moreover, many of my classmates at the University of New Mexico were *hispanos*, and even some of my professors. I thought that would obtain at UCLA, were I began graduate studies in 1960. Los Angeles had a very large Mexican population and that population was visible even in and around Westwood and on the campus. Many of the groundskeepers and food-service personnel at UCLA were Mexican. But Mexican-American students were few and mostly invisible, and I do not recall seeing or knowing a single Mexican-American (or, for that matter, African-American, Asian, or American Indian) professional on the staff or faculty of that institution during the five years I was there. Needless to say, people like me were not present in any capacity at

Dartmouth College, the site of my first teaching appointment, and of course were not even part of the institutional or individual mind-set. I knew then that we—a we that had come to encompass American Indians, Asian-Americans, African-Americans, Puerto Ricans, and women—were truly missing persons in American institutional life.

Over the past three decades the *de jure* and *de facto* types of segregation that have historically characterized American institutions have been under assault. As a consequence, minorities and women have become part of American institutional life. Although there are still many areas where we are not to be found, the missing persons phenomenon is not as pervasive as it once was. However, the presence of the *other*, particularly minorities, in institutions and in institutional life resembles what we call in Spanish a *flor de tierra* (a surface phenomenon): we are spare plants whose roots do not go deep, vulnerable to inclemencies of an economic, or political, or social, nature.

Our entrance into and our status in institutional life are not unlike a scenario set forth by my grandmother's pastor when she informed him that she and her family were leaving their mountain village to relocate to the Rio Grande Valley. When he asked her to promise that she would remain true to the faith and continue to involve herself in it, she asked why he thought she would do otherwise. "Doña Trinidad," he told her, "in the Valley there is no Spanish church. There is only an American church." "But," she protested, "I read and speak English and would be able to worship there." The pastor responded, "It is possible that they will not admit you, and even if they do, they might not accept you. And that is why I want you to promise me that you are going to go to church. Because if they don't let you in through the front door, I want you to go in through the back door. And if you can't get in through the back door, go in the side door. And if you are unable to enter through the side door I want you to go in through the window. What is important is that you enter and stay."

Some of us entered institutional life through the front door; others 15 through the back door; and still others through side doors. Many, if not most of us, came in through windows, and continue to come in through windows. Of those who entered through the front door, some never made it past the lobby; others were ushered into corners and niches. Those who entered through back and side doors inevitably have remained in back and side rooms. And those who entered through windows found enclosures built around them. For, despite the lip service given to the goal of the integration of minorities into institutional life, what has frequently occurred instead is ghettoization, marginalization, isolation.

Not only have the entry points been limited, but in addition the dynamics have been singularly conflictive. Gaining entry and its corollary, gaining space, have frequently come as a consequence of demands made on institutions and institutional officers. Rather than entering institutions more or less passively, minorities have of necessity entered them actively, even aggressively. Rather than waiting to receive, they have demanded. In-stitutional relations have thus been adversarial, infused with specific and generalized tensions.

The nature of the entrance and the nature of the space occupied have greatly influenced the view and attitude of the majority population within those institutions. All of us are put into the same box; that is, no matter what the individual reality, the assessment of the individual is inevitably conditioned by a perception that is held of the class. Whatever our history, whatever our record, whatever our validations, whatever our accomplish-ments, by and large we are perceived unidimensionally and dealt with ac-cordingly. I remember an experience I had in this regard, atypical only in its explicitness. A few years ago I allowed myself to be persuaded to seek the presidency of a well-known state university. I was invited for an interview and presented myself before the selection committee, which included members of the board of trustees. The opening question of that brief but memorable interview was directed at me by a member of that august body. "Dr. Madrid," he asked, "why does a one-dimensional person like you think he can be the president of a multidimensional institution like ours?"

Over the past four decades America's demography has undergone significant changes. Since 1965 the principal demographic growth we have experienced in the United States has been of peoples whose national ori-gins are non-European. This population growth has occurred both through birth and through immigration. A few years ago discussion of the national birthrate had a scare dimension: the high—"inordinately high"—birthrate of the Hispanic population. The popular discourse was informed by words such as "breeding." Several years later, as a consequence of careful tracking by government agencies, we now know that what has happened is that the birthrate of the majority population has decreased. When viewed histori-cally and comparatively, the minority populations (for the most part) have also had a decline in birthrate, but not one as great as that of the majority.

There are additional demographic changes that should give us some-thing to think about. African-Americans are now to be found in significant numbers in every major urban center in the nation. Hispanic-Americans now number over 15 million people, and although they are a regionally con-centrated (and highly urbanized) population, there is a Hispanic community in almost every major urban center of the United States. American Indians, heretofore a small and rural population, are increasingly more numerous and urban. The Asian-American population, which has historically consisted of small and concentrated communities of Chinese-, Filipino-, and Japanese-Americans, has doubled over the past decade, its complexion changed by the addition of Cambodians, Koreans, Hmongs, Vietnamese, et al.

Prior to the Immigration Act of 1965, 69 percent of immigration was from Europe. By far the largest number of immigrants to the United States since 1965 have been from the Americas and from Asia: 34 percent are from

20

Asia; another 34 percent are from Central and South America; 16 percent are from Europe; 10 percent are from the Caribbean; the remaining 6 percent are from other continents and Canada. As was the case with previous immigration waves, the current one consists principally of young people: 60 percent are between the ages of 16 and 44. Thus, for the next few decades, we will continue to see a growth in the percentage of non–European–origin Americans as compared to European-Americans.

To sum up, we now live in one of the most demographically diverse nations in the world, and one that is increasingly more so.

During the same period social and economic change seems to have accelerated. Who would have imagined at mid-century that the prototypical middle-class family (working husband, wife as homemaker, two children) would for all intents and purposes disappear? Who could have anticipated the rise in teenage pregnancies, children in poverty, drug use? Who among us understood the implications of an aging population?

We live in an age of continuous and intense change, a world in which what held true yesterday does not today, and certainly will not tomorrow. What change does, moreover, is bring about even more change. The only constant we have at this point in our national development is change. And change is threatening. The older we get the more likely we are to be anxious about change, and the greater our desire to maintain the status quo.

Evident in our public life is a fear of change, whether economic or moral. Some who fear change are responsive to the call of economic protectionism, others to the message of moral protectionism. Parenthetically, I have referred to the movement to require more of students without in turn giving them more as academic protectionism. And the pronouncements of E. D. Hirsch and Allan Bloom are, I believe, informed by intellectual protectionism. Much more serious, however, is the dark side of the populism which underlies this evergoing protectionism—the resentment of the *other*. An excellent and fascinating example of that aspect of populism is the cry for linguistic protectionism—for making English the official language of the United States. And who among us is unaware of the tensions that underlie immigration reform, of the underside of demographic protectionism?

A matter of increasing concern is whether this new protectionism, and the mistrust of the *other* which accompanies it, is not making more significant inroads than we have supposed in higher education. Specifically, I wish to discuss the question of whether a goal (quality) and a reality (demographic diversity) have been erroneously placed in conflict, and, if so, what problems this perception of conflict might present. *25*

As part of my scholarship I turn to dictionaries for both origins and meanings of words. Quality, according to the *Oxford English Dictionary*, has multiple meanings. One set defines quality as being an essential character, a distinctive and inherent feature. A second describes it as a degree of excellence, of conformity to standards, as superiority in kind. A third makes reference to social status, particularly to persons of high social status. A fourth talks about quality as being a special or distinguishing attribute, as being a desirable trait. Quality is highly desirable in both principle and practice. We all aspire to it in our own person, in our experiences, in our acquisitions and products, and of course we all want to be associated with people and operations of quality.

But let us move away from the various dictionary meanings of the word and to our own sense of what it represents and of how we feel about it. First of all we consider quality to be finite; that is, it is limited with respect to quantity; it has very few manifestations; it is not widely distributed. I have it and you have it, but they don't. We associate quality with homogeneity, with uniformity, with standardization, with order, regularity, neatness. All too often we equate it with smoothness, glibness, slickness, elegance. Certainly it is always expensive. We tend to identify it with those who lead, with the rich and famous. And, when you come right down to it, it's inherent. Either you've got it or you ain't.

Diversity, from the Latin *divertere*, meaning to turn aside, to go different ways, to differ, is the condition of being different or having differences, is an instance of being different. Its companion word, diverse, means differing, unlike, distinct; having or capable of having various forms; composed of unlike or distinct elements. Diversity is lack of standardization, of regularity, of orderliness, homogeneity, conformity, uniformity. Diversity introduces complications, is difficult to organize, is troublesome to manage, is problematical. Diversity is irregular, disorderly, uneven, rough. The way we use the word diversity gives us away. Something is too diverse, is extremely diverse. We want a little diversity.

When we talk about diversity, we are talking about the *other*, whatever that other might be: someone of a different gender, race, class, national origin; somebody at a greater or lesser distance from the norm; someone outside the set; someone who possesses a different set of characteristics, features, or attributes; someone who does not fall within the taxonomies we use daily and with which we are comfortable; someone who does not fit into the mental configurations that give our lives order and meaning.

In short, diversity is desirable only in principle, not in practice. Long live diversity . . . as long as it conforms to my standards, my mind set, my view of life, my sense of order. We desire, we like, we admire diversity, not unlike the way the French (and others) appreciate women; that is, *Vive la différence!*—as long as it stays in its place. 30

What I find paradoxical about and lacking in this debate is that diversity is the natural order of things. Evolution produces diversity Margaret Visser, writing about food in her latest book, *Much Depends on Dinner,* makes an eloquent statement in this regard:

> Machines like, demand, and produce uniformity. But nature loathes it: her strength lies in multiplicity and in differences. Sameness in biology means fewer possibilities and therefore weakness.

The United States, by its very nature, by its very development, is the essence of diversity. It is diverse in its geography, population, institutions, technology; its social, cultural, and intellectual modes. It is a society that at its best does not consider quality to be monolithic in form or finite in quantity, or to be inherent in class. Quality in our society proceeds in large measure out of the stimulus of diverse modes of thinking and acting; out of the creativity made possible by the different ways in which we approach things; out of diversion from paths or modes hallowed by tradition.

One of the principal strengths of our society is its ability to address, on a continuing and substantive basis, the real economic, political, and social problems that have faced and continue to face us. What makes the United States so attractive to immigrants is the protections and opportunities it offers; what keeps our society together is tolerance for cultural, religious, social, political, and even linguistic difference; what makes us a unique, dynamic, and extraordinary nation is the power and creativity of our diversity.

The true history of the United States is one of struggle against intolerance, against oppression, against xenophobia, against those forces that have prohibited persons from participating in the larger life of the society on the basis of their race, their gender, their religion, their national origin, their linguistic and cultural background. These phenomena are not consigned to the past. They remain with us and frequently take on virulent dimensions.

If you believe, as I do, that the well-being of a society is directly re-   35
lated to the degree and extent to which all of its citizens participate in its institutions, then you will have to agree that we have a challenge before us. In view of the extraordinary changes that are taking place in our society we need to take up the struggle again, irritating, grating, troublesome, unfashionable, unpleasant as it is. As educated and educator members of this society we have a special responsibility for ensuring that all American institutions, not just our elementary and secondary schools, our juvenile halls, or our jails, reflect the diversity of our society. Not to do so is to risk greater alienation on the part of a growing segment of our society; is to risk increased social tension in an already conflictive world; and, ultimately, is to risk the survival of a range of institutions that, for all their defects and deficiencies, provide us the opportunity and the freedom to improve our individual and collective lot.

Let me urge you to reflect on these two words—quality and diversity—and on the mental sets and behaviors that flow out of them. And let me urge you further to struggle against the notion that quality is finite in quantity, limited in its manifestations, or is restricted by considerations of class, gender, race, or national origin; or that quality manifests itself only in leaders and not in followers, in managers and not in workers, in breeders and not in drones; or that it has to be associated with verbal agility or elegance of personal style; or that it cannot be seeded, nurtured, or developed.

Because diversity—the *other*—is among us, [it] will define and determine our lives in ways that we still do not fully appreciate, whether that other is women (no longer bound by tradition, house, and family); or Asians, African-Americans, Indians, and Hispanics (no longer invisible, regional, or marginal); or our newest immigrants (no longer distant, exotic, alien). Given the changing profile of America, will we come to terms with diversity in our personal and professional lives? Will we begin to recognize the diverse forms that quality can take? If so, we will thus initiate the process of making quality limitless in its manifestations, infinite in quantity, unrestricted with respect to its origins, and more importantly, virulently contagious.

I hope we will. And that we will further join together to expand—not to close—the circle.

The Responsive Reader

1 What does it mean to Madrid to be the "other"? What is or was the role of such factors as history, genealogy, appearance (or "physiognomy"), and language in his sense of being different?
2 What was Madrid's experience with or perception of the *Americanos*?
3 What was Madrid's experience with the school as the institution most directly representing American society? What was its goal? What was its governing myth? Did it fail or succeed?
4 What are different ways of dealing with minority identity or minority status? How did (and does) Madrid react or cope? Did his attitude or awareness change at different stages in his life?
5 What is Madrid's account of the changes as American colleges and universities try to deal with the issue of diversity? Have the changes been for the better?
6 What is Madrid's last word on the role of diversity in American society?

Talking, Listening, Writing

7 On balance, what do you think predominates in this essay—the "discontents" of the past or the challenges of the future?
8 Have you ever tried to put yourself in the shoes of someone with a history or with grievances and aspirations very different from your own? Tell the story of an experience that opened up for you a new perspective or opened a new window on the world. What did you learn from the experience?
9 Have you ever had difficulty answering the question "Who are you?" or "What are you?"

Collaborative Projects

10 Have the hiring and retention of minority faculty been an issue at your own institution? You and classmates may want to arrange interviews with people who are in a position to know.

THE SPIRITUALLY DIVERSE SOCIETY

Jeremiah Creedon

The transition to a spiritually diverse society has led to a "new perception of religion: a personalized, customized form of faith views which meets personal needs."

The author of the following selection, condensed in 2002 from a longer earlier article for the Utne Reader, *focuses on a growing search for spiritual meaning that may cross the borders between traditional faiths.*

He sees increased immigration, especially from Asia, bringing many Americans face to face with religious philosophies from other parts of the world. Spiritual teachers or gurus from other cultures extend their influence beyond their original followers to American popular culture, and the information explosion has brought religious and spiritual texts from around the world into the nation's bookstores. Ministers report that outsiders not committed to the basic beliefs of the congregation attend because they like its work with AIDS or the homeless or because they love its tradition of church music. The result, the author claims, is a "robust spiritual marketplace" and a rise in "do-it-yourself spirituality."

Thought Starters: Have you been exposed to religious teachings or sacred art from other parts of the world?

We're living in what observers call an age of extreme "religious pluralism." The same cultural forces that have driven many to leave their inherited faiths have also affected others who have stayed. Almost all the major denominations now contain internal movements that are trying to transform them. Many traditionalists, of course, are fighting to block reforms. Syncretism, the formal term for the blending of rituals and beliefs from different faiths, is a dirty word to conservative worshipers, dreaded like a plague of locusts—and maybe as hard to stop. New hybrid modes of worship are constantly appearing, from the new Christian megachurches, whose mammoth services can resemble arena rock, to tiny garage religions hardly bigger than the average band.

The latest edition of the *Encyclopedia of American Religions* lists more than 2,100 religious groups, a figure that has almost doubled in 20 years. They range from the most straightlaced forms of Judaism and Christianity to UFO cults awaiting deliverance by flying saucer. The influx of Asian religions is clearly mirrored in the *Encyclopedia*, and so is the recent rapid rise of Islam, which other sources put at about 3.5 million adherents. With about 750,000 believers, including 100,000 American converts, Buddhism is said to be the country's fastest-growing faith.

The statistics ultimately yield a portrait full of contradictions. One certainty is that we live in a very religious country—in fact, the United States is generally considered to be the most religious country in the Western industrial world. Though nine out of ten American adults believe that God exists, there's growing disagreement about how God should be described. God is Michelangelo's bearded old man in the Sistine Chapel. God is pure intelligence. God is cosmic energy. God is a Goddess. At least eight out of ten American adults consider themselves to be Christians, but most are hazy about the basic tenets of their faith. The pollsters say that Americans pray more often than they have sex, but no one knows how many consider sex and prayer to be the same thing.

The undeniable reality, concludes George Barna in *The Index of Leading Spiritual Indicators* (Word Publishing, 1996), "is that America is transitioning from a Christian nation to a spiritually diverse society." One result of this spiritual upheaval is a "new perception of religion: a personalized, customized form of faith views which meet personal needs, minimize rules and absolutes, and bear little resemblance to the 'pure' form of any of the world's major religions."

John H. Berthrong, associate dean at Boston University's School of   5 Theology and director of the Institute for Dialogue Among Religious Traditions, has seen this trend unfold in his classroom. "When I talk to students about their own sense of religious identity, I find that more and more of them have been brought up in homes that are post-Christian," he says. "So to say that they are reacting against Christianity is wrong; they've never been Christians. Even some of the ones who are Christian will say, 'But I really like Taoism and Buddhism too, and my meditation is Vipassana, but I also do a lot of work at my local church because I like the choir.'"

A Christian theologian and scholar of Confucianism, Berthrong has spent 20 years fostering communication among different religions. His observations on the modern fluidity of belief are the basis of a new book he's writing called *The Divine Deli*, to be published by Orbis. "I think a lot of traditional boundaries for many people are simply dissolving," he says. Berthrong sees a trend toward "multiple citizenship" in a number of separate faiths—and no complete allegiance to any one. In terms of basic issues like child rearing and church fund-raising, the trend's potential impact is profound. And that's before anyone raises the touchy matter of doctrine. "Many of the more conservative Christian theologians don't find any of this either amusing or profitable," he adds. "It's one of the areas that really defines the difference between liberal theology and conservative theology."

Chenyang Li, associate professor of philosophy and religious studies at Monmouth College, and author of the forthcoming book, *The Tao Encounters the West*, looks to his native China for an example of how multiple religious participation can work. In China, he explains, an individual's religious life may be a harmonious interplay among Confucianism, Taoism, and Buddhism. Even though their basic value systems may not always be perfectly aligned, aspects of each faith can be useful in different areas of life, or even in the same area. Confucianism and Buddhism, for example, may be at odds about worldly success, says Li, but this play of opposites can be used to achieve breadth (a kind of enlightened tolerance) and balance, which are important Chinese cultural ideals.

The Responsive Reader

1 Have you had personal contact with current trends in religious life the author mentions—such as the "new Christian megachurches" with "mammoth services"? "tiny garage religions"? the rise of Islam? How was the experience different from your experience with more traditional forms of worship?
2 What for you is striking or new about the author's statistics? Do you agree that the picture they paint is "full of contradictions"?

Talking, Listening, Writing

3 Do you think "we live in a very religious country"?
4 The founding teacher of a meditation center said, "Wide experimentation in spiritual life is symptomatic of the growing recognition that the things we thought would make us happy aren't working, and there is a deep need to connect to what is sacred in our lives." Have you seen evidence of "wide experimentation in spiritual life"? When and where?

Collaborative Projects

5 Scholars from nineteenth-century anthropologists to today's feminists have explored the possibility of a religious stage before patriarchy— before the rule of male gods. They have examined evidence of a prehistoric cycle where worship centered on earth goddesses or mother goddesses—with some still surviving into historic times, like the Babylonian Ishtar or the Greek Demeter, goddess of the harvest. You may want to team up with classmates to report on current research on this subject.

INDIAN MOVIE, NEW JERSEY
Chitra Divakaruni

Nostalgia movies take first-generation immigrants from India back to a world without hostile neighbors or ungrateful offspring.

Born in Calcutta in India, Chitra Banerjee Divakaruni came to America when she was nineteen and became a college teacher and a widely published writer of poems and stories. She has been fascinated with the "rich cosmopolitan mix" of contemporary America and with the way not only race but also economics and gender shape our multicultural society

Divakaruni has a Ph.D. in English literature from the University of California at Berkeley. She has published several volumes of poetry, including Black Candle *(1991), and a collection of stories,* Arranged Marriage *(1996). She edited a collection of multicultural readings,* Multitude *(1993), which a colleague called "a new kind of anthology altogether, with a virtual multitude of converging, creative possibilities and perspectives." Like the following example, Divakaruni's poems have often centered on the life journey of Asian immigrants adapting to their new culture. She has been much involved in women's issues and was one of the founders of MAITRI, a service that offers support to South East Asian women.*

Thought Starters: Where have you seen examples of nostalgia or a strong sentimental attachment to Old Country ways and memories?

Not like the white filmstars, all rib
and gaunt cheekbone, the Indian sex-goddess
smiles plumply from behind a flowery
branch. Below her brief red skirt, her thighs
are satisfying-solid, redeeming
as tree trunks. She swings her hips
and the men-viewers whistle. The lover-hero
dances in to a song, his lip-sync
a little off, but no matter, we
know the words already and sing along.
It is safe here, the day
golden and cool so no one sweats,
roses on every bush and the Dal Lake
clean again.
        The sex-goddess switches
to thickened English to emphasize

a joke. We laugh and clap. Here
we need not be embarrassed by words
dropping like lead pellets into foreign ears.
The flickering movie–light
wipes from our faces years of America, sons
who want mohawks and refuse to run
the family store, daughters who date
on the sly.

        When at the end the hero
dies for his friend who also
loves the sex–goddess and now can marry her,
we weep, understanding. Even the men
clear their throats to say, "What *qurbani!*°   *sacrifice*
What *dosti!*"° After, we mill around   *friendship*
unwilling to leave, exchange greetings
and good news: a new gold chain, a trip
to India. We do not speak
of motel raids, cancelled permits, stones
thrown through glass windows, daughters and sons
raped by Dotbusters.
        In this dim foyer,
we can pull around us the faint, comforting smell
of incense and *pakoras,*° can arrange   *ethnic food*
our children's marriages with hometown boys and girls,
open a franchise, win a million
in the mail. We can retire
in India, a yellow two–storeyed house
with wrought–iron gates, our own
Ambassador car. Or at least
move to a rich white suburb, Summerfield
or Fort Lee, with neighbors that will
talk to us. Here while the film–songs still echo
in the corridors and restrooms, we can trust
in movie truths: sacrifice, success, love and luck,
the America that was supposed to be.

The Responsive Reader

1 What hints, scattered in the poem, does the poet give at of the *realities* of immigrant life from which the movie provides an escape? (Who are the "Dotbusters," and why are they given that name? What role do language difficulties play in the immigrants' lives?)

2 What comment does the poem offer on the *vision* of America that brought the immigrants here?

3 We are often told today that *ideals of beauty* are relative—they are culturally conditioned. How does the poem support this view?

Talking, Listening, Writing

4 What ideals of beauty—female and male—do the mass media promote? Is it true, as many feminists claim, that our ideal of female beauty is damaging to women? (Is something similar true of the image of the handsome male created by the media?)
5 What kind of fantasy world created by the media is your own favorite retreat from reality?

FORUM: *Redeeming Past Injustice*

For many immigrants, the story of America has been the story of the distant golden shore. In America, things would be different. People living in wretched conditions, exploited by greedy landlords or brutalized by repressive governments, dreamed of a country where people could be free and equal. People persecuted because they dissented on points of doctrine dreamed of a New Jerusalem where they could worship according to the dictates of their conscience.

Much current rewriting of American history has moved beyond the myth of America as the land of promise. Much current writing takes into account the point of view of the conquered, the dispossessed, the enslaved. The tide of white invaders that swept over the Americas did not fill an empty space—"virgin land." In the Caribbean islands, the native population, doomed to extinction by the arrival of Columbus and the Spaniards, is variously estimated to have numbered as much as ten million. Millions of people were brought to the land of the free in chains to work as slaves. California and the Southwest were Mexican before they were annexed to the United States.

In recent years, much discussion has focused on injustices in the nation's past. Should a current generation feel guilty for past abuses? Should white Americans feel obligated to compensate members of minorities for treaties broken by their ancestors? Should American society today indemnify descendants of slaves? Should we apologize to Japanese Americans whose parents or grandparents were stripped of their property and confined in relocation camps in World War II?

Today courts are reexamining ancient treaty rights that a tribe may be trying to recover. Powerful television series and movies have retold the story of slavery and of the aftermath of slavery from the point of view of the victims. At the same time, influential voices are saying that preoccupation with the injustices of the past is divisive. Is it true that dwelling on their history as victims keeps people from shaping their own destiny?

THE DAY THE SLAVES GOT THEIR WAY

Matthew Kauffman

The seizure of the *Amistad* touched off a two-year legal battle by a small group of abolitionists "determined to prove that the Africans were enslaved illegally and should be freed."

Slavery has been the great trauma of America's experience as a nation. An estimated half a million African slaves were in the country at the time of the American Revolution in 1776. The slave trade was revived after the War of Independence, with an estimated 80,000 people a year carried out of Africa as slaves, many of them in American ships. Slaves mixed prisoners coming from different ethnic groups and speaking different languages so that organized group resistance could not materialize. Nevertheless, a number of slave mutinies or slave rebellions are on record, rediscovered by modern writers and historians as forgotten pages from American history.

The following selection focuses on the legal aftermath of a slave rebellion that is also treated in Robert Hayden's poem "Middle Passage" and in a book that Howard Jones wrote in 1987. The article was first published in Hartford, Connecticut, in the Hartford Courant. *It appeared on the occasion of the 150th anniversary of the court case that lined up American abolitionists in support of Africans who had staged a successful mutiny on a slave ship bound for Cuba. In 1998, the* Amistad *movie powerfully dramatized the story of the rebels.*

Thought Starters: What shaped your own views of slavery and abolition? What was the role of teachers, books, the media?

For weeks in the summer of 1839, seafarers along the East Coast had spotted a sleek, black schooner with no national flag waving above its tattered sails. The ship moved slowly, seemingly with no destination, and those who approached the mysterious vessel reported that the crew was composed almost entirely of half-naked black men.

When the crew of a Coast Guard cutter boarded the vessel near Montauk Point, N.Y., on Long Island, they found that the men were slaves who had overpowered their captors at sea, killed four white men and commandeered the schooner. The captain ordered the ship towed to New London, Conn., where, he expected, the slaves would be tried as murderers and mutineers.

But the seizure of the Amistad, as the schooner was called, touched off a two-year legal battle that pitted the governments of two nations against a small group of feisty abolitionists determined to prove that the Africans were enslaved illegally and should be freed.

A celebration of the 150th anniversary of that legal struggle has been planned in New Haven, where the Africans were jailed for much of the time their fate was argued in the courts. The city has scheduled lectures, exhibits, school essay contests, artistic performances, outdoor events and a community dinner.

5

The case will be celebrated as the first major court victory for the anti-slavery forces and as an early example of the involvement of blacks on the frontline of the battle against slavery.

Americans were riveted by the case, but the fate of the Africans is less well-known today. In the early 1970s, Amistad House opened in Hartford as a group home for troubled teenage girls, but the house closed in 1983. One of the men who kidnapped Patricia Hearst 15 years ago called himself Cinque after Joseph Cinque, the leader of the rebellion.

Organizers hope the celebration will revive interest in the saga.

"What I would love to see is that it become an integral part of Connecticut history," said Alfred Marder, a New Haven peace worker and a member of the 100-member committee planning the celebration.

The 52 slaves aboard the schooner undoubtedly had little concern for their place in history when they rose up against their Cuban captors. They wanted to go home, so they spared the lives of two men and ordered them to sail east toward Africa. But during the night, the Cubans secretly turned the ship around, and spent nearly two months zig-zagging north along the East Coast, hoping to be rescued.

10

The Cubans had documents indicating that the Africans were ladinos, Africans taken to Cuba before the importation of slaves to the island was outlawed in 1817, but abolitionists suspected that the papers were fraudulent. If the blacks had been illegally imported from Africa, the abolitionists argued in court, then they were not slaves guilty of murder, but kidnap victims who acted reasonably to regain their liberty.

The case became a lightning rod for those who opposed slavery, including Roger Sherman Baldwin, who later became governor of Connecticut and a U.S. senator, and former President John Quincy Adams, who argued the case before the U.S. Supreme Court. A leading abolitionist declared the Amistad case a "providential occurrence" delivered to force a nationwide hearing on the evils of slavery.

Abolitionists, who were determined to keep the Africans, and the issue of slavery, on the minds of Americans, embarked on a tremendous public relations drive, inviting people to visit the Africans in jail, delivering lectures across the country and arranging to have life-size wax dummies made of Cinque and others.

Hundreds and sometimes thousands of people visited the Africans in jail each day. In Hartford, an especially entrepreneurial jailer charged visitors 12½ cents each for a peek at the captives.

Despite the excitement, lawyers for the Africans knew they had an uphill battle. The administration of President Martin Van Buren, bowing to pressure from the Spanish government and pro-slavery forces in America, worked against the Africans.

Despite Van Buren's inclinations, the Africans won in the lower court. But the case was appealed to the Supreme Court, and lawyers for the Africans knew that only two of the nine men on the court opposed slavery. Nevertheless, in March 1841, the court granted the Africans the wish expressed by Cinque, who knew only enough English to utter in court the simple plea, "Give me free." 15

The Africans, the court ruled, were not slaves and were not criminals.

The Africans from the Amistad returned to their homeland 10 months later, but before leaving, the prominent New Haven lawyers who had arranged their defense sought to turn the Africans into Christian missionaries. Cinque and the others took up residence in Farmington, Conn., and spent six hours a day in a classroom. They also cultivated a 15-acre farm and participated in a nationwide tour to help raise money for their voyage home.

The Amistad rebellion rates only a few paragraphs in most encyclopedias and is rarely taught in schools or included in textbooks, said Howard Jones, a University of Alabama history professor who wrote a 1987 book on the case.

New Haven schools, however, are ordering 2,000 booklets on the Amistad affair, and an effort is under way to have the Amistad rebellion featured on a U.S. postage stamp during the sesquicentennial of the Supreme Court decision.

New Haven also hopes to raise $100,000 for a statue of Cinque, which would be erected on the street where the town jail stood. 20

The Responsive Reader

1   How much do you learn from this article about the Amistad rebellion and its legal aftermath? (What are some of the "hard facts"?)
2   How much knowledge of slavery and the abolitionist movement does the writer assume? How much does he add to your understanding of slavery and of the antislavery forces? (One hundred fifty years later, can you get into the spirit of the abolitionist movement?)

Talking, Listening, Writing

3   Prepare a defense (or an indictment) of the accused "murderers and mutineers."

4   As a member of a school board or similar body, would you vote in favor of commemorating the Amistad affair or similar historical episodes? Why or why not?

Collaborative Projects

5   You may want to team up with classmates to stage a mock trial of the Amistad group. (You may want to turn to the Hayden poem and the Jones book or to other sources—history books, encyclopedias—for additional information.)

JEFFERSON, HEMINGS AFFAIR CAN'T BE DENIED

Cynthia Tucker

"Black Americans are not only integral to the American experience. We are also in the family."

Thomas Jefferson symbolizes both the promise and the contradictions of the American heritage. He was a plantation owner from Virginia who helped formulate the rallying cries of the American Revolution, and he became the third president of the new country.

Jefferson drafted the Declaration of Independence when a new revolutionary ideology was challenging the "divine right" of kings and the privileges of a hereditary aristocracy. Jefferson's document, finalized with the assistance of Benjamin Franklin and John Adams, declared that all were "created equal" and entitled to human dignity. However, although Jefferson denounced the slave trade in an early draft of the Declaration, he owned slaves and is being criticized by recent historians for his compromises with or support of the slave-holding society of his time.

Political enemies in his time had already accused him of a relationship with a female slave who was a half sister of his deceased wife, but traditionalist or mainstream historians had long defended him against the charge. Other biographers and historians slowly came to accept it as fact. In a book about Jefferson, Fawn M. Brodie described the liaison with Hemings as a "serious passion that brought Jefferson and the slave woman much private happiness over a period lasting over thirty-eight years." In 1998, an article in the prestigious science magazine Nature *claimed that DNA tests proved conclusively that at least one of Sally Hemings' children was Jefferson's.*

Cynthia Tucker, writing for the Atlanta Journal-Constitution, *was one of many columnists and commentators who discussed what the new research meant for the historical record and the self-image of Americans as a nation.*

Thought Starters: Have your history teachers and history books tended to be admiring of the founders and early leaders of the country? Or have they reflected critical reexaminations of the great figures of American history?

The strangest thing about the Jefferson–Sally Hemings controversy   1
has always been just that: the controversy. It has been downright surreal to hear historian after mainstream historian vehemently deny even the possibility of a sexual relationship between a founding father and one of his slaves.

Any black American could have told you that that sort of relationship was part and parcel of the experience of slavery. Countless blacks have among their genetic forebears some slavemaster(s).

That story is as common as dirt. How else do you account for the millions of black Americans with light skin and straightish hair, some with blue or green eyes? The existence of these light-skinned blacks was evident well before the Civil War, when most black Americans were still bound in slavery.

Backed by reams of circumstantial evidence, a handful of writers and historians, including Barbara Chase-Riboud and law professor Annette Gordon-Reed, have insisted that Jefferson engaged in a long-term affair with Hemings. They note that Hemings was the half-sister of Jefferson's dead wife and bore a striking resemblance to her.

Jefferson never remarried, and was presumably lonely after his wife   5
died. Still, the denials of a Jefferson-Hemings affair from the majority of modern-day historians were furious, almost as savage as the tongue-lashings unleashed upon 19th-century Richmond journalist James Thomson Callender, who first reported the affair in 1802. And the denials came from highly regarded sources. Just last year, Joseph J. Ellis won the National Book Award for a Jefferson biography, "American Sphinx: The Character of Thomas Jefferson," that rejects the notion of a Jefferson-Hemings affair.

But in a plot worthy of William Faulkner, the truth of the Jefferson-Hemings relationship has come crashing into the front parlor, where it can no longer be denied. Newly revealed DNA evidence strongly suggests that Jefferson fathered at least one of Hemings' children. And that brings us back to the more interesting part of this story: What were those historians thinking?

The defenders of Jefferson's image as a paragon of principle and virtue claimed that his noble character would have prevented such a liaison. What a strange moral hierarchy those historians must hold. It ought to be clear that once a man's basic character has permitted him to own other human beings, sexual exploitation of those human beings is no stretch.

Jeffersonites insist, however, that it is unfair to judge a founder of American democracy by modern moral standards, which hold slavery reprehensible. In Jefferson's world, they point out, slavery was commonplace.

While they are right, that hardly disentangles Jefferson from Hemings. Judging Jefferson by the standards of his time, when women (of all colors) of lesser social status were often sexually exploited by more powerful men, the likelihood of an affair should have been obvious.

So another truth has been revealed: Some rather commonplace prejudices kept prominent historians from seeing what should have been obvious even before science intervened. How many other history texts have been written inaccurately and how many other historic episodes wrongly interpreted because of those same prejudices?   10

This overdue acknowledgment of the truth about Thomas Jefferson ought to hurry the long-delayed business of setting the rest of the historical record straight: Black Americans are not only integral to the American experience, we are also in the family.

The Responsive Reader

1   According to Tucker, what is the history of the controversy about Jefferson and Sally Hemings? Who were major players? How does she describe the role of mainstream historians? How does she explain their attitude? What for Tucker is "surreal" about the controversy?
2   What is a sphinx? Why did one biographer call Jefferson an "American Sphinx"?
3   What for Tucker is the "truth about Thomas Jefferson"? How does she want you to "set the historical record straight"?

Talking, Listening, Writing

4   Should we apply today's standards of sexual morality to the leaders of the past? Is it fair "to judge a founder of American democracy by modern moral standards" regarding slavery and the exploitation of women?
5   Many Americans believe in the principles of Jeffersonian democracy: universal public education, an educated citizenry as the cornerstone of democracy, respect for the individual, equal opportunity for all, and tolerance for dissent. For you, would the revelations about Jefferson undermine his role as a moral authority and as a source of guidance and inspiration?

Separate Cemeteries for Jefferson Heirs

In 2002, an Associated Press report said that Thomas Jefferson's officially recognized heirs had proposed the creation of a separate cemetery on the grounds of Jefferson's Monticello estate for the descendants of Sally Hemings. They were not ready to let her offspring into the family association. One member of the officially recognized family had caused a furor some years earlier when he invited Hemings' descendants to the annual family gathering.

A Hemings descendant said yesterday that the proposal is just another example of separate but unequal. "Nothing has changed in 200 years, has it?" Julia Westerinen of New York City said after learning of the recommendation by the Monticello Association's membership advisory committee. "They're still saying the same thing: You've got to sit in the back of the bus."

Hemings' descendants have been trying for years to gain official recognition that the nation's third president and author of the Declaration of Independence fathered at least some of Hemings' children. Their argument was bolstered in 1998, when DNA tests found that a male in Jefferson's family fathered Hemings' last child, Eston.

A 24-page report by the family committee, however, concluded that there is not sufficient evidence to prove Eston Hemings' lineal descent from Jefferson, a strict requirement for burial in the family plot at Monticello.

—Allen G. Breed, *Associated Press*

YOUR TURN:

1 Do you think that in another five or ten years a new generation will still recognize what memories allusions like "separate but unequal" or "sit in the back of the bus" bring into play?

2 Sally Hemings was half-white and her child Eston three-quarters white. Would you call them white or black?

3 If you were part of a panel approving applicants for membership in a social organization, what kind of people would you try to keep out?

I WON'T BE CELEBRATING
COLUMBUS DAY

Suzan Shown Harjo

"Native people will memorialize those who did not survive the invasion of 1492. It is fitting for others to join us to begin an era of respect and rediscovery."

Suzan Shown Harjo is of Cheyenne and Muskogee ancestry. She wrote the following guest column for Newsweek *as the coordinator of a coalition of Native American groups. In 1991, plans for celebrating the 500th anniversary, or quincentenary, of Columbus's first voyage to America brought into collision radically different visions of America's past.*

To those organizing the celebrations, Columbus Day meant an occasion to commemorate the discovery of a new continent, leading eventually to the birth of a new nation. Harjo writes from a very different point of view. She sets out to commemorate the native inhabitants of the "New World," who were subjugated, driven from their lands, stripped of their culture and religion, and decimated by wholesale extermination and the white man's diseases. As you read the following article, do you find yourself taking sides between the "Columbus-bashers" and the organizers of "Columbus hoopla"?

Thought Starters: Are you aware of controversies surrounding Columbus Day, Martin Luther King Day, Presidents' Day, or similar commemorative occasions? What is at issue?

Columbus Day, never on Native America's list of favorite holidays, *1* became somewhat tolerable as its significance diminished to little more than a good shopping day. But this long year of Columbus hoopla will be tough to take amid the spending sprees and horn blowing to tout a five-century feeding frenzy that has left Native people and this red quarter of Mother Earth in a state of emergency. For Native people, this half millennium of land grabs and one-cent treaty sales has been no bargain.

An obscene amount of money will be lavished on parades, statues and festivals. The Christopher Columbus Quincentenary Jubilee Commission will spend megabucks to stage what it delicately calls "maritime activities" in Boston, San Francisco and other cities with no connection to the original rub-a-dub-dub lurch across the sea in search of India and gold. Funny hats will be worn and new myths born. Little kids will be told big lies in the name of education.

The pressure is on for Native people to be window dressing for Quincentennial events, to celebrate the evangelization of the Americas and to denounce the "Columbus-bashers." We will be asked to buy into the thinking that we cannot change history, and that genocide and ecocide are offset by the benefits of horses, cut-glass beads, pickup trucks and microwave ovens.

The participation of some Native people will be its own best evidence of the effectiveness of 500 years of colonization, and should surprise no one. But at the same time, neither should anyone be surprised by Native people who mark the occasion by splashing blood-red paint on a Columbus statue here or there. Columbus will be hanged in effigy as a symbol of the European invasion, and tried in planned tribunals.

The United Nations declared 1993 the "Year of the Indigenous   5
People." Perhaps we can begin to tell our own stories outside the context of confrontation—begin to celebrate the miracle of survival of those remaining Native people, religions, cultures, languages, legal systems, medicine and values. In the meantime, it should be understood that, even in polite society, voices will be raised just to be heard at all over the din of the celebrators.

Native people will continue marking the 500th anniversary of 1491, the good old days in our old countries. There was life here before 1492—although that period of our history is called "pre-history" in the European and American educational systems.

We would like to turn our attention to making the next 500 years different from the past ones; to enter into a time of grace and healing. In order to do so, we must first involve ourselves in educating the colonizing nations, which are investing a lot not only in silly plans but in serious efforts to further revise history, to justify the bloodshed and destruction, to deny that genocide was committed here and to revive failed policies of assimilation as the answer to progress.

These societies must come to grips with the past, acknowledge responsibility for the present and do something about the future. It does no good to gloss over the history of the excesses of Western civilization, especially when those excesses are the root cause of deplorable conditions today. Both church and state would do well to commit some small pots of gold, gained in ways the world knows, to bringing some relief to the suffering and some measure of justice to all.

The United States could start by upholding its treaty promises—as it is bound to do by the Constitution that calls treaties the "Supreme law of the Land." Churches could start by dedicating money to the eradication of those diseases that Native people still die from in such disproportionately high numbers—hepatitis, influenza, pneumonia, tuberculosis.

Church and state could start defending our religious freedom and stop   10
further destruction of our holy places. The general society could help more of our children grow into healthy adults just by eliminating dehumanizing images of Native people in popular culture. Stereotypes of us as sports mas-

cots or names on leisure vans cannot be worth the low self-esteem they cause.

Native people are few in number—under 2 million in the United States, where there are, even with recent law changes, more dead Indians in museums and educational institutions than there are live ones today. Most of us are in economic survival mode on a daily basis, and many of us are bobbing about in the middle of the mainstream just treading water. This leaves precious few against great odds to do our part to change the world.

It is necessary and well past time for others to amplify our voices and find their own to tell their neighbors and institutions that 500 years of this history is more than enough and must come to an end.

Native people will memorialize those who did not survive the invasion of 1492. It is fitting for others to join us to begin an era of respect and rediscovery.

The Responsive Reader

1   How does Harjo employ the rhetoric of protest, the language of dissent? How are the terms she uses to describe this nation's early history different from what you remember from your schooling or early reading? What grievances does she stress? What are major points in her indictment?

2   For you, is there any part of the article that is particularly telling or thought-provoking? Is there any part that you think is particularly unfair?

3   Which of Harjo's charges and arguments are familiar, and which are new to you?

Talking, Listening, Writing

4   What has been your experience with the current rewriting of American history? Have you encountered examples of history revised to reflect the point of view of the exploited, the dispossessed? Explore the contrast between what you might have been taught earlier and the changes now seen in many courses and textbooks.

5   Would you vote to rename "Columbus Day" and call it "Indigenous People's Day"?

Collaborative Projects

6   The current rethinking of the nation's early history has produced reevaluations of figures like Christopher Columbus, Thomas Jefferson, and Father Junípero Serra. For use in a future research project, you may want to look for a recent book or article on one of these or a similar figure. How do current attitudes compare with earlier, more worshipful, ones? (Your class may want to organize a panel discussion to pool findings on one or several of these figures.)

Exploring Internet and Nonprint Sources

Much effective writing draws on a mix of print sources, on-line sources, and live community or campus input.

How computer literate are you and your classmates? How much time do you spend surfing the Internet? Are you using the full range of Internet resources for writing projects and other college work? Informal research goes into most writing that aims at the educated reader. On issues ranging from gender parity in college athletics to vouchers authorizing tax money for private schools, you will be able to tap into a vast storehouse of resources recently published or earlier archived on the Internet.

- Leading **search engines** like Google and Yahoo compete in helping researchers find the most useful, most reliable, or most frequently consulted material. They compete in helping you focus your search.

- **Websites** of institutions and organizations often combine background information and advocacy of programs or agendas. They often provide numerous links to subtopics and FAQs (Frequently Asked Questions).

- Specialized **databases** list and often provide access to material in special fields. They provide in-depth guidance to current activity in major areas of study and research such as psychology, political science, history, and education. Often the material will challenge you

201

to become familiar with the specialized technical terminology of an academic discipline or with specialists' customary or conventional procedures for organizing information.

Triggering

Let current questions or unresolved issues activate your search.

Your interest in a current local or national issue will send you to a range of sources. Who makes a strong plea for support or for a course of action? Who has checked out the facts? Who has listened to witnesses, experts, or insiders? Here is a sampling of questions that might activate your search:

■ *"Are we moving toward a color-blind society?"* What is behind current initiatives to ban the use of racial or ethnic categories in public records? You may find promising material in publications available online ranging from national newspapers like the *New York Times* and the *Washington Post* to regional and local news sources like the *Boston Globe*, the *Sacramento Bee*, or the *Las Vegas Review-Journal*. You will find articles with titles like the following:

"Using Race as a Label"

"The California Battle over Racial Identification"

"Color-blind or Just Blind?"

"Racial Segregation and Public Health"

"The Rise of 'Whiteness' Studies"

■ *"Who controls the media?"* Because the "media system is fed by corporate advertising" and advertisers want "good demographics," do the media reach out mostly the affluent upper middle class? Are there efforts to promote grassroots citizens' media ownership or to support independent news sources? Websites like the following will guide you to a wealth of background information:

Fairness and Accuracy in Reporting   **www.fair.org**
a media watchdog organization committed to tracking bias in the mainstream press and issuing weekly media alerts

Alliance for Community Media   **www.alliancecm.org**
provides a guide to local media centers (often connected to local libraries) that prove training in radio and television work

Nation media ownership chart
                www.thenation.com/special/bigten.html
a Big Ten listing of holdings and media outlets controlled by the ten biggest media corporations

Free Press   **www.mediareform.net**
a Massachusetts-based group aimed at promoting greater public involvement in the shaping of media ownership

- *"What are the root causes of gun violence in our schools?"* Where would
you find expert commentary? Can you go beyond sensational news coverage of Columbine-style massacres? On issues like school shootings or juvenile violence, you may want to turn to magazines of opinion now mostly
available online. They range from the traditional *Harper's* and *Atlantic* to
more strongly political periodicals, ranging across the political spectrum
from the *National Review* to the *New Republic* or the *Nation.*

- *"Are we saving the nation's remaining forests?"* Is it true that more than
80 percent of the planet's natural forests have already been destroyed? Is it
true that in the United States between one and two percent of the original
forest cover are left? You may want to consult in-depth studies of the long-
range issue sponsored by independent agencies or published in scientific
journals. You may find sources with titles like the following:

"Productivity of Forest Ecosystems"
a report from an early UNESCO (United Nations) Congress

"The Mother of the Rainforest"
an article published in the *American Forests* journal in 2002

"Deforestation: Humankind and the Global Ecological Crisis"
a detailed study of key sources published on the Aqua Pulse website in
2003 ,http://www.aquapulse.net/knowledge/deforestation.

Gathering

**Turn to the Internet for hard data, background informa-
tion, informed commentary, and expert testimony on many current issues.**

Major national newspapers and newsmagazines are available online,
and back issues are available in the online archives of the publications. Many
articles on current medical advances and science issues published in health
or science magazines for the general reader are available online. Increasingly, technical and scholarly journals will be available to you not only on
the periodical shelves of your library but also online.

SIFTING YOUR SOURCES   How do you select promising material
from the mass of material often identified by a search? How do you make
sure to go beyond the first five or ten items listed in response to an Internet query?

Recent initiatives, lawsuits, and the appointment of a national commissions reopened the discussion of Title IX. The federal law had greatly

SURFING THE NET

Guidelines for Users

Experienced users of the Internet pride themselves on being up-to-date on the latest or most powerful search engines guiding them to material useful for their project. Remember advice from editors and instructors:

- *Become familiar with how your search engine functions.* Some search engines will search for different versions of a key word. If you include in your query *educat** with the asterisk, the search will yield items including different versions of your key word: *education, educational, educator, educators, educating.* If you include the question mark in *glamo(?)r,* your search will yield items with titles using either *glamor* or *glamour,* regardless of the variation in spelling. However, other search engines will search only for complete words you actually type in.

- *Become familiar with online resources available by subscription or through your college library.* Cost and availability may become factors when you want to use reference sources like the *Encarta* encyclopedia or specialized databases.

- *Be wary of anonymous or near-anonymous material on the Internet.* Who wrote or assembled the material? Is the author or sponsoring institution clearly identified? Who sponsors and maintains a website? Whose agenda does it serve?

- *Check authenticity of integrity of the material.* How reliable and complete is the current version? Has it been shortened or excerpted, and by whom? Was it copied, recycled, or pirated from somewhere? Can you trace it to the original source?

- *Check for permanence or continued availability.* How long will this material be accessible? Has it been archived? Will other people be able to retrieve and verify it at a later date?

increased the participation of women in college sports and the number of women's collegiate teams. At the same time, the media were covering a backlash from supporters of endangered men's collegiate sports, from football to wrestling. Legislators and government agencies were listening to a range of complaints, and recommendations. How do you pick and check out the most promising items that have Title IX in the title?

In a tentative source list, you may begin to sort out promising articles under headings like the following:

Wrestling with Title IX

STRONGLY DEFENDING TITLE IX:
"Women's Groups Worry about Title IX Review"

(This is an article from *The Philadelphia Inquirer* that quotes a vice president of the National Women's Law Center and the executive directory of
the National Association for Girls and Women in Sports. Women's rights
groups fear that recent initiatives "would widen the still-sizable gap between men's and women's collegiate sports programs.")

"Stacking the Deck against Women's Programs"

(This is an article from the *San Francisco Chronicle* archives. A recent
national commission was stacked with representatives of Division I football
schools, which pour huge financial resources into their football teams, with
million dollar salaries for coaches.)

STRADDLING THE FENCE ON TITLE IX:
"NCAA Official Mulls Title IX"

(This is an Associated Press article in the middle-of-the road *New York
Times:* Does there need to be a change in the way Title IX is applied? The
article carefully balances opinions from a strong supporter of Title IX and
from athletic directors attacking or litigating against the legislation.)

"Giving Title IX a Sporting Chance"

(This is an article in the national *USA Today* with a huge circulation:
Supporters celebrate Title IX as a civil rights law in a "volatile atmosphere,"
whereas opponents call the regulations "a blunt instrument that kills men's
teams.")

STRONGLY ATTACKING TITLE IX:
"Bad Coaches, Bad Players—Thank You, Title IX"

(This is from the aggressively conservative *Washington Times:* Colleges
have women's basketball teams because there is a law and not because girls
want to play. Much heated prejudicial language: "Watch the incompetence
soar." "dinosaur" male coaches; most of these people "probably would be
sweeping floors if not for Title IX.")

As you sort out early leads and follow up your most promising sources,
you start building a computer file of supporting data and key quotations.
Here are two sample entries, focused on one of the key issues that may have
emerged from your reading.

FOCUS: PROPORTIONALITY Much of the debate focuses on **proportionality,** "which courts historically have used to determine an institution's compliance under Title IX. It says a school's athletic population must closely reflect the gender makeup of its student body."
Article posted on the website of an Oklahoman news organization

FIND IT ON THE WEB

The Range of Online Sources

The following were included in results from one student's first search for background on the topic of political correctness.

Language Stereotypes, "Put-downs" and "Politically-Correct" Reference Index. Department of Translation Studies. University of Tampere. 15 Nov. 2001. 28 Jan. 2003. <http://www.uta.fi/FAST/US81PCI>

This website, maintained at the University of Tampere, Finland, is a list of links to discussions of and research into politically correct language. It guides users to research into the origins of the term "politically correct" and discussions of the political correctness of certain words, as well as issues and events relating to Political Correctness. The sources include material such as Purdue University's *Purdue Writing Lab Guide to Non-Sexist Language.*

Codgill, Sharon. *Being Politically Correct.* 28 Oct. 1999. 21 Feb. 2003. <http.//www.stcloudstate.edu/~scogdill/339/polcor.html>

This website, by an English professor at St. Cloud State, provides her list of recommended "politically correct" terms and expressions for use by students. It contains sections on pronoun use and salutations, and an extensive vocabulary of Politically Correct terms.

O'Riordian, Michael. "Politically Correct Journalism." *Thunderbird Magazine* 1 Mar. 2000. 18 Feb. 2003. <http://wwwjournalism.ubc.ca/thunderbirdI 20001march/correct.html>

This article, from the official magazine of the Sing Tao School of Journalism at the University of British Columbia, summarizes a presentation by journalist Chris Wood, attacking Political Correctness as an instrument of censorship.

Ross, Kelley L. "Against the Theory of 'Sexist Language'". 1996. 17 Feb. 2003. <http://www.triesian.com/language.htm>

This article examined the theory that gender differences in language correlate with the status of women in society. There is also an extensive discussion on whether "femaleness" in language is regarded as more or less valuable than "maleness."

"We support Title IX . . . But what we don't support is the interpretation that makes **proportionality** a quota."

Mike Moyer, executive directory of the National Wrestling Coaches Association, which filed a lawsuit against the U.S. Department of Education seeking to overturn the proportionality standard.

DRAWING ON ORAL SOURCES *Draw on interviews and other live oral sources.* Live oral sources can bring in real-life material to bridge the gap between theory and practice. What do current issues or arguments mean in the lives of the people concerned? You can provide a reality check for your writing by interviewing a local sheriff on gun control issues, a teenager from a low-income neighbood on false arrest, or a Peace Corps volunteer about working to promote literacy.

PLANNING THE INTERVIEW Suppose you are visiting an area high school or returning to your own high school. You interview one or more teachers. Here are questions you may prepare to ask:

Leaving No Child Behind

- Is discipline a problem at the school? What are the most serious discipline problems? How do teachers and administrators deal with them?
- Has violence been a problem at the school? What brings on violent incidents? Do they follow a pattern?
- Do the teachers think in terms of "good kids" and "bad kids"? Do they have thoughts about who is a "good influence" and who is a "bad influence"?
- What is the racial or ethnic mix at the school? Is race an issue or cause of tension? Is there good communication between different groups?
- Do they think the conditions at the school are improving or deteriorating?
- What is the morale of teachers at the school? Would they choose teaching again at a profession?
- What do you think of curent slogans like "leaving no child behind"?

A reporter from *Rolling Stone* magazine visited a school after a violent incident. As part of his investigation, the reporter interviewed teachers who had taught at the school for many years. Here is how the reporter used selections from one interview:

Back in the days when he was a student at South Eugene High, Kessinger said, "probably ninety to ninety-five percent of the kids were 'good kids.' They went to class and believed in trying to treat people and institutions with respect. Maybe two percent were the ones who hung out, skipped school, got in trouble.

"Today, sixty to sixty-five percent of the kids are in trouble, and maybe forty percent at most are 'good kids.' And they're good only because they are real careful about who they hang out with. Seeing how careful these kids have to be to stay out of trouble really gets to you.

"In my day, it was hard to find a bad influence. Today, it's hard to find a good influence, and the good influences that are out there, they're very careful to protect themselves. It's not just that we seem to be getting worse and worse . . . By the time your kids are fifteen or sixteen, the percentage of good kids could be down to five or ten percent."

from Randall Sullivan, "A Boy's Life," Rolling Stone

Shaping

Organize your material under major headings to support a unifying thesis.

Tracking and organizing your search materials are intertwining, intermeshing steps. Suppose that you are investigating the celebrity cult that made figures like Elvis Presley and Marilyn Monroe icons of the media culture. You choose as your central example Lady Diana, who rose from obscurity through a storybook marriage to the heir to the British throne. Is she going to be remembered like other heroes or heroines for a large popular audience before her? Or has the outpouring of public interest and sympathy focused on her divorce, her troubled later years, and her violent death already faded from public memory?

In sorting out a range of promising material, you will be attending to two key steps in the writing process:

- *You start looking for the connecting thread.* Overall, what does the story of Lady Di show? What may be your overarching thesis? What does her story show about the cult of celebrity? Or what does it show about today's popular culture? You move beyond an open-ended noncommittal trial thesis. What have you really learned and want to share with your readers?

TRIAL THESIS: Lady Diana provides an important example of the role the celebrity title entails in today's popular culture.

(So what is that role? How do you see it? Sum it up here?)

REVISED THESIS: **The constant pressure of unrelenting media scrutiny makes it impossible for today's celebrities to lead a normal life.**

■ *You start marking off major stages or sections of your paper.* As you develop and support your overall point, how are you going to lay out the material that led you to your conclusion? Each of the following theses already sets up an organizing strategy for the paper as a whole. The first one promises a paper that would first focus on the idealized image of Lady Diana that attracted her many fans and admirers. It would then go on to the "darker side." It would look at the scandals that attracted the tabloids, the sensation-mongering press, and the paparazzi—the celebrity-hounding free-lance "journalists from hell":

THESIS: **Lady Diana attracted an abundance of fans with her charm and charisma; however, like other icons of popular culture she had a dark side that was long kept hidden from the public.**

The following possible thesis also already sets up a program for the rest of the paper. This thesis sets up a three-point program: the celebrity as admired ideal, the celebrity as victim, and finally the celebrity as humanitarian or philanthropist.

THESIS: **A combination of contradictory qualities coexisting within the same individual helped create the media image of Lady Diana.** She was a natural beauty, much photographed like a classic fashion model. At the same time her admirers sympathized with her role as a victimized mother and her struggle with eating disorders and divorce. Her humanitarian work took her to encounters with starving children and with AIDS patients.

The thesis and the sentences that follow it provide a preview creating expectations that the rest of the paper will fulfill.

Revising

Draw on your sources when revising and rethinking.

Welcome feedback from instructor's comments and peer reviews. Sharpen your thesis, adjusting it to what the material you have collected has really shown. Do more to highlight your overall plan. Fill in missing links, showing the connection between major sections of your paper. If necessary, shuffle major parts of the paper for a better flow. Rearrange material so your readers can progress from the more easily understood to the more challenging, or from safe areas of agreement to the more controversial.

If possible, return to online sources for additional support. A student revising a paper on an outstanding example of the cult of celebrity might respond to recommendations like the following:

■ *Capture the reader's attention with a more dramatic introduction.* Bring the issue to life. Look in contemporary reports for a striking incident or attention-getting quotation.

The Legacy of Princess Diana

Elton John sang, "And your footsteps will always fall here, along England's greatest Hills; your candle burned out long before your legend ever will" at the funeral of Princess Diana. The divorced wife of the possible successor to the English throne had become the most outstanding example of our modern celebrity worship since Elvis Presley's fans started traveling to Graceland keeping the spirit of the King alive.

> ■ *Go back to your sources for a key quotation that could serve as your thesis.* Which writer best summed up the quasi-religious devotion popular culture idols inspire in their fans?

People around the world were devastated when Diana Spencer, former Princess of Wales, was killed in a terrible accident on August 31, 1997. **The author of one of many articles on the first anniversary of her death found in the online archives of a major publication said that Lady Diana "was an obsession for Britons in her lifetime and has been raised to the status of demigod."**

> ■ *Strengthen supporting testimony.* Fill in striking real-life examples. Give your readers concrete details that will help them visualize a scene or get into the spirit of an event:

As with other popular culture idols, the cult of Diana found its shrine comparable to Elvis Presley's Graceland. Writing about her burial site at Althorp, her childhood home, **T. R. Reid writes, "If there is a cult of 'Diana' this is its cathedral. On top, the Temple has a large cross and a single word: DIANA. Inside, where the altar would be is a marble silhouette of the late princess and a stone slab etched with a quotation of hers that reads like something from the New Testament: 'Whoever is in distress call on me.'"**

> ■ *Acknowledge and deal with damaging charges or misunderstandings.* Final revision may offer you a chance to anticipate and defuse questions that might undercut the generally positive perspective of your paper.

The media's constant presence in Lady Diana's life contributed to many of her personal problems and even her untimely death. Her supporters defended her against the continuous harassment by the media. Her children were almost always off to boarding school. However, despite her children's absence, Princess Diana made every effort to show affection towards her children. **According to Michael Johnston, the creator of the website called "Prince William," she defied the royal establishment to do so: "Princess Diana broke royal protocol by hugging the boys in public and taking them to amusement parks and McDonald's." In an online article by Renora Licata for a website called *Death of a Princess*, Princess Diana is described as "beloved by the public for her warmth and humanity. . . . She was spontaneous in manner, happily**

ignoring royal protocol to bestow a kiss on a child in a crowd and writing letters to members of the public signed "love Diana."

A Paper for Peer Review

The following student paper could be the revision of a paper that drew on both Internet sources and oral sources. Where and how well are they used? Study the student's range and use of source materials. What is the overall point? What is the plan?

Censorship with a Halo?

Offensive language is a touchy topic. No one will deny that some measure of control of language must be enforced. Violent language breeds violence in real life. **News reports in online newspaper sources** followed up the story of a baseball fan who kept calling the players of the visiting team crudely insulting names until the pitcher of the visiting team threw a chair at the fan and his wife. **On the Internet,** the proliferation of hate groups calls on us to enforce some sort of restraint in our speech and writing. On the other hand, some conventions **published by institutions** in the name of political correctness have been criticized as misguided and some have been questioned by the very groups they aim to protect. ——————>>>>>>>>>>>>>>

(The **introduction** uses a lively current incident repeated in online news sources to bring the topic to life and prepares the reader for a cautious "yes-but" discussion of the "touchy topic.")

A backlash against censorship perceived as political correctness has received much media attention. **Chris Wood, guest lecturer at the Sing Tao School of Journalism at the University of British Columbia,** said, "Political correctness has become censorship with a halo." The use of political correctness as a reason to justify censorship, he said, robbed journalists of their ability to observe and report truthfully, regardless of the consequences. **Kelley L. Ross, a linguist** attacked the theory that gender conventions in the English language are sexist, using examples of other languages to show that sexual equality in a culture and the sexual neutrality of its language are not meaningfully correlated. She drew on examples from English, Greek, and Spanish to show how apparently sexist language may be more neutal or benign than it is portrayed to be.

The achievement of perfect gender equality in language is no guarantee of gender equality in society. ——————>>>>>>>>>>>>>>

(This paragraph illustrates the current backlash against "political correctness" with **two academic sources.**)

A testing ground for language reflecting changing attitudes has been the language of disability, which has moved slowly over the years from *crippled* to *handicapped* to *disabled* or *impaired*. Branches of the government wanted to adopt new approved terms for referring to the blind. **The National Federation of the Blind drafted a resolution, available on its website,** objecting to the terms that were being chosen to refer to the blind. The resolution distinguished questionable terms under three major headings. First, it objected to terms such as "visually impaired" or "hard of seeing," on the grounds that such terms should only be used to distinguish between people with limited sight and those with none. It objected to awkward new terms such as "sightless." Finally, it objected to using a phrase such as "person who is blind" instead of "blind person," if the reason for that use is meant to emphasize that a blind person is first and foremost a person. All such terms may achieve the opposite of the purported goal, portraying blindness as a condition that requires special treatment and portraying the blind as demanding or belligerent.

————>>>>>>>>>>>>>>

(This paragraph pays detailed attention to an important **test case,** documenting the difficulties or obstacles of trying to legislate "approved" terms from above.)

However, many people who object to censorship and complain about the spread of political correctness fail to understand the reasons behind it. The continued existence of racism, sexism, and hate in our culture requires that some measure of control be present. **The following online quote, from "On Tactics and Strategy for USENET" by Milton John Kleim Jr.,** shows us what exists when speech is not policed enough:

> USENET offers enormous opportunity for the Aryan Resistance to disseminate our message to the unaware and the ignorant. It is the only relatively uncensored (so far) free-forum mass medium which we have available. The State cannot yet stop us from "advertising" our ideas and organizations on USENET . . . NOW is the time to grasp the WEAPON which is the Net, and wield it skillfully and wisely while you may still do so freely.

Radicals such as Kleim, a holocaust denier and member of a White Power organization, are allowed to convey whatever message they choose. Calling the Nazi genocide of the Jews the "legend of the Holocaust," Kleim says:

> The Holocaust Myth is peddled by both professional liars, and well-meaning but misguided historians. Enormous amounts of material have been produced and hundreds of millions of dollars have been expended in this campaign to disseminate the "acceptable" version of the plight of the Jews under the Third Reich.

While our constitution protects our right to free speech, the issue is not the denial of free speech but how to deal with individuals such as Kleim, whose

words perpetuate race hate and tension in our society.
————>>>>>>>>>>>>>

(The paper reaches its turning point with two detailed **block quotations** of hate speech material circulated on the Internet.)

A **survey of fellow students at a private college** on topics related to language issues yielded discouraging results. When asked if they agreed with revising the Bible to remove sexist language, 80 percent aid it should remain unchanged, 13.3 percent said it could be revised, and 6.7 percent were undecided. On the topic of whether using ethnic slurs such as the N- word in recreations to create a greater sense of realism was appropriate, 93.3 percent said that it was appropriate, while 6.7 percent said that it was inappropriate. On the question of whether having a Native American as a team mascot was demeaning to Native Americans, 73.3 percent said it was not demeaning, while 26.7 percent said that it was. The question that evoked the most different responses, however, was whether people should be allowed greater freedom of expression even if it meant allowing people to air offensive views. Sixty percent said that people should be allowed to air extreme views.
————>>>>>>>>>>>>>

(A **student survey** at a private school demonstrates the gap betwen officially approved guidelines and attitudes of the "next generation.")

There is no simple solution to the issue of political correctness. There are too many people, with too many different views, for any single plan to satisfy them all. The best we can hope for is a compromise that pleases most people. While there must be a degree of restraint in language, a widespread impression is that political correctness has gone beyond its mandate. Despite this there is a large, and still growing, amount of **hate rhetoric circulating, particularly on the Internet.** A plan to combat hateful and discriminatory language should focus on restraining these fonts of race rhetoric and hate speech, rather than going after relatively minor issues.

(The **conclusion** returns to the original dilemma, leaving it largely unresolved.)

YOUR TURN:

1   How would you sum up the overall message of the paper? Does the paper need a stronger thesis? Is the student writer too cautious, "hedging his bets"?

2   What is the plan or organizing strategy for the paper implied in the opening paragraph? How well or successfully is it carried out?

3 What is the range of Internet sources? How well are they identified? How effectively are they used?

4 How well is the student survey set up? How informative are the results?

5 Where does the student writer draw the line between what is unnecessary and necessary restraint of free speech? Do you think the distinction the writer makes can be implemented in practice?

Writing Options 3: Using Internet and Oral Sources

1 Who tracks current immigrants' assimilation or "Americanization"? Do today's immigrants tend to be slower to assimilate than previous generations? Do they tend to stay separate from the mainstream?

2 What current online sources focus on arguments for or against raising the minimum wage? Who supports raising the minimum wage? Who opposes raising the minimum wage and why?

3 What online sources tell the story of workfare? What has been the experience of people who have moved from welfare to workfare? Are there reliable statistics? Can you draw on personal testimonies from online sources or personal interviews?

4 Can you track current discussions of "voluntary segregation" in today's schools? Is there a true mixing of students in today's schools, or do students tend to divide along ethnic, racial, or cultural lines?

5 What agencies or organizations investigate the current status of the single-parent family? How many young Americans grow up in single-parent homes? Do they face special challenges? Can you bring in live personal testimonies on how they cope?

6 Have women arrived in big-time, big-money sports? What sources could provide reliable or credible information? What is the visibility of women in today's professional sports? How do men's sports and women's sports compare in attendance, publicity, earnings, or influence on the lives of young people?

7 What is the self-image of police officers today? How do they cope with the dangers and traumas of police work? How they respond to charges of police misconduct or police brutality? Where do you find authentic testimony or discussion?

8 What current research or discussion focuses on today's mixed marriages? What is the experience of Americans marrying someone from a different cultural, ethnic, or racial background? What is it like to be in a "cross-cultural" marriage?

9 Where can you find out about Americans abroad? What is the story of expatriate Americans? What is it like to live as an American in a foreign country? What stereotypes about Americans are Americans likely to encounter? What attitudes or reactions should an American expect?

10   Are there stirrings of reform or dissent in a major branch of today's or-
     ganized religion? What media outlets or online sources would give
     them a voice? For instance, how orthodox are today's orthodox Jewish
     families? Are there debates or current issues in the Mormon church, or
     in the Catholic church, or among Baptists or Episcopelians?

Chapter 4
IDENTITY
Rethinking Race

Gordon Parks: Gloria Vanderbilt, Department Store, Birmingham, Alabama

VISUAL LITERACY 4

IMAGE AS DOCUMENT:
ALABAMA DEPARTMENT STORE

Documentary photography developed in time to record shattering images of the Civil War or War between the States. It showed bodies of poorly trained and poorly equipped soldiers, the walking wounded with blood-encrusted bandages, the ruins of burnt cities. War photographers in two world wars and in Korea and Vietnam documented the face of war not seen in wartime progaganda or in history books focused on military strategy. During the Civil Rights struggle, photographers documented the realities of segregation and repression in images that stirred the conscience of the nation.

Gordon Parks was an outstanding photojournalist who was one of the first African American graphic artists breaching the color barrier to gain national recognition and reach a wide audience. He was a highly successful photographer of the world of fashion and privilege. At the same time, he never forgot those shut out from the American Dream. The editor of a collection of modern photography said that Parks's images from the segregated Old South opened the eyes of white Americans to their divided country.

Reading the Image

1   What images "speak for themselves"? Sometimes a strong image needs no comment, no explanation. To understand the two images juxtaposed here, does the viewer need to see them in the *historical context* of the segregated South before the Civil Rights era? How much do viewers need to know about the history of their "divided country"?

2   Photographers like Parks know how to *focus* on the strong revealing image. Of the hundreds of customers passing through the entrance of the store, Parks selected this woman and this child. How would you describe these two to someone who wasn't there? Spell out in your own words what these two figures say to the viewer. What is their story?

3   How much *biographical background* may be needed to help viewers? Parks was the youngest of 15 children of a day laborer, and he was on his own at 16 working as a busboy and a musician. He bought a used camera and eventually became a photographer for *Life* magazine and an acclaimed movie producer. Do you think knowing these biographical data affects the reaction of viewers? Why or why not? Do you think viewers knowing about Parks and his work are likely to respond differently from others?

4   Do you have a strong *visual imagination?* Has a strong image or set of images ever brought historical facts or a historical idea to life for you? What did it show? What did you learn from it?

5   When do images become *dated?* Trend watchers claim that many young people today live in the present. Many issues that agitated their parents are for them ancient history. Do you think documentary photographs like these still have a meaning for today's generation?

Chapter 4

IDENTITY: RETHINKING RACE

"Everyone of us could write a book about race. The text is already imprinted in our minds and evokes our moral character."

—ANDREW HACKER

Throughout American history, the promise of equality before the law and in the eyes of God has been invoked by groups claiming their place in the sun. Harriet Beecher Stowe's novel *Uncle Tom's Cabin,* which was read by millions around the world, asserted that the African captives who were brought to this country in chains were our sisters and brothers. Therefore, slavery was an abomination in the sight of God.

For anthropologists, the concept of race has no scientific standing. All human beings are members of the same species, capable of intermarrying. In that sense, all human beings are "created equal." Skin color varies from dark in some tropical climates to pale in some countries of the North. Members of some ethnic groups in Africa tend to be very short; members of other ethnic groups tend to be very tall (and may be sought after by basketball teams).

Nevertheless, the *perception* of race has played a crucial role in human history. It has been a powerful divisive influence in the history of this country. Slavery was built on the assumption that some races were created inferior. In the minds of many, the bloodiest war in American history was fought to abolish the institution. Whether and how racism survives in contemporary American society is the subject of much debate and of charges and countercharges. A Jewish student reports that in high school she was called "every name that anti-Semites have created: cheap, smart, rich, stuck up, big-nosed, and JAP" (Jewish American Princess).

Race is one of the factors, and in recent history perhaps the most deadly one, that keep us from being judged by the "content of our character." Being identified as a member of a group, we encounter expectations, pressures, or barriers visible and invisible. Sometimes, these barriers are crudely obvious, as when a country club does not accept Jews. Sometimes, they are more subtle, as when a prominent journal of opinion devalues or undercuts the black leadership. Many feel that race continues to be the great unresolved challenge to traditional American values.

HOW IT FEELS TO BE COLORED ME

Zora Neal Hurston

"The terrible struggle that made me an American out of a potential slave said 'On the line!' The Reconstruction said 'Get set!'; and the generation before said 'Go!'"

Zora Neal Hurston was part of an early generation of African American writers and artists who asserted their independence and sense of self-worth in a largely segregated society. The following selection from her The World Tomorrow *was first published in 1928.*

Hurston once said about the idea of democracy that she was all for trying it out. In fact, she couldn't wait to do so as soon as the Jim Crow laws that legalized discrimination against African Americans were a thing of the past. Hurston was born in Eatonville, an all-black town in Florida, and was working as a domestic when she managed to attend college. She finally went on to Howard University, which has been called "a center of black scholarship and intellectual ferment." As a scholarship student at Barnard College in New York City, she became an associate of the anthropologist Franz Boas, who asked her to return to the South to collect black folk tales. She had earlier published earthy slice-of-life sketches of black life; her classic collection of African American folklore, Mules and Men, *appeared in 1935. Like other students of black dialect and folk tradition, she was accused of perpetuating stereotypes of African Americans as uneducated and unsophisticated. Like other minority artists and writers dependent on white patronage, she was accused of selling out to the white establishment.*

Although for a time one of the best-known voices of the Harlem Renaissance of the twenties and thirties, she died in a county welfare home and was buried in an unmarked grave. In recent years, feminists have rediscovered her fiction; her masterpiece, the novel Their Eyes Were Watching God *(1937), is now widely read in college classes.*

Thought Starters: How aware are people you know of their separate racial or ethnic identity? Is it constantly on their minds?

I remember the very day that I became colored. Up to my thirteenth year I lived in the little Negro town of Eatonville, Florida. It is exclusively a colored town. The only white people I knew passed through the town going to or coming from Orlando. The native whites rode dusty horses, the Northern tourists chugged down the sandy village road in automobiles.

The town knew the Southerners and never stopped cane chewing when they passed. But the Northerners were something else again. They were peered at cautiously from behind curtains by the timid. The more venturesome would come out on the porch to watch them go past and got just as much pleasure out of the tourists as the tourists got out of the village.

The front porch might seem a daring place for the rest of the town, but it was a gallery seat to me. My favorite place was atop the gate-post. Proscenium box for a born first-nighter. Not only did I enjoy the show, but I didn't mind the actors knowing that I liked it. I usually spoke to them in passing. I'd wave at them and when they returned my salute, I would say something like this: "Howdy-do-well-I-thank-you-where-you-goin'?" Usually the automobile or the horse paused at this, and after a queer exchange of compliments, I would probably "go a piece of the way" with them, as we say in farthest Florida. If one of my family happened to come to the front in time to see me, of course negotiations would be rudely broken off. But even so, it is clear that I was the first "welcome-to-our-state" Floridian, and I hope the Miami Chamber of Commerce will please take notice.

During this period, white people differed from colored to me only in that they rode through town and never lived there. They liked to hear me "speak pieces" and sing and wanted to see me dance the parse-me-la, and gave me generously of their small silver for doing these things, which seemed strange to me for I wanted to do them so much that I needed bribing to stop. Only they didn't know it. The colored people gave no dimes. They deplored any joyful tendencies in me, but I was their Zora nevertheless. I belonged to them, to the nearby hotels, to the county—everybody's Zora.

But changes came in the family when I was thirteen, and I was sent to school in Jacksonville. I left Eatonville, the town of the oleanders, as Zora. When I disembarked from the river-boat at Jacksonville, she was no more. It seemed that I had suffered a sea change. I was not Zora of Orange County any more, I was now a little colored girl. I found it out in certain ways. In my heart as well as in the mirror, I became a fast brown—warranted not to rub nor run.

But I am not tragically colored. There is no great sorrow dammed up in my soul, nor lurking behind my eyes. I do not mind at all. I do not belong to the sobbing school of Negrohood who hold that nature somehow has given them a lowdown dirty deal and whose feelings are all hurt about it. Even in the helter-skelter skirmish that is my life, I have seen that the world is to the strong regardless of a little pigmentation more or less. No, I do not weep at the world—I am too busy sharpening my oyster knife.

Someone is always at my elbow reminding me that I am the granddaughter of slaves. It fails to register depression with me. Slavery is sixty years in the past. The operation was successful and the patient is doing well, thank you. The terrible struggle that made me an American out of a potential slave said "On the line!" The Reconstruction said "Get set!"; and the generation before said "Go!" I am off to a flying start and I must not halt in the stretch to look behind and weep. Slavery is the price I paid for civilization, and the choice was not with me. It is a bully adventure and worth all that I have paid through my ancestors for it. No one on earth ever had a greater chance for glory. The world to be won and nothing to be lost. It is thrilling to think—to know that for any act of mine, I shall get twice as much praise or twice as much blame. It is quite exciting to hold the center of the national stage, with the spectators not knowing whether to laugh or to weep.

The position of my white neighbor is much more difficult. No brown specter pulls up a chair beside me when I sit down to eat. No dark ghost thrusts its leg against mine in bed. The game of keeping what one has is never so exciting as the game of getting.

I do not always feel colored. Even now I often achieve the unconscious Zora of Eatonville before the Hegira. I feel most colored when I am thrown against a sharp white background.

For instance at Barnard. "Beside the waters of the Hudson" I feel my race. Among the thousand white persons, I am a dark rock surged upon, overswept by a creamy sea. I am surged upon and overswept, but through it all, I remain myself. When covered by the waters, I am; and the ebb but reveals me again.   10

Sometimes it is the other way around. A white person is set down in our midst, but the contrast is just as sharp for me. For instance, when I sit in the drafty basement that is The New World Cabaret with a white person, my color comes. We enter chatting about any little nothing that we have in common and are seated by the jazz waiters. In the abrupt way that jazz orchestras have, this one plunges into a number. It loses no time in circumlocutions, but gets right down to business. It constricts the thorax and splits the heart with its tempo and narcotic harmonies. This orchestra grows rambunctious, rears on its hind legs and attacks the tonal veil with primitive fury, rending it, clawing it until it breaks through to the jungle beyond. I follow those heathen—follow them exultingly. I dance wildly inside myself; I yell within, I whoop; I shake my assegai above my head, I hurl it true to the mark *yeeeeooww!* I am in the jungle and living in the jungle way. My face is painted red and yellow and my body is painted blue. My pulse is throbbing like a war drum. I want to slaughter something—give pain, give death to what, I do not know. But the piece ends. The men of the orchestra wipe their lips and rest their fingers. I creep back slowly to the veneer we call civilization with the last tone and find the white friend sitting motionless in his seat, smoking calmly.

"Good music they have here," he remarks, drumming the table with his fingertips.

Music! The great blobs of purple and red emotion have not touched him. He has only heard what I felt. He is far away and I see him but dimly across the ocean and the continent that have fallen between us. He is so pale with his whiteness then and I am *so* colored.

At certain times I have no race, I am *me*. When I set my hat at a certain angle and saunter down Seventh Avenue, Harlem City, feeling as snooty as the lions in front of the Forty-Second Street Library, for instance. So far as my feelings are concerned, Peggy Hopkins Joyce on the Boule Mich with her gorgeous raiment, stately carriage, knees knocking together in a most aristocratic manner, has nothing on me. The cosmic Zora emerges. I belong to no race nor time. I am the eternal feminine with its string of beads.

I have no separate feeling about being an American citizen and col-   *15* ored. I am merely a fragment of the Great Soul that surges within the boundaries. My country, right or wrong.

Sometimes, I feel discriminated against, but it does not make me angry. It merely astonishes me. How *can* any deny themselves the pleasure of my company! It's beyond me.

But in the main, I feel like a brown bag of miscellany propped against a wall. Against a wall in company with other bags, white, red and yellow. Pour out the contents, and there is discovered a jumble of small things priceless and worthless. A first-water diamond, an empty spool, bits of broken glass, lengths of string, a key to a door long since crumbled away, a rusty knifeblade, old shoes saved for a road that never was and never will be, a nail bent under the weight of things too heavy for any nail, a dried flower or two, still a little fragrant. In your hand is the brown bag. On the ground before you is the jumble it held—so much like the jumble in the bags, could they be emptied, that all might be dumped in a single heap and the bags refilled without altering the content of any greatly. A bit of colored glass more or less would not matter. Perhaps that is how the Great Stuffer of Bags filled them in the first place—who knows?

The Responsive Reader

1   There has been much talk about the need for self-esteem—the need for women and minorities to overcome culturally conditioned feelings of inferiority and inadequacy. What is the secret of Hurston's self-esteem?

2   What were major stages in Hurston's awareness of race? (For instance, when was it that she "became" colored? How does she distance herself from other definitions of "Negrohood"? When is she least aware of racial difference?)

3   What is Hurston's last word on the role of race in her life and in the larger society? Do her words seem dated or still valid today?

Talking, Listening, Writing

4 How does Hurston's attitude toward race compare with what you think is predominant in today's generation?

5 What efforts have you observed to restore people's pride in their own racial or ethnic identity? Have you personally participated in such efforts? How successful are they?

6 Have you experienced self-doubt, feelings of inadequacy, or feelings of inferiority? What causes them? How do you cope with them?

Collaborative Projects

7 How much do you know about the art and literature of diverse ethnic or cultural traditions? Your class may want to organize a presentation of poems, tales, songs, or music. (Will you encounter any questions about what is authentic, what is exploitative, or what is offensive or demeaning?)

SUCCESS BOUGHT AT HIGH COST

Rebecca Wingers

> *Brown* v. *Board of Education:* **What is the legacy of what** *Time* **magazine calls "a historic Supreme Court decision"?**

In May 2004, retrospectives in sources like *Time* magazine honored the fiftieth anniversary of the Supreme Court decision in *Brown* v. *Board of Education of Topeka, Kansas.* Ruling in a case that had combined four separate lawsuits protesting gross inequalities in educational opportunity for black and white young Americans, the court ruled that "separate educational facilities are inherently unequal." All-white schools found they were under court order to admit nonwhite students.

In the backlash against the court decision, some of the black parents and pastors who initiated the court cases were fired from their jobs and run out of town or out of the state. A pastor's church was burned. A famous battleground during the desegration battle was Central High in Little Rock, Arkansas, where the first nine black students to enroll had to be protected by federal troops called in by President Eisenhower. The students (including the young girls that the poet Gwendolyn Brooks called "bright madonnas") defied spitting and jeering white townspeople and abuse from fellow students. For a year, in a last-ditch stand, the governor of Arkansas closed all public schools.

Sociologists attributed the "white flight" from the cities to the desire of parents to live near suburban schools without large minority enrollment. Court-ordered busing to take students from neighborhood schools in an effort to create schools with racial balance became a bitterly divisive political issue. Fifty years after *Brown* v. *Board of Education,* state officials and school districts were still fighting off lawsuits challenging gross inequalities in funding and educational resources for America's public schools.

Thought Starters: During the Civil Rights struggle, terms like *integration, desegregation, forced busing,* and *black pride,* were watchwords everywhere echoing in the media. For you or your generation, are these words ancient history? Or do they still have a special meaning or current significance?

Of all the communities among the *Brown* cases, this rural, Black Belt county in Virginia may have suffered the deepest scars—but not from bombs, cross burnings or any of the other violence desegregation sparked in much of the rest of the South. While today educators call its schools a model of integration, in 1959, Prince Edward County locked its school-houses for five long years rather than comply with *Brown*. "It turned our lives completely around," says Rita Moseley, a slender, soft-spoken school secretary and grandmother who was 12 the year the schools closed. "I will always wonder what I would have done, who I would have been."

Prince Edward is the only place where the students themselves launched the drive for integration. Before *Brown,* the county's black high school was so over-crowded, some pupils attended class in leaky, tar-papered shacks outside. Their outdated textbooks and buses were hand-me-downs from the white schools. One spring day in 1951, more than 450 students walked out to demand a new school. The student strikers wrote to N.A.A.C.P. lawyers in nearby Richmond, who took on their cause, and the case *Davis* v. *County School Board* was launched.

Despite the Supreme Court's ruling three years later, county supervisors refused to fund public schools serving all races. When a federal district court reaffirmed *Brown* in 1959, Prince Edward chained its schools' doors. White families attended a new private school in the county, with scholarships for those who couldn't afford it. Black families like Moseley's either sent their children away to stay with relatives or studied in small groups in churches and homes. Many simply went without schooling at all, as Moseley did at first. After two years of sitting at home, Moseley got an opportunity to stay with a family 140 miles away in Blacksburg, Va., and attended an all-black school there. "I used to cry in silence at night for my family," Moseley remembers. She returned to Prince Edward two years later to attend the privately funded "free schools" created as a temporary remedy by local black leaders. "They threw us all in together, taught a little of this, a little of that. It was a big confusion," Moseley recalls. When the public schools finally reopened under court order in 1964, Moseley went back, graduating two years later than she would have. She says she felt uncomfortable about walking in the ceremony and so didn't attend.

Starting in the early '70s, Prince Edward gradually integrated over the next three decades, thanks to an ambitious superintendent who improved academics and to liberal faculty at two local colleges who began sending their children to public school. Today Prince Edward's public schools are 59% black, 40% white and 1% other. Without violence, busing or magnet schools, the community that once chose no schools over racially mixed ones has achieved a level of integration far above the national average—typically, a white child attends a school that is 79% white. At the same time, Prince Edward's students are raising their state test scores. Black students are still slightly less likely to graduate than whites, but they fare better here than elsewhere in the state. "What they have accomplished in Prince Edward County is stunning," says Gary Orfield, of Harvard University's Civil Rights Project. "In the '60s, no one would have thought it possible."

And yet there is a group of people in the county who still pay for those gains. African Americans whose education was interrupted by the school

closings are called Prince Edward's "crippled generation." Many never returned to school, and those who did often found their dreams derailed by
the lost time. As secretary at the county's high school, Moseley, 57, often
visits the guidance office to use the computers and chat with students.
"That's where I would have liked to have been," she says, gesturing at the
counselor's desk.

But Moseley and her husband, who also missed years of school, were
pleased with the education their two children got in Prince Edward's integrated system, and were able to send them to college. One now works for
a pharmaceutical company, and the other is pursuing a real estate license.
Last spring, with about 400 other graying graduates, both the elder Mose-
leys crossed the stage of the Prince Edward High School auditorium to receive honorary diplomas. Rita Moseley recently testified in the state legislature on a bill that would give scholarships to African Americans who
missed school during the closings. With the money, she would like to take
some college courses and then write a book about what happened in Prince
Edward County after *Brown*. The ending will be bittersweet.

The Responsive Reader

1 Important court decisions are often hailed as milestones in the struggle
for social justice. However, how was the intent of the Supreme Court
decision defeated in this case? What would you include in a candid account of how the court decision was circumvented when "the schools
closed"?

2 The *Time* writer tells the largely untold story of a "lost generation" of minority students affected by the court decision. Critical observers remind
their audiences of the law of "unintended consequences." It is illustrated
when people with the best intentions produce disastrous result. What
were the disastrous consequences of the Brown decision for the generation of students whose parents and teachers brought the original suits?

3 The *Time* magazine reporter turns the schooling or educational opportunities of the next generation in a "Black Belt county in Virginia" into
a success story of the opportunities for a new generation. What are the
key statistics? How do they compare with national and state averages
cited in the article? According to this article, what made the difference—upgrading of facilities? less discriminatory funding? teacher
training and motivating teacher salaries? preschool and outreach programs? What was the role of the individuals the reporter mentions?

Talking, Listening, Writing

4 Does this *Time* magazine article put a positive spin on unresolved social
issues? Does it allude to the physical violence the *Brown* decision ignited?
Does it recognize the lawsuits still being initiated and fought across
the country to challenge unequal funding and facilities? Does it offer

suggestions for dealing with violence both in the neighborhood and the actual schools?

5   Is what happened in the *Brown* case "ancient history" for today's young Americans? Have you heard voices asking us to let bygones be bygones and move on beyond the injustices of the past? Revisiting the struggles of the civil rights era may reopen old wounds. Other voices tell us that we have to remember and understand the past to deal with the challenges of the present. We have to honor those who fought the battles and made the sacrifices whose fruits we now enjoy. Your class or group may decide to organize a panel discussion debating these alternatives.

Collaborative Projects

6   For its issue commemorating the Brown decision, *Time* investigators checked the current status of integration in schools involved in the original litigation. Results varied. In Topeka, the city's largest high school has an ethnic blend of 61 percent white, 20 percent black, 14 percent Latino, and 5 percent other. Working with a group, can you get similar statistics on the racial mix in a range of schools in your area?

OTHER VOICES

Resegregating the Schools

"By some measures public schools have now been resegregating for more than a decade. Partly as a consequence, white children today have access to much better educational opportunities than do their minority counterparts."

Jeannie Oakes, the Director of the Institute for Democracy, Education, and Access at UCLA, collected data on a range of "opportunity to learn" indicators for schools in Los Angeles County. She identified schools that had a serious problem with its teachers ("fewer than 80 percent are certified by the state"), its curriculum ("fewer than two-thirds of the available courses prepare students for a four-year college"), or its facilities ("buildings are so crowded that students must attend school in shifts, effectively shortening the academic year by seventeen days or more"). She concluded that problems are more common in schools located in predominantly black and Hispanic neighborhoods. The schools exhibiting serious problems with teachers, curricula, and facilities "collectively educate a population that is 94 percent black and Hispanic. Meanwhile, not a single L.A. County school that is more than 90 percent white and Asian exhibits any serious problems with teachers, curricula, or facilities."

AFFIRMATIVE ACTION OR NEGATIVE ACTION

Miriam Schulman

"However imperfect, affirmative action has made a small dent in the inequities that have characterized the distribution of jobs and educational opportunities in the United States."

For several decades, affirmative action to correct injustices suffered by minorities and by women was official government policy. In government employment, government contracts, and college admissions, programs were instituted to step up the representation of underrepresented groups. As part of a conservative backlash, however, affirmative action programs came under attack for giving "special preferences" on the basis of race and gender. A widely publicized initiative campaign in California, inspiring similar efforts elsewhere, made it illegal for any state institution to take race or gender into account in dealing with its citizens. According to Nicholas Lemann writing in Time *magazine, the initiative was predicted to "wipe out a host of programs . . . from magnet schools to science tutoring for girls" and to "decrease the minority presence at the University of California's two flagship schools, Berkeley and UCLA." According to some estimates, the admission rate of African American students to be trained as members of the country's educational and professional elite was cut in half.*

During the following years, colleges like the University of California tried to take account of "color-blind" criteria like socioeconomic status in their effort to increase representation of students from struggling schools and poor minority neighborhoods. In 2003, a divided Supreme Court gave mixed signals by ruling out race as a factor in undergraduate admissions but not for admission to law schools, recognizing affirmative action as a "compelling state interest."

The following article is from the newsletter of a center for applied ethics at a Catholic university. The author was trying to go beyond political exploitation of the race issue and the vicissitudes of court cases to the ethical and political issues at the heart of the controversy. After this article was published in the fall of 1996, affirmative action for a time seemed a lost cause. Today, courts and educational institutions again grapple with the issues the author raised.

Thought Starters: Do you still hear references to "affirmative action hires"? Have you or people you know benefited from affirmative action or related programs? Have you or people you know been hurt or disadvantaged by affirmative action?

I was having a discussion with my freshman composition class at Santa Clara University about racial preference. Several white students were telling me about friends who should have gotten into SCU but didn't because the University was accepting so many "affirmative action students." Others were assuring me that they would have been accepted at Stanford if some minority student had not gotten their slot.

There were no African American students in the class; at that time, the freshman African American population at Santa Clara stood at 24 out of the total 886 freshmen. When I tried to get my students to look at the numbers and explain why they felt so threatened, they regarded me with the half-indulgent look college students used to reserve for '60s children such as myself and shrugged. They knew what they knew.

And me? As much as I liked my students, I found it easy to write off their opinions as racist, or at the least, paranoid.

Ten years later, as the issue of affirmative action threatens to fracture the state of California, I think back on that conversation. It has come to represent for me what is wrong with the public dialogue on this subject: We throw out anecdotal evidence, mixed with a few facts and figures, and then we all retreat into our preconceived ideas without any empathetic consideration of the other side. At least I know I was not really listening to what my students had to say.

I do not mean to suggest that I have changed my mind about affirmative action. I still support it, which may seem a strange admission in the introduction to an article that I hope will be seen as an evenhanded exploration of the ethical issues involved. But I have come to believe that—in the affirmative action debate, at least—we cannot move forward unless we understand the justice of the other side's position.

At its heart, the controversy over affirmative action is a controversy about justice. When we try to judge the justice of a social policy, we start with the basic premise that everyone should be treated similarly unless there is a morally relevant reason why they should be treated differently. Whatever benefits and burdens the society has to distribute, justice requires them to be allocated on this basis.

For simplicity, I'll confine myself to exploring how this premise applies to race (which, by the way, is how the debate over affirmative action is usually couched, despite the fact that such programs include women and other minorities). Most people agree that the history of slavery and Jim Crow in this country violated the first premise of justice. The color of someone's skin is not a morally justifiable reason for treating people differently.

Ah, but if that's so, say opponents of affirmative action, why is it acceptable to *favor* people because of their skin color? If everyone were treated similarly, wouldn't we have a colorblind society? Indeed, the California Civil Rights Initiative, the ballot proposition that sought to overturn affirmative action, reads like this:

The state shall not discriminate against, or grant preferential treatment to, any individual or group on the basis of race, sex, color, ethnicity, or national origin in the operation of public employment, public education, or public contracting.

To clarify the values that make us come down on one or the other side in this debate, we must address the justice of preference. In the case of affirmative action, we must decide if there are ever circumstances that make it fair to favor one race over another when it comes to jobs or university admissions.

One answer to that question might be found in the principle of compensatory justice, which states that people who have been treated unjustly ought to be compensated. No reasonable person would argue with the fact that African Americans have suffered more than their share of injustice over the course of U.S. history. Many proponents of affirmative action defend the programs as a kind of reparation for the terrible wrongs of slavery and segregation. The white majority, in this view, must compensate African Americans for unjustly injuring them in the past.

A related concept brings this argument into the present: Affirmative action, proponents hold, neutralizes the competitive disadvantages that African Americans continue to experience because of past discrimination; segregated neighborhoods served by poor schools would be an example.

President Johnson had this justification for preferential treatment in mind when he signed the 1964 Voting Rights Act and said: "You do not take a person who, for years, has been hobbled by chains and liberate him, bring him up to the starting line of a race, and then say, 'You are free to compete . . .' and still justly believe that you have been completely fair."

While the argument for compensatory justice seems persuasive to me, I find that it often plays differently with the folks who are called upon to do the compensating. First of all, many people are not ready to concede their complicity in the wrongs of the past. It's very hard to persuade a young Asian college applicant, whose parents did not arrive in this country for a century after abolition, that she must take responsibility for slavery. Others cannot see how their race puts them at a competitive advantage. Most Appalachian out-of-work coal miners don't see themselves as the beneficiaries of past favoritism.

Even the average white male—who has weaker grounds for rejecting the compensatory argument—is beginning to rebel against racial preference. While it may fall outside the realm of morality to consider whether an argument is popular or not, those of us who want affirmative action to continue must confront the fact that many Americans believe these programs are asking them to take their punishment like . . . well, like a man. A lot of them are refusing to bend over.

I believe there's an equally valid moral argument for affirmative action that avoids the punitive overtones of the justice approach, focusing instead on why these programs are in everyone's best interest. In resolving the affirmative action question for myself, I find the best guidance in a common-good approach to ethics: The common good consists primarily in "ensuring that the social policies, social systems, institutions, and environments on which we depend are beneficial to all. Appeals to the common good urge us to view ourselves as members of the same community, reflecting on broad questions concerning the kind of society we want to become and how we are to achieve that society."

I look around me—at the poverty, crime, and alienation that so disproportionately afflict our minority communities—and I ask myself, Is this the kind of society I want to live in or the world I want my children to grow up in? The answer to that question is much clearer to me than deciding where justice resides in the affirmative action debate.

This is not simply a matter of feeling compassion or guilt, though neither of those responses strikes me as inappropriate. But beyond how I feel, I have a stake in addressing these problems. I know that social blights cannot be confined to a particular neighborhood or community; eventually, I will pay for every angry, jobless, poorly educated person—through the welfare system and through the prison system (the cost of which is fast surpassing schools in California).

However imperfect, affirmative action has made a small dent in the inequities that have characterized the distribution of jobs and educational opportunities in the United States. According to *The New York Times,* "The percentage of blacks in managerial and technical jobs doubled during the affirmative action years. During the same period, as Andrew Hacker pointed out in his book *Two Nations* [Ballantine Books, 1992], the number of black police officers rose from 24,000 to 64,000 and the number of black electricians, from 14,000 to 43,000."

Abolition of affirmative action would clearly reverse these gains. Cities that have dropped minority set-aside programs, for example, have experienced a sharp drop in the percentage of government contracts going to minorities. To say that these programs should be retained is not, however, to ignore the claims of fairness and justice raised by opponents of affirmative action. But I wonder if we need to define these in the competitive manner that has characterized so much of the debate—"You got my spot," as my students might have put it. Wouldn't it be better to create a vision of a society in which my good fortune did not mean your suffering?

Much of the threat my students felt, I now believe, came from the realistic assessment that they faced a dearth of employment and educational prospects. The best way to foster their support for affirmative action would be to address the underlying scarcity. *20*

That was the experience in Atlanta, which, in preparation for the Olympic Games, awarded almost a third of $387 million in construction and vending contracts to women- and minority-owned businesses. "Grumbling has been minimal during Olympic preparations, largely because Atlanta's economy is so strong that work has been plentiful," writes Kevin Sack in *The New York Times.*

A common-good argument for affirmative action is part of a broader approach that envisions a society with plentiful work and good education for everyone. I can imagine the eyeballs rolling as I write these lines. Naive. Utopian. But, really, every ethical system is utopian in that it suggests an ideal. Why is my concept any more idealistic than the California Civil Rights Initiative, which is premised on a colorblind society where no one is ever discriminated against on the basis of race?

The Responsive Reader

1 In the introduction to her article, how does Schulman show that she will try to listen to the other side?
2 What is her basic definition of *justice?* (Is it the same as yours?) How does she apply it to the history of the race issue in this country?
3 What is "compensatory justice"? According to Schulman, what are its limitations as an argument for affirmative action? What is "punitive" about it?
4 What is the essence of the author's "common-good" approach to ethics? How does it apply to the current situation in our society and the prospects for its future?
5 What is the author's estimate of the past record or accomplishments of affirmative action? On balance, does she seem to think of it as a success or as a failure?
6 What do you think of Schulman's "Utopian" vision of a future when affirmative action would work without anyone getting hurt?

Talking, Listening, Writing

7 Do you think ethics means a concern with what is good for other people, or can it mean an enlightened concern with what is good for oneself, one's family, or one's group?
8 According to a *Time* article on the history of affirmative action, the idea behind it was that "custom, ethnocentrism, poverty, bad schools, old-boy networking, and a host of other factors would conspire against the new civil rights of African Americans and any real socioeconomic advancement." What is "ethnocentrism"? What is "old-boy networking"? Which of the "factors" listed here are still playing a major role, and which may have become less relevant? How much closer are we to the ideal of a "color-blind" society?

Collaborative Projects

9 Working with a group, you may want to check the current status of affirmative action or anti–affirmative action initiatives or legislation. You may want to focus on one major area, such as college admission, government employment, or government contracts.

FIND IT ON THE WEB

Student researchers looking for background of the "resurgence of debate" over affirmative action have found that "preferential selection" on the basis of race, gender, or ethnicity again "generates intense controversy." The following sample sources from a Google search range from a detailed program for a new approach to affirmative action to an in-depth study of the controversy in an educational reference source and to a sample of aggressive argument pro and con.

Affirmative Action: *DiversityInc's* Vision for Success.
http://www.diversityinc.com/public/5641 print.cfm

Affirmative Action. *Stanford Encyclopedia of Philosophy.*
http://plato.stanford.edu/entries/affirmative action/

Against Affirmative Action.
http://www.snc.edu/socsci/chair/336/agaffir.htm

Working alone or with a group. you may search for updates on the affirmative action controversy.

MIXED LIKE ME

David Bernstein

"I was always good for a sound bite in the school newspaper, and as a unique case—a black Jewish conservative—I had opportunities to comment with some authority on a range of issues."

It was long assumed that students from minority backgrounds were likely to align themselves with progressive or liberal causes. Increasingly, however, on campus as in the larger society, members of a new generation began to form new alliances, leaving traditional claims of discrimination or forms of protest behind.

David Bernstein was a twenty-six-year-old magazine editor in Washington, D.C., when he wrote the following essay. He was one of the "Generation X," or "twenty-something," group of writers included in a collection called Next: Young American Writers on the New Generation *(1994). These writers were born after the great events that had shaped the outlook of an earlier generation: the traumas and divisions of the lost Vietnam War; the struggles and triumphs of the civil rights movement; the militant early years of the women's movement. Living in a post–Cold War world, many of these authors write about outgrowing the think schemes and stereotypes of the past.*

As Bernstein says, the opening statement of his essay might have sounded provocative thirty years ago; readers today may find it only mildly interesting and "move along." Because of his mixed ethnic parentage, Bernstein is in a unique position to reexamine this country's "way of thinking about race." What is his perspective on the future of race relations in America?

Thought Starters: What do you think and know about "mixed marriages"? Has intermarriage been an issue in your family or among people you know? Are you aware of changing social attitudes on this topic?

I am a twenty-six-year-old man, half black and half Jewish, who   *1* founded and edits a conservative magazine that deals with race relations and culture. Such a statement would have been extraordinary thirty years ago; today we treat it with mild interest and move along. No one would argue that my life has been typical—typical of the "black experience," of the "Jewish experience," or of any other dubious paradigm associated with a particular race or ethnicity. I have not overcome racism or poverty, and people become visibly disappointed when I tell them that my mixed background has not been a cause of distress, or any other difficulty for that matter.

However, my story may be of some interest. For better or worse, America is going to look more and more like me in the next century—that is to say, individuals are going to be walking embodiments of the melting pot. The argument over whether America is more like cheese dip or the multiculturalist "tossed salad" (Are you getting hungry yet?) will be made moot by the increasing incidence of mixed marriage and of the growing class of mutts like me who have more ethnicities than the former Yugoslavia.

My parents married in 1965, in Washington, D.C. If they had lived then in the comfortable suburb where they now reside, they would have been breaking the law—miscegenation, as marriage between blacks and whites was known in those days, was still illegal in Maryland. My mother was a native Washingtonian who, until her teen years, felt sorry for the few white people who lived near her, her mother, and two siblings; she thought they were albinos. Her parents—both of whom had moved from the country to Washington when they were teenagers—were separated when my mother was just a toddler. She was raised, along with an older sister and brother, in a small brownstone apartment in downtown D.C. Her brother, the oldest child, went off to fight in the Korean War, one of the first black airmen to participate in the integrated armed forces. While in Korea, he fell in love with and married a Korean girl. Meanwhile, my mother attended segregated public schools until senior high school, when she was in the first class that integrated Eastern Senior High School in the wake of the Supreme Court's *Brown* decision. After graduation, she opted not to attend college, because she didn't know what she wanted to do—and "didn't want to waste" my grandmother's money.

My father grew up in North Philadelphia, one of those old working-class neighborhoods where there were Jewish blocks, Italian blocks, Irish blocks, and so on. His parents were second-generation Americans: Grandpa Bernstein's family was from Poland; my grandmother's family from Leeds, England. (I understand the Blasky family still lives there, apparently running a successful wallpaper-hanging business.) My grandfather and my father's two brothers fought in World War II; my father, who was too young to go, became a paratrooper soon after the war ended. After leaving the Army in the early 1950s, he moved to Washington, where he and my mother eventually ended up working at the same furniture-rental place.

Despite the rich possibilities for mischief making presented by their union, my parents did not marry to make a political statement. While their contemporaries marched for civil rights and held sit-ins, they hung out with a mixed-race group of cool cats at various jazz nightclubs in downtown D.C. Most of these establishments were burned to the ground after Martin Luther King's assassination in 1968, bringing to an end that unique era of naive integration. Since those riots, race relations in this country have been tinged with guilt, fear, and lies.

In 1970, my father's company transferred him to the redneck mill town of Reading, Pennsylvania. My mother hated it; my father tolerated it; and I went about the business of growing up. I went to a mostly white private school and Monday afternoons attended Hebrew school with the children of Reading's prosperous and assimilated Jewish community. My Cub Scout group and summer camp were at the local Jewish community center, which had been bombed recently by Reading's prominent community of neo-Nazis.

It was also at the center that I was first called a "nigger." My mother had been preparing me my entire life for that to happen, but when it did, I was hardly bothered at all. I actually felt sorry for the kid who shouted it at me during a softball game; he genuinely felt bad afterward and apologized about six times. (Even though it's out of sequence in our little narrative, I should recount the only other time I have been called a "nigger." A couple of years ago, I was riding on D.C.'s Metro with two white liberal friends when a white homeless person approached me and stated, "You niggers get all the jobs." My friends were horrified and silent. I laughed and told the bum that he was right; that was how it should be.)

We moved back to Washington in 1977. Again, I attended private school, this time at Georgetown Day School, a place founded in the 1940s as Washington's first integrated school. Despite the forty-year tradition, there were still not many blacks at GDS. The students were largely from well-to-do, secular Jewish families with traditions of liberal political activism. My family, though secular, was not well-to-do or politically active. My parents were somewhat liberal, but it was a liberalism of function rather than form; in other words, they might be considered budding neoconservatives. I inherited from my parents a healthy suspicion of conventional wisdom—which, in the case of my teachers and peers, was overwhelmingly on the left. By 1980, I was one of six kids in my junior-high class to vote for Ronald Reagan in our mock election.

My "political awakening" was just beginning. In high school I cowrote a piece in the school newspaper on what it meant to be conservative, an awfully crafted piece of literature that nearly caused a riot, despite its (by my standards today) extremely mushy conservatism. I started to realize that you could make liberals mad just by saying the "c" word. On election day 1984, I wore a jacket and tie to school to celebrate President Reagan's impending victory. One friend didn't talk to me for a week.

It never dawned on me that, as a "person of color," I ought to be   *10* "mortally" opposed to this Reagan guy. All I ever heard come out of his mouth just sounded like good sense to me. I heard over and over again on TV that the man was a racist and that he was bad for black people. But what stuck with me from all this was that the people who repeated this charge were buffoons. Early on, the idea of race was not central to my view of politics. This would change rather sharply later on.

My freshman year in college was spent at Allegheny College in lovely Meadville, Pennsylvania. Within weeks, it was apparent to me and several of my friends there that the school was lousy. A group of us dedicated our lives to the idea of transferring out of that freezing mud hole of a campus. In one of our brainstorming sessions on how to make our trans-fer applications look beefier, we locked onto the idea of starting a "Con-servative Club," which would be a forum for discussing ideas on the right. It sounded like fun, and more importantly, we would all be made vice pres-idents of the club, an ideal way to bolster our extracurricular résumés.

Once again, just using the word *conservative* nearly brought the cam-pus down around our ears. Two of the conspirators in our résumé-building scheme went before the student government in order to get the necessary recognition, supposedly just a formality. Forty-five minutes later, after shrieks of outrage from the so-called student leaders of this $13,000-a-year institution of higher learning, we were told that the student government was afraid to get involved in "neo-Nazi" groups and that we should come back in a month with a detailed statement of just what we stood for. Only one member of the SG stood up for us—a young woman who pointed out that on a campus with absolutely no political activity, people who showed some initiative to do something, anything, ought to be encouraged.

But this was a college where political discourse was typified by this statement from the school's chaplain: "We should divest from South Africa. Harvard and Princeton already have, and if we want to be as good as them, we must do so as well." In this kind of environment, which is now typical at liberal-arts colleges around the country, it should have come as no sur-prise that conservatism was associated with evil. It wasn't the last time that the supposed characteristics of conservatives like me—that we were nar-row-minded, ignorant, and shrill—were to be embodied better by our critics.

I did finally escape from Allegheny College, going back home to the University of Maryland. At UM, I decided to make politics a full-time vo-cation. I worked in Washington afternoons and evenings at various political jobs, first at the Republican National Committee and later at a small, con-servative nonprofit foundation. In between, I took a semester off to work for Senator Bob Dole's ill-fated presidential campaign. Returning to Mary-land, I was soon elected president of the campus College Republicans, a po-sition that occasionally put me at the center of campus political attention.

This was not because I was a vocal, articulate (some would say loud-   15
mouthed) conservative but because I was a *black* conservative. Conservatives are a dime a dozen, smart ones are common, but a black one? "Nelly, wake the kids! They have to *see* this!"

Other conservatives loved having me around. After all, most of them were presumed to be Nazis from the get-go by the ultrasensitive P.C. crowd; having a black person say you're okay was temporary protection from the scholastic inquisition. Further, as a black conservative, I was thought to have special insight into why more blacks didn't identify with the Republican party. Again and again, I was asked how conservatives could find more blacks (or African-Americans, if the petitioner wanted to be sen-sitive). After a while, I think I actually began to believe that, somehow, I had special understanding of the souls of black folk, and with increasing confidence I would sound off about the political and social proclivities of African-Americans.

In a perverted way, liberals and left-radicals liked having me around as well—because I helped justify their paranoia. I was living proof that imperialist, racist forces were at work, dividing black people and turning us against one another. How else, they theorized, could a black person so obviously sell out both his race and the "progressive" whites who were the only thing standing between him and a right-wing lynch mob? The ardor (and obvious pleasure) with which they alternatively ignored and condemned me demonstrated their belief that I was more than just the opposition: I was a traitor, a collaborator in my own oppression. Finally, one particularly vitriolic black militant suggested in the school newspaper that black conservatives ought to be "neutralized." I took it personally.

And I got fired up. There comes a time in every conservative activist's life when he gets the heady rush of realization at how much fun (and how easy) it is to annoy liberals. Indeed, it was something I had been doing for years. People on the left, with their self-righteousness, humorless orthodoxies, and ultrasensitivity to their own and everyone else's "oppression" are only fun at parties if you get them pissed off. Naturally, then, it is something that conservatives spend a lot of time doing.

Rush Limbaugh, R. Emmett Tyrell, P.J. O'Rourke, hundreds of editors of conservative college newspapers like the *Dartmouth Review,* and thousands of College Republican activists turned the 1980s into one long laugh for conservatives at the expense of the P.C. crowd. The staleness of liberal beliefs, the inability of the campus activists to move beyond sloganeering to real thought, and the creation of a regime on campus by college professors and administrators that treats open discussion as anathema offered fertile ground for conservative humorists.

But it also allowed many conservatives to dismiss leftism as a political 20 force, and they were unprepared when it was resurrected as such in the person of Bill Clinton—thus in 1992, it was the right that too often degenerated into empty sloganeering. The intellectual stagnation of liberalism contributed to the intellectual sloth of too many conservatives, concerned more with one-liners than actually formulating policy.

I was no exception. I slipped easily into the world of leftist haranguing. I was always good for a sound bite in the school newspaper, and as a unique case—a black Jewish conservative—I had opportunities to comment with some built-in authority on a range of issues. Controversy with the Black Student Union? I would have a comment. Someone wants the university to divest from South Africa? I would be there with other conservatives holding a press conference presenting the other side. Controversy between Arab students and Jewish students? The College Republicans would uphold the Reagan tradition of unswerving support for Israel as long as I was in charge.

I tried not to lose sight of why I was doing this; that annoying liberals was just a means, not an end. But like every young right-winger, I'm sure that more than once I've annoyed just for annoyance's sake. There are worse sins, but this is the only one I'll admit to in print.

Since those heady college days, I have become a magazine editor. *Diversity & Division* looks at race relations in America from the perspective of young people, particularly of its black Jewish editor and white male managing editor. Do I still go after liberals? Yeah, sure. But the issues we talk about—those bearing on the future, on how we are all going to get along—are not very funny. And the things that leftists advocate on these issues, from radical multiculturalism to quotas, promise to make it next to impossible for us to survive as a multicultural society.

There are two lessons, I think, that my little autobiography teaches. First is my comfort in moving between worlds of different cultures and colors. The conventional wisdom about us mixed-race types, that we are alienated, never feeling comfortable in either culture, is baloney. I am black. I am Jewish. I am equally comfortable with people who identify themselves as either one, or neither one. Why? Because to me the most defining characteristic of who I am is not my race, ethnicity, religious beliefs, political party, or Tupperware club membership. Rather, I see myself as an individual first, part of the larger "human family," with all the suballegiances reduced to ancillary concerns.

This is obviously a very romantic and idealistic notion. It is also, equally as obviously, the only ideology that will allow us to overcome prejudice and bigotry and enable everyone to get along. In me, the melting pot the idea has become the melting pot the reality, with (I must immodestly say) reasonably positive results. My commonality with other people is not in superficial appeals to ethnic solidarity—it is far more fundamental. 25

That is why I am sickened by people who continue to insist that we must all cling to our ancestors' "cultures" (however arbitrarily defined at that moment) in order to have self-awareness and self-esteem. The notion of "self" should not be wrapped up in externalities like "culture" or "race"—unless you want to re-create the United States as Yugoslavia, Somalia, or any other such place where people's tribal identities make up their whole selves. Indeed, true self-awareness stands opposed to grouping human beings along arbitrary lines like race, gender, religion, weight, or preferred manner of reaching orgasm. Groupthink is primitive. It is not self-awareness; rather it is a refuge for those afraid of differences.

Those who preach about diversity believe that tolerance means not exulting one class of human being over another, by recognizing that every race and culture has made a contribution to modern civilization: a worthy goal, especially if this were true. But this way of thinking ignores a powerful truth, an obvious solution to the bigotry and suspicion that these sensitivity warriors say they are out to eliminate. The reality is that groups aren't equal; individuals are. If it is "self-evident that all men are created equal" isn't it even more self-evident that blacks and whites, men and women, Christians and Jews are created equal?

Granted, we haven't lived up to this absolute ideal. But we are beginning to see the implications of setting our aspirations below what we know to be the best. Here's the second lesson I think my story tells.

Despite my obvious distaste for the entire notion of group politics, I have become wrapped up in it. By editing a magazine that deals primarily with racial issues, I am not doing what I would most like to be doing. But I am doing what is expected. Under our phony system of racial harmony, college-educated blacks are expected to do something that is, well, black. Black academics are concentrated in Afro-American studies, sociology, and other "soft" fields where they can expound at length about the plight of the American Negro. Everyone, it seems, needs an expert on what it means to be black. Corporations need human-relations specialists to tell them about the "special needs" of black employees. Newspapers need "urban beat" reporters. Foundations, political parties, unions, and any other organizations you can name all need black liaisons to put them "in touch with the community." And, of course, conservatives need a magazine that reassures them that many of the ideas that they have about race relations are not evil and fascistic. These jobs are generally somewhat lucrative, fairly easy to do, and carry just one job requirement—you have to be black.

No one is forced to follow this course; there should be no whining about that. But in life, as in physics, currents flow along the path of least resistance. As long as it is easy to make a living as a professional race man, the best and brightest blacks will be siphoned off into this least-productive field in our service economy. The same is true, of course, of Hispanics, Asians, or whatever minority group is in vogue in a specific region or profession. Our educational system, our country's entire way of thinking about race, is creating a class of professionals whose entire raison d'être is to explore and explain—and thus perpetuate—the current regime. All the preaching of sensitivity, all the Afrocentric education, all the racial and ethnic solidarity in the world will not markedly improve race relations in America. Indeed, the smart money says that this obsession with our differences, however well-meaning, will make things much, much worse.

But this is a point that, blessedly, may well be rendered moot for the next generation. Intermarriage is the great equalizer; it brings people of different races together in a way that forced busing, sensitivity training, and affirmative action could never hope to—as individuals, on equal footing, united by common bonds of humanity. Four hundred years ago Shakespeare wrote of intermarriage:

> Take her, fair son, and from her blood raise up
> Issue to me; that the contending kingdoms . . .
> May cease their hatred; and this dear conjunction
> Plant neighbourhood and Christian-like accord
> In their sweet bosoms . . .

Eventually, if all goes well, America's melting pot will be a physical reality, bringing with it the kind of healing Shakespeare had in mind. Let's just hope we don't file for an ethnic divorce before then.

30

The Responsive Reader

1   What is Bernstein's perspective on the strife-ridden racial legacy of the past? What glimpses do you get in his essay of racism or race-related violence in the society around him? In his and his family's history, what was the role of miscegenation laws, segregation, and the movement toward integration?

2   Bernstein questions "dubious" paradigms, or theoretical models, associated with race or ethnicity. Where and how does he go counter to the reader's stereotypes and conventional expectations about race?

3   What were major factors in Bernstein's "political awakening"? Does his conservatism seem as wrong-headed to you as it did to many on campus? Why was his role as a black conservative of special interest to both conservatives and liberals?

4   Liberal-bashing has become a favorite conservative pastime in the days of Rush Limbaugh. What do you learn from Bernstein about its motivation or psychological workings? *Political correctness* became a buzzword as a conservative groundswell gained force. What are Bernstein's key criticisms of the "P.C. crowd"?

5   How or why does Bernstein rehabilitate the "melting pot" metaphor that many others have left behind? What does he see as the dangers of multiculturalism? What for him are the shortcomings of "group politics"?

Talking, Listening, Writing

6   On the basis of Bernstein's essay, what would you include in a capsule portrait of a young conservative? What are key positions or telltale features?

7   Have you seen evidence that harping on differences can be a mistake?

8   Do you think it inevitable that members of minority groups will turn politically conservative as they become affluent and move into the middle class?

9   Do you think of yourself as conservative, liberal, radical, or none of the above? Explain and defend your position.

Collaborative Projects

10   What statistics concerning race and ethnicity are kept at your school and in your community? Who collects them? Who uses them, and for what purpose? How are racial or ethnic criteria employed? What are the pitfalls in collecting and interpreting them? Your class may want to parcel out different aspects of this question to small groups.

WHY THEY EXCEL

Fox Butterfield

"The academic success of many Asian Americans has prompted growing concern among educators, parents, and others students."

The following article about the model minority was first published in January 1990, at a time when the term was becoming a buzzword in the national media.

Fox Butterfield won the National Book Award for his book China: Alive in the Bitter Sea *(1982). He first became intrigued by the motivation and academic performance of Asian students when he was a young journalist in Taiwan. The young Vietnamese student he interviewed for the following article had left Vietnam ten years earlier and had not heard from her parents, who stayed behind, for three years. However, their admonitions to be a good daughter and a good student were still ringing in her ears. One of the sayings she remembered from her childhood was "If you don't study, you will never become anything. If you study, you will become what you wish." In his article about why Asian students excel, Butterfield draws on a mix of personal experience, firsthand investigation, and expert opinion. Asians have been called the "model minority" because they work hard, study hard, and enter college and graduate in large numbers. How does this article support and explain the idea of the model minority?*

Thought Starters: How much of what you know about Vietnamese or Chinese or other Asian students is based on personal contact or observation? How much is hearsay or media stereotype?

Kim-Chi Trinh was just 9 in Vietnam when her father used his savings to buy a passage for her on a fishing boat. It was a costly and risky sacrifice for the family, placing Kim-Chi on the small boat, among strangers, in hopes she would eventually reach the United States, where she would get a good education and enjoy a better life. Before the boat reached safety in Malaysia, the supply of food and water ran out.

Still alone, Kim-Chi made it to the United States, coping with a succession of three foster families. But when she graduated from San Diego's Patrick Henry High School, she had a straight-A average and scholarship offers from Stanford and Cornell universities.

"I have to do well—it's not even a question," said the diminutive 19-year-old, now a sophomore at Cornell. "I owe it to my parents in Vietnam."

Kim-Chi is part of a tidal wave of bright, highly motivated Asian-Americans who are surging into our best colleges. Although Asian-Americans make up only 2.4 percent of the nation's population, by 1990 they had come to constitute 17.1 percent of the undergraduates at Harvard, 18 percent at the Massachusetts Institute of Technology and 27.3 percent at the University of California at Berkeley.

With Asians being the fastest-growing ethnic group in the country—   *5*
two out of five immigrants are now Asian—these figures will increase. At the University of California at Irvine, in a recent year, a staggering 35.1 percent of the undergraduates are Asian-American, but the proportion in the freshman class is even higher: 41 percent.

Why are the Asian-Americans doing so well? Are they grinds, as some stereotypes suggest? Do they have higher IQs? Or are they actually teaching the rest of us a lesson about values we have long treasured but may have misplaced—like hard work, the family and education?

Not all Asians are doing equally well. Poorly educated Cambodian and Hmong refugee youngsters need special help. And Asian-Americans resent being labeled a "model minority," feeling that is just another form of prejudice by white Americans, an ironic reversal of the discriminatory laws that excluded most Asian immigration to America until 1965.

But the academic success of many Asian-Americans has prompted growing concern among educators, parents and other students. Some universities have what look like unofficial quotas, much as Ivy League colleges did against Jews in the 1920s and '30s. Berkeley Chancellor Ira Heyman apologized for an admissions policy that, he said, had "a disproportionately negative impact on Asian-Americans."

I have wondered about the reason for the Asians' success since I was a fledgling journalist on Taiwan in 1969. That year, a team of boys from a poor, isolated mountain village on Taiwan won the annual Little League World Series at Williamsport, Pa. Their victory was totally unexpected. At the time, baseball was a largely unknown sport on Taiwan, and the boys had learned to play with bamboo sticks for bats and rocks for balls. But since then, teams from Taiwan, Japan or South Korea have won the Little League championship in 16 out of the 21 years. How could these Asian boys beat us at our own game?

Fortunately, the young Asians' achievements have led to a series of intriguing studies. "There is something going on here that we as Americans need to understand," said Sanford M. Dornbusch, a professor of sociology at Stanford. Dornbusch, in surveys of 7000 students in six San Francisco–area high schools, found that Asian-Americans consistently get better grades than any other group of students, regardless of their parents' level of education or their families' social and economic status, the usual predictors of success. In fact, those in homes where English is spoken often, or whose families have lived longer in the United States, do slightly less well.   *10*

"We used to talk about the American melting pot as an advantage," Dornbusch said. "But the sad fact is that it has become a melting pot with low standards."

Other studies have shown similar results. Perhaps the most disturbing have come in a series of studies by a University of Michigan psychologist, Harold W. Stevenson, who has compared more than 7000 students in kindergarten, first grade, third grade and fifth grade in Chicago and Minneapolis with counterparts in Beijing; Sendai, Japan; and Taipei, Taiwan. On a battery of math tests, the Americans did worst at all grade levels.

Stevenson found no differences in IQ. But if the differences in performance are showing up in kindergarten, it suggests something is happening in the family, even before the children get to school.

It is here that the various studies converge: Asian parents are able to instill more motivation in their children. "My bottom line is, Asian kids work hard," said Professor Dornbusch.

In his survey of San Francisco–area high schools, for example, he reported that Asian-Americans do an average of 7.03 hours of homework a week. Non–Hispanic whites average 6.12 hours, blacks 4.23 hours and Hispanics 3.98 hours. Asians also score highest on a series of other measures of effort, such as fewer class cuts and paying more attention to the teacher. *15*

Don Lee, 20, is a junior at Berkeley. His parents immigrated to Torrance, Calif., from South Korea when he was 5, so he could get a better education. Lee said his father would warn him about the danger of wasting time at high school dances or football games. "Instead," he added, "for fun on weekends, my friends and I would go to the town library to study."

The real question, then, is how do Asian parents imbue their offspring with this kind of motivation? Stevenson's study suggests a critical answer. When the Asian parents were asked why they think their children do well, they most often said "hard work." By contrast, American parents said "talent."

"From what I can see," said Stevenson, "we've lost our belief in the Horatio Alger myth that anyone can get ahead in life through pluck and hard work. Instead, Americans now believe that some kids have it and some don't, so we begin dividing up classes into fast learners and slow learners, where the Chinese and Japanese believe all children can learn from the same curriculum."

The Asians' belief in hard work also springs from their common heritage of Confucianism, the philosophy of the 5th-century B.C. Chinese sage who taught that man can be perfected through practice. "Confucius is not just some character out of the past—he is an everyday reality to these people," said William Liu, a sociologist who directs the Pacific Asian-American Mental Health Research Center at the University of Illinois in Chicago.

Confucianism provides another important ingredient in the Asians'   *20*
success. "In the Confucian ethic," Liu continued, "there is a centripetal
family, an orientation that makes people work for the honor of the family,
not just for themselves." Liu came to the United States from China in 1948.
"You can never repay your parents, and there is a strong sense of guilt," he
said. "It is a strong force, like the Protestant Ethic in the West."

Liu has found this in his own family. When his son and two daughters
were young, he told them to become doctors or lawyers—jobs with the
best guaranteed income, he felt. Sure enough, his daughters have gone into
law, and his son is a medical student at UCLA, though he really wanted to
be an investment banker. Liu asked his son why he picked medicine. The
reply: "Ever since I was a little kid, I always heard you tell your friends their
kids were a success if they got into med school. So I felt guilty. I didn't have
a choice."

Underlying this bond between Asian parents and their children is yet
another factor I noticed during 15 years of living in China, Japan, Taiwan
and Vietnam. It is simply that Asian parents establish a closer physical tie to
their infants than do most parents in the United States. When I let my baby
son and daughter crawl on the floor, for example, my Chinese friends were
horrified and rushed to pick them up. We think this constant attention is
overindulgence and old-fashioned, but for Asians, who still live through the
lives of their children, it is highly effective.

Yuen Huo, 22, a senior at Berkeley, recalled growing up in an apartment above the Chinese restaurant her immigrant parents owned and operated in Millbrae, Calif. "They used to tell us how they came from Taiwan
to the United States for us, how they sacrificed for us, so I had a strong sense
of indebtedness," Huo said. When she did not get all A's her first semester
at Berkeley, she recalled, "I felt guilty and worked harder."

Here too is a vital clue about the Asians' success: Asian parents expect
a high level of academic performance. In the Stanford study comparing
white and Asian students in San Francisco high schools, 82 percent of the
Asian parents said they would accept only an A or a B from their children,
while just 59 percent of white parents set such a standard. By comparison,
only 17 percent of Asian parents were willing to accept a C, against 40 percent of white parents. On the average, parents of black and Hispanic students
also had lower expectations for their children's grades than Asian parents.

Can we learn anything from the Asians? "I'm not naïve enough to think   *25*
everything in Asia can be transplanted," said Harold Stevenson, the University of Michigan psychologist. But he offered three recommendations.

"To start with," he said, "we need to set higher standards for our kids.
We wouldn't expect them to become professional athletes without practicing hard."

Second, American parents need to become more committed to their
children's education, he declared. "Being understanding when a child does-

n't do well isn't enough." Stevenson found that Asian parents spend many more hours really helping their children with homework or writing to their teachers. At Berkeley, the mothers of some Korean-American students move into their sons' apartments for months before graduate school entrance tests to help by cooking and cleaning for them, giving the students more time to study.

And, third, schools could be reorganized to become more effective — without added costs, said Stevenson. One of his most surprising findings is that Asian students, contrary to popular myth, are not just rote learners subjected to intense pressure. Instead, nearly 90 percent of Chinese youngsters said they actually enjoy school, and 60 percent can't wait for school vacations to end. These are vastly higher figures for such attitudes than are found in the United States. One reason may be that students in China and Japan typically have a recess after each class, helping them to relax and to increase their attention spans. Moreover, where American teachers spend almost their entire day in front of classes, their Chinese and Japanese counterparts may teach as little as three hours a day, giving them more time to relax and prepare imaginative lessons.

Another study, prepared for the U.S. Department of Education, compared the math and science achievements of 24,000 13-year-olds in the United States and five other countries (four provinces of Canada, plus South Korea, Ireland, Great Britain and Spain). One of the findings was that the more time students spent watching television, the poorer their performance. The American students watched the most television. They also got the worst scores in math. Only the Irish students and some of the Canadians scored lower in science.

"I don't think Asians are any smarter," said Don Lee, the Korean-American at Berkeley. "There are brilliant Americans in my chemistry class. But the Asian students work harder. I see a lot of wasted potential among the Americans."   30

The Responsive Reader

1   Have you encountered the idea of the "model minority"? Do you remember any evidence, ideas, explanations? (Have you encountered challenges or rebuttals to this idea?)
2   The author dramatizes the issue by using Kim-Chi Trinh as a case in point. What key details and key ideas does the author want you to take in and remember?
3   How does the author use key statistics, expert testimony, and his "insider's" knowledge of the Confucian heritage to support his points?
4   What recommendations is Butterfield's article designed to support? Are they surprising or predictable? Which are strongest or most convincing? (Who has the last word in this article?)

Talking, Listening, Writing

5   Does this article change your ideas or preconceptions? Does it make you think? Why and how—or why not?

6   Do you want to take issue with all or part of this article? On what grounds? Where would you turn for supporting evidence?

7   What has shaped your own ideas about success and failure in our system of education? In your experience as a student, what have you learned about learning?

8   Some people support admission quotas to ensure fair representation of minority students in colleges and universities. Do you agree with them? Do you think there should be quotas to prevent *over*representation of groups like the Asian students described in Butterfield's article?

Collaborative Projects

9   Why do model students do well? Why do dropouts fail? How many dropouts are really pushouts—pushed out by educational policies or economic pressures that defeat them? How many dropouts drop back in for a second (or third) chance? You may want to focus on one of these questions. Working with a group, quiz students, teachers, counselors, or others in a position to know. Find some current articles or new reports. What conclusions do your explorations suggest? Is there a consensus among your sources?

THE MYTH OF THE MODEL MINORITY

Noy Thrupkaew

"Southeast Asian immigrants have started to embrace that most American of activities, political protest."

Many observers have challenged the umbrella label Asian *for people from the many regions and cultures of a huge continent with billions of inhabitants. Many articles about Asians as the model minority have focused on the large growing number of Chinese American students at elite universitiies. They have focused on the growing number of professionals who have come from China and India in the sciences and areas like information technology. The author of the following article focuses on Asian immigrants who do not fit the model minority stereotype.*

During the 90s, "Welfare Reform" legislations had cut off welfare benefits and food stamps for all noncitizens. These included many immigrants who had been persecuted in their homelands after having worked with the Americans during their losing war in Southeast Asia. Many other refugees had been brutalized and had barely escaped with their lives after being associated by the new Communist rulers with American-style ideas, business success, or education. According to the following excerpt from an American Prospect *article first published in 2002, many of these refugees spoke little English, lived in linguistically isolated living areas, and were largely cut off from contact with public agencies or support groups. How does this article challenge the myth of the model minority?*

Thought Starters: When you hear the term *Asian,* what are the first images that come to mind? Do you think of *A* students at Berkeley or Harvard, or do you think of teenage members of gangs? Do you think of Asian doctors and other professionals or of Korean or Vietnamese cleaning establishments and neighborhood groceries?

Mali Keo fled Cambodia with her husband and four children in 1992. Several years later, she was still haunted by searing memories of "the killing fields," the forced-labor camps where millions of Cambodians died, victims of Communist despot Pol Pot's quest for a perfect agrarian society. Because of the brutal beatings she suffered at the hands of Pol Pot's Khmer Rouge, she was still wracked with physical pain as well. Traumatized and ailing, uneducated, unskilled, and speaking very little English, Mali Keo (a pseudonym assigned by researchers) could barely support her children after her husband abandoned the family.

And now she may not even have public assistance to fall back on, because the 1996 welfare-reform act cut off most federal benefits to immigrants and subsequent amendments have not entirely restored them. In what was supposed to be the land of her salvation, Mali Keo today is severely impoverished. Living in a hard-pressed neighborhood of Philadelphia, she struggles with only mixed success to keep her children out of trouble and in school.

The Southeast Asia Resource Action Center (SEARAC), an advocacy group in Washington, estimates that more than 2.2 million Southeast Asians now live in the United States. They are the largest group of refugees in the country and the fastest-growing minority. Yet for most policy makers, the plight of the many Mali Keos has been overshadowed by the well-known success of the Asian immigrants who came before and engendered the myth of the "model minority." Indeed, conservatives have exploited this racial stereotype—arguing that Asians fare well in the United States because of their strong "family values" and work ethic. These values, they say, and not government assistance, are what all minorities need in order to get ahead.

Paradoxically, Southeast Asians—supposedly part of the model minority—may be suffering most from the resulting public policies. They have been left in the hands of underfunded community assistance programs and government agencies that, in one example of well-intentioned incompetence, churn out forms in Khmer and Lao for often illiterate populations. But fueled by outrage over bad services and a fraying social safety-net, Southeast Asian immigrants have started to embrace that most American of activities, political protest—by pushing for research on their communities, advocating for their rights, and harnessing their political power.

The model-minority myth has persisted in large part because political conservatives are so attached to it. "Asian Americans have become the darlings of the right," said Frank Wu, a law professor at Howard University and the author of *Yellow: Race beyond Black and White*. "The model-minority myth and its depiction of Asian-American success tells a reassuring story about our society working."

The flip side is also appealing to the right. Because Asian Americans' success stems from their strong families and their dedication to education and hard work, conservatives say, then the poverty of Latinos and African Americans must be explained by their own "values": They are poor because of their nonmarrying, school-skipping, and generally lazy and irresponsible behavior, which government handouts only encourage.

The model-minority myth's "racist love," as author Frank Chin terms it, took hold at a sensitive point in U.S. history: after the 1965 Watts riots and the immigration reforms of that year, which selectively allowed large numbers of educated immigrants into the United States. Highly skilled South and East Asian nurses, doctors, and engineers from countries like India and China began pouring into the United States just as racial tensions were at a fever pitch.

Shortly thereafter, articles like "Success Story of One Minority in the U.S.," published by *U.S. News & World Report* in 1966, trumpeted: "At a time when it is being proposed that hundreds of billions be spent to uplift Negroes and other minorities, the nation's 300,000 Chinese Americans are moving ahead on their own, with no help from anyone else." *Newsweek* in 1971 had Asian Americans "outwhiting the whites." And *Fortune* in 1986 dubbed them a "superminority." As Wu caricatures the model-minority myth in his book:

> Asian Americans vindicate the American Dream. . . . They are living proof of the power of the free market and the absence of racial discrimination. Their good fortune flows from individual self-reliance and community self-sufficiency, not civil-rights activism or government welfare benefits.

A closer look at the data paints another picture, however. If Asian-American households earn more than whites, statistics suggest, it's not because their individual earnings are higher but because Asian Americans live in larger households, with more working adults. In fact, a recent University of Hawaii study found that "most Asian Americans are overeducated compared to whites for the incomes they earn"—evidence that suggests not "family values" but market discrimination.

What most dramatically skews the data, though, is the fact that about half the population of Asian (or, more precisely, Asian-Pacific Islander) Americans is made up of the highly educated immigrants who began arriving with their families in the 1960s. The plight of refugees from Cambodia, Laos, and Vietnam, who make up less than 14 percent of Asian Americans, gets lost in the averaging. Yet these refugees, who started arriving in the United States after 1975, differ markedly from the professional-class Chinese and Indian immigrants who started coming 10 years earlier. The Southeast Asians were fleeing wartime persecution and had few resources. And those disadvantages have had devastating effects on their lives in the United States. The most recent census data available show that 47 percent of Cambodians, 66 percent of Hmong (an ethnic group that lived in the mountains of Laos), 67 percent of Lantians, and 34 percent of Vietnamese were impoverished in 1990—compared with 10 percent of all Americans and 14 percent of all Asian Americans. Significantly, poverty rates among Southeast Asian Americans were much higher than those of even the "non-model" minorities: 21 percent of African Americans and 23 percent of Latinos were poor.

Yet despite the clear inaccuracies created by lumping populations together, the federal government still groups Southeast Asian refugees under the overbroad category of "Asian" for research and funding purposes. "We've labored under the shadow of this model myth for so long," said KaYing Yang, SEARAC's executive director. "There's so little research on us, or we're lumped in with all other Asians, so people don't know the specific needs and contributions of our communities."

To get a sense of those needs, one has to go back to the beginning of the Southeast Asian refugees' story and the circumstances that forced their migration. In 1975, the fall of Saigon sent shock waves throughout Southeast Asia, as communist insurgents toppled U.S.-supported governments in Vietnam and Cambodia. In Laos, where the CIA had trained and funded Hmong to fight Laotian and Vietnamese communists as U.S. proxies, the communists who took over vowed to purge the country of ethnic Hmong and punish all others who had worked with the U.S. government.

The first refugees to leave Southeast Asia tended to be the most educated and urban, English-speakers with close connections to the U.S. government. One of them was a man who wishes to be identified by the pseudonym John Askulraskul. He spent two years in a Laotian re-education camp—punishment for his ability to speak English, his having been educated, and, most of all, his status as a former employee of the United States Agency for International Development (USAID).

"They tried to brainwash you, to subdue you psychologically, to work you to death on two bowls of rice a day," Askulraskul told me recently.

After being released, he decided to flee the country. He, his sister, and his eldest daughter, five and a half years old, slipped into the Mekong River with a few others. Clinging to an inflated garbage bag, Askulraskul swam alongside their boat out of fear that his weight would sink it.

After they arrived on the shores of Thailand, Askulraskul and his daughter were placed in a refugee camp, where they waited to be reunited with his wife and his two other daughters.

It was not to be.

"My wife tried to escape with two small children. But my daughters couldn't make it"—he paused, drawing a ragged breath—"because the boat sank."

Askulraskul's wife was swept back to Laos, where she was arrested and placed in jail for a month. She succeeded in her next escape attempt, rejoining her suddenly diminished family.

Eventually, with the help of his former boss at USAID, they moved to Connecticut, where Askulraskul found work helping to resettle other refugees. His wife, who had been an elementary-school teacher, took up teaching English as a second language (ESL) to Laotian refugee children. His daughter adjusted quickly and went to school without incident.

Askulraskul now manages a project that provides services for at-risk Southeast Asian children and their families. "The job I am doing now is not only a job," he said. "It is part of my life and my sacrifice. My daughter is 29 now, and I know raising kids in America is not easy. I cannot save everybody, but there is still something I can do."

Like others among the first wave of refugees, Askulraskul considers himself one of the lucky ones. His education, U.S. ties, and English-

language ability—everything that set off the tragic chain of events that culminated in his daughters' deaths—proved enormously helpful once he was
in the United States.

But the majority of refugees from Southeast Asia had no such advantages. Subsequent waves frequently hailed from rural areas and lacked both
financial resources and formal schooling. Their psychological scars were
even deeper than the first group's, from their longer years in squalid refugee
camps or the killing fields. The ethnic Chinese who began arriving from
Vietnam had faced harsh discrimination as well, and the Amerasians—the
children of Vietnamese women and U.S. soldiers—had lived for years as
pariahs.

Once here, these refugees often found themselves trapped in poverty,
providing low-cost labor, and receiving no health or other benefits, while
their lack of schooling made decent jobs almost impossible to come by. In
1990, two-thirds of Cambodian, Laotian, and Hmong adults in America
had less than a high-school education—compared with 14 percent of
whites, 25 percent of African Americans, 45 percent of Latinos, and 15 percent of the general Asian-American population. Before the welfare–reform
law cut many of them off, nearly 30 percent of Southeast Asian Americans
were on welfare—the highest participation rate of any ethnic group. And
having such meager incomes, they usually lived in the worst neighborhoods,
with the attendant crime, gang problems, and poor schools.

But shouldn't the touted Asian dedication to schooling have overcome
these disadvantages, lifting the refugees' children out of poverty and keeping them off the streets? Unfortunately, it didn't. "There is still a high number of dropouts for Southeast Asians," Yang said. "And if they do graduate,
there is a low number going on to higher education."

Their parents' difficulty in navigating American school systems may
contribute to the problem. "The parents' lack of education leads to a lack
of role models and guidance. Without those things, youth can turn to delin-
quent behavior and in some very extreme cases, gangs, instead of devoting
themselves to education," said Narin Sihavong, director of SEARAC's Successful New Americans Project, which interviewed Mali Keo. "This underscores the need for Southeast Asian school administrators or counselors
who can be role models, ease the cultural barrier, and serve as a bridge to
their parents."

"Sometimes families have to choose between education and employment, especially when money is tight," said Porthira Chimm, a former
SEARAC project director. "And unfortunately, immediate money concerns often win out."

The picture that emerges—of high welfare participation and dropout
rates, low levels of education and income—is startlingly similar to the situation of the poorest members of "nonmodel" minority groups. Southeast
Asians, Latinos, and African Americans also have in common significant
numbers of single-parent families. Largely as a result of the killing fields,

nearly a quarter of Cambodian households are headed by single women. Other Southeast Asian families have similar stories. Sihavong's mother, for example, raised him and his five siblings on her own while his father was imprisoned in a Laotian re-education camp.

No matter how "traditional" Southeast Asians may be, they share the fate of other people of color when they are denied access to good education, safe neighborhoods, and jobs that provide a living wage and benefits. But for the sake of preserving the model-minority myth, conservative policy makers have largely ignored the needs of Southeast Asian communities. . . .

Southeast Asians are disproving the model-minority myth not just with their difficult lives but with their growing insistence that it takes more than "traditional values" and "personal responsibility" to survive in this country. It takes social supports and participation in the legacy of civil rights activism as well.

The refugees and their children are forging their identities as new Americans and are starting to emerge as a political force. At first, Yang said, "we had no time to think about anything else but our communities—and no one was thinking about us. But now we know that what we were grappling with [affects both] me and my neighbor, who might be poor black, Latino, or Asian. We are no longer refugees, we are Americans. And we know what being 'successful' is: It's being someone who is truly aware of the meaning of freedom to speak out."

The Responsive Reader

1   Both Butterfield in his article "Why They Excel" and Thrupkaew start with a human-interest story about the refugee experience. How are the two *introductions* similar? How are they different?
2   The author claims that the "model-minority" myth has been used for political purposes. What are his *sources* for this claim? What evidence does he present? What are the alleged purposes? Do you think the author's claims are believable? Are you shocked by them?
3   How does the author *contrast* the different waves of Asian refugees? Why were early waves of refugees more successful in America? What were the obstacles or handicaps encountered by later waves of immigrants from Southeast Asia?
4   Overall, what is the purpose of Thrupkaew's article—recrimination or finger-pointing? setting the record straight? fighting stereotypes? a call to action? Can you find a *thesis* that sums up the author's purpose?

Talking, Listening, Writing

5   Would you call the denial of welfare support, health care, or education to noncitizen refugees who had worked for or fought with Americans a betrayal?

Collaborative Projects

6 The twentieth century was the century of the refugee. Millions were uprooted from their homes, fled from persecution, and were often shunted from one refugee camp to another. Have today's young Americans forgotten the boat people of Vietnam? Working alone or with a group, collect and edit testimonies of refugees from Southeast Asia, from Central America, or another area of conflict where the American presence played a major role.

EVERYDAY USE

Alice Walker

The quilt as a symbol of African American tradition has a different meaning for the traditional mother and her city sophisticate daughter.

In 2004, Alice Walker, whose Color Purple *had made her a national and international celebrity, had returned to her current home in California after an extensive book tour for her latest novel,* Now Is the Time to Open Your Heart. *A multimillion-dollar musical adaptation of* The Color Purple, *earlier made into a Spielberg movie, had opened in Atlanta and was headed for Broadway. Evelyn C. White published a full-length biography,* Alice Walker: A Life, *based on years of study of Alice Walker's life and work. The biographer said about the central message of Walker's writing that hard issues "having to do with the oppression of women and the wounding of people of African descent could be only be changed by telling the truth about them."*

Alice Walker's novel The Color Purple *(1982) established her as a dominant voice in the search for a new black identity and black pride. In her Pulitzer Prize—winning novel, as in 33 of her short stories, her heroines are black women struggling to emerge from a history of oppression by white society and abuse by black males who "had failed women—and themselves." Walker's women find strength in bonding with other women, and they turn to the African past in the search for alternatives to our exploitative technological civilization. Walker's novel* The Temple of My Familiar *(1989) has been called a book of "amazing, overwhelming" richness, with characters "pushing one another towards self-knowledge, honesty, engagement" (Ursula K. Le Guin).*

Born in Eatonton, Georgia, Walker knew poverty and racism as the child of sharecroppers in the South. While a student at Spelman College in Atlanta, she joined in the rallies, sit-ins, and freedom marches of the civil rights movement, which, she said later, "broke the pattern of black servitude in this country." She worked as a social worker for the New York City Welfare Department and as an editor for Ms. *magazine.*

In the following short story, first published in 1973, the older generation holds on to its hard-won pride and independence, while members of a younger generation assert their break with the past by adopting Muslim names and African greetings. What do the quilts symbolize in the story?

Thought Starters: Stereotyping lumps together diverse members of a group. Have you observed striking contrasts between members of the same ethnic, racial, or religious group?

---

for your grandmama

I will wait for her in the yard that Maggie and I made so clean and   1
wavy yesterday afternoon. A yard like this is more comfortable than most
people know. It is not just a yard. It is like an extended living room. When
the hard clay is swept clean as a floor and the fine sand around the edges
lined with tiny, irregular grooves, anyone can come and sit and look up into
the elm tree and wait for the breezes that never come inside the house.

Maggie will be nervous until after her sister goes: she will stand hope-
lessly in corners, homely and ashamed of the burn scars down her arms and
legs, eyeing her sister with a mixture of envy and awe. She thinks her sister
has held life always in the palm of one hand, that "no" is a word the world
never learned to say to her.

You've no doubt seen those TV shows where the child who has
"made it" is confronted, as a surprise, by her own mother and father, tot-
tering in weakly from backstage. (A pleasant surprise, of course: What
would they do if parent and child came on the show only to curse out and
insult each other?) On TV mother and child embrace and smile into each
other's faces. Sometimes the mother and father weep, the child wraps them
in her arms and leans across the table to tell how she would not have made
it without their help. I have seen these programs.

Sometimes I dream a dream in which Dee and I are suddenly brought
together on a TV program of this sort. Out of a dark and soft-seated limousine I am ushered into a bright room filled with many people. There I
meet a smiling, gray, sporty man like Johnny Carson who shakes my hand
and tells me what a fine girl I have. Then we are on the stage and Dee is
embracing me with tears in her eyes. She pins on my dress a large orchid,
even though she has told me once that she thinks orchids are tacky flowers.

In real life I am a large, big-boned woman with rough, man–working   5
hands. In the winter I wear flannel nightgowns to bed and overalls during
the day. I can kill and clean a hog as mercilessly as a man. My fat keeps me
hot in zero weather. I can work outside all day, breaking ice to get water
for washing; I can eat pork liver cooked over the open fire minutes after it
comes steaming from the hog. One winter I knocked a bull calf straight in
the brain between the eyes with a sledge hammer and had the meat hung
up to chill before nightfall. But of course all this does not show on television. I am the way my daughter would want me to be: a hundred pounds
lighter, my skin like an uncooked barley pancake. My hair glistens in the
hot bright lights. Johnny Carson has much to do to keep up with my quick
and witty tongue.

But that is a mistake. I know even before I wake up. Who ever knew
a Johnson with a quick tongue? Who can even imagine me looking a
strange white man in the eye? It seems to me I have talked to them always
with one foot raised in flight, with my head turned in whichever way is farthest from them. Dee, though. She would always look anyone in the eye.
Hesitation was no part of her nature.

"How do I look, Mama?" Maggie says, showing just enough of her thin body enveloped in pink skirt and red blouse for me to know she's there, almost hidden by the door.

"Come out into the yard," I say.

Have you ever seen a lame animal, perhaps a dog run over by some careless person rich enough to own a car, sidle up to someone who is ignorant enough to be kind to him? That is the way my Maggie walks. She has been like this, chin on chest, eyes on ground, feet in shuffle, ever since the fire that burned the other house to the ground.

Dee is lighter than Maggie, with nicer hair and a fuller figure. She's a woman now, though sometimes I forget. How long ago was it that the other house burned? Ten, twelve years? Sometimes I can still hear the flames and feel Maggie's arms sticking to me, her hair smoking and her dress falling off her in little black papery flakes. Her eyes seemed stretched open, blazed open by the flames reflected in them. And Dee. I see her standing off under the sweet gum tree she used to dig gum out of; a look of concentration on her face as she watched the last dingy gray board of the house fall in toward the red-hot brick chimney. Why don't you do a dance around the ashes? I'd wanted to ask her. She had hated the house that much.

I used to think she hated Maggie, too. But that was before we raised the money, the church and me, to send her to Augusta to school. She used to read to us without pity; forcing words, lies, other folks' habits, whole lives upon us two, sitting trapped and ignorant underneath her voice. She washed us in a river of make-believe, burned us with a lot of knowledge we didn't necessarily need to know. Pressed us to her with the serious way she read, to shove us away at just the moment, like dimwits, we seemed about to understand.

Dee wanted nice things. A yellow organdy dress to wear to her grad-   10
uation from high school; black pumps to match a green suit she'd made from an old suit somebody gave me. She was determined to stare down any disaster in her efforts. Her eyelids would not flicker for minutes at a time. Often I fought off the temptation to shake her. At sixteen she had a style of her own: and knew what style was.

I never had an education myself. After second grade the school was closed down. Don't ask me why: in 1927 colored asked fewer questions than they do now. Sometimes Maggie reads to me. She stumbles along good-naturedly but can't see well. She knows she is not bright. Like good looks and money, quickness passed her by. She will marry John Thomas (who has mossy teeth in an earnest face) and then I'll be free to sit here and I guess just sing church songs to myself. Although I never was a good singer. Never could carry a tune. I was always better at a man's job. I used to love to milk till I was hooked in the side in '49. Cows are soothing and slow and don't bother you, unless you try to milk them the wrong way.

I have deliberately turned my back on the house. It is three rooms, just like the one that burned, except the roof is tin; they don't make shingle roofs any more. There are no real windows, just some holes cut in the sides, like the portholes in a ship, but not round and not square, with rawhide holding the shutters up on the outside. This house is in a pasture, too, like the other one. No doubt when Dee sees it she will want to tear it down. She wrote me once that no matter where we "choose" to live, she will manage to come see us. But she will never bring her friends. Maggie and I thought about this and Maggie asked me, "Mama, when did Dee ever *have* any friends?"

She had a few. Furtive boys in pink shirts hanging about on washday after school. Nervous girls who never laughed. Impressed with her they worshiped the well-turned phrase, the cute shape, the scalding humor that erupted like bubbles in lye. She read to them.   15

When she was courting Jimmy T she didn't have much time to pay to us, but turned all her faultfinding power on him. He *flew* to marry a cheap city girl from a family of ignorant flashy people. She hardly had time to recompose herself.

When she comes I will meet—but there they are!

Maggie attempts to make a dash for the house, in her shuffling way, but I stay her with my hand. "Come back here," I say. And she stops and tries to dig a well in the sand with her toe.

It is hard to see them clearly through the strong sun. But even the first glimpse of leg out of the car tells me it is Dee. Her feet were always neat-looking, as if God himself had shaped them with a certain style. From the other side of the car comes a short, stocky man. Hair is all over his head a foot long and hanging from his chin like a kinky mule tail. I hear Maggie suck in her breath. "Uhnnnh," is what it sounds like. Like when you see the wriggling end of a snake just in front of your foot on the road. "Uhnnnh."

Dee next. A dress down to the ground, in this hot weather. A dress so   20
loud it hurts my eyes. There are yellows and oranges enough to throw back the light of the sun. I feel my whole face warming from the heat waves it throws out. Earrings gold, too, and hanging down to her shoulders. Bracelets dangling and making noises when she moves her arm up to shake the folds of the dress out of her armpits. The dress is loose and flows, and as she walks closer, I like it. I hear Maggie go "Uhnnnh" again. It is her sister's hair. It stands straight up like the wool on a sheep. It is black as night and around the edges are two long pigtails that rope about like small lizards disappearing behind her ears.

"Wa-su-zo-Tean-o!" she says, coming on in that gliding way the dress makes her move. The short stocky fellow with the hair to his navel is all grinning and he follows up with "Asalamalakim, my mother and sister!" He moves to hug Maggie but she falls back, right up against the back of my chair. I feel her trembling there and when I look up I see the perspiration falling off her chin.

"Don't get up," says Dee. Since I am stout it takes something of a push. You can see me trying to move a second or two before I make it. She turns, showing white heels through her sandals, and goes back to the car. Out she peeks next with a Polaroid. She stoops down quickly and lines up picture after picture of me sitting there in front of the house with Maggie cowering behind me. She never takes a shot without making sure the house is included. When a cow comes nibbling around the edge of the yard she snaps it and me and Maggie *and* the house. Then she puts the Polaroid in the back seat of the car, and comes up and kisses me on the forehead.

Meanwhile Asalamalakim is going through motions with Maggie's hand. Maggie's hand is as limp as a fish, and probably as cold, despite the sweat, and she keeps trying to pull it back. It looks like Asalamalakim wants to shake hands but wants to do it fancy. Or maybe he don't know how people shake hands. Anyhow, he soon gives up on Maggie.

"Well," I say. "Dee."

"No, Mama," she says. "Not 'Dee,' Wangero Leewanika Kemanjo!"   *25*

"What happened to 'Dee'?" I wanted to know.

"She's dead," Wangero said. "I couldn't bear it any longer, being named after the people who oppress me."

"You know as well as me you was named after your aunt Dicie," I said. Dicie is my sister. She named Dee. We called her "Big Dee" after Dee was born.

"But who was *she* named after?" asked Wangero.

"I guess after Grandma Dee," I said.   *30*

"And who was she named after?" asked Wangero.

"Her mother," I said, and saw Wangero was getting tired. "That's about as far back as I can trace it," I said. Though, in fact, I probably could have carried it back beyond the Civil War through the branches.

"Well," said Asalamalakim, "there you are."

"Uhnnnh," I heard Maggie say.

"There I was not," I said, "before 'Dicie' cropped up in our family, so   *35* why should I try to trace it that far back?"

He just stood there grinning, looking down on me like somebody inspecting a Model A car. Every once in a while he and Wangero sent eye signals over my head.

"How do you pronounce this name?" I asked.

"You don't have to call me by it if you don't want to," said Wangero.

"Why shouldn't I?" I asked. "If that's what you want us to call you, we'll call you."

"I know it might sound awkward at first," said Wangero.   *40*

"I'll get used to it," I said. "Ream it out again."

Well, soon we got the name out of the way. Asalamalakim had a name twice as long and three times as hard. After I tripped over it two or three times he told me to just call him Hakim-a-barber. I wanted to ask him was he a barber, but I didn't really think he was, so I didn't ask.

"You must belong to those beef-cattle peoples down the road," I said. They said "Asalamalakim" when they met you, too, but they didn't shake hands. Always too busy: feeding the cattle, fixing the fences, putting up salt-lick shelters, throwing down hay. When the white folks poisoned some of the herd the men stayed up all night with rifles in their hands. I walked a mile and a half just to see the sight.

Hakim-a-barber said, "I accept some of their doctrines, but farming and raising cattle is not my style." (They didn't tell me, and I didn't ask, whether Wangero (Dee) had really gone and married him.)

We sat down to eat and right away he said he didn't eat collards and   45
pork was unclean. Wangero, though, went on through the chitlins and corn bread, the greens and everything else. She talked a blue streak over the sweet potatoes. Everything delighted her. Even the fact that we still used the benches her daddy made for the table when we couldn't afford to buy chairs.

"Oh, Mama!" she cried. Then turned to Hakim-a-barber. "I never knew how lovely these benches are. You can feel the rump prints," she said, running her hands underneath her and along the bench. Then she gave a sigh and her hand closed over Grandma Dee's butter dish. "That's it!" she said. "I knew there was something I wanted to ask you if I could have." She jumped up from the table and went over in the corner where the churn stood, the milk in it clabber by now. She looked at the churn and looked at it.

"This churn top is what I need," she said. "Didn't Uncle Buddy whittle it out of a tree you all used to have?"

"Yes," I said.

"Uh huh," she said happily. "And I want the dasher, too."

"Uncle Buddy whittle that, too?" asked the barber.   50

Dee (Wangero) looked up at me.

"Aunt Dee's first husband whittled the dash," said Maggie so low you almost couldn't hear her. "His name was Henry, but they called him Stash."

"Maggie's brain is like an elephant's," Wangero said, laughing. "I can use the churn top as a centerpiece for the alcove table," she said, sliding a plate over the churn, "and I'll think of something artistic to do with the dasher."

When she finished wrapping the dasher the handle stuck out. I took it for a moment in my hands. You didn't even have to look close to see where hands pushing the dasher up and down to make butter had left a kind of sink in the wood. In fact, there were a lot of small sinks; you could see where thumbs and fingers had sunk into the wood. It was beautiful light yellow wood, from a tree that grew in the yard where Big Dee and Stash had lived.

After dinner Dee (Wangero) went to the trunk at the foot of my bed   *55*
and started rifling through it. Maggie hung back in the kitchen over the dishpan. Out came Wangero with two quilts. They had been pieced by Grandma Dee and then Big Dee and me had hung them on the quilt frames on the front porch and quilted them. One was in the Lone Star pattern. The other was Walk Around the Mountain. In both of them were scraps of dresses Grandma Dee had worn fifty and more years ago. Bits and pieces of Grandpa Jarrell's Paisley shirts. And one teeny faded blue piece, about the size of a penny matchbox, that was from Great Grandpa Ezra's uniform that he wore in the Civil War.

"Mama," Wangero said sweet as a bird. "Can I have these old quilts?"

I heard something fall in the kitchen, and a minute later the kitchen door slammed.

"Why don't you take one or two of the others?" I asked. "These old things was just done by me and Big Dee from some tops your grandma pieced before she died."

"No," said Wangero. "I don't want those. They are stitched around the borders by machine."

"That'll make them last better," I said.   *60*

"That's not the point," said Wangero. "These are all pieces of dresses Grandma used to wear. She did all this stitching by hand. Imagine!" She held the quilts securely in her arms, stroking them.

"Some of the pieces, like those lavender ones, come from old clothes her mother handed down to her," I said, moving up to touch the quilts. Dee (Wangero) moved back just enough so that I couldn't reach the quilts. They already belonged to her.

"Imagine!" she breathed again, clutching them closely to her bosom.

"The truth is," I said, "I promised to give them quilts to Maggie, for when she marries John Thomas."

She gasped like a bee had stung her.   *65*

"Maggie can't appreciate these quilts!" she said. "She'd probably be backward enough to put them to everyday use."

"I reckon she would," I said. "God knows I been saving 'em for long enough with nobody using 'em. I hope she will!" I didn't want to bring up how I had offered Dee (Wangero) a quilt when she went away to college. Then she had told me they were old-fashioned, out of style.

"But they're *priceless!*" she was saying now, furiously; for she has a temper. "Maggie would put them on the bed and in five years they'd be in rags. Less than that!"

"She can always make some more," I said. "Maggie knows how to quilt."

Dee (Wangero) looked at me with hatred. "You just will not under-   *70*
stand. The point is these quilts, *these* quilts!"

"Well," I said, stumped. "What would *you* do with them?"

"Hang them," she said. As if that was the only thing you *could* do with quilts.

Maggie by now was standing in the door. I could almost hear the sound her feet made as they scraped over each other.

"She can have them, Mama," she said, like somebody used to never winning anything, or having anything reserved for her. "I can 'member Grandma Dee without the quilts."

I looked at her hard. She had filled her bottom lip with checkerberry   75
snuff and it gave her face a kind of dopey, hangdog look. It was Grandma Dee and Big Dee who taught her how to quilt herself. She stood there with her scarred hands hidden in the folds of her skirt. She looked at her sister with something like fear but she wasn't mad at her. This was Maggie's portion. This was the way she knew God to work.

When I looked at her like that something hit me in the top of my head and ran down to the soles of my feet. Just like when I'm in church and the spirit of God touches me and I get happy and shout. I did something I never had done before: hugged Maggie to me, then dragged her on into the room, snatched the quilts out of Miss Wangero's hands and dumped them into Maggie's lap. Maggie just sat there on my bed with her mouth open.

"Take one or two of the others," I said to Dee.

But she turned without a word and went out to Hakim-a-barber.

"You just don't understand," she said, as Maggie and I came out to the car.

"What don't I understand?" I wanted to know.   80

"Your heritage," she said. And then she turned to Maggie, kissed her, and said, "You ought to try to make something of yourself, too, Maggie. It's really a new day for us. But from the way you and Mama still live you'd never know it."

She put on some sunglasses that hid everything above the tip of her nose and her chin.

Maggie smiled; maybe at the sunglasses. But a real smile, not scared. After we watched the car dust settle I asked Maggie to bring me a dip of snuff. And then the two of us sat there just enjoying, until it was time to go in the house and go to bed.

The Responsive Reader

1   What kind of person is the mother? What role do her daydreams play in the story? How does her initial self-portrait as the narrator, or person telling the story, prepare you for what happens later?

2   What is the contrasting history of the two sisters? What is most important in their earlier history?

3   What do Dee and her companion stand for in this story? Do you recognize their attitudes and way of talking?

4   How does the confrontation over the quilts bring things to a head? What is the history of the quilts and their symbolic meaning? How does the climactic ending resolve the conflict in this story?

Talking, Listening, Writing

5   If you had to choose a role model from this story, would you opt for the mother or for Dee? Defend your choice.

Collaborative Projects

6   Do you ever chafe at being a passive reader—who cannot enter into the story to help it steer one way or another? Write a passage in which one daughter or the other tells her side of the story. Or rewrite the ending the way you would have preferred the story to come out. Or write a sequel to the story bringing it up to date. Arrange for members of the class to share their imaginative efforts.

FORUM: *Educating about Race*

> Kwame Ture (Stokely Carmichael) was my friend for 40 years. The thing that touched me most about him was that he loved his black people. He was deeply committed to their plight and worked all his 57 years to improve conditions for African Americans. One of his greatest contributions was his 1966 wake-up call to black Americans, saying that they are "a mighty people" who can and must determine and define their own destiny.
>
> Marion Barry, Jr., mayor of Washington, D.C.,
> in the eulogy of his former coworker in the
> Student Nonviolent Coordinating Committee

The civil rights movement of the sixties and seventies, inspired by the eloquence of the Reverend Martin Luther King, Jr., and fueled by the enthusiasm of black activists and white liberal sympathizers, broke the shackles of legalized segregation in America. It established the principle of equal access to education. It helped create a new African American middle class of lawyers, educators, scholars, and public officials. It made demeaning racial stereotypes unacceptable on television screens and in boardrooms, if not in locker rooms.

Has the civil rights movement run its course, leaving many questions about race in America unresolved? Politicians—supported by prominent conservative black Americans—exploit a backlash against affirmative action programs, rechristened as "racial preferences." Pundits pore over income statistics, test results, and surveys, drawing widely differing conclusions.

On the one hand, conservatives marshal statistics showing that the income gap between black and white is narrowing and that we can no longer put the blame on racism in an increasingly "color-blind" society. Alternatively, conservatives focus on the breakdown of moral values in the black community, blaming black Americans for their own plight.

In the meantime, is it true that more young African Americans are in jail than in college? Is it true that sentences for cocaine use are five times as severe for blacks as they are for whites? In many of America's inner cities, no one—white liberal, black neoconservative, or closet racist—would walk at night. What are we going to tell the next generation about race in America? How are we going to educate them for what lies ahead?

OUR CHILDREN ARE OUR FUTURE— UNFORTUNATELY THEY'RE BIGOTS

Richard Cohen

"Younger Americans apparently know little about— and did not see on television—the civil rights struggles of the 1950s and 1960s, everything from the police dogs of Birmingham to the murder of civil rights workers."

During the era of the civil rights movement, many Americans believed in progress toward better race relations. They envisioned a future where African Americans and other minorities would emerge from poverty and deprivation to become fully integrated into American life. However, in the nineties, trend watchers like the Washington Post *columnist who wrote the following selection noticed a growing backlash against official policies of tolerance, integration, and affirmative action. "Forced busing" to achieve better racial balance in the schools had proved bitterly divisive and contributed to "white flight" from public education. The media sensationalized racial incidents like the beating by Los Angeles police of the black motorist Rodney King and the killing of a black youth by a white mob in Bensonhurst. Journalists started to give prominent treatment to racial incidents on college campuses. Was the nation backsliding in the fight against racism?*

Thought Starters: Would you call your campus integrated or divided along ethnic and racial lines? Can you cite incidents that point to racial animosity or racial harmony? Do friends and acquaintances sound prejudiced to you?

There's hardly a politician in the land who, when children are mentioned, does not say they are our future. That's true, of course—and nothing can be done about it—but the way things are going we should all be worried. A generation of bigots is coming of age.

The evidence for that awful prognostication can be found in a recent public opinion survey conducted for the Anti-Defamation League by the Boston polling firm of Marttila & Kiley—two outfits with considerable credentials in the field of public opinion research. For the first time, a trend has been reversed. Up to now, opinion polls have always found that the more schooling a person has, the more likely he is to be tolerant. For that reason, older people—who by and large have the least education—are the most intolerant age group in the nation.

1

But no longer. The ADL found a disturbing symmetry: Older and younger white Americans share the same biases. For instance, when white people were asked if blacks prefer to remain on welfare rather than work, 42 percent of the respondents 50 years old and over said the statement was "probably true." Predictably, the figure plummeted to 29 percent for those 30 to 49. But then it jumped to 36 percent for respondents under 30.

Similarly, a majority of younger respondents thought blacks "complain too much about racism" (68 percent) and "stick together more than others" (63 percent). For both statements, the young had a higher percentage of agreement than any other age category. The pattern persisted for the other questions as well—questions designed to ferret out biased attitudes. In the words of Abraham Foxman, the ADL's national director, the generation that's destined to run this country is either racist or disposed to racism to a degree that he characterized as "a crisis." It's hard to disagree with him.

What's going on? The short answer is that no one knows for sure. But some guesses can be ventured and none of them is comforting. The first and most obvious explanation has to do with age itself: The under 30 generation is pathetically ignorant of recent American history. Younger people apparently know little about—and did not see on television—the civil rights struggles of the 1950s and 1960s, everything from the police dogs of Birmingham to the murder of civil rights workers. They apparently do not understand that if blacks tend to see racism everywhere, that's because in the recent past, it *was* everywhere and remains the abiding American sickness. 5

But historical ignorance is not the only factor accounting for the ADL's findings. Another, apparently, is affirmative action. It has created a category of white victims, either real or perceived, who are more likely than other whites to hold prejudicial views. For instance, the ADL asked, "Do you feel you have ever been a victim of reverse discrimination in hiring or promotion?" Only 21 percent said yes. But the percentage rose to 26 percent for college graduates and 23 percent for people with post-graduate degrees. Since the ADL found that "about one third" of the self-described victims of reverse discrimination fell into the "most prejudiced" category, these numbers are clearly worth worrying about. Too many of the American elite are racially aggrieved—although possibly some of them were bigoted in the first place.

One could argue that not all of the statements represent proof of bigoted attitudes. For instance, white college students who witness voluntary self-segregation on the part of black students—demands for their own dorms, for instance—have some reason to think that blacks "stick together more than others." Nevertheless, the data strongly suggest that progress on racial attitudes is being reversed—with contributions from both races. Worse, this is happening at a time when the economic pie is shrinking and competition for jobs increasing. If the economic trend continues, racial intolerance is likely to grow.

No one I spoke with at either the Anti-Defamation League or at Marttila & Kiley thought their findings were definitive or could offer concrete explanations. But the numbers conform to what you and I know—or think we do—about racial friction on the nation's campuses and a growing uneasiness about affirmative action. After all, most of those programs were instituted during a period of sustained economic growth, a boom time especially for college graduates, when jobs were plentiful. That's no longer the case.

Given the ADL's findings, it's clear that something has to be done. It's nothing less than a calamity that a generation has come of age without a deep appreciation of the recent history of African Americans. At the same time, black leaders who advocate or condone separatism had better appreciate the damage they are doing. And finally, affirmative action programs, as well-intentioned as they may be, need to be re-examined—and without critics automatically being labeled as racist. No doubt these programs have done some good. But there's a growing body of evidence—of which the ADL poll is only the latest—that they also do some bad.

The Responsive Reader

1   According to this columnist, how does the survey he cites reverse traditional assumptions about intolerance?

2   What test questions did the survey use to determine whether young people were "disposed to racism"? Which to you seem most relevant or important? Would you challenge any of them? Does Cohen question any of them?

3   Why and how, as in other, similar discussions, does affirmative action become a central issue in this column?

Talking, Listening, Writing

4   Cohen concludes that "something has to be done." What? How useful or convincing are his suggestions?

5   Do you agree that racism is on the rise in our society? What evidence can you cite to support your opinion?

6   Do you or institutions or organizations you know have a concrete program for addressing the problem Cohen examines?

Collaborative Projects

7   Working with a group, explore questions like the following: How much attention do people pay to opinion polls? How much confidence do they place in them? What role have opinion polls played in recent elections or policy decisions by officials?

THE TINY, BROWN PROFESSOR

Patricia Smith

**"Here, I was assured, teaching tolerance was a priority.
Well, that took care of the kids. The parents were
another story."**

*The following article, first published in Ms. magazine in the summer of
2000 by a parent in search of a good preschool experience for her daughter,
raises a key question about the next generation.*

*Young Americans increasingly have cross-cultural experiences. How do they
learn positive or negative attitudes toward children from other ethnic, racial, or
religious backgrounds? Some observers claim that parents pass on negative attitudes to the next generation. Some studies show that children may be influenced by their peers as much as or more than by their parents. And some
psychologists claim that children have spontaneous impulses of rejection toward
those perceived as different that they have to unlearn. The following account
was written by a woman of color who is a successful journalist and who is committed to ideas of diversity and tolerance widely accepted in the media and by
educators. She records some of the conflicting impressions and mixed emotions
encountered by those translating their liberal ideas into everyday practice.*

Thought Starters: Have you always been part of the in-group? If not,
what were your earliest experiences with being treated as an outsider or
feeling like an outsider? When were you first part of a group that treated
someone else as an outsider? What did you learn from the experience?

I plotted to skip the Purim Carnival this year, even though it meant
passing up the enticingly interactive reading of the megillah and the crooning of Purim songs by Rabbi David and Cantor Margot. I finally had to admit that I felt acute discomfort at the Jewish temple where my granddaughter attends preschool. Even in the midst of an idyllic crossing of
cultures, the real world was bound to intrude.

When we relocated to New York State last summer, our timing
couldn't have been worse. Most of the preschools were packed to bursting
for the upcoming fall session. The one with space for a four-year-old came
highly recommended, boasted an innovative curriculum, and was affiliated
with Temple Beth Abraham. And every student in the school was white.
This was initially a concern, since we'd just moved from Ridgefield, Connecticut—the home of SUVs, A-line skirts, and the world's whitest
women—where the only blacks, browns, reds, and yellows Mikaila encountered were crammed in a box marked "Crayola." I wanted a school

that reflected our new community's diversity. Here, I was assured, teaching tolerance was a priority. Well, that took care of the kids. The parents were another story.

To be fair, several of the moms and dads were welcoming from the start. But once the realization set in that I was not one of the West African or Caribbean nannies who deliver and collect their charges, my relationship with many of them was strained, at best. I kept right on speaking to people who kept right on staring past me. At school events, I was marginalized, stuck at the nerd table, an oddity viewed with resentful curiosity and suspicion. What was I doing there? What did I want? Weren't there other places I could go?

Nope, I'm not imagining things. When Mikaila clamors for a play date with a classmate, or vice versa, the kid's mom undergoes an intriguing transformation. Her eyes flutter, she stammers, suddenly there's a very interesting something else at the other end of the hall. Since I am a stickler for personal hygiene and don't drool in conversation, I can only conclude that there's some misunderstanding about playtime at our place. Perhaps it's assumed that the kids will be force-fed a diet of fried pig parts and gangster rap while they make fun with my collection of loaded pistols. Oh, and don't forget the warm malt liquor in the Tigger juice cup. Calms the little buggers right down.

The urge to scoop up my granddaughter and skedaddle to someplace more receptive was tempered by the change in Mikaila. Her world grew. 5

Dressed in a satiny black tutu, my high heels, and a ratty pair of wool leg warmers, she stomps purposefully in circles in the living room, banging a spoon on the bottom of an empty Pringles potato chip can for backbeat. Her chant is insistent, filled with new-found passion: "Shabbat Shalom—HEY! Shabbat Shalom—HEY! Shabbat Shalom—HEY!" Each "HEY!" is punctuated by a dramatic surge in volume.

This is now Mikaila's favorite song, surpassing the "Macarena" by miles. There may be other words besides the three, but she doesn't care to know them. It's got beat. It's got rhythm. It's got the cool "s" sound, every preschooler's favorite. You can boogie to it. It's got that "HEY!" to top things off. And if you're tiny, brown, and sing it in public, you get lots of attention.

At home in the evenings, I am often urged to sit still for my dose of Judaic culture. My miniature professor instructs me in the Hebrew alphabet. She knows how to craft a menorah with marshmallows and pretzels. Her handmade Torah hangs from a special hook in her room. We make a racket with our groggers, and a bright purple dreidel sits atop my computer monitor.

Mikaila is energized by her instructors, but she, too, is a teacher, sharing as much as she learns, barreling her way through any pesky intolerance her playmates may have picked up from their parents. She is brown, not afraid to say so, and an expert at getting everyone in range to see how special her difference is. I believe wholeheartedly in her ability to rock the world.

So am I devastated by this selective snub, this slice of reality? Initially, I was flooded with those ol' colored-girl terrors, those stark slaps of exclusion. In response, I did exactly what I shouldn't do, what never even occurred to Mikaila. I cowered, folded into myself, grew silent. I made myself unapproachable so I had an excuse for not being approached. 10

I spent a lot of time dealing with only the kids. They're way cooler anyhow, and it will be some time before any of life's perceived badness seeps through. I chatted with them even as their mothers glowered. We winked, giggled, and whispered when no one was listening. They taught me to be much bigger than I am. I may have even pried open their vistas a bit. Little Jared, fascinated from the first by my crinkly braids, finally got up the nerve to reach out and touch. His single flabbergasted word: "Wow."

But living life fully means never letting the inhabitants of the world keep you away from the world. And sometimes clinging to that tenet pays off.

I resolutely planned to skip the Purim bash, but I didn't. We checked it out, and we had a ball. For some reason, parents ventured forth with friendly, if clipped, overtures. A week later, at a birthday party for one of the kids, more adults initiated conversations, and Mikaila's play-date dance card began to fill up. Although my granddaughter had attended the school for eight months, I was just learning many of the parents' names, and they were just learning mine. The picture that kept coming to mind was that of a mountains' resolute stone face being blasted away.

So what happened? Did I "prove" myself in some fashion, maybe simply by always being there, chipping away at that mountain of resistance? Did Mikaila's relentless charm shame our would-be detractors into surrender? If I had to guess, I'd say that my perceptive four-year-old taught me that there's no place I don't belong—and with a shake of her grogger and a little help from her friends, she pulled open yet another door and beckoned me through.

The Responsive Reader

1 What made Smith enroll her granddaughter in the temple preschool? Was she naive in not anticipating the "discomfort" and the problems she encountered? Was this her first experience with being the only person of color in a predominantly white or all-white setting?

2 Smith is torn between her belief in diversity and "those ol' colored-girl terrors, those stark slaps of exclusion." When she felt marginalized by the parents at the preschool, was she feeling too defensive? Do you think she was "imagining things"?

3 Have you had experience with being exposed to the music, folklore, history, or rituals of another culture the way Mikaila is in this account? Do

you think such experiences have a lasting influence or result? Why or why not?

4   Was there a breakthrough in Smith's relationship with the parents, or was what happened a natural development? Although the author's tone is lighthearted most of the time, where does she turn most serious in sizing up what took place?

Talking, Listening, Writing

5   Smith describes Mikaila as "barreling her way through any pesky intolerance her playmates may have picked up from their parents." Based on your own experience or your observation of those you know well, do you think parents or peers influence children's views more strongly? Do you think that children are generally more "innocent" and more tolerant than their parents about racial, ethnic, and religious differences?

6   Smith's testimony is what social scientists call **anecdotal**—it is one person's story or one person's observation. It may mean something, and it may not. It may be representative, or it may not be. What in her account seems to you to be part of larger patterns? What do you think people who, like her, believe in diversity and tolerance can learn from her account?

7   As a parent, would you basically wish your children to go to school with others mostly of their own kind, or do you believe in the educational value of children mixing with others of a different background?

HOME TRUTHS ABOUT RACE

Joan Ryan

"I invited readers to share their views on how 'to instill in our children the ideal that color doesn't matter.'"

Joan Ryan is a columnist who represents the "well-meaning white liberal" position in the debate about racism. In preparing for the following column, she had invited readers to comment on how to teach young Americans that "color doesn't matter." Do you think her informal opinion poll would today yield significantly different results from when she first published it in 1998?

Thought Starters: Suppose a youngster—son or daughter, niece or nephew, kindergarten pupil—asked you what all the talk of race is about or what racism is. Where would you start? What would you say?

Two weeks ago, in a special . . . issue on race, I invited readers to share   1
their views on how "to instill in our children the ideal that color doesn't
matter."

The response has made me feel frighteningly stupid (an emotion always close to the surface anyway)—but also uplifted. Reading the letters
and e-mails was like sitting in on the kind of frank and unvarnished discussion you hear at family dinner tables, where the real-life issues of the world
are hashed out.

Of course color matters, readers said. "I get angry with all this talk
about our having achieved a color-blind society," wrote one Chinese
American man with two children. "I feel that is a lie that really just sets up
people of color to work harder at an unachievable goal. . . . Color-blind
means we all have to pretend that we can be white . . ."

An African American woman with a 12-year-old son wrote: "You
posed the wrong question. I've often thought that this premise . . . is at the
core of the problem of race relations. Color matters because, it's who we
are."

Another African American, a 32-year-old man in Berkeley, wrote: 5
"Being told (by my parents) that 'People are people' was not helpful when
I was consistently receiving the message from others that I was, in fact, dif-
ferent."

A Japanese American woman pointed out that kids "have enough
brains to look around and see that we live in a white-dominated society."
It's important, she says, to "give children the vocabulary for naming what
they see, so that racial hurts are not locked away inside them in silence."

Many also felt I gave my son a bad answer when, as we read a book
about Abraham Lincoln, he wanted to know why people were slaves. I told
him that white Americans used their power and prejudice to enslave blacks
for free labor.

"You taught him it's better to be white than to be black. I would have
been ashamed to do that to my kids," wrote one.

Others said I should have explained that slavery is not a uniquely
American horror. "Tell your son that other people of different skin colors
have also been held in slavery over history," one man said.

Another wrote: "Slavery, you might have said, is a bad thing no mat-   10
ter who does it. In this way, you would have put the focus where it belongs:
on slavery (rather than race)."

One father in Sonoma said I could have broadened the discussion
from slavery to oppression. "Kids understand that the powerful take advantage of the less powerful—they see it in the schoolyard and in the playing
fields. It was more important for us that our kids understand they should
never allow themselves to be oppressors. . . . The virtue we hoped to instill
was compassion."

Several parents said they tried to teach their children racial tolerance
by moving into racially diverse neighborhoods and sending their children to

diverse schools. "Then we raised them with the Golden Rule, simply to treat all people as they would like to be treated," wrote a mother in Berkeley.

A white Oakland mother of two who is married to an African-Caribbean man says the key is to talk. When her daughters asked why flesh-colored Band-aids didn't come in their "cafe au lait" skin color and why the good people on TV were white and the bad people weren't, "we discussed it so that it wouldn't become some kind of shameful secret."

"When our daughters were very young," the mother wrote, "we told them that people are like the flowers in the garden. They all come in different colors, and no color is better than any other."

Thanks for the lessons.

15

The Responsive Reader

1   In the liberal tradition, Ryan believes in the virtues of a "frank and unvarnished discussion." She believes in listening to a range of views. What is the range of views in the comments she reprints? Do any of them seem familiar or predictable to you? Are any of them particularly new or thought-provoking for you? Is there a latent consensus or common center?

Talking, Listening, Writing

2   How do *you* feel about trying to teach young Americans that "color doesn't matter"? Would you call this goal admirable? unrealistic? doomed to failure? the only hope for a better future?

3   What would have been your own response to Ryan's invitation to share views on how to instill the ideal of a "colorless" society in our children? Write a "Letter to the Future" to be read at a future time by a young relative or other young American.

DOUBLE STANDARD ON DRUG SENTENCES

Cynthia Tucker

"We have created laws designed to make the streets safe. And we have designed laws whose only result is to ensure that entire neighborhoods regularly send their young men off to prison."

As a syndicated columnist and the editorial page editor for the Atlanta Journal-Constitution, *Cynthia Tucker became known for her outspoken discussion of issues concerning "average working folk." She has written about the fraying social safety net, the need for jobs with decent pay, the need for ex-*

tending unemployment benefits, and access to health care. (In a recent column she cited figures from a Tax Policy Center claiming that during recent years of tax cuts for Americans the top 1 percent of income earners had received a 24.2 share.)

As one of America's best-known African American journalists, Tucker never expected much from presidential advisory boards, commissions on race relations, or "national conversations on race." However, she for a time saw hopeful new beginnings when voters elected a president who counted African Americans among his closest associates and whose childhood in Arkansas had given him "the cross-cultural training to eat and worship and pray with blacks with an ease that was natural." At the same time, good times economically could be expected to make whites more generous and less hostile and minorities less resentful.

However, the politics of personal destruction and lack of resolve on the part of white politicians squashed her hopes for a real conversation among the races that would address crime, cultural patterns that contribute to poverty, drug abuse, and "continuing race consciousness, if not outright racism." Tucker first published the following column in November 1998.

Thought Starters: Do you know Americans who have the "cross-cultural training to eat and worship and pray" with natural ease with Americans of a different racial background or ethnicity?

There are forgotten neighborhoods in America where the holiday season imposes a distinct and peculiar ritual: Mom and the kids, or Grandma and the grandkids, pack up a few goodies in tin plates and paper bags, carefully wrapped in foil. They set out early for a visit preordained to be brief and circumscribed, its joy limited by the setting. They go to visit a relative in prison.

The places in America already decimated by poverty and economic collapse—the black and brown inner-cities—are also places where many of the young men are out of circulation. They cannot become taxpayers or decent parents or reasonable prospects for marriage. They will leave prison with criminal records that guarantee them limited job opportunities.

Lacking decent incomes, they will never marry the mothers of their children. And that, in turn, will guarantee another generation of children who have had little contact with their fathers.

America has succeeded in locking up more of its citizens than any other country on the planet. The state of California alone has more inmates than France, Britain, Germany, Japan, Singapore and the Netherlands combined, according to a report by Eric Schlosser in the December issue of the *Atlantic Monthly*.

We have incarcerated violent, dangerous felons as well as non-violent   5
drug abusers. We have created laws designed to keep the streets safe. And
we have designed laws whose only result is to ensure that entire neighborhoods regularly send their young men off to prison.

And we have confused the one with the other.

Let's make some distinctions. Many convicted felons are thugs and
punks. Some of them practiced their violent tendencies on their families
and friends first—beating a girlfriend, robbing a neighbor, abusing a child.
They deserve to be in prison.

But a substantial portion of the 850,000 black Americans behind bars
are there for non-violent drug offenses. Marc Mauer of the Washington,
D.C.–based Sentencing Project estimates the number at 216,000—about
one-fourth. With drug treatment of the sort routinely available to drug-ad-
dicted actors and athletes, or to white-collar employees with good health
insurance, many of them would become tax-paying citizens, able to support
a family, own a home.

To avoid being labeled "soft" on crime, even politicians who know
better have refused to acknowledge a simple truth: We waste money, as well
as lives, when we lock up non-violent drug offenders.

"Among those arrested for violent crimes, the proportion who are   10
African-American men has changed little over the past 20 years. Among
those arrested for drug crimes, the proportion who are African-American
men has tripled. Although the prevalence of illegal drug use among white
men is approximately the same as that among black men, black men are five
times as likely to be arrested for a drug offense," Schlosser wrote.

We ought to be able to talk about alternative sentences for non-violent drug abusers—free drug treatment, with participation a condition of
probation, for example.

The streets may be safer because we have succeeded in locking away
for good many of the most dangerous predators, the gangbangers and serial
killers, the robbers and rapists and car-jackers. But the country is no better
off for a shameless double standard that celebrates the privileged athlete, actor or businessman who licks his drug habit in a ritzy sanitarium, while imprisoning the crackhead too broke to afford drug treatment.

That policy guarantees a permanent underclass.

The Responsive Reader

1   Tucker pounds home a familiar thesis: America keeps "locking up more
    of its citizens than any other country on the planet." Does she bring this
    central point to life for you? Where and how?
2   In discussing the huge prison population, Tucker emphasizes the price
    society pays beyond the cost of incarceration. What is the effect on fam-
    ilies and on the community? What are the aftereffects for the black com-
    munity and for society in general?
3   Tucker makes a basic distinction between violent and nonviolent of-

fenders. Do you think politicians could label her "soft" on crime? Why or why not?

4   According to Tucker, what is the "shameless double standard" society applies in the war on drugs?

5   Much of the dialogue on race in this country has been long on analysis of problems or diagnosis of social pathologies. It has been short on workable suggestions or positive advice. Do you find workable suggestions or positive advice in this column?

Talking, Listening, Writing

6   Sentimentality is a warm, self-approving feeling that allows us to feel generous and compassionate at no real cost to our own comfort or established routines. Do you think our tendency to remember the homeless, the poor, or prisoners at holiday times is sentimental? Do you think you are sentimental about the poor and unfortunate?

FIND IT ON THE WEB

You may want to search for articles on social and political trends in the black community like those published in *The Black Scholar,* a journal by Manning Marable and other African American intellectuals. You may want to check for websites of organizations like the NAACP, the Urban League, the Nation of Islam, or the Black Radical Congress.

Pushing Toward a Thesis

The Writing Process

1 Drawing on Your Experience
2 From Reading to Writing
3 Exploring Internet and Nonprint Sources
4 **Pushing Toward a Thesis**
5 Organizing Your Writing
6 Feedback and Revision

Make your thesis state the answer that your paper gives to the question or questions you have raised.

In much effective writing, readers look for the **thesis** or main idea. What is the point? What is the message? What key idea or challenge are the readers expected to remember?

As you finish exploring a current issue, what main point stood out for you after you explored the subject and gathered material? What is the main idea that the evidence you sifted will support? Your thesis is the central message that you want your readers to think about and perhaps act on—taking or supporting appropriate action. It is often most effective if it follows a brief introduction that dramatizes the issue or brings a central question into focus. The following introduction early shows readers that the thesis will be followed up by strong convincing examples:

Where Are You From?

"Latinos are hot-blooded." "Asian women are terrible drivers." "Mexicans come here to live on welfare." "Arab Americans support terrorists." "Sikhs wear turbans because they do not care enough to become real Americans." **As a greater range of immigrants comes into our country, prejudice is increasingly directed at a wider range of ethnicities.**

This thesis makes a claim that the rest of the paper will support. It creates expectations: Readers will expect that the writer will look in turn at several major groups of newcomers and show how they have become the target of negative stereotypes.

278

EDITOR'S TIP! It is true that a writer may choose to present valuable information or lay out data first. Then the writer may guide the reader through processing the information. However, effective writing often has a strong early thesis that makes a claim, answers a central question, sums up a trend, or presents a call for action.

Triggering

A paper with a strong thesis often sums up and defends your answer to a question in your readers' minds.

A paper may send a strong message when you take a stand on a current issue or alert you readers to an important current trend. For instance, for Americans of a current generation, is the Cold War or the Civil Rights struggle already ancient history? (Are we failing to learn from the past?) Will tests and more tests help "failing schools"? (Or will they penalize teachers and fail students?)

TAKING A STAND *Much writing takes a stand on a debated community issue.* You have a strong motive for writing when you want to testify or to make your voice count on a "hot-button" issue in your area or community.

KEY QUESTION: **Are big national chains driving out small community-based small businesses?**

Your current **test case** may be a "run-down" neighborhood shopping center that the city government was trying to shut down. The city was going to use the right of "eminent domain" to take over the run-down "eyesore" place long familiar to local residents. An anonymous "deep-pockets" national organization would then tear down the cheap jewelry store, mom-and-pop stores, and the tatoo parlor and put in a state-of-the-art shopping mall. Who initiated or supported the proposed takeover? Why did the city lose in court? Who mobilized opposition in the community? What were striking testimonies from the local business people and their customers?

WATCHING A TREND *Much writing anwers questions about current trends.* When do isolated examples begin to point toward an important change?

For instance, what are current trends related to the growing recognition of diversity in our lives? Are the traditional melting pot image and the goal of assimilation outdated? What has taken their place? The following is a choice of questions that could trigger your search for your answer as you focus on an ethnic, a cultural, or a linguistic group that you know well from personal experience and recent study or observation:

KEY QUESTIONS:
How "assimilated" were earlier or recent generations of immigrants? What was or is their relation to the old-country culture and their first language?

Is the current generation of "Generation 1½" immigrants or children of immigrants less assimilated or more assimilated than earlier generations?

Is the current generation of "Generation 1½" immigrants or children of immigrants becoming truly bilingual or bicultural?

Is our society headed for increasing separatism, de facto segregation, or ghettoization?

Gathering

Formulate your thesis after sifting and interpreting material from firsthand observation or close study.

Effective writers often present their pointed thesis "up front" as a guide and a promise to the reader, However, remember that a strong thesis is the result of careful data gathering or investigation.

For example, when a student writer claims that the United States long restricted immigration from Asia, we expect the writer to have done serious **fact-finding** to support this claim.

THESIS: It is only during last half century that the U.S. government has loosened restrictions on Asian immigration to allow Asian immigrants to show that they can be an asset to the nation. **For over 200 years, our government tried to close our borders to Asians.**

This thesis is a signal to the reader that the writer's claim is anchored in widely accepted historical fact. The student established the following timeline, drawing on sources including an encyclopedia of world history (updated in a new current edition edited by Peter N. Stearns):

TIMELINE:

1790 The Supreme Court upholds legislation making Asian immigrants ineligible for citizenship.

1882 The Chinese Exclusion Act bars Chinese laborers from entering the country.

1907 A "Gentlemen's Agreement" with the Japanese government limits Japanese immigration to the United States.

1917 Immigration Act bans virtually all immigration from Asian Pacific countries.

Shaping

Practice summing up your message or central claim in a thesis statement.

When you ask yourself: "What is my thesis?" you are preparing yourself to answer readers who ask: "What is the point?" How are you adding up your investigation and your thinking about your topic?

Study examples of writing that presents and follows up a strong thesis statement. For instance, parents, educators, and political leaders have witnessed years of heated debate on the national level and on the local grassroots level about what is happening to the nation's schools. The following might be the thesis statements of articles or editorials focusing on basic trends and developments. What is the key point that each writer is contributing to the debate? What supporting material or follow-up does the thesis statement make you expect?

> **THESIS: Schools remain under intense pressure to raise test scores with fewer dollars.**
>
> Ordering prepackaged tests is cheaper than hiring teachers and funding programs, and it holds out to administrators the promise of being able to satisfy the public demand for documented results.
>
> **THESIS: Charter schools have been promoted as more motivating and as more concentrated on academics than ordinary public schools.**
>
> Although recent studies show mixed results, charter schools have raised parents' hopes by attracting motivated students from a larger area and by being freer to use innovative approaches to learning than ordinary public schools.
>
> **THESIS: Science education in secondary schools has fallen behind, with problems ranging from a shortage of qualified teachers to inadequate lab equipment and other resources.**
>
> Science teachers can find better paying jobs in private industry, and adequate science facilities have been hard to fund.

THE PREVIEW THESIS   The last thesis in the sampling above is an example of a **preview thesis.** It already previews or programs the major sections of the paper. It sketches out the major waystations of the itinerary the writer is planning for the readers.

> **THESIS: Determined campaigns by parents and educators can reverse political decisions regarding teacher layoffs, library closings, and canceled programs.**
>
> Active citizen involvement is needed in campaigns to reverse the firing of teachers and counselors and other support staff, the dismissal of librarians and curtailed library hours, and the axing of the art and music actitivies that for many former students are among the most cherished memories of their high school years.

Revising

Revise a trial thesis to state what your observation or your evidence really shows.

A key step in revision is to go back to your trial thesis to make it truly sum up what your completed paper will tell the reader. Will your thesis take into account what you learned at a late stage of your search? Will it make allowance for exceptions or objections? Has your trial thesis proved premature? You may need to adjust it in the light of later findings. Does your conclusion show a more advanced stage of your thinking than the original thesis? Does it seem to contradict what you originally claimed?

Check for familiar reasons to sharpen your thesis:

- *A trial thesis may be too open or noncommittal.* It may still sound too much like a "fishing expedition."

TOO OPEN: The court ruled in favor of driving licenses for illegal aliens but questions remain.

(What key questions remain, and how are we going to find the answer?)

TOO OPEN: As with everything, there are two sides to the question, and there are advantages or disadvantages.

(What are the key points of either side, and which side will outweigh the other?)

- *A trial thesis is often too sweeping.* It may claim more than your evidence really shows. In final revision, you may have to scale down a trial thesis, making it less vulnerable to doubting questions by your readers.

TOO SWEEPING: Women are serving in the Armed Forces in increasing numbers and are proving the equals of male soldiers.

(Checking a report from an Army Research Institute, the student writer found that at the time the army was still restricting assignments in armor and in field and air defense artillery, and the navy excluded women from submarine warfare.)

REVISED: Although some combat roles and sensitive security roles are still closed to them, women in the Armed Forces are increasingly sharing duties and leadership roles.

EDITOR'S TIP! A thesis that has words like *all* or *never* in it is likely to be questioned by doubting readers. The same is true for a thesis that uses *they* and *them* as if all members of a whole group or a whole nation think the same.

A Paper for Peer Review

How does the following slightly shortened student paper support its thesis? What is the range of material that backs up the writer's central claim?

SHARPENING YOUR THESIS

Do peer reviewers or instructor comments ask you for a stronger thesis? Keep in mind advice like the following:

- *Spell out your thesis.* What exactly are you claiming? Did your trial thesis say that "certain factors" play a role in prejudice or homelessness? What are these factors? Which are the most important?

- *Claim what you can support or defend.* The following might be your thesis of a paper about the lack of political involvement among fellow students. Make sure you have the evidence that led to this charge:

THESIS: A pervasive apathy about political issues marks my cohort of students.

Turnouts for controversial speakers invited to your campus have been small.

Turnout for elections for student government has been dismal.

Debates scheduled on topics like AIDS and safe sex have fizzled.

Few students turned out for special events scheduled to honor minority authors or to recognize outstanding women on campus.

- *Limit your generalizations.* Guard against "jumping to conclusions." Readers will reject claims that people of one nationality or religion are more gifted or generous than another. Neither will educated readers listen to claims that members of any one group are inherently lazy or violence-prone. Less provocative generalizations—about voter apathy or about immigrants on welfare—may also have to be reworded and checked against the evidence you are actually able to present.

- *Follow up with representative examples.* Try to present a cross section of relevant instances. Try to listen to a cross section of witnesses, pro and con. Do not build your case on one outstanding case that might turn out to be an isolated example.

How real or convincing are the observations and commentary that led the writer to formulate her thesis?

The Thin Look

"I would do anything to look like a skinny model or a Barbie doll. I used to starve myself for days at a time. I lost a lot of weight, but when I started getting sick, I started eating and gained it all back." The anonymous seventeen-year-old who made this comment represents a feeling and experience

common to many young women in the United States. **Many women grow up with a fear of gaining weight and being criticized or belittled by society.**
————>>>>>>>>>>>>>>

(The **opening quotation** that serves as a preview of major emphases in the paper leads up to the **thesis.**)

A health pamphlet says "guilt about gaining too much weight may develop into fear." Many forms of social pressure give young women a standard of beauty to which they feel they need to aspire. Parents might be surprised to know that some simple gifts are psychologically harmful to children, like Barbie dolls. Little girls may compare their own bodies with those of the dolls and even begin to compete. Studies have been performed to translate the size of a Barbie doll into a real woman. While the doll's figure varies slightly in size, her waist measurement would not exceed twenty-three inches if human, and would, on average, be closer to seventeen. Her long legs would give her a height ranging from six feet, two inches to seven feet, five inches. A seven foot, five-inch Barbie woman would have a bust measurement of thirty-six inches. When a twelve-year-old compares her body to this popular standard, she is going to be very disappointed and may feel inadequate at a young age. ————>>>>>>>>>>>>>

(In this substantial paragraph, the writer starts her **support** of the thesis with a look at impressions formed at an **early age** and a graphic analysis of the Barbie anatomy.)

As young women mature, they are affected more by the media and by the incessant advertisement of images portraying unnaturally thin women. The media define "what forms of femininity are acceptable and desirable," in the words of a media consultant. Women are faced with models that symbolize how women should look, how they should behave, and how women can expect to be seen by others. Perfection is the ultimate goal. In a Chanel No. 5 perfume ad, there was a picture of French movie idol Catherine Deneuve beside an enlarged bottle of the perfume. She is an ageless, skinny woman with high cheek bones, beautiful eyes, and gold colored hair. She also looks very elegant. "What Catherine Deneuve's face means to us in the world of magazines and films, Chanel No. 5 seeks to mean and comes to mean in the world of consumer goods. It signifies flawless French beauty, which makes it useful as a piece of linguistic currency to sell Chanel," notes Judith Williamson in her piece on decoding advertisments. ————>>>>>>>>>>>>>

(Moving on to adolescence as a **second major stage,** the writer illustrate her point about the role of advertising with a detailed **case in point.**)

Various studies (including my own) have concluded that the ideal figure envisioned by a woman is slimmer than her own; this is also the figure that is most appealing to men. The models in the media often have a hard time portraying the supreme female image because there has been an "image-slimming effect" of over fifty percent since the turn of the century. One fashion model was quoted as saying it took a crew of people to get her into a pair of size three designer jeans and to carry her into position to be photographed: "To look as I did in that ad, you would have to fast for two months and hold your breath for twenty minutes."

Using an illustration of ten different female body types numbered from one to ten in size (excluding height), I asked ten women between the ages of sixteen and twenty to show me how they perceive their own body and how they would like to look. Eight out of ten said they would like to have the second to skinniest figure on the chart and the other two, already thin, said they would like to remain the same. ———>>>>>>>>>>>>>>

(In these two paragraphs, **live testimonies** on the artificiality of the media image and on the self-image of fellow students offer real-life support.)

As long as women continue to be bombarded with unhealthy standards of nearly unattainable slimness, the number of victims of eating disorders will steadily increase. Colleges have distributed pamphlets on anorexia and bulimia because of the problem with eating disorders among their students. Specialists blame mostly social pressures for the eating disorders suffered almost exclusively by young women. According to one study, a little over ten percent of college women had "a pattern of bingeing and purging." Many young women were taking unsafe "fat burning" pills. ———>>>>>>>>>>>>>

(The writer moves on to **serious effects**—the health hazards of the Thin Look.)

"When I watch a commercial or a news broadcast and I see a normal looking spokeswoman, it's shocking!" said a student. Not only have the media caused major health problems and sentiments of insufficiency on the part of women, but they have also begun to measure success, in part, in terms of beauty. Women have to learn to resist this media lure. If a woman does not interfere with her body's true chemistry is she neither successful nor beautiful? No. She is an individual who recognizes that beauty comes in all forms, shapes, and sizes.

(This **conclusion** moves beyond earlier points to challenge the connection between stereotypical ideals of beauty and success in our world.)

YOUR TURN:

1 Do you think the writer's *thesis* is too sweeping? Does she over-generalize?

2 How live or current are her *examples?* What is the mix of personal experience or testimony and outside sources?

3 Can you track the *network* of many phrases and expressions that keep the paper focused on the "look" or the "image" and its effects?

4 Do you think the paper should include more of the gross *details* of "bingeing and purging" for their deterrent effect? Why or why not?

5 Do you think the *conclusion* is limited to "good intentions"? Could the conclusion do more to suggest how women could resist the "media lure"? As a peer reviewer, could you recommend concrete steps or initiatives that the writer might endorse?

Writing Options 4: Formulating Your Thesis

1 In school or college today, is there such a thing as "in-group" status and "outgrouping" of others? For instance, were cliques a problem in high school, or are they now in college? Have you observed a "jock culture"? Is there a common pattern in the behavior of cliques or other "insider" groups?

2 Do you observe "voluntary segregation" by students from diverse ethnic, racial, or cultural groups? On your campus, do students of the same racial or ethnic background tend to flock together? How much mingling is there of people from diverse backgrounds?

3 To judge from your observation and experiences, is the current generation of "Generation 1 1/2" immigrants or children of immigrants less assimilated or more assimilated than earlier generations?

4 Is it true that current "Generation 1 1/2" immigrants or children of immigrants are becoming truly bilingual or bicultural? Do people you know or observe cross over easily from one language to the other? Do they function equally well in two different cultural contexts?

5 Is our society headed for increasing separatism, *de facto* segregation, or "ghettoization"? Who sounds such warnings? What questions do they raise? What would be your answer?

6 To judge from your contact with members of an older generation, how diverse were Americans of an earlier era? Political candidates appealing to patriotic sentiment claimed there was no room in this country for "hyphenated Americans." How fully assimilated were earlier or recent generations of immigrants? How would you describe their relation to the old-country culture and their first language?

7 To judge from your observation, reading, and viewing, is our society headed toward more "foreigner-bashing" or anti-foreign sentiment? Or are we becoming more "open to the world"?

8 Have you observed common traits in young people who are alienated from school or mainstream society? Have you observed a recurrent pattern in young people who get into trouble with the law?

9 To judge from personal experience, reading, or viewing, what immigrant group has the least (or the most) difficulty in adjusting to the new environment? Do you believe in the "myth of the model minority"?

10 Is your college, your community, or your generation becoming "color-blind"?

5
ROLES:
Constructing Gender

VISUAL LITERACY 5:

CULTURE WATCH: WHAT MEETS THE EYE

Do clothes "make a statement"? Like skin color, do they divide society into separate kinds of people? Different cultures have their own ways of emphasizing or playing down the differences in appearance that set apart men and women. If it is still true that "clothes make the man," is it also still true that the way she dresses makes a woman? Part of the emancipation of women in modern societies has been their freedom to wear slacks or jeans or tailored suits — clothing less obviously distinct than in the past from that of men. In many traditional societies, older women especially in rural areas dressed entirely in black. In fundamentalist societies, women still today wear burkas that completely shield the body and the face.

Reading the Image

1   How completely does *outward appearance* signal gender? Outward appearance by definition is the first thing that meets the eye. Look at the woman seated at the desk in the foreground of the picture. How many signals can you list that tell the viewer: "I am a woman"? Look at the two men seated across the aisle from the woman. How many signals can you point out that tell the viewer: "We are men"?

2   When does clothing become an issue in the *classroom?* At various times in different countries, school authorities have banned or tried to ban articles of clothing with a strong religious significance: the Muslim headscarf for women, or the Jewish yarmulke, the Sikh turban. What do you think is the reasoning justifying such initiatives? In a similar situation, would you support or oppose a similar policy?

3   How much does outward appearance affect your *first impressions* of people? For you, does a characteristic mode of dress make a statement? What does a black suit with a dress shirt and tie say to you? What message do cast-off army fatigues convey? What kind of person do you expect to wear a dress with a large flower pattern? Do you react negatively to a grunge look?

4   Have gender differences become less visible in the way Americans dress? Do you see evidence of a *Unisex trend* in clothing both in school and at work? How far has it gone in your generation? From what you observe, do you think it has peaked or been reversed? Do you think it is a good thing?

5   Do you think images like this one have a *universal meaning?* In many parts of the world, there has been a backlash against Western (American and European) influences. Do you think that when Americans try to decode the signals from other cultures they are like aliens from outer space — lacking a common language?

5

ROLES

Constructing Gender

The legal subordination of one sex to another is wrong in itself and now one of the chief hindrances to human improvement.

—JOHN STUART MILL

Many cultures have had assumptions about what it means to be a man and what it means to be a woman. What parents, counselors, teachers, and employers expect of a young woman may steer her toward options very different from those open to a young man. How much is biology—how true is it that "biology is destiny"? How much is culture—with boys taught from the beginning to be tough and adventurous, and girls taught from the beginning to be dainty and play with dolls? How much is genetic; how much is learned?

In recent decades, there has been a seismic shift in how we think about gender roles and how we define "masculine" and "feminine" traits. Today we no longer take it for granted that the judge will be male and the court clerk female, the physician a man and the nurse a woman, the manager a male and the secretary a female, and the police officer a male and the meter maid a female. Medical schools and law schools enroll large numbers of female students, pointing to something closer to parity down the road. All-male businessmen's clubs and military academies survive only in backwaters.

At the same time, while highly visible female CEOs and top managers are today less of a rarity, the top-level executive suites and boardrooms of American business are still largely peopled by males. Congress remains largely a white male preserve. The star athletes in many big-money sports are predominantly male. Women in pink-collar occupations are paid less than construction workers and truck drivers. Public school teachers are far from receiving pay comparable to that of other professionals.

Whether or not women consciously identify with the women's movement, they are likely to be involved in women's issues: There is growing concern about sexual abuse of women and children, with rape victims and women in battered women's shelters demanding less cavalier treatment by law enforcement and the justice system. The integration of women into the military has led to charges of sexual harassment and exploitation. Abortion rights are contested by male-dominated legislatures.

How do we become aware of the limits and opportunities that await us when we are identified according to such factors as gender or sexual orientation? What chance do we have to shape our own destiny, to forge our own identity?

FEW WOMEN PICK COMPUTER SCIENCE

Lisa M. Krieger

"Many female Internet users repeatedly say the digital world still heavily reflects male perspectives."

The author of the following article says that "the number of women online has increased rapidly." Is there nevertheless a gender gap in the age of information technology? A study by the Information Technology Association found that the number of women working in information technology had decreased from 41 percent of the workforce in 1996 to 34.9 percent in 2002. A 2003 report by the American Association of University Women reported that women were earning college degrees and entering the job market at a higher rate than ever. According to the AAUW report, however, most of them still opted for traditionally female careers. "Only 28 percent of women study subjects related to science, engineering or information technology—some of the highest paying and fastest growing fields." Krieger's article was one of many newspaper and newsmagazine articles reporting on initiatives designed to reverse these trends. Lisa Krieger wrote this article in 2002 for the San Jose Mercury News, *published in the city that advertises itself as the Capital of Silicon Valley.*

Thought Starters: Sally Ride, the first American woman to travel in space, has said. "More girls than boys start to drift away from science in middle school." In your own schooling, have you observed a gender gap in math and science classes? From what you have seen in classes you or friends have taken, is the gap narrowing or widening? What do you think accounts for the gap or for current trends?

One of the most troubling trends to emerge in higher education is the marked decline in women's participation in college-level computer science study.

In 1984, when computer science was relatively new, women earned 37 percent of undergraduate computer science degrees. In 1999, women earned fewer than 20 percent of computer science degrees, according to a study by Tracy Camp, an associate professor at Colorado School of Mines.

If this trend continues, by next year women will constitute only 16 percent of all computer science graduates.

Anita Borg, a pivotal figure in the field of computer science and the founder of the Institute for Women and Technology at Xerox's Palo Alto Research Center, explained the trend in the report "Balancing the Equation: Where Are Women and Girls in Science, Engineering and

Technology?" released last summer. A conference last week at Barnard College used the report to explore strategies to open the highest levels of science, engineering and technology to women.

"Part of the image of working on computers is working to create gadgets—techie stuff having nothing to do with people's lives," she said. "Young women want to have a positive impact on people. If we can get across that there are powerful ways to have a hugely positive impact on people, then maybe we can turn that image around."

Male Perspectives

The shortage of women in computer science hits everything from recruiting in the high-tech industry to software, Web sites and other computer-related products that eventually wind up in the hands of consumers. The number of women online has climbed rapidly, for example, but many female Internet users repeatedly say the digital world still heavily reflects male perspectives.

"Women are not there filling the slots, and the companies are too shortsighted to go out of their way to recruit them," Borg said. "Even when human resources people ask, 'How do we get the women? How do we bring in the minority people?' they only want to know how to get them this week. They are unwilling to consider their environment and their advertising.

Call for Perseverance

But some women working in computer-related fields also stress that working in a highly competitive area such as computer science requires resolve and a thick skin. To change computer science, they say, women will have to persevere and not abandon their research.

"It's really, really hard—but somehow women have gotten the message that it's OK to give up," said Teresa Meng, 41, a professor of electrical engineering at Stanford University and founder of the Sunnyvale-based wireless networking company Atheros Communications.

Meng's company now has 83 employees and is a leader in the race to develop computer chips that send and receive data over the airwaves—offering the promise of surfing the Web from anywhere, without wires.

"I don't know why—it's not biology—that when things get really hard, men are more likely to stick with it," she said.

The Responsive Reader

1   Young women's "disinterest" in science and technology is a matter of serious concern to trend watchers like Krieger. What were Krieger's *sources?* Where did she turn for informed opinion and reliable data? How and how fully does she identify them? How impressive or authoritative do they seem to you?

2 Where does Krieger most strongly state her overall *thesis?* Which of her data most strongly support her thesis? She says that the shortfall or short-age of women in the computer science field "hits everything." What are some of the areas affected? What are some of the repercussions?

3 According to Krieger, what *stereotypes* or contrasting expectations concerning the computer and the computer age divide the genders? How does what young women expect from life affect their attitudes?

4 Where in her article does the author recognize *countertrends?* What is the positive message or advice for young women that emerges from her article?

Talking, Listening, Writing

5 Some educators and corporations are promoting girls-only science camps or classes for female-students-only to motivate and prepare young women for the computer science and information technology fields. Critics have questioned the limiting or segregating effects of single-sex education. What do you think are the advantages and disavantages?

6 A researcher for the AAUW said, "Girls approach the computer as a tool—it's useful primarily for what it can do." On the other hand, "boys more often view the computer as a toy or an extension of themselves—what they can make of it, what they can do with it." Do you think this is true? If it is true, does it go counter to the familiar assumption that males are more practical-minded than females?

7 Writers tracking current trends are sometimes criticized for having re-lied too much on "anecdotal evidence." They have drawn mainly on what they have heard or seen, often including comments from by-standers or participants in events. Critics of anecdotal evidence say that it may or may not be truly representative. They look for scholarly stud-ies, for solid "facts and figures." As a trend watcher, which would you trust or rely on more, and why?

THE JOY OF WOMEN'S SPORTS

Ruth Conniff

"The effect of Title IX is evident in the freedom, strength, and joy of a whole generation of young women."

The author of the following article wrote it as the Washington editor of the Progressive *magazine. She traces the changes in women's collegiate sports since the passing of the 1972 Education Amendments Act, whose Title IX stated: "No person in the United States shall on the basis of sex be excluded from participating in, be denied the benefits of, or be subjected to discrimination under any educational program or activity receiving Federal financial assistance." Before Title IX, Division I colleges spent two percent of their athletic budgets on women's sports, and there were virtually no athletic scholarships for women. Title IX required colleges to allot an equal or proportionate share of money spent on athletic programs to women's sports—or risk losing all federal funding. In spite of challenges and reverses, and in spite of fitful enforcement, Title IX led to vastly increased participation of women in collegiate sports. The August 1998 issue of the* Nation *magazine that printed this article included an article by the author of a book on a women's basketball team, Lauren Kessler's* Full Court Press.

Thought Starters: Do you think women students are less interested in sports than men?

It has been my generation's great good fortune to grow up in the era of Title IX. Never before has a single law made it possible for so many previously disfranchised people to have so much fun. Since Title IX of the Education Amendments Act passed in 1972, requiring publicly funded schools to offer equal opportunities to male and female athletes, the number of American high school girls who play sports has jumped from one in twenty-seven to one in three. The effects are visible everywhere: an explosion of female Olympic stars, college and professional women's teams playing to packed stadiums, new magazines aimed at female athletes. But most of all, the effect of Title IX is evident in the freedom, strength and joy of a whole generation of young women.

In June I went to Buffalo, New York, to watch the NCAA track championships with Kamila Hoyer-Weaver, a young woman I coached when she was a high school runner, and her mother, Joan.

"What must it be like to get this far—to be ready at this level?" Joan mused, as we stood near the starting line before the women's 1,500-meter race. College runners in ponytails and racing flats were doing their warmup strides and nervously shaking out their legs. Behind us, a high jumper made the best attempt of the meet so far, and the stands erupted in cheers.

"For women my age it's a foreign thing to understand this competition," she said. "We weren't even raised to be competitive."

Kamila, a freshman at the University of Wisconsin, has an entirely different point of view. She came to watch her teammates who have made it to this elite level—some of the best athletes in the country. She has been steeped in competition, as a high school runner and basketball player, and now as part of a Division I college program.

I watched Kamila and her friends grow up during the six years I spent coaching runners at nearby Madison East High School—my alma mater. It was a joy to see those saucer-eyed kids on the starting line, pale and sometimes sick with nerves, propel themselves into accomplished, self-assured womanhood. This, it seems to me, is the whole project of adolescence—testing yourself, facing your fears, discovering what you can do. Sports provide the natural arena for it. Instead of turning inward, nurturing the crippling self-consciousness that often afflicts adolescent girls, these female athletes thrust themselves into the world. Along the way, they shed some of their peer group's cloying affectations and picked up an appealing jocky swagger. Kamila blossomed from a shy back-of-the-packer to a consistent varsity scorer in cross-country and track. At the end of her high school career, I traveled with her to the state meet where she ran a lifetime best in the 800, taking eighth place at 2:20.14. Now, she is reaching the next stage.

"She gets to run with the big girls," Kamila said admiringly of Kathy Butler, the NCAA cross-country champion from Wisconsin. The "big girls" are a group of Olympic hopefuls, including the famous Suzy Favor Hamilton, UW graduates who still train full time with their former college coach, Peter Tegen. "It's inspiring to see them on the track with us," Kamila says.

At Wisconsin, Kamila is in the center of women's track history. Coach Tegen, who founded the Wisconsin women's program twenty-five years ago, has nurtured a series of Olympians, beginning with Cindy Bremser, Wisconsin's first female All-American. In a speech at our girls' city banquet one year, Bremser told us how she began jogging for exercise in college and ended up at the Olympics, where she took fourth in the 1,500 meters in 1984.

"The talent that was developed while I was at Wisconsin has had an impact on the rest of my life," she said. "It's opened doors for me that I never would have dreamed of."

In the eighties, when I was running for East, Suzy Favor was starting her career on one of our rival teams, Steven's Point Area High School. She and her teammates would warm up together, a pack of fierce-looking girls with French braids and black-and-red windsuits. At the start of each race their fans chanted "SPASH! SPASH! SPASH!" Their coach blew a horn you could hear for miles as his runners came charging over hills and through the woods. Favor, who was a rocket even then, went on to become the four-time NCAA champion in the 1,500 and the American record-holder in the 1,000 meters.

All this is ancient history to Kamila, who is well beyond the gee-whiz era of women's sports. She takes it for granted that there is a long line of female champions in whose footsteps she can follow. She says her heroes are Amy Wickus, a 1995 graduate of Wisconsin and the indoor collegiate record-holder in the 800 (2:01.65), Hazel Clark of Florida, this year's winner of the outdoor NCAA women's 800 (2:02.16) and Michael Jordan ("but I guess he's everybody's hero").

After the meet, back at the hotel, she talks with ABC track commentators Carol Lewis, the Olympic long jumper, and Dan O'Brien, Olympic gold medalist in the decathlon. It's nice to see how easily she moves among these female and male stars. For much of the weekend, she has been hanging out with Gabe Jennings, her classmate from high school, now a freshman at Stanford. Gabe took second in the men's 1,500 and made the national news. The day before his final race, he was sitting in the stands with Kamila and her mom, watching the men's and women's races, trading track stories.

One of the best things about the rise of women's sports is the friendship and camaraderie it engenders between boys and girls. In track and other individual sports, male and female athletes travel together, support each other and have fun as a team. Because the goal of each athlete is to improve his or her own best performance, and because men and women go through the same workouts and races, there is a feeling of equality.

"It's easier to build friendships with guys who do track," says Avrie Walters, Kamila's teammate, who made it to the 1,500 trials at the nationals. "There's a kind of respect," Stephanie Pesch, another Wisconsin runner, adds. "It's like they understand what you've achieved."

"I like it, even if you're just training at the track and the guys yell for you," says Kamila.   *15*

At East High, the boys' and girls' cross-country runners were particularly close. They took turns hosting spaghetti dinners at their houses before meets. They ran along the course to cheer for each other during races. When both teams won the city meet, they did a victory dance together, beating on drums some of the boys had brought along, hopping around the finish chute, forming a crazy, mismatched can-can line and swinging each other by the arms in a spontaneous outburst of celebration.

These moments of coeducational enthusiasm are part of what's precious to me about my own experience in sports. Both in college and in a postcollegiate track club, I made lifelong friends with the men and women I ran with, shared the ups and downs of training and competition, and partied afterward. Hearing the encouraging words of my male track coaches, seeing my male teammates pound each other on the back and yell when my female teammates and I sprinted across the finish line to win, made an indelible impression on me. To the great benefit of us all, sports have changed how men look at women, and how women view themselves.

That's not to say there's no more conflict between the sexes when it comes to sports.

The *Washington Post* ran a story recently about the forty-six-year-old World Series for boys, which the Babe Ruth League is holding this August in Loudoun County, Virginia. In keeping with a musty tradition, tournament organizers have been advertising for local teenage girls to be "hostesses" to escort the players, entertain them and cheer for them during the tournament. Each girl, the *Post* reported, is supposed to wear a kind of modified baseball uniform with a skirt.

This idea went over like a ton of bricks with the female high school   20
athletes of Loudoun Country.

"You can consider me a feminist . . . when they told me about that, I said 'Nope,'" Brooke Hoeltzel, a junior at Loudoun Valley High School, said. "A lot of my friends are athletes, and they have the same view I did."

Tournament organizers were quoted blaming the culture of Washington, with all its professional women, for the problems their hostess-recruitment effort encountered. "In Kentucky and Arkansas it does fine," said Erik Zimmerman, who heads the Loudoun organizing committee for the boys' World Series.

But girls like Hoeltzel say they don't have time to jump around in a little skirt. They have their own summer-league games to play. After getting a taste of playing, it seems, there's no going back.

"I'm an athlete," Hoeltzel told me. "I'm not a cheerleader, I know that. This would make me a cheerleader."

"What's the big difference?" I ask.   25

"With an athlete I think of an equal, a guy and a girl," she says. "And with a cheerleader it's sitting on the sidelines. I'm not one to sit there and watch."

Joy Miller, a Loudoun County mother of two daughters, ages 9 and 12, agrees. Her 9-year-old, who plays fast-pitch ball in a 10-and-under league, has been hitting and catching since she was 4. And both girls are now trying out for a summer travel team. They've been all fired up since they attended a clinic put on by Olympic softball player Dot Richardson.

"My daughters would rather be out swinging a bat than being a hostess for the boys," Miller told me.

When I get hold of Erik Zimmerman on the phone, he sounds weary from the media attention his event has been getting, first from the *Post,* then from the local television stations. "It's interesting, they've all been women interviewing me," he says dryly. He wants to set the record straight: For one thing, the hostess uniforms are not skirts. "We figured out a long time ago that skirts were not appropriate. After all, they're going to a ball game. So what they're wearing are skorts," he says.

Skorts?

"It's a pair of shorts that look like a skirt."   30

I try to picture the girl athletes' reaction to this.

Zimmerman seems nice enough. He tells me about his 15-year-old daughter, who played three sports last year. "I'm the last person to denigrate women's sports," he says. But when I ask him if the Babe Ruth League has considered adding a girls' program, he says no. "I don't think girls are interested in playing baseball."

In spite of the boom in women's sports, a backlash is brewing against Title IX. Opponents of the law say it forces schools to cut men's programs in order to give women money and facilities they don't want or need.

Earlier this year, John Stossel of ABCs *20/20* offered one tale of the   *35* ravages of what he called "the equality police." At the Merritt Island High School in Florida, he reported, the boys' baseball team had a stadium with lights, bleachers, a concession stand and fancy scoreboard. The girls' softball team had a field just the other side of a locked fence, with patchy grass and no lavatories. Two softball players, Jennifer and Jessica Daniels, sued the school board for discrimination under Title IX.

"So the school board proposed a solution," Stossel intoned. "They would unplug the boys' scoreboard, shut down the concession stand and the press box and rope off the bleachers so no one could sit here. That would make things equal."

This scorched-earth response was not what the girls had in mind, of course. Stossel didn't bother to explain that their lawyer, Lisa Tietig of the ACLU, argued that it was unconstitutional to rope off the bleachers, since this would be discriminating against the boys. A judge agreed, and the boys got to keep their facilities.

I talked to Tietig after the *20/20* show aired, "I was so mad about that," she said. "It really distorted things. And of course everyone would hate the girls after seeing it."

The lawsuit, which has expanded to include all of the public schools in the county, is not scheduled for trial until the year 2000. But already for the girls in Merritt Island, the results of their legal action have been good. The school took down the locked fence between the boys' and girls' fields, so the girls and their fans can use the toilets. (Before the lawsuit, according to Tietig, the school had refused to consider unlocking the fence.) The school board paid for outdoor lights for the girls, and the community arranged to buy the girls a scoreboard and fix the grass. "The kids on the boys' and girls' teams have banded together," says Tietig. "And the parents of both teams helped each other out. They've been down on their hands and knees weeding the girls' field. It's a lot better."

In general, parents no longer accept the idea that their sons deserve a   *40* better shot at sports than their daughters. That is the transformative effect of Title IX.

Still, according to Billie Jean King, who started the Women's Sports Foundation when she retired from tennis, after twenty-five years schools have come only about halfway to compliance with Title IX. Overall, boys still have almost twice as many opportunities to play in school athletic programs as girls do.

"The Office of Civil Rights has been incredibly ineffective in executing its responsibility" to enforce the law, King writes in a foundation report. "Moms and dads are being forced to go to court and suffer the expense and animosity generated by such judicial solutions. While they have won their cases, it is clear that the promises of Title IX will not be realized in my lifetime if each school not in compliance must be taken to court to force them to 'do the right thing.'"

Lately, opponents of Title IX have been trying to persuade people that you can be in favor of girls' sports and still be against Title IX. Leo Kocher, a wrestling coach who heads the National Coalition for Athletics Equity, argued this case on *20/20*. "We're just perpetrating an awful thing against the men," he said. "We're saying we're punishing you because you have more interest in sports than women."

It's true that Division I colleges across the country have been eliminating men's minor sports, from wrestling to gymnastics to baseball. And many coaches blame Title IX. But budget figures from the colleges don't support the argument that women's teams are the cause. The NCAA's latest gender-equity study shows that budget increases over the past five years for Division I-A men's sports was more than three times larger than the increase for women. More important, at the same time that Division I-A colleges have been cutting minor men's teams, spending on the big programs— mainly football—has increased dramatically.

Sixty-three percent of the $1.7 million increase in funding for Division I-A men's sports over the past five years went to football. Just that extra money for football exceeded the total operating budget for *all* Division I-A women's sports combined. 45

"The real problem is that schools are refusing to hold the line on men's football and basketball budgets," says Donna Lopiano, executive director of the Women's Sports Foundation.

Football is the Pentagon of athletic department budgets. Big schools continue to pour the bulk of their money into it, leaving the other, small-budget sports to fight it out over the scraps.

Interestingly, the smaller Division II and III schools have actually added men's teams over the same period that Division I schools have been cutting them. As a result, men's participation in college sports is at an all-time high. When you count all men's teams in all divisions, men have seen a net increase of seventy-four teams since the advent of Title IX. "The poor schools are adding sports for men," Lopiano says. "The richest schools are dropping sports. Why? Because they're fueling the football monster."

Schools have a lot of control over how they allocate their sports budgets. And, contrary to popular belief, Title IX does not require that girls get the exact number of slots on a team as boys, nor the same amount of funding. Instead, it gives schools three options for meeting the requirements of the law. They can show (1) that female athletes are getting an opportunity to play sports proportional to their representation in the student population; or (2) that, even if female athletes are underrepresented, the school is making progress by gradually expanding the female sports program; or (3) that, even if female athletes are underrepresented, women and girls are getting as much opportunity to play as their interests demand.

It's a shame to see men's and women's minor sports pitted against each other, because they have a lot in common. They are less about entertainment for sedentary fans than about participation. They are more inclusive than the big-time, quasi-professional programs. And they are subversive in a way, because they are driven by something other than the values of the market. You often hear the word "pure" bandied about to describe college women's teams. It's part of their charm that, as in minor men's programs, the athletes are playing for the love of it, not because they're raising revenue or planning on a multimillion-dollar professional career.

"Sports are the laboratory of the human spirit," says Anson Dorrance, the coach of one of the winningest teams in women's soccer, the University of North Carolina Tar Heels. He says he's learned to enjoy his sport more by coaching the women's game. In his book, *Training Soccer Champions,* he talks about how his coaching style has evolved. As a men's coach at UNC for thirteen years, Dorrance says, he used a lot of negative techniques, yelling at and bullying his athletes, waging a constant battle of egos with his players. "You basically have to drive men, but you can lead, women," he writes. "And, in my opinion, the way you coach women is a more civilized mode of leadership."

Dorrance's female athletes responded badly to bullying, which forced him to become a more reasonable coach. On the flip side, he had to teach his players to overcome their training as girls to be sweet and passive. "They have this internal war going on between wanting to prove they are great soccer players and the social agenda of wanting to be accepted by the group," Dorrance writes of his younger players. "So when they go into direct confrontation with a veteran, it's almost like they feel they have to acquiesce."

To drill this out of his players, Dorrance throws them into what he calls a "competitive cauldron" at practice: "They sort of beat it into each other that it's okay to compete."

Clearly his athletes have got the message, winning national championship after national championship. Some have gone on to the world-champion US women's team, including April Heinrichs, the US team's assistant coach in 1996.

"I think women bring something incredibly positive to athletics," Dorrance told me. "They are wonderfully coachable and so appreciative of

50

55

anything you give them. If men could draw something from the women's model, their image would improve."

Out of the interaction of male and female athletes and coaches arises the prospect of a better approach to sports, and to life. That's good news not just for women but also for men. My colleague at East High, Ty Prosa, who switched from being a boys' coach to coaching the girls' track team, says this about his experience: "With boys, the old-fashioned idea is that coaches give orders, and the athletes are supposed to accept it. You're like a drill sergeant in the Marines. Girls have more questions. I was unprepared to deal with this questioning at first. It took me a lot of effort to overcome my feeling that it was a challenge to my authority. But now I really enjoy coaching girls. I'm more invested in their success, because they give me more feedback, and I've become a better coach."

Sports bring out the most fundamental parts of human nature. There's the potential for cruelty, cowardice and unethical behavior, as in any other social sphere. But sports can also put us in touch with the greatest parts of being human—our own courage, compassion and capacity for the sheer physical enjoyment of life.

The happiness and freedom sports bring us, as participants, is a radical notion in consumer culture. There's all that pleasure to be had, from ourselves and each other, without buying anything. That potential slips away when, instead of participants, we become only spectators. We let professional athletes become stand-ins for ourselves.

The Responsive Reader

1   For Conniff, what are dramatic outward signs of the "explosion" of women's sports? How does she dramatize the contrast between today's expectations and those of an earlier generation? What are some outstanding success stories she includes in her article?

2   According to Conniff, what role do sports play in helping adolescent women deal with the challenges and obstacles of growing up? How does the vastly expanded participation of young women in athletic programs help them move toward "self-assured womanhood"?

3   Does Conniff see the growth of women's sports as driving a wedge between the boys and girls she observes?

4   From the beginning, supporters of Title IX attracted much hostile attention from the defenders of traditional men's sports, in particular football and basketball. What kind of backlash does Conniff describe? What examples does she give of the initiatives or maneuvers of the opposition? On what grounds does she criticize the spin and methods of hostile media coverage?

5   How does Conniff counter charges that the growth in women's sports is a danger to traditional male sports? What figures does she use to support her position? What misconceptions does she try to counter?

6   In Conniff's view, why and how should supporters of men's and women's collegiate sports be natural allies against the influence of professional sports and the role of heavily commercialized programs? How is the growing influence of women having a positive influence on men's sports? What new ideal vision of the role of sports does Conniff sketch when she talks about "the prospect of a better approach to sports, and to life"?

Talking, Listening, Writing

7   Have you seen evidence that a commitment to women's sports can "transform" women's lives? What evidence have you seen that the increased visibility of women athletes is changing the way we think about sports?

8   Do you know people who see the push toward women's sports by the "equality police" as a threat to traditional male sports? What are their arguments or concerns? Do most people you know accept or support growing support for women's athletics?

9   One supporter of women's sports said, "There are too many magazines out there that tell us how to do our hair, what to wear." In the treatment of women's sports, have you seen a shift in emphasis from looking good or "aesthetically pleasing" to performing well? (Are cheerleaders passé?)

Collaborative Projects

10   You may want to team up with classmates to investigate how women's sports are prospering in local schools and area colleges. What can you find out about funding, morale, media coverage, unresolved issues?

FIND IT ON THE WEB

Fitness magazines for women—with titles like *Shape, Fit,* and *Self*—tend to focus more on weight loss, aerobics, or trends in workouts than on team play and athletic competition. *Sports Illustrated* started to develop a spinoff focused on women and sports, and Condé Nast created a publication called *Women's Sports and Fitness* aimed at the same market. At the time this article was written, *Girljock* magazine focused on "hard-core" sports—like hockey, rugby, kickboxing, rock climbing. Websites recommended to sports and fitness enthusiasts included *Go, Girl* (www.gogirlmag.com) and *W.I.G.* (www.wigmag.com).

FACING DOWN ABUSERS

Im Jung Kwuon

"A criminal charge plus 52 classes encourages an abuser to give up violence and intimidation as control strategies."

The following account was first published in August 1998 as part of a Newsweek *tradition of allotting space to candid personal testimonies.*

Im Jung Kwuon is a Korean American woman who works in Los Angeles as a counselor in a domestic-violence-prevention program. The women's movement has everywhere raised public awareness of violence against women: Communities today have domestic-violence hotlines, shelters for battered women, and more effective police intervention. Kwuon is one of the countless anonymous dedicated professionals who make it their life's work to help others. At the same time, Kwuon's article makes it clear that there are no quick fixes or cheap solutions for the social pathologies that impact people's lives.

Thought Starters: If you were to observe or witness a case of domestic violence, what would be your reaction? Would you be likely to intervene? Would you stay out of it? Would you tell others not to "get involved"?

I always wanted a safe life after recovering from alcoholism, two suicide attempts and abusive relationships. But could I truly be safe if others were in danger? Helping families became part of my recovery. Now I work with men who beat and sometimes kill the women they love. I counsel those who are court-ordered attendees to a yearlong domestic-violence prevention program. Some people hearing this step back startled, cringing at a familiar memory of abuse. Others glare, accusing me of coddling bad guys by teaching them anger-management skills.

Even cops twice my size say they would be scared to go into my classes. They say that domestic calls are the worst, too dangerous. I tell them, "Hey, my groups are as safe as you'll get. Come see what it's like. I'll protect you." They look skeptical since I'm a petite, 40-year-old, Korean-American woman. My bravado hides the fact that I've shopped for a bulletproof Kevlar vest. I've fingered the high-tech, impenetrable material, wondering if it would be a good investment. I choose not to buy one, because fear is my worst enemy.

I wish I had been wearing a vest when enrolling some batterers into the classes. They scream curses and pace threateningly. They rarely admit to having beaten their partners or children. When they do, most cling to a justification. "She made me punch her." I always suggest they take a timeout to cool off until the next class. When they choose to de-escalate, both classmates and family are less likely to get hurt.

Recovery begins when men can express anger without intimidating others. It continues when they can recount how often they saw their mothers slapped, choked or hit with a two by four. I encourage them to share painful childhood experiences, but remind them there is no excuse for abuse.

I remain on guard even after healing days. When a group member *5* shakes my hand or brings flowers in gratitude, I remember that emotional intimacy is dangerous for both victims and victimizers. Batterers usually injure only those they care about. Getting close to one is like building a home on the slopes of a dormant volcano. Occasionally, I hear encouraging reports from partners of former clients. One joyful wife called a year after her husband finished the class. She gushed, "We had a big fight and he didn't hit me. I should've called the police 10 years ago."

After working with batterers for four years, I no longer have unrealistic expectations of success. I remember a young man I'll call Joey. He attended 14 classes, entertaining us with clever jokes and reassuring us that he was getting along with his girlfriend. Then he dropped out. Two months later, I saw on TV that Joey had shot her in the chest and killed her. Six months earlier, she had given birth to their second son.

For weeks I cried and lost sleep, wondering if I could have saved her life. I pored over the newspaper, looking for names of former clients charged with homicide. Can the chain of domestic violence ever be broken? Recovery frequently includes relapse. So it wasn't surprising when a man called me after getting my number from his cellmate, a former client doing hard time for a second spousal-abuse charge. I reflected back to a decade ago when domestic-violence calls were less frequent and counseling haphazard. Today, an arrest often follows a 911 call. A criminal charge plus 52 classes encourages an abuser to give up violence and intimidation as control strategies. Families benefit because batterers can learn to become safer partners and fathers.

Without help abusers can also lose their lives. Last year after Father's Day weekend, one group talked about who among them got drunk, who picked a fight, who walked away for a timeout. Near the end of that session, a man I'll call John revealed how he had lost his father that past Sunday. "Just before midnight, my mom called me for help. Dad was drinking and beating her. Like times before, he pointed a shotgun at her, but this time they wrestled with it and she shot him." John choked up. "I got there too late," he explained.

John stayed behind to confess, "I know it was an accident. This has been going on since I was a kid, but even at Dad's funeral I couldn't forgive her. I couldn't look at my mom's face." He added, "I can't come back for a while." I hugged him goodbye, encouraging him to return soon.

I knew he needed our support as much as the group needed him. *10* John's courage in telling other batterers about his loss could help prevent tragedy in their lives now. Confronting abusers with the consequences of their behavior increases the chance their families will survive and recover. Unfortunately, counseling cannot save or heal people who never try it. As a young adult, I took up with increasingly abusive boyfriends. I remember standing mute when a boyfriend punched a wall. He said my anger provoked him. I felt I was going to be hit next. Being a paralyzed victim or witness supports abusers. I learned this the hard way.

After salvaging my life through counseling, I've realized how powerful batterers are. They scare the world, because no one wants to face them. Often they are our family leaders. We still struggle to love and be loyal to them. I teach abusers how to be safe physically and emotionally. But no one is safe until every batterer is held accountable for his behavior.

For me, safety means that I'm prepared to call the police if anyone gets violent. This rule applies even to family and friends. But strengthening this basic security doesn't shield me from sadness and pain.

When I watched John walk away, I realized I had embraced someone experiencing my ultimate nightmare. No one in his family called 911 for the domestic violence, just the death. Breaking the chain of family abuse is a good job, even if it hurts.

The Responsive Reader

1   What would you include in a sketch of the counselor's own personal history? Do you think a person with her history would find it hard to be objective or professional, or do you think it is essential that a counselor or therapist should have lived through some of the experiences that she deals with in her professional capacity?

2   Kwuon talks about abusers on the basis of close personal observation and extended professional involvement. To judge from her article, what are major constants or predictable factors in the psychology of abusers? What are likely to be common elements in their background? What are recurrent patterns of behavior? What causes them to be the way they are, and what makes them act the way they do?

3   Kwuon says she no longer has "unrealistic expectations of success," and she offers no panacea. What is she trying to tell her readers about the successes and limits of counseling or therapy? What is the "bottom line" in the advice she gives to victims or to families?

4   What for you is the most revealing or thought-provoking case history in this article?

Talking, Listening, Writing

5   Kwuon works in a court-ordered program for offenders. Overall, how much good do you think her kind of work does? (Do you think she is "coddling bad guys"? Would you rather not hear about her kind of work in the first place?)

6   Do you think there is too much or not enough emphasis in our society today on women as victims?

WHAT'S LOVE GOT TO DO WITH IT?

Anjula Razdan

"Who hasn't at some point—at the end of an ill-fated relationship or midway through a dinner with the third 'date from hell' this month—longed for a matchmaker to find the right partner"?

In many traditional cultures, marriages were arranged between the two families, often with the help of a matchmaker or go-between. Often a younger generation influenced by Western ideas began to defy tradition by winning approval for love marriages. In a hugely successful Bollywood movie from India, the oldest son defies his stern traditional father and leaves the country to marry the woman he loves. "It is too bad God did not give you a heart," the younger son tells the patriarch.

In the following article published in the Utne Reader *for May/June 2003, Anjula Razdan asks her readers to take a second look at the failures of Western Romantic love. Half of the marriages in the cultures of the West fail, and the average duration of a marriage is estimated at seven years. Are we ready to consider the idea of marriage as a more lasting practical arrangement? Razdan weighs the the pro and con of marriage based on the illusions of romantic love and marriage based on more realistic practical assumptions.*

Razdan was born and raised in the American heartland as the daughter of immigrants from India, and she is a careful observer of cross-cultural encounters. She has written about the isolation of Americans from much of the rest of the world as a result of the lost art of translation. Few literary works from countries other than perhaps France or Germany are published in English translations. "We live in a tremendous isolationist bubble," says a publisher of books from other cultures who is trying to help Americans "get to know our neighbors in the world."

Thought Starters: What do today's marriage vows say? What promises do they make? What do they say about the hopes and expectations of the couple?

One of the greatest pleasures of my teen years was sitting down with a bag of cinnamon Red Hots and a new LaVyrle Spencer romance, immersing myself in another tale of star-crossed lovers drawn together by the heart's mysterious alchemy. My mother didn't get it. "Why are you reading that?" she would ask, her voice tinged with both amusement and horror. Everything in her background told her that romance was a waste of time.

Born and raised in Illinois by parents who emigrated from India 35 years ago, I am the product of an arranged marriage, and yet I grew up under the spell of Western romantic love—first comes love, *then* comes marriage—which both puzzled and dismayed my parents. Their relationship was set up over tea and samosas by their grandfathers, and they were already engaged when they went on their first date, a chaperoned trip to the movies. My mom and dad still barely knew each other on their wedding day—and they certainly hadn't fallen in love. Yet both were confident that their shared values, beliefs, and family background would form a strong bond that, over time, would develop into love.

"But, what could they possibly know of *real love?*" I would ask myself petulantly after each standoff with my parents over whether or not I could date in high school (I couldn't) and whether I would allow them to arrange my marriage (I wouldn't). The very idea of an arranged marriage offended my ideas of both love and liberty—to me, the act of choosing whom to love represented the very essence of freedom. To take away that choice seemed like an attack not just on my autonomy as a person, but on democracy itself.

And, yet, even in the supposedly liberated West, the notion of choosing your mate is a relatively recent one. Until the 19th century, writes historian E. J. Graff in *What Is Marriage For?: The Strange Social History of Our Most Intimate Institution* (Beacon Press, 1999), arranged marriages were quite common in Europe as a way of forging alliances, ensuring inheritances, and stitching together the social, political, and religious needs of a community. Love had nothing to do with it.

Fast-forward a couple hundred years to 21st-century America, and you see a modern, progressive society where people are free to choose their mates, for the most part, based on love instead of social or economic gain. But for many people, a quiet voice from within wonders: Are we really better off? Who hasn't at some point in their life—at the end of an ill-fated relationship or midway through dinner with the third "date-from-hell" this month—longed for a match-maker to find the right partner? No hassles. No effort. No personal ads or blind dates.

The point of the Western romantic ideal is to live "happily ever after," yet nearly half of all marriages in this country end in divorce, and the number of never-married adults grows each year. Boundless choice notwithstanding, what does it mean when the marital success rate is the statistical equivalent of a coin toss?

"People don't really know how to choose a long-term partner," offers Dr. Alvin Cooper, the director of the San Jose Marital Services and Sexuality Centre and a staff psychologist at Stanford University. "The major reasons that people find and get involved with somebody else are proximity and physical attraction. And both of these factors are terrible predictors of long-term happiness in a relationship."

At the moment we pick a mate, Cooper says, we are often blinded by passion and therefore virtually incapable of making a sound decision.

Psychology Today editor Robert Epstein agrees. "[It's] like getting drunk and marrying someone in Las Vegas," he quips. A former director of the Cambridge Center for Behavioral Studies, Epstein holds a decidedly unromantic view of courtship and love. Indeed, he argues it is our myths of "love at first sight" and "a knight in a shining Porsche" that get so many of us into trouble. When the heat of passion wears off—and it always does he says—you can be left with virtually nothing except "lawyer's bills."

Epstein points out that many arranged marriages result in an enduring love because they promote compatibility and rational deliberation ahead of passionate impulse. Epstein himself is undertaking a bold step to prove his theory that love can be learned. He wrote an editorial in *Psychology Today* last year seeking women to participate in the experiment with him. He proposed to choose one of the "applicants," and together they would attempt to fall in love—consciously and deliberately. After receiving more than 1,000 responses, none of which seemed right, Epstein yielded just a little to impulse, asking Gabriela, an intriguing Venezuelan woman he met on a plane, to join him in the project. After an understandable bout of cold feet, she eventually agreed.

In a "love contract" the two signed on Valentine's Day this year to seal the deal, Epstein stipulates that he and Gabriela must undergo intensive counseling to learn how to communicate effectively and participate in a variety of exercises designed to foster mutual love. To help oversee and guide the project, Epstein has even formed an advisory board made up of high-profile relationship experts, most notably Dr. John Gray, who wrote the best-selling *Men Are From Mars, Women Are From Venus*. If the experiment pans out, the two will have learned to love each other within a year's time.

It may strike some as anathema to be so premeditated about the process of falling in love, but to hear Epstein tell it, most unions fail exactly because they aren't intentional enough; they're based on a roll of the dice and a determination to stake everything on love. What this means, Epstein says, is that most people lack basic relationship skills, and, as a result, most relationships lack emotional and psychological intimacy.

A divorced father of four, Epstein himself married for passion—"just like I was told to do by the fairy tales and by the movies"—but eventually came to regret it. "I had the experience that so many people have now," he says, "which is basically looking at your partner and going, 'Who are you?'" Although Epstein acknowledges the non-Western tradition of arranged marriage is a complex, somewhat flawed institution, he thinks we can "distill key elements of [it] to help us learn how to create a new, more stable institution in the West."

Judging from the phenomenon of reality-TV shows like *Married By America* and *Meet My Folks* and the recent increase in the number of professional match-makers, the idea of arranging marriages (even if in non-traditional ways) seems to be taking hold in this country—perhaps nowhere more powerfully than in cyberspace. Online dating services attracted some 20 million people last year (roughly one-fifth of all singles—and growing), who used sites like Match.com and Yahoo Personals to hook up with potentially compatible partners. Web sites' search engines play the role of patriarchal grandfathers, searching for good matches based on any number of criteria that you select.

Cooper, the Stanford psychologist and author of *Sex and the Internet: A Guidebook for Clinicians* (Brunner-Routledge, 2002)—and an expert in the field of online sexuality—says that because online interaction tends to downplay proximity, physical attraction, and face-to-face interaction, people are more likely to take risks and disclose significant things about themselves. The result is that they attain a higher level of psychological and emotional intimacy than if they dated right away or hopped in the sack. Indeed, online dating represents a return to what University of Chicago Humanities Professor Amy Kass calls the "distanced nearness" of old-style courtship, an intimate and protected (cyber) space that encourages self-revelation while maintaining personal boundaries.

And whether looking for a fellow scientist, someone else who's HIV-positive, or a B-movie film buff, an online dater has a much higher likelihood of finding "the one" due to the computer's capacity to sort through thousands of potential mates. "That's what computers are all about—efficiency and sorting," says Cooper, who believes that online dating has the potential to lower the nation's 50 percent divorce rate. There is no magic or "chemistry" involved in love, Cooper insists. "It's specific, operationalizable factors."

Love's mystery solved by "operationalizable factors"! Why does that sound a little less than inspiring? Sure, for many people the Internet can efficiently facilitate love and help to nudge fate along. But, for the diehard romantic who trusts in surprise, coincidence, and fate, the cyber-solution to love lacks heart. "To the romantic," observes English writer Blake Morrison in *The Guardian,* "every marriage is an arranged marriage—arranged by fate, that is, which gives us no choice."

More than a century ago, Emily Dickinson mocked those who would dissect birds to find the mechanics of song:

> Split the Lark—and you'll find the Music—
> Bulb after Bulb, in Silver rolled—
> Scantily dealt to the Summer Morning
> Saved for your Ear when Lutes be old.
>
> Loose the Flood—you shall find it patent—
> Gush after Gush, reserved for you—

Scarlet Experiment! Skeptic Thomas!
Now do you doubt that your Bird was true?

In other words, writes Deborah Blum in her book, *Sex on the Brain* (Penguin, 1997), "kill the bird and [you] silence the melody." For some, nurturing the ideal of romantic love may be more important than the goal of love itself. Making a more conscious choice in mating may help partners handle the complex personal ties and obligations of marriage; but romantic love, infused as it is with myth and projection and doomed passion, is a way to live *outside* of life's obligations, outside of time itself—if only for a brief, bright moment. Choosing love by rational means might not be worth it for those souls who'd rather roll the dice and risk the possibility of ending up with nothing but tragic nobility and the bittersweet tang of regret.

In the end, who really wants to examine love too closely? I'd rather curl up with a LaVyrle Spencer novel or dream up the French movie version of my life than live in a world where the mechanics of love—and its giddy, mysterious buzz—are laid bare. After all, to actually unravel love's mystery is, perhaps, to miss the point of it all.

The Responsive Reader

1   How does Razdan explain and defend the traditional arranged marriages to a *skeptical audience?* Many of her readers are likely to consider them fully outmoded, and they had offended her own "ideas of love and liberty" as a teenager. How does she describe the marriage of her immigrant parents? How did it work? What values did it embody?

2   How does Razdan *contrast* the tradition with a trend toward failure or disappointment in modern marriage? How familiar are her data? Are her explanations familiar, or do they throw new light on the subject for you?

3   How has online dating challenged *traditional assumptions* about dating and marriage? How does it work, and how widely has it spread? What does Razdan see as its attraction and advantages?

4   What is Razdan's *definition* of Romantic love? What are key elements in Razdan's profile of the "die-hard Romantic"? Which of them do you recognize? Could you initiate a newcomer into the traditional vocabulary of Romantic love recognized by Razdan: "love at first sight," "star-crossed lovers," fate myth, "doomed passion," "tragic nobility," and "bittersweet" regret? Does she leave out important concepts, feelings, or expectations? What would you include in your own extended definition?

5   What is Razdan's mix of *sources?* How credible or informative do they seem? How does she blend material from her sources and from personal observation?

Talking, Listening, Writing

6   Do you think computer dating involves no magic or "chemistry"?

7   Have you experienced or observed proposed ways of strengthening modern marriage? Could you report on "love contracts" stipulating rights and obligations? marriage counseling? support groups? other activities or initiatives?

THE NEW MOMISM

Sue Hutchison

"Stories about the mom debate usually focus on the narrow segment of the population that can afford to stay home."

For years political candidates and media voices have talked about "family values" and "defending the traditional family." At the same time, the media have given much coverage to the social changes that are the focus of the following article. Women in large numbers have joined the workforce. Growing numbers of single mothers are supporting families. Many families are two-income families so they can plan to buy a home or send children to college. There is growing recognition of the need for accessible and affordable child care for mothers working outside the home.

Is there a backlash against these trends? Is there a backlash against the trend toward growing numbers of women in the workforce? Is it good or bad for children if mothers spend much of the day at work? Sue Hutchison, who published this column in March 2004, is a columnist for a Knight-Ridder newspaper who sees the "new momism" as a threat to gains made by the women's movement.

Thought Starters: In your own everyday world, which is the most typical or most common kind of household—a couple with both working outside the home, a couple with one working outside the home, a single mother working outside the home, househusband as homemaker while partner works outside the home?

For the past several years, I've noticed a new defensiveness among the working mothers I know who've been subjected to the Office Mom/Day Care Guilt Trip.

Often it's camouflaged as sympathy: "Isn't it sad that there are so many kids in day care? I hope they're not scarred for life." Even working mothers who have excellent child care are likely to snap, "Hey, I can't afford to stay home! You think I work 60-hour weeks to feel 'fulfilled'?"

No Apology Needed

Of course, most mothers have to work because their husbands' incomes aren't enough to support the family or because they're supporting their families alone. But why are mothers with satisfying careers apologizing for putting their kids in day care and having office jobs that are important to them for reasons beyond their paychecks?

According to authors Susan J. Douglas and Meredith W. Michaels, the answer is the "new momism." In their recently published book, *The Mommy Myth,* Douglas and Michaels define this as a tyrannical philosophy promoted in the media: "To be a remotely decent mother, a woman has to devote her entire physical, emotional and intellectual being, 24/7, to her children." The tenets of new momism imply that any woman who has an outside career is failing her family.

Douglas, a University of Michigan professor who has one child, and Michaels, a teacher of philosophy at Smith College who has five children, blast new momism as hostile to working mothers and a thinly disguised attack on the women's movement.

"Now mothers have seen the error of their ways, and supposedly seen that the June Cleaver model, if taken as a *choice,* as opposed to a requirement, is the truly modern, fulfilling, forward-thinking version of motherhood," they write. "In other words, ladies, the new momism seeks to contain and, where possible, eradicate, the social changes brought on by feminism."

But what's happening in the workforce reflects the changes brought on by feminism. According to a study released last fall by the Families and Work Institute, women are more likely to work as managers or professionals than men—38 percent of women compared to 28 percent of men. Is it likely that all of those women are pursuing high-powered careers only so they can bring in big salaries? Would they all rather be staying home with their kids if they had a choice?

That's what the cover of a recent issue of *Time* magazine would have us believe. The headline: "The Case For Staying Home/Why More Young Moms are Opting Out of the Rat Race," was accompanied by a photo of a blond moppet clutching the legs of an unseen mother. But many of the mothers profiled in the story said that though they were leaving their office jobs to stay home with their kids, they intended to return to the workforce eventually. And their careers are important to them.

What About Fathers?

Stories about the mom debate usually focus on the narrow segment of the population that can afford to stay home—and rarely on how fathers factor into the equation.

But even many mothers I've spoken with over the years who have lower-income jobs say they wouldn't want to quit. They like what they do and think they're better parents when they're not with their kids all day. Is that heresy?

Mothering in the 21st century isn't one-size-fits-all. Mothers shouldn't have to apologize for staying home with kids or for having an office job. We need better child care options, more enlightened corporate attitudes about flex-time, part-time and sabbaticals for women *and* men—and no guilt trips.

We haven't come this far just to be bullied by the new momism.

The Responsive Reader

1 The working mothers and career women Hutchison champions in her article do not fit a single *profile*. They come from various social levels. They have different needs, motives, and attitudes. They find themselves at different stages in their lives or in their careers. However, can you identify and describe several major types or kinds of "women at work" from this article?

2 What *evidence*—what sources and examples—does Hutchison cite of the "guilt trip" laid on women in the current "mom debate"? Have you seen evidence of the media or politicians laying a guilt trip on mothers working outside the home? Have you observed something like it in your own experience?

3 What *initiatives* are designed to help mothers working outside the home deal with child care and other demands of parenting? How would measures like "flex-time, part-time, and sabbaticals for women and men" help mothers reconcile the demands of family and work? How widespread and how realistic are these and other proposed initiatives?

Talking, Listening, Writing

4 What is the *media image* of the "working mother"? The cover for a *Time* magazine issue featuring a major story about "staying home" showed a blond moppet clutching the mother's leg. What pictures of mothers do you see in the news media? How realistic or representative are they? In your real world, have you observed women bringing small children to school or to work? How do they manage? What is the attitude of management or coworkers?

Collaborative Projects

5 Working alone or with a group, can you check out relevant facts and figures? How many mothers support their families alone? Hutchison contrasts them with "the narrow segment of the population that can afford to stay home." How narrow is the segment? Are there statistics on affluent families where women do not need to work outside the home?

THE COMMUNITY OF MEN

Robert Bly

"The journey many American men have taken into softness, or receptivity, or 'development of the feminine side,' has been an immensely valuable journey, but more travel lies ahead."

The following selection is an excerpt from a widely read and debated book claiming that the women's movement and the resulting reexamination of gender roles had left many young men disoriented or confused.

Robert Bly is an award-winning poet, storyteller, showman, translator, and guru who lives on a lake in Minnesota. He grew up as his mother's favorite and as the son of a kindly but distant alcoholic father. He has traveled around the country doing sold-out poetry readings that bring back the days when poetry, interwoven with song and story, was a communal experience that helped shape people's views of themselves and of the world. He became a leader of the men's movement with his book Iron John: A Book about Men *(1990), which looked in myth and popular tradition for heroic archetypal figures who could serve as inspiration and role models for the disoriented modern male. He explored rites of initiation that would bring young males closer to their natural and instinctual roots and turn the overmothered boy into a man.*

One reviewer of Iron John *said, "No poet in the United States in recent years has commanded so much attention. As a popularizer of archetypal psychology Bly has found a growing audience through public readings and lectures and more recently through a Bill Moyers television program which highlighted the wilderness 'gatherings' of men who have engaged with Bly on a ritualized variant of the 'talking cure.'" (Stephen Kuusiso).*

Thought Starters: If you were to nominate a living contemporary as a role model for young boys, who would it be? How would you justify your choice?

We are living at an important and fruitful moment now, for it is clear   1
to men that the images of adult manhood given by the popular culture are worn out; a man can no longer depend on them. By the time a man is thirty-five he knows that the images of the right man, the tough man, the true man which he received in high school do not work in life. Such a man is open to new visions of what a man is or could be.

The hearth and fairy stories have passed, as water through fifty feet of soil, through generations of men and women, and we can trust their images more than, say, those invented by Hans Christian Andersen. The images the old stories give—stealing the key from under the mother's pillow, picking up a golden feather fallen from the burning breast of the Firebird, finding the Wild Man under the lake water, following the tracks of one's own wound through the forest and finding that it resembles the tracks of a god—these are meant to be taken slowly into the body. They continue to unfold, once taken in.

It is in the old myths that we hear, for example, of Zeus energy, that positive leadership energy in men, which popular culture constantly declares does not exist; from King Arthur we learn the value of the male mentor in the lives of young men; we hear from the Iron John story the importance of moving from the mother's realm to the father's realm; and from all initiation stories we learn how essential it is to leave our parental expectations entirely and find a second father or "second King."

The dark side of men is clear. Their mad exploitation of earth resources, devaluation and humiliation of women, and obsession with tribal warfare are undeniable. Genetic inheritance contributes to their obsessions, but also culture and environment. We have defective mythologies that ignore masculine depth of feeling, assign men a place in the sky instead of earth, teach obedience to the wrong powers, work to keep men boys, and entangle both men and women in systems of industrial domination that exclude both matriarchy and patriarchy.

Most of the language in my book speaks to heterosexual men but does not exclude homosexual men. It wasn't until the eighteenth century that people ever used the term *homosexual;* before that time gay men were understood simply as a part of the large community of men. The mythology as I see it does not make a big distinction between homosexual and heterosexual men.   5

We talk a great deal about "the American man," as if there were some constant quality that remained stable over decades, or even within a single decade.

The men who live today have veered far away from the Saturnian, old-man-minded farmer, proud of his introversion, who arrived in New England in 1630, willing to sit through three services in an unheated church. In the South, an expansive, motherbound cavalier developed, and neither of these two "American men" resembled the greedy railroad entrepreneur that later developed in the Northeast, nor the reckless I-will-do-without culture settlers of the West.

Even in our own era the agreed-on model has changed dramatically. During the fifties, for example, an American character appeared with some consistency that became a model of manhood adopted by many men: the Fifties male.

He got to work early, labored responsibly, supported his wife and children, and admired discipline. Reagan is a sort of mummified version of this dogged type. This sort of man didn't see women's souls well, but he appreciated their bodies; and his view of culture and America's part in it was boyish and optimistic. Many of his qualities were strong and positive, but underneath the charm and bluff there was, and there remains, much isolation, deprivation, and passivity. Unless he has an enemy, he isn't sure that he is alive.

The Fifties man was supposed to like football, be aggressive, stick up *10* for the United States, never cry, and always provide. But receptive space or intimate space was missing in this image of a man. The personality lacked some sense of flow. The psyche lacked compassion in a way that encouraged the unbalanced pursuit of the Vietnam war, just as, later, the lack of what we might call "garden" space inside Reagan's head led to his callousness and brutality toward the powerless in El Salvador, toward old people here, the unemployed, schoolchildren, and poor people in general.

The Fifties male had a clear vision of what a man was, and what male responsibilities were, but the isolation and one-sidedness of his vision were dangerous.

During the sixties, another sort of man appeared. The waste and violence of the Vietnam war made men question whether they knew what an adult male really was. If manhood meant Vietnam, did they want any part of it? Meanwhile, the feminist movement encouraged men to actually look at women, forcing them to become conscious of concerns and sufferings that the Fifties male labored to avoid. As men began to examine women's history and women's sensibility, some men began to notice what was called their *feminine* side and pay attention to it. This process continues to this day, and I would say that most contemporary men are involved in it in some way.

There's something wonderful about this development—I mean the practice of men welcoming their own "feminine" consciousness and nurturing it—this is important—and yet I have the sense that there is something wrong. The male in the past twenty years has become more thoughtful, more gentle. But by this process he has not become more free. He's a nice boy who pleases not only his mother but also the young woman he is living with.

In the seventies I began to see all over the country a phenomenon that we might call the "soft male." Sometimes even today when I look out at an audience, perhaps half the young males are what I'd call soft. They're lovely, valuable people—I like them—they're not interested in harming the earth or starting wars. There's a gentle attitude toward life in their whole being and style of living.

But many of these men are not happy. You quickly notice the lack of *15* energy in them. They are life-preserving but not exactly life-giving. Ironically, you often see these men with strong women who positively radiate energy.

Here we have a finely tuned young man, ecologically superior to his father, sympathetic to the whole harmony of the universe, yet he himself has little vitality to offer.

The strong or life-giving women who graduated from the sixties, so to speak, or who have inherited an older spirit, played an important part in producing this life-preserving, but not life-giving, man.

I remember a bumper sticker during the sixties that read "WOMEN SAY YES TO MEN WHO SAY NO." We recognize that it took a lot of courage to resist the draft, go to jail, or move to Canada, just as it took courage to accept the draft and go to Vietnam. But the women of twenty years ago were definitely saying that they preferred the softer receptive male.

So the development of men was affected a little in this preference. Nonreceptive maleness was equated with violence, and receptive maleness was rewarded.

Some energetic women, at that time and now in the nineties, chose and still choose soft men to be their lovers and, in a way, perhaps, to be their sons. The new distribution of "yang" energy among couples didn't happen by accident. Young men for various reasons wanted their harder women, and women began to desire softer men. It seemed like a nice arrangement for a while, but we've lived with it long enough now to see that it isn't working out.   20

I first learned about the anguish of "soft" men when they told their stories in early men's gatherings. In 1980, the Lama Community in New Mexico asked me to teach a conference for men only, their first, in which about forty men participated. Each day we concentrated on one Greek god and one old story, and then late in the afternoons we gathered to talk. When the younger men spoke it was not uncommon for them to be weeping within five minutes. The amount of grief and anguish in these younger men was astounding to me.

Part of their grief rose out of remoteness from their fathers, which they felt keenly, but partly, too, grief flowed from trouble in their marriages or relationships. They had learned to be receptive, but receptivity wasn't enough to carry their marriages through troubled times. In every relationship something *fierce* is needed once in a while: both the man and the woman need to have it. But at the point when it was needed, often the young man came up short. He was nurturing, but something else was required—for his relationship, and for his life.

The "soft" male was able to say, "I can feel your pain, and I consider your life as important as mine, and I will take care of you and comfort you." But he could not say what he wanted, and stick by it. *Resolve* of that kind was a different matter.

In *The Odyssey,* Hermes instructs Odysseus that when he approaches Circe, who stands for a certain kind of matriarchal energy, he is to lift or show his sword. In these early sessions it was difficult for many of the younger men to distinguish between showing the sword and hurting someone. One man, a kind of incarnation of certain spiritual attitudes of the sixties, a man who had actually lived in a tree for a year outside Santa Cruz, found himself unable to extend his arm when it held a sword. He had learned so well not to hurt anyone that he couldn't lift the steel, even to catch the light of the sun on it. But showing a sword doesn't necessarily mean fighting. It can also suggest a joyful decisiveness.

The journey many American men have taken into softness, or recep- *25* tivity, or "development of the feminine side," has been an immensely valuable journey, but more travel lies ahead.

The Responsive Reader

1 In recent years, males have come in for much negative criticism. How does Bly in his opening paragraphs acknowledge "the dark side of men"?

2 What are some models for the true American that Bly finds in the nation's early history? Do you recognize these early models of the typical American? (What is the meaning of *Saturnian* and *cavalier?*)

3 Do you recognize the fifties male as described by Bly? What are his key features? What are his strengths? What are his weaknesses?

4 Do you recognize the sixties male? What are his key qualities? What about the sixties male appeals to Bly? What does Bly think is lacking?

5 What is Bly's own vision of the ideal male? Do you recognize the mythical or literary precedents on which he draws?

Talking, Listening, Writing

6 Is the fifties man extinct? Do you identify with or feel attracted to the sixties man?

7 Are critics right who charge that Bly is merely in his own way rehabilitating the traditional patriarchal male?

8 Do you agree that our popular culture denies the existence of "positive leadership energy"? Is it true that we tend to debunk our leaders, cutting them down to size?

9 What would you include in your own portrait of the ideal male?

Collaborative Projects

10 Have images of American womanhood undergone a transformation similar to that of the images of manhood identified by Bly? Working with a group, you may want to prepare composite portraits of the fifties woman, the sixties woman, and the nineties woman.

A GLIMPSE

Walt Whitman

The "poet of democracy," who in sweeping nineteenth-century poems celebrated America as a "nation of nations," embracing all ethnic origins, races, and social classes, records a quiet tender moment between gay lovers surrounded by a noisy smutty heterosexual world.

Through most of the history of our culture, gay men and lesbian women had to keep their sexual orientation secret. When it became a matter of public record, as in the case of the nineteenth-century poet and playwright Oscar Wilde, it wrecked careers and lives. (When Wilde came back from prison, one of his first acts was to write to the press pleading the cause of three children kept in the same brutal, dehumanizing jail where he had been confined.)

In recent decades, gay and lesbian artists and writers have slowly emerged from the twilight in which they were kept by societal repression. Many of them admire the American poet Walt Whitman (1819–1892), author of Leaves of Grass *and the "poet of democracy," as a precursor and pioneer. Although he did not openly acknowledge his homosexuality, his celebration of the male human form and the love of comrades made him a prophet of gay liberation.*

Thought Starters: When did you first become aware of the gay lifestyle? How were your early impressions shaped?

A glimpse through an interstice caught,
Of a crowd of workmen and drivers in a bar-room around the stove
   late of a winter night, and I unremark'd seated in a corner,
Of a youth who loves me and whom I love, silently approaching and
   seating himself near, that he may hold me by the hand,
A long while amid the noises of coming and going, of drinking and
   oath and smutty jest,
There we two, content, happy in being together, speaking little,
   perhaps not a word.

The Responsive Reader

1 How does this poem go counter to stereotypes about gays?
2 Whitman uses the word *love* twice in this poem. Can you define love in such a way that it includes both heterosexual and homosexual love?
3 How do you think this poem should be read? How should it sound? (What should be the volume, speed, tone of voice?)

Talking, Listening, Writing

4 What prominent gays or lesbians are you aware of in contemporary American life? What do you know about them? How are they treated by the media?

5 What have you read or heard about gay-bashing or homophobia? What have you observed of it at first hand? What psychological or cultural mechanisms are at work?

FORUM: Gay in America

In America, are all "created equal" regardless of race, ethnic origin, gender, age, or sexual orientation?

Are gays and lesbians becoming more widely accepted in American life? Or is a conservative backlash slowing down the movement toward gay rights?

■ Openly gay or lesbian Americans have become a familiar feature of American politics and entertainment. In sitcoms, the squirming of family and friends when introduced to the gay lover of one of theirs became a tired joke. Tom Hanks played a gay AIDS victim treated shabbily by a homophobic establishment. Gay rights initiatives asked voters to ban discrimination against gays in housing and employment. Communities and corporations extended health benefits and pension rights to the domestic partners of gay employees. States including California, Connecticut, Hawaii, Massachusetts, Minnesota, Nevada, New Hampshire, New Jersey, Rhode Island, and Vermont forbade employers to discriminate on the basis of sexual orientation.

■ At the same time, television evangelists and conservative political leaders mounted a counterattack. State legislatures passed laws declaring same-sex marriages invalid. "Defense of Marriage" legislation moved through state legislatures and through Congress. In the United States Senate, a majority leader from Mississippi classed homosexuals with alcoholics and kleptomaniacs (people driven by a pathological urge to steal). A multi-millionaire television evangelist claimed that God was sending hurricanes to punish young people and families for loving gay siblings or family members. Brutal and at times fatal violence against gays, as in the case of the Shepard murder in Wyoming, was on the rise.

■ At the beginning of the new century, the gay rights movement gathered momentum as courts ruling on the legality of same-sex marriages began to affirm the right of gays and lesbians to participate on equal terms and with equal rights in American life. A Massachusetts court legalizing same-sex marriages based its decision on the equal protection clause of the the U.S. Constitution and of state constitutions. The core goal of the equality principle was to prevent the government from creating a "caste system" that would make a whole group of Americans "second-class citizens."

A DAY TO LEAVE THE CLOSET

Elizabeth Birch

"We are conservative and liberal, often people of faith, of all races and socioeconomic classes. We are, and always have been, an integral part of America."

Elizabeth Birch wrote the following column in 1998, at a time when gays and lesbians were being urged to "come out of the closet" and openly acknowledge their sexual orientation. She published the column in the "Perspectives" section of a metropolitan newspaper as the executive director of the Human Rights Campaign, described as the largest U.S. gay political organization.

She was the director of litigation at the Apple Computer corporation in Silicon Valley in California, where she pushed for domestic partner benefits. She focuses her article on a basic choice that she says has faced millions of gay Americans. One alternative has traditionally been to stay in the closet—to deny or hide one's sexual orientation. It has been to conform to the heterosexual lifestyle of the majority, leading a furtive, guilt-ridden life. The other alternative, increasingly chosen in recent years, has been to come out—to live one's life with "integrity," even if at the risk of facing rejection, discrimination, and anti-gay violence.

Thought Starters: Have you seen evidence of increased visibility of gays and lesbians as the result of efforts by gay activists? Have you seen or read about Gay Pride parades or similar activities?

WASHINGTON—Since the inaugural National Coming Out Day a decade ago, millions of Americans have taken the bold step of emerging from the closet. As more and more people realize their friends and family members are gay, their attitudes are changing, and they are joining the demand for basic fairness. Polls show more than two-thirds of Americans believe no one should lose a job or job opportunity because of sexual orientation.

This broad-based support for fairness is directly linked to individuals coming out and challenging misconceptions about gay people.

But it wasn't always this way—even in Silicon Valley, now recognized as progressive on gay and lesbian issues.

In 1992, as chief litigator at Apple Computer, I and colleagues in a gay employee group (led by Bennett Marks) began a push for health benefits for our domestic partners. We did not know how we would be received. Some feared that, by coming out, they would be jeopardizing their careers.

When we met with Chairman John Scully, he was magnificent. He immediately saw the wisdom of instituting a fair policy. In 1993, Apple announced it would offer equal benefits to partners of gay and lesbian employees.

Following Apple's lead, many other employers came to recognize that treating all employees equally is good for business: It deepens commitment, boosts morale and inculcates the culture with a sense of fairness. Today, more than half of Fortune 500 companies offer domestic-partner benefits.

This success story underscores the impact of a simple tool for educating society and irreversibly improving the lives of gay Americans. Through the bold act of coming out at Apple, we helped blaze a trail.

Unfortunately, not everyone who comes out is embraced as we were.

Each year, thousands are fired, kicked out of their homes or even brutalized for being gay. It is still legal in 40 states to fire people for being gay, and gay Americans are the victims of 11.6 percent of all hate crimes reported. Attempts to pass federal legislation to remedy these problems are met with open hostility on Capitol Hill.

A Marathon Effort

Under these circumstances, coming out is like running a marathon. It can be excruciating, exhausting and painful—and just when you think the race is over, you realize you aren't even at the halfway mark. Yet it is also liberating and empowering, and can provide some of life's most rewarding experiences. 10

The most difficult part of coming out is the constant anticipation of rejection. Sometimes those we thought would be accepting have deserted us. Other times, friends and relatives who we expected to snub us have opened their hearts and minds, resulting in new closeness. This constant foray into the murky, and scary, world of the unknown is what makes coming out a monumental act of courage.

National Coming Out Day, which falls on Oct. 11 this year, is a celebration for those who have successfully made this difficult journey. And it is a time of hope for those still struggling to love themselves in an often-hostile society.

But the decision to be honest does not end after a single declaration on a specific day. Coming out is a lifelong process that requires even the most open gay people to find new reservoirs of courage and fortitude daily.

Every time a gay person meets someone new, questions of sexuality come up directly or indirectly. Simple questions that the average heterosexual takes for granted, such as "Are you married?" or "What are you doing this weekend?" can cause great anxiety. We must decide whether to conjure up a tortured fiction or evasion, or simply tell the truth and potentially face the consequences.

Despite the constant juggling act—"Should I be brave today?" vs. "Should I be safe today?"—I and millions of others have found that the closet is not a safe place. It is a prison that produces self-hatred and validates those who would deny us our basic human dignity 15

Coming out is the ultimate weapon against politically motivated assaults on gay people in the guise of love or religion. And whatever the obstacles, gay people continue to come out in record numbers. Fear of societal reprisals cannot suppress the human need to live freely and with integrity.

A Diverse Community

We are military heroes, like Vietnam Bronze Star recipient Col. Grethe Cammermeyer. We are successful entrepreneurs, like Quark founder and chairman Tim Gill.

We are conservative and liberal, often people of faith, of all races and socioeconomic classes. We are, and always have been, an integral part of America.

When I look back at what we accomplished at Apple, I marvel. I think, "How did we do it?" The answer is simple. We had the courage to come out, to take an immense risk to improve our lives and offer hope to the next generation of gay people.

Each day, and especially on National Coming Out Day, more people   20
are choosing to "risk it all"—because in the emptiness of the closet, surrendering self-respect and freedom, "all" can seem like nothing.

The Responsive Reader

1   What made her experience at Apple a *test case* for Birch? What features of the story stood out for her, and what did she learn from it?
2   Birch views society's progress toward acceptance and equal rights of gays or lesbians with *mixed emotions*. What developments for her stand out in the "success story" of improving conditions for gay Americans? What evidence does she cite of positive changes in public opinion? On the downside, how does she sum up the negatives in recent developments?
3   According to Birch, what was the *psychological price* homosexual Americans paid for staying "in the closet"? What did it mean in everyday life? For her and many of her contemporaries, what were the pros and cons of "coming out"?
4   Have you observed *difficult transitions* as gays are becoming more open about sexual orientation? Have you seen evidence that social encounters and family relations between gays and straights can cause "great anxiety"? Have you seen evidence of the meeting of gay and straight causing strain or embarrassment in school? In the workplace?

Talking, Listening, Writing

5   You may decide to team up with classmates to draft a "Miss Manners" set of guidelines for straight Americans interacting with gays and lesbians in social situations, in family relations, and in the workplace. You may want to draft a similar set of guidelines advising gay or lesbian Americans on how to act in the same situations.

Collaborative Projects

6 You may want to team up with classmates to investigate the role of
openly gay and lesbian Americans in public life—in Congress, in local
politics, in the news media. What is the role or influence of public
figures like Frank Rich or Richard Rodriguez?

OTHER VOICES

"I only pray that you will be a good man."

Richard Rodriguez is the Mexican American writer who first became
known for his autobiographical *Hunger of Memory* (1982), which talked of
immigrants and their children leaving their old-country language behind as
a necessary rite of passage in the process of joining fully in the American
experience. In recent years, Rodriguez has written about the meeting of
cultures as a two-way street. with American life absorbing much from the
lifestyles of immigrant cultures.

Writing about legal challenges to laws banning discrimination against
gays, Rodriguez said:

> What I see is an astonishing change. I meet homosexual men and
> women now in every corner of American life. Everywhere people are
> "out" and, more remarkably, they are being accepted by their families
> and their friends and their coworkers. I know, like you, stories of par-
> ents who no longer speak to their children. But I am more impressed
> by the accommodation taking place throughout America. I think of
> two Catholic families in California. They have been united in recent
> years by the love of two dying men—lovers dying of AIDS. There
> they all were—50 smiling faces in a Christmas photograph. Three of
> four generations, standing alongside the two thinning men. That is the
> way the sexual revolution is taking place—by the Christmas tree,
> within the very family that Pat Buchanan and Pat Robertson invoke
> for their own purposes as unchanging and rigid. . . .
>
> I am not being overly optimistic. I suspect that the great, perhaps
> even calamitous struggle in the next century will be a cultural war, pit-
> ting the secular against the fundamentalist. Do I think there will be
> more anti-gay legislation passed? Yes. Are we in for dangerous times?
> Yes. Do I think that there are many judges in America who will re-
> main preoccupied by what I do in the dark? But the other day I re-
> ceived a letter from my first-grade teacher, a Catholic nun now in her
> 80's. "About your being gay," she writes, "I don't have any problem
> with it. I only pray that you will be a good man."

YOUR TURN:

Have you seen evidence of an anti-gay backlash in your community or in society at large? Or have you seen evidence of growing tolerance or acceptance?

LOVE, MARRIAGE, AND THE LAW

William Bennett

"I believe that overall, allowing same-sex marriages would do significant, long-term social damage."

William Bennet has long been one of the country's most prominent conservatives, marching under the banner of traditional values. With pundits like George Will and Roger Rosenblatt, he was a leader of the attack on multiculturalism, feminism, gay rights, and other mainstays of a liberal agenda. He originally published the following article in 1996 in The Wall Street Journal, *which was becoming a leading voice of a pro-business neoconservative movement.*

A chief initiator of the current culture wars, Bennett signed on as President Reagan's Secretary of Education at a time when the Reagan administration was trying to abolish the U.S. Department of Education. He has published tracts like The Book of Virtues *to admonish Americans to adopt higher moral standards. According to figures published in* Harper's *magazine, the author of* The Book of Virtues *earned $1,800,000 in speaking fees in a single year. Bennett briefly made the headlines in 2004 when establishment newspapers reported that he had lost 8 million dollars as a gambler in Las Vegas. A lead conservative columnist for a Hearst newspaper explained that what Bennett had done was perfectly legal.*

Thought Starters: What does the term "family values" bring to mind? Where do you hear or see it used? Who uses it and on what occasions or for what purposes?

We are engaged in a debate which, in a less confused time, would   1
be considered pointless and even oxymoronic: the question of same-sex marriage.

But we are where we are. The Hawaii Supreme Court has discovered a new state constitutional "right"—the legal union of same-sex couples. Unless a "compelling state interest" can be shown against them, Hawaii will become the first state to sanction such unions. And if Hawaii legalizes same-sex marriages, other states might well have to recognize them because of the Constitution's Full Faith and Credit Clause. Some in Congress recently introduced legislation to prevent this from happening.

Now, anyone who has known someone who has struggled with his homosexuality can appreciate the poignancy, human pain and sense of exclusion that are often involved. One can therefore understand the effort to

achieve for homosexual unions both legal recognition and social acceptance. Advocates of homosexual marriages even make what appears to be a
sound conservative argument: Allow marriage in order to promote faithfulness and monogamy. This is an intelligent and politically shrewd argument. One can even concede that it might benefit some people. But I
believe that overall, allowing same-sex marriages would do significant,
long-term social damage.

Recognizing the legal union of gay and lesbian couples would represent a profound change in the meaning and definition of marriage. Indeed,
it would be the most radical step ever taken in the deconstruction of society's most important institution. It is not a step we ought to take.

The function of marriage is not elastic; the institution is already frag-   5
ile enough. Broadening its definition to include same-sex marriages would
stretch it almost beyond recognition—and new attempts to broaden the
definition still further would surely follow. On what principled grounds
could the advocates of same-sex marriage oppose the marriage of two con-
senting brothers? How could they explain why we ought to deny a marriage license to a bisexual who wants to marry two people? After all, doing
so would be a denial of that person's sexuality. In our time, there are more
(not fewer) reasons than ever to preserve the essence of marriage.

Marriage is not an arbitrary construct; it is an "honorable estate"
based on the different, complementary nature of men and women—and
how they refine, support, encourage and complete one another. To insist
that we maintain this traditional understanding of marriage is not an attempt to put others down. It is simply an acknowledgment and celebration
of our most precious and important social act.

Nor is this view arbitrary or idiosyncratic. It mirrors the accumulated
wisdom of millennia and the teaching of every major religion. Among
worldwide cultures, where there are so few common threads, it is not a coincidence that marriage is almost universally recognized as an act meant to
unite a man and a woman.

To say that same-sex unions are not comparable to heterosexual marriages is not an argument for intolerance, bigotry or lack of compassion (although I am fully aware that it will be considered so by some). But it is an
argument for making distinctions in law about relationships that are themselves distinct. Even Andrew Sullivan, among the most intelligent advocates
of same-sex marriage, has admitted that a homosexual marriage contract
will entail a greater understanding of the need for "extramarital outlets."
He argues that gay male relationships are served by the "openness of
the contract," and he has written that homosexuals should resist allowing
their "varied and complicated lives" to be flattened into a "single, moralistic model."

But this "single, moralistic model" is precisely the point. The marriage commitment between a man and a woman does not—it cannot—
countenance extramarital outlets. By definition it is not an open contract;

its essential idea is fidelity. Obviously that is not always honored in practice. But it is normative, the ideal to which we aspire precisely because we believe some things are right (faithfulness in marriage) and others are wrong (adultery). In insisting that marriage accommodate the less restrained sexual practices of homosexuals, Sullivan and his allies destroy the very thing that supposedly has drawn them to marriage in the first place.

There are other arguments to consider against same-sex marriage— for example, the signals it would send, and the impact of such signals on the shaping of human sexuality, particularly among the young. Former Harvard professor E. L. Pattullo has written that "a very substantial number of people are born with the potential to live either straight or gay lives." Societal indifference about heterosexuality would cause a lot of confusion. A remarkable 1993 article in the *Washington Post* supports this point. Fifty teen-agers and dozens of school counselors and parents from the local area were interviewed. According to the article, teen-agers said it has become "cool" for students to proclaim they are gay or bisexual—even for some who are not. Not surprisingly, the caseload of teen-agers in "sexual identity crisis" doubled in one year. "Everything is front page, gay and homosexual," according to one psychologist who works with the schools. "Kids are jumping on it . . . (counselors) are saying, 'What are we going to do with all these kids proclaiming they are bisexual or homosexual when we know they are not?'"

If the law recognizes homosexual marriages as the legal equivalent of heterosexual marriages, it will have enormous repercussions in many areas. Consider just two: sex education in the schools and adoption. The sex education curriculum of public schools would have to teach that heterosexual and homosexual marriage are equivalent. "Heather Has Two Mommies" would no longer be regarded as an anomaly; it would more likely become a staple of a sex education curriculum. Parents who want their children to be taught (for both moral and utilitarian reasons) the privileged status of heterosexual marriage will be portrayed as intolerant bigots; they will necessarily be at odds with the new law of matrimony and its derivative curriculum.

Homosexual couples will also have equal claim with heterosexual couples in adopting children, forcing us (in law at least) to deny what we know to be true: that it is far better for a child to be raised by a mother and a father than by, say, two male homosexuals.

The institution of marriage is already reeling because of the effects of the sexual revolution, no-fault divorce and out-of-wedlock births. We have reaped the consequences of its devaluation. It is exceedingly imprudent to conduct a radical, untested and inherently flawed social experiment on an institution that is the keystone in the arch of civilization. That we have to debate this issue at all tells us that the arch has slipped. Getting it firmly back in place is, as the lawyers say, a "compelling state interest."

The Responsive Reader

1 For Bennett, what are the *key values* marriage represents? What for him is the essence of marriage as a traditional institution? What in his praise of marriage seems idealized? What seems valid to you?

2 What *language* does Bennett use about gay people? His "I'm-not-a-bigot" stance keeps him from repeating vulgar abuse directed at gays by homophobes. How does he talk about gays at the beginning of his article? Later in the article, what use does he make of anti-gay charges such as their proselytizing for homosexuality among the impressionable young or their encouraging of promiscuity (or "less restrained sexual practices," in Bennett's words)?

3 What *related evils* does Bennett envision once same-sex marriages open the door? Conservatives see trends they oppose as part of a threatened general breakdown of Western civilization. Besides gay marriage, what other items in Bennett's catalogue of societal evils signal the decay (or "deconstruction") of traditional values? A "slippery slope" argument attacks people not for what they advocate but for what else their success might bring in its wake. Where does Bennett see us headed as we start sliding on the slippery slope?

Talking, Listening, Writing

4 Do you think same-sex marriages are a threat from which the institution of marriage has to be protected?

5 The controversy about gay rights triggers highly emotionally charged rhetoric or loaded language. What is a "fundamentalist"? Do you think Bennett is a "bigot"? What kind of people use the words *faggot* and *queer*?

6 Do you think the press reports about Bennett's gambling addiction should disqualify him from lecturing others about morality? Or do you think bringing up these charges against him is an example of *ad hominem*—an inappropriate attack "on the person" rather than staying focused on the issue?

GAY PAIRS WED IN MASSACHUSETTS

Carolyn Lochhead

"Lesbian and gay couples lined up at city halls to register their intent to marry, allowed to do so with the full legal sanction of their state's highest court."

In May 2004, after a long court battle, the state of Massachusetts was everywhere in the headlines. Massachusetts is widely considered the most progressive state of the Union. Along the Freedom Trail in Boston and in much of the surrounding area, reminders of the early skirmishes and confrontations of the American Revolution are everywhere. Harvard University and MIT (Massachusetts Institute of Technology), two of the world's leading universities, are in Cambridge across the river from downtown Boston. Political leaders from John F. Kennedy to Edward Kennedy and John Kerry have gone to the U.S. Senate from Massachusetts.

A November 2003 ruling by the highest Massachusetts court had legalized same-sex marriages, and officials started issuing the first licenses for legal same-sex marriages at 12:01 A.M. May 17, 2004, the launch date set by the court. At the time, only a few countries in the world allowed gay or lesbian couples to wed. The state of Vermont had set a hotly contested precedent when it authorized civil unions for same-sex couples without the full rights of marriage. Early in 2004, the mayor of San Francisco had taken a step further, authorizing hundreds of same-sex marriages while claiming that the equal protection clause of the state constitution overrode a voter-approved "Defense of Marriage" initiative.

In Massachusetts, gay and lesbian couples as well as town clerks defied the Republican governor's invoking a 1913 law to keep out-of-state couples from flocking to the state to be married there. (The law may originally have been designed to keep mixed-race couples from being married in a liberal northern state.) In state legislatures and in Congress, proposed constitutional amendments to ban same-sex marriage were working their way slowly through an often long-drawn-out process with uncertain outcome.

Thought Starters: Lochhead says that in the Massachusetts statehouse the court's gay marriage decision set off a "vitriolic cultural debate." Have you ever followed or been close to a verbal confrontation that turned "vitriolic"—poisonous and violently abusive? What was the occasion or the issue?

BOSTON—Julie and Hillary Goodridge, together 17 years and mothers of 8-year-old Annie, were legally wed Monday under authority granted by the Commonwealth of Massachusetts after a 3½-year court battle, marking a turning point in the history of gay civil rights.

The tiny, spartan hall of the Unitarian Universalist Association headquarters, next door to the Statehouse where the decision that bears the Goodridges' name invoked a vitriolic cultural debate, erupted in cheers and applause as the Rev. William G. Sinkford declared at about 2:30 P.M, "By the power vested in me by the Commonwealth of Massachusetts, I now pronounce you fully and legally married."

Across Massachusetts, in large cities and small towns, lesbian and gay couples lined up at city halls to register their intent to marry, allowed to do so with the full legal sanction of their state's highest court for the first time in U.S. history.

The usual three-day waiting period was waived for the seven plaintiff couples whose 4–3 victory before the state Supreme Judicial Court last November—which the U.S. Supreme Court refused to block last Friday—paved the way for same-sex couples to marry in Massachusetts.

The marriages proceeded despite a fierce struggle led by the Catholic Church in this very Catholic state, evangelical Christians and the state's Republican Gov. Mitt Romney, a Mormon, to amend the state's constitution and override the court's decision.

Those who opposed the court decision narrowly won legislative approval of a ban on same-sex marriage that also would grant civil unions for same-sex couples in Massachusetts. But that process cannot be completed before November 2006. It requires a second legislative approval and a vote of the people.

Same-sex marriage opponents view the existence of potentially thousands of marriages in Massachusetts for at least two years as an enormous and possibly irreversible setback.

President Bush issued a statement from a campaign stop saying the "sacred institution of marriage should not be redefined by a few activist judges," and he reiterated his call on Congress to pass an amendment to the U.S. Constitution that would ban same-sex marriages in all states. The amendment has languished in Congress despite heavy lobbying by conservative religious groups.

The issue, which has spurred proposals for state constitutional bans in many states, could affect the outcome of the presidential election. The president's Democratic challenger, Sen. John Kerry of Massachusetts, has said he opposes same-sex marriage but also opposes a federal constitutional ban.

At a news conference outside the Capitol in Sacramento, a leading opponent of same-sex marriage decried the Massachusetts legal action as "sexual and judicial tyranny" and predicted that a new wave of photographs of happy couples getting married will rouse opposition nationally.

"This is San Francisco all over again," said Randy Thomasson, executive director of the Campaign for California Families, referring to the four weeks in February and March when more than 4,000 gay and lesbian couples were married in the city before a legal challenge stopped the weddings.

Celebrants and opponents alike widely predicted that the Massachusetts decision soon will migrate to other states and begin to erode the legal and cultural barriers that have long separated lesbians and gays from mainstream American life. Marriage, they said, is the ultimate civil grant of full equality and the ultimate badge of social acceptance.

It was in the most mundane municipal setting—the registry division of Boston's City Hall, tucked amid the windows for parking stickers, tax forms and other routine civil business—that the ordinary became extraordinary.

Couple after couple, many of them together for decades, many accompanied by their children, filed for their marriage licenses on Monday and made history.

As Mary Bonauto—who won the Goodridge case as the lead attorney for Gay and Lesbian Advocates and Defenders—said in Cambridge just after midnight Sunday, when the first license applications were granted, there was something heroic in the profound ordinariness of the act. As each couple emerged waving their stamped piece of paper, cheers rose from the crowds outside. Protesters were few. One of the leading opposition groups, the Massachusetts Family Institute, chose not to disrupt the day.

The Goodridge wedding was filled with laughter, tears and a sense of validation. "We are absolutely no different from any couple who loves each other," Julie Goodridge, 46, said after the ceremony. "We intend to uphold our marriage the rest of our lives."

The couple walked up the aisle as the guests sang the traditional wedding march to the words, "Here come the brides, so gay with pride . . . lovely to see, legally free, finally hitched by a 4−3 decree."

Their friend who first introduced the couple 17 years ago, Amy Domini, joked, "You introduce two people, you encourage them a little bit, and what happens? A national crisis!" as the room broke out in laughter.

A few hours earlier and few blocks away at the Arlington Street Church, also part of the liberal Unitarian Universalist denomination, a much more solemn and formal ceremony, but equally tearful and joyous, united another plaintiff couple, Robert Compton, 55, and David Wilson, 60.

The Rev. Kim Crawford Harvie, who had performed a commitment ceremony for the couple, declared that the couple's nine-year relationship meant they were already married by "a far higher authority than we answer to today." But when she said the words, "And now, by the power invested in me by the Commonwealth of Massachusetts," a huge roar went up from the crowd, stamping the polished wooden floors with their feet, cheering, applauding and crying. "I hereby pronounce you partners for life, legally married," Harvie concluded.

Wilson's grandchildren, Tyler and Colby Wilson, served as ring-bearers, and their father, Wilson's son Scott, stepped out of the church wiping tears from his eyes, telling the assembled media throng, "It was awesome."

A San Francisco couple, Joe Alfano, 30, and Frank Capley, 29, who live in the Castro neighborhood, came to witness history in the making, having been married in February during San Francisco's brief but historic act of civic rebellion, which still awaits court resolution.

"It's about equality," Alfano said. "Until now, we've been belittled and oppressed and made to be second-class citizens. In Massachusetts now, we're equal."

Capley predicted deep changes in gay culture from the act of opening marriage to gays and lesbians.

"We won't have to be in dark alleys any more," he said. Opponents "don't believe we deserve marriage and long-term relationships. As a result of society acknowledging our relationships, I think we're going to see stronger relationships."

Tim McCarthy, a Provincetown, Mass., publisher of the gay *Lip* magazine, said, "No professional gay ever thought this was going to be the one that would win us our equality," referring to marriage. "We thought it would come piece by piece, through employment law or pension law. Not marriage, not a moral institution. But that's the best place to have won, because the basis of all arguments and all laws is morality. Yes, we are equal. Yes, we are."

Chronicle staff writer John Hubbell
contributed to this report from Sacramento.

The Responsive Reader

1   What is the *legal situation?* Are advocates of gay marriage entering into a "legal labyrinth"? Do the legal complications seem like a maze to you? From what you read here and have read elsewhere, can you reconstruct some of the legal history? Can you track key legal complications and uncertainties for an outsider?

2   What is the *constitutional argument?* The founders based their promise that America would be different on the "self-evident" principle that all are created equal. There would be no second-class citizens, no untouchables. The parting shot or punchline in the conclusion of this article is "Yes, we are equal. Yes, we are." Where is the "equality principle" alluded to or invoked in this article?

3   What made the gay-marriage initiatives a great *human interest* story? According to an eyewitness, the packed congregation at Boston's Arlington Street Church burst into tears when the minister pronounced two of the original plaintiffs in the suit for gay marriage rights "partners for life." The news media gave extended coverage to scenes of tears and laughter and hymn singing from communities around the state and the country. They showed couples waiting patiently in long lines, with flowers, wedding cakes, and teary-eyed friends and relatives waiting for them as they emerged after trading vows. Do you think this kind of coverage will permanently alter the attitudes and stereotypes of the straight majority? Why or why not?

Talking, Listening, Writing

4   Students of the marriage institution enumerate several hundred special rights and obligations. These include shared insurance benefits, continuing health coverage after the death of a spouse, tax deductions or lower tax rates, and the right to hospital visits in the event of serious illness. How do these affect people's lives, and how important are they?

5   Opponents of gay marriage describe marriage as a sacred institution. Supporters of gay marriage counter that marriage is an institution created by governments. Marriage traditions and marriage laws vary greatly from one culture and one legal system to another. Do you think that when the government defines marriage as a sacred institution it breaches the separation of church and state?

6   Some observers claim that topics like gay marriage bring into play deep-rooted attitudes that defeat any attempts at rational discussion or attempts to find common ground. Do you agree?

Collaborative Projects

7   What is the definition of civil unions? What is the difference between civil unions or domestic partnerships and same-sex marriage? Are there key differences in areas like property rights, tax obligations, insurance benefits, survivor benefits, or inheritance arrangements? What are some of the most important differences? How important are they?

ATTITUDES ON MARRIAGE CHANGE SLOWLY

L. A. Chung

"You don't recognize the problems or the harm unless you've lived it."

The following newspaper article was part of an outpouring of media discussion of the gay marriage issue in the early months of 2004. Major social or cultural developments that are turns in the road for society stimulate the public dialogue. Commentators and private individuals seriously thinking about or "ruminating" on the charges and counter charges talk and write extensively about precedents, parallels, and arguments pro and con. Media watchers tracking the "chatter" both in print and on the Web activated by milestone events have stressed the importance of what readers and viewers bring to what they read, hear, or view. What explains different perspectives and different points of view? Much depends on personal background, social level, area of the country, and political or religious affiliation.

A close friend quoted by the author is a West Coast feminist "raised as an Irish Catholic." Another friend is Chinese American with a white husband. The author remembers legal barriers against miscegenation or racially mixed marriages, and in her extended family there have been numerous interracial couples.

Thought Starters: The author counsels patience and asks readers to trust in slow change. How do you react when you are waiting for an important decision and are told "people are not ready for this" or "this is not the right time"? Do you tend to believe in "acting now," or do you trust in slow change?

If there's one thing some couples who got married in Massachusetts should count on, it's change.

Very slow, but nonetheless steady, change. Especially when it comes to attitudes about marriage.

Today, marriage among couples of the same sex can be a joyful or scandalous event, depending on your point of view. My answer, with any wedding, is it depends on the couple. But tomorrow and 40 years from tomorrow, patience and change are the bywords.

I was reminded of this in a moment of sudden seriousness, interrupting some vacation banter with friends last January.

I'd asked my friend Samantha why she and her husband travel to Kauai winter after winter, all the way from Washington, D.C.

Hawaii had a level of total ease she didn't find at home. They are an interracial couple, she said. Her husband is white. She is Chinese-American. "And D.C.," she reminded me, "is still the South."

From a Californian's perspective, it sounded utterly weird. But I'd heard that once before. Another friend, Esther, had mentioned something similar about Dallas. There's something you still feel, quite palpably.

Finding Family Acceptance

Thirty-seven years after interracial marriage bans were swept away by the U.S. Supreme Court, 56 years after the California Supreme Court ruled them invalid in this state, the vestiges of old attitudes are still felt.

That is the nature of change. Much has been made of the similarities and differences in the debates over marriage of people of different races and now over the marriage of people of the same sex. People point to polls showing 90 percent were against interracial marriage in 1948, when the state overturned miscegenation laws.

My own extended family has had numerous interracial marriages mirroring California's diverse makeup. My cousins have dealt with different levels of acceptance inside the family and outside — just as many interracial couples have done.

But like many people, unless something affects me directly, I don't have a true appreciation for it. You don't really recognize the problems or harm unless you've lived it.

As a heterosexual woman, coming of age long after both rulings, I'd given little thought to what it meant not to be able to marry the person I chose.

My friend Karen and I talked as the same-sex marriage debate unfolded on both coasts in February. Back in the Bay State after more than 15 years, she marveled at the changes.

She's a feminist with Bay Area loyalties. But she was raised as an Irish Catholic.

Should a court move faster than the attitudes of the people, she asked, ruminating on the accusations that the Massachusetts Supreme Judicial Council had taken an activist approach? Wouldn't it be better to wait?

Not Ready in 1940s

Then it struck me. Activist court? That's been one characterization of the Supreme Court that made the landmark *Brown* vs. *Board of Education* decision 50 years ago. How would the civil rights movement have proceeded without the Brown decision? I asked her. Wasn't public opinion starting to move along from the accumulation of various court challenges?

Was it activist or weighing in at the right time in history? Justice Felix Frankfurter later indicated that the court thought the time was not right before the 1954 case. Once they decided, it paved the way for accelerating change of attitudes.

The light went on. "Maybe you're right," she said.

Sure, I got a call from an anonymous guy on Friday who commented that "Latinos and blacks need to be segregated. . . . I don't want them in school with my kids." But just one.

So, huzzahs to the Massachusetts Supreme Judicial Court. My blessings to the couples marrying.

As with all couples, I counsel patience for a good marriage—and good, slow change, as well.

The Responsive Reader

1 Does Chung have a special *credibility* in writing about diversity and exclusion? What does Chung tell her readers about the "diverse makeup" of her friends and extended family? Does it give her a special credibility in writing about same-sex marriage? Why or why not?

2 Is there a *geography* of basic attitudes and core values? Do controversial decisions concerning race or gender tend to originate or gain traction in particular parts of the country? Why does Chung point to Washington D.C. and Dallas as places that are "still the South"? Are such references based on unfair stereotypes or on still widely existing reality? (Kauai is one of the Hawaiian islands. Apart from the climate, why would Chung's friend and her husband feel at "total ease" or at home there— thousands of miles from where they actually live?)

3 How did the activist judge become *a negative stereotype?* Judges responsible for landmark decisions in cases involving race or gender have been accused of being "activist judges." What are Chung's key examples of

activist courts being ahead of public opinion? In key examples, how far ahead was the court, and how significant was the court's decision?

Talking, Listening, Writing

4 African-American pastors have objected to comparing the struggle for gay rights to the struggle for racial equality. They say that gay marriage is "not a civil right." Do you think comparisons between the earlier struggle for civil rights and the struggle for gay rights are legitimate? Why or why not?

5 Have you ever dreamed of spending time in a place where the stresses or issues of your current life could be forgotten or pushed aside? Have you been able to spend time in such a place? You may want to devote a **journal entry** or a class presentation to your ideal real or imaginary place "without cares."

Organizing Your Writing

The Writing Process

1 Drawing on Your Experience
2 From Reading to Writing
3 Exploring Internet and Nonprint Sources
4 Pushing Toward a Thesis
5 Organizing Your Writing
6 Feedback and Revision

Work out an overall plan for your paper.

How good are you at organizing your writing? Effective writers know how to lay things out. They present information and ideas in such a way that we say: "Now I see how this works." To organize your material, you may have to sort out a set of data—like statistics on temporary employment or teenage pregnancy. Or you may have to mark off the stages in a process to show us how to get from point A to points B and C. You may have to set up categories to show what goes with what.

Major organizing strategies prove useful again and again as you try to help readers make sense of a confusing or challenging situation. In organizing your writing, you will often ask yourself one or more questions like the following:

- What are the major steps in the process? (What does it take to produce the desired end result?)

- When we read about challenges to an institution, like marriage, what is the range—from a traditional nuclear family to other kinds of family living? (Do traditional classifications fit the current situation—or should we adjust our mental categories?)

- In a confusing situation, can you help readers make the right choice? (Can you line up the advantages or disadvantages for different plans of action?)

- Can you help readers see what brought about a current problem? (Can you isolate some of the causes of a difficult situation—and work toward a solution?)

Triggering

Recognize tasks that require you to organize your thinking.
Dealing with any writing task, effective writers think about how to steer the reader's attention and how to direct the flow of ideas on the page. However, your ability to sort things out will be put to the test in situations like the following:

PROCESS Are you good at showing readers how to make things work? Can you show people dissatisfied with additive-laden supermarket food how to grow their own vegetables? Can you help others to organize and streamline their computer files or to make sophisticated new software work for them? [15]

CLASSIFICATION Do you feel that current discussion about immigrants tends to lump together a whole range of people? Who are these people? Do they all fit the same stereotype? Or are there major kinds of immigrants representing different facets of the "new immigrant" population? Can you show that legal status, voting rights, and entitlements vary for different classifications of immigrants?

CHARTING THE TREND Have you followed conflicting claims about job creation and job loss? What is the general trend? Can you bring in real-life examples and believable facts and figures to show that the trend toward temporary work without benefits is continuing?

WEIGHING OPTIONS If the city council is debating different plans for zoning or development, and if you are strongly opposed to one of the alternatives, can you show the consequences of adopting plan A and of adopting plan B?

[15]

Gathering

Build up and start sorting out a solid base of related material.
The first step toward a well-organized paper is to build up a solid base of material: first-hand observation, reliable information, insiders' testimony, or trustworthy data. You will need substantial input before you try to explain how things fit together or how things work.

BUILDING A FILE Immigration has resurfaced in recent politics as a subject of heated debate. How much is campaign talk? How much is directed at alienated white males worried about immigrants taking their jobs? How much is directed at taxpayers worried about spiraling welfare costs for aliens? The following might be a sampling of notes you type in or jot down during your material-gathering stage:

The Immigrant Economy

- Several small businesses in this community are run by Korean grocers or liquor store owners. Both spouses and maybe older children work in the store. The store is open from early in the morning till late at night.

- The local newspaper reports on a new city ordinance concerning day workers who everyone knows line up along a street every morning where employers pick them up for a day's work. Many of these workers are probably illegals? The city council is going to prohibit workers looking for temporary work from lining up along the street.

- A pharmacy downtown is now run by a Vietnamese family. The business is a family operation. Little kids run around the store even late in the evening. What used to be a dead part of town has come back to life with little stores, ethnic restaurants, and colorful shop signs.

- I had high school friends whose parents were from Australia and worked in a high-tech company. They never took out citizenship papers and always talked about going back because of the threat of unemployment and poor health insurance.

- The immigration authorities raid sweatshops in New York City.

- A visiting professor talks about visiting a migrant camp that is on no map and that the sheriff said he knew nothing about. The people worked for local growers on a seasonal basis, living in shacks without sanitation.

SETTING UP MAJOR HEADINGS Early in the process of collecting your material, you are likely to start thinking in terms of of major categories. It looks as if you will need separate sections of your paper for "foreigners" with very different status. There is a big difference between legal immigrants building a future for their families and illegals who work in a twilight zone, exploited by employers and facing deportation when denounced.

Your first **scratch outline** may look like this:

Looking for Work

- small-business legal immigrant entrepreneurs
- menial labor for illegals
- highly trained professionals on special visas

As you dig in, you may remember additional details from personal observation and check out more recent news coverage. An intermediate **working outline** might look like this:

The Immigrant Economy

FIRST CATEGORY: *Established immigrants*—many of these are legal immigrants who came as refugees or as relatives of earlier immigrants and are tax-paying hard-working small-scale entrepreneurs

SECOND CATEGORY: *The migrant population*—many of these are illegals employed in sweatshops or by agribusiness as part of a black market economy; many live from day to day and from job to job, at risk of being reported to the migra

THIRD CATEGORY: *The "brain-drain" professionals*—many of these are highly qualified high-tech workers who come here on special visas and work here when times are good but may not have established permanent ties

When you present your classification of the new immigrants in your paper, you will flesh out each category with convincing real–life examples. Your readers will not have to agree with you, but you are giving them a basis for discussion.

Shaping

Adapt major organizing strategies to your own purposes.

Among the thinking and writing strategies that can help you organize your writing, several prove useful again and again. For instance, you may trace the stages in a process, so you can show what leads to what. What is first, and what is the next step? You may classify, putting things that belong together in the same bin. What goes with what? You may analyze cause and effect: What are the consequences if we do A, and what will happen if we do B?

TRACKING A PROCESS *To get a handle on how something works, we often mark off stages.* We trace a **process**—whether to help readers understand evolution or to help them raise chickens. When you mark off major stages, you will be able to focus on one thing at a time. You do justice to what seems important during a particular phase while yet seeing it as part of a larger whole. Marie de Santis, in a later chapter of this book, charts the life cycle of the salmon as follows:

The Last of the Wild Salmon

THESIS: The upstream journey of the salmon to its spawning grounds is a symbol of the indomitable force of life.

PHASE ONE: THE SALMON RUN Salmon fight their way upstream, motivated by a powerful instinctual drive. In prodigious leaps, they overcome waterfalls and manmade obstacles.

PHASE TWO: THE SPAWNING GROUNDS Lacerated by their upstream fight, the salmon reach the spawning grounds. They lay and fertilize a myriad eggs.

PHASE THREE: NEW LIFE The parents die, but after an interval fingerlings are in evidence everywhere, which eventually begin their journey downstream.

PHASE FOUR: TRANSITION The young salmon stay in the delta—they live in a sweetwater environment for a time, until they are ready for the saltwater environment of the ocean.

PHASE FIVE: RETURN TO THE OCEAN The adult salmon live in the ocean for a number of years—until a powerful urge propels them to seek the spawning grounds of their birth and the cycle begins anew.

SETTING UP CATEGORIES *Sorting things out into categories is a basic way of interpreting data.* **Classification** requires us to ask: What goes with what? Schools track students according to IQ, aptitude, or test results. Mortgage companies classify potential home buyers as low–risk, high–risk, and need–not–apply.

To place people on a socioeconomic scale, sociologists used to rely on the traditional upper class—middle class—lower class scheme. Today, a sociologist might set up a more realistic updated scheme of classification like the following:

Are You Upwardly Mobile?

- upper class (families of large inherited wealth and the corporate elite)
- upper middle class (mid-level managers, professional people, successful business people)
- lower middle class (lower-echelon employees, office workers; teachers, nurses, owners of small marginal businesses)
- underclass (dropouts, chronically unemployed, long-term public assistance cases)

EXAMINING CAUSE AND EFFECT *Trying to understand what goes on in our world, we often focus on causes and their consequences or results.* We focus on **cause and effect.** Once we understand what caused a problem, we may be able to work toward a solution. If we understand the factors that contributed to success, we may be able to make them work for us again. After we recognize the causes of a bad situation, we may be able to keep from repeating the same mistakes.

For instance, why are some commentators today reopening the question of no-fault divorce? No-fault divorce seemed to promise relief from court battles traumatizing the family members and enriching lawyers. However, many women found themselves with insufficient child support. Alimony was often required for only a few years or proved hard to collect. The family home often had to be sold so property could be divided, uprooting the woman and children. Many divorced women reported a drastic decline in their standard of living. Why?

Drawing on an article by Lenore J. Weitzman, a professor of sociology at Harvard, on other sources, and on personal observation, a student might identify major causes as follows:

The Unintended Consequences of Divorce

THESIS: Many divorced women have experienced a decline in their standard of living.

FIRST CAUSE: While treating women as theoretical equals, courts tended to ignore the unequal future earning power of the man and the woman. The man had often built a career, whereas the woman had been a homemaker or part-time worker, now trying to enter the labor force after many years of marriage. . . .

SECOND CAUSE: The "equal" division of property was in fact unequal if the property was divided between one person (usually the male) and three or four other people—the mother and the children who often stayed with her. . . .

THIRD CAUSE: Dividing tangible property such as money and real estate did not, at least at first, take into account more intangible assets. How do you estimate the value of advanced degrees or business contacts? . . .

A close look at cause and effect can make readers think about why people facing a similar challenge succeeded while others failed. Much writing about social issues probes underlying causes and long-range effects. If we can identify the most common causes of domestic violence, maybe we can institute educational programs or legal remedies that would help. If we can pinpoint the causes for high dropout rates in local schools, perhaps we can support remedial action.

Revising

Use your revision to provide needed help for your reader.
In a first draft, you may have concentrated on getting your facts right or on working in the right kinds of material. In a revision, you have a chance to ask yourself: Have I done enough to make my readers find their way? Will this paper make them say: "Now I see"? Here are questions you may want to keep in mind in reworking a paper:

PURPOSE *Should you do more to show why your explanations matter?* You may be able to add a quote from an authority on nutrition testifying to the value of baking your own bread or raising free-range chickens. You may be able to show how a realistic estimate of the current immigrant population can help voters make informed decisions about welfare policy.

PLAN *Should you do more to make your readers see your overall strategy?* Should you do more to give a preview or overview so that readers know how parts of your paper fit into the larger picture? Make sure they have a sense of what the whole process is as you close in on details. As you develop major categories, make sure readers see how these relate to one another.

SUPPORT *Should you bring in more real-life examples or real people?* Categories you set up without convincing examples can remain lifeless and theoretical.

BALANCE *Should you aim at more balanced treatment of different parts or stages?* Is any part of your paper too skimpy—because you were hurried, or because you did not have the right kind of support ready at the time?

AUDIENCE *Should you provide more help for your readers?* Do you need to fill in more technical background or remind readers of key historical facts?

A Paper for Peer Review

In the following paper, how effectively has the student writer brought a familiar problem into focus? How clearly does he identify key factors contributing to the situation? How convincing are the answers or the solutions he suggests?

Why AIDS Education Has Failed

I remember walking into a locker room where students were crowding around a radio. "Magic Johnson has AIDS!" In the following months, AIDS awareness peaked all over the country. Magic Johnson's misfortune sparked an interest and a new-found curiosity in the youth of America, who felt they could relate to the basketball star. The media had specials on AIDS and on the HIV virus daily. Misconceptions were being answered about the virus and the disease. ——>>>>>>>>>>>>>

(The above **media event,** illustrating the often short-lived attention the media pay to crucial issues, brings the subject to life.)

Nevertheless, according to an article in the *New York Times,* the number of teenagers with AIDS increased 70 percent in the course of two years, and AIDS was the fifth leading cause of death among people 15 to 24 years old. Although many schools now require AIDS education, many teenagers continue to have unprotected sex. **The blame for the failure of AIDS education can be placed on typically adolescent attitudes, on the attitudes of school boards and parents in local communities, and on the general conservative nature of our political world.** ——>>>>>>>>>>>>

(A strong **preview thesis** sets up a clear three-point program, promising a candid look at major causes of the failure to educate young Americans about the epidemic.)

Teenagers at this age feel immortal; the attitude is "it will not happen to me." Although studies show that as many as half of sexually active students use protection, their main motivation is to avoid pregnancy. Vivian Sheer, in an article in *Human Communication Research,* calls teenagers who put themselves at risk "sensation seekers" who like the immediate gratification that unprotected sex provides. My own friends and aquaintances see protection as a hassle; it can "ruin an intimate mood, destroy spontaneity, and reduce the partner's pleasure." ——>>>>>>>>>>>>

(This paragraph follows up the **first basic cause** of the failure of education about the epidemic: typical adolescent attitudes.)

Often the community needs as much education as the students. Schools have been slow to address the issues raised by the presence of an HIV-infected student or even a faculty member. Although experts say that "comprehensive, open discussion about sexuality" is the most effective way of educating people about AIDS, this "open discussion" type of teaching has had to do battle against conservative communities. Parents as well as political leaders preach abstinence and the promotion of moral conduct as the answer. In the words of one school board member, children should be taught what is right and wrong; "they shouldn't be presented with options." ———>>>>>>>>>>>>>>

(This paragraph follows up the **second basic cause** of the failure of education about the epidemic: Parents and school boards fight open discussion of the issue and the threat is poses.)

Advocates of sex education find themselves hampered by moralistic restrictions on explicit information about high-risk practices. Often the giving of explicit information is prohibited outright by a politically dominant faction. A Surgeon General of the United States was forced from office for her outspoken discussion of adolescent sexuality and advocacy of condom use. Are political leaders more concerned with their image than with saving the lives of young people? I could find no evidence of a coordinated government effort that targets adolescents or collects research data concerning teenagers, a situation that one observer called "a national disgrace." ———>>>>>>>>>>>>>>

(This paragraph follows up the **third basic cause** of the failure of AIDS education: The political climate nationwide prevents effective government programs.)

Non-government efforts like the AIDS education project for the National Coalition of Advocates for Students try to make people see the AIDS crisis from a public health perspective. How many lives must be put at risk before another superstar is infected and the media for a short time again keep the AIDS issue in the limelight? In the meantime, students are beginning to develop their own initiatives to protect themselves. In a high school in Massachusetts, students fought and negotiated for a year to make condoms available with counseling. In Connecticut, HIV testing was made available to students without a parent's consent. These battles fought and won show the maturity and capability of teenagers to deal with this topic and their desire to slow the epidemic down.

(This **conclusion** counteracts the defeated tone of much of the paper by paying tribute to positive initiatives.)

YOUR TURN:

1 Do you think the description of "immature" adolescent attitudes is fair or unfair?

2 In your experience, was sex education explicit? nonexistent? effectual — or ineffectual?

3 Do you think local student-based initiatives can make a real difference?

Writing Options 5: Organizing Your Thinking

1 Bookstores sell books like *Internet for Dummies*. Can you write clear and helpful instructions for a task that might be difficult for readers challenged by today's fast-moving world? For instance, can you give your readers help with upgrading a computer, programming a cell phone, cruising the Internet, or a similar task?

2 Defenders of tradition complain that many special old-time skills are dying out — from cabinet building to tortilla making or raising free-range chickens. Can you initiate readers into the world of a craft or traditional calling kept alive by people proud of their work?

3 Do schools still track students? What criteria do they apply — or should they apply — for sorting out students? Do or should they classify them by academic ability? career goals? English language proficiency? other?

4 What is the ethnic or racial mix at your school? Or what was the mix at your high school? Can you sort out major groups? What sets them apart?

5 A large number of immigrants have come into the country in recent years. How would you sort them out, setting up major categories? Are there major distinct immigrant communities, representing different world views or lifestyles?

6 What kind of marriage are "defense of marriage" initiatives defending? What are major current alternatives to the traditional family? In recent decades, what alternative living arrangements and lifestyles have come to compete with the traditional nuclear family?

7 Teachers and parents worry about teenagers who seem alienated from what schools have to offer or who see no point in trying hard in school. To judge from your own experience or observation, what causes young people to tune out teachers and school? What makes youngsters drop out?

8 Are Americans accepting high divorce rates as a fact of life? Is it still worthwhile to look at major causes of divorce and talk about possible answers?

9 From what you have seen, what makes some people bigots? Why are some people more prejudiced or narrow-minded than others? What makes the difference — for instance, family, peers, school, media exposure?

10 What have you learned about programs to fight the spread of drugs among young people? Do the programs or initiatives work? Why or why not?

6

OUTSIDERS:
Hearing the
Unheard Voices

VISUAL LITERACY 6:
HONOR LABOR: VOICES FROM THE FIELDS

David Bacon
Stoop Labor and Migrant Shelter

Much effective photojournalism translates statistics and campaign soundbites into human realities. During a Thanksgiving week, a socially committed photojournalist published a photo essay paying tribute to the 400,000 farm workers who toil in California's fields, producing more than half of the fruit and vegetables for the nation, and generating an estimated $29 billion in net annual revenue for growers. Earning an average $10,000 a year, many of the farm workers live in makeshift encampments that show on no map. Many workers are illegals. Increasingly the undocumented migrant workers from Mexico include many non-Spanish-speaking immigrants from surviving indigenous cultures.

Reading the Image

1 What do you see in these photographs? What first meets the eye? If you were a visitor from outer space whose spaceship has just landed close by, what detailed factual *description* of what you saw would you send to your home planet?

2 What *information* do you glean about the work and lives of these laborers? What do you learn about stoop labor? The first photograph shows a young migrant constructing a temporary shelter of the kind his people traditionally constructed in his indigenous village. What do you learn about living conditions for the workers in the fields?

3 What is your *response* to these photographs? Where are you in these pictures? Are you one of the people driving by on a highway? Can you identify with the workers? Why or why not?

4 What was the *intention* of the photographer? Was he recording a "slice of life"—capturing reality? Or did he have a personal or public agenda? Did he have a message for the viewer?

5 What was the *intended audience*? Was the photographer aiming at a limited audience or at a larger audience? Who would make a good audience for these photographs?

6 Do you agree with the *editorial judgment* that approved these images for publication in a major newspaper? Are they "newsworthy"? Why or why not?

Collaborative Projects

7   How much do North Americans or *Norte Americanos* know about the non–Spanish–speaking indigenous populations of Central and South America? Who are the survivors of pre–Columbian peoples? Where and how do they live? What is their role in the politics and culture of Latin American countries? You may decide to collaborate on a **research report,** with different dimensions of the topic farmed out to participants.

6

OUTSIDERS

Hearing Unheard Voices

**"This is where poor peoples *lives,*" she says.
"Where else you think poor peoples goin to be?
You a professor?"**

—JONATHAN KOZOL

The promise of America to successive waves of immigrants was that it had created a new classless society. No longer would society be run for the benefit of a small privileged elite. The blessings of liberty would be available to all. No longer would the many toil so that the few could squander the fruits of honest labor. In some of the great movements of our history, the unfree and disenfranchised reminded American society of its unkept promise. Abolition of slavery, the civil rights movement, and the women's movement aimed to make the promise of equal rights come true.

Today, however, observers find much evidence of inequality and the failure of human hopes. The gap between the rich and the poor is widening, with millions of American children growing up in poverty. The United States has a larger percentage of its population in jail than any other country. The gulf that separates a homeless encampment from the digs of a billionaire is as wide as the one that separated the hut of the French peasant from the Sun King's palace at Versailles. The dropout rates for minority students in high school and college are an unanswered challenge to the Jeffersonian ideal of an educated citizenry, of free universal education. Sections of some American cities have turned into war zones, with guns and drugs out of control.

At the same time, affluent American society seems to be turning its back on its poor and sick. The social safety net, the war on poverty, and food stamps for the needy have been made to seem part of a discredited vocabulary of "tax-and-spend" liberalism. Is our society going to heed those who ask us to listen to the unheard voices of the disenfranchised and the dispossessed, or are the affluent going to insulate themselves from the marginalized, the outsiders?

IS THERE LIFE AFTER WELFARE?

Annie Downey

"I call the welfare office, gather old bills, look for day care, write for my degree project, graduate with my son slung on my hip, breast-feeding."

In the nineties, a push toward welfare reform aimed at "ending welfare as we know it" and moving welfare recipients from welfare to workfare. Political leaders and media voices talked about ending welfare dependency and the "cycle of poverty." Federal legislation set the maximum amount of time welfare mothers and their children could receive welfare support at five years. Articles from authors in think tanks like the Hoover Institute argued against raising the minimum wage. The author of the following article tells the story of welfare not from the point of view of the affluent well-fed and well-insured but from the point of view of the recipient. With few outlets for her kind of story, she first published her account in a zine (Hip Mama) *in 1997—zines being the marginal underground cousins and poor relations of America's glossy commercialized magazine culture. Her story was reprinted in the* Utne Reader *and in* Harper's *magazine.*

Thought Starters: In recent years there has been much discussion of "profiling"—drawing up composite portraits of types or groups of people as an aid to law enforcement, social workers, and others. If before reading the following article you were asked to prepare a profile of a welfare mother, what would you include in your composite portrait? Compare your own welfare-mother profile with those prepared by fellow students.

I am a single mother of two children, each with a different father. I am a hussy, a welfare rider—burden to everyone and everything. I am anything you want me to be—a faceless number who has no story.

My daughter's father has a job and makes over two grand a month; my son's father owns blue-chip stock in AT&T, Disney, and Campbell's. I call the welfare office, gather old bills, look for day care, write for my degree project, graduate with my son slung on my hip, breast-feeding.

At the welfare office they tell me to follow one of the caseworkers into a small room without windows. The caseworker hands me a packet and a pencil. There is an older woman with graying hair and polyester pants with the same pencil and packet. I glance at her, she looks at me, we are both ashamed. I try hard to fill out the packet correctly, answering all the questions. I am nervous. There are so many questions that near the end I start to get careless. I just want to leave. I hand the caseworker the packet in an envelope; she asks for my pencil, does not look at me. I exit unnoticed. For five years I've exited unnoticed. I can't imagine how to get a job. I ride the bus home.

After a few weeks a letter arrives assigning me to "Group 3." I don't even finish reading it. I put my son in his stroller and walk to the food shelf.

My grandmother calls later to tell me that I confuse sex with love. I   5
tell her that I am getting a job. She asks what kind. I say, "Any job."

"Oh, Annie," she says. "Don't do that. You have a degree. Wait."

I say, "I can't, Gram, I've got to feed my kids, I have no one to fall back on." She is silent. I grasp the cord. I know I cannot ask for help.

It is 5 A.M. My alarm wakes up my kids. I try nursing my son back to sleep, but my daughter keeps him up with her questions: "Don't go out without telling me. Who's going to take care of us when you leave? What time is it?" I want to cry. It is still dark and I am exhausted. I've had three hours of sleep. I get ready for work, put some laundry in the washer, make breakfast, set out clothes for the kids, make lunches. I carry my son; my daughter follows. They cling to me. They cry when I leave. I see their faces pressed against the porch window and the sitter trying to get them inside.

I slice meat for $5.50 an hour for nine hours five days a week. I barely feed my kids, I barely pay the bills.

I struggle against welfare. I struggle against this faceless number I have   10
become. I want my story. I want my life. But without welfare I would have nothing. On welfare I went from teen mom to woman with an education. I published two magazines, became an editor, a teacher. Welfare, along with Section 8 housing grants and Reach Up, gave my children a life. My daughter loves and does well in school. My son is round, and at 20 months speaks wondrous sentences about the moon and stars. Welfare gave me what was necessary to be a mother.

Still, I cannot claim it. There is too much shame in me. The disgusted looks in the grocery lines, the angry voices of *Oprah* panelists, the unmitigated rage of the blue and white collar. I never buy expensive ice cream in pints. I don't do drugs. I don't own a hot tub. But the voices won't be stilled.

I am one of 12 million who are 1 percent of the federal budget. I am one of the 26 percent of AFDC recipients who are mothers and the 36.6 percent who are white. I am one of the 68 percent of teen mothers who were sexually abused. I am $600 a month below the poverty level for a family of three. I am a hot political issue. I am 145-65-8563. Group 3.

I have brown hair and eyes. I write prose. My mother has been married and divorced twice. I have never been married. I love Pablo Neruda's poetry, Louise Gluck's essays. I love my stepfather but not my real father. My favorite book is *Love in the Time of Cholera* by Gabriel García Márquez. My favorite movie, *The Color Purple*.

I miss my son's father. I love jazz. I've always wanted to learn how to ballroom dance. I am not a number. I have a story, I have a life, I have a face.

The Responsive Reader

1 If you were a social worker investigating Downey's case, what key facts in her personal history and family background would you note? Which to you would seem most relevant or important? Why? Which to you seem familiar or predictable? Which seem unusual and why?

2 What is Downey's history as a welfare recipient and job seeker? What stages and what details would you include in a résumé of her record as a single mother below the poverty line?

3 As early as the days of the Great Depression, Americans struggling against poverty have rebelled against the paperwork, the obscure classifications, the bureaucratic language, and the failure to deal with applicants as human beings. According to Downey, what is it like to be a faceless number in the welfare bureaucracy? How does it make her feel or react?

4 What light does Downey shed on how society shames welfare recipients? What evidence have you personally seen of strong negative feelings toward welfare recipients? How are they shown or expressed? Do you share them? Why or why not?

5 At the end, Downey does another verbal self-portrait that seems to have nothing to do with her economic situation or welfare status. What does she include there and why? What kind of send-off does her conclusion provide for her article?

Talking, Listening, Writing

6 Drawing on input from Downey's essay, prepare a journal entry titled "A Day in the Life of a Welfare Mother."

7 Have you ever been on welfare or accepted charity? If so, what is the most important lesson you learned from the experience? Would you accept welfare if you were unable to make ends meet?

8 Have you ever felt that people viewed you as "a faceless number who has no story"?

9 What was the worst job you ever held? Why did you take the job? How long did you keep it? What made it the worst job you ever held? For you, what would be the best possible job?

Collaborative Projects

10 Working with a group, investigate how welfare-to-work programs are faring in your area or community. What is required of former welfare recipients? What problems have the programs encountered? How successful are they? If possible, talk to former welfare recipients, social workers, employers.

MOTHER'S DAY IN FEDERAL PRISON

Amanda Coyne

"That boyfriend talked and he got three years. She didn't know anything. Had nothing to tell them. They gave her ten years."

Do you tend to feel that prison, like a serious accident or catastrophic illness, is something that happens to others—to people who are different from you and from people you care for? Amanda Coyne is a writer who tries to put a human face on the mind-numbing numbers of America's growing prison industry. Americans have grown used to staggering statistics about an exploding prison population. Coyne takes you to a visiting room at a women's prison to make you look at the faces of real people—both the women incarcerated there and the families they left behind. Coyne was a graduate student at the University of Iowa when she wrote this article for Harper's *magazine in 1997.*

Thought Starters: Do you ever visit a jail, a hospital, a juvenile home, a homeless shelter, or a similar institution? What is the routine? What goes through the visitor's mind? How does the visitor behave—or how should the visitor behave?

You can spot the convict-moms here in the visiting room by the way they hold and touch their children and by the single flower that is perched in front of them—a rose, a tulip, a daffodil. Many of these mothers have untied the bow that attaches the flower to its silver-and-red cellophane wrapper and are using one of the many empty soda cans at hand as a vase. They sit proudly before their flower-in-a-Coke-can, amid Hershey bar wrappers, half-eaten Ding Dongs, and empty paper coffee cups. Occasionally, a mother will pick up her present and bring it to her nose when one of the bearers of the single flower—her child—asks if she likes it: And the mother will respond the way that mothers always have and always will respond when presented with a gift on this day. "Oh, I just love it. It's perfect. I'll put it in the middle of my Bible." Or, "I'll put it on my desk, right next to your school picture." And always: "It's the best one here."

But most of what is being smelled today is the children themselves. While the other adults are plunking coins into the vending machines, the mothers take deep whiffs from the backs of their children's necks, or kiss and smell the backs of their knees, or take off their shoes and tickle their feet and then pull them close to their noses. They hold them tight and take in their own second scent—the scent assuring them that these are still their children and that they still belong to them.

The visitors are allowed to bring in pockets full of coins, and today that Mother's Day flower, and I know from previous visits to my older sister here at the Federal Prison Camp for women in Pekin, Illinois, that there is always an aberrant urge to gather immediately around the vending machines. The sandwiches are stale, the coffee weak, the candy bars the ones we always pass up in a convenience store. But after we hand the children over to their mothers, we gravitate toward those machines. Like milling in the kitchen at a party. We all do it, and nobody knows why. Polite conversation ensues around the microwave while the popcorn is popping and the processed-chicken sandwiches are being heated. We ask one another where we are from, how long a drive we had. An occasional whistle through the teeth, a shake of the head. "My, my, long way from home, huh?" "Staying at the Super 8 right up the road. Not a bad place." "Stayed at the Econo Lodge last time. Wasn't a good place at all." Never asking the questions we really want to ask: "What's she in for?" "How much time's she got left?" You never ask in the waiting room of a doctor's office either. Eventually, all of us—fathers, mothers, sisters, brothers, a few boyfriends, and very few husbands—return to the queen of the day, sitting at a fold-out table loaded with snacks, prepared for five or so hours of attempted normal conversation.

Most of the inmates are elaborately dressed, many in prison-crafted dresses and sweaters in bright blues and pinks. They wear meticulously applied makeup in corresponding hues, and their hair is replete with loops and curls—hair that only women with the time have the time for. Some of the better seamstresses have crocheted vests and purses to match their outfits. Although the world outside would never accuse these women of making haute-couture fashion statements, the fathers and the sons and the boy-friends and the very few husbands think they look beautiful, and they tell them so repeatedly. And I can imagine the hours spent preparing for this visit—hours of needles and hooks clicking over brightly colored yards of yarn. The hours of discussing, dissecting, and bragging about these visitors—especially the men. Hours spent in the other world behind the door where we're not allowed, sharing lipsticks and mascaras, and unraveling the occasional hair-tangled hot roller, and the brushing out and lifting and teasing . . . and the giggles that abruptly change into tears without warning—things that define any female-only world. Even, or especially, if that world is a female federal prison camp.

While my sister Jennifer is with her son in the playroom, an inmate's 5
mother comes over to introduce herself to my younger sister, Charity, my brother, John, and me. She tells us about visiting her daughter in a higher-security prison before she was transferred here. The woman looks old

and tired, and her shoulders sag under the weight of her recently acquired bitterness.

"Pit of fire," she says, shaking her head. "Like a pit of fire straight from hell. Never seen anything like it. Like something out of an old movie about prisons." Her voice is getting louder and she looks at each of us with pleading eyes. "My *daughter* was there. Don't even get me started on that place. Women die there."

John and Charity and I silently exchange glances.

"My daughter would come to the visiting room with a black eye and I'd think, 'All she did was sit in the car while her boyfriend ran into the house.' She didn't even touch the stuff. Never even handled it."

She continues to stare at us, each in turn. "Ten years. That boyfriend talked and he got three years. She didn't know anything. Had nothing to tell them. They gave her ten years. They called it conspiracy. Conspiracy? Aren't there real criminals out there?" She asks this with hands outstretched, waiting for an answer that none of us can give her.

The woman's daughter, the conspirator, is chasing her son through the   10
maze of chairs and tables and through the other children. She's a twenty-four-year-old blonde, whom I'll call Stephanie, with Dorothy Hamill hair and matching dimples. She looks like any girl you might see in any shopping mall in middle America. She catches her chocolate-brown son and tickles him, and they laugh and trip and fall together onto the floor and laugh harder.

Had it not been for that wait in the car, this scene would be taking place at home, in a duplex Stephanie would rent while trying to finish her two-year degree in dental hygiene or respiratory therapy at the local community college. The duplex would be spotless, with a blown-up picture of her and her son over the couch and ceramic unicorns and horses occupying the shelves of the entertainment center. She would make sure that her son went to school every day with stylishly floppy pants, scrubbed teeth, and a good breakfast in his belly. Because of their difference in skin color, there would be occasional tension—caused by the strange looks from strangers, teachers, other mothers, and the bullies on the playground, who would chant after they knocked him down, "Your Momma's white, your Momma's white." But if she were home, their weekends and evenings would be spent together transcending those looks and healing those bruises. Now, however, their time is spent eating visiting-room junk food and his school days are spent fighting the boys in the playground who chant, "Your Momma's in prison, your Momma's in prison."

He will be ten when his mother is released, the same age my nephew will be when his mother is let out. But Jennifer, my sister, was able to spend the first five years of Toby's life with him. Stephanie had Ellie after she was incarcerated. They let her hold him for eighteen hours, then sent her back to prison. She has done the "tour," and her son is a well-traveled six-year-old. He has spent weekends visiting his mother in prisons in Kentucky, Texas, Connecticut (the Pit of Fire), and now at last here, the camp—minimum security, Pekin, Illinois.

Ellie looks older than his age. But his shoulders do not droop like his grandmother's. On the contrary, his bitterness lifts them and his chin higher than a child's should be, and the childlike, wide-eyed curiosity has been replaced by defiance. You can see his emerging hostility as he and his mother play together. She tells him to pick up the toy that he threw, say, or to put the deck of cards away. His face turns sullen, but she persists. She takes him by the shoulders and looks him in the eye, and he uses one of his hands to swat at her. She grabs the hand and he swats with the other. Eventually, she pulls him toward her and smells the top of his head, and she picks up the cards or the toy herself. After all, it is Mother's Day and she sees him so rarely. But her acquiescence makes him angrier, and he stalks out of the playroom with his shoulders thrown back.

Toby, my brother and sister and I assure one another, will not have these resentments. He is better taken care of than most. He is living with relatives in Wisconsin. Good, solid, middle-class, churchgoing relatives. And when he visits us, his aunts and his uncle, we take him out for adventures where we walk down the alley of a city and pretend that we are being chased by the "bad guys." We buy him fast food, and his uncle, John, keeps him up well past his bedtime enthralling him with stories of the monkeys he met in India. A perfect mix, we try to convince one another. Until we take him to see his mother and on the drive back he asks the question that most confuses him, and no doubt all the other children who spend much of their lives in prison visiting rooms: "Is my Mommy a bad guy?" It is the question that most seriously disorders his five-year-old need to clearly separate right from wrong. And because our own need is perhaps just as great, it is the question that haunts us as well.

Now, however, the answer is relatively simple. In a few years, it won't   15
be. In a few years we will have to explain mandatory minimums, and the war on drugs, and the murky conspiracy laws, and the enormous amount of money and time that federal agents pump into imprisoning low-level drug dealers and those who happen to be their friends and their lovers. In a few years he might have the reasoning skills to ask why so many armed robbers and rapists and child-molesters and, indeed, murderers are punished less severely than his mother. When he is older, we will somehow have to explain to him the difference between federal crimes, which don't allow for parole, and state crimes, which do. We will have to explain that his mother was taken from him for five years not because she was a drug dealer but because she made four phone calls for someone she loved.

But we also know it is vitally important that we explain all this without betraying our bitterness. We understand the danger of abstract anger, of being disillusioned with your country, and, most of all, we do not want him to inherit that legacy. We would still like him to be raised as we were, with the idea that we live in the best country in the world with the best legal system in the world—a legal system carefully designed to be immune to political mood swings and public hysteria; a system that promises to fit the punishment to the crime. We want him to be a good citizen. We want him to have absolute faith that he lives in a fair country, a country that watches over and protects its most vulnerable citizens: its women and children.

So for now we simply say, "Toby, your mother isn't bad, she just did a bad thing. Like when you put rocks in the lawn mowers' gas tank. You weren't bad then, you just did a bad thing."

Once, after being given this weak explanation, he said, "I wish I could have done something really bad, like my Mommy. So I could go to prison too and be with her."

We notice a circle forming on one side of the visiting room. A little boy stands in its center. He is perhaps nine years old, sporting a burnt-orange three-piece suit and pompadour hair. He stands with his legs slightly apart, eyes half-shut, and sways back and forth, flashing his cuffs and snapping his fingers while singing:

> . . . Doesn't like crap games with barons and earls.
> Won't go to Harlem in ermine and pearls.
> Won't dish the dirt with the rest of the girls.
> That's why the lady is a tramp.

He has a beautiful voice and it sounds vaguely familiar. One of the visitors informs me excitedly that the boy is the youngest Frank Sinatra impersonator and that he has been on television even. The boy finishes his performance and the room breaks into applause. He takes a sweeping bow, claps his miniature hands together, and points both little index fingers at the audience. "More. Later. Folks." He spins on his heels and returns to the table where his mother awaits him, proudly glowing. "Don't mess with the hair, Mom," we overhear. "That little boy's slick," my brother says with true admiration.

Sitting a few tables down from the youngest Frank Sinatra is a table of Mexican-Americans. The young ones are in white dresses or button-down oxfords with matching ties. They form a strange formal contrast to the rest of the rowdy group. They sit silently, solemnly listening to the white-haired woman, who holds one of the table's two roses. I walk past and listen to the grandmother lecture her family. She speaks of values, of getting up early every day, of going to work. She looks at one of the young boys and points a finger at him. "School is the most important thing. *Nada mas importante.* You get up and you go to school and you study, and you can make lots of money. You can be big. You can be huge. Study, study, study."

The young boy nods his head. "Yes, *abuelita*. Yes, *abuelita*," he says.

20

The owner of the other flower is holding one of the group's three infants. She has him spread before her. She coos and kisses his toes and nuzzles his stomach.

When I ask Jennifer about them, she tells me that it is a "mother and daughter combo." There are a few of them here, these combos, and I notice that they have the largest number of visitors and that the older inmate, the grandmother, inevitably sits at the head of the table. Even here, it seems, the hierarchical family structure remains intact. One could take a picture, replace the fast-food wrappers with chicken and potatoes, and these families could be at any restaurant in the country, could be sitting at any dining room table, paying homage on this day to the one who brought them into the world.

Back at our table, a black-haired, Middle Eastern woman dressed in 25 loose cottons and cloth shoes is whispering to my brother with a sense of urgency that makes me look toward my sister Charity with questioning eyes and a tilt of my head. Charity simply shrugs and resumes her conversation with a nineteen-year-old ex-New York University student—another conspirator. Eight years.

Prison, it seems, has done little to squelch the teenager's rebellious nature. She has recently been released from solitary confinement. She wears new retro-bellbottom jeans and black shoes with big clunky heels. Her hair is short, clipped perfectly ragged and dyed white—all except the roots, which are a stylish black. She has beautiful pale skin and beautiful red lips. She looks like any midwestern coed trying to escape her origins by claiming New York's East Village as home. She steals the bleach from the laundry room, I learn later, in order to maintain that fashionable white hue. But stealing the bleach is not what landed her in the hole. She committed the inexcusable act of defacing federal property. She took one of her government-issue T-shirts and wrote in permanent black magic marker, "I have been in your system. I have examined your system." And when she turned around it read, "I find it very much in need of repair."

The Responsive Reader

1 What would you include in capsule portraits or thumbnail sketches of the women inmates Coyne describes in her article? What kind of people are they? (You and your classmates may want to stage a miniproduction in which you and your fellow students assume the identity of the inmates, with each telling her story.)

2 Is there a common element or common denominator in the histories of the inmates? Is there anything to be learned from their stories?

3 In what ways is the jail Coyne visited a woman's world? Which of the scenes or details Coyne records do you think would be missing or different in the visiting room of a prison for men?

4 Do you tend to think that imprisonment, like a serious accident, is

something that happens to others—not to people like you and those you care for? Or do you recognize yourself or people close to you in any of the inmates you see in this article?

Talking, Listening, Writing

5 Do you believe it is possible in our justice system for the main offender to get off with three years in prison while a friend or lover serves ten? When it happens, is it a fluke? What makes it possible?

6 People who go into prisons to teach or befriend inmates or who agitate for prisoners' rights are sometimes called "do-gooders" or "bleeding hearts" by self-styled "hard-nosed" individuals. Temperamentally, are you inclined to be "hard-nosed" or to be a "bleeding heart"? How and where does the difference show in how you act and talk? What do you think accounts for the difference?

Collaborative Projects

7 Growing numbers of women are involved with the justice system or go to jail. You may want to team up with classmates to investigate current trends in your area or your state. Your group may try setting up interviews with insiders in law enforcement or the court system whose jobs bring them into close contact with female offenders. Will Hermes's article "Jailhouse Lawyer" (*Utne Reader* January/February 1999), about a woman who won a MacArthur Foundation award for her work as an advocate for women in prison, may help your group identify current issues and initiatives.

TIME

Nathan McCall

"I'd heard white people brag about being free, white, and twenty-one. There I was, black, twenty-one, and in the penitentiary. It seemed I'd gotten it all wrong."

During the decade spanning the Reagan and first Bush presidencies, the population of America's prison Gulag archipelago tripled from half a million to an estimated million and a half human beings. In some communities, prison construction was one of the few growth industries left. Three-strike laws were projected to swell prisons to the point where money spent on jails would outstrip the money the nation spends on schools.

Nathan McCall is an African American journalist who went to hell and back in the American prison system and told his story in Makes Me Wanna Holler *(1994). Growing up in a black working-class neighborhood in Portsmouth, Virginia, he had a stepfather who brooked "no hustling, gambling in the streets, or carrying on" and who believed in "work, work, work." McCall says he and his brothers "saw my old man working hard, and he had nothing." Like many young black males, McCall was carrying a gun by the time he was fifteen and was in jail by the time he was twenty. After serving three years for armed robbery, he studied journalism at Norfolk State University. He became a reporter for the* Virginia Pilot-Ledger Star *and the* Atlanta Journal and Constitution *and joined the prestigious* Washington Post *in 1989.*

Thought Starters: Is America's large prison population invisible in the American media?

I was standing in my cell doorway, checking out the scene on the floor 1 below, when a white convict appeared in the doorway across from mine. He stood stark still and looked straight ahead. Without saying a word, he lifted a razor blade in one hand and began slashing the wrist of the other, squirting blood everywhere. He kept slashing, rapid-fire, until finally he dropped the razor and slumped to the floor, knocking his head against the bars as he went down.

Other inmates standing in their doorways spotted him and yelled, "Guard! Guard! Guard!" Guards came running, rushed the unconscious inmate to the dispensary, and ordered a hallboy to clean up the pool of blood oozing down the walkway. Later, when I asked the hallboy why the dude had tried to take himself out, he said, "That *time* came down on him and he couldn't take the pressure. You know them white boys can't handle time like us brothers. They weak."

It was a macho thing for a guy to be able to handle his time. Still, every once in a while, time got to everybody, no matter how tough they were. Hard time came in seasonal waves that wiped out whole groups of cats, like a monsoon. Winter was easiest on everybody. There was the sense that you really weren't missing anything on the streets because everyone was indoors. Spring and summer were hell. The Dear John letters started flowing in, sending heartbroken dudes to the fence for a clean, fast break over and into the countryside. Fall was a wash. The weather was nice enough to make you think of home, but winter was just ahead, giving you something to look forward to. Time.

I saw the lifers go through some serious changes about time. Some days, those cats carried theirs as good as anybody else, but other days, they didn't. You could look in their eyes sometimes and tell they had run across a calendar, one of those calendars that let you know what day of the week your birthday will fall on ten years from now. Or you could see in the wild way they started acting and talking that they were on the edge. Then it was time to get away from them, go to the other side of the prison yard, and watch the fireworks. They went *off*. Especially the brothers. They were determined not to go down kicking and screaming and slashing their wrists like the white boys. The brothers considered themselves too hard for that. When the time got to be too much for them, they'd go fuck with somebody and get themselves in a situation where there was no win. It was their way of saying, "Go on, kill me. Gimme a glorious way to get outta this shit."

My time started coming down on me when I realized I'd reached the one-year mark and had at least two to go. I tried to cling tighter to Liz, but that didn't work. After I was transferred from the jail to Southampton, it seemed we both backed out on the marriage plans. She didn't bring it up, and neither did I. Liz's visits and letters slacked off, and I felt myself slipping out of touch with the outside world. When Liz did visit, she seemed distant and nervous, like there was something she wanted to tell me but couldn't get out. That drove me crazy, along with about a hundred thousand other irritations that constantly fucked with my head.

I thought a lot about the irony of the year 1976: It was the year Alex Haley published the slave epic *Roots* and the country was celebrating the two hundredth year of its freedom from tyranny. It seemed that every time I opened a magazine or walked past a TV set, there was talk about the year-long bicentennial celebration. I'd heard white people brag about being free, white, and twenty-one. There I was, black, twenty-one, and in the penitentiary. It seemed I'd gotten it all wrong.

It's a weird feeling being on the edge and knowing that there's not much you can do about it but hang on. You can't get help for prison depression. You can't go to a counselor and say, "Look, I need a weekend pass.

This punishment thing is taking more out of me than I think it was intended to take."

I didn't want to admit to myself that the time was getting to me that much, let alone admit it to anybody else. So I determined to do the macho thing: suffer quietly. Sometimes it got so bad I had to whisper to myself, "Hold on, Nate. Hold on."

Frustrated and depressed, I went to the prison and bought a green spiral-bound tablet and started a journal, partly out of a need to capture my fears and feelings, and partly to practice using the new words I learned. I adopted a journal theme—a quote I ran across by the writer Oliver Wendell Holmes—as encouragement to keep me pushing ahead and holding on:

> I find the great thing in this world is not so much where we stand as in what direction we are moving. To reach the port of heaven, we must sail, sometimes with the wind and sometimes against it—but we must sail, and not drift, nor lie at anchor.

It made me feel better sometimes to get something down on paper just like I felt it. It brought a kind of relief to be able to describe my pain. It was like, if I could describe it, it lost some of its power over me. I jotted down innermost thoughts I couldn't verbalize to anyone else, recorded what I saw around me, and expressed feelings inspired by things I read. Often, the thoughts I wrote down reflected my struggle with time.

> *Each day I inspire myself with the hope that by some miracle of God or act of legislature I will soon regain my freedom. However, from occasional conversations, I find that many other inmates have entertained the same hope for years. May 21, 1976*

Even the guys doing less than life had a hard time. Anything in the double digits—ten years to serve, twenty, forty, sixty—could be a back-breaker. I had a buddy, Cincinnati. Real outgoing cat. Every time you saw him, he was talking beaucoup trash. But Cincinnati was doing a hard forty, and it drove him up a wall at least twice a week. He fought it by trying to keep super-busy. With a white towel hung loosely over his shoulder and several cartons of cigarettes tucked under his arm, Cincinnati (we called him that because that's where he was from) would bop briskly across the yard, intent on his missions. He'd stop and jawbone with a group of guys hanging out near the canteen, then hand a carton of cigarettes to one of them and hurry off to the next meeting.

Cincinnati was one of several major dealers at Southampton who used the drug-peddling skills they'd learned on the streets to exploit the crude prison economy. In that economy, cigarettes replaced money as the medium of exchange. Favors and merchandise were negotiated in terms of their worth in packs of cigarettes. For twelve cartons of cigarettes, a guy could take out a contract to have somebody set up on a drug bust, or get them double-banked or shanked. Eight packs could get you a snappy pair of prison brogans from one of the brothers on the shoe-shop crew. For three packs each week, laundry workers would see to it your shirts and pants were crisply starched. Cincinnati liked to get his gray prison shirts starched so that he could turn up the collar and look real cool.

The really swift dealers found ways to convert a portion of their goods to forbidden cash, which they used to bribe guards to get them reefer and liquor, or saved for their eventual return to the streets.

Cincinnati, who was about two years older than me and had logged a lot more street time, was penitentiary-rich. He decorated his cell with plush blue towels and stockpiled so much stuff that the rear wall of his cell looked like a convenience store. It was stacked from floor to ceiling with boxes of cookies, cigarettes, and other stuff he sold, "two for one," to inmates seeking credit until payday.

Watching cats like him, I often thought about Mo Battle and his the- *15* ory about pawns. Cincinnati handled time and played chess like he lived: He failed to think far ahead and he chased pawns all over the board. In his free time off from the kitchen, where he worked, he busied himself zigzagging across the prison yard, collecting outstanding debts and treating his petty "bidness" matters like they were major business deals.

Cincinnati was playful and cheery most of the time. He was as dark as night and had a shiny gold tooth that gleamed like a coin when he smiled. Short and squat, he had a massive upper body and a low center of gravity, like Mike Tyson. In fact, his voice, high-pitched and squeaky, sounded a lot like Tyson's, too. It was the kind of voice that sounded like it belonged to a child. But nobody mistook Cincinnati for a child. He was a tank, and could turn from nice guy to cold killer in a split second.

He addressed everybody as "bro'." I'd see him on the yard and say, "Yo, Cincinnati, what's happ'nin'?" And if he was in a good mood, he'd say, "Bro' Nate, life ain't nothin' but a meatball."

But time came down on Cincinnati, like it did on everybody else. He had to do at least ten of his forty years before going up for parole. I could tell when he was thinking about it. I'd run into him on the yard and say, "What's happ'nin', Cincinnati?" He'd shake his head sadly and say, "Bro' Nate, I'm busted, disgusted, and *can't* be trusted."

Cincinnati was so far away from home that he never got visits. On visiting days, he usually went out to the main sidewalk on the yard and looked through the fence as people visiting other inmates pulled into the parking lot.

Other times, I could tell how depressed he was by the way he handled *20* defeat on the chessboard. I beat him all the time and taunted him, but sometimes he didn't take it well. Just before I put him in checkmate, he'd get frustrated and knock one of his big arms against the board, sending the pieces crashing to the floor. Then he'd look up with a straight face and say, "Oh, I'm sorry, Bro' Nate. I didn't mean to do that."

We were playing chess one day when Cincinnati stared at the board a long time without making a move. I got impatient. "Go on and move, man! You gonna lose anyway!"

Ignoring me, Cincinnati kept his eyes glued to the board and didn't speak for a long time. After a while, he said, "Bro' Nate, I'm gonna make a break for the fence. I been thinking about it a long time. I got a lotta money saved up. I can get outta state. You wanna come?"

Any inmate who says he's never thought about escaping is either lying or telling the sad truth. The sad truth is, the only dudes who don't think about making a break are those who are either so institutionalized that their thoughts seldom go beyond the prison gates, or who were so poor in the streets that they had been rescued and are glad to be someplace where they are guaranteed three hots and a cot.

There were a few desperate, fleeting moments when I thought half-seriously about making a run. Southampton is ringed by a tall barbed-wire fence with electrical current running through it, but everybody knew the heat was turned off much of the time. Sometimes, I'd stare at that fence and think about how to scale it. I pictured myself tossing my thick winter coat on top of the barbed wire to test the heat and protect my hands, climbing quickly to the top, and leaping to the other side to make my dash before tower guards could get off a good shot. I'd mapped an escape route based on what I'd seen of the area while traveling with the gun gang. I'd thought it through like a chess match, move for move. That's why I didn't try. When I thought it through, I always saw a great chance of getting busted or leading such a miserable life on the run that it would be another form of imprisonment.

Looking at Cincinnati, I jokingly turned down his offer to run. "Naw, brother-man. I'm gonna squat here. I'm expecting a visit from my lady this weekend. I'd hate for her to come and find me gone. Besides, I can handle my bid. You do the crime, you gotta do the time, Jack!"   25

I forgot about our conversation until a week or two later, when the big whistle at the guard tower sounded, signaling all inmates to go to their cells to be counted. The whistle blew at certain times every day, but on this day, it sounded at an odd hour, meaning there was something wrong. After we went to our cells, the word spread that Cincinnati had made a break. He'd hidden in the attic of the school building, then scrambled over the fence after a posse left the compound to hunt for him.

Following the count, guys in my building (I was in C–3 by then) grew real quiet. Every time someone escaped, I got quiet and privately rooted for him to get away. I sat on my bunk thinking about Cincinnati, trying to picture him out in the pitch dark, his black face sweating, ducking through bushes, hotly pursued by white men with guns and barking dogs. I imagined him low-running across some broad field, dodging lights and listening for suspicious sounds. I imagined the white country folks, alerted to the escape, grabbing their shotguns and joining the hunt.

Some weeks after Cincinnati made his break, he got caught somewhere in the state. It saddened me. He was shipped to a maximum-security prison more confining than Southampton, and he got more time tacked on to the forty years that was already giving him hell.

> *Prison paranoia is a dangerous thing. It can affect a person to the extent that he becomes distrustful of anyone and everyone. Even though my woman has displayed no signs of infidelity, I find myself scrutinizing her behavior each week (in the visiting room), searching her eyes for the slightest faltering trait. I search in hope that I discover none, but hope even more that if there is, I will detect it before it discovers me and slithers back into some obscure hiding place. June 4, 1976*

I walked into the crowded visiting room and took a seat at the table with Liz. My intuition told me that something was up. She'd come alone, without my parents or my son, and her brown eyes, usually bright and cheery, were sad and evasive. In a letter she'd sent to me earlier in the week, she had said there was something she wanted to discuss. I sensed what it was, and I'd come prepared.

We exchanged small talk, then there was this awkward silence. Finally, I spoke, relieving her of a burden I sensed was killing her. "You're seeing someone else, aren't you?"

She nodded. "Yes."

There was a long pause as she waited for my reaction. I looked down at the floor and thought about what I'd just heard. My worst fear had come true. Liz couldn't hang. I'd have to do the time alone. I understood. She'd done the best she could. She'd been a helluva lot more supportive and reliable than I would have been under the circumstances. The best I could do was be grateful for what she'd done. Take it and grow, as she used to say. I tried to put on a brave face, and I said, "I understand, really. . . . Well, nothing I can do about that but wish you the best. I would like you to hang in there with me, but really, I don't know when I'm gettin' outta here."

She listened quietly and nodded as I talked. When I finished, she didn't say much. We sat there, bummed out, looking at each other. Mr. and Miss Manor. Liz wished me well. Her eyes watered. Then she said goodbye, and left.

I practically ran back to my cell that Saturday morning. I wanted to get back there before the tear ducts burst. It was like trying to get to the bathroom before the bladder gives out. I made it, went inside, and flopped down on a stool. I turned on the stereo, slid in one of my favorite gospel tapes, *Amazing Grace,* by Aretha Franklin, and closed my eyes. The tape opened with a song called "Mary, Don't You Weep." The deep strains of a full gospel choir, comforting the sister of Lazarus after his death, sang in a rich harmony that sent shivers through me:

Hush, Mary, don't you weep.
Hush, Mary, don't you weep.

When I heard those words, the floodgate burst and the tears started   35
streaming down my face. Streaming. The pain ran so deep it felt physical,
like somebody was pounding on my chest. I'd never been hurt by a woman
before. I had never cared enough to be hurt by one. I sat there, leaning on
the cell door, listening to Aretha and crying. Inmates walked past and I did-
n't even lift my head. I didn't care who saw me or what they thought. I was
crushed. Wasted. I cried until tears blurred my vision. Then I got up,
picked up my washcloth, rinsed it in the sink, held it to my face, and cried
some more. Liz was gone. I remembered that she had once told me, "I'll
follow you into a ditch if you lead me there." Well, I had led her there, but
she'd never promised to stay.

Sometimes I'd get grinding migraines that lasted for hours on end. I
figured it was caused by the pain of losing Liz, and the stress and tension
hounding me. When the frequency of the headaches increased, I came up
with ways to relieve the stress. I'd leave the place. I'd stretch out on my
bunk, block out all light by putting a cloth over my eyes, and go into deep
meditation or prayer. Starting with my toes, I'd concentrate hard and command every one of my body parts to chill. Often, by the time I reached my
head the tension was gone.

Then I'd take my imagination and soar away from the prison yard. I'd
travel to Portsmouth or some faraway, fictional place. Or I'd venture beyond the earth and wander through the galaxy, pondering the vastness of
what God has done. I developed a hell of an imagination by doing those
mental workouts, and it put me in touch with my spirit in wondrous ways.
When the concentration was really good, I'd lose all feeling in my body,
and my spirit would come through, making me feel at one with the universe. It was like being high: It felt so good, but I couldn't figure out a way
to make it last.

> *I just witnessed a brutal fight in the cafeteria. The atmosphere was certainly*
> *conducive to violence: hot, odorous air filled with noise and flies. The two com-*
> *batants went at each other's throats as if their lives meant nothing to them. Af-*
> *ter being confined for an extended period of time, life does tend to lose its value.*
> *I pray that I can remember my self-worth and remain cool.*
> *July 27, 1976*

A group of us from Tidewater were sitting around, sharing funny tales
from the streets and telling war stories about crazy things we'd done. When
my turn came, I told a story about a near stickup on Church Street in Norfolk. "Yeah, man, we ran across a dude who had nothing but chump change
on him. We got mad 'cause the dude was broke, so we took his change and
started to take his pants. He had on some yellow, flimsy-looking pants, so

we made him walk with us under a streetlamp so we could get a better look at them. When we got under the streetlamp, we could see the pants were cheap. And they were dirty. So we let the dude slide, and keep his pants . . ."

Everybody was laughing. Everybody but a guy from Norfolk named Tony. Squinting his eyes, he leaned over and interrupted, "Did you say the guy had on yellow pants?"

"Yeah."

"Goddammit, that was *me* y'all stuck up that night!" he said, pointing   40 a finger at me.

Everything got quiet. The guys looked at me, then at Tony, then back at me. Somebody snickered, and everybody else joined in. I laughed, too, until I looked at Tony and realized he still wasn't laughing. He was hot. He looked embarrassed and mad as hell.

To lighten the mood, I extended my hand playfully and said, "Wow, man, I'm sorry 'bout that. You know I didn't know you then."

Tony looked at my hand like he wanted to spit on it. "Naw, man. That shit ain't funny." The way he said it, I knew he wasn't going to let the thing drop. I knew that stupid macho pride had him by the throat and was choking the shit out of him.

A week or two after the exchange, he came into the library, where I   45 was working, sat in a corner, and started tearing pages out of magazines. The library was filled with inmates. I walked over to the table and said, "Yo, Tony, you can't tear the pages outta the magazines, man. Other people have to read 'em."

He looked up, smiled an evil smile, then ripped out another page and said. "What you gonna do 'bout it? You ain't no killer." The room grew quiet. I felt like all eyes were on me, waiting to see what I would do. I started thinking fast. Tony was stout and muscular and I figured he'd probably do the moonwalk on me if he got his hands on me. He was sitting down and I was standing. I glanced at an empty chair near him. I thought, *I could sneak him right off the bat, grab that chair, and wrap it around his head.* Then I thought about the potential consequences of fighting at work. I could lose my job, get kicked out of the library. I thought, *I gotta let it slide. I have to.* I looked at Tony, shrugged my shoulders, and said, "I ain't gonna do nothin', man. The magazines don't belong to *me.*"

Tony sat there, staring at me, and tore more pages out of magazines. I walked away.

Later that night, I thought about it some more. I thought about how he'd come off. I thought, *He disrespected me.* I was too scared to let that man get away with disrespecting me. I felt I had faith that God would take care of me, but whenever I got that scared about something, I relied on what I knew best—faith in self. So I prayed, then set God aside for the time being and put together a shank like I'd learned to make while in the Norfolk jail. I melded a razor blade into a toothbrush handle, leaving the sharp edges sticking out, like a miniature tomahawk. I told one of my buddies what I intended to do. "I gotta get that niggah, man. He disrespected me and tried to chump me down."

The next day, we went looking for Tony on the yard. We spotted him leaving the dispensary with a partner. While my friend kept a lookout for guards, I approached Tony. Without saying anything, I pulled the razor blade and swung it at his throat. He jumped back. I lunged at him again and he flung his arms in front of his face, blocking the blow. The razor slashed his coat. He held up his hands and said, "Hold it, hold it, hold it, man! Be cool. Everything's cool. We all right, man. I ain't got no beef with you."

I pointed the razor at him. "Niggah, don't you *never* take me to be no   50
chump!"

"All right, bro', I was just playing with you yesterday."

I turned and walked away, relieved that he'd backed down and grateful that none of the guards standing on the yard had seen what went down.

My parents came to see me that afternoon. I went into the visiting room still hyper from the scene with Tony. As we talked, I looked at them and wondered what they'd say if they knew I had just risked everything I'd worked for to prove a manhood point. I wondered if Tony was going to try to get some get-back or pay somebody to try to shank me when my back was turned. I wondered if the time was coming down on me so badly that I was losing my grip.

At chow time that evening, my homie Pearly Blue came to the table and sat next to me. There was a slight smirk on his face. I sensed he was feeling a certain delight in knowing he'd warned me to hang tight with my homies to keep hassles away. "Yo, man, I heard you had a run-in with Tony."

"Yeah, a small beef."   55

"I told you these old rooty-poot niggahs will try you if they think you walk alone. . . . You know if you need to make another move on him, the homies can take care of it."

I kept looking straight ahead as I ate. "Naw, man. I got it under control."

I had no problems from Tony the remainder of the time I was at Southampton.

The one thing that seemed to soothe everybody in the joint was music. The loudest, most fucked-up brothers in the place chilled out when they had on a set of headphones. Some white inmates had musical instruments—guitars, saxophones, flutes—and they practiced in their cells at night. Most of the brothers didn't like hearing white music. The brothers would holler through the cell bars, "Cut that hillbilly shit out!"

But one white guy, from some rural Virginia town, was exempt from   60
the hassles. He was a fairly good guitar player, and an even better singer. Every night, before the lights went out, he calmed the building with music. He sang the same song, and it reverberated throughout the place. He strummed his guitar and sang the John Denver tune "Take Me Home,

Country Roads." He sang it in a voice so clean it sounded like he was standing on a mountain crooning down into one of those luscious green valleys he was singing about:

> *Country rooaads,*
> *Take me hoomme,*
> *To the plaaace*
> *Where I beloooonng. . .*

When those lyrics floated into my cell, I'd sit quietly, lean my head against the concrete wall, and listen. That song reminded me of how lonely I was and made me think of home. It made me think of Liz. It made me think of my son, my family, my neighborhood, my life. Sometimes, when he sang that song, tears welled in my eyes and I'd wipe them away, get into bed, and think some more.

That song seemed to calm everybody in the building, even the baadasses who were prone to yell through their cells. It had the soothing effect of a lullaby sung by a parent to a bunch of children.

The Responsive Reader

1 Can you empathize with the author of this account of prison life? Why or why not? What kind of person is he? How did the prison experience affect him? How did it shape his attitude toward life?

2 How do the different inmates McCall remembers deal with "doing time"? How do they cope? What strategies do they develop, and how successful are these?

3 Many stories of prison life focus on trying to survive in a brutally violent environment. For the author, what is the point of the story he tells about his confrontation with Tony? What is the point or the lesson of the story for you?

4 How do white people look as seen through the eyes of black inmates? Does McCall think whites and blacks deal differently with the prison experience? Is race a major segregating factor or dividing line in McCall's prison?

5 What is the role of music in McCall's story?

Talking, Listening, Writing

6 Do you tend to think people in jail are a different breed from ordinary law-abiding citizens? Do you know anyone who is doing or has done time? What is the person's story?

7 Critics of the American justice system claim that in our society poor people go to jail. People of color go to jail. Poor people of color go to jail. To judge from McCall's account, are the critics right?

8 What is the racial or ethnic mix and social status of defendants in your local courts?

Collaborative Projects

9   The cost of prison construction and of housing ever-growing numbers
    of inmates has soared in recent years. What is the bottom line? What sta-
    tistics are available on the actual and projected costs of the prison indus-
    try? How does the cost of confining a young person for most of his or
    her life compare, say, with the cost of supporting a welfare family or
    with the average funds spent in poor neighborhoods on educating a
    child?

WHY THE ABLE-BODIED STILL DON'T GET IT

Andre Dubus

"I wanted to yell at someone, wanted above all to put someone in a wheelchair for one long pushing, pulling, muscle-aching, mind–absorbing day."

The following article challenging our complacency about society's treatment of the disabled was first published in the Epoch *periodical in 1997.*

Society has come a long way in its treatment of and attitudes toward people with disabilities. Ramps and special elevators facilitate wheelchair access to schools, public buildings, and restaurants. Public transit provides special lifts or alternative transportation. Employers are finding new ways of allowing people with disabilities to use their skills. The media tout breakthroughs in space-age technologies that promise to help physically impaired people to see, to hear, or to walk. Nevertheless, the author of the following article and other voices speaking for the disabled express their rage and frustration at deep-seated engrained attitudes and unresolved issues. Why?

Thought Starters: Like other spokespersons for people with physical or mental impairments, the author of the following article assumes the existence of two worlds: the world of the fully enabled and the world of the impaired. What has been your own experience with that second universe? Where do you come into contact with or confront disability? What attitudes, expectations, or obligations does it bring into play?

In my sixth year as a cripple, I read a newspaper story about a 34–year–old man who, while he was playing rugby, received an injury that changed his body, and so his life, forever—he is a quadriplegic. The newspaper story focused on the good effect he had on his friends and other people in the city where he lived. They raised money for him; they visited him in the hospital; they said they drew strength from his courage. The injured man said he had regained the use of his hands and that someday he would walk again and play golf. He was still in the hospital.

I was hit by a car on the highway, and lost my left leg above the knee; my right leg was too damaged to use. On the night of my injury I was 49 years old and my sixth child was in her mother's womb. Friends visited me, phoned, wrote letters. Eight writers raised money for me with readings; I didn't even know five of them till we met at the readings. The quadriplegic was talking about playing a game on grass in summer, and his injury was far

1

worse than mine. As he lay on the ground after being hurt, he said *I'm still single*.

So why, as I ate cereal and read this story, did I feel rage instead of gratitude? I wanted to yell at someone, wanted above all to put someone in a wheelchair for one long pushing, pulling, muscle-aching, mind-absorbing day. But who? The reporter and his editor? That newspaper gives favorable reviews to restaurants that the quadriplegic cannot go into, and it doesn't tell you whether or not the restaurant is accessible to people in wheelchairs. This means the reviewers and editors don't think of us as people. They wouldn't review a restaurant that was accessible only to Caucasians or only to men.

Who will carry the quadriplegic up even one step to a restaurant? And why would he want to be carried, when his helplessness, his very meatness, slaps his soul? Chairs with motors cost around $8,000, and if you plan to leave your home you need a van with a lift, and someone to drive it. The quadriplegic will not walk. He will forever be dependent on someone. He cannot sit on a toilet, he cannot wipe himself, or shave, shower, make his bed, dress. He will use a catheter. He cannot cook. He will not feel the heat of a woman, except with his face.

When I was a graduate student at the University of Iowa Writers' Workshop, I had a friend in a wheelchair. I met him in late afternoon on a cold winter day. There was snow on the ground and the sidewalks, and he was pushing his chair up a long steep hill. I was walking at the bottom of the hill when I heard his voice. I stopped and saw him looking over his shoulder at me, calling, "Can you give me a push?"

He couldn't make it any farther up the hill. I felt the embarrassment of being whole while he was not, and went up to him and pushed. In this way we introduced ourselves: I spoke to the back of his head, and he spoke into the cold air in front of him. The hill led to a street that was flat, and he told me I could stop pushing. Across the street was a bar, and we went in. I don't remember how he got down to the street, over the sidewalk's curb, and back up again on the other side. He did it alone. His crippling, he said, came from polio, while he was in the army. In rehabilitation he had learned to lean his chair backward, bring the small front wheels down on the curb, and push and lift the big rear wheels onto it.

He had broad shoulders and a deep voice that I loved hearing. I do not remember how much of his lower body was paralyzed. He had a girl-friend and, one evening in a bar, he said to me *I can have intercourse*. I don't remember pulling him up the steps to our house when he came for dinner or a party, but we had more than one step and my wife and I must have helped him. He told me of learning to use a wheelchair, how the instructors took the men on wheels out of the hospital and raced to a nearby bar. *You had to keep up and get over the curbs* he said. *If you fell on your back, tough shit*. He laughed and I laughed with him, and that's how I thought of people in wheelchairs until I became one: stout-hearted folk wheeling fast on side-

5

walks, climbing curbs, and of course sometimes falling backward, but that seemed to me like slipping and falling on the outfield grass while you're chasing a fly ball. That is, until over 20 years later, when I fell backward in my chair, and slammed my head against the floor, and I lay helpless and hurt. It was summer and the windows were open and my neighbor, in his house 30 yards away, heard my head striking wood.

My friend was very skillful in his wheelchair, and I lacked imagination. Or I lacked the compassion and courage to imagine someone else's suffering. I never thought of my friend making his bed, sitting on a toilet, sitting in a shower, dressing himself, preparing breakfast and washing its dishes, just to leave his house, to go out into the freezing Iowa air.

In my freshman year of college in Louisiana, I studied journalism. If I had become a reporter, and if one day I had walked into a hospital and interviewed a quadriplegic, I would have written the same kind of story I read in the newspaper that morning. It's good story. The human spirit is strong, and the heart is capable of such hope that, even when we know the truth and it's not the truth we want, we still persevere. I would have celebrated this, as a reporter; and that night, after writing my story about the brave and hopeful quadriplegic, I would have climbed four steps to a restaurant.

And I wouldn't have imagined sitting in a 250-pound wheelchair star-   *10* ing at those few steps leading to the restaurant's door; or looking into a woman's eyes and, in my chest, feeling passion my body could no longer release.

A friend of mine who was a Marine lieutenant in Vietnam was blown into the air by a mine and lost his left leg below the knee. He had been a quarterback in school. When he came home to his small town, limping on an artificial leg, he saw his coach. The coach asked what happened to his leg, and my friend said, "I twisted my knee."

I met him nearly 20 years later, and less than a month before I was injured. We were at a writers' conference, and he didn't limp. When he told me about his leg, I said I never would have known. A long time after my injury, when I was still working with a physical therapist, I talked with this friend on the phone and reminded him of what I had said that summer. "You pissed me off," he said. "People don't know how tiring it is, and how much it hurts."

We were talking on the phone again when he told me about his coach. "You didn't tell him you were in the war?" I asked.

"I was afraid of his reaction."

I sing of those who cannot. To view human suffering as an abstrac-   *15* tion, as a statement about how plucky we all are, is to blow air through brass while the boys and girls march in parade off to war. Seeing the flesh as only a challenge to the spirit is as false as seeing the spirit as only a challenge to the flesh. On the planet are people with whole and strong bodies, whose wounded spirits need the constant help that the quadriplegic needs for his body. What we need is not the sound of horns rising to the sky but the steady beat of the bass drum. When you march to a bass drum, your left foot touches the earth with each beat, and you can feel the drum in your body: *boom* and *boom* and *boom* and *pity people pity people*.

The Responsive Reader

1 One of the first words Dubus uses is the word *cripple*. Media people, teachers, and politicians years ago learned not to use this word, because it is demeaning, abusive, outgrouping, or insensitive. Why does Dubus use it?

2 Dubus is a writer who uses a powerful personal narrative to make his points. In the opening paragraphs, he tells the story of the rugby player and his own story. What in both of these stories would make readers experience positive feelings or make them expect gratitude? Why does the author instead feel a growing rage?

3 In the flashback to his graduate student days, Dubus reverses the perspective: He looks at a disabled person from the point of view of the enabled person. How does he make you see and come to know the other person as a fellow human being? Why does he nevertheless feel that he failed or fell short in befriending the other person?

4 What does the story of the Vietnam veteran add to Dubus's essay? What added dimension or broader perspective does it bring to the essay? Would you feel differently about a disabled veteran than you would about other people with disabilities? Why or why not?

5 Dubus is a writer who lets authentic personal experience speak for itself before he strongly makes his points. How does his conclusion sum up his central message? How does it go beyond what he has already said?

Talking, Listening, Writing

6 Do you think Dubus's article would keep media people from creating "brave and hopeful" articles or programs about disability? Would you defend the positive slant the media often give to reporting about disability? What would you say?

7 When Dubus describes his encounters with people with disabilities before he himself became disabled, he says, "I lacked imagination. Or I lacked the compassion and courage to imagine someone else's suffering." How do you think we could show that imagination, that compassion, or that courage? What does Dubus want from able-bodied readers?

8 After reading and discussing Dubus's article, write a letter to the editor, a chat room posting, or a communication asking your readers to rethink their attitudes toward people with disabilities.

FIND IT ON THE WEB

What promising leads can you identify for an investigation of technological advances designed to help disabled or impaired people see, hear, or walk? Which seem to raise realistic hopes for future progress? Pool your findings with coworkers' in preparation for a possible class presentation or written report.

The following are sample entries from one student's annotated search report:

Dellio, Michael. "A Wheelchair for the World." *Wired News*. 27 July 2000.   10   Jan.   2003   <http://www.wired.com/news/technology/ 0,1282,37795-2,00.html>

This website is a review of a technologically advanced wheelchair, designed to help those with disabilities move around in a more normal fashion. It is controlled by an array of small computers that automatically adjust to allow it to cross uneven ground, remain upright in almost any circumstances, and even climb stairs as quickly as a nondisabled person.

Johansen, Anders S. "ALS Computer Solutions FAQ." 9 Jan. 2003. <http://www.secondguess.dk/techfaq.html>

This FAQ (frequently asked questions) provides a discussion of the symptoms of ALS (amyotrophic lateral sclerosis), the problems experienced by those affected by it, and a list of technological devices designed to mitigate those problems. It lists common types of technological aids, along with pros and cons for most solutions.

Hammett, Corinne F. "Quietly Making Life Better with One-of-a-Kind Inventions for Persons with Disabilities." *Tapping Technology*. May 2000. 9 Jan. 2003. <http://www.mdtap.org/tt/2000.05/art_2.html>

This article describes the efforts of Gordon Herald, a retired electrical engineer, and of other members of the VME (Volunteers for Mechanical Engineering) to make life better for the disabled. The VME is a group of individuals who work on a volunteer basis to provide free, individualized solutions to meet the needs of disabled individuals. It provides solutions when mainstream equipment is overly expensive or simply not available.

Solomon, Karen. "Smart Biz: Enabling the Disabled." *Wired News*. 3 Nov. 2000. 9 Jan. 2003. <http://www.wired.com/news/print/ 0,1294,39563,00.html>

This article focuses on the business reasons and new legislation pushing companies to become accessible to the disabled. Using examples, statistics, and legal precedents, the author outlines both the current lack of accessibility and the many compelling reasons for companies to become accessible to the disabled.

FERRYING DREAMERS TO THE OTHER SIDE

Tomas Robles

"Americans are never going to stand a chance of controlling illegal immigration until they're honest with themselves about what really causes it."

—RUBEN NAVARETTE JR., *DALLAS MORNING NEWS*

Millions of immigrants live in the United States illegally. A 2003 estimate put the number of illegal Americans nationwide at 9.7 million, with 2.8 million in California. Tens of thousands of others try to cross the border from Mexico, driven by extreme poverty, unemployment, or failing institutions.

Illegal aliens fill the need of employers and private citizens for cheap labor with no benefits, health care, or union protection. In border states like California and Texas, illegal undocumented immigrants are part of a large black market economy, working as maids, nannies, restaurant help, construction workers, and sweatshop employees. Many work as migrant workers in the fields, often living under substandard conditions, sending money to their families in Mexico. Undocumented workers live at risk of being rounded up and deported by the migra *or U.S. Immigration Service.*

The journey north, crossing the great river or the deadly desert, has been called a life-and-death attempt. In the West, a huge border fence and a border patrol whose numbers have tripled in ten years force the migrant farther inland into desert country where temperatures reach 100 degrees. They encounter rifle-wielding bandits who rob them of their money and at times even their shoes. Armed vigilantes in paramilitary camouflage uniforms have begun to intimidate and discourage the illegals when they reach the American side. The migrants keep coming, some crossing over finally on their third or fourth attempt. According to incomplete official statistics, 409 undocumented aliens died from exhaustion or dehydration in 2003.

The following article is the testimony of a Mexican patero *or guide who makes a living helping illegal immigrants cross the border. The editor who published the following testimony in 1998 was teaching at the Irvine campus of the University of California, an hour's drive from the Mexican border. Irvine is located between San Diego and Los Angeles, two large cities where the majority of the population is now Spanish-speaking or of Mexican descent.*

Thought Starters: How far back can you trace your family history? When or how did your ancestors come to America or become part of America? What were their needs or motives? What obstacles or challenges did they have to overcome? Were any of them "illegals" or in conflict with the law either here or in the old country?

TOMAS ROBLES

Ferrying Dreamers to the Other Side

1

First I look at you. I study you. Then I know whether or not you're going to cross to the other side.

When people arrive, they're afraid. If I see that you've just stepped off the bus and I ask if you want to get to the other side, you're not going to say yes. You're uncertain. You'll think to yourself, "Who is this guy? Is he a criminal? A policeman?" So you'll tell me, "No, I am not going to cross. I'm just here to visit some relatives." Now, when a lot of *pateros* hear this, they'll just walk away. Not me. I say, "You know what? Whatever you want to do, my job is to cross people over to the other side, and I won't charge you a nickel until we get there."

I just keep talking. I don't stop. It's the *patero* who talks the best that gets the most people. I say, "It doesn't matter to me if you've got no money. All you need is a telephone number of someone over there, a relative or some-one else who can pay your way. Here, I'll cover your food and lodging. I'll give you a place to sleep and everything. I won't charge you a penny until we've crossed over. Do you have the number of someone on the other side?"

Then you'll look at me and say, "Okay, I want to cross. How much do you charge?"

5

"Six hundred dollars from here to Houston. Everyone charges the same. But listen, we can't talk here. It's dangerous with all these police. I live just one block away. Let's go to my house. You can wash up. I'll buy you something to eat and we can talk some more."

Then you follow me, see, and we keep talking. Once you're at my house, you're mine. That's how it works. Before we cross the border, you give me the telephone number of someone on the other side, and we call. If they say, "We don't have any money" or "We don't know him," that's it, there's no deal. That's how we arrange things.

We put you up in a hotel until we've gathered ten, twelve, or fifteen people. Sometimes it takes two or three days. We won't carry just two or three people across. It isn't worth it. We need at least eight, because we never work alone. We usually cross over with three or four *pateros*. When we've got everyone together, we tell them, "At four o'clock we're going to cross the river. You'll have to leave your suitcases here. This isn't a vacation. You're going to cross with just a shirt and a pair of pants. Okay?"

Then we say, "If they catch us, don't tell them who's carrying you across. If they ask who helped you cross or which one's the coyote, you just say, 'Nobody's carrying us across. We're all just looking for work.' That way, if Immigration finds us, they'll just send us back across the border, back to Matamoros. They won't jail us and we'll cross over again. If Immigration catches us, they'll ask for our names. We'll give them fake names, and if they catch us again, we'll give them different names. They never remember us."

Once we've talked this over and everyone understands, we take a taxi that drops us off close to the river. On the Mexican side, the police patrol the river on horseback. If they see us, they'll come over to check us out.

"Listen, we're just going over to Brownsville to earn a little money." 10

"Okay, just give us a little something so we can buy a drink."

So we give them a little money and they let us pass. If we're caught by police who know we're *pateros,* we're screwed. They'll make us pay them one, two, maybe three hundred dollars. If we don't pay them, they'll arrest us for some crime we've never committed. They won't just charge us with being *pateros.* They'll charge us with assault and really screw us. They're tough, so we have to work with them. After we give them their *mordida,* they'll let us pass.

Then we go on to the river. We take off our clothes and put them in a bag. We get in the water and cross the river naked. If we crossed wearing clothes, when we got to the other side we'd be wet and people would notice. If La Migra sees that, they'll say, "Look, there goes another wetback," and they'll nail you.

Sometimes we cross people who don't know how to swim. We buy inner tubes and put the people inside. They get nervous, but I tell them, "Don't worry if you can't swim. Just hold on tight to one of my feet." They'll grab on to my foot, and I'll swim across the river using my hands. It's about thirty feet across, but when the water's high, the current gets strong. If you know what you're doing, it's easy, but if not, it can be dangerous. Lots of people drown.

On the American side of the river, there are bandits who carry knives and guns. They'll wait for you and catch you as you get out of the water, naked. They'll tear open your bag looking for money. They'll check your socks and your shoes. They look everywhere. If you've got good boots, nice pants, or a decent shirt, they'll steal them. Sometimes they take everything. Other times they beat you up or threaten you with knives. That's happened to me many times. I've got a knife wound on my leg, another one over there, and another here. Look at all these scars. Look at how they've sliced me up.

Once we've crossed the river, we walk calmly into Brownsville. Then 15 we call up some friends who drive taxis. We put five people in each taxi and carry them to a hotel. We get one room for everybody. The next day, around three or four in the morning, we wake everyone up. We divide the group between three cars. That way if the police or Immigration stop us on the way, they'll only catch one group and the other two will make it through to Houston. We lose less money if we split up, because when they catch you, they arrest the driver, confiscate the car, and send everyone back to the other side.

Before we get to the immigration checkpoint, we get out of the car and let the driver continue north. The drivers have their papers, so they can pass through the checkpoint. Then we walk into the countryside. It's dark, but we know where we're going. There are power lines that we use to guide us. We go on together, walking and walking, for five or six hours. There are lots of rattlesnakes, and you can die if they bite you. We walk on through the brush until we get to a place to rest. Then one person—only one—goes out to the road to see if the drivers are there yet. When they arrive, we get back in the cars and off we go to Houston.

Then we drive to a special house. Our boss meets us there. We gather everyone into the house, park the cars, close the door, and then start calling the phone numbers, one by one. "Okay, we've got your nephew here"—or your son, your brother, whoever. "Come on over with the money." They come over and pay us. We give them the person and off they go. There's times when they don't want to pay or when they only have three or four hundred dollars. Sometimes they'll give us rings, watches, or bracelets. If they don't have anyone who can pay and nothing to give us, we take the people back to Matamoros. If there's someone who'll buy the people off of us, we'll sell them.

I know that what I do is illegal, but it's man who invented these laws, not God. It's the American government that doesn't want us to pass people to the other side. They don't want us to be with you, the gringos. I'm not doing anything wrong. I'm not robbing, beating, or killing anyone. I'm not working against God. Where these people are from, they earn so little they can't even support their families. So even though what I do is illegal, in the end it's actually good. I'm helping people to better themselves, to realize their dreams.

I'm ready for whatever might happen. If today or tomorrow they kill me, or a snake bites me, or they crush the life out of me, my kids will have money in the bank. Every day, I risk my life for my family. It's an adventure being a *patero,* a beautiful life—to know the road, to cross the river. If tomorrow something were to happen to me, who cares? In the end, every man suffers for the life he leads.

The Responsive Reader

1   What is the *job decription* of a coyote? As Robles describes it, his work is not a hit-or-miss operation but a carefully planned and tested procedure. What are major steps or stages in the kind of drill he describes? What are key requirements to make his operation work? What would he include in a brief guide for an apprentice *patero* or coyote?

2   Who are the *players* in the drama of illegal immigration? Much law-and-order rhetoric lines up law-abiding people against lawbreakers. Robles

shows a more complicated, less black-and-white picture. He identifies several types of participants on both sides of the border. Who are major players? What roles do they play? What does Robles think of them? What do you think of them?

3 Whose *code of morality* applies to the border crossers? Robles says that laws are not made by God but by men. Would you call him a criminal? People or groups others labeled criminal may have their own value system or their own code of honor. How would you describe his value system? Does he have loyalties or commitments?

Talking, Listening, Writing

4 Are you able to identify with testimonials from across a cultural or linguistic divide? Reading this account, can you feel empathy—sharing others' feelings? Can you "walk a mile in someone else's shoes"? Which of the people involved are you most likely to identify with, and why— the illegal immigrants? the coyote (or *patero*)? the police or government agents on either side? readers who object to a rising tide of illegal immigration?

5 Where do you draw the line between hard-nosed realism and cynicism? Robles says matter-of-factly that in the crossing of the river many drown. He says that if no one pays or provides compensation for the illegal border crossers he takes them back to Mexico. Would you call him callous or cynical?

Collaborative Projects

6 In a reverse migration, U.S. corporations in search of cheap and nonunionized labor have crossed the southern border to create *maquiladoras*. What are they? What kind of businesses or industries have relied on them? What do their supporters say? What do their critics say?

OTHER VOICES

Undocumented in America

For a column on illegal immigration for the *Dallas Morning News* (June 1, 2004), Ruben Navarette Jr. interviewed immigrants waiting for work on street corners, and he listened to voices from both anti-immigration organizations and Latino advocacy groups. He made the following points:

- "Clearly for some Americans, hiring illegal immigrants is a really good deal. . . . hiring these people is the next best thing to having free labor." Would you discourage employers and private citizens from hiring illegals?

- The illegals "come because they are virtually assured of finding a job—perhaps a dangerous, low-paying, highly exploitative job, but a job nevertheless." At the same time, the nation's largest Spanish-television network put together a report titled "Latino Slaves in the United States." Should authorities in Mexico or other countries discourage their citizens from trying to reach the United States in search of a better life?

- Navarette says that people have emigrated to the United States "for generations—many of them illegally." They were "determined and courageous and sometimes ingenious." Do you tend to honor America's immigrants, or do you tend to be negative or suspicious about foreigners?

STAMPS

Bethlyn Madison Webster

**In a society that begrudges the food stamps helping the
working poor and the unemployed feed their families,
a poet rebels against the smug superiority of the
affluent.**

*Bethlyn Madison Webster was working as a part-time teacher when she
published the following poem in 1995. Like many modern poets, she focuses
on what she observes and lets it largely speak for itself. She finds meaning in
what a more casual observer might have considered just a very ordinary
event—a routine transaction in the checkout line at the grocery store. The
poem tells a story with a point. However, the reader has to do any overt editorializing or spell out more fully the message that is implied in the poem.*

Thought Starters: Have you ever had to accept charity? Have you ever
had to ask others for support? What were your feelings? What went through
your mind? In retrospect, how do you feel about the experience?

I'm watching the woman   1
who is watching my groceries
rolling along the conveyor belt.
She stands Cheerio-mouthed
in a pink and white dress   5
sporting a crisp, curled hairdo
and staring as much as she pleases
while I stand behind my husband,
hiding behind him and the baby.
She has seen him produce   10
a book of foodstamps
from his pocket, and I think she wants
to see how her tax dollars
are being wasted today.
Eggs, milk, peanut butter, bread   15
root beer and a bag of store brand
chocolate chips. She looks
at those the longest.
I want to tell her that we work
for ten cents above minimum.   20
I want to explain

that it's Friday, we're tired,
and our chocolate is none of her business.
Somehow, we're on display
along with the tabloids and gum.   *25*
With long pink-nailed fingertips,
she puts her stuff up now:
a big red rib-eye steak
a head of green lettuce,
the leafy kind, and a bottle of merlot.   *30*
Our total is rung
and my husband pays.
The checker lays the coupons upside-down,
like a blackjack hand,
and pounds them with a rubber stamp.   *35*

The Responsive Reader

1   People complaining about dull reading often say that it is as dull as a gro-
    cery list or a laundry list. How can you tell that the poet did not intend
    the grocery lists in this poem to be dull or irrelevant? For you, what are
    the most telling or the most striking details in this poem?
2   Who are you in this poem—the food stamp recipient, the affluent cus-
    tomer, or the checker? Or do you see yourself as an outside observer
    who is not "involved"? Why do you identify the way you do?

Talking, Listening, Writing

3   Poets often focus on something that has a larger symbolic meaning. Are
    the food stamps a symbol in this poem? How would you spell out their
    symbolic meaning?

Collaborative Projects

4   Much welfare reform has meant the loss of benefits to large numbers of
    Americans. The food stamp programs that for many years helped feed
    poor families were cut back. *Time* magazine reported that 40 percent or
    more of disabled children stood to lose the supplementary social secu-
    rity payments that helped their families. You may want to team up with
    classmates to investigate the history, the politics, and the impact of cut-
    backs in one major area of the welfare state or the social safety net in our
    society.

FORUM: *Class in a Classless Society*

Are we accepting huge differences in wealth and privilege as an inevitable fact of life in our society? Are critics challenging the concentration of wealth and power in the hands of a new upper class waging "class warfare"?

In 1848, the great conservative British politician Benjamin Disraeli published a book warning that England was becoming "two nations." New technologies and expanding trade had created a newly rich upper class living in magnificent mansions. Increasingly, an impoverished industrial working class lived in crowded slums. Today, in a new era of free-for-all economic competition, many observers again see a widening gulf between the rich and the poor. They see the CEO of a large bank taking successive ten-million-dollar bonuses after reducing his tellers to part-time jobs, taking away their pension rights and health benefits, defeating their hopes of owning a home or helping their children share in the American Dream. They see ballplayers signed to multimillion-dollar contracts while food stamps are taken away from poor families.

After the spectacular bankruptcy of a major energy-producing company, chief executives walked away with hundreds of millions of dollars in last-minute bonuses and insiders' stock sales while loyal employees—who had invested their lives and their savings in the company—found that their stock was worth nothing and that their retirement plans were worth less than five cents on the dollar. A high government official who had consulted with top executives of the now-defunct company had earned a reported $58 million during his last year in private industry. At the same time, a scholar in a conservative think tank funded from industry sources published an article on the adverse results of raising the minimum wage.

CLASS STRUGGLE
ON THE REFRIGERATOR

Adair Lara

**"A boyfriend who was watching me decorate the house
for Christmas once informed me that it was very
working class of me to hang holiday cards from a
string across a mantel."**

*Adair Lara is a columnist who writes in an amusing, informal way about
the challenges of everyday life—family, school, work, relatives. In this column,
she looks at indicators of social status—telltale signs revealing the underlying
class structure of a society that prides itself on not having rigid social barriers.
In this column first published in 1998, she makes us think about distinctions
for which Americans may not always have sociological labels or official categories, but that people sense nevertheless and that shape their behavior and
channel their aspirations.*

Thought Starters: Do you think of some people as "low class"? Do you
think there is an "upper class" in this country? Do you think of yourself and
your friends as "middle class"? Why or why not? If not, do you want to be
"middle class"?

I was reading an article Steve Rubenstein wrote about a new $6,000   1
refrigerator that is so fancy it can be told to stop producing ice cubes on the
Sabbath. But when Steve pointed out that refrigerator magnets wouldn't
stick to its designer wood panels, the salesman sniffed, "We're in a niche.
The people who can afford one of our refrigerators may not be the same
people who use refrigerator magnets."

I glanced over at our fridge. We bought it new about a year ago for
$600. It's white, I think—I really can't be sure because just about every inch
of it is covered with photo magnets. I buy the magnets at Office Depot
(they're really designed for business cards) and cut up photos to fit them.
Over the magnets are invitations, clippings, New Yorker cartoons, movie
listings, poems, report cards.

I sighed. Every time I think I've made a successful escape from the
working-class thing, there it is again.

I still collect those Cashmere Bouquet soaps from motel rooms. When
I worked at a posh style magazine, my boss circled the words "kitchen
table" in the lead of a story I was working on and scrawled in the margin,
"Our readers don't have kitchen tables."

And I wondered, where then do they read the paper? When I was lit-   5
tle, we had not only a kitchen table in our kitchen—it looked suspiciously
like the redwood picnic benches down the road at Samuel Taylor Park—
but also a couch. I still miss that couch.

I'm a have with the soul of a have-not.

I shop at garage sales, trying on brown leather jackets and pointing out
the boxes of wineglasses to Bill, elbowing aside teenagers to offer 15 cents
for a 25-cent pair of used Van sneakers.

It's embarrassing, but it's not my fault. My mother did our shopping
at a thrift store called the Bargain Box. She liked bargains. "It was only $75
for the pair of you," she told my twin and me once, referring to the bill for
our birth at the public clinic.

So I think nothing of wearing other people's castoffs. I only think,
"What a perfectly good pair of black Gap jeans. And only a dollar." Two of
my sisters opened secondhand clothing shops when they grew up, just
switching the side of the counter they were on.

All of us Daly kids are better off than our parents were when we were   10
kids, but it hasn't sunk in. We all still stockpile toilet paper as if we might
run out. My sister Connie just Fed-Ex'ed me a nicely wrapped box of presents in return for a favor, and I unwrapped them to find a toothbrush
holder, a knitted grandma hat, a pair of too-small white slippers and a Dick
Francis audiotape.

It looked exactly like the stuff you see left over at the end of the day
at a garage sale—probably is.

We still kind of go nuts when anything's free. When another sister and
I went wine tasting, I noticed her slipping the free chocolates into her
pocket and urging me to load up on the free apples. I ignored her, being
preoccupied with getting my share of the thimblefuls of wine they were
pouring, the cheapskates.

You can take the girl out of the class, but you can't take the class out
of the girl. Or, in this case, get anything resembling class into the girl. A
boyfriend who was watching me decorate the house for Christmas once informed me that it was very working class of me to hang holiday cards from
a string across the mantel.

I saw what he meant, but privately I wondered how else I was supposed to demonstrate to visitors that I had received all of these cards. I did-
n't have enough magnets to put them all on the fridge.

The Responsive Reader

1 For Lara, what are telltale signs of her working-class origins? How does
the refrigerator in the title come to play its role as an indicator of social
class? What do garage sales and the kind of presents her sister sends have

to do with class status? What other indicators of her social background and class status keep cropping up in her essay?

2   Like many Americans of an earlier generation, Lara became an example of social mobility—being "better off than our parents were." Where in her article do you see her in contact with or moving on a new, higher, social level, and with what result?

3   What behaviors explained by their past have Lara and her sister carried over into their new lives? Are they all just amusing? Or might some become a handicap in a career or in social situations?

Talking, Listening, Writing

4   What telltale indicators of social class or social status would you include in pegging the social status of your family or of friends you know well? What is most important or most revealing—for instance, cars, home furnishings, favorite pastimes, shopping habits, personal habits?

5   Americans have often prided themselves on living in a classless society, without the rigid class barriers of traditional societies. Are Americans becoming more class conscious? Are they becoming more separated according to family background, level of schooling, or job opportunities? What major dividing lines or class barriers have you observed?

6   Are most of your friends from the same class or social background as you? Do you feel uncomfortable in the presence of people whose class is different (whether higher or lower), or do you mix easily with people from different backgrounds?

7   Lara says, "I'm a have with the soul of a have-not." What does she mean? Try your hand at writing a journal entry that starts with a line like the following:

> I'm a commuter with the soul of a cowboy.
>
> I'm an art student on the outside but a farm girl on the inside.
>
> I just started to play the guitar, but I imagine myself as a rock star.

Collaborative Projects

8   Is America predominantly a middle-class society? Do most people you know think of themselves as middle class? If not, do they aim at becoming middle class? Working with a group, poll or interview classmates, family, or friends. What ideas or criteria do they associate with the term *middle class?* What for them are middle-class homes, jobs, neighborhoods, and people like?

YOU CAN'T GET BY
ON NICKELS AND DIMES

Molly Ivins

> **"Working more than 40 hours a week at $6-to-$7 an hour in variously priced markets. . . . Ehrenreich found she could not make a no-frills living."**

Molly Ivins is a sharp-tongued Texas columnist who has been a sharp-eyed critic of the good-ole-boy Texas legislature. A favorite target of her biting sense of humor is what she sees as a basic issue in America—the way we rely on Big Money to finance elections. In her view, what's wrong with American government is the extent to which rich people and their paid operatives run the country. In the following 2001 review, Ivins pays tribute to a fellow social critic.

Barbara Ehrenreich has published widely in opinion makers' publications from Ms. *and* Mother Jones *to the* New York Times, *the* New Republic, *the* Atlantic Monthly, *and the* Nation. *She has long been an effective voice of the women's movement, chronicling the progression from the image of an independent woman as a "disheveled radical" to the new stereotype of the career woman, carrying an attaché case and "skilled in discussing market shares and leveraged buyouts." In one of the two books recommended in this review, Ehrenreich reports on her experience trying to live on the wages of America's pink-collar workers.*

Thought Starters: Have you or people you know well ever been part of the "service industries"? What is it like to work as a server, maid, gardener, house cleaner, or other kind of helper or attendant? What do you think would be the best and the worst of the job?

What a glorious year for the summer reading list! Enough gems to stock any list—fiction and non-, funny and tragic, sometimes both simultaneously; plus a perfect plethora of peppy public policy books. 1

But there are two books I especially want to recommend, both by women I admire and know slightly: "Nickel and Dimed" by Barbara Ehrenreich and "Washington" by the late Meg Greenfield of the Washington Post. If you read them in conjunction, it more than doubles the strength of each.

Ehrenreich's book, it seems to me, is the stronger of the two. She did what reporters used to do before they became so unbearably self-important:

She reports what the society actually looks like from the bottom. Starting in 1998, she went out and got successive and sometimes simultaneous no-skills, close-to-minimum wage jobs and tried to make it from one month to the next. She couldn't do it. As she so painfully shows, the joker in the deck for low-wage workers is the cost of housing.

The reason you don't hear much about it is that the official poverty rate has remained, as Ehrenreich puts it, "at a soothingly low 13 percent" for several years. Trouble is, the official poverty rate is calculated by the cost of food, which is relatively inflation-proof. The living-wage movement—to establish a minimum wage based on the true cost of living—puts the true minimum at about $14 an hour. Ehrenreich was working for between $6 and $7, living in everything from trailer parks (an upscale option), to not-so-low-rent apartments, to a dorm.

This is where the system is seriously gamed against low-income work-   5
ers. Ehrenreich observes: "It did not escape my attention, as a temporarily low-income person, that the housing subsidy I normally receive in my real life—over $20,000 a year in the form of a mortgage-interest deduction—would have allowed a truly low-income family to live in relative splendor. . . . If rents are exquisitely sensitive to market forces, wages clearly are not."

She points out that when the rich and poor compete for housing in the same market, the rich always win—thus we get fancy downtown con-dos, McMansions in the suburbs and golf courses galore, but nowhere for low-income workers to live, especially since they are clumped in inner cities and the new jobs are in the "edge cities."

The increase in the cost of housing has been neatly matched by a si-multaneous drop in government support. Expenditures on public housing have fallen since the 1980s, when that prince of social services Ronald Rea-gan was president.

Working more than 40 hours a week at $6-to-$7 an hour in variously priced markets (including a faintly hilarious stint with the Merry Maids housecleaning service in Maine), Ehrenreich found she could not make a no-frills living. She thinks she might have done so in Minneapolis had things fallen out so that she could work weekends as well.

In theory, the working poor have some weapons in what is in fact class warfare in this country: They can organize, and they can vote. Why, in re-ality, they A, can't, and B, don't, is part of the degeneration of democracy.

For a fascinating read on how this works at the other end of the power   10
scale, try Meg Greenfield's posthumous book, "Washington." Greenfield had a great b.s. detector. Her central metaphor for the Capital of the World's Only Remaining Superpower is high school, and it is eerily apt—the same cliques, rivalries, obsession with popularity, peer pressure and eternal presidents of the student council.

The Responsive Reader

1   As summarized by Ivins, what are the basic economics and statistics of the "no-skills, close-to-minium wage" jobs that Ehrenreich researched? Why is the cost of housing "the joker in the deck"? How do the realities of the housing market work against the poor?

2   Have you seen any evidence of the "working poor" trying to organize or of the difficulties they encounter? Do you think it is true that the poor are the least likely to vote? Who do you think are the people most likely to vote? Do you and your friends vote? Why or why not?

3   Meg Greenfield was a respected senior nationally syndicated columnist. Do you think it is disrespectful to say that she had "a great b.s. detector"? From what you see of Washington politics in the media, can you see any parallels between the world of high school and the world of national politics? Can you cite some recent examples or cases in point?

Talking, Listening, Writing

4   In your area, does much construction activity produce luxury apartments, upscale custom homes, and posh fitness clubs or golf clubs? Is there any evidence of a push toward affordable or low-cost housing?

5   Terms like *class warfare* and *the working poor* date back to an earlier period of social conflict, but they have recently come back into use. The term *class warfare,* once a slogan of the political left, is today also used by the political right. How or why? You may want to do a quick-search on the Internet to track current or recent uses of these terms.

Collaborative Projects

6   Working with a group, try to draw up a hypothetical budget for a single mother—with or without child—trying to make it by working forty hours or more at $6 to $7 an hour in your area or community. If you can, draw on the help of accounting or business majors to help you figure deductions from the paycheck and job expenses. Try to be specific about the housing you would try to rent and the food you would be able to buy.

FIND IT ON THE WEB

Congressional, statewide, or citywide initiatives to raise the minimum wage or to establish a "living wage" trigger heated debates. Who are the advocates, and what are their arguments? Who are the opponents, and what are their arguments?

The following were sample entries from one student's preliminary source list:

Kuttner, Robert. "Boston's Living Wage Law Highlights New Grassroots Efforts to Fight Poverty." *The American Prospect*. 1997. 14 Jan. 2003. <http://www.prospect.org/columns/kuttner/bk970818.html>

Berg, John. Rev. of *A Living Wage: American Workers and the Making of Consumer Society*. John Berg's Book Reviews. 2000. 15 Jan. 2003. <http://world.std.com/˜jberg/living wage.html>

"Cost of Living." *The Columbia Encyclopedia*. 6th ed. July 2001. 15 Jan. 2003, <http://www.bartleby.com/65/co/costlivi.html>

OTHER VOICES

The Race to the Bottom

Who speaks for America's working class? Do major newspapers in your area have a Business section, a Home and Gardens section, or a Fine Food section? However, do they have a Labor section? The following is a shortened reprint of a full-page advertisement taken out in a metropolitan newspaper by the Building and Construction Trades Council of the area. In times of economic prosperity, the blue-collar workers of the skilled trades—such as carpenters, plumbers, and electricians—have profited from construction booms, overtime rules, and strong union protection. How are they faring in today's and tomorrow's economy?

(Paid Advertisement)

IN A RACE TO THE BOTTOM, WE ALL LOSE

T.M. lost a job because a local shopping center brought in low-wage laborers from another area. His wife and daughter and our entire community lost the wages he would have earned.

America is a stronger and better place for the freedom it allows working people to improve collectively their circumstances. Our institutions and our way of life depend on having a highly skilled workforce that earns a living wage, provides for its health care and retirement, contributes to community organizations and pays taxes.

The building trades make a special contribution, for they provide the training, organization, and discipline that eleváte construction from itinerant job to chosen career. We represent the only pool of skills required by contractors to build increasingly complex, reliable, and safe structures.

WE NEED YOUR SUPPORT

We are seeing the same race to the bottom that has cost millions of other Americans their jobs. Like companies that shift jobs among overseas sweatshops in perpetual pursuit of the cheapest labor, there are now employers who bring in low-wage, low-skilled workers to undercut and displace local workers.

The new owner of an eastside shopping center has hired an out-of-state contractor who has brought in low-paid workers from other areas for a $32 million remodeling project. Many of them are working out of pickups and bunking in motels.

PLEASE DON'T SHOP AT THE CENTER

Support responsible employers, local workers, and quality construction in our community. Take your business to a responsible owner at other area shopping centers.

YOUR TURN:

1 How effective is this plea for support? What appeals and arguments does it use to appeal to the readers? How effective are they?

2 As a local resident, would you stop shopping at the center targeted in this advertisement? Why or why not?

3 What is a sweatshop? What is a boycott? (For instance, have you heard of movements to boycott lettuce or grapes? Have you heard of calls to boycott French wines and cheese? What were the issues in each case?)

4 Do you think this ad is antibusiness?

EDUCATING FOR PRIVILEGE

Gene Nichol

"Educating for privilege is powerfully at odds with who we say we are."

Who governs this nation? Who writes and administers the laws? Who presides over the administration of justice? Who conducts court cases, instructs juries, and sentences offenders? Gene Nichol is a professor and law school dean at the prestigious University of North Carolina. According to his statistics, a "stunning" 74 percent of the students leading law schools select to train for careers in law and the justice system come from the top quarter of the income scale in our society.

In an earlier cycle, affirmative action programs were developed to improve access to college educations for students held back by race, gender, or poverty. These programs were widely attacked and largely abandoned after successful lawsuits forced institutions to base admissions on strictly academic qualifications, including especially test scores and grades. In a closely followed and widely debated apparent reversal, a divided Supreme Court in 2003 allowed the University of Michigan to recognize considerations of racial representation in admissions to its law school, although not in admissions to undergraduate study. This article published in the Nation *magazine in October 2002 was part of an outpouring of editorial comment in the national media.*

Thought Starters: Who gets student aid? Who gets students loans? What are the terms? How are student loans paid back?

As a law school dean, I was much taken with a statement from Justice Sandra Day O'Connor's landmark opinion in the University of Michigan case: "Law schools represent the training ground for a large number of our nation's leaders . . . it is necessary that the path to leadership be visibly open" to every segment of society.

In a powerful way, that sentiment breaks new ground. It recognizes that more is at stake in our affirmative-action battles than the quality of the classroom experience. The graduates of the country's strong law schools enjoy a hugely disproportionate access to opportunity and authority in the private and public sectors of our economy. Selective professional schools constitute distinctive pipelines to our principal corridors of power. The processes designed to distribute these remarkable resources, Justice O'-Connor reminded, must be open to all.

The Michigan case, of course, explored the accessibility of selective higher education when it comes to race. The Justices concluded, thankfully, that universities need not be agnostic about the effective integration of their halls. But what if we cast O'Connor's inquiry more broadly? What if we asked about the diversity of selective student bodies on the basis of class? I think we'd find that the great institutions of American higher education, and their law schools, are constructed on a foundation of economic advantage that is bad—and getting worse. We aren't doing much about it. And we're behaving in ways to widen the breach.

Here's what I mean.

The Educational Testing Service recently published a study of the nation's 146 most selective colleges and universities. This is the pool into which law schools cast their nets. ETS concluded that only 3 percent of those students come from the bottom economic quartile. Only about 10 percent of the cohort comes from the bottom 50 percent. A stunning 74 percent hails from the top quarter. The pool of undergraduates from which we choose is badly skewed toward the economically privileged.

And the bias is increasing. A 2003 Education Department study found that the lion's share of the past decade's financial aid increases has gone to students in the top economic quarter. In 1995, 41 percent of private university aid went to high-income students. By 1999 it was 51 percent. The Lumina Foundation's recent study of tuition discounting draws similar conclusions. Eight years ago, students from families making $20,000 or less received, on average, 2 percent more than students from families making $60,000 or more. Today, wealthier children get 29 percent more than poorer ones. The high tuition, high aid model is backfiring.

And then there are the law schools. Tuition increases have dramatically outpaced inflation over the past decade. Public school tuition rose a staggering 141 percent. Inflation was 31 percent. The average private law school tuition bill is now about $25,000 a year. Public ones charge about $19,000 for nonresidents, $10,000 for residents; 86 percent of law students borrow to pay for their studies. Last year, the median private law graduate debt burden was $84,000. And that doesn't include undergraduate loans, which can also be daunting. The typical starting salary for public-sector jobs nationally is about $35,000—requiring an impossible 40 percent of monthly income for debt repayment.

As private law school tuition has skyrocketed, some of the best public law schools have, in effect, privatized—Michigan and Virginia being ready examples. Average per-student expenditures at American Bar Association–approved schools quadrupled over the past two decades—rising from about $5,000 to $20,000 per student. The money fueled what one dean calls "a positional arms race." We compete on *U.S. News & World Report*'s terms—offering more high-end and fewer need-based scholarships; paying extraordinary salaries to star faculty and deans; spending huge sums on facilities, technology and brochures bragging about our accomplishments—raising the price of education for everyone. No one even thinks of expanding our student bodies or reducing the costs of instruction. That would be heresy. This elevator only goes up.

This crescendo of rising costs and expenditures cannot be thought acceptable. It fences out a huge segment of our community on the basis of wealth. It allows students' dreams to be swamped by their debts—forcing them into career paths they wouldn't otherwise choose. It increases the ultimate cost of representation in a legal regime that already prices too many out. It results in a system of legal education that radically penalizes the bottom half, in the service of a system of justice that has long done exactly the same thing.

No single formula will push back the mounting exclusion. But altered admissions and financial aid practices could work to assure that poor students matter. And meaningful loan forgiveness programs, at both state and federal levels, could help return public-sector jobs to viability. State legislators must recall that even given budget difficulties we face, an economically polarized democracy can't afford to abandon public higher education. And the academy itself has to remember that professional education is a public good, not merely a private one. After all, educating for privilege is powerfully at odds with who we say we are.

The Responsive Reader

1 In the Michigan case, Justice O'Connor, in an eloquently worded opinion, said the "path to leadership" should be "visibly open" to all. How do Nichol's detailed *statistics* compare with Justice O'Connor's goal?

2 What does Nichol tell his readers about the *financing* of a law-student's education? Who is assisted by student loans? Do they go mainly to poor students? What burdens do they impose on graduates?

3 Why do you think social critics like Nichol have changed their *strategy* by shifting the emphasis from questions of race to questions of social class? Why does he emphasize considerations of income level and social status applying to Americans regardless of whether they are black, brown, or white?

4 Does Nichol offer a *positive program* for action? How would he help make access to elite professions and positions of privilege "open to all"?

Talking, Listening, Writing

5 Elite universities train the nation's political, economic, and educational elite. What is an elite university? What is a "prestige university"? What clientele does it serve? Is education at top-level schools reserved for the offspring of the rich?

6 Have you seen challenges to the privileges of wealthy Americans described as class warfare? Have you seen them described as calls for a more democratic America? Who makes these claims? How do you respond to them?

POVERTY UP, WOMEN STILL DOWN

Mary Bridges

**"Readjusting statistics is unlikely to improve the
condition of those 34.6 million people who live on
poverty wages, still unable to afford basic necessities."**

*Have current discussions of poverty in the world's richest country moved
away from blaming "welfare mothers" and the "culture of dependency" or from
accusations of "welfare cheats"? Mary Bridges focuses on a major phenomenon
in the class structure of this country: the working poor. Especially, she discusses
growing poverty among women as the result of divorce, of becoming single mothers, of the retrenching of government programs, and of lacking funding for educational advancement. Bridges published this article in* Ms. *magazine in the
winter of 2003–04.* Ms. *has long been the leading American feminist publication, dedicated to breaking down the barriers in the path of women's rights,
paying tribute to achievements, and reminding readers of the unfinished agenda.*

Thought Starters: Has poverty disappeared from the radar screen of the
establishment media? Do the media serve affluent readers and viewers?
Where or when do you see poor people on television?

A four-person family earning $18,392 is considered poor, but one   1
making $18,393 isn't. How does the U.S. Census Bureau draw this line?
The formula is surprisingly simple: Estimate the cost of food for a given year
and multiply by three.

Why this formula? The answer has more to do with history than logic:
In 1963 a researcher at the Social Security Administration needed a quick
way to estimate poverty levels and reasoned that families usually spent a
third of their annual income on food. The Lyndon B. Johnson administration adopted the formula, and no administration since has changed it.

Critics from the left and right agree that the calculation has flaws. For
one, it doesn't account for regional differences in living expenses—uptown
Manhattan and rural Mississippi are considered to have the same poverty
threshold. Also, the formula is based on the belief that families' spending
habits are dominated by the expense of food, but in recent years the costs
of health care, housing and transportation have consumed a greater percentage of families' budgets.

This year the Census Bureau has used an additional 15 formulas to determine poverty rates, factoring in geography, health care and non-cash
benefits from government programs.

Life below the poverty line isn't a statistical abstraction to Jane Eleey, project director for Pathways, PA—a Pennsylvania non-profit that provides services to low-income women and their families. Each day she meets with clients who can't afford basic necessities for themselves and their children. That means "skipping meals, losing housing and having their utilities cut off," she says.

An additional 1.7 million Americans fell into such a position in the year 2002, according to a late-September report on poverty rates from the U.S. Census Bureau. On the surface, the bureau's report was encouraging for women: Poverty rates remained relatively flat between 2001 and 2002 for households led by single women. But beyond the numbers lurks the unpleasant fact that single mothers continue to bear a disproportionate share of the poverty burden in the United States. While they represent only 17 percent of total households, the households led by single mothers comprise nearly half of those below the poverty line.

Vicky Lovell of the Institute for Women's Policy Research in Washington, D.C., explains that recent initiatives to reduce poverty haven't reached these women. "We have been successful at bringing other groups out of poverty—such as the elderly—but we haven't been as successful for single moms and their children," she says.

Single mothers face enormous barriers that keep them impoverished, particularly in times of a faltering economy. Often they rely on state-sponsored programs for assistance with child care, food and housing, but as state governments try to trim budget deficits, many of these programs have been reduced or eliminated. As Lacey Siegel of the Community Service Society of New York (CSS) points out, "What are single mothers going to do with their kids when an after-school program gets cut?"

A second obstacle is the recent change in the welfare system that pushes recipients to "get a job, any job," says Lovell. The emphasis on finding immediate employment tends to be a shortsighted response to poverty because, as a study by CSS reveals, the kinds of jobs women must take usually involve "high turnover, low pay and few employer-provided benefits."

Activists insist that helping women pull themselves out of poverty requires a more long-term approach: namely, improving women's access to education. A high school diploma or college degree reduces the likelihood from 26.9 percent to just 4.6 percent that a family will fall below the poverty line.

But without government programs that provide support, single mothers get stuck in a double bind, says Eleey. They don't have the skills to get more stable jobs, but they can't afford the education and training necessary for stable jobs while taking care of their children. Until government programs address this central problem, the burden of poverty will continue to weigh most heavily on those for whom our society purports to have the most concern.

The Responsive Reader

1 According to Bridges, what was wrong with the Census Bureau's traditional *definition* of the poverty line? What adjustments were necessary to redefine poverty?

2 What does Bridges do to remind her readers of the *realities* of poverty beyond the "statistical abstractions"? What does poverty mean in real life for poor mothers and their children?

3 What are the *barriers* that keep women from rising above the poverty level? What economic and political trends have affected funding for government programs? What changes in the welfare system have worked against them?

4 What *statistics* does Bridges offer to support the claim that education is for poor women the major escape route from poverty? But what is the "double bind" that causes single mothers to "get stuck"?

Talking, Listening, Writing

5 What real-life examples of poverty can you provide to dramatize the issue? How close to or how distant from the realities of poverty has your own experience been?

6 Bridges calls poor people poor. Do you prefer euphemisms ("beautiful or unthreatening words") that soften the impact of harsh realities? Would you prefer for instance "low-income" or "economically disadvantaged" or "lowest quartile of income distribution"? Why or why not?

Feedback and Revision

The Writing Process

1 Drawing on Your Experience
2 From Reading to Writing
3 Exploring Internet and Nonprint Sources
4 Pushing Toward a Thesis
5 Organizing Your Writing
6 **Feedback and Revision**

During revision, you build on the strengths and work on the weaknesses of an early draft.

Much strong professional writing and effective student writing has gone through several drafts. Revision is your chance to build on the strong points of an early draft and shore up weaknesses. What worked well, and what needs work? What will help you make your revision a solid step forward? What kind of rewriting will make your revision more than a cosmetic touch-up of minor points?

Triggering

Learn equally from feedback that is strongly supportive and from comments that may seem negative to you.

Make good use of the whole range of readers' responses that may be available to you. These might include talking early about your plans with a classmate or a friend. They might include informal reactions in discussions in a small group. Writing instructors annotate student papers, using formats ranging from a **running commentary** in the margin to overall comments on the paper. Peer reviewers may be asked to respond to a detailed **peer review** questionnaire. They may be asked to write a **review-critique,** focusing on such questions as the writer's purpose, the overall plan, or the intended audience.

Revision is often set in motion when the writer receives written or oral **feedback** and wants to say:

"That's not what I meant!"

"I thought everybody knew this."

"I'm not sure where I learned this. Maybe it's just hearsay—let me check this out."

"I did not mean to insult members of the group."

Remember that the original meaning of the Greek word *critic* was "skilled in judgment." Think of the critical reader as a thinking reader.

- *Study feedback from an editor or your instructor.* We all hope for positive encouragement. However, we also need to learn from readers who were disappointed by a paper or article. Why did they react negatively to what they read? What is needed to make them reconsider?

- *Listen to the reactions of fellow writers in group discussion or read peer reviews.* Some peer reviewers may try to spare a fellow student's feelings. Others may be very critical in a competitive academic environment. Do both friendly and unfriendly readers agree on what is needed or lacking?

- *Become your own critic.* Experienced writers already know what a doubting reader is likely to ask. They provide the explanations needed to prevent misreading. They know how to defuse a hot-button topic. They remember where perhaps they moved too quickly in a first draft or postponed checking evidence till later.

The categories in the following sample of instructions for a peer review cover basic questions in a critical reader's mind.

PEER REVIEW

Trend Watcher's Paper

author _____   reviewer _____

1 BEGINNINGS—How do the title and introduction focus on the issue? How do they bring the topic to life or dramatize the issue?

2 THESIS—What is the thesis? How does it sum up what the paper as a whole shows or is trying to show? Does it serve as a preview, setting up a program or pattern for the paper to follow?

3 ORGANIZATION—What is the organizing strategy or overall plan? What are major stages or subdivisions of the paper? How or in what order are they followed up?

4   SOURCES—Where in the paper do you find unsupported opinion? What sources were used by the writer for support? What kind of material is it—for instance, live personal contact or testimony, popular journalism, government statistics, scholarly study? How is each identified or introduced? What does it contribute to the paper?

5   REAL-LIFE EXAMPLES—What use does the writer make of real-life examples or case histories? How detailed and how convincing are they? How representative do they seem to you?

6   CONCLUSION—Does the conclusion add anything to the paper? Does it conclude the paper on a strong note? Is there a punchline, a clincher quotation, or a positive recommendation? How concrete or helpful are any suggestions for change or future action?

7   READER RESPONSE—Who would be the ideal reader? Are you a good audience for this paper? Did you learn something from it? Did it change your mind? Did you at any point strongly agree or disagree?

Gathering

Look for material to help you build up a promising but underdeveloped paper.

Each paper is different. The needs and opportunities for revision vary accordingly. However, the subtext of much guidance for revision is the same: If you raise a point, try to do it justice. Follow up key points more. Try not to move on too quickly. When you make an important statement, follow it up with key examples, informed opinion, expert testimony, or selected statistics.

- *Build up real-life examples.* Fill in convincing examples from firsthand experience and observation. Try to avoid hypothetical (made-up) examples.

FIRST DRAFT: **Asian Americans on the Rise**

In spite of racism, in many fast-growing cities, especially in California, Asian Americans have become a model minority.
Young Asian Americans have the **fast track in education** because first-generation parents push their children to the right track. They push their chil-

dren to strive for excellence so that they may have a better life than their parents. Studies show that when parents teach their children at an early age, they are more likely to succeed.

Racism just causes minorities to push hard to succeed in life. In the town where I grew up, I saw many Asian Americans opening **their own businesses.** There are areas with many Asian American business owners. There are whole neighborhoods that have become Japantowns or Bombay by the Bay or Little Saigons.

Many immigrants were well educated before they came to this country. I see many caretakers like nurses and doctors who are Asian American. . . .

FEEDBACK: You already have identified three major factors that help make Asian Americans a "model minority": honoring education, business enterprise, and professional training. Do more to help your readers see that in your experience the model minority idea has not just been a buzzword or a stereotype?

SECOND DRAFT: **Asian Americans on the Rise**

In spite of racism, in many fast-growing cities, especially in California, Asian Americans have become a model minority.

Young Asian Americans have the **fast track in education** because first-generation parents push their children to the right track. They push their children to strive for excellence so that they may have a better life than their parents. Studies show that when parents teach their children at an early age, they are more likely to succeed. **My math and science teachers always had a large percentage of Asian American students in their classes. One teacher showed me a report claiming that Asian students averaged up to 50 percent more hours spent on homework than other students.**

Racism just causes minorities to push hard to succeed in life. In the town where I grew up, I see many Asian Americans opening **their own businesses.** There are areas with many Asian American business owners. There are whole neighborhood that have become Japantowns or Bombay by the Bay or Little Saigons. There are dental offices, photography studios, and many other popular stores. **Not far from my college there is a cluster of crowded and busy stores with a jewelry store and a store selling colorful traditional clothing next to an India-style vegetarian restaurant with special produce and favorite sweets and an electronics store stacked with videos and CDs from the Indian subcontinent.**

Many immigrants had **medical or clinical training** before they came to this country. I see many caretakers like nurses and doctors who are Asian American. **My mother is a nurse and has her own business taking care of mentally disabled elderly people** . . .

■ *Move in for a closer look.* Do more to make your subject real for your readers. Help them see what you saw. Show them the actual steps in a process or task.

THE CLOSER LOOK

Building Up Detail

In our society today, much of what we consume comes to us prefabricated, prepackaged, or ready to assemble. How many people are still good at working with their hands—whether as professionals or as weekend amateurs? Do you see why the author of the following paper might have a bumper sticker that says "Honor Labor"? Look at how feedback from a peer reviewer or instructor might encourage the student writer to rework the first draft in order to give readers a closer look.

The Tricks of the Trade

1 FIRST DRAFT: Like other youngsters I knew, I early became fascinated with how things are made and how they work. Ever since I was about five years old, I spent many afternoons in a relative's or older sibling's shed or workshop, watching them at work.

(You focus effectively on an important strand in your life. Can you make it real for your reader? Do you remember something especially vividly? Can you bring your topic to life by sharing with your readers something you actually saw or took part in?)

REVISED: Like other youngsters I knew, I early became fascinated with how things are made and how they work. Ever since I was about five years old, I spent many afternoons in a relative's or older sibling's shed or workshop, watching them at work. **The first real present I ever received was a large wooden rocking horse that I watched the carpenter craft for me. I learned the secrets of how it was built. I remember the final touches: a dab of superglue to attach the tail, a leather strap nailed to the side for a handle, a small marble carefully placed in a slot in the wood for an eye, and a final coat of glaze for a good looking finish.**————->>>>>>>>>>>>>>>>>>

2 FIRST DRAFT: What started off as casual bonding often eventually became years of important experiences that I am thankful for now.

(This does provide a unifying trial thesis. However, "important experiences" sounds too interchangeable. It could appear in the thesis sentences of other papers on very different subjects? Spell out more strongly what made your actual experiences important?)

REVISED: I would pester the workers I watched to teach me the tricks of the trade. **I learned much of the basics of the trade of building and construction, but I also built lasting friendships through the bonds that develop when people work together.**————->>>>>>>>>>>>>>>>>>

3   FIRST DRAFT: I learned to see that workers in the crafts and trades are proud of their tools. They buy them carefully and devote much time to their

care and maintenance. They would arrange sets of implements of different caliber carefully according to their different sizes.

(The pride of experienced workers in their tools is a very important point in your paper. Provide a stronger **transition?** Fill in the link that shows you are moving ahead in your timeframe? Then build the point up more by showing that pros do not just call a tool a "gismo." They know their tools and the names of their tools.)

REVISED: **When I was old enough to understand and handle tools,** I began to see that workers in the crafts and trades are proud of their tools. They buy them carefully and devote much time to their care and maintenance. They would arrange sets of implements of different caliber carefully according to their different sizes. **I learned about the differences between a hammer and a mallet, a regular wrench and a socket wrench. I early learned simple sayings, like the one helping me remember which way to turn a screwdriver: "Right to make tight. Left to turn loose." Eventually I learned the difference between a mitre saw and a chainsaw, an axe and a hatchet.** ————>>>>>>>>>>>>

4   FIRST DRAFT: I eventually was trusted to drive a pick-up truck when hauling lumber to and from a work site and work on a number of projects. An important value I learned was that safety was always first. The summer before my senior year in high school, I was a helper in a project to renovate a basement. The basement project took us about a month to complete, and it included drywalling, plumbing, electrical wiring, lighting, tiling, carpentry, and painting. My associates tolerated no shoddy work. Just when I thought I knew so much about these fields of work, I realized I only knew very little and there was much more to learn.

(Your **conclusion** covers important points. However, you begin to sound as if you are running out of time! Should not pride in the quality of work deserve a separate paragraph? And maybe a separate conclusion could focus on concern for fellow workers' safety. Is this not part of the bonding that you said early was an important reward of working with other people? This way you could circle back to the beginning.

REVISED: I eventually was trusted to drive pick-up truck when hauling lumber to and from a work site and work on a number of projects. The summer before my senior year in high school, I was a helper in a project to renovate a basement. The basement project took us weeks to complete, and it included drywalling, plumbing, electrical wiring, lighting, tiling, carpentry, and painting. My associates tolerated no shoddy work. **I was amazed how much exact measuring and cutting and careful fitting together was required to produce a smooth tiled surface. Even a small mistake had to be corrected.**

An important value I learned was that safety was always first. **It was important to wear safety goggles when required by the job. It was very important to doublecheck the safety of scaffoldings and to be doubly careful when backing a truck out of or into a construction site. What creates a strong bond of fellowship among buddies is that you trust your coworkers to put the other person's safety first. That means you.**

■ *Look for backup that will make readers respect your findings.* To show that a claim you make is more than one person's opinion, can you bring in authoritative support?

For instance, you may be discussing claims that the remaining woodlands adjacent to expanding development or urban sprawl suffer from pervasive negative effects affecting the wildlife of the spared or protected habitats. You may have quoted a news report about starving elks driven from their feeding area by a neighboring new ski resort. You may have quoted another report about a plague of mice infesting a whole area abandoned by small predators such as weasels and foxes. Can you bring in supporting material like expert testimony? Can you cite data from an official report? Should you quote a key passage from a court decision?

Shaping

Use your revision to check the flow of material in your paper as whole.

An early draft may have good material, but it may have remained scattered. Your readers may find it hard to follow. Check for missing links or missed connections. Look for apparent backtrackings or sidesteppings. Much feedback on your writing will ask you to give clearer or stronger answers to questions like the following:

■ What is going to be your key issue?

■ What is your main point?

■ What are the the major steps in your overall plan?

■ What are the key examples that support your general claims?

■ Is this a digression—why is this in here?

■ At the end, what do you want your reader to think about or to do?

BECOMING YOUR OWN CRITIC   Some writers use the opportunity for revision to work their way through a draft from start to finish. The following will often be part of your revision agenda. Attending to basic needs like the following, you should increasingly become your own critic and reviewer, anticipating the frequently asked questions and frequently made comments from critical readers.

1   SHARPENING YOUR TITLE

FIRST DRAFT TITLES:

Police-Community Relations

Racial Profiling

Homelessness in America

(FEEDBACK: Sharpen your title to focus your reader's attention on your central issue or question. Make your title informative—what is this really about? However also make it inviting or provocative. Rework sweeping open-ended titles that do not zero in your key question or main point. On a topic like racial profiling or homelessness, have the title already give a strong hint from what side of the issue you are going to approach the subject.)

REVISION:

> **Teenagers against Police**
>
> **What's Your Racial Profile?**
>
> **Living on the Streets**

2   USING YOUR INTRODUCTION TO DRAMATIZE THE ISSUE

FIRST DRAFT:

> Teenagers against Cops

I remember attending local parades and city events as a girl when police officers were my heroes. However, this attitude was lost somewhere during adolescence. On Saturday nights, the police department apparently had nothing better to do than to follow teenagers around, waiting for them to do something illegal.

(FEEDBACK: Do more to bring the topic to life for your readers? Try to start with a striking real-life example. Use it to bring the central question in your paper into focus. Maybe include a striking quotation or statistic.)

REVISION:

> Teenagers against Cops

I remember attending local parades and city events as a girl when police officers were my heroes. However, this attitude was lost somewhere during adolescence. **One August evening my friends and I were driving around, as many teenagers do on long summer nights, looking for something to do and people to meet. We wound up at the park near our high school chatting with friends. We could not help noticing a black police car circling the park, and one of us started saying: "I hate cops!"** Everyone chimed in to agree. The consensus was that the police department apparently had nothing better to do than to follow teenagers around, waiting for them to do something illegal. **Finally the police car pulled up. An officer rolled down the window, and there was a cordial conversation. The bottom line was that we needed to move our car because the park was closing.** I learned something that night about the mutual distrust between teenagers and their local police.

3 USING A STRONG THESIS TO GIVE DIRECTION TO YOUR PAPER

FIRST DRAFT:

Foreigner-Bashing on the Increase

After the September 11 attack on the World Trade Center, people from the Middle East became frequent targets of verbal abuse. Immigrants from India and Pakistan are becoming a more visible minority and encounter prejudice or misunderstanding. Hate speech used to mean mainly racial slurs directed at African Americans. Chinese American parents still complain that their children are called ugly names.

(FEEDBACK: By the end of your introduction, zero in on your key point. What is your paper as a whole going to show or to claim? State your answer to this question as your thesis, which the rest of your paper will follow up and support. Try to make your thesis a preview of what your paper will present.)

REVISION:

Foreigner-Bashing on the Increase

Hate speech used to mean mainly racial slurs directed at African Americans. After the September 11 attack on the World Trade Center, people from the Middle East became frequent targets of verbal abuse. Immigrants from India and Pakistan are becoming a more visible minority and encounter prejudice or misunderstanding. Chinese American parents complain that their children are called ugly names. **With more diverse immigrants flowing into the country, hate speech is increasingly directed at a "rainbow coalition" of minorities.**

4 AIMING AT A STRONGER, CLEARER OVERALL PLAN:

FIRST RAFT:

Young Males Today

Young men today increasingly see women in positions of authority. They encounter female doctors and judges and are even stopped by female police officers. This teaches young males to show respect to women and avoid inappropriate sexist jokes.

Many young boys grow up in households with single mothers or divorced mothers. They are exposed to values different from those of the "tough-guy" macho male. . . .

And of course young boys associate earlier than in the past with girls. They learn that the jokes and rough behavior of all-boy activities often alienate young women . . .

(FEEDBACK: You have ample material from personal observation, from your reading, and from the media. Can you sort it out better? Can you set up maybe a three-point or four-point program for covering major stages or subheadings of your topic? For instance, writing about the sensitive male, can you take up in turn three major reasons for greater sensitivity on the part of young men—tracking them in their growing up? You could then structure your paper by following up each point in turn with examples. Include the links or transitions that take the reader from one stage to the next.)

REVISION:

Sensitizing the Young Male

First of all, from early childhood on, mothers increasingly play a dominant role in educating young males. Many young boys grow up in households with single mothers or divorced mothers and are exposed to emotions and values different from those of the "tough-guy" macho male. . . .

As adolescents, young boys associate earlier than in the past with girls. They learn that the jokes and rough behavior of all-boy activities often alienate young women . . .

As young adults, young men increasingly see women in positions of authority. Encountering female doctors, judges, and police officers teaches young males to show respect to women and avoid inappropriate sexist jokes. . . .

5   ENDING YOUR PAPER ON A STRONG NOTE

FIRST DRAFT:

. . .Prejudice survives today and has found many new targets. Immigrants from India, Vietnam, and China are excluded or shunted aside by those who want them to stay "with their own kind."

(FEEDBACK: Try not to use your conclusion to repeat one more time your general point. Leave your readers with a strong final impression. Maybe save a thought-provoking example for the last. Or end with a clincher quotation. If you can, end on a positive or constructive note that is not just wishful thinking. Even if you cannot, try to end with a punchline.)

. . . Prejudice survives today and has found many new targets. Immigrants from India, Vietnam, and China are excluded or shunted aside by those who want them to stay "with their own kind."

Something took place in my life yesterday. that may seem a small issue, but for me it has a wider meaning. I was sitting at one of the tables in our college restaurant, having my lunch. The hall was filled with students coming in for their meals, and there was no additional place for anyone to sit except at my table. There were students waiting to be seated so they could begin their meal. Not one of them sat down at the table where I was munching my lunch. The only reason I can think of is that I am Asian.

The Final Check

If you have time for a final check, act on editor's tips like the following:

- Adjust your thesis to take into account any late additions or second thoughts.
- Check if you should acknowledge exceptions or dissenting views to keep your paper from seeming opinionated or one-sided.
- Edit for expressions that might intentionally or unintentionally give offense: *welfare mother; RINO* (Republican in name only); *tree hugger; politically correct.*

A PAPER FOR PEER REVIEW

The first draft of the following paper had a strong overall plan and made good use of sources to support major points. The focus in final revision could then be on strengthening **transitions.** The student may have been asked to review familiar transitions or thought links to see if they are being used where needed to show logical connections between ideas. The student may also have been encouraged to strengthen the connecting phrases or transitional sentences taking the reader from one paragraph to the next.

first, second, third These show a clear sorting out, although they may not show an overall plan. (*Why* are some things first and others second or third?)

for example, for instance, to illustrate These alert the reader that the writer is backing up general statements with needed examples and cases in point.

in addition, moreover, furthermore, in fact These and similar links signal "more of same," often bringing in additional supporting examples or arguments to support a major point. *In fact* puts special emphasis on an important reinforcing example or point.

however, nevertheless, on the other hand These often bring in an exception or recognize an objection, but they can also signal a major **turning point** as the writer begins to look "at the other side."

therefore, as a result These show cause and effect or lead from an argument to a logical conclusion. Use these and similar logical links to keep weak links like **another** from giving your paper a merely "added-on" or stitched–together effect.

EDITOR'S TIP! **in conclusion** This is an overused routine ending. It gives no hint whether the conclusion will add anything new.

Study the mix of short transitional words or phrases and longer connecting sentences or parts of sentences. On the basis of the strengthened thought links or transitions, can you chart the flow of ideas in the paper?

Generation 1½: Cheung Sam and Jeans

Nearly one in five Americans speaks a language other than English at home, the Census Bureau says, an increase of nearly 50 percent during the past decade. "Most speak Spanish, followed by Chinese, with Russian rising fast," says Genaro C. Armas in his article for *The Boston Globe*, "Percentage of Non-English Speaking Americans Surges." **Although there are more bilingual Chinese Americans now, many children of Chinese immigrants have been very Americanized, and they may not be truly bilingual.**

Most basically, the current "Generation 1 1/2" of Chinese immigrant progeny is educated in American schools, or they work in American companies, where English is the only norm of communication. As a result, they have no means of learning the Chinese language. **As a result,** many Chinese Americans speak English more frequently or all the time instead of their native language, especially when most friends or colleagues speak English.

Because of the constant exposure to the American environment, many lose their Chinese cultural identity and are pressured to adopt a more American lifestyle and cut off ties with their cultural roots. **In fact,** Iris Chang says in her book, *The Chinese in America*, that many Chinese American children "had so deeply absorbed the toxin of racism that they grew to loathe everything Chinese, even their own looks."

The weakening of cultural ties is accelerated when families are isolated from a larger ethnic community. Many Chinese Americans worked in small towns or rural areas where there were few other Chinese; thus their children had little exposure to the Chinese culture and in turn lost their ties to Chinese culture. Iris Chang states in her book that some American-born Chinese simply viewed themselves as white. "Such individuals tended to live in rural areas, where the absence of an established ethnic Chinese community made them less threatening to whites and encouraged their participation in the mainstream."

Without an established cultural community, passing on the language to the next generation is difficult. Kevin Simpson states in his article for *The Denver Post*, "Kids Dive into Chinese Language, Roots," that while some organizations offer weekend classes to strengthen Chinese cultural ties, there remains a language void for kids who were born in China but have grown up speaking English. Plus, some Chinese-American parents may speak Chinese at home but have little time to teach their children to read or write the language."

Regardless of the parents' ties with tradition, Chinese American children are inevitably exposed to the American culture, which would definitely have a strong influence on a child. Thus, many Chinese Americans choose to speak only English and drop their Chinese cultural values, as they are greatly influenced by the American media. As Iris Chang states in her book,

> Popular culture permeated even the most isolated ethnic ghettos, shaping the desires of ethnic Chinese youths, exposing them to new values, new ideas, beyond the reach of parental control. The children listened to the radio for entertainment, read English language newspapers, pored over comic books and pulp novels bought from neighborhood drugstores, spent Saturday afternoons at the local nickelodeons watching movies.

Nevertheless, despite the weakening of cultural ties, there has been a growing counter trend especially with the growing importance of China and the need to know the language to do business there. **In fact,** many schools are now offering Chinese language classes to students. For example, the St. Edward's Upper School in Vera Beach, Florida, has exchange teachers from China who spend a year teaching Chinese in their school. It is the first southeastern school in the United States to get a Chinese teacher through the program.

We are witnessing a revival or return to Chinese language schools, where Chinese Americans enroll their children to learn the Chinese language and culture. **For example,** at the Quincy Chinese Language School students attend weekly three-hour lessons. Terisa Hsiao states in her article, "Chinatown South; Weekend Training" in *The Patriot Ledge,* that the school "sets aside a half hour for students in first through sixth grade to learn conversational Mandarin, the official language of China." She **also** quotes a teacher explaining its importance, saying, "For the future, when they grow up, if they want to do business and talk with Chinese people, Mandarin is the most important language."

Traditional patterns of family life and a revival of ethnic pride combine to slow down assimilation. Families continue to speak Chinese at home, because they have grandparents that baby-sit the children or live with the family. **As a result,** the children are forced to learn Chinese in order to communicate with their grandparents, or they inevitably learn the language from constant exposure to its use. How many immigrants choose to preserve their Chinese culture in their homes? **One example** is Steve Wong, whose family was featured in the article "N.C.'s Immigrants Cling to Ties of Family, Culture" by Morgan Josey for *The Gason Gazette.* He was quoted as saying, "In my case, I am very strong willed. I don't speak English to [my children] at all. If they try to talk to me in English, I just ignore them."

In the future, will more young Americans be bilingual? Children learn much faster than their immigrant parents; **therefore** they are more able to be fluent in both English and Chinese if they are taught the Chinese language when they are young. "They acquire the ability to communicate with members of the host society much sooner and consequently are often called upon to serve as interpreters and translators when their parents deal with the outside world," as stated by K. Scott Wong in his book *Claiming America*. **As a result,** these bilingual young Americans become what K. Scott Wong calls "mediators between the two cultures."

YOUR TURN:

1   What sentence in this paper would you pick as the *thesis* of the paper? How does it sum up the main point or intention of the paper?

2   Prepare a *paragraph outline* summing up in one sentence each how each paragraph moves the paper one step forward.

3   Does all of the input for this paper come from *inside sources*— sources within the Chinese American community? What "outside" references or sources are included?

4   Where and why did the writer choose to use an extended *block quotation?* What major lasting impression does it drive home or reinforce?

5   Would a good *audience* for this paper have to be from a Chinese American background? from an Asian background? from an immigrant background?

6   How does the conclusion and the clincher quotation go beyond a mere summary of the ideas in the paper?

Writing Options 6: From Quick Draft to Revision

Many writing programs today obtain writing samples from students as entrance or exit exams. The following are examples of current issues you may be asked to write about on short notice or in a limited time period. Choose an issue that you think would be of concern to an audience of your fellow students. Take a few minutes at the beginning to jot down notes or prepare a scratch outline. In writing your draft, aim at supporting a central idea or thesis, and try to follow an overall plan that your readers can follow. Bring in supporting examples or other backup material.

After feedback that may include peer reviews and commentary from your instructor, revise your draft in accordance with revision guidelines.

1   Are you aware of the issue of hate speech on campus or in your community? Do you hear hateful or abusive language? For your revision, can you investigate attitudes or concerns of students and faculty? Do students on your campus undergo orientation on language issues?

2   Are current media images like the "soccer mom," "the single mother," or the "career woman" helping or hurting young women charting their own course?

3   Are today's young males more sensitive than a previous generation? Are they more attuned to the feelings and needs of others? Or is the new sensitive male mostly a media image? In your revision, can you include commentary from women's magazines or feminist publications?

4   Do people in your community tend to be friendly or hostile toward the police? Do people support or distrust the police? Why? For your revision, you may conduct an informal neighborhood survey but also look for articles in local publications.

5   Is America becoming a more religious nation? Do you see signs of a religious revival in your community, your area, or your campus? Do you follow coverage of religion or religious issues in local media, a campus newspaper, or national publications?

6   Have you or people you know well witnessed censorship efforts from a "morality police"? For instance, have you observed initiatives from a movement for public decency? What was the issue or the agenda? For your revision, can you find sources shedding light on the issue?

7   Have the homeless disappeared from the radar screens of the media? Have the homeless been shunted aside in your community? Do you remember news coverage of how city authorities are dealing with the issue? Do you know people who have worked in shelters or soup kitchens?

8   Should Americans traveling or working abroad promote American ideas or ideals? For instance, do you think foreign-born Americans should try to be a good influence when they revisit their native countries? Why or why not?

9   Do you or your friends ever put on a "public face" or public appearance different from your private self? Why and how? Does a public persona make a person a hypocrite?

10 Have you or your friends or relatives considered military service? Were there arguments for and against? Where would you turn for candid testimony and advice?

7

MEDIA WATCH
Virtual Reality

LAYOUT: FORMATING YOUR MESSAGE

SCIENTIFIC AMERICAN PROMOTION JULY 2004

How do advertisers design text messages to keep them from getting lost in a flood of commercial mail? How do graphic artists design and lay out a commercial message to make it stand out? How do graphic artists arrange text material on a page for optimal effect? What do graphic artists do to get attention, to make their message exceptionally visually attractive, and to make sure it stays focused on the essentials of the message?

Reading the Image

1   Promotions and sales campaigns are often built around a single major concept or *central theme*. In this ad from a direct mail promotion, what is the key word? How often is it echoed or repeated directly? How many occurrences can you or your classmates track? What related words vary or reinforce the same basic concept? Can you identify current buzzwords used here to help project the central idea?

2   What *strategies* support or drive home the message? Which examples most directly or most strongly illustrate the central idea of the ad? How much repetition is there of the name of the publication for strong product identification?

3   Design or *layout* enlists highly qualified talent in commercial promotions. How aware are you of the resources of the printer's art? How and how effectively does this layout use variation in print size or font? How does it use capital letters? Where does it use underscoring, shading, and framing or boxing? How effective is the side bar using sample covers of the magazine?

4   Who is the intended *audience*? What knowledge is expected of the readers? What interests or attitudes are they expected to share? How limited or self-selecting is the audience expected to be? Alone or with a group, you may want to draw up an audience profile of the ideal target audience for this sales promotion.

5   What is your *response* as a viewer and reader? Do you respond well to the upbeat, positive tone of the ad? In addition to *front-row seat, uncanny*, and *unveiled*, what other words or labels can you track that are designed to create a sense of excitement?

6   What is the *bottom line*, and how effectively does the ad address it? What action is the customer supposed to take? Where and how effectively is the actual sales pitch spilled out? Do you think this is an aggressive or intrusive ad? Why or why not?

7

MEDIA WATCH

Virtual Reality

On the front page of the daily fivestarfinal edition a child is dying in the rubble of newsprint.

—OLGA CABRAL

Many Americans are media-dependent, spending hours each day looking at a screen or hand-held device. How do the media shape or distort our view of reality? Many centuries before television, the Greek philosopher Plato claimed that most human beings do not see true reality. They perceive reality indirectly, at second hand. They see flickering images that are like moving shadows cast on the wall of a cave. Do image-makers and image builders in our modern world have many us living in a virtual reality comparable to Plato's shadows on the wall of the cave?

Do the modern mass media merely skim the surface, in sound bites that allow for no real thinking? Do they mostly serve the commercial interests or political commitments of the large corporations who own them? In the age of the celebrity cult, are the faces we see on screen—Madonna, Arnold Schwarzenegger, Michael Jackson, or a favorite quarterback—more real and interesting to many of us than our coworkers or neighbors? Are we helpless target audiences, or can we influence the steady stream of images and ideas that the media aim at us?

The media have a vast potential for educating us and broadening our views. Independent readers and viewers can follow events in Russia or Haiti as easily as the proceedings of their county Board of Supervisors. They can surf the Internet or tune in to public broadcasting stations for independent dissenting voices.

However, the media also have the power to channel our thinking or manipulate our minds. We choose political leaders in campaigns conducted in large part in the newspapers and on television with a constant barrage of polls, sound bites, and attack ads. These campaigns are orchestrated by consultants and spin doctors who are at times willing to work both sides of the political street. What gets reported depends on editors' and network executives' judgment on what is newsworthy or "fit to print." Editorial and often marketing judgment decide what goes on page one and what is lost in the back pages.

We know some of our world at first hand and much of it through the media. Our views on race relations may have been shaped by TV images of violence and riots in places that few viewers have actually visited. Our fears about child molestation, street crime, or rape are aroused and fueled (and often again allowed to fade) by the media. People who have never been in a court room get their ideas about how the justice system works from watching trials on the screen—whether as fictional crime-as-entertainment or as sensationalized long-running courtroom-reality TV. Viewers remote from the true diversity of multicultural America may have their mental images of minorities shaped by media stereotypes: the kindly ever-smiling African American entertainer or else the African American star athlete in trouble with the law; the Mexican military massacred and humiliated as the enemy in a movie glorifying the Anglo defenders of the Alamo.

The news in both the print media and on radio or television may play out in loving detail the personal disasters, heroic rescues, and petty scandals that viewers love. However, it may provide little insight into the politics of race, immigration, education, the national debt, recession, sexism, mental health, or unemployment. What does it take to become a critical viewer and reader?

GAME OVER

Amanda Fazzone

"Unlike most reed-thin models and actresses, Cybermodels have no need for breast augmentation, airbrushing, padded bras."

In her spectacularly successful book The Beauty Myth: How Images of Beauty Are Used against Women *(1990), Naomi Wolf attacked "the icon of the anorexic fashion model" that drives out "most other images and stories of female heroines, role models, villains, eccentrics, buffoons, visionaries, sex goddesses and pranksters." She marshaled formidable statistics, insiders' testimony, and official reports in support of her charges against fashion magazines, the cosmetic surgery industry, the dieting industry, and other forces promoting an ideal of female beauty that robs women of their sense of self-worth. In the decade that followed, the "impossibly beautiful" stereotypical fashion model encountered formidable competition from a new kind of computer-generated video-game heroine that co-opted the new fashion of strong independent female characters while carrying the media cult of the "unnaturally perfect body" to a new extreme. Amanda Fazzone wrote the following article for the "Washington Diarist" column of the* New Republic *in July of 2001.*

Thought Starters: The simulated reality of video games became a huge marketing success. Are you or people you know well part of the target audience? For a journal entry, can you give a synopsis or vivid plot outline of a current favorite?

I have more than a few things in common with Lara Croft, the gun-toting, Bigfoot-slaying, back-flipping, treasure-hunting, aristocratic English heroine who stars in the video game Tomb Raider, [. . .] spun off into [. . . a] movie in the United States, *Lara Croft: Tomb Raider*. We both have dark hair and dark eyes. We both enjoy music and the arts. We both like corgis. We both write for a living. And we both have breasts. But while Lara's 34Ds unwaveringly float mid-bicep, I, like most women, rely on an armada of brassieres to ballast what nature never intended skin to buoy. The 5-foot-9-inch, 130-pound Lara—even with the enviable measurements of 34D-24-35—seems not to have any breast-control issues at all. Whether she's fighting giant lizards or rappelling in the Himalayas, they invariably stay put.

Her secret? Lara Croft isn't real. She doesn't actually weigh in at 130 pounds (and her breasts don't weigh anything at all), the "stats" in her

1

lengthy promotional "bio" notwithstanding. She's a synthespian: a computer-generated virtual woman with the pixels and the moxie to engender crushes in the hearts of the millions of gamers who made Tomb Raider one of the most successful video game series of all time. The game's tag line: "Sometimes a killer body just isn't enough."

But not being human hasn't kept Lara from taking heat for her unnaturally perfect body. Feminists say that, with the advent of computer-generated cybermodels and synthespians, the bar for real women has been raised even higher. Asks Germaine Greer: "How many women do you know with broad chests and narrow waists like [Lara Croft]? Men should wake up to the fact that women have big bums. Whatever these characters are, they're not real women." Princeton University Professor Elaine Showalter claims that "Croft and the cybermodels epitomise the era of power grooming. No longer can women depend on a dab of powder and lipstick before they face the public." Today's woman, Showalter writes, employs "[l]iposuction, exfoliation, laser-blasting, Botox and collagen [to] take the skin to pix[e]lated smoothness and tautness." Life imitating art.

The outrage isn't surprising. Feminists have long decried the alchemy employed to create women of Barbie doll proportions, charging that such images cause men to objectify women, and contribute to the lack of female self-esteem that leads to depression, eating disorders, and the operating table. And with Lara and her virtual compatriots, that alchemy—and presumably the suffering it spawns—has taken a giant technological leap forward. Still, there may be an upside to all this pixelation. After all, feminists aren't the only ones infuriated by the emergence of cybermodels—the "real" modeling industry has good reason to be upset as well. Cybermodels may do more than put human models out of work; their explicit fakeness might just force people to admit that the whole modeling enterprise has been fake from the start.

From *Toy Story* to *Titanic* to *Shrek*, we're growing increasingly accustomed to recognizing synthespians for the man-made products they are. On the Internet, cybernewscasters Vandrea (modeled on British newscaster Andrea Catherwood) and Ananova have become celebs. And Webbie Tookay (that's "2-K"), the first virtual model, was dubbed "the most valuable model in the world" with an estimated market value last year of $15 million, thanks, in part, to contracts with Nokia and Sony. (By contrast, Gisele Bundchen, the world's highest-paid human model, earns a mere $5 million per year.) But cybermodel celebrity is a consciously cynical phenomenon. Their creators aren't trying to *trick* us into believing these images are real. They're just simulating reality.

What's more, even as girls' magazine *mary-kateandashley* dubs Lara "an Indiana Jones–esque girl" and as Angelina Jolie, the 26-year-old Academy Award–winning actress, doubles for Lara on film, it's almost impossible not to notice that Croft and her cyberpeers aren't real. It's true, as Naomi Wolf wrote in her 1991 book *The Beauty Myth*, that "'Computer imaging'—the controversial new technology that tampers with photographic reality—has been used for years in women's magazines' beauty advertising." But the whole point of computer imaging was that magazine readers didn't know—or at least didn't think much about the fact—that the woman on the cover didn't look that way in real life. And so young girls could aspire to look the way Gisele looks on this month's cover of *Vogue*. But they can't ignore Lara's inauthenticity, because her inauthenticity is central to her fame. "When I first played the game, I thought [Lara's breast size] was ridiculous," said one 15-year-old girl I interviewed after the film. "How could she run and jump dressed like that?" And you can see it on the video screen. Lara barely speaks, is controlled by the player, and is primarily seen from behind. A clear case of art trying—and failing—to imitate life.

Of course it's possible that, as technology improves, it will become increasingly difficult to distinguish real women from their computer-generated counterparts. And if that's the case, beauty-industry handlers will have even more reason to prefer synthetic women. "She is the perfect model," cheers Webbie Tookay's agent, John Casablancas—the founder of Elite Model Management who left his post [. . .] to found the first-ever cyber-model agency, Illusion 2K. "Webbie can eat nothing and keep her curves. . . . [S]he will never get a pimple or ask for a raise." With a Screen Actors Guild strike looming, speculates a recent *Entertainment Weekly* article, the demand for synthespians may grow even higher. And, unlike most reed-thin models and actresses, cybermodels have no need for breast augmentation, airbrushing, padded bras, or industrial-strength double-stick tape.

Still, would it be so bad if technology grew sophisticated enough to trump reality, if synthespians replaced women in all those forms of entertainment feminists have historically derided—modeling, beauty pageants, pornography? Who would protest if we no longer expected women to look like models, just as we never expected anyone to climb walls like Spider-Man or have supersonic hearing like the Bionic Woman?

Perhaps cybermodels and synthespians will help us admit that what men have been getting off on all these years—and what women have been emulating at unrecoupable cost—are, like Lara Croft, little more than cartoon characters. And with that admission might come a more natural definition of what's sexy, by which the genuine confluence of health and DNA is deemed preferable to the handiwork of a Photoshop virtuoso. Were that truly to come to pass, of course, it wouldn't only be the human supermodels whose careers would suffer: Presumably, Lara's would as well. But she'd manage. After all, she'll always have her writing.

The Responsive Reader

1 In the course of her essay, Fazzone touches on many of the methods women employ to emulate the ideal created by the Beauty Myth. These range from the traditional "dab of powder and lipstick" to much more

strenuous and costly methods and procedures. On which of these could you serve as somewhat of an expert to fill in your fellow students on the mysteries of the beauty trade?

2   What were the traditional objections of feminists to the Barbie doll image and to modeling shows and beauty pageants? What for them makes the new computerized synthetic "thespians," or virtual actors, an even more formidable challenge? How do they raise the bar for women "even higher"?

3   Fazzone several times touches on the question of whether video game users really at some point confuse fantasy and reality. Overall, what seems to be her answer to the question? Do you think attitudes from the virtual reality of video games do in some way or to some extent carry over from the fantasy world into the real world of human behavior and human relationships?

Talking, Listening, Writing

4   Have you ever made a conscious effort to make yourself over or improve your appearance? What made you do it? What did you do? What was the result?

5   Do you or people you know object to makeup, perfume, or other beauty helps? Can you help with a presentation lining up arguments pro and con?

6   As Fazzone indicates, feminists have long agitated against fashion shows, beauty pageants, and Barbie dolls. Do you think their objections have had an impact?

Collaborative Projects

7   Working with a group, collect images from advertisements or commercials aimed at you and your peers or others of your age group. What kinds of faces, bodies, and clothes do you see? Do you think the grunge look, for instance, could be a rebellion of the young against the stereotypes of the Beauty Myth?

FIND IT ON THE WEB

Much controversy has swirled about the Barbie doll as an icon of American popular culture. Studies have focused on the impact of the stereotypical Barbie doll image on young girls and on the manufacturer's initiatives designed to overcome charges of racism. Can you track some of the controversy in current or archived Internet sources?

UNGOOD FELLAS

George de Stefano

"Although real mafiosi are venal and violent, films and TV too often have presented them far more sympathetically than they deserve—*The Sopranos* is just the latest case in point."

When The Sopranos *television series returned for yet another season, media critic Jeremiah Creedon said, "The Sopranos began in 1999 when Tony, a mob boss, blacked out beside his swimming pool in suburban New Jersey. He promptly hired a therapist." According to this article first published in February 2000 and many other media watchers' commentary, years later and untold episodes later, "Dr Jennifer Melfi had dredged up all there is to know about her thuggish but complicated client."*

The Godfather, *Mario Puzo's original Mafia epic with Marlon Brando as Don Corleone, spawned countless sequels and spinoffs. In some of the most popular American film and television entertainment, evil comes not from outer space or from the designs of a mad scientist but from your Italian neighbors around the block in the Bronx or other American city with a large ethnic population.* The Sopranos, *a trendy updating of the Godfather mystique, has became one of the most widely watched and critically acclaimed show on American television. Criminals still bully, conspire, and kill, but they share their concerns with a psychiatrist and operate in a society where brutal violence is no longer news.*

George de Stefano is a media watcher and culture critic for Nation *magazine and other publications. As an Italian American author, de Stefano objects to the turning of ruthless criminals into audience favorites and to the continuing stereotyping of the Italian American community as a hotbed for organized crime.*

Thought Starters: Do you watch Mafia epics on television or on the big screen? Which of the *Godfather, GoodFellas,* or similar mafia epics are you familiar with? What identifies the gangsters and criminals as Italians or as Americans of Italian descent?

The last decade of the twentieth century was not a happy one for the   *1* Mafia. During the nineties both the United States and Italy made remarkable strides in curbing organized crime, imprisoning gangsters and dismantling their business interests. Though it would be premature to declare either the Italian or the American Mafia dead, both have been wounded, the latter perhaps mortally. But if the Mafia is a shadow of its former self, you'd hardly know it from pop culture. In fact, media images of La Cosa Nostra seem to be proliferating in direct proportion to the decline of organized crime. Not since Francis Ford Coppola's *The Godfather* reinvented the gangster genre in the early seventies have there been so many wiseguys on screen. The past year brought the films *Analyze This* and *Mickey Blue Eyes*, and with *i fratelli* Weinstein, Harvey and Bob, having acquired the rights to the late Mario Puzo's final novel, *Omertà*, for their Miramax Films, there's at least one other high-profile Mafia movie on the way. Another may well be the fourth installment of Coppola's *Godfather* saga. According to the *Hollywood Reporter*, Leonardo Di Caprio and Andy Garcia (Al Pacino's nephew in *Godfather III*) are keen to sign on to the project, pending a suitable script.

On television, gangsters with Italian surnames have been a surefire audience draw, from the days of *The Untouchables* to contemporary cop shows like *NYPD Blue*. A very partial list of recent programs includes the network miniseries *The Last Don* and *Bella Mafia*, as well as biopics about John Gotti and his turncoat lieutenant Sammy "The Bull" Gravano, and, on Showtime cable, an absurdly hagiographic one about Joseph Bonanno produced by his son, Bill. But no mob-themed show has generated the critical accolades and viewer enthusiasm accorded *The Sopranos*, the Emmy Award–winning HBO comedy-drama that has become the cable network's most-watched series, its recent second-season premiere attended by an avalanche of hype.

Moving from *The Sopranos'* suburban New Jersey turf to Palermo, HBO last fall premiered *Excellent Cadavers*, a feature-film adaptation of Alexander Stille's 1995 book about the anti-Mafia campaign launched by two courageous Sicilian magistrates. Why is Italian-American (and Italian) organized crime such a mainstay of American pop culture, and do these images reflect the reality of the Mafia? And does the persistence of the Mafioso as a pop-culture archetype constitute ethnic defamation of Italian-Americans?

That many of today's depictions of the American Mafia are in the comic mode—*The Sopranos, Analyze This, Mickey Blue Eyes*, the parody *Mafia!*—is possible only because organized crime is much less fearsome than in its heyday. Both *The Sopranos* and *Analyze This* feature Mafiosi on the verge of a nervous breakdown, their psychological crackups reflecting the disarray of their criminal enterprises under the pressure of law enforcement and the breaking of *omertà*, the code of silence, by gangsters who'd rather sing than serve time. V. Zucconi, a commentator for the Italian newspaper *La Repubblica*, analyzed this development in an article titled "America: The Decline of the Godfather." Zucconi claims that in the United States the Mafia survives mainly in its pop-culture representations, and that while it used to generate fear, today it is a source of humor. He says that in America one can observe "the funeral of the dying Mafia," an outcome he hopes one day will occur also in Italy. Is Zucconi overoptimistic?

Criminologist James Jacobs reaches a similar conclusion in his study *Gotham Unbound: How New York City Was Liberated from the Clutches of Cosa Nostra* (NYU Press). Organized-crime-control strategies "have achieved significant success in purging Cosa Nostra from the city's social, economic, and political life," he writes. Gangsters in New York, and also in other large and small cities, are losing their foothold in the labor and industrial rackets that have been the source of their power and influence; and there is a dearth of younger, rising stars to replace aging or incarcerated leaders. The decline, says Jacobs, has been so marked that "Cosa Nostra's survival into the next millennium . . . can be seriously doubted." It's a different story in Italy. The Sicilian Mafia's economic might, its alliances with politicians and indifferent law enforcement enabled it to grow so powerful that it threatened Italy's status as a modern nation. As Alexander Stille observed in *Excellent Cadavers*, the war against the Mafia in Sicily is not a local problem of law and order but the struggle for national unity and democracy in Italy. HBO's film based on Stille's book promised to tell that story, but, at barely ninety minutes, it ended up too compressed to offer more than a skim on the events he reported and analyzed so compellingly. Talk about missed opportunities: Instead of the Z-like political thriller it could have been, *Cadavers* is a rather routine *policier*.

In the eighties, Mafia killings accelerated as ambitious upstarts from Corleone (a real place, *Godfather* fans) challenged the Palermo old guard for the control of organized crime. The body count included not only Mafiosi but also police officials, magistrates and politicians, who came to be called, with fine Sicilian mordancy, excellent cadavers. Two magistrates, Giovanni Falcone and Paolo Borsellino, began to pursue the Mafia with unprecedented persistence. Their efforts culminated in the historic "maxi-trials," which resulted in the imprisonment of hundreds of Sicily's most powerful gangsters.

The Mafia, of course, retaliated, assassinating Falcone in May 1992 and, two months later, Borsellino. The murders, however, ignited the simmering rage of Sicilians against the Mafia and the officials who protected it. The government was forced to respond, and the subsequent crackdown resulted in the arrest of numerous Mafiosi and connected businessmen and politicians.

Italians overwhelmingly regard Mafiosi as the other; they do not identify or empathize with criminals, nor do they feel that portrayals of organized crime in movies, television and other media tar them with the brush of criminality. Many Italian-Americans, however, regard the seemingly endless stream of Mafia movies and TV shows as a defamatory assault. In mid-January a coalition of seven Italian-American organizations issued a joint statement condemning *The Sopranos* for "defaming and assassinating the cultural character" of Americans of Italian descent.

It's undeniable that the dominant pop-culture images of Italian-Americans have been the mobster and the related, anti-working class stereotype of the boorish *gavone*. But there are important differences between these skewed portrayals and other forms of ethnic stereotyping. If the Mafia has been conflated with Sicilian / Italian culture, it's in large part because Italian-American filmmakers and writers have so expertly blended the two. Coppola's memorable and authentic depiction of an Italian–American wedding in *The Godfather* comes to mind. *The Sopranos*, created by veteran TV writer David Chase (né De Cesare), similarly gets many details right about *nouveau riche* suburban Italian-Americans, the eponymous mob family's noncriminal neighbors.

The Sopranos cleverly acknowledges Italian-American indignation   10
over Mafia stereotyping only to try to co-opt it. In an episode from the show's first season, Dr. Jennifer Melfi, Tony Soprano's psychiatrist, and her family have a lively dinnertime debate about the persistence of the mob image. The scene ends with the Melfis toasting the "20 million Italian Americans" who have nothing to do with organized crime. But Jennifer also mocks her ex-husband, an ethnic activist, for being more concerned about "rehabilitating Connie Francis's reputation" than with ethnic cleansing. The line neatly skewers the tunnel vision of conservative Italian-Americans who ignore forms of bias and social injustice that don't affect them. But it also poses a false dichotomy: caring passionately about the image of one's group need not preclude a broader perspective. At other times, the show suggests that Tony, a murderous criminal, is an Italian-American everyman. He's aware of his people's history—he informs his daughter that the telephone was invented not by Alexander Graham Bell but by Antonio Meucci—and he's depicted as more honest and vital than his snooty neighbors, or, as he calls them, the "Wonder-Bread wops."

The Mafia has become the paradigmatic pop-culture expression of Italian-American ethnicity for several reasons: the aura of glamour, sometimes tragic, surrounding the movie mobster, exemplified by Coppola's Corleones; the gangster genre's embodiment of the violent half of "kiss kiss, bang bang," Pauline Kael's famous distillation of the essential preoccupations of American movies; and, perhaps most important, the enduring appeal of the outlaw—the guy who, in a technocratic, impersonal society, has the personal power to reward friends, and, more important, whack enemies. Although real Mafiosi are venal and violent, films and TV too often have presented them far more sympathetically than they deserve—*The Sopranos* is just the latest case in point.

Italian-Americans, whose forebears fled *la miseria*, the crushing poverty of Southern Italy and Sicily, in numbers so vast that their departure has been likened to a hemorrhage, constitute one of the United States' largest ethnic groups. An Italian-American film critic and author told me some years ago that it was "selfish" of our *paesani* to complain about Mafia stereotyping given their largely successful pursuit of the American Dream and the more onerous discrimination faced by other minorities. He also insisted that most Americans are smart enough to realize that gangsters constitute only a tiny minority of the Italian-American population.

But it is dismaying—no, infuriating—to see one's group depicted so consistently in such distorted fashion. Unlike racist stereotyping of blacks, portrayals of Italian-American criminality don't reflect or reinforce Italian-American exclusion from American society and its opportunities. (Faced with a threatened NAACP boycott, both the NBC and ABC networks recently agreed to increase the hiring of blacks, Latinos and Asians, in front of and behind the TV cameras.) The pervasiveness of these images, however, does affect the perception of Italian-Americans by others. Surveys indicate that many Americans believe that most Italian-Americans are in some way "connected" and that Italian immigrants created organized crime in the United States, even though the Irish, Germans and others got there first.

Besides fostering such attitudes, the Mafia mystique also serves to obscure other, more interesting and no less dramatic aspects of the Italian-American experience. In 1997 the City University of New York hosted a conference on "The Lost World of Italian American Radicalism." Scholars discussed the immigrant anarchists Sacco and Vanzetti (executed by the US government), other major figures like the labor organizer Carlo Tresca, the New York City Congressman Vito Marcantonio and such icons of sixties activism as civil rights advocate Father James Groppi and Mario Savio of the Berkeley Free Speech movement. The conference also highlighted unsung men and women who were labor militants, anti-Fascist organizers and politically engaged writers and artists.

Besides such efforts to recover and understand the radical past, there   15
has been a surge of cultural production and activism among Italian-Americans. In recent years the American-Italian Historical Association, a national organization of academics and grassroots scholars, has held conferences on such hot-button topics as multiculturalism and race relations. Fieri, an association of young Italian-American professionals, last year commemorated the life and work of Vito Marcantonio—an amazing choice given the far less controversial figures they could have honored. The New York-based Italian-American Writers Association and journals such as *Voices in Italian Americana* (VIA) and *The Italian American Review* promote and publish fiction, poetry and critical essays by writers whose vision of *italianità* flouts the pop-culture clichés. Italo-American gays and lesbians have come out with *Hey, Paisan!*, a new anthology, and *Fuori!*, a folio of essays published by VIA. Actor/playwright Frank Ingrasciotta's *Blood Type: Ragu*, currently enjoying a successful run at the Belmont Italian American Theater in the Bronx (several of whose productions have moved to Off Broadway), offers an exploration of Sicilian-American identity and culture free of *goombahs* with guns.

Ethnicity remains a powerful and contentious force in American life, and popular culture should illumine its workings. Italian-Americans who want to promote more diverse depictions might not only protest Hollywood film studios and TV production companies. They might put some of the onus on Italian-American creative talents who have built careers on the Mafia. And they could also support the alternative, community-level work being done. Other stories from Italo-America can and should be told.

The Responsive Reader

1 De Stefano mentions milestones and key features of the traditional gangster genre. What would you include in a description of the literature and media fare that feeds the public's appetite for entertainment with a Mafia or Cosa Nostra theme? (What is the Cosa Nostra? What is *omertà*?)

2 According to de Stefano, how has the gangster genre evolved in recent years? Does it show us the same types but seen from a more sophisticated, updated point of view? Does it reflect changes in the world of organized crime?

3 Media critics often accuse the mainstream media of co-opting voices of protest of criticism. They silence or undercut protest by adopting some of the protesters' language—"talking the talk without walking the walk." De Stefano claims that a recent media success co-opted the indignation of Italian Americans at the continued use of the gangster stereotype. How did it do so?

4 De Stefano mentions the "memorable and authentic depiction of an Italian-American wedding" in the original *Godfather* movie. If you remember the movie or similar scenes in other gangster movies, what makes such scenes so memorable or authentic for viewers like de Stefano? Other media critics are especially troubled by the role of family, and of the gangsters' wives and children, in the pop-culture Mafia movies. What do you think disturbs them?

Talking, Listening, Writing

5 De Stefano says that many Italian Americans "regard the seemingly endless stream of Mafia movies and TV shows as a defamatory assault." Do you think these media products defame or slander a whole group of Americans? Do you think Americans that are not of Italian descent should be concerned? Why or why not?

6 Producers and media executives often justify violent gangster epics as "just entertainment." Do you think they are just entertainment? Do you think that in the gangster genre criminals are glorified?

7 Do you think the trend in American popular entertainment is toward more brutal and more cynical violence?

8 Have you or people you know well felt you or they were the target of ethnic stereotyping in the media? What form did it take? How serious was it? What recourse do targeted groups have?

FIND IT ON THE WEB

Have Americans come to think of organized crime as entertainment? De Stefano reminds them of the brutal realities of the struggle in his tribute to the murdered Italian crime fighters Falcone and Borsellino. What can you find out about Falcone, Borsellino, or other real-life crime fighters— their struggle against organized crime, their murders, and the attacks on their families? What would you include in an update on Italy's fight against organized crime?

A BATTLE BETWEEN CITIZENSHIP, ANCESTRY

Edmund Tijerina

A new film about the Battle of the Alamo revives the discussion about the divided loyalties of Mexican Americans whose ancestors fought on "both sides of the wall."

Edmund Tijerina wrote the following article for the San Antonio Express News *in March 2004. A new Alamo movie was being premiered in San Antonio, Texas, with much media fanfare and attendance of celebrities. San Antonio is the home of the famed church-fortress of the Alamo, still a landmark and a shrine there, where a few hundred defenders were overwhelmed by a superior Mexican force commanded by General Santa Anna. "Remember the Alamo!" was long the patriotic rallying cry for Texans whose ancestors wrested the territory from a newly independent Mexico and established a Republic of Texas that became part of the United States.*

In the movie, Colonel William Travis, Davy Crockett, Jim Bowie, and Sam Houston, in frontierman's garb, live up to their legendary status as American folk heroes with defiant patriotic speeches and heroic deeds. The defenders fire a cannon into a meeting where negotiators arboring a white flag hope to explore the chances for a truce or surrender. The tea-drinking Mexican officers in garish costume-shop uniforms are commanded by an evil bad-tempered Santa Anna ("the peacock") who executes prisoners. Hundreds or thousands of the badly trained Mexican conscript soldiers are blown up in the carnage of the battle scenes, but the camera never seems to dwell on their mortal agony or their last words for their mothers or wives who will mourn their loss. A movie critic for the New York Times *called the movie "a bafflingly upbeat take" on the second-most famous defeat in American history.*

Tijerina asks his readers: What side are you on? Or are there really two sides?

Thought Starters: Have you seen movies about Mexican history or about the Mexican revolution or revolutions?

Don't expect to find too many Mexican Americans celebrating over   1
the new Alamo movie and suddenly fueling a wave of interest in the historic battle site.

And whether or not Disney manages to portray the Mexican perspective of the Alamo, it almost doesn't matter.

After all, even now, there are still waves of conflicted feelings swirling inside us about this battle.

It's not that our ancestors happened to be on the wrong side of the battle. Instead, it's that our ancestors were on both sides of the wall, and that sense of conflicted loyalties gives many of us very mixed feelings about the battle and its ultimate meaning.

On the one hand, we're Americans and grew up in this country. Most Mexican Americans in San Antonio speak English far better than Spanish and know the history of George Washington crossing the Delaware better than the story of Hernán Cortez and Cuauhtémoc.

Even if we didn't see the 1960 movie, we know the John Wayne version of the Alamo, and many Mexican Americans feel an identification with, of all people, many of the Texian—or Anglo—defenders of the Alamo. William Barret Travis and David Crockett belong to us, too.

We also know that there were Tejano defenders of the Alamo, our direct ancestors who fought for a free Texas. People who looked like us also held off wave after wave of Mexican troops. Only they didn't get movies made about them.

There were also hundreds of families who lived on this land when it was Mexico and who can truthfully say that the border crossed them.

And there were Tejano patriots such as Juan Seguin and José Antonio Navarro, who made it possible for Texas to break free of Mexico. They fought for freedom, too.

At the same time, we feel a kinship with the Mexican side of the battle. After all, far from the stories of "battle hardened" troops, too many of the Mexican soldiers were conscripts who were firing their rifles for the first time.

Santa Anna didn't give many of these young men a chance or a choice about whether to join the march to San Antonio.

A generation later, young men in Northern Mexico were given the choice to join the federales or the forces of Pancho Villa or be shot. Their families formed the biggest wave of migration into San Antonio, when thousands of families fled the Mexican Revolution nearly a century ago. Being forced to fight at gunpoint is something many of us know about from family stories.

Because the Alamo stirs both the Mexican and American sides of us, it makes many of us feel like we have to choose sides between our ancestry and our citizenship. Most of us don't want to have to do that.

But even more than the battle itself that causes so much uneasiness is the aftermath. Yes, "Remember the Alamo" has served not only as a rallying cry for the soldiers at the Battle of San Jacinto and has been adopted in other parts of the world.

But it has also been used as a very thin veneer to discriminate against Mexican immigrants and Mexican Americans. For second- and third-generation Mexican Americans here, nearly all of us have parents or grand-parents who can tell stories about hearing "Remember the Alamo." They're not pleasant.

In a very real way, those of us of Mexican descent here in South Texas carry the blood and memories from both sides of the walls of the "Shrine of Texas Liberty." We also helped to build this state and this country into what it has become.

So maybe this movie will be a commercial and critical success and help erase the images of bloodthirsty, dirty Mexicans and pristine Anglo Texans as the only heroes of the battle.

Even if it does, it's going to take a lot more than just a movie.

The Responsive Reader

1   Tijerina says of the mixed feelings and "conflicted loyalties" of Mexican Americans about the Alamo story: "It's not that our ancestors happened to be on the wrong side of the battle." So what is his *thesis*? What is the central point he makes about the "Mexican perspective" early in his review? Toward the end of his review, where and how does he again take up and reinforce his central theme?

2   "On the one hand, we are Americans." How does Tijerina follow up this *transition* setting up the first part of his *on the one hand* and *on the other hand* organizing strategy? What key points does he recall for his readers about the history and allegiance of Mexican-American tejanos?

3   "At the same time, we feel a kinship with the Mexican side of the battle." What key points does Tijerina include after this *turning point* transition taking readers to the other side of the divided loyalties of many in his South Texas audience?

4   Tijerina talks about the "uneasiness" caused by the *aftermath* and subsequent history of the Alamo story for many of his readers. What role has the Alamo history played in discrimination against Mexican Americans? What stereotypes about Americans of Mexican descent and Anglos has it served to perpetuate?

Talking, Listening, Writing

5   Do you know Americans, or have you known about Americans, who felt they had to choose sides between their ancestry and their citizenship?

6   Tijerina says it will take much "more than just a movie" to erase discrimination and stereotypes encountered by Mexican Americans. What will it take? What evidence of progress or of backsliding have you been able to observe or to track?

OTHER VOICES

Film as Document

How much documentary film-making is fiction, and how much is a truth-telling look at reality?

Michael Moore became a world-famous independent filmmaker with low-budget documentaries. In 1989, Moore launched his *Roger & Me*, his indictment of General Motors management for abandoning its Flint, Michigan, headquarters and the Michigan base that was the heart and soul of the American automobile industry. His Oscar-winning *Bowling for Columbine* received wide attention as it dramatized a national tragedy when the violence of *Terminator* movies and killer video games spilled over into the local high school. In 2004, Moore won an Oscar for *Fahrenheit 9/11*, his indictment of the political establishment's response when terror invaded America and of the subsequent invasion of Iraq. His film won the *Palme d'Or* at the Cannes Festival in France, generally considered the height of critical acclaim. An attempt by the giant Disney corporation to hinder distribution of the movie and attempts to protect teenagers from its "violent and disturbing images" helped create an avalanche of advance publicity.

1   Hostile critics of Moore's *Fahrenheit 9/11* attacked it as propaganda. Have you seen movies or television programs you would consider propaganda? For what were they propaganda? How did you respond? Did they change your mind or make you support a cause?

2   Should the media show the grim realities of war? Moore showed footage "like nothing seen on American television." He showed the boy with the severed arm, and he talks to a mother whose son was killed. Was he "manipulating" viewers? At the other end of the political spectrum, are media sources that gloss over the horrible realities of war distorting the truth?

3   The Walt Disney coorporation invited conservative groups to screenings of a rival documentary that they claimed was nonpartisan. A reporter for a Hearst Corporation newspaper described the film as "stitching simple, positive vignettes of everyday Americans with sweeping vistas and up-tempo music." Compared with *Fahrenheit 9/11*, the journalist said,

> the messages in "America's Heart and Soul"—which will begin playing on 100 screens Friday—are more thematic, general and affirming. Besides their espoused patriotism, Puritan work ethic and shared can-do-it-ness, Disney's mini-profile subjects give voice to no particular political philosophy. . . . "You get a horse to trust you, and you have a wonderful thing," says

Roudy Roudebush, an on-the-wagon cowboy who a few minutes into the film rides his steed into a Telluride, Colo., saloon
for a deep drink of water. He soon adds: "We've experienced
being free . . . because there aren't many people, and there is-
n't much government. And so it's hard to have your freedoms
even infringed a little bit. Cherish your freedom."

What would be your reaction if early in a film about "everyday
Americans" you saw an "on-the-wagon cowboy" take a horse
into a saloon for a drink of water and then segue into a speech
about freedom?

4 Do you think one political party has the right to call itself more
patriotic than another?

RETURN OF THE CLICHÉ EXPERT

Roger Angell

"None of this is rocket science. But, yes, my plate is full."

Viewers and listeners hear the same buzzwords and canned phrases again and again. The language of campaign ads and political talk shows is shot through with ready-made phrases: "tax-and-spend liberals," "faith-based initiatives," "failing schools." Viewers who don't mute commercials hear familiar appeals: "absolutely free," "no obligation," "limited time only," "more doctors (or dentists) recommend," "guaranteed!"

In the following article first published in the New Yorker *in 1996, Roger Angell reminds media watchers that the habit of falling back on ready-made phrases or clichés is a time-honored practice dear to people "from all walks of life." "They speak and write in clichés—tired and predictable phrases that sound as if they came to the speaker all ready-made and strung together ready for use:* a run for their money, throw in the towel, only the tip of the iceberg, the window of opportunity, the cutting edge, and the bottom line. *Some of these may at one time have been clever or imaginative, but they have lost their flavor, like stale bread. To say it in the language of clichés:* To be brutally frank, and not to put too fine a point on it, the bloom is off such expressions (to coin a phrase), and in this day and age they are far from being a sure winner in the hearts and minds of men and women from all walks of life, and in the final analysis, when all is said and done, they do more harm than good.

The New Yorker *magazine for many years ran a feature with the cliché expert parodying contemporaries who fall back on trite, ready-made expressions rather than using fresh language to communicate some fresh thinking of their own. Recently, the cliché expert returned to take stock of the buzzwords of a new, proactive, computer-literate generation.*

Thought Starters: How aware are you of changing fashions in the way people use words? Do you or your friends use expressions like, "You don't want to go there," or, "It doesn't get any better than this"? Do you ever say, "No problema"? Does anyone still say, "You've made my day"?

Q: Good morning, Mr. Arbuthnot. It's a pleasure to see you again, and to hear further testimony from you on the subject of clichés.

A: Wrong man. You're thinking of my uncle, Dr. Magnus Arbuthnot, who is no longer with us. Bought the farm, checked out, fumed out, popped off, slipped his cable, went over the pass, hit the throughway. I mean, he's gone-zo. I'm Chip Arbuthnot, his heir. His *spiritual* heir.

Q: But you are here to give us your views on current and established clichés, are you not?

A: No way.

Q: You're not?   5

A: I'm here to share my views.

Q: I see. And you are an expert in the field, are you not?

A: Arguably.

Q: You wish to argue with the court?

A: No, I'm arguably an expert. The adverb allows me to say some-   10
thing and then partly take it back.

Q: I think I understand.

A: Don't worry about it. This stuff isn't written in stone.

Q: You're very kind.

A: There's a reason for that.

Q: I can almost guess what it is. It's on the tip of my tongue.   15

A: I'm a people person.

Q: I knew it! Now, Mr. Arbuthnot, may I ask a strange question? What's that on your head?

A: This is my other hat.

Q: Your *other* hat?

A: This is the hat I wear when I'm being the cliché expert. When   20
I'm doing something else, I wear a different other hat, not this one.

Q: Hmm. Are you telling us that being a cliché expert is not a full-time occupation?

A: As if. Get a grip.

Q: You must be a busy man, holding so many demanding jobs.

A: None of this is rocket science. But, yes, my plate is full.

Q: And you must have to maintain a constant schedule of travels to   25
different parts of the country, if not the world, to keep up with regional as well as occupational clichés, is that not the case?

A: Been there, done that.

Q: Tell me, do most people know when they're speaking in clichés? Or is that a dumb question?

A: I'm not comfortable with it. If I said it was a no-brainer, I'd be sending the wrong message. Let's say that some folks who think they're pushing the envelope conversationwise ain't.

Q: Mr. Arbuthnot, are there specific occupations that produce a greater preponderance of clichés in daily human intercourse than others do?

A: "Daily human intercourse" is very fine. Congratulations.   30

Q: Shall I repeat the question?

A: No, because I'm going to pass. This is a slippery slope.

Q: What about the sexes? Are women more likely than men to—

A: Whoa. Back off, Mister. Don't go there. It's a no-win situation.

Q: Oh, I'm sorry.   35

A: You're putting me between a rock and a hard place.

Q: I didn't mean to upset you. I apologize.

A: You mean you empathize.
Q: That's what I meant to say.
A: You feel my pain.   *40*
Q: Yes, I do, I do!
A: Historically, you have concerns.
Q: That's right!
A: Unless I miss my guess, you're also pro-active.
Q: Yup.   *45*
A: At the same time, you're a very private person.
Q: Absolutely. How did you know?
A: Trust me, it's easy. All you have to do is listen to your inner child.
Q: So any of us can become a cliché expert—is that what you're
saying?
A: How did we end up here? Hello?   *50*
Q: Oop, I'm going too fast again, aren't I? Just *using* clichés doesn't
do the trick—is that right?
A: No. You have to talk the talk and walk the walk.
Q: But of course. I wish we could go on with this and perhaps find
out how you got to ask all the questions, instead of the court. But our time
is up. I hope you've enjoyed our little meeting.
A: You've made my day.
Q: You have enlightened us all.   *55*
A: It doesn't get any better than this.
Q: Thank you, Mr. Arbuthnot.
A: No problema.

The Responsive Reader

1 How up-to-date are you on buzzwords and current clichés? Have you
   heard people talk about wearing different hats? When do people talk
   about a no-win situation? What do people mean when they use the
   terms *no-brainer, counter-intuitive, pushing the envelope,* and a *full plate*?

2 People may pick up new buzzwords because they fit in well with the
   way they think or with their personal agendas. Who uses the expression
   the bottom line—when, where, and for what purpose? When do people
   use expressions like, "It's not written in stone," or, "This is not rocket
   science"? Why do they say, "I'm not comfortable with it"? What signal
   do they give when they say, "We have concerns"? What purposes does
   the expression *slippery slope* serve? What's the difference between giving
   your views and sharing your views? Why does Angell think there is
   something wrong with the term *arguably*?

Talking, Listening, Writing

3 Do you use one kind of language when you are trying to impress people
   and another kind of language when relaxing with your friends? Can you
   give examples of the two contrasting ways of saying things?

Collaborative Projects

4   The language of politics and political campaigns is shot through with buzzwords and clichés. For instance, when and why did politicians start to talk about a color-blind society? When and how did "preferences" get to be a dirty word? Working with a group, you may want to investigate current trends in political rhetoric.

5   One African–American playwright said that productions about black singers or musicians or other entertainers have "left the lives of millions of black people who don't sing and dance for a living unattended to" in the theater or in the media. Is the media treatment of African Americans still tilted toward entertainers? Where and how?

SISTER FROM ANOTHER PLANET PROBES THE SOAPS

Andrea Freud Loewenstein

"All of my sample were hostile toward their own gender, whom they perceived as rivals in their never-ending fight to possess the opposite sex."

The ancient art of satire holds our human weaknesses and vices up to ridicule. The satirist's art is like a funhouse mirror that exaggerates our short-comings for all to see. It employs humor as a weapon to shame us into acting more responsible or humane. Satire may be gentle and affectionate, but it may also turn cutting and bitter when ignorance, deviousness, or callousness offend the satirist's standards of acceptable behavior.

The women's movement, at first stereotyped as humorless, increasingly pro-vided a stage for women's satirical humor. (Women's Glibber: State-of-the-Art Women's Humor appeared in 1993.) In the following example of fem-inist satire, a contributor to Ms. *magazine directs her satirical barbs at a time-honored American institution. She has a visitor from outer space marvel at the strange rituals of courtship and "copulation" in the universe of the soaps. Andrea Freud Loewenstein is the author of* The Worry Girl, *published by a women's press in the United Kingdom. This collection of interconnected sto-ries, with its echoes of an Austrian Jewish past and the Holocaust, has been described as re-creating "the sorrows and terrors that inform a Jewish child's dreams." Loewenstein's study* Loathsome Jews and Engulfing Women *was published by New York University Press.*

Thought Starters: Why do people watch soap operas? Is it true that soap opera plots and a soap opera mentality are increasingly infiltrating prime-time television?

Dear Professor:

Enclosed is my research paper. As you may remember, I attended every one of your lectures (I float at a right angle in the front row; last Thursday I was an iridescent green with other spots) on that most fascinating subject, the hu-man species North Americanus Soapus. For my research project, I viewed sev-eral weeks' worth of documentary videotapes from four different "Soaps," cho-sen because they were among the most widely watched programs in the Earthling year 1993, with some 50 million viewers combined. I will hereafter refer to the humanoids whose acquaintance I made in "The Young and the Restless," "The Bold and the Beautiful," "All My Children," and "General Hospital," as "Soapoids."

1

The name "Soaps," by the way, appears to derive from the obsessional re-currence of the cleanliness theme in the "commercials," which occur at rhythmic intervals throughout the tapes. These are short, ritualized hymns of thanks-giving and praise to selected objects of worship, such as toilet bowl cleaners and vaginal deodorants.

I must admit that during the first week of viewing, in which I used all 17 of my sensors, I was unable to distinguish one Soapoid from another. The only distinction I was immediately able to make was between male and female—the Soapoids' preoccupation with ritual ownership of the oppo-site sex causes them to go to amazing lengths to signal gender distinction. These signals include the compulsory arrangement and selective removal of facial and head hair, distinctive body coverings, and (for the adult female) symbolic facial markings and mutilations.

This species, in contrast to our own, is subdivided into a mere two fixed gender groupings: male and female. Contrary to the lecture in which you informed us that occasionally both male and female choose to couple with their own kind and that those humanoids tend to be ostracized by the majority, I observed no variation in gender identity or object choice. On the contrary, all of my sample were hostile toward their own gender, whom they perceived as rivals in their never-ending fight to possess the opposite sex. Although this goal appears to be the Soapoids' overwhelming motiva-tional force, the humans in my sample spent almost no time actually copu-lating. Instead, their main behavior consisted of endless discussions of, preparations for, and references to the act.

Nevertheless, copulation, when it does occur, often leads to trouble and confusion, even for the viewer. I spent a great deal of time attempting to determine the name of the young woman from *All My Children* who works in a police station, is the daughter of one of the two possible fathers of Mimi's unborn child, and nosily looked up information to determine the date of conception. Since the records revealed that she had copulated with both men during the same week, Mimi was forced to confess and call off her wedding the day it was scheduled. I never did get the young woman's name.

Copulation does allow the females to exert ownership over the males. You had informed us that males are the dominant gender, and that their in-ability to express their feelings verbally leads to frequent acts of violence. I regret to inform you that this conclusion is no longer valid. Soapoid males are quite gentle and verbally expressive. Their preferred behavior consists of lengthy expositions on their feelings toward the females. The male is es-pecially prone to elaborate courtship rituals in preparation for copulation. These include the repetition of such submissive phrases as: "I love you so much," "You're my whole life," and "You were amazing last night, dar-ling!" In one typical behavior, a male in *The Bold and the Beautiful* prepared for intercourse by placing at least 20 floating water lilies containing small lit candles in a pool of water upon which floated an inflatable rubber raft, the intended scene of sexual activity.

5

The far more complex females are the actual aggressors. In a lecture, you had mentioned that some women, referred to as "feminists," join with one another toward a common goal. No such movement was evident in this sample. In fact, the females' most favored posture was the standoff, a highly aggressive position in which two women position themselves from one to two feet apart and emit such statements as "I hated you the first time I saw you." This is accompanied by a full range of physical expressions, including crossing of the arms, curling of the lip, and advancing in a menacing manner.

Unlike the male, the female can be classified into several subtypes, all arranged around the notions of "good" and "evil." These inborn tendencies emerge at puberty, apparently along with the mammary glands. The Good Female mitigates her natural dominance by an exaggerated concern for the welfare and nourishment of "her" male. She is especially solicitous of his title—Writer, Actor, Businessman, Doctor, Lawyer, or Policeman—and is always ready to abandon her own title to have more time to support his efforts. In *The Young and the Restless*, for example, Nikki, a Businesswoman, repeatedly interrupts her own work to service Cole, a Writer who is also a Groomer of Horses. Attired in a series of low-cut red evening gowns, she waits on him at his workplace in the horse stable, serving him champagne and caviar, assuring him that publishers from the mythical city of New York will turn his novel into a "best-seller."

It is important to note, however, that these work titles are symbolic. Soapoids, who possess a limited will to action and often require several hours of "processing" conversation to accomplish a simple task, must limit themselves to the all-important Preparation for Copulation. They have neither the time nor the energy to engage in actual "work." (The now meaningless title *General Hospital* indicates that Soapoids did work at one time.)

Good Females can be recognized by their wide-open, forward-gazing   10
eyes, modest demeanor, and light pink lip-paint. In old age they become wrinkled. Evil Females, on the other hand, remain slim, highly polished, and brightly painted throughout life, a certain tautness of the facial skin being the only visible sign of aging. The Evil Females' characteristics include unfaithfulness, sexual rapacity, and the need to manipulate others. Most Evil Females confine their ambition to collecting a large number of men, but a few exhibit a further will to power through the ownership of Titles, Land, Factories, Businesses, or Patents. These women, whom I call Controllers, have destroyed the lives of generations of Soapoids.

In your lecture on racial and ethnic diversity, you brought us almost to jellification with your tale of the oppression of darker-hued or "African American" humanoids at the hands of the lighter ones whom you labeled the subspecies "European American." I am happy to inform you that no such oppression exists among modern-day Soapoids. In fact, there seems to be no difference between the darker and lighter types. All hues mix and converse on terms of perfect equality and good-will and hold titles of equal symbolic significance. Dark-skinned females (who exhibit a wide range of coloration, unlike the more muted light-skinned humanoids) wear their head hair in the same fashion as all other females—raised two or three inches from the head, then flowing to the shoulders. Darker and lighter humanoids do not mate, and appear to have no desire to do so. Whether this is because of the force of taboo or physical incompatibility cannot be determined at this juncture. It should be noted, however, that none of the African American females had attained the status of Controller, perhaps because they lack the necessary icy blue eyes.

Saul, an elderly male from *The Bold and the Beautiful*, speaks with an accent, wears a pink shirt, highly ornamented necktie, and thick spectacles; he appears to be a eunuch. My ethnosensor identified him as a member of the subspecies "Jew." Whether these characteristics are an honest reflection of this identity is hard for me to determine—he was the only member of the group in this sample. Maria from *All My Children* was identified as a member of the subspecies "Latina"; as far as I can tell from my viewing, this group is notable for wavy head hair and the ability to ride a Horse without a saddle. Unlike African Americans, these Latinas appear able to mate with the "European Americans."

The photographs you showed us of the unsavory dwelling places (known as "Ghettos") of some humanoids also appear to be out of date. As of now, all Soapoids inhabit spacious, carefully color-coordinated cubes, filled with plastic flowers and bright modular furniture, in which they engage in their activities of arguing, preparing for copulation, and discussing their feelings for one another. Since eating, cleaning, and evacuation are not part of these sequences (being reserved for the "commercials"), no rooms are provided for these activities. It is unclear whether this is by choice or necessity (perhaps the atmosphere outside these cubes is not pure enough to breathe).

No analysis of Soapoid society would be complete without a mention of the interlacing "commercials." These mini-documentaries demonstrate the Soapoids' unique ability to encapsulate and split off areas of behavior and their need to control their errant bodies. The mini-docs also provide a neat solution for any scholars who may, thus far in my narrative, have been puzzled by the absence of ingestion and excretion in the lives of these living organisms. All such functions are reserved for the mini-docs, during which Soapoids frantically ingest prepackaged slimness-controlling nourishments and rid their cubes, their eating utensils, their garments, and their bodies of all superfluous liquids and imperfections. "Dirty on the outside!" exclaims a voice-over as a female handles her mate's garment in horror. "Uh oh, what about the inside!" A typical hour in the lives of Soapoids contains countless mini-docs that utilize not only a cleaning fluid that will purify garments on the inside, but also: a garment that can absorb the excretions of even the most wiggly of infant young; a tablet that cleans the excreting instrument by providing 2,000 flushes; another tablet to be ingested by the enemy species Cockroach; and yet another to be taken by the female Soapoid in order to soften her stools and ease excretion.

The lower body of the female seems to be especially in need of such   15 devices. A sequence that begins with the frightening words "Out of control!" introduces tablets that will "take control" of diarrhea in one day. The vaginal area is serviced by a pellet that cures yeast infections, a deodorant designed to "intercede" between the female's odor and her undergarments, and—for those who would seem to have the opposite problem—an ointment for vaginal dryness. Is it because the female Soapoid's vagina is the seat of her dominance over the male, and thus the location of her power, that it requires such constant servicing? Or is the female's verbal aggression yet another mark of her need to "stay in control" of her wayward body?

I end this paper with a confession: I entered my research project with a certain amount of bias against humanoids, whom I had been taught to regard as primitive, quarrelsome creatures, frozen in their limited natures and bodily forms, unable to regulate their own lives and affairs. But slowly, I grew increasingly susceptible to the charm of these beings. Before long, I found myself growing impatient with the time spent in my ordinary occupations. As I went about my daily tasks, I couldn't wait to join those beings who, never challenging, always predictable, asked nothing more from me than to watch them. Now that the viewing is over, I feel empty.

As I beam this paper to your neurotransmitters and project it into the ozone, it is with both fondness and regret that, amid the busy whirl of my life, I pause to remember the Soapoids, a matriarchal people whose lives drag out in long luxurious segments lived within color-coordinated cubes, and who relegate the more messy business of life to quick one-minute segments, thus freeing themselves for a stress-free, germ-free, moisture-controlled existence.

The Responsive Reader

1   What trappings of research and science fiction help make this space visitor's field trip to the land of the humanoids humorous?

2   What is exaggerated and what is true to life in the visitor's naive observations of gender distinctions and gender roles? As here observed, what is revealing and funny about the treatment of sex in the soaps? about the treatment of "courtship"? What are some telling satirical touches on these subjects in this space traveler's log?

3   Does the episode about Mimi's intended marriage and unborn child from *All My Children* ring true? What does it show about the moral universe of the soaps?

4   What are Loewenstein's targets when she satirizes the treatment of race, ethnicity, or class differences in soapland?

5   How does life in the soaps go counter to what the visitor had been taught about the impact of feminism in the real human world? How else

does the humanoid world of the soaps contradict what the visitor had been led to expect?

Talking, Listening, Writing

6   How much in the soaps as described here mirrors life? How much is fantasy? What kind of fantasy is it? Why is it so popular? What, if anything, is its central appeal?

7   Many college students reportedly are avid followers of the soap operas. What would you say or write in defense of the soaps? Or what would you say or write to wean people from this kind of entertainment?

8   Do male humor and female humor reflect different ways of looking at the world? Is what is funny to men often not funny to women, and vice versa?

Collaborative Projects

9   Working with a group, study typical plots of current soaps and examine what they show about the emotional and moral world of soap opera.

FORUM: *The Fencing In of Cyberspace*

Freedom remains the essence of the innovation at the heart of Silicon Valley.

Sòlveig Singleton

Cyberspace—the world of electronic communication—opened up vast new uncharted areas. As in the Old West, the vast new spaces attract enterprising people staking out sites in the new territories—some of which prosper and some of which turn into ghost towns. The new opportunities attract empire-building entrepreneurs who make millions (or billions) as well as a fair share of adventurers, pirates, and scam artists. They also attract organizations and vigilantes trying to establish law and order—to regulate and fence in the free-for-all, anything-goes brave new world of the Internet.

Sòlveig Singleton, director of information studies at the Cato Institute, warns of continued pressure to impose regulations and require monitoring devices, sifting and blocking mechanisms, and rating systems:

> High-tech products will continue to be the focus of regulatory efforts because decentralized networks like the Internet give individuals unprecedented power of choice, a sure-fire way to irritate regulators. Consumers everywhere perversely seek out Web sites devoted to sex, gambling, bizarre political commentaries, off-label uses of medications . . . Silicon Valley can expect continued pressure to build certain choices out of its networks.

Some attempts to regulate, restrict, channel, or censor the flow of information and ideas on the Net take the form of highly visible legislation debated in the media and contested in the courts. Other initiatives take the form of stealth legislation—riders attached quietly to unrelated high-priority legislation that other lawmakers want. First Amendment watchdogs like the American Civil Liberties Union (ACLU) fight restrictive legislation as an infringement of constitutionally guaranteed free speech.

Since electronic communication ignores national borders, the attempts to regulate have become a world-wide phenomenon. According to news reports, the successor organization to the Soviet secret police (KGB) asked for legislation that would require Internet providers to install black-box surveillance devices. These Big Brother devices would allow Russian law enforcement to track tax evasion and illegal economic activities. Law enforcement agencies of several countries have collaborated to track down Internet users accused of downloading child pornography.

Do you side with those trying to control harmful or abusive uses of the Net or with those defending free access?

ON THE INTERNET, WE ALL OWN A PRESS

Adair Lara

"The little guy has a voice now."

While the "talking heads" of television news programs debate national trends or celebrity trials, Adair Lara is a columnist who talks to her readers about the issues and annoyances of every day. She published the following column in 1998, when the excitement or euphoria of earlier days of the Internet revolution was making more and more of her readers marvel at a bright new future. E-mail and the Internet were changing the way people communicate, do business, and cope. In the brave new electronic world, independent individuals were finding new ways to publish and communicate, bypassing and eluding the control of the huge depersonalized corporate media.

Thought Starters: Have you used Internet messages to make contact with people who may share your needs or concerns? Have you used electronic messages to enlist support for a cause? Have you used Internet messages to vent bad feelings or a sense of injustice?

The other day my friend Bob noticed a new Nissan Sentra advertised in the paper for $10,000. He called the dealer. "Is that the real price?" he asked. It was.

When he got to the lot, though, the salesman told him that price had been a typo.

Furious, Bob said fine. But he wanted the dealer to know that he taught English at Santa Rosa Junior College and that on Monday morning 1,200 of his colleagues on various campuses were going to know this whole story.

He got the Nissan for the advertised price.

Another story: A 12-year-old is missing in Tennessee. She has brown hair and eyes, stands 5 foot 3 and left home in the company of two teenage boys. They were in a green Ford F-150 extended-cab pickup. Her name is Emily Marie Tiger. She was last seen in Nashville on January 4. If anyone has seen her, please call. Her mother is worried.

I read this story on my e-mail, and there were a hundred addresses listed above mine. It was going out to a lot of people.

In recent months, I've read other messages like this. One came from a frantic woman whose husband had kidnapped their teenage son; she was imploring people to visit her Web site and look at the pictures posted there.

A woman named Jessica is using e-mail to search for donors for her friend Sachi, who has leukemia and desperately needs a bone-marrow transplant. She's half Caucasian and half Japanese, and people who think they might provide a match can call (800) 59-DONOR.

I got another one from a man who says he was plucked from a crowd of drivers on eastbound Highway 80, few of them wearing seat belts, and cited for violation of the seat belt law. He felt he received the citation because he was black, yet he could do nothing—except describe the incident over the Internet to hundreds of, he hoped, sympathetic fellow drivers.

Yet another was from a man in Forestville fuming because AOL was charging him a $5 monthly service charge because he had no Visa card. *10*

Before e-mail, when somebody did something mean to us, we just raged impotently and stormed up and down in our own kitchens and kicked the dog. We could threaten to sue, and sometimes did, but that was like punishing ourselves, exposing ourselves to years of the expenses and continued bad feelings of a lawsuit—with no certainty that the other side's lawyers would not in the end squash us and our little plea for justice like a bug.

But now. Now we can do what we wanted to do when we were little. We can tell on them.

Even Kate Millett, author of the groundbreaking book "Sexual Politics," writes from her farm in Poughkeepsie—or allows her piece to be circulated, I can't tell which—that she can hardly support herself. "I cannot earn money. Except by selling Christmas trees, one by one, in the cold in Poughkeepsie. I cannot teach and have nothing but farming now. And when physically I can no longer farm, what then? Nothing I write now has any prospect of seeing print. I have no salable skill, for all my supposed accomplishments. I am unemployable."

Millett is probably telling the truth, but some of these stories may be false. The classic story—you must have seen it by now—is the Internet version of the urban legend about the woman who ordered cookies at Neiman Marcus, asked for the recipe, was charged hundreds of dollars for it and in retaliation printed the recipe on the Web. That is bunk, but people keep forwarding it because they like the idea of it, getting back at the big companies. *15*

And because they like this feeling: The little guy has a voice now.

And, in at least one case, a new Nissan Sentra.

The Responsive Reader

1 What Internet stories does Lara tell to support her thesis that "the little guy has a voice now"? Which of her accounts seem most significant or convincing to you? Why?

2 What is an "urban legend"? How typical do you think is the one Lara mentions?

Talking, Listening, Writing

3 Do you sometimes respond to negative experiences with impotent rage? Have you observed people who punished themselves by exposing themselves to "years of the expenses and continued bad feelings of a lawsuit"? Do you think the Internet can provide people with valid alternatives?

4 Has the Internet broadened your range of contact with other people? Are you or people you know well interacting with others in new and different ways? Or do you agree with people who claim that the virtual reality of the Net tends to isolate people from real human contact?

FIND IT ON THE WEB

Becoming a Blogger

"These days it costs nothing to become a publisher, editor and star reporter."

The rapidly growing popularity of blogging is demonstrating the power of the Internet to democratize communication, bypassing control by the impersonal "old media" and institutions. Blogs have been described as the medium of amateur journalists recording freely their news and their thoughts at their personal Internet address. They often attract a wide range of candid personal responses, with bloggers sharing information, floating their ideas, and challenging each other's facts.

Joanne Jacobs was for a long time an editorial writer and columnist for the mainstream press. She then started to run an education blog with links to current news, with her own analysis and commentary, and with comments from a wide range of readers. She says about blogs that "there are so many—even if you stick just to political blogs—that readers have choices."

> People looking for political news and commentary go back to the blogs that are sane, well-written, and amusing . . . you have to prove you're worth reading and believing by providing links to your credential or to your source material or to your credentials and by making sense. If a blogger makes an error, there will be plenty of people to point it out.

At the time she wrote these comments, Jacobs said she blogged at www.JoanneJacobs.com.

YES, VIRGINIA, THERE IS A FIRST AMENDMENT

Rob Morse

"The First Amendment protects against prior restraint of speech on the basis of content. There's no restraint as capricious as a machine looking for key words."

Both in Britain and in the American colonies, the printing press was a key weapon in the struggle to assert the rights of the people against an oppressive government. For civil libertarians, resistance to censorship of the press, of the media, and of teaching has always been a cornerstone of the defense of liberty. Adopted as part of the Bill of Rights in 1791, the First Amendment to the U.S. Constitution stipulates that "Congress shall make no law . . . abridging the freedom of speech, or of the press." Justice Hugo L. Black stated long-observed judicial doctrine when he said, "The Federal Government is without any power whatsover under the Constitution to put any type of burden on free speech and the expression of ideas of any kind (as distinguished from conduct)."

The leapfrogging growth of access to printed and visual material on the Internet opened up a new front in the struggle between First Amendment "absolutists" and censorship forces. New legislative initiatives focused on restricting Internet access to adult material in libraries, schools, and private homes. A Communications Decency Act was passed by Congress but found by the Supreme Court to violate First Amendment rights. Various new initiatives aimed at imposing severe penalties on providers allowing access to material harmful to minors. Libraries and colleges began to rely on filtering software or censoring services to block offensive or objectionable material.

Rob Morse is an outspoken West Coast columnist who found that his columns were caught in the censorship web in 1998 while he was working for the conservative Hearst news organization.

Thought Starters: During your high school or college years, were you aware of any censorship controversy involving student publications, teaching content, library resources, or Internet access? What were the issues? Who were the key players? What was the outcome?

A guy from National Public Radio called me at home wanting to talk about my lawsuit against the Loudoun County, Va., public libraries.

"You won," he said.

Alas, I hadn't won any money. This was not a lawsuit over hot coffee in the lap.

It was more important than that. It was about the First Amendment, and what you as an adult may or may not read on the Internet in a public library.

It wasn't just my lawsuit. I was one of eight plaintiffs whose Web sites   5 had been blocked by a filtering device called X-Stop meant to block pornography from computers used by both adults and children in the Loudoun County public libraries.

I don't know what pornography the filter stopped, but it kept Loudoun County safe from a safe-sex Web page, as well as Web sites belonging to the Quarkers, Beanie Baby collectors, the American Association of University Women and The San Francisco Examiner and the Chronicle.

That means me. I joined the suit to defend the First Amendment.

And we won. Now adults and children in Loudoun County libraries will be able to read about all the latest San Francisco perversions, such as pies being thrown in the faces of the mayor and other public figures.

Judge Leonie M. Brinkema of the United States District Court for Eastern Virginia decided last Monday that Loudoun County's Internet censorship policy violated the First Amendment because it blocked adults from accessing a wide variety of constitutionally protected material.

The guy from NPR asked a strange question: "When you found out   10 the newspapers were blocked, why didn't you just call the filtering company and ask to be unblocked?"

Maybe he was trying to goad me into a flip answer, so I gave one: "Yeah, and I could ask the guy who's burning my books to put out the match."

At least there's smoke when someone burns your book. When someone blocks your Web site in a faraway county's libraries, you don't even know it—unless you hear about it from a friend of a friend, as I did.

When I heard that the San Francisco newspapers were being electronically blocked from Loudoun County libraries, I thought it was a great joke.

Then I talked to lawyers at the American Civil Liberties Union, which had joined a group of Loudoun County citizens in bringing the suit against their libraries. I learned how Internet filtering devices work—or don't work.

Internet filters are stupid. The First Amendment protects against prior   15 restraint of speech on the basis of content. There's no restraint as capricious as a machine looking for key words.

The people who make X-Stop, Log-on Data Corp. of Anaheim, won't say how their filter works, but most filters involve punching in key words like "bondage." Then low-paid drones go through blocked sites and decide whether to unblock them. Thus Somerset Maugham's "Of Human Bondage" may or may not get through.

Lots of nonpornographic sites get blocked, while many pornographic sites go unblocked.

Harper's magazine has an excerpt from "Confessions of a Smut Blocker," which ran originally in Yahoo! Internet Life. This anonymous former employee for an Internet-filtering company (not Log-on Data) wrote:

"The main computer created a list of sites for us to check. . . . It was really an entry-level job. You didn't have to be computer-literate. They just showed you which buttons to push. We could choose to block a site, not block it, or even unblock it."

Just before I joined the suit against Loudoun County 10 months ago,   20
I wrote, "If the Supreme Court can't define obscenity, how can some computer programmers in Anaheim do it?"

Or entry-level button pushers.

Some officials in Loudoun County complained that Judge Brinkema's decision overrode local standards of decency.

Local, where? In Loudoun or in Anaheim? The makers of X-Stop won't even tell Loudoun officials the criteria they use for blocking Web sites. It's proprietary information.

So how do public libraries deal with the Internet? They could just shut it off. However, the Internet is increasingly where information is to be found.

Judge Brinkema, a former librarian, cited some suggestions for keep-   25
ing kids from Internet porn in public libraries while not violating adults' First Amendment rights—for example, filters that can be turned on or off for adult use.

Perhaps the most important thing is not to pass unnecessary and unconstitutional Net censorship laws, or otherwise get caught up in what Mike Godwin, author the book "Cyber Rights," calls "Net backlash," or "fear and loathing of the Net."

Loudoun County could point to only a single complaint arising from Internet use in a library in another Virginia county, and reports of three incidents in other libraries across the country.

It's not worth blocking the First Amendment for that.

The Responsive Reader

1 Who were the other plaintiffs joining Morse in his suit? What was the purpose of the X-Stop filter that the plaintiffs challenged? What are Morse's examples of communications or messages the filter blocked? Can you explain or speculate on why or how some of the examples were among those blocked?

2 Why would a journalist in California join in a lawsuit against a library system across the country in Virginia? How does Morse explain why he did not just ask to have his material unblocked?

3 Like much self-censorship or media censorship, the people running the filtering operation worked anonymously behind the scenes (and appar-

ently not in Virginia but in Anaheim in southern California). What did Morse find out about the personnel and the MO, or operating mode, of the enterprise? According to Morse, what was wrong with the operation? What were the criteria they applied? (Why does he use Somerset Maugham's classic *Of Human Bondage* as a key example? Why does he object to censors appealing to local standards? What support did Loudoun County officials offer for their adoption of the filtering method?)

4   Morse writes for an audience that likes his amusing sidelights on the follies and weird happenings he observes in day-to-day politics of the city (like the incident when activists expressed their displeasure with the city's power structure by throwing a pie in the mayor's face). However, many of the topics he touches on in his informal, half-amused manner have serious undertones and implications, such as his "flip" reference to book burnings. What do you know about book burnings? Do they take place abroad or also in the United States? How are they similar to or different from current censorship initiatives?

5   Whistleblowers and other critics of prevailing practices are often dismissed as malcontents or "disgruntled" individuals. Does Morse offer any constructive suggestions for dealing with the issues causing the controversy? What for him is the most important lesson or warning we should heed?

Talking, Listening, Writing

6   If you were a member of a school board, library commission, or similar body, what stand would you take on the issues Morse raises? What arguments would you present to the opposing side? What counterarguments would you anticipate? What constructive suggestions would you offer?

7   In the early years of euphoria, the Internet was hailed as ushering in the era of the knowledge explosion and the information highway. Today many observers claim that we have entered an era of lowered expectations and second thoughts. What does Morse mean when he contends that the public libraries were succumbing to "Net backlash"? Have you observed second thoughts or a backlash concerning the promise of the Internet?

Collaborative Projects

8   Many controversies over censorship have hinged on definitions of key terms like *obscenity, community standards,* or *indecency.* Morse claims that even the "Supreme Court can't define obscenity." Working with a group, you may want to study media coverage of court cases, legislation, or local controversies to see whether and how in your judgment one or more of these terms can be successfully defined.

OTHER VOICES

Censorship and the High Court

After the Supreme Court found a 1996 law regulating sexual content on the Internet unconstitutional, Congress in 1998 passed a new revised law aimed at banning material "harmful to minors." In 2004, in a decision crossing the Court's ideological lines, the Supreme Court ruled against the new law also, banning enforcement of its provisions until further deliberation in a lower court. The following excerpts from a newspaper article about the court decision show some of the range of commentary.

A Attorney Ann Beeson of the American Civil Liberties Union, which challenged the law, said the ruling "has made it safe for artists, sex educators and Web publishers to communicate with adults about sexuality without risking jail time."

B "Our society has reached a broad consensus that child obscenity is harmful to our youngest generation and must be stopped," said Justice Department spokesman Mark Corallo. "Congress has repeatedly attempted to address this serious need, and the court yet again opposed these common sense measures to protect America's children."

C "It's as close as the court was willing to go in saying that broad wholesale regulations of Internet content probably will never pass muster," said Christopher Wolf, a Washington attorney and president of an organization called Hands Off the Internet.

D The court said a government commissioned study indicated that Internet filters, calibrated to screen out sexually explicit content, were more effective than proof-of-identity requirements in shielding minors from "harmful" material. Last year the court upheld another federal law that requires libraries and schools to use filters on Internet terminals or lose federal funding.

E The 1998 law "presumes that parents lack the ability, not the will, to monitor what their children see," said Justice Anthony Kennedy in the majority opinion. "By enacting programs to promote use of filtering software, Congress could give parents that ability without subjecting protected speech to severe penalties."

Bob Egelko, "High Court and Internet Law," *San Francisco Chronicle* [June 23, 2004]

1 Court decisions by the High Court are often described as sending mixed signals. Do you see any "loud and clear" message emerging from the news report? Do you see mixed signals?

2 What players in the struggle over Internet censorship are identified or mentioned in these excerpts? How would you identify them and their agendas?

7 WAYS TO SQUELCH THE NET

Jessie Scanlon

"Censors rely on software filters. e-cops, and loyalty oaths. Here's a look at the surveillance technologies in use today—and how to get around them."

Wired *magazine emerged as a large glossy magazine serving as a guide and advocate for the leapfrogging developments in Information Technology (IT). It featured a range of articles on developments taking us into the electronic future: Voice recognition software will make the keyboard obsolete. Computers will be taking dictation, turning the spoken word into a printout. Highspeed wireless will make obsolete the hugely expensive optic-cable connections that were wiring schools and homes. Corporations and individuals will be encrypting messages—encoding them in a secret code that cannot be deciphered by government agents or hackers. Government agencies and private user will continue to guard against viruses that infect programs and files and cause million-dollar or billion-dollar damage.*

Americans increasingly take access to the Internet and e-mail communication for granted. The following are excerpts from a graphic published in Wired *magazine in August of 2003, at a time when attempts to fence in cyberspace were gathering momentum here and abroad. The author reminds American readers that in many parts of the world the information highway is still far from open to all. What are the roadblocks, and who is putting them up?*

Thought Starters: How hard is it to keep up with developments in electronic communication? Have you seen breakthroughs in information technology become first dated and then obsolete? Have you seen new equiment turn old? Have you seen old problems solved and seen new problems arise?

CENSORS RELY ON SOFTWARE FILTERS, E-COPS, AND LOYALTY OATHS

FIREWALLS

Saudi Arabia has a firewall that monitors the kingdom's only bridge to the Internet. Proxy servers – computers that act as intermediaries between the Net and users on private networks – scan email for offensive content and review all Web traffic, checking requested URLs against a constantly updated blacklist. The United Arab Emirates and Yemen use similar tactics.

WORKAROUND: Decentralized programs like Triangle Boy and Peekabooty allow surfers to access the Internet through a dynamic network of nodes – the PCs of individuals in noncensoring countries who've set up their machines as Web servers. Banned sites also frequently change IP addresses.

ROUTERS

The firewall approach isn't feasible in countries with high-volume Web traffic and where multiple ISPs have established myriad routes onto the Net. China, for instance, would need thousands of proxy servers to monitor all incoming and outgoing traffic. So those nations require ISPs to install routers capable of blocking offending IP addresses and even filtering content.

WORKAROUND: The same tools used to circumvent firewalls can be used to slip by router-level censors.

SOFTWARE FILTERS

These are the staples of censorship. Some filters are list-based, vetting requested URLs against a roster of banned sites. Others look for keywords and block messages or Web pages that contain offensive terms or phrases. (A few combine both approaches.) Word filters are notoriously stupid – for instance, they blocked former Congressman Dick Armey's Web site and an AOL chat room for breast cancer survivors.

WORKAROUND: Censored groups outwit filters by changing Web addresses frequently, using creative spelling, or encoding text as an image.

The Responsive Reader

1   *Government surveillance* has often employed large numbers of human spies monitoring and listening in on the communications of their citizens. According to this graphic, how and where has the monitoring become computerized? To judge from the examples given here, why does this guide to net censorship call computerized filters "notoriously stupid"? How and where is electronic surveillance still entrusted to human personnel?

2   Much censorship is *self-censorship*. Government intimidation has a "chilling" effect. How do government encourage self-censorship? What is the role of "loyalty oaths"? What historical memories or precedents does the term bring to mind?

Talking, Listening, Writing

3   Will the information revolution break down barriers and take us into a wired (or wireless) future of instant unlimited communication? Are you a good audience for voices promoting such a very optimistic view of the electronic future? Do you encounter more pessimistic voices warning us that the forces of censorship and surveillance may get the upper hand?

Collaborative Projects

Alone or working with a group, investigate limited Internet access for According to a recent estimate, only one fourth of the nation's elderly had computers. Are they left out of government programs offering choices of providers for drugs at discount prices? Information and application forms for programs assisting poor and disabled Americans are increasingly offered over the Internet. Is much of the target population going to be left out?

Comparing and Contrasting

Comparison and contrast can alert us to important similarities and differences.

Writers use comparison and contrast to make us see connections we might otherwise overlook. For instance, they may help readers understand something new by showing how it built on or adapted something already familiar. Or they may show in detail how it differs from something familiar, concentrating on new or different features. For example, gentrification became a buzzword for efforts to rehabilitate decaying sections of a city. It was similar to earlier patterns of urban renewal because it promised to restore decaying neighborhoods. However, it did not raze existing structures. It aimed at renovating and upgrading them instead, using them to lure affluent buyers back to the city.

ORGANIZING STRATEGIES FOR WRITERS

An Overview

Comparison/contrast serves as one of the major organizing strategies that writers adapt or combine to accomplish their purposes. Here are major strategies that help you organize your thinking and your writing:

CHRONOLOGY Writers develop a timeline for showing stages in a person's development, for tracking major phases of a process, or for following a process of gradual evolution.

GENERALIZATION AND EXAMPLES Trend watchers and people watchers form cautious generalizations and follow them up with detailed convincing examples that lead them to their conclusions.

CLASSIFICATION Writers set up major categories or update existing ones to help us sort out data or identify groups that share important features and may call for different kinds action.

CAUSE AND EFFECT Writers trace the causes that explain events or help us understand current problems. They make us see the consequences of different courses of action.

COMPARISON/CONTRAST Comparing and contrasting help writers organize their data or observations to help readers understand changes or to help them make choices.

WEIGHING ALTERNATIVES Decisions that come to a vote often force the voters to weigh the arguments pro and con. On many issues, the writer needs to examine several possible solutions to explain a choice.

DEFINITION Writers define key terms to help us use weighty words carefully or to give real-life meaning to large umbrella labels.

PERSUASION Writers appeal to shared values or basic needs of a target audience to change attitudes or enlist support.

ARGUMENT Writers present carefully verified evidence and logical arguments to convince readers ready to listen to reason.

Triggering

Writers making comparisons typically have an agenda.
Writers compare and contrast with a purpose. They may be writing to justify a preference, to influence our buying patterns or our votes, or to

nudge us toward needed change. They often aim at helping us make tricky choices between cars to buy, places to live, or careers to pursue.

    ■ An architecture critic may be contrasting the stark boxy glass–and–steel high rises of Manhattan early modern architecture with the curves, step patterns, and curlicues of more recent postmodern buildings. The critic is not likely to be a neutral observer. He or she is likely to consider the earlier style too impersonal or sterile and the newer style more imaginative and more human—creating a more people-friendly environment for the people working or living there.

    ■ A medical researcher may be comparing the cost and traumatic experience of an elderly relative's terminal illness under two different systems of health insurance. In a country with a largely privately operated system of health insurance the illness and death of an elderly relative might leave a family bankrupt and in disarray. In a country like Canada that aims at providing universal health care, major costs might be assumed by the publicly financed system. How does the quality of care compare? What are the key differences in how the systems are financed?

Gathering

To trace similarities or differences, you need to be an alert observer.

    For an informative comparison and contrast, the preliminary stock-taking will be especially important. As a key part of your prewriting, you are likely to be jotting down features that will prove important as you chart similarities and differences. Suppose you are working on a paper that will show how changing gender roles have transformed traditional assumptions about marriage. After jotting down brainstorming notes or comparing notes in a group, the following may be your list of possibly relevant points:

Tying the Knot

TRADITIONAL

church wedding

till death do us part

compliant wife

husband works

husband handles finances

housewife cleans and cooks

talk about sex is taboo

marry your own kind

feminine wife

————>>>>>>>>>>>>>

MODERN

live together first

family planning

both work

backyard weddings

equal relationships

male shares chores

mixed marriages

marriage contract

discuss problems

Even while you jot down these items, you will be mentally making connections. Revealing contrasts emerge as you connect contrasting items:

(traditional) the wife cooks and cleans/
                           (modern) both share chores
(traditional) the husband works/
                           (modern) both work
(traditional) compliant wife/
                           (modern) equal partners.

What other items should be linked to show the contrast between the old and the new?

Shaping

Choose among different strategies for organizing your points of comparison.

How would you organize your prewriting notes about changing gender roles in the modern marriage?

■ Your notes might lead naturally to a **point-by-point** comparison. As you raise each question, you could first show the traditional answer and then the contrasting modern one. The following sequence might prove workable as an organizing strategy for the point-by-point paper:

POINT ONE: Who is considered an "eligible" marriage partner?
POINT TWO: Who supports the family financially? Who "provides"?
POINT THREE: Who is the dominant partner? Who is "in charge"?
POINT FOUR: Who does the housekeeping? Who is the homemaker?
PONT FIVE: Who makes key decisions or handles finances?

■ However, sometimes a **parallel-order** comparison proves more workable or instructive. To give your readers a clear picture of two things you are comparing, you might decide to give them a complete, rounded picture of first the one and then the other. However, you help your readers see the connections. You take up key points in the same or very similar order—in parallel order. The following excerpts are from a parallel-order comparison of two day care centers:

Day Care: It's Your Choice

In a world of two-career or single-parent families, day care is going to be part of growing up for thousands of children. Instead of dropping a child off at the nearest center, parents must shop around to find a place designed to help children grow. Working parents should suspend some of their feelings of guilt and instead concentrate on the hardest task: finding the right place for their children.

THESIS: **Three important qualities to look for in a day care center are a stable staff, the right activities, and an active role for the parents.**

EXAMPLE A

point 1   I have worked at two different centers. The first one I consider a bad example. The staff changed every few months, mainly because we were paid minimum wage. The teachers who stayed did so because they did not feel qualified to work for a higher salary elsewhere. . . .

point 2   The children's day was as follows: TV—inside play—outside play—lunch—nap—outside play—TV—parents pick up. The main goal was to make the children follow the rules and keep quiet. I remember one small girl particularly who was a very active child. . . .

point 3   Parents were not encouraged to participate; their role was to drop off the children and pick them up. . . .

————>>>>>>>>>>>>>

EXAMPLE B

point 1   The second school I worked at was quite different. There was a very low turnover of staff. . . .

point 2   The children's schedule was as follows: Play—story time—work time—music—outside play—lunch—nap—independent work or play—story time—outside play—art—parents pick up. . . .

point 3   Parents joined in all the outside activities and often stopped for lunch with the children. Parents should be wary of any school that does not allow drop-in visits. . . .

■ Instead of the classic point-by-point or parallel-order patterns, a **similarities-first** or **differences-first** strategy may prove right for your topic. You may want to start with strong but misleading similarities. You then alert your reader to important differences that may not meet the eye. Or you may want to start with deceptive surface differences. For instance, race relations today are different from the days of overt legalized segregation. Minorities are part of the mix in photographs promoting a company or an institution. However, you might then go on to show that similarities remain, though their current version may take a more subtle form. For instance, there is no longer legal but instead *de facto* segregation in many schools. Minorities may be hired, but they may hit a "glass ceiling" on their way up the promotion ladder.

Revising

Make major points of comparison or key contrasting features stand out.

Organizing a comparison-and-contrast paper presents more of a challenge than a paper that states a main point and then lines up supporting examples. As you reread and revise a first draft, see whether you have taken your readers with you—or whether you may have lost them along the way. You may need stronger **transitions**—stronger signposts to keep pointing your readers in the right direction.

- *Spell out clearly the main point of your comparison.* Have you summed up in a unifying thesis what your paper as a whole is trying to show? You may also need a stronger conclusion to pull together various points you made along the way.

- *Give your readers a preview of the itinerary.* Try to word your thesis in such a way that it gives away your overall plan. Give your readers a hint: point-by-point? parallel-order? similarities first? differences first?

- *Strengthen your network of transitions.* Signal turning points. **Transitions** signaling similarities are phrases like *similarly* or *in parallel fashion.* Signal contrasts by phrases like *however* or *by contrast* or *on the other hand.*

SIMILARITIES:	similarly, in parallel fashion, as an exact counterpart, pointing in the same direction, along the same lines
DIFFERENCES:	however, by contrast, on the other hand, as the direct opposite, providing a counterweight, pointing in the opposite direction

A Paper for Peer Review

What is the overall plan in the following sample paper? How does the plan become clear to the reader? How effectively has the student writer followed through?

The Sensitive Male: Reality or Myth?

Hollywood has come a long way from depicting super macho characters. A decade or two ago, the action hero was brazenly and fearlessly shooting his way through the plot, not offering much dialogue other than a few grunts and moans. Many male characters in the movies have undergone dramatic transformations. Movies today more often bestow on their heroes moral consciences as well as physical prowess. In a *Terminator* movie, the hero listened patiently and sympathetically to a young boy who lamented about growing up without his mother's presence. Moreover, at the end of the movie, the hero sacrificed his own life to save the world from nuclear disaster.
———>>>>>>>>>>>>>

(This introduction dramatizes a **then–and–now contrast** between media images of the past and present.)

How accurately do the media reflect the changing attitudes of men? Have men's attitudes, especially toward women, really changed? **Some experts question that men will achieve a successful balance between their nurturing sides and their masculinity**. Psychologist Mathilda Carter is quoted in an article in the *U.S. News and World Report* as saying that "many men are confused and searching for their identity, as they struggle to blend vestiges of traditional masculinity with what are regarded as softer, or feminine traits." Psychologist Phyllis Bronstein, a psychologist quoted in the same article, maintains that "a less rigid definition of masculinity will emerge that enables men to be more at ease with whatever paths they choose. We're at the awkward stage right now."
———>>>>>>>>>>>>>

(Early in this second paragraph, the **thesis** sets up a program for examining both sides of the central issue.)

Movies and television shows started to capture the current awkwardness that some men grapple with. **Men responded to pressure from women to be more open and show their emotions more**. Sensitive male characters portrayed in television programs began to share their most intimate feelings. In fact, one of the men I interviewed, a retired police officer, claims that such male characters produce a "manufactured emotion." He said that the camera unnecessarily zooms in on Brad Pitt whenever he cries. Commercials followed the trend: In one commercial, an empathetic husband tenderly looked at the camera and earnestly told the audience how his wife, a dedicated gymnast coach, overcame her muscle pain by taking the advertised pain medication.
———>>>>>>>>>>>>>

(This first major follow–up paragraph focuses on the first major **point of comparison**.)

Males were shown discovering their nurturing side. In one example the lead character was shown being urged by his girlfriend to bond with his baby brother by reading a nursery story to him. After a few moments of discomfort, he put down the book and achieved intimacy with his brother by reading an electrical manual to him instead. In an episode from another program, the oldest brother, who was appointed legal guardian to his brothers and sisters after his parents were killed in a car accident, was shown taking his baby brother to an all-fathers' group. At this gathering, each father, teary-eyed and voice wavering with emotion, recalled the extraordinary moment when he first bonded with his baby. ———>>>>>>>>>>>>>>

(This paragraph brings in the second major **point of comparison.**)

Researchers quoted in an article in *Time* magazine reported that men's contribution to household chores "increased dramatically." Newspaper reporters interviewed househusbands who let women be the providers while they took care of the home and children. ———>>>>>>>>>>>>>>

(This paragraph focuses on the third major **point of comparison.**)

Did television and Hollywood exaggerate the trend toward the sensitive male? Some men complain that the media sensationalized or exaggerated the trend. **Some males react to the current confusion over the changes of gender roles by rejecting pressure from women to be more open.** Many of my male friends assert that men in real life are nothing like the sensitive male characters portrayed in television programs, who reveal their most intimate feelings. "Although I consider myself sensitive, I'd say that over half of my male friends do not want to show any of their emotions," claims a twenty-eight-year-old accountant, "because they are afraid of being branded wimps." ———>>>>>>>>>>>>

(The above paragraph provides the **turning point** of the paper, starting the second part of the writer's **parallel-order comparison** highlighting the major contrasts.)

Are fathers doing the dishes? According to one study, young two-income couples without children tended to divide household chores, including laundry and grocery shopping, fairly evenly. However, "many new fathers—55 percent—actually started spending *more* time at work after a child is born." According to psychology professor Carter, interviewed for the article in the *U.S. News and World Report,* some men take refuge in what has been called the new macho. . . . They contend that real men don't eat quiche or change diapers but instead swig beer." ———>>>>>>>>>>>>>

(The paragraph focuses on a second major **contrast** in the parallel-order comparison.)

While some men may modify their behavior in the public eye, others openly flaunt a hostile attitude toward women. Programs continue to feature male characters who act like sarcastic jerks. Traces of old machismo could be

found in popular sitcoms such as *Married with Children*. In this show, the husband was a shoe salesman who preferred to hang around the television set,
drinking beer rather than conversing with his wife. In one episode he totally
ignored his wife while conspicuously ogling other women at the supermarket.
————>>>>>>>>>>>>>>

(The above paragraph departs from a strict parallel-order comparison by addressing a major **underlying contrast** between the myth and the
reality.)

Although there is debate over how realistic the entertainment industry
portrays men in society, clearly men have come some distance from their traditional roles as breadwinners and providers. As men and society adjust to
these changes perhaps we should examine the way that we define strength and
masculinity. **As Art Bohart, Professor of Psychology at a California State University campus, observes in *USA Today*, "to be sensitive you have to be open
and vulnerable. So to be strong at the same time means you have to develop a
different kind of strength."**

(The strong **concluding quotation** points forward to an ideal future
resolution of the contrast.)

YOUR TURN:

1   Do you think that in Terminator or Robocop movies, there is
    room for compassion, tenderness, or other human qualities?

2   Do you think that in sitcoms or current movies there has been a
    return to the leering sexist male?

3   In couples you have a chance to observe, have you seen a ma-
    jor shift toward more genuine partnering and equal sharing of
    responsibilities?

Writing Options 7: Taking Time to Compare

1   Do workers and managers tend to be two different kinds of people?
    What do they tend to have in common? What are key qualities that tend
    to set them apart?

2   In movie or television fare, have you observed the change from earlier
    "sex symbol" female leads or stereotypically feminine stars to "strong
    woman" characters? Can you choose one or more striking examples of
    each to dramatize the contrast?

3   Have you ever lived in a homogeneous neighborhood (with people of
    very similar backgrounds or social status)—but also in a more diverse,
    mixed neighborhood? Or, have you ever attended a school with a ho-
    mogenous student body—but also a school with a more diverse popu-
    lation? Write a paper working out the contrast between the two settings.

4 Have you experienced the difference between blue-collar and white-collar jobs?

5 Have you experienced a major change in your lifestyle? Write a before-and-after paper on the subject.

6 In the men you have a chance to observe, do you find both the macho and the sensitive male? What sets them apart?

7 Have you observed a difference in outlook and values between recent immigrants (or Americans from recent immigrant families) and Americans from earlier cycles of immigration?

8 In your family or in other areas of your experience, is there a generation gap? Have you observed a contrast in values or outlook between the older and the younger generation?

9 Have you changed or converted from one political or religious group to another? Or have you had a chance to observe closely two such groups? How did they compare?

10 Do men and women feel differently about love?

8
ROLE MODELS
Searching for Heroes

VISUAL LITERACY 8
UNSUNG HEROES: FEMALE FIREFIGHTER

Does our society honor those who serve the public? Does it recognize and value those who protect the public, fight fires, battle disease, prevent or control violence, rescue disaster victims, or tend the sick? Does it honor those who feed the homeless, go into the prisons to teach, rehabilitate ex-convicts, care for the aged, or teach the young? How often do you see media images of real-life individuals who serve the public in dangerous or challenging occupations? Are they our society's "unsung heroes"? Are they remembered mainly when a natural disaster or terrorist attack causes them to risk their lives?

Reading the Image

1   As a first impression, what do you think was the photographer's *purpose* or intention in creating this image? Why do you think an editor decided to reprint this image?

2   What are the major parts or elements that together make up this image? Which are most important? How do the elements of this image work together to contribute to the *composition* of this image? Students of design study the way important elements are set off against a background. They study the way strong lines direct the viewer's attention or frame the most important part of the image. How does this photograph center attention on the face of the firefighter?

3   Are you a good *audience* for this photograph? Have you been an eye witness to a serious emergency or disaster? Are you close to or distant from people in public service occupations? Have you had experiences as a volunteer firefighter or other kind of public service volunteer that might help you identify with the person in the picture?

4   What is your *personal evaluation* as a viewer? Does this image look like a posed photograph to you—of the kind used for publicity purposes? Do you think this was a spontaneous candid shot? Why or why not?

5   How do we *commemorate* people who gave their lives? Have you read or heard about initiatives to honor the firefighters and police officers who lost their lives in the terrorist attack of September 11? Working alone or with a group, find information about the proposed memorial or memorials and the questions the initiatives raised.

8

ROLE MODELS
Searching for Heroes

When I hear the people praising greatness, then I know that I too shall be recognized; I too when my time comes shall achieve.

—FROM THE CHIPPEWA

Who is your hero? What does it take to be a hero in today's America? In our diverse culture, what role models do we have who are not star athletes, generals, or astronauts? In the aftermath of the September 11 attack on the World Trade Center in Manhattan, Americans rediscovered everyday heroes who risk their lives in the service of the public: firefighters, police officers, or rescue workers. An American tradition surviving from earlier days honors the mavericks, whistleblowers, or investigative reporters who challenge the powerful or go on against misguided public opinion. What do we hear when we do not merely put people we admire on a pedestal but listen to what they have to say?

Modern society has often found it hard to worship heroic figures or to find heroes to worship. Americans have a tradition of debunking—of exposing the disreputable or shady side of the lives of leading figures past and present. Biographers and offspring of famous people lay bare the private traumas or meanness behind the glamorous or warmhearted façade. Scandal-hungry media sensationalize crimes involving big names in the worlds of sports or entertainment. The media show in handcuffs executives who were once celebrated on the business pages but are now accused of insider trading, accounting fraud, or fleecing investors. Celebrities endorse products they don't use.

Nevertheless, people who are struggling or faced with barriers have a need for someone to look up, to admire. They look for someone who can serve as an example to emulate. They look for role models that can symbolize for them their hopes and aspirations. Public television programs honor pioneers who overcame barriers or ridicule to achieve breakthroughs in science or medicine. Many Americans admire volunteers who work for organizations like Doctors Without Borders or Amnesty International. They admire teachers or preachers who work with the homeless or go into the jails to help convicts believe in a second chance. Students cross the borders to help fight poverty and disease.

The poet Eve Merriam said in her poem dedicated to Elizabeth

Blackwell, who braved centuries of precedent to become a female MD, "don't let it darken,/the spark of fire;/keep it aglow." Before she left on the flight around the world from which she did not return, Amelia Earhart said in a letter:

> Please know that I am quite aware of the hazards. I want to do it be- cause I want to do it. Women must try to do things as men have tried. When they fail, their failure must be but a challenge to others.

Thousands of Americans each year visit the Martin Luther King Memorial in Atlanta to remind themselves of the eloquence and vision of the preacher who spoke of his dream that "the rough places will be made plain, and the crooked places will be made straight, and the glory of the Lord shall be revealed, and all flesh shall see it together."

A BLACK ATHLETE LOOKS AT EDUCATION

Arthur Ashe

"There must be some way to assure that those who try but don't make it to pro sports don't wind up on street corners or in unemployment lines."

Arthur Ashe was widely quoted as an early voice warning young African Americans not to let the lure of big-time sports make them ignore the need for a solid education.

Ashe was one of the first African Americans to achieve an international reputation in tennis, until then often thought of as a sport for white players with money and social aspirations. Althea Gibson had been the first black woman to win the English Wimbledon tournament, in 1957 and 1958. Ashe defeated the seemingly invincible Jimmy Connors for the Wimbledon title in men's tennis in 1975. Ashe was ranked first in the world at the time, but injuries and finally a heart attack cut short his career. He used his influence as a sports celebrity to promote civil rights causes; he helped get South Africa banned from the Davis Cup when its government was still identified with apartheid policies.

The following is one of the articles he wrote for the New York Times *and the* Washington Post, *trying to convince "not only black athletes but young blacks in general to put athletics in its proper place." Ashe said about this article, "Some teacher probably read it and put it on the bulletin board. . . . The people who have the problems may not read it, but the ones who are in a position to influence them will." Do you think the kind of advice Ashe gives in this article influences people? Do you think attitudes and policies have changed since he wrote the article?*

Thought Starters: Have you ever read or heard enough about an outstanding athlete to make you feel you knew the person behind the media image?

Since my sophomore year at UCLA, I have become convinced that we blacks spend too much time on the playing fields and too little time in the libraries. Consider these facts: for the major professional sports of hockey, football, basketball, baseball, golf, tennis and boxing, there are roughly only 3170 major league positions available (attributing 200 positions to golf, 200 to tennis and 100 to boxing). And the annual turnover is small.

There must be some way to assure that those who try but don't make it to pro sports don't wind up on street corners or in unemployment lines. Unfortunately, our most widely recognized role models are athletes and entertainers—"runnin" and "jumpin" and "singin" and "dancin."

Our greatest heroes of the century have been athletes—Jack Johnson, Joe Louis, and Muhammad Ali. Racial and economic discrimination forced us to channel our energies into athletics and entertainment. These were the ways out of the ghetto, the ways to get that Cadillac, those regular shoes, that cashmere sport coat.

Somehow, parents must instill a desire for learning alongside the desire to be Walt Frazier. Why not start by sending black professional athletes into high schools to explain the facts of life?

I have often addressed high school audiences and my message is always   5
the same: "For every hour you spend on the athletic field, spend two in the library. Even if you make it as a pro athlete, your career will be over by the time you are 35. You will need that diploma."

Have these pro athletes explain what happens if you break a leg, get a sore arm, have one bad year or don't make the cut for five or six tournaments. Explain to them the star system, wherein for every star earning millions there are six or seven others making $15,000 or $20,000 or $30,000. Invite a bench-warmer or a guy who didn't make it. Ask him if he sleeps every night. Ask him whether he was graduated. Ask him what he would do if he became disabled tomorrow. Ask him where his old high school athletic buddies are.

We have been on the same roads—sports and entertainment—too long. We need to pull over, fill up at the library and speed away to Congress and the Supreme Court, the unions and the business world.

I'll never forget how proud my grandmother was when I graduated from UCLA. Never mind the Davis Cup. Never mind the Wimbledon title. To this day, she still doesn't know what those names mean. What mattered to her was that of her more than thirty children and grandchildren, I was the first to be graduated from college, and a famous college at that. Somehow, that made up for all those floors she scrubbed all those years.

The Responsive Reader

1   Where does Ashe state his central thesis? How does he echo or reinforce it? How does he support it with examples, explanations, statistics?
2   Does Ashe look at the larger political or cultural context of the issue? Does he try to get at underlying causes?

Talking, Listening, Writing

3   Do you think this article persuaded its intended audience? Why or why not?
4   Some observers say that the lionizing of black athletes and entertainers perpetuates damaging stereotypes: African Americans can succeed only

as ballplayers, singers, or comedians. Others answer that successful athletes from nonwhite backgrounds give both nonwhite and white youngsters people from other backgrounds to admire. Widely admired athletes thus help break down the barriers of prejudice. What do you think? How would you defend your stand on this issue?

5   In 1992 Ashe announced at a news conference that he had been infected with the AIDS virus, apparently as the result of a blood transfusion during open-heart surgery. He made the announcement reluctantly, after *USA Today* confronted him with a rumor of his condition and asked him to confirm or deny. Anna Quindlen examined the question of journalistic ethics involved when she wrote in her column in the *New York Times*:

> Anyone who tries to make readers believe the questions are simple ones, who automatically invokes freedom of the press and the public's right to know, is doing a disservice to America's newspapers. . . . Naming rape victims. Outing gay people. The candidate's sex life. The candidate's drug use. Editors are making decisions they have never made before, on deadline, with competitors breathing down their necks. . . . Like victims of rape, perhaps the victims of this illness deserve some special privacy. . . . The white light of the press and the closed doors of our homes are two of the most deeply prized assets of our lives as Americans. It just so happens that they are often in direct opposition.

Toward the end of her column, Quindlen asked: "Need we know the medical condition of every public figure? . . . What are the parameters?" How would you answer the questions raised by her column?

Collaborative Projects

6   Critics attack the passive role of the audience in the popular spectator sports, which the fans follow from their seats in the stadium or from the couch in front of the small screen. On your campus or in your community, is there a trend away from spectator sports and toward more active participation in sports? Working with other students, you may want to organize an investigation or survey to find answers to this question.

WHISTLEBLOWER:
A QUESTION OF CONSCIENCE

Ambre Brown Morley and Nicole Ostrow

Microbiologist David Franklin said conscience made him blow the whistle on Pfizer Inc.'s Warner–Lambert unit over promoting the epilepsy drug Neurontin for off-label uses.

The maverick has long been an admired figure of American folklore. The maverick is the sturdy individualist who listens to the voice of conscience when it is at odds with popular opinion or official policy. The maverick refuses to "play ball" and does not follow advice "not to make waves."

A modern version of the maverick is the whistleblower—blowing the whistle on wrongdoing by the whistleblower's employer, which may be a corporation, a government agency, or the U.S. military. Often the whistleblower exposes abuses when it might be more prudent to keep quiet. The whistleblower may challenge a high-tech company exposing employees to dangerous chemicals. The whistleblower may expose accounting frauds that mislead shareholders or the IRS. The whistleblower may expose abuse of prisoners in jails at home or in prisoner-of-war camps abroad.

Although whistleblowers may for a time be folk heroes in the media, they may also face retribution. They may be reassigned to lesser jobs or be fired after negative job evaluations. They may face lawsuits pitting their limited financial resources against the formidable legal talent and "deep pockets" of a megacorporation. The following article from a national news service was first published in 2004 when lawsuits involving whistleblowers and critics of corporate practices were much in the news.

Thought Starters: Have you ever been advised "not to make waves"? Have you or friends and relatives ever been warned "not to rock the boat"? What was the occasion? What was the outcome?

Microbiologist David Franklin said conscience made him blow the whistle on Pfizer Inc.'s Warner–Lambert unit over promoting the epilepsy drug Neurontin for off-label uses including hiccups. His reward will be about $26.6 million. 1

In a news conference Thursday in Boston after Warner–Lambert agreed to plead guilty to criminal charges that it misbranded the medication, Franklin, 42, said, "I actually had training for it. It was ridiculous."

Warner–Lambert will pay more than $430 million to settle with the Justice Department, from which Franklin's award comes, the government said Thursday. Franklin sued the company in 1996 under a U.S. law that encourages employees to report illegal activities at their companies.

Also known as the False Claims Act, the law was passed in 1863 to crack down on war profiteering during the Civil War. It allows individuals to bring lawsuits on behalf of the federal government and receive part of any settlement or judgment.

· · ·

The Justice Department recovered $2.1 billion under the False Claims   5
Act in the year that ended Sept. 30, up from $1.1 billion the previous year, said Charles Miller, a Justice Department spokesman in Washington.

· · ·

Franklin's award is far from the largest. In 2001, Douglas Durand, a former vice president of sales at Tap Pharmaceuticals, got $77 million for triggering a suit that revealed the company gave doctors free samples, cash, trips to Hawaii and Rolling Stones concert tickets to promote the company's drugs. The company also was charged with encouraging doctors to seek reimbursement from Medicare.

Tap, a joint venture of Abbott Laboratories and Takeda Chemical Industries Ltd., agreed in 2001 to pay $875 million to settle criminal and civil charges, the largest criminal settlement under the whistle-blower law, Miller said. Thursday's Warner-Lambert case was the second-largest criminal settlement, he said.

Franklin also asked for Pfizer to pay legal fees, according to his lawyer, Thomas Greene of the Boston firm Greene & Hoffman.

· · ·

Warner-Lambert, which Pfizer acquired in 2000 for about $120 billion, paid doctors to attend conferences in Hawaii, Florida and the 1996 Atlanta Olympics, where Neurontin was touted as a treatment for such ailments as migraines and bipolar mental disorder, the government said.

· · ·

Franklin, who received a doctorate in microbiology from the Uni-   10
versity of Rhode Island in 1992, was a research fellow at the Harvard Medical School from 1992 through 1996, his law firm said. Warner-Lambert hired him for a medical liaison position in 1996, and company officials soon began introducing him as "Dr. Franklin" to enhance his credibility in visits with physicians, he said.

"We were made very much aware that the patent life on Neurontin was very short," he said on a conference call with reporters. "I was trained very quickly to adjust from being a cardiology expert to a neurology expert."

Franklin, who is now vice president of marketing science at Boston Scientific Corp. in Natick, Mass., outside Boston, said he was blackballed from working in the pharmaceutical industry.

"This has been the most disruptive thing I can imagine can take place in anyone's life," he said.

Franklin said he plans to continue working at Boston Scientific, even as a newly minted millionaire.

"My wife and I have struggled over the years to not make this a defin- 15
ing moment in our lives," he said. At the same time, he said, "a vacation would be good."

Franklin does have advice for other potential whistle-blowers.

"People who are in the position I was need to think about their own futures and how they feel about themselves and what their kids look up to and why they got into this business in the first place," he said. "That's where the endurance of this thing comes into play."

The Responsive Reader

1 What was the *basic issue* that made Franklin blow the whistle? New medications often go through long-drawn-out tests and evaluations before they are approved. What are "off-label uses"? What is wrong with them? What is "misbranding"?

2 What do you learn from the parallel *case history* of the Durand case? What is the "False Claims Act," and how did it apply in this case? Do you read this account as an exposure of a few "rotten apples"? Or do you read it as an example of a pervasive problem in today's business ethics?

3 Watchdog media sources have tracked the cases of whistleblowers having their careers destroyed or being killed in suspicious accidents. Franklin and Durand were apparently vindicated and received huge financial rewards. In this article, are there nevertheless hints of second thoughts and of the *retribution* that whistleblowers may experience?

Talking, Listening, Writing

4 Do you think the next generation of business majors will think strictly in terms of economic advncement and the "bottom line"? Or will they worry about "how they feel about themselves and what their kids look up to"?

5 Are you amazed at the size of the damage awards? Is there any mention in this news report of restitution to patients misled or hurt by corporate malfeasance or deception?

JESSICA LYNCH: THE INTERVIEW

Nancy Gibbs and Richard Stengel

"If women can't be in the military, you're going to have your son or your grandson or your father or your brother that's out there, who may not want to be there and who may still get hurt."

Jessica Lynch's rescue after nine days in an Iraqui hospital as a prisoner of war became an international media event. Lynch had enlisted hoping to be able to earn a college degree after serving her country. (She had hopes of becoming a kindergarten teacher.) Her truck was part of a supply column that was attacked after it missed a detour around a city considered too dangerous to pass through. Eleven of her fellow G.I.s were killed, and others captured. She herself was severely injured and was taken by Iraquis to a hospital. An army report attributed the events on "a navigational error caused by the combined effects of the operational pace, acute fatige, isolation and the harsh environmental conditions."

American media sources reported that "she had been fighting to the death." A columnist for the Washington Times *celebrated her as a true American heroine. Her own account was that her sand-clogged rifle wouldn't fire. Her column had already lost many vehicles because of breakdowns, and she was afraid to be left behind. Army sources said that she had possibly been sexually assaulted while a prisoner. The Iraqui physician who saved her life on the first day with emergency surgery and blood transfusions said he saw no such evidence.*

Lynch's best friend Lori Piestewa, a Hopi from Arizona, had picked her up in her Humvee when Lynch's own truck left her stranded. Lori, who was also badly injured in the attack, had been taken by the Iraquis to the same hospital, which had also taken in hundreds of Iraqui casualties. She died there because doctors did not have the resources for the brain surgery required by her head wound. The following interview with Lynch accompanied a cover story in Time *magazine in November 2003.*

Thought Starters: Are you part of the potential audience for recruitment commercials for the military? Why or why not?

1 TIME: *When the Army recruiter came to your house, what did he say?*

JESSICA LYNCH: He talked about how you could travel and see all these different kinds of places. And then he was like, "You can get an education while you go there." And I was like, "Yeah, you know that would be cool if I could have a job plus go to school at the same time. Yeah, that would be cool."

TIME: *You were still here in Palestine, W. Va., on Sept. 11, right? What was that like?*

JL: I was scared, actually, myself because I knew that a week later I would be going off to the Army, and that scared me. So I did try to back out of it. But then I thought, Nah. I still wanted to go and serve my country, even if it did mean going over there, but I never actually thought I'd get hurt or anything.

5   TIME: *And you re-enlisted a year ago while still stationed in Texas?*

JL: Yes, I signed a paper saying they would have to send me to Hawaii if I re-enlisted.

TIME: *And then, in between, you learned you were going to Iraq?*

JL: That just happened. It was time for deployment.

TIME: *What did they tell you to expect? What you trained for [maintenance and supply] obviously wasn't what happened.*

10   JL: We had to do the whole weapons qualification again to make sure that we knew how to operate a weapon, but also we did a lot of training with gas masks. In a sense we were ready, but we weren't ready for an ambush attack.

TIME: *Did you feel your commanding officer had the training and equipment he needed to do his job?*

JL: Yeah, I think he did. I think it was just all a big mistake that happened. Just fatigue, sleepiness, the whole thing—we were just not prepared.

TIME: *What were your impressions when you got there?*

JL: It was completely not what I was expecting.

TIME: *What were you expecting?*   15

JL: At least roads. But all that was really there was sand.

TIME: *here is a certain point at which people are firing on you.*

JL: It was scary. It was one of the most scary times you could possibly be in. I mean it was like, Oh, God, you know, help me get through it. There was nothing you could do but fire back. But since my weapon jammed, there was nothing I could do to defend myself. I couldn't defend the four other people in my vehicle. It just felt like it was never going to end.

TIME: *If your weapon hadn't jammed, you would have been . . .*

JL: Firing, of course. But it would   20
still have been nervous and scary.

TIME: *You said they hadn't trained you for an ambush?*

JL: Yeah, well, I don't really know how you could train someone for an ambush. I guess it was just more, Defend yourself, get out of there alive.

TIME: *Why do you think they didn't kill you like they killed the others?*

JL: They could have. I don't know. God saved me. That's one of God's prayers, I guess.

TIME: *At one point at the Nasiriyah hospital, some of the orderlies put you in   25 an ambulance. Did you know that they were trying to take you back to the Americans then?*

JL: No, I actually thought they were taking me out to kill me, to hurt me. Once we got back, they told me, "We tried to deliver you to the Americans, but they started to shoot at us." They started talking to me about how they were wanting to give me back.

TIME: Was there any pain medicine they could give you?
JL: No, they weren't giving me stuff like that. There was this old lady, though. She would come, and she would rub my back with some kind of powder, and she would sing me a song. And that would kind of calm me down and make the back stop hurting for a little bit, but it was still so much pain.

TIME: At that point, what could you move?
30 JL: Nothing. I couldn't move either leg or this arm, of course, and plus my back. I couldn't sit up or anything.

TIME: Did you think you were going to die there?
JL: No, I wouldn't let myself think that. If it happened, it was go-ing to happen but not because I gave up or because I wanted to die. There was no way I was going to give up hope that I was going to get back to America.

TIME: Where you trying not to show that you were in pain?
JL: Of course, they could see I was in pain—that was obvious—but I was afraid that if I showed them extreme pain and anger, that would show them that I was completely weak—I was weak in my head. I wasn't—I was bound to get out of there.

35 *TIME: What did you think when you saw the American soldiers who came to get you?*
JL: I was kind of scared, thinking, Well, maybe this isn't real. Maybe they're just trying to trick me to go with Iraqis dressed in our soldiers'

suits that they killed, you know? But once the guy started talking to me, explaining stuff, I thought, Wow, yeah, it's true. It's amazing! And once that guy gave me his hand, I would not let go. I was not going to be left behind, not again.

TIME: Do you feel lucky?
JL: I do feel lucky that I survived or that I can even sit up, that I am not paralyzed or that I am walking. I mean, it's such a great feeling. I feel lucky that I am here.

TIME: How does it feel to be treated like a hero?
JL: Overwhelming. It's just unbe- 40 lievable the things people want to do, to take a picture of my house or something that I own. It makes them feel good, and I don't know what to say. I'm still the same per-son, you know.

TIME: Who are the people you con-sider heroes?
JL: Well, obviously the ones that came and rescued me—they're my big heroes. And Lori. She could have gave up right there, said, "You know, I can't do this." But no, she stayed calm and cool had everything together.

TIME: Has this all affected your view of women in the military?
JL: You know, women are equal to men. We may not be physically strong or something, but if women can't be in the military, you're going to have your son or your grandson or your father or your brother that's out there, who may not want to be there and who may still get hurt.

TIME: Do you follow what's going on 45 *in Iraq now?*

JL: I flip through the channels, and [news] will catch my eye, and I watch it. But I try not to too much because I am trying to move past this. It's kind of hard not to watch — but yet at the same time, I don't want to sit there and constantly watch it. I can't deal with that.

TIME: You still think you might want to leave Palestine?
JL: Yeah, but only because I want to travel. I know I'll always keep roots here, always be here. But I just want to get out and see different things. I am still planning on going back to college. I would still like to see Hawaii.

The Responsive Reader

1   The Iraq war focused media attention on *army recruiting* and the people who serve in the army. What does this interview tell you about the recruiter's methods or approaches and the mindset of people like Lynch?

2   The *enemy profile* — the image of the enemy each side creates — plays a major role in war reporting and war progaganda. What image of the enemy emerges from this interview? Lynch says she doesn't know why the attackers didn't kill her the way they killed the others G.I.s. What do you think are possible reasons?

3   Did the Jessica Lynch story reopen the issue of the role of *women in the military?* The interviewers ask Lynch: "Has this all affected your view of women in the military?" What is her answer? What would be your answer to the same question?

Talking, Listening, Writing

4   In a quick current-issue book about Lynch published by journalist Rick Bragg, she is quoted as saying: "I am not a hero. If it makes people feel good to say it, then I am glad. But I'm not. I'm just a survivor." Do you think she is a hero?

5   Are the recently wounded or permanently injured in military hospitals the forgotten heroes of the nation's wars? Have you ever visited such a facility? What did you see and hear? Can you track some recent informative and candid reports? What do they say?

6   In his book about Lynch, Bragg says that the soldiers recruited with her were

> sons and daughters of endangered blue-collar workers, immigrant families and single mothers — a United States Army borrowed from tract houses, brick ranchers and back roads. . . . they had traded uncertain futures for dead-certain paychecks and a place in the adventure that they had heard their ancestors talk of as they twisted wrenches, pounded IBM Selectrics and packed lunches for the plants that closed their doors before the next generation could build a life from them.

How much contact do you have with people in the military or with military families? From what segments or layers in the class structure of American society do they come?

GET MOTIVATED!

Steven Win

"Anyone with a computer can get rich by spending 10 minutes a day buying and selling stocks online. Seventeen percent is totally doable in any market."

Steven Win wrote the following article as the art and culture critic for the San Francisco Chronicle *in May 2004, at a time of escalating conflict during the war in Iraq. The promotional events he describes took place in huge halls usually hosting major sports events or trade shows and had been promoted in full-page ads featuring photographs of celebrities. These included Ronnie Lott, millionaire former football star and sports commentator from 49ers Superbowl glory; ex-mayor Giuliani of New York, who became a media hero after the terrorist attack on the World Center; and a Hollywood movie star.*

Win is part of a tradition of culture critics challenging the use of "positive thinking," patriotism, and religion in support of a sales effort. They challenge using God and the flag in the service of a political party, business philosophy, or self-promotion.

Thought Starters: Have you attended a pep rally that made an impression on you? What was your reaction? Have you attended an inspirational event meant as a moral-booster? How did it affect you?

"For the first time in history," a crowd of 12,000 learned the other   *1*
day at the HP Pavilion, "the little guy has the advantage."

So sayeth Phil Town, a former river-rafting guide who has abandoned Colorado whitewater to share his wisdom with throngs of historically advantaged little guys. His message: Anyone with a computer can get rich by spending 10 minutes a day buying and selling stocks online. "Seventeen percent is totally doable in any market, guys," Town said in his brisk, commonsensical cadence. "Click, click, click—you could have done it, too."

Taken out of context, Town's spiel sounds like, well, like what it was—a bells-and-whistles prelude to a sales pitch that was plainly too good to be true. Sure enough, after a teasing whirl through covered calls, group rotation, market timing and other investment legerdemain, Town offered a daylong class with breakfast and lunch included, DVDs and online support—a $6,000 value, he said—at the deeply discounted price of $995.

People lined up three deep at sign-up tables around the arena to take him up on it during a break. And somehow, under the circumstances, you could understand why they did.

Town's presentation came at a marathon Get Motivated program that   *5*
played the HP Pavilion and the Cow Palace last week. Tickets sold for $49

to $89. For more than nine hours, speakers from various rooms of life's success mansion poured out a stream of platitudes, pep talks, canned-ham humor, live infomercials, prefab patriotism, Bible Belt Christianity and the barest smattering of concrete advice. Signing up for something—anything—was like an involuntary reflex action to being repeatedly, numbingly hammered in the knee.

"In this huddle of life we play hard," ex-49er Ronnie Lott said after tossing a few autographed footballs into the stands. Motivational superstar Zig Ziglar turned another old sports truism, about where nice guys finish, on its ear. "The good guys and the good gals ultimately do win," he said in his broad Mississippi drawl. "Who you are is different from who you are when skill and will come together," offered Ziglar disciple Krish Dhanam, in one of his perky koans. By the time freed prisoner of war Jessica Lynch, quarter back Joe Montana and comedian Jerry Lewis finished off the proceedings, in a bizarre late-afternoon sequence, the day had acquired its own transfixing logic.

It was a cross of boot camp and revival meeting, pep rally and a very large group therapy session. Behind all the hard-sell optimism and draining, calculated energy—there were original (but dreadful) songs and indoor fireworks, red-white-and-blue confetti storms and a beach ball toss—this motivational "seminar" seemed strangely attuned to a mordant American mind-set in 2004.

By serving up a self-referential belief system that was finally about nothing other than its own miasma of "success," the day radiated that gnawing sense of unease so many people feel now. These market-minded Get Motivated! hucksters were selling what people were ready to hear, at least for a day off from work in San Jose—an escapist fantasy of personal empowerment and consumer comforts that would somehow create a shield against the very real and vividly imagined terrors of life in 2004.

With its promises of financial potency for the working single mothers, go-get-'em pluck for salespeople squeezed by the economy and a bullish determination for the rest of us—this feel-good-athon built a shining bridge to some mythical, impregnable suburban Xanadu. There everyone lives in big houses and drives nice cars, plays golf or rides horses, sits down for quiet cups of coffee with spouses of 57 years who love them more than ever and enjoys a casual proximity to the immortals.

"A neighbor of mine is Wayne Gretzky," noted author Tom Hopkins ("How to Master the Art of Selling"). "America's Success Strategist" Peter Lowe was introduced, by his wife, Tamara, the day's master of ceremonies, as a friend to quarterbacks, four U.S. presidents and Mother Teresa.

There was even a shimmer of noblesse oblige. Real estate wizard James Smith told a heartwarming tale of helping his garbage man buy a house. "And he wasn't even of my race," Smith added. The guru of assumed mortgages, foreclosures and U.S. marshal sales then offered his training seminar, reduced from $999 to $99. "For the next 10 minutes only," he said. For all its PowerPoint projections, wireless mikes and headline speakers (Rudolph

10

Giuliani spoke on leadership a day before his testimony at the federal Sept. 11 commission in New York), the Get Motivated! managers work a classic American vein that runs from Melville and Twain to P.T. Barnum and Norman Vincent Peale. It's the archetype of the American confidence man, who mirrors back our own native spirit of optimism and trust.

Dropping to one knee in secular prayer, Ziglar, 77, put it this way: "There's something I can do to make my future better or make it worse. I choose to make it better." The baby-faced Lowe followed up later with a rhetorical question that rejected a vengeful God and endorsed an upbeat one: "How could a negative creator create a positive living success?" Accentuate the positive, and so it shall be.

In a keen study of "The Confidence Man in American Literature," Gary Lindberg identifies this "essential quality in the confidence man's situation: Everyone around him believes in some larger promise." Adds Lindberg, "What the confidence man celebrates in American life is the delight of entering a series of roles and making them work." Real estate, the stock market, a good marriage, belief in God: Bring 'em all on.

"Have you competed to be the best mother, the best husband, the best worker?" Lott asked the hushed crowd. "Otherwise, why play the game?"

The weird procession from war heroine (Lynch) to football hero 15 (Montana) to King of Comedy (Lewis) at the end of the day underscored the point: Success isn't so much a matter of mastering a specific skill set as it is a fungible state of mind that can be applied to anything. Somehow, through all the smoke and mirrors, what people may be hearing are the durable American mantras of individualism and self-transformation. For a day inside the HP Pavilion, they can let themselves believe that anything is possible.

Not that there isn't plenty of static along the way. A lot of the attendees in San Jose grumbled about all the hawking of stock market and real estate seminars and Ziglar's books and videotapes. "Sell, sell, sell," one woman said. "I feel like I've been trapped inside a live infomercial," muttered another. But here and elsewhere it works. According to *Potentials* magazine, Americans spend more than $22 billion a year on motivational "products." Many are repeat users. "This is lifelong learning," as a market-minded Dhanam says.

In a half-dozen conversations, people offered testimony that was both specific and abstract. Leland Nicholes, who works in a Palo Alto law firm, lost 80 pounds after his first Ziglar seminar. "He's some motivator," Nicholes said. Deana Gerhard, a collections manager at San Jose State University, was back for her third motivational session. "I appreciate teamwork more now," she said. Some people came as individuals; others were there on office outings. The parade of speakers on and off the fern-banked stage had a narcotic effect after a while. Dyan Cannon: "We gotta be an attorney for our own case." Giuliani: "You have to love people." Real estate man Smith: "You gotta get in the game." Montana: "Strive for perfection."

Emerson, St. Augustine, Jim Rome and Dr. Laura were among the sages invoked.

Then suddenly, into this tepid bath, came a refreshing cold slap of reality from super-salesman Hopkins. Like a defecting Soviet scientist, he revealed a rush of trade secrets. Never say "down payment," he instructed a class of 12,000 prospective real estate agents. Say "initial investment." Buyers instinctively balk at "signing" a "contract," he advised. But they're pleased as puppies to "OK, approve, authorize or endorse" the "paperwork, agreement or form."

Hopkins explained the strategy of the "inverted tie-down question" or "alternate of choice" ("Would you prefer a five or 10 percent deposit?"). His example of a "porcupine" to snare a female house buyer was pure David Mamet, a sun-splashed glimpse inside "Glengary Glen Ross." Get the woman to commit to the swing set out back, Hopkins explained, and she's got to buy the house that goes along with it. The crowd murmured its approval.

Here, for the first and only time of the day, the little guy finally did   20
get the advantage: He got to see how the little guy gets handled all the time.

The Responsive Reader

1   For this inspirational, motivational event, what is the *bottom line?* To judge from this account of the event, what were its promoters actually selling? What were they marketing? What would motivate the promoters to invest in the expensive advertising and high-profile talent?

2   Would you be a good *audience* for the promotions covered here? (How would you react to invitations to help you get rich by spending ten minutes a day trading stocks online? How would you react to an offer of a $6,000 value marked down to $995? How do you react to before-and-after pictures of an obese person losing 50 or 60 pounds?)

3   Culture critics like Win have often identified the confidence man as an American *archetype*—fitting a pattern deeply rooted in the collective national psyche. (Why is he called the "confidence man"?) In Win's account, what parts of the program come closest to the stereotype of the promoter as the rainmaker, the peddler of miracle cures, the promoter of Get-Rich-Quick schemes, the financial analyst touting lifetime-opportunity insiders' stock tips? (Why did the promoters call this a "seminar"?)

4   Win complains that there was little concrete *usable advice* in the presentations he attended. What do you learn from the detailed example of the advice for aspiring real-estate agents? What is the difference between saying "down payment" and "initial investment"? What is the difference between saying "sign the contract" and "endorse the agreement"? In the scenario sketched out by the real-estate agent, where do you imagine yourself? Do you imagine yourself as a hotshot real-estage agent? Or in-

stead do you identify with the "little guy" getting the spiel? Or do you think of yourself as a consumer advocate warning low-income people against familiar ploys?

5 Win keeps up a drumbeat of *connotative language*. He uses emotionally weighted terms and comparison to drive home his negative view of the promoters' resolutely positive pitch. What are "platitudes"? How is a "spiel" or a "sales pitch" different from a sales presentation? How are "hucksters" different from ordinary salespeople? How much of what he describes is truly "escapist" or "fantasy"? How would a belief system be "self-referential"?

Talking, Listening, Writing

6 Win attacks an alliance of "hard-sell" marketing, stock market or real estate promotion, religious ideology, sports as a national pastime and quasi-religion, and patriotism. How for you are major areas of American life connected? How did they get combined or intertwined? (For you, is there anything wrong with salespeople using red-white-and-blue confetti?)

FREDERICK DOUGLASS

Robert Hayden

During the Civil Rights era, writers and artists like Robert Hayden rewrote American history by honoring leaders in the struggle against injustice.

During much of the nineteenth century, American political life was dominated by the issue of slavery as against abolition and the emancipation of the slaves. Even in states where slavery was illegal, the issue of slavery was kept before people's consciences by the arrival of runaway slaves—the "runagates" of one of Robert Hayden's poems and the targets of "fugitive slave" laws.

In the 1960s and 1970s when the following poem was first printed, Hayden was an outstanding member of a movement of poets, novelists, religious leaders, and artists causing the nation to reexamine and update its history books to honor leaders in the struggle for freedom. Students studied the testimonies or read the life stories of Harriet Tubman, Sojourner Truth, Frederick Douglass, and W.E.B. DuBois. Frederick Douglass was one of the leaders speaking and writing most eloquently about the aspirations of black Americans. In his Autobiography *(1845), he told the story of his own rebellion against and escape from slavery. As a journalist and powerful public speaker, he became a leader of the anti-slavery movement in the United States. His Independence Day speech of 1852 ("What to the American slave is your Fourth of July?") is still widely reprinted in documentary histories of the country and in collections of American oratory.*

As recently as 2003 and 2004, the "rewriting of history" in textbooks was still a hotly contested issue in large states like Texas and California that set a pattern for the rest of the country to follow. The movement away from "white men on great horses" toward greater inclusiveness in dealing with the history and contributions of America's minorities was still being challenged and debated by educators, journalists, and politicians.

Thought Starters: Is it true that "hero-worship" has gone out of style? What inspirational figures or national leaders did you come to know best during your study of American history? Which would you recommend to others for role models?

When it is finally ours, this freedom, this liberty, this beautiful
and terrible thing, needful to man as air,
usable as earth; when it belongs at last to all,
when it is truly instinct, brain matter, diastole, systole,
reflex action; when it is finally won; when it is more

than the gaudy mumbo jumbo of politicians:
this man, this Douglass, this former slave, this Negro
beaten to his knees, exiled, visioning a world
where none is lonely, none hunted, alien,
this man, superb in love and logic, this man
shall be remembered. Oh, not with statues' rhetoric,
not with legends and poems and wreaths of bronze alone,
but with the lives grown out of his life, the lives
fleshing his dream of the beautiful, needful thing.

The Responsive Reader

1   The *rhetoric* paying homage to American ideals of freedom may threaten
    to become routine or perfunctory, used at times dutifully or without real
    conviction. Part of a poet's task is to use language that is not trite or
    overused but instead compels our attention, making us listen again. Why
    does the poet call freedom "beautiful" and "terrible" and "needful as
    air" and "usable as earth"?
2   The diastole and systole are two phases of the heartbeat—expansion and
    contraction. Do you you think allegiance to an ideal can become as nat-
    ural as the heartbeat? For the poet, is the ideal of freedom mainly a mat-
    ter of the heart?
3   In a few lines about Douglass' vision of the future, the poet evokes *ma-
    jor themes* of a history of persecution. How real or vivid are these themes
    or memories for a current generation? Are they alive for today's young
    Americans, or have they become ancient history?
4   For the poet, what are the *limitations* of statues, legends, poems, and
    memorials as ways of honoring the legacy of heroic figures of the past?

Collaborative Projects

5   Does your college or community schedule observances like a Black His-
    tory Month or Hispanic Heritage Week? Working with a group, you
    may want to prepare a sound-and-image presentation using readings
    from the writings or speeches of major historical figures for a com-
    memoration of a strand in American history.

FORUM: Exceptional Lives

The most popular stories in American lore are not about someone who inherited a fortune or was chauffeured to a private school in a limousine. Instead, they are the biographies of people who started in life without money or privilege and became a legend in their own time. They may be the stories of people whose families arrived penniless from a war-torn country and who became movie moguls or advisers to presidents. Among American presidents in the twentieth century, one came from a family that ran a corner grocery store, one had taught Mexican American children in a country school in Texas, and one was born after his father died, leaving the son to grow up with an abusive alcoholic stepfather. One of the great American myths is the log cabin myth—the story of those making it on their own.

What does it take? What admiration, envy, or resentment do people who stand out inspire?

THE AUTOBIOGRAPHY
OF BILLY GRAHAM

Andrew Delbanco

"They had a camera there, and as you walked by, you could see yourself on the screen. We never thought it would amount to anything, though. It seemed too incredible!" The rest is evangelical history.

In this book review first published in a longer version in the New Republic *magazine in 1997, the reviewer responds to the publication of an autobiography by one of America's best-known public figures by assessing the author's life story and life work.*

If name recognition is a test of success, the evangelist Billy Graham is one of the great success stories of American history. Adviser to presidents, he has been organizer of megacrusades around the globe, earning his reputation "as having preached Christianity to more people than anyone in history." He transplanted to the world of today's media the American tradition of the revival tent, the itinerant or traveling preacher, and the converts swearing off a life of sin. Graham has been admired for not allowing religion to become a divisive force. He has said that although homosexuality is a sin, God's love extends to homosexuals.

Thought Starters: Do you watch religious broadcasts? Have you ever attended a revival meeting? What do you think of evangelists?

There is a striking moment in Benjamin Franklin's *Autobiography* in   1
which two main currents of American life converge. Skeptical Ben, a man who "seldom attended any public worship," and for whom "Revelation had indeed no weight," goes out one day in 1739 to hear a famous evangelical preacher whom he regards as a holdover from the age of credulity. The place is Philadelphia, the preacher is the visiting English Methodist George Whitefield, and the charity on Whitefield's mind that day is an orphanage in Georgia. Before the appeal, Franklin "did not disapprove of the design" for an orphans' home. Ever the booster of local interests, he "thought it would have been better to have built the House here & [to have] Brought the Children to it." By the time Whitefield finished his soaring plea, however, Franklin had "emptied my pocket wholly into the collector's dish, gold and all." A wealthy friend, whose wariness of the preacher's blandishments had led him to attend the service without a cent on his person, found himself begging in the crowd for a loan with which he could make a gift of his own.

If Whitefield was the first great practitioner of itinerant revival preaching in America, Billy Graham is its modern master. His story begins fifty years ago, when Americans outside the South first came to know this dentally impeccable farmboy from North Carolina with a taste for Dr Pepper and goofy suits, who traveled with a supporting cast of musicians, notably George Beverly Shea, the baritone who sings what Graham's biographer Marshall Frady aptly calls the "lanolin-lubricated solos" that are a standard part of a Graham service. In 1949, Billy and his Crusade Team (the initial letters are always capitalized) made their first incursion into the urban Northeast. Preaching on the Boston Common in a city full of theological liberals, Catholics and egghead unbelievers, he borrowed his topic from a sermon that Whitefield had preached there some two centuries before: "Shall God Reign in New England?" The result was a "harvest" of contributions and converts, and a sense among some in the infidel city that God's messenger had come to town. Even some latter-day skeptics, in the tradition of Franklin, were impressed.

Journey, Arrival, Doubt, Triumph: this is the four-part movement of Billy Graham's autobiography, which bears the belligerently modest title *Just As I Am*. It is a monotonous tale—how the ministry went national and then international, how it reached out through radio, film and (most of all) television—that makes for a book with a repetitive structure rather like the structure of pornography. Virtually every chapter tells the same story in the same vocabulary. Billy flies into town in a rickety chartered plane that is running low on fuel or in the hands of an unlicensed pilot or buffeted by a thunderstorm. At first, the press as well as local civic and religious leaders are dubious or hostile (Billy's handlers are always fretting that the plane is late or the weather bad), but the great man remains undaunted, the rally goes on, and it ends with a throng of converts approaching the sundrenched or moonlit platform to declare their "decisions for Christ."

Billy Graham probably deserves his reputation as having preached Christianity to more people than anyone in history. Pastor to presidents, inventor of (in Garry Wills's phrase) "golf course spirituality," author now of a bestselling memoir, he has been on the lists of most admired Americans for most of the last forty years. But who is this Elvis of the evangelicals? What does he believe? And what kind of religious experience does he offer his followers?

Just As I Am does not help much with these questions. Despite its   5
length, it is not really a book. It is what Robert Giroux used to call an "ook": a gesture toward an idea or a sentiment or a story that is packaged as a book, but never quite becomes one. Considering how important strenuous self-reflection is in the religious tradition to which Graham belongs, one of its oddest features is how little it reveals of its author's inner life. We do catch glimpses of Billy in times of edginess and exhaustion; we learn that on tour he misses his wife and children; we witness a fleeting moment of doubt about the inerrancy of scripture. He expresses regret over a few public gaffes—such as when he and the Team, after a chilly visit with President

Truman, knelt in posed prayer for photographers on the White House lawn. Put together with help from various writers, secretaries and "editorial co-ordinators," this memoir has the feeling of having been dictated on the run. There are flashes of self-deprecating humor, as when Billy looks back and discovers his youthful resemblance to Li'l Abner; but most of the humor is unwitting, as when we encounter "Bev" Shea at the Helsinki Crusade crooning "I'd Rather Have Jesus" in Finnish.

"To be honest," Graham says, "I never thought I would write this book . . . and one of the hardest parts has been deciding what to leave out." It is not always easy to grasp just what has guided him in choosing what to put in. Skipping quickly over the war years (he was 23 when Pearl Harbor was bombed), he says little more than that his hopes for an army chaplaincy were thwarted when he turned out to be underweight. Yet certain small childhood incidents are carefully preserved for their allegorical value, as when the future preacher of love and reconciliation shuts up the family col-lie in the doghouse overnight with a cat—an experiment by which he learns, presumably, that creatures who go into a situation as enemies can come out friends.

Graham's first stirrings of conviction came when he was turning 16, in response to the voice and the gaze of a traveling preacher with the splen-did name of Mordecai Ham, who had come to Charlotte to denounce sin. Dr. Ham seemed especially attuned to the dark secrets of the young, and Billy, whose participation in the local Presbyterian church had until then been merely dutiful, found himself feeling accused by the man's state. "Billy was always a ladies man," as one friend (quoted not in *Just As I Am*, but in an admiring biography by William Martin) has put it. "He was quite a thinker, too. That's all he thought about." Surprising himself in feeling drawn to the revival meeting for a second night, he and his lifelong friend Grady Wilson decided to join the choir so they could mouth the words (neither could sing) while using their hymn books to hide from Ham's dread gaze.

Evidently, Graham came to his faith out of standard adolescent anxi-ety. "As a teenager, what I needed to know for certain was that I was right with God." *Just As I Am* does not elaborate on this quest for certainty, which concluded successfully when he was 16 and seems never to have fal-tered in the ensuing sixty-four years. It was a conversion of what William James called the "volitional type," a spiritual event without much sense of upheaval. "No bells went off inside me," Billy says. "No signs flashed across the tabernacle ceiling. No physical palpitations made me tremble." Now, nearly 80, he indulges in scant retrospective analysis of his adolescent self, but he does recall that after being smitten by Dr. Ham, he worried about ridicule from his peers. "How could I face school tomorrow? . . . There seemed to be a song in my heart, but it was mixed with a kind of pounding fear as to what might happen when I got to class." There are hints that even before his conversion he may already have been regarded as over-scrupulous:

Once in my senior year, when we were in a night rehearsal of a school play at Sharon High, one of the girls in the cast coaxed me aside into a dark classroom. She had a reputation for "making out" with the boys. Before I realized what was happening, she was begging me to make love to her. My hormones were as active as any other healthy young male's, and I had fantasized often enough about such a moment. But when it came, I silently cried to God for strength and darted from that classroom the way Joseph fled the bedroom of Potiphar's philandering wife in ancient Egypt.

What Mordecai Ham gave to this boy was a new sense of the dignity of his scruples. To this was added the gift of a vocation: Billy would be a preacher. At Bible school and college, Graham discovered his own oratorical gifts and developed chaste friendships with several pious girls, eventually courting Ruth Bell, the daughter of missionaries, to whom he has now been married for more than fifty years. While studying to be a purveyor of the gospel, he spent some time hawking Fuller brushes door to door, an experience by which he tested and refined his salesman's knack. In 1940, at the New York World's Fair, Graham saw his first television. "They had a camera there, and as you walked by, you could see yourself on a screen. We never thought it would amount to anything, though. It seemed too incredible!" The rest is evangelical history.

The Responsive Reader

1   In the beginning of this review, you hear echoes of the *vocabulary* of old-time religious crusades, which pitted "infidels," "skeptics," and "unbelievers" against "Revelation" or else "credulity." Is this language obsolete or old-fashioned today, or are people still using it? Where and how? (What is the "inerrancy of scripture"? Is it an issue for you or people you know?)

2   According to this review, how does Graham describe the basic *scenario* or MO, of his traveling ministry? Do you find it inspirational or self-admiring?

3   What key traits of Graham's *personality* emerge for you from this portion of a longer review? What were key factors in his conversion or major stages in his spiritual history? What temperament suited him for his life work? For you, what about his personality was predictable, and what was surprising?

Talking, Listening, Writing

4   Do you think that the ministry of the individual crusading evangelist is more American than the organization and ritual of a traditionally structured church? Why or why not?

5   Many television evangelists have built business empires and become millionaires. Do you think large personal wealth is compatible or incompatible with the teachings of the gospels?

6   What major experiences or what influences played a role in your own
spiritual or intellectual history?

THE DIGITAL AMAZON

Leslie Gornstein

**She became the founder of Digital Amazon, a Web
consulting firm, and also "the brain behind Amazon
City, an online women's community, and one of the
driving forces behind the growing women's presence in
cyberspace."**

A standard feature of feminist publications like Ms. *or minority-oriented
publications like* Ebony *has been tributes to Americans from unconventional
backgrounds who succeeded against odds. Often the journalist writing about an
outstanding woman will ask: What set her on the path to success? What did
she consider her mission? What obstacles did she have to overcome? How can
she serve as an inspiration to others? The following article focuses on an outstanding woman making her way in the "brutally male" medium of cyberspace. When she published this article in 1998, Gornstein encouraged readers
to check out Amazon City at www.amazoncity.com*

Thought Starters: What do you know about the original Amazons? Have
you encountered current revivals of the word or the concept? Where or in
what context?

Five-feet-eight and skinny as a model, ramrod-poised in DKNY sun-   1
glasses and high-heeled mules, the 28-year-old blond in stretch pants is
blowing away the burns along the Venice Beach boardwalk. They tell her
she looks "just fi-i-ne," but her head never turns. The mules maintain their
clip as she heads back to the candlelit apartment that doubles as the worldwide headquarters for her unlikely online empire.

Stephanie Brail is a digital Amazon.

More specifically, she's the founder of Digital Amazon, a Web consulting firm with clients ranging from healthcare giant Kaiser Permanente
to the nonprofit Los Angeles Commission on Assaults Against Women.
She's also the brains behind Amazon City, an online women's community,
and one of the driving forces behind the growing women's presence in
cyberspace.

The whole idea behind Digital Amazon, she says, is to support and
promote women as they strive for success. That's a daunting mission, given
the testosterone coursing through the net, and Brail knows firsthand how

brutally male the medium can be. In 1993 she found herself in the middle of a flame war that morphed into a case of e-mail stalking so terrifying that she began practicing martial arts for self-defense. "That's when I decided that I wanted to get more women on the Internet, to even things out," she says.

Five years later, things *are* beginning to even out—more women are getting online—partly because of Brail's work. Like any young entrepreneur with no venture capital, she logs 60- to 80-hour workweeks. She also fights a constant battle with chronic fatigue immunodeficiency syndrome, which requires daily naps and causes occasional bouts of "brain fog." Still, Brail has managed, on a shoestring, to develop some of the most successful women-oriented sites on the net. Her Amazon City Radio, launched last year, is the only radio station on the Web offering women-oriented music, talk, news, and public affairs programming. The Amazon City online community attracts as many as half a million page views a month.

Meanwhile, women-oriented sites are attracting corporate sponsors. "This is not a bad thing," Brail says, "but I think a lot of women are downright suspicious of glitzy, advertisement-driven Web sites."

And many of these sites avoid political content at all costs. "Say the word *bitch* on your Web site and that's enough for an ad campaign to be pulled," Brail says. "Sometimes you'll actually find more controversial stuff in the traditional women's magazines."

Brail, who grew up in Jackson, Michigan, got turned on to computers at 10, when her father brought one home and told her she'd be needing it if she wanted a career. Her feminist leanings also began at an early age. "I grew up in an environment where I was always told I could be whatever I wanted to be," she says.

By 1993—when most of the world still didn't know what the Internet was—Brail was typing away on cyberspace bulletin boards. At 24, she was teaching Internet classes. But with chronic fatigue occasionally draining her energy, she knew she couldn't fit into a 9-to-5 grind. So she started building Web pages for pay, mooching a free Internet connection from a friend and sharing a server with a few colleagues.

Today, her Digital Amazon empire is profitable and supports seven part-time off-site employees. She's hoping to move the entire operation into an office next year.

But is all this enough to revitalize the women's movement? "I don't think technology is the key to advancing feminist goals," she explains. "It is certainly, helpful, but not essential. It is more important that women, individual women, have a shift in their perceptions of themselves, that they start to believe in their dreams and follow them."

The Responsive Reader

1 What key details would you include in a portrait of the cyberspace entrepreneur featured in this article? Do any of the biographical data seem especially significant? Do any seem surprising or nonstereotypical?

2   What concrete evidence do you see in this article of the success or promise of Brail's business venture? If you were a budding cyberspace entrepreneur, what key points—or what sidelights—would you note especially?

3   How much does this article focus on obstacles in Brail's path?

4   Where in the article do Brail's feminist convictions or commitments come through most strongly? What kind of feminist is she? What is her advice to other feminists?

Talking, Listening, Writing

5   The magazine where this article was printed included a picture of Brail with the caption "Maverick." What makes her a maverick, or what kind of maverick is she?

6   Would you turn to articles like this one for inspiration and guidance? Or are you a reader suspicious of too much hype that might create unrealistic expectations?

PUBLIC INTEREST LAWYER

Dave Ford

"You have to keep moving forward. I guess the point is not to lose heart."

—IRMA HERRERA

The following article is a tribute to a lawyer providing legal help to women "in low-wage service jobs, non-traditional occupations, sweatshops, and academia."

Irma Herrera is a lawyer of Mexican American descent who says she has enjoyed working for both commercial and public interest law firms. She became the executive director of Equal Rights Advocates, a nonprofit law firm that provides legal aid and advocacy to women who cannot afford them. The firm's 15-member staff provides legal counseling and representation in cases of sexual harassment, family and medical leave conflicts, and workplace safety issues. It works on cases of discriminatory hiring, unfair treatment in advancement or promotion, and unequal pay. One of Herrera's law professors became the first female professor to be hired at the Stanford University law school, at a time when law school attendance by women was going up up from 2 to 20 percent.

For some groups she addressed earlier in her career, Herrera was the first Latina lawyer they had seen. When the author of the following article talked to Herrera about her background and her work in 2004, women made up half of the students at highly ranked law schools.

Thought Starters: Have you observed or read about lawyers serving as advocates in cases involving community issues? Have you observed or been close to a court case or legal situation where people from a "low-wage" sector of society won?

Herrera, who lives in El Cerrito with her husband, Mark Levine, and   1
their son, Antonio Levine, 11, sits behind a simple desk in her office and tells the story of how a girl raised poor in South Texas wound up a successful public interest lawyer. The tale likely resonates for many in her generation whose values were formed and lives were shaped by the 1970s women's movement.

Herrera grew up in what she describes as a "low-income, working-class family" in Alice, a town then of 17,000 south of San Antonio. Her father was a barber, her mom a homemaker. She has a brother and two sisters. The family spoke Spanish in the home, which was in the town's heavily Mexican-American area.

It was in Alice that Herrera had her first taste of the apartness that would one day drive her to consider public interest law. She recalls being 7 or 8 years old and shopping with her mother at a department store. She overheard two white girls her age mocking her mother's accented English. "I remember telling them that 'at least my mother can speak two languages,'" she says, adding, "I remember being so infuriated that here were these little girls who thought they had the right to mock a grown-up. That was so insulting."

Her community had no sidewalks, while the "Anglo" side of town boasted a public swimming pool and the town's nicest park. Parochial schools were segregated: Herrera and her Hispanic classmates saw the "Anglo kids" once a year, during an intramural volleyball game. "When I was a child I could see in the world around me that things weren't fair," she says.

For some, that might have set off a cycle of despair. But Herrera says   5
watching her parents aid relatives in dire straits—when her family had few resources—taught her the value of lifting those in trouble. "I grew up in a home where it was expected that you always helped people in worse situations that you were," she says.

At 16, Herrera, something of a prodigy, entered Texas A&M University at Kingsville. In her junior year, she transferred to St. Mary's University, in San Antonio. Both experiences challenged her perceptions of race. "I guess I expected that people who were not like me were really, really different, and (I had) the realization that people all have the same issues." She graduated in 1971 with a degree in political science, and then dropped out of a graduate urban studies program at Trinity University, also in San Antonio, to work for a New Orleans architecture firm.

"But I was always interested in doing something directly related to serving my community and fighting discrimination," she says, so she decided to attend law school at Notre Dame University, in South Bend, Ind. To her surprise, she discovered Mexican-American communities there and in Michigan composed of migrant workers who had drifted north to pick cranberries—from South Texas, her home.

While at Notre Dame, Herrera worked for the nonprofit Michigan Migrant Legal Services. After graduating, she moved to eastern Washington to work for another legal services group. She represented Spanish-speaking migrant farm workers in cases involving benefits conflicts, work injury compensation and labor camp raids.

Equal Rights Advocates addresses some of the same challenges today. "If you don't keep doing it again and again, you'll roll backwards," Herrera says. "You have to keep moving forward. I guess the point is not to lose heart."

The very thing that made her stand out in eastern Washington — she 10 was the only Mexican-American in the area—also isolated her, she says. In 1980, she moved to San Francisco to become a staff attorney at the local office of the Los Angeles-based Mexican-American Legal Defense and Education Fund, commonly known as MALDEF, a nonprofit Latino rights group.

Despite some successes, Herrera felt frustrated that the work might not be doing any long-term good. "You could win the lawsuits, but if you didn't change public perception, those decisions wouldn't be as effective as they could be," she says. She left MALDEF in 1983 to travel, write and teach.

She returned to law practice three years later at two San Francisco commercial firms. To her surprise, she enjoyed the work and her colleagues. Still, subtle forms of discrimination sometimes popped up. At one firm, a receptionist asked Herrera to have her friends who called "pronounce their names in English." Herrera set about educating her colleagues. "Many activists do that," she says. "You work in institutions and become a thorn in their side."

The lure of public interest law once again drew her, and she went to the San Francisco offices of the Boston-based legal group Multicultural Educational Training and Advocacy, which specializes in the educational rights of Hispanics and migrant children. In 1995, she took the executive director post at Equal Rights Advocates.

Hobbies such as gardening, cooking and reading help Herrera maintain balance in the face of potentially draining advocacy work, but she says it's the positive responses to what she does that really fuels her engines. She mentions speaking to a middle school class of girls who had never seen a Latina lawyer.

"I feel that they see a possibility in me that they haven't thought of," 15 Herrera says, at peace in her office with the deep blue walls. "And that's very important to me."

The Responsive Reader

1   What would you include in a short *synopsis* or summary devoted to Herrera in a publication like *Who's Who among American Women*? Compare your entry with that prepared by a classmate.

2   What *first-hand testimony* does Herrera offer about her personal experiences with discrimination? Do you think the kind of experiences she describes are a thing of the past?

3   Who would be the ideal *audience* for Herrera's story? Who could or should choose her as a role model? Should the right person

   - be female?
   - be from a minority background?
   - come from a low income background?
   - be interested in the law?
   - be exceptionally motivated academically?
   - believe in the American Dream?
   - (other)?_____

Talking, Listening, Writing

4   Do you think your community or the larger society offers young Americans opportunities to work *pro bono*—literally "without pay" but more generally "for the public good"? Is devotion to the "public interest" impractical idealism?

5   If you were involved in a legal case, would you prefer to be presented by a male or a female lawyer? Do you think it would make a difference? Would you prefer to have a woman or a man preside as the judge? Would you care one way or the other? Why or why not?

Collaborative Projects

6   A national magazine published a study claiming that the meat-packing industry is the most dangerous among unsafe workplace environments. Working alone or with a group on a **research project**, you may want to study the worker safety record of a major industry.

Weighing Your Options

To convince fair-minded readers, show that you have listened to more than one point of view.
Thinking the matter through often means listening to different views. On many contested issues, it means sorting out the pro and con. When we face a difficult issue, we weigh the arguments for and against. We may lean to one side, but then we listen to those who disagree. We often find that there is something to be said for the other side. Sometimes, we have to weigh three or more different positions. Ideally, after giving due weight to opposing views, we reach a balanced conclusion. When we give others the benefit of the doubt, we don't make up our minds ignoring crucial facts or dismissing valid objections.

Writing that weighs different points of view invites the reader to share in an intellectual journey. Writer and reader together embark on a journey of discovery. They look at conflicting evidence together, trying to sort it out and make sense of it. Ideally, writer and reader will arrive at the same or similar conclusion. Readers then do not have to feel that they were taken advantage of or manipulated. When we listen to dissenting voices, fair-minded readers cannot accuse us of being one-sided, of having a closed mind.

Triggering

Get involved in issues on which reasonable, fair-minded readers will disagree.

Many people's minds are set on controversial subjects. They may voice their opinions confidently, sometimes at the top of their voice. However many other people are genuinely challenged by issues where there is something to be said on both sides. Here are some issues that you may want to ask your readers to think about:

- Traditionally, Americans have prided themselves on their opposition to censorship. However, we encounter situations that test our commitment to constitutional guarantees of freedom of speech. How serious a problem is hate speech on campus or hate literature on the Internet? Do we have to protect hate literature circulated by "Aryan" groups? Do we have to tolerate rap songs endorsing the killing of cops or violence against women? Should we defend provocative modern art that seems blasphemous to religious groups?

- Most Americans endorse equal educational opportunity. However, what happens when students reach college age whose previous schooling has been hampered by poverty, a violent environment, and substandard schools? What if they come from schools with much turnover among burnt-out teachers and no money for up-to-date textbooks or enrichment programs? Do we apply the same admission standards to them as to those who had the benefit of well-funded schools, tutoring programs for those falling behind, and much coaching for today's "high-stakes" tests?

- Traditionally, Americans have prided themselves on freedom of choice. If someone continues to smoke in spite of health warnings, is that the person's choice? However, nonsmokers who inhale secondary smoke in offices, restaurants, or airplanes did not make that choice. Do smokers have rights, and how do we balance them off with those of nonsmokers?

Gathering

Give the other side or opposing points of view equal time.
As with any other substantial paper or even more so, input has to come before output. You need to explore the issue—listening, reading, and taking notes. Develop the mental habit that will help you profit from the play of differing points of view:

- *Learn to listen to people even if at first you think they are wrong.* Resist the impulse to say that their position is ridiculous or "ludicrous" and that your own position is obvious to informed people of good will. What are others actually saying? Why do they disagree with you? What do they know that you don't know? What do they value that you may have disregarded?

- *Try playing the devil's advocate.* To come to know an opposing view from the inside, try to present your opponents' position as if you were on their side.

■ *Look for the informed impartial observer.* Listen to some voices that do *not* represent opposing factions. Is there someone who is knowledgeable but above the fray? Can you find someone who might care but not have an axe to grind? Much of what you encounter will be "facts" and arguments presented by interested parties or by PR people promoting an agenda. Who might be unbiased and yet be in a position to know?

The following file of entries shows a promising mix of sources for a projected paper examining the pros and cons of large-scale reliance on cheap immigrant labor.

Reformers Target Immigration

SOURCE 1
Websites of groups advocating "immigration reform" have started to re-fer to "European Americans" and the "values of European civilization."

SOURCE 2
Opponents of increasing immigration question the need of the American economy for large numbers of low-paid immigrant workers. **In a letter sent to the Op-ed page of a large metropolitan newspaper, the correspondent said,** "As for farm work, such as picking crops, we will put the engineers back to work designing modern-day equipment to handle this chore, and with all this high technology available, it would be a simple thing to replace the migrants."

SOURCE 3
Joe Rodriguez is a columnist in a state employing large numbers of mi-grant workers in agricultural areas like the San Joaquin Valley or the Salinas Valley. He writes, "Mechanized farming can reduce agriculture's dependence on imported farmhands. But domestic service, not agriculture is the largest employer of illegal immigrants. Until scientists invent an android nanny or gardener, the mechanization of low-wage labor won't dent the problem. But Americans can't retire with the quality of life they expect without large num-bers of immigrant workers to pay for it."

SOURCE 4
A new report from the Census Bureau points out that as our country ap-proaches 300 million people, whites are aging rapidly while Latinos and Asians, who are the fastest growing groups primarily through immigration, are generally younger. The median age of whites is nearly 40. It is 34 for Asians, 31 for blacks, and 27 for Latinos.

SOURCE 5
William Frey, a demographer at the Brookings Institution in Washington, predicts that immigrant Latinos and Asians will replenish the workforce. . . .

The children and grandchildren of immigrants will no longer settle for the low-end jobs or grunt jobs that their parents took without complaint. They will be better educated. They will be working better jobs enabling them to contribute to Social Security and private retirement funds.

Shaping

To organize your material, line up differing views clearly in your mind.

As with other kinds of papers, there is no standard formula for writing a pro-and-con paper. Line up pro and con arguments in two separate facing columns. Preparing these two contrasting lists will help clarify the issue for you. It will be a big step toward structuring your paper.

Here is a tentative lining up of the pro and con on the issue of drug testing on the job: As a condition of employment, should people in sensitive occupations agree to submit to unannounced testing for illegal drugs? Or is unreliable and often contested drug testing an intrusion?

Are You Testing Positive?

PRO	CON
Pilots, engineers, and operators of heavy equipment literally take others' lives into their hands.	The "war on drugs" makes no distinction between recreational drug users and addicts.
Drug users are responsible for absenteeism, low productivity, and high injury rates on the job.	The tests are notoriously inaccurate (sesame seeds cause false positives) and ruin the careers of people falsely accused.
"Recreational" drug users support a lethal drug trade responsible for unprecedented levels of crime.	Employers become agents of a police state, poisoning employer-employee relations.
Drug users in prestigious occupations are the worst possible role models for endangered American youth.	Drug testing undermines basic American traditions of due process and protection against self-incrimination.
Testing is above-board and better than snooping and spying.	We already have too much government meddling in people's private lives.

By looking at what points you have on each side of the issue, you can decide what organizational strategy might be more effective.

PARALLEL ORDER *You may decide to present the position of each side in its entirety.* You present and explain major arguments on one side first, and then you look at those on the opposing side. This way the inner logic of each opposing position might become clear. Your readers would first see how major planks in the first of the opposing positions are related, how they fit together. They then see the logic of the different or opposing points of view. If each time you can cover similar points in roughly the same order, your reader can see the contrast between differing ideas or courses of action.

POINT-BY-POINT ORDER *You may decide to present the pro and con point by point.* You present one argument on one side at one time—and then immediately show what the other side would say in return. This way your readers can share in the excitement of the debate. They can become involved in the give-and-take of statement and counterstatement—of assertion and rebuttal.

Revising

Use your revision to make your paper a balanced weighing of the alternatives.

Although you have checked out conflicting opinions and opposing views, your early draft may still be one-sided. It may be too aggressive or polemical—pushing your own side of the argument while giving only a nod to the other. Do the following to make your paper read more like a true weighing of the options:

- *Apply the equal time rule.* Your treatment of an opposing side may be too brief—or too biased. Are you giving the arguments for the other side roughly as much space as the arguments against?

- *Lower the emotional thermostat.* Use your revision to tone down heated statements—to make your treatment more objective, more balanced. A sentence like "Again our First Amendment rights are encroached upon, ignored, and violated by the pro-censorship forces" is not likely to make the other side listen to your arguments. (It may merely make them angry.)

- *Edit out outright invective or abuse.* Check for terms like *extremists, lunatic fringe, loco left, baby killers, gun nuts, femlibbers.* If such labels appear in your paper, show that you are merely quoting them and that they are not yours.

The following are questions for peer reviews of a pro and con paper:

PEER REVIEW

Weighing Your Options

author_____   reviewer_____

Write a *review critique* addressing most or all of the following questions. Take prewriting notes on a separate sheet of paper. Do not write on the student's paper.

1 Is the introduction effective? What does the writer do to bring the issue into focus and to bring it to life?

2 Does the paper have a thesis or initial overview? Does it alert you to the author's intention or agenda? What does it say? Does it set directions or suggest a plan for the paper as a whole?

3 How well does the writer present the alternatives or the pro and con? Has the writer listened to "the other side"? Do opposing views or alternative views seem to get a fair hearing or "equal time"?

4 Can you line up opposing arguments or major options? Can you briefly summarize the arguments or major points weighed in the paper?

5 What supporting material does the author use? What is the range or mix of material? Does it seem reliable, informative, or convincing?

6 Has the writer tried to reach a balanced conclusion? Are there signs of an emerging consensus? If not, why not?

7 Are you a good audience for this paper? Why or why not? Did you learn something here or change your mind? Who would be the ideal reader?

A Paper for Peer Review

Study the following sample student paper. How successful is it? Does it make you see that there is more than one side to the question it raises? How good a model does it make?

Saving the Trees

While in high school, I watched a movie on endangered animals called, *Say Goodbye*. The narrator stated, "In nature, each creature takes only what it needs to survive." For most nonhuman creatures, this is true. However, humans have tended to deplete the earth's resources beyond what they truly need. This is the issue in the arguments over whether loggers should be allowed to cut old-growth forests. Should these old-growth forests be sacrificed for human needs? **Only strong public support for conservation and for alternatives to current logging practices will save the trees.**
————————>>>>>>>>>>>>>>>>

(This **introduction** raises the issue of the destructive exploitation of our natural resources and leads into a **thesis** highlighting the search for alternatives.)

Those that argue that old-growth forest logging should be banned have strong arguments. For some, these forests are a spiritual place. An article in *BusinessWeek* said that in the California Lost Coast the redwoods serve as a home to a monastery. Mother Myriam explained, "We came to this place to turn ourselves toward God. God is not just a spirit within but is also in nature. Nature is a gift to be respected, not exploited." Even the owner of a local construction company opposed clear cutting and said, "That a tree is big and old doesn't mean it should be cut." ——————>>>>>>>>>>>>>>>>

(The second paragraph starts with a **transition** signaling that the pro side will come first, and it then presents the first argument supporting restrictions.)

Perhaps these old trees are even more special than younger ones. Many animals reside only in old-growth forests. The most famous example was the spotted owl, which faced extinction if the loggers removed their homes. In a *U.S. News & World Report* article, "A War in an Ancient Forest," Michael Satchell, described the Tongass National Forest and the adjoining coastal waters as teeming with "bald eagles, seabirds, grizzly bears, wolves, humpback whales, and migrating salmon. The Tongass is one of the world's most diverse and fecund ecosystems." Indeed, forests are homes to many different species of animals and plants. The older trees play a vital role in this delicate ecosystem. ——————>>>>>>>>>>>>>>>

(This paragraph presents the second major point on the pro side, supporting it with a look at the Tongass forest as a **test case**.)

Some environmental activists view the whole world as a delicate ecosystem. The Earth First! organization taught that we must place the "Earth first

in all decisions, even ahead of human welfare if necessary." The preservation of wilderness was their fundamental goal. Activists argue that the environment as a whole is more important than human welfare.
——————————>>>>>>>>>>>>>>>>

(The above paragraph goes beyond the limited example of one ecosystem to the larger environmentalist view.)

Those who oppose the ban on logging argue that thousands of jobs will be lost. These loggers have been logging all their lives and do not have another trade to fall back on. Many of these loggers have families to support. Why should human families suffer for the sake of "a few old trees"? The logging industry does not just provide jobs for those operating the chainsaws but provides employment in the lumber mills and many supporting trades.
——————————>>>>>>>>>>>>>>>>

(At this **turning point** of the paper, a strong transition takes the readers to the other side of the argument.)

The logging industry provides the wood that supplies the construction industry and furniture manufacturing. These industries are less vulnerable than others to job loss from outsourcing manufacturing to foreign countries. Modern technology has given us the means to use plants for our purposes, and as humans we may shape them however we like. Therefore, the trees are here for us to do with as we see fit. Humans need timber for shelter and for many other purposes—trees can grow back. ——————————>>>>>>>>>>>>>>>>

(The above paragraph takes the argument on "the other side" from the regional economy to the larger national economy.)

In addition, many of the logging companies have legal, binding contracts that allow them to cut the trees. Often the legal arrangements are worked out between private owners, the industry, and government agencies.
——————————>>>>>>>>>>>>>>>>

(This final paragraph on the other side reminds readers that conflicts like these are often decided in courts of law rather than in the court of public opinion.)

In the end, the loggers may be doomed even if they are allowed to clear cut the old-growth forests. Peter H. Raven, the author of a book on the environment, predicted that at current rates of logging, "all of the old-growth forest would disappear within 20 years." The loggers will be forced to find new jobs or focus on tree-harvesting as opposed to clear cutting old-growth forests.

Long-term solutions to the logging problem include retraining many loggers in a different field of work, perhaps one that will help to preserve the environment. Public opinion and government regulation will force more lumber companies to practice tree-harvesting. Tree-harvesting is similar to running a tree farm, where the trees are grown especially for lumber. In the movie I saw in my high school years, the most powerful line was "Share, or say goodbye."

YOUR TURN

1   How and how well does the student writer set up the issue?

2   Do you think both sides are fairly represented in this paper?

3   Can you draw up a con-and-pro listing of the major points on each side?

4   Do you think the writer's conclusion points the way toward a balanced, rational solution? Why or why not?

Writing Options 8: Weighing Alternatives

1   Are efforts to bring back predators like coyotes, wolves, mountain cats, or grizzlies misguided? What are the arguments on either side? Which side do you think has the better arguments?

2   When laws deny driver's licences to illegal immigrant workers, are we making the roads unsafe? Should we force illegals to drive unlicensed, untested, and uninsured? What are possible alternatives?

3   Are "activist" judges justified in banning school prayer? Do they have the right to ban invocations at ceremonies at public colleges or universities?

4   Should colleges enforce speech codes aimed at controlling hate speech or offensive language? What are the arguments pro and con?

5   Should colleges have special admission standards for members of minorities? Should they modify or lower their requirements for special groups?

6   Should public funds be used to support art that is offensive to the majority?

7   Convicts, male and female, in the nation's jails are doing hard time as the result of having been led into committing an illegal act by an undercover agent. Are you in favor of sting operations, or do they constitute entrapment?

8   Should anything be done to stem escalating violence in movies or television programs? Or should anything be done to restrict video games featuring extreme violence?

9   Do public figures have a right to privacy? Are there limits to the public's right to know? Or are the private lives and past histories of public servants or political candidates fair game for the news media?

10 Advice columns in newspapers debate the merits of staying in a troubled marriage or terminating it. To judge from what you have seen or read, what is preferable—a problem marriage or a divorce?

11 Should bookstores remove from their shelves magazines or calendars criticized as being sexist or exploitative of women?

9

LANGUAGE
Bond or Barrier?

FRIDAY, JULY 23, 2004

415-777-1111   46 CENTS   PLUS TAX

'We do believe both presidents could have done more.'

U.S. safer – but not safe, 9/11 commission says

WWW.MERCURYNEWS.COM

THE SEPT. 11 INVESTIGATION

JULY 23, 2004 | FRIDAY
THE NEWSPAPER OF SILICON VALLEY

Panel's searing look at government failure

REPORT TRACES TERRORISM CATASTROPHE

HEADLINES: SPINNING THE NEWS

As the datelines indicate, the contrasting headlines reproduced here are from newspapers published on the same day. The news stories they head-lined were the same: Both reported on the identical newsworthy event. A congressional panel with members from both major parties had been inves-tigating alleged breakdowns in intelligence gathering and prevention of ter-rorist attacks. The panel had just published a second voluminous report of its findings.

Reading the Image

1   What is the basic *contrast* between the front-page headlines repro-duced here? What makes one more reassuring and the other more alarming? Papers with these contrasting headlines were on sale on newspaper racks next to each other. If you wanted to buy only one morning paper, which would you have bought?

2   How aware are you of the *spin* that news sources give to current events? On controversial subjects, do you tend to look for news sources that give a positive spin to the news? Or do you look for information that does not gloss over disturbing facts? Are you suspi-cious of news sources that use scare tactics to influence the reader or viewer?

3   Do you consider yourself an alert *critical reader* or an easy mark for those who know how to sway the audience? Do you ever feel satis-faction when something you considered fake or misleading is exposed and you can say: "I told you so"?

4   Is it true that many Americans track important current events mostly through *headlines?* Do you ever get the gist of the news from head-lines without reading all or most of the article? Do you think loyal newspaper readers go on to finish reading important articles contin-ued on the back pages?

5   Is it true that Americans increasingly depend for news coverage on one major *limited source?* Has your community or city become a one-newspaper town? Working along or with a group, can you still collect contrasting headlines giving a different spin to the same events or the identical issues?

9

LANGUAGE
Bond or Barrier?

**Languages are far-reaching realities. They go far
beyond those political and historical structures we call
nations.**

—OCTAVIO PAZ

Many of the readings in this chapter raise a crucial question about language: Is it a blessing or too often a curse in relationships between individuals or groups? Does it more often help human beings bond with others—helping them understand one another and work together? Or does it more often serve to divide or antagonize us, stirring up passions or reinforcing prejudice? In our modern society, does it provide a forum for the honest sharing of information? Or is it too easy for the wealthy and powerful to use language as an instrument for manipulating and taking advantage of the public?

Language gives us more than neutral information of the kind that could be stored in a computer or recited by a computerized voice. Words do not just give directions ("This way to the center of the city"). They also tell us something about the speaker—as if a telephone while carrying a message were to tell us whether it liked what the message said. *Bureaucrat, labor leader, politician, welfare mother, activist,* and *woman driver* are not neutral informative labels like *detergent* or *soap.* They give vent to the speaker's feelings or serve the speaker's intentions. They carry messages of support, dislike, or antagonism.

We like to think of language as a bond. It helps people to break out of their isolation, to break down the wall of separateness. In the prehistoric past, language enabled human beings to band together, to make plans, to coordinate their efforts. Language enables us to offer other human beings help and comfort. ("Be of good cheer; we will not abandon you" is chalked on a message board held up on a rescue vessel to comfort the people on a shipwrecked ship in one of Walt Whitman's poems.) However, language also carries messages of rejection, condescension, or contempt, as with words like *stud, punk, foreigner, wetback, greaser, cracker,* and racial or ethnic slurs too ugly to mention. Language often reinforces divisions; it serves to outgroup people who are "not one of us." Language is a medium of love and affection, but it is also the medium of quarrels, of hate speech, and of incitement to violence.

Many people in our modern world have been suspicious of language—wary of its potential for abuse. They warn of Big Brother governments and dominant ideologies that try to channel our thinking by limiting us to approved uses of language. Others have maintained their faith in the capacity of language to help human beings communicate. The critic Margaret Laurence said about the Nigerian novelist Chinua Achebe, author of *Things Fall Apart,*

> In lbo villages, the men working on their farm plots in the midst of the rain forest often shout to one another—a reassurance, to make certain the other is still there, on the next cultivated patch, on the other side of the thick undergrowth. The writing of Chinua Achebe is like this. It seeks to send human voices through thickets of our separateness.

TALK IN THE INTIMATE RELATIONSHIP: HIS AND HERS

Deborah Tannen

"Male-female conversation is cross-cultural communication."

Deborah Tannen is a language scholar who says her marriage broke up because of a classic breakdown in communication: She employed a literal style, trying to say exactly what she meant, whereas her husband used the indirect style of people who hint at what they want and expect other people to pick up the hints.

Tannen, who studied at Berkeley under linguists focusing on language as an interactive social medium, reached a large public with two books on the undercurrents and hidden messages in how people talk: You Just Don't Understand: Women and Men in Conversation *and* That's Not What I Meant: How Conversational Style Makes or Breaks Relationships *(1986). Her focus is on the metamessages we send—the messages that go beyond what we say outright. Literal-minded people miss much of the subtext of communication—what lies below surface meanings. The mere fact that people bother to talk to us already sends a message (they care enough to give us some of their time), just as their refusal to talk to us also sends a message.*

Tannen's later book is Talking from 9 to 5 *(1994), on the role of language in the workplace. A reviewer of the book said that much of the secret of her success is "that she is writing about the single most common social activity in the world; everyone talks, although not everyone reads, writes, or reasons." Dr. Tannen's scholarly essays have been collected in* Gender and Discourse, *published by Oxford University Press.*

Thought Starters: Is it true that as far as language goes, boys and girls "grow up in different worlds"? Is a conversation between a man and a woman truly "cross-cultural" communication?

Male-female conversation is cross-cultural communication. Culture is [1] simply a network of habits and patterns gleaned from past experience, and women and men have different past experiences. From the time they're born, they're treated differently, talked to differently, and talk differently as a result. Boys and girls grow up in different worlds, even if they grow up in the same house. And as adults they travel in different worlds, reinforcing patterns established in childhood. These cultural differences include different expectations about the role of talk in relationships and how it fulfills that role.

Everyone knows that as a relationship becomes long-term, its terms change. But women and men often differ in how they expect them to change. Many women feel, "After all this time, you should know what I want without my telling you." Many men feel, "After all this time, we should be able to tell each other what we want."

These incongruent expectations capture one of the key differences between men and women. Communication is always a matter of balancing conflicting needs for involvement and independence. Though everyone has both these needs, women often have a relatively greater need for involvement, and men a relatively greater need for independence. Being understood without saying what you mean gives a payoff in involvement, and that is why women value it so highly.

If you want to be understood without saying what you mean explicitly in words, you must convey meaning somewhere else—in how words are spoken, or by metamessages. Thus it stands to reason that women are often more attuned than men to the metamessages of talk. When women surmise meaning in this way, it seems mysterious to men, who call it "women's intuition" (if they think it's right) or "reading things in" (if they think it's wrong). Indeed, it could be wrong, since metamessages are not on record. And even if it is right, there is still the question of scale: How significant are the metamessages that are there?

Metamessages are a form of indirectness. Women are more likely to   5
be indirect, and to try to reach agreement by negotiation. Another way to understand this preference is that negotiation allows a display of solidarity, which women prefer to the display of power (even though the aim may be the same—getting what you want). Unfortunately, power and solidarity are bought with the same currency: Ways of talking intended to create solidarity have the simultaneous effect of framing power differences. When they think they're being nice, women often end up appearing deferential and unsure of themselves or of what they want.

When styles differ, misunderstandings are always rife. As their differing styles create misunderstandings, women and men try to clear them up by talking things out. These pitfalls are compounded in talks between men and women because they have different ways of going about talking things out, and different assumptions about the significance of going about it.

Sylvia and Harry celebrated their fiftieth wedding anniversary at a mountain resort. Some of the guests were at the resort for the whole weekend, others just for the evening of the celebration: a cocktail party followed by a sit-down dinner. The manager of the dining room approached Sylvia during dinner. "Since there's so much food tonight," he said, "and the hotel prepared a fancy dessert and everyone already ate at the cocktail party anyway, how about cutting and serving the anniversary cake at lunch tomorrow?" Sylvia asked the advice of the others at her table. All the men agreed: "Sure, that makes sense. Save the cake for tomorrow." All the women disagreed: "No, the party is tonight. Serve the cake tonight." The men were focusing on the message: the cake as food. The women were thinking of the metamessage: Serving a special cake frames an occasion as a celebration.

Why are women more attuned to metamessages? Because they are more focused on involvement, that is, on relationships among people, and it is through metamessages that relationships among people are established and maintained. If you want to take the temperature and check the vital signs of a relationship, the barometers to check are its metamessages: what is said and how.

Everyone can see these signals, but whether or not we pay attention to them is another matter—a matter of being sensitized. Once you are sensitized, you can't roll your antennae back in; they're stuck in the extended position.

When interpreting meaning, it is possible to pick up signals that 10 weren't intentionally sent out, like an innocent flock of birds on a radar screen. The birds are there—and the signals women pick up are there—but they may not mean what the interpreter thinks they mean. For example, Maryellen looks at Larry and asks, "What's wrong?" because his brow is furrowed. Since he was only thinking about lunch, her expression of concern makes him feel under scrutiny.

The difference in focus on messages and metamessages can give men and women different points of view on almost any comment. Harriet complains to Morton, "Why don't you ask me how my day was?" He replies, "If you have something to tell me, tell me. Why do you have to be invited?" The reason is that she wants the metamessage of interest: evidence that he cares how her day was, regardless of whether or not she has something to tell.

A lot of trouble is caused between women and men by, of all things, pronouns. Women often feel hurt when their partners use "I" or "me" in a situation in which they would use "we" or "us." When Morton announces, "I think I'll go for a walk," Harriet feels specifically uninvited, though Morton later claims she would have been welcome to join him. She felt locked out by his use of "I" and his omission of an invitation: "Would you like to come?" Metamessages can be seen in what is not said as well as what is said.

It's difficult to straighten out such misunderstandings because each one feels convinced of the logic of his or her position and the illogic—or irresponsibility—of the other's. Harriet knows that she always asks Morton how his day was, and that she'd never announce, "I'm going for a walk," without inviting him to join her. If he talks differently to her, it must be that he feels differently. But Morton wouldn't feel unloved if Harriet didn't ask about his day, and he would feel free to ask, "Can I come along?," if she announced she was taking a walk. So he can't believe she is justified in feeling responses he knows he wouldn't have.

These processes are dramatized with chilling yet absurdly amusing authenticity in Jules Feiffer's play *Grown Ups*. To get a closer look at what happens when men and women focus on different levels of talk in talking things out, let's look at what happens in this play.

Jake criticizes Louise for not responding when their daughter, Edie,   *15*
called her. His comment leads to a fight even though they're both aware
that this one incident is not in itself important.

Jake: Look, I don't care if it's important or not, when a kid calls its
mother the mother should answer.
Louise: Now I'm a bad mother.
Jake: I didn't say that.
Louise: It's in your stare.
Jake: Is that another thing you know? My stare?

Louise ignores Jake's message—the question of whether or not she
responded when Edie called—and goes for the metamessage: his implication that she's a bad mother, which Jake insistently disclaims. When Louise
explains the signals she's reacting to, Jake not only discounts them but is an-
gered at being held accountable not for what he said but for how he
looked—his stare.

As the play goes on, Jake and Louise replay and intensify these
patterns:

Louise: If I'm such a terrible mother, do you want a divorce?
Jake: I do not think you're a terrible mother and no, thank you, I do
not want a divorce. Why is it that whenever I bring up any difference between us you ask me if I want a divorce?

The more he denies any meaning beyond the message, the more she
blows it up, the more adamantly he denies it, and so on:

Jake: I have brought up one thing that you do with Edie that I don't
think you notice that I have noticed for some time but which I have deliberately not brought up before because I had hoped you would notice it for
yourself and stop doing it and also—frankly, baby, I have to say this—I
knew if I brought it up we'd get into exactly the kind of circular argument
we're in right now. And I wanted to avoid it. But I haven't and we're in it,
so now, with your permission, I'd like to talk about it.
Louise: You don't see how that puts me down?
Jake: What?
Louise: If you think I'm so stupid why do you go on living with me?
Jake: Dammit! Why can't anything ever be simple around here?!

It can't be simple because Louise and Jake are responding to different
levels of communication. As in Bateson's example of the dual-control electric blanket with crossed wires, each one intensifies the energy going to a
different aspect of the problem. Jake tries to clarify his point by overelabo-
rating it, which gives Louise further evidence that he's condescending to
her, making it even less likely that she will address his point rather than his
condescension.

What pushes Jake and Louise beyond anger to rage is their different perspectives on metamessages. His refusal to admit that his statements have implications and overtones denies her authority over her own feelings. Her attempts to interpret what he didn't say and put the metamessage into the message makes him feel she's putting words into his mouth—denying his authority over his own meaning.

The same thing happens when Louise tells Jake that he is being manipulated by Edie:

Louise: Why don't you ever make her come to see you? Why do you always go to her?

Jake: You want me to play power games with a nine year old? I want her to know I'm interested in her. Someone around here has to show interest in her.

Louise: You love her more than I do.

Jake: I didn't say that.

Louise: Yes, you did.

Jake: You don't know how to listen. You have never learned how to listen. It's as if listening to you is a foreign language.

Again, Louise responds to his implication—this time, that he loves Edie more because he runs when she calls. And yet again, Jake cries literal meaning, denying he meant any more than he said.

Throughout their argument, the point to Louise is her feelings—that Jake makes her feel put down—but to him the point is her actions—that she doesn't always respond when Edie calls:

Louise: You talk about what I do to Edie, what do you think you do to me?

Jake: This is not the time to go into what we do to each other.

Since she will talk only about the metamessage, and he will talk only about the message, neither can get satisfaction from their talk, and they end up where they started—only angrier:

Jake: That's not the point!

Louise: It's *my* point.

Jake: It's hopeless!

Louise: Then get a divorce.

American conventional wisdom (and many of our parents and English teachers) tell us that meaning is conveyed by words, so men who tend to be literal about words are supported by conventional wisdom. They may not simply deny but actually miss the cues that are sent by how words are spoken. If they sense something about it, they may nonetheless discount what they sense. After all, it wasn't said. Sometimes that's a dodge—a plausible defense rather than a gut feeling. But sometimes it is a sincere conviction. Women are also likely to doubt the reality of what they sense. If they don't doubt it in their guts, they nonetheless may lack the arguments to support their position and thus are reduced to repeating, "You said it. You did so." Knowing that metamessages are a real and fundamental part of communication makes it easier to understand and justify what they feel.

An article in a popular newspaper reports that one of the five most *20* common complaints of wives about their husbands is "He doesn't listen to me anymore." Another is "He doesn't talk to me anymore." Political scientist Andrew Hacker noted that lack of communication, while high on women's lists of reasons for divorce, is much less often mentioned by men. Since couples are parties to the same conversations, why are women more dissatisfied with them than men? Because what they expect is different, as well as what they see as the significance of talk itself.

First, let's consider the complaint "He doesn't talk to me."

One of the most common stereotypes of American men is the strong silent type. Jack Kroll, writing about Henry Fonda on the occasion of his death, used the phrases "quiet power," "abashed silences," "combustible catatonia," and "sense of power held in check." He explained that Fonda's goal was not to let anyone see "the wheels go around," not to let the "machinery" show. According to Kroll, the resulting silence was effective on stage but devastating to Fonda's family.

The image of a silent father is common and is often the model for the lover or husband. But what attracts us can become flypaper to which we are unhappily stuck. Many women find the strong silent type to be a lure as a lover but a lug as a husband. Nancy Schoenberger begins a poem with the lines "It was your silence that hooked me, so like my father's." Adrienne Rich refers in a poem to the "husband who is frustratingly mute." Despite the initial attraction of such quintessentially male silence, it may begin to feel, to a woman in a long-term relationship, like a brick wall against which she is banging her head.

In addition to these images of male and female behavior—both the result and the cause of them—are differences in how women and men view the role of talk in relationships as well as how talk accomplishes its purpose. These differences have their roots in the settings in which men and women learn to have conversations: among their peers, growing up.

Children whose parents have foreign accents don't speak with accents. *25* They learn to talk like their peers. Little girls and little boys learn how to have conversations as they learn how to pronounce words: from their playmates. Between the ages of five and fifteen, when children are learning to have conversations, they play mostly with friends of their own sex. So it's not surprising that they learn different ways of having and using conversations.

Anthropologists Daniel Maltz and Ruth Borker point out that boys and girls socialize differently. Little girls tend to play in small groups or, even more common, in pairs. Their social life usually centers around a best friend, and friendships are made, maintained, and broken by talk—especially "secrets." If a little girl tells her friend's secret to another little girl, she may find herself with a new best friend. The secrets themselves may or may not be important, but the fact of telling them is all-important. It's hard for newcomers to get into these tight groups, but anyone who is admitted is treated as an equal. Girls like to play cooperatively; if they can't cooperate, the group breaks up.

Little boys tend to play in larger groups, often outdoors, and they spend more time doing things than talking. It's easy for boys to get into the group, but not everyone is accepted as an equal. Once in the group, boys must jockey for their status in it. One of the most important ways they do this is through talk: verbal display such as telling stories and jokes, challenging and sidetracking the verbal displays of other boys, and withstanding other boys' challenges in order to maintain their own story—and status. Their talk is often competitive talk about who is best at what.

Feiffer's play is ironically named *Grown Ups* because adult men and women struggling to communicate often sound like children: "You said so!" "I did not!" The reason is that when they grow up, women and men keep the divergent attitudes and habits they learned as children—which they don't recognize as attitudes and habits but simply take for granted as ways of talking.

Women want their partners to be a new and improved version of a best friend. This gives them a soft spot for men who tell them secrets. As Jack Nicholson once advised a guy in a movie: "Tell her about your troubled childhood—that always get 'em." Men expect to *do* things together and don't feel anything is missing if they don't have heart-to-heart talks all the time.

If they do have heart-to-heart talks, the meaning of those talks may be 30 opposite for men and women. To many women, the relationship is working as long as they can talk things out. To many men, the relationship isn't working out if they have to keep working it over. If she keeps trying to get talks going to save the relationship, and he keeps trying to avoid them because he sees them as weakening it, then each one's efforts to preserve the relationship appear to the other as reckless endangerment.

If talks (of any kind) do get going, men's and women's ideas about how to conduct them may be very different. For example, Dora is feeling comfortable and close to Tom. She settles into a chair after dinner and begins to tell him about a problem at work. She expects him to ask questions to show he's interested; reassure her that he understands and that what she feels is normal; and return the intimacy by telling her a problem of his. Instead, Tom sidetracks her story, cracks jokes about it, questions her interpretation of the problem, and gives her advice about how to solve it and avoid such problems in the future.

All of these responses, natural to men, are unexpected to women, who interpret them in terms of their own habits—negatively. When Tom comments on side issues or cracks jokes, Dora thinks he doesn't care about what she's saying and isn't really listening. If he challenges her reading of what went on, she feels he is criticizing her and telling her she's crazy, when what she wants is to be reassured that she's not. If he tells her how to solve the problem, it makes her feel as if she's the patient to his doctor—a metamessage of condescension, echoing male one-upmanship compared to the female etiquette of equality. Because he doesn't volunteer information about his problems, she feels he's implying he doesn't have any.

His way of responding to her bid for intimacy makes her feel distant from him. She tries harder to regain intimacy the only way she knows how—by revealing more and more about herself. He tries harder by giving more insistent advice. The more problems she exposes, the more incompetent she feels, until they both see her as emotionally draining and problem-ridden. When his efforts to help aren't appreciated, he wonders why she asks for his advice if she doesn't want to take it. . . .

When women talk about what seems obviously interesting to them, their conversations often include reports of conversations. Tone of voice, timing, intonation, and wording are all re-created in the telling in order to explain—dramatize, really—the experience that is being reported. If men tell about an incident and give a brief summary instead of re-creating what was said and how, the women often feel that the essence of the experience is being omitted. If the woman asks, "What exactly did he say?," and "How did he say it?," the man probably can't remember. If she continues to press him, he may feel as if he's being grilled.

All these different habits have repercussions when the man and the woman are talking about their relationship. He feels out of his element, even one down. She claims to recall exactly what he said, and what she said, and in what sequence, and she wants him to account for what he said. He can hardly account for it since he has forgotten exactly what was said—if not the whole conversation. She secretly suspects he's only pretending not to remember, and he secretly suspects that she's making up the details.

One woman reported such a problem as being a matter of her boyfriend's poor memory. It is unlikely, however, that his problem was poor memory in general. The question is what types of material each person remembers or forgets.

Frances was sitting at her kitchen table talking to Edward, when the toaster did something funny. Edward began to explain why it did it. Frances tried to pay attention, but very early in his explanation, she realized she was completely lost. She felt very stupid. And indications were that he thought so too.

Later that day they were taking a walk. He was telling her about a difficult situation in his office that involved a complex network of inter-relationships among a large number of people. Suddenly he stopped and said, "I'm sure you can't keep track of all these people." "Of course I can," she said, and she retraced his story with all the characters in place, all the details right. He was genuinely impressed. She felt very smart.

How could Frances be both smart and stupid? Did she have a good memory or a bad one? Frances's and Edward's abilities to follow, remember, and recount depended on the subject—and paralleled her parents' abilities

35

to follow and remember. Whenever Frances told her parents about people in her life, her mother could follow with no problem, but her father got lost as soon as she introduced a second character. "Now who was that?" he'd ask. "Your boss?" "No, my boss is Susan. This was my friend." Often he'd still be in the previous story. But whenever she told them about her work, it was her mother who would get lost as soon as she mentioned a second step: "That was your tech report?" "No, I handed my tech report in last month. This was a special project."

Frances's mother and father, like many other men and women, had honed their listening and remembering skills in different arenas. Their experience talking to other men and other women gave them practice in following different kinds of talk. 40

Knowing whether and how we are likely to report events later influences whether and how we pay attention when they happen. As women listen to and take part in conversations, knowing they may talk about them later makes them more likely to pay attention to exactly what is said and how. Since most men aren't in the habit of making such reports, they are less likely to pay much attention at the time. On the other hand, many women aren't in the habit of paying attention to scientific explanations and facts because they don't expect to have to perform in public by reciting them—just as those who aren't in the habit of entertaining others by telling jokes "can't" remember jokes they've heard, even though they listened carefully enough to enjoy them.

So women's conversations with their women friends keep them in training for talking about their relationships with men, but many men come to such conversations with no training at all—and an uncomfortable sense that this really isn't their event.

Most of us place enormous emphasis on the importance of a primary relationship. We regard the ability to maintain such relationships as a sign of mental health—our contemporary metaphor for being a good person.

Yet our expectations of such relationships are nearly—maybe in fact—impossible. When primary relationships are between women and men, male-female differences contribute to the impossibility. We expect partners to be both romantic interests and best friends. Though women and men may have fairly similar expectations for romantic interests, obscuring their differences when relationships begin, they have very different ideas about how to be friends, and these are the differences that mount over time.

In conversations between friends who are not lovers, small misunder- 45 standings can be passed over or diffused by breaks in contact. But in the context of a primary relationship, differences can't be ignored, and the pressure cooker of continued contact keeps both people stewing in the juice of accumulated minor misunderstandings. And stylistic differences are sure to cause misunderstandings—not, ironically, in matters such as sharing values and interests or understanding each other's philosophies of life. These large and significant yet palpable issues can be talked about and agreed on. It is far harder to achieve congruence—and much more surprising and trou-bling that it is hard—in the simple day-to-day matters of the automatic rhythms and nuances of talk. Nothing in our backgrounds or in the media (the present-day counterpart to religion or grandparents' teachings) pre-pares us for this failure. If two people share so much in terms of point of view and basic values, how can they continually get into fights about in-significant matters?

If you find yourself in such a situation and you don't know about dif-ferences in conversational style, you assume something's wrong with your partner, or you for having chosen your partner. At best, if you are forward thinking and generous minded, you may absolve individuals and blame the relationship. But if you know about differences in conversational style, you can accept that there are differences in habits and assumptions about how to have conversation, show interest, be considerate, and so on. You may not always correctly interpret your partner's intentions, but you will know that if you get a negative impression, it may not be what was intended—and neither are your responses unfounded. If he says he really is interested even though he doesn't seem to be, maybe you should believe what he says and not what you sense.

Sometimes explaining assumptions can help. If a man starts to tell a woman what to do to solve her problem, she may say, "Thanks for the ad-vice but I really don't want to be told what to do. I just want you to listen and say you understand." A man might want to explain, "If I challenge you, it's not to prove you wrong; it's just my way of paying attention to what you're telling me." Both may try either or both to modify their ways of talk-ing and to try to accept what the other does. The important thing is to know that what seem like bad intentions may really be good intentions ex-pressed in a different conversational style. We have to give up our convic-tion that, as Robin Lakoff put it, "Love means never having to say 'What do you mean?'"

The Responsive Reader

1 Tannen once said that readers of her work reported an "Aha!" response. They found that what they thought was their personal problem was ac-tually part of a larger pattern. Did you have an "Aha!" response to any part of this selection? Can you give examples from your own experience for the clashing assumptions or expectations that Tannen ascribes to men and women?

2 What are key examples that Tannen gives for the difficulties of commu-nication between men and women? How real or convincing do they seem to you? (How convincing are the examples from the Feiffer play?) Do you interpret the examples the same way she does?

3 How does Tannen explain how misunderstandings "intensify" or escalate?

4 How familiar are the stereotypes about males that Tannen claims are widespread in our culture and shape male behavior? How strong are they?

5 Is there hope for miscommunicating couples? What is the gist of the positive advice, explicit or implied, that Tannen would give to couples who have trouble communicating?

Talking, Listening, Writing

6 There is much debate over what is truly gender-specific in our culture. Do you think Tannen exaggerates the differences between the talking styles of the sexes? Where and how?

7 Tannen has challenged the feminist claim that men dominate women in conversation. Is it true that men tend to interrupt women, cutting them off or brushing off their opinions? Or are women right who claim that "men never talk"?

8 Have you ever rebelled against a style of talking expected of you? Have you ever found yourself using language that was not "you"? What was the occasion or situation? What was the problem? What was the outcome?

Collaborative Projects

9 Working alone or in a group, you may want to investigate the "women's language" of fashion sections or society pages or the "men's language" of the sports pages. Or you may want to work out significant contrasts between the two.

MEN AND WOMEN TALKING

Bernice Sandler

"Women's behavioral style—listening, clarifying and providing affirmative verbal and nonverbal feedback such as nodding—encourages others to speak and participate."

Pioneering studies in the eighties and nineties had highlighted the role of language in "making or breaking relationships." More recent studies have focused on the role of language in the workplace. What role do language differences between the genders play in competition for jobs and advancement? How do these patterns show in competition for leadership or influence? What role do language differences play in the public dialogue? How do gender differences affect the use of language in the classroom and more generally on campus?

Bernice Sandler, who became famous for her studies of the communication problems experienced by couples, moved on to the role of workplace language in her later book Talking from Nine To Five. *Like the educators who compiled the following research summary, she moved on from interaction in a private space to interaction in a public space. The following guide to gender-specific public uses of language has been condensed and adapted from* The Chilly Climate, *edited by Sandler, Silverberg, and Hall, and published by the National Association of Women in Education. The study here summarized focused on language patterns that work against women in education and the public sphere.*

Thought Starters: Many teachers encourage active student participation in the classroom. Do you speak up? Are you ever impatient when others talk? Do you interrupt other students? Do you think the way you talk in class or in the workplace reflects gender differences?

Numerous researchers have noticed that men and women use language and speech differently and that speech behavior is often interpreted and perceived differently according to gender. Research on speech helps us understand how people interact with each other, why certain forms of speech may silence women and others, and how women's tendency to use more tentative speech may be perceived as a lack of knowledge or commitment. However, like other research, most of the examinations of men's and women's speech have been conducted primarily on white people, so that we have little information about differences by race. The generalities in this section, as in others, may not apply to many women of color.

Here are some ways in which women and men may use speech differently:

Females generally learn to use speech for developing and maintaining relationships.

Many . . . females . . . demonstrate communication skills that promote linking. These women reach out, verbally and non-verbally, and make an effort to cultivate collegial relationships. They try to keep conversations going, add a thought, do the interaction work, nurture others and accommodate. In short, they want to connect. Many of the men, on the other hand, seem more preoccupied with trying to achieve personal rank. . . . They try to control by maneuvering conversations to topics in which they are interested and turning off topics they do not care for.

Thus women learn to give criticism in a helpful rather than competitive manner; they learn to interpret the speech of others. When they respond to another's comments, they often enlarge upon the person's ideas rather than challenge his or her assumptions. In contrast, males generally learn to use speech to express dominance in a competitive manner. They seek to attract and maintain an audience and to assert themselves when others have the floor. Men's speech is more likely to be direct and authoritative ("This room is hot."), while women's speech often seems indirect and tentative ("Is this room hot?" or "It's hot in here, isn't it?" or "Do you think it's hot in here?"). Persons who use "feminine" speech are typically perceived as less competent and less persuasive than those who use more "masculine" speech, whether the speaker is male or female.

Women are more likely to start conversations and keep them going; men are more likely to interrupt.

The conversational "rule" is that the more powerful can interrupt the less powerful. Women use more "minimal responses" such as "uh-huh," by which they mean "I'm listening to you," while men, who use them less, usually mean "I agree with what you are saying."

Women's speech is typically more tentative, polite, and deferential,

while men's speech generally is more assertive and definitive. Men are more likely to make declarative statements, while females make more qualifying and inquiring statements. The tentativeness of women's speech may be partly related to the power difference between men and women.

Women's speech is often hesitant,

characterized by false starts ("I was wondering . . ." or "I think . . .") and more likely to include qualifiers ("perhaps," "maybe," "somehow," "there is a possibility that in some instances . . ."). This, like other kinds of women's speech, can be an effort to include others and to encourage others to state their ideas.

Women's speech is generally more apologetic.

("I don't know if I ought to say this, but . . .") Women are also more likely to use tag questions, such as "It's cold in here, isn't it?" This may occur for a number of reasons, including power differences and the expectations of women's greater politeness. Women, like men, adapt to try to "fit in." Often the best way to do so is by not challenging, at least in speech patterns, stereotypes about appropriate behavior. Tag questions can be used to emphasize something in a "polite" and less assertive manner.

Women's voices are more likely to exhibit rising inflection at the end of a sentence.

Although there are regional differences and a possibly increasing tendency for many to "rise" at the end of a sentence, rising inflection may also reflect a sense of powerlessness, uncertainty, or seeking of agreement.

Women are more likely to use questions to maintain a conversation,

even if they know the answer. ("Is it cold in here?" or "Do you think the Revolution was caused by ——?") Men are more likely to answer questions and use them to obtain information. Although women are more likely to ask questions as a way of making a point, they may use them to avoid making a definitive statement, i.e., speaking in a "masculine" way. One of the authors of this report recalls how she spent her undergraduate years never making a definitive statement but always looking instead for the "clever" question to ask.

Men are more likely to control the topic of conversations.

In mixed gender interactions; women often defer to men's choices.

Women's verbal comments are often accompanied by non-verbal behaviors

such as smiling (sometimes seemingly inappropriately) or averting their eyes, especially when dealing with men or any person in authority.

Contrary to the myth that women talk more than men, **men speak more often than females in mixed gender interactions.**

Often faculty members are surprised to find, after an observer counts the times men and women speak, that men speak more, because this revelation contradicts their perception that women and men had been speaking equally. Usually women speak about one-third of the time. Should women speak more than that, they are typically perceived as rude, domineering, and aggressive. A male professor at a law school described what happened when he went out of his way to encourage women students to speak.

> I actually kept a journal on how long women and men spoke . . . and at the end of the year, women had spoken 40 – 45 percent of the time. . . When I asked the men, they said that the class was dominated by women [so] it was completely unfair. They thought women were speaking about 80 percent of the time.

Women and men may respond to disagreement differently, men being more likely to view verbal aggression as positive, except when women engage in it.

As mentioned earlier, men may use aggressive, challenging, critical, and argumentative behavior as a way to organize and maintain a conversation. Tannen and others have noted that men seem to enjoy controversy more and to perceive it as energizing and interesting. In contrast, many women may view such behavior as negative, unappealing, even distressing, and as aimed at them personally. The competitive organization of many of our classrooms may well have a differential effect on women and men students: men are more likely to consider such an environment demanding but positive; women may view the same environment as inhospitable and negative.

Men are more likely to use sports and military analogies,

which many women and some men may not understand. One of the authors of this report remembers her puzzlement when, during one of the Gulf War briefings, General Schwartzkopf referred to the Army's use of a "Hail Mary play." She wondered if the Army was engaging in religious activity, but knew that did not make sense. "Everyone" else seemed to know what the General meant, but to her it was as if he was speaking in a foreign tongue which others understood and she did not. She felt that asking about the meaning of the comment might expose her to ridicule.

Even when men and women speak in the same manner, they may be perceived as speaking differently. Women speaking in an assertive manner, sounding and acting knowledgeable, using clear and definitive speech, acting in a nonsubordinate manner, may be labeled "arrogant" or "bitchy," even though they may be speaking no differently than their assertive male peers. Faculty members and male and female students may be less comfortable with female students whose behavior does not fit their expectations of how female students should act.

Because of their discomfort, some faculty members may unknowingly withhold attention or praise from an assertive female student and not call on her. Many people experience discomfort with women who do not use the stereotyped softer, more polite, more deferential speech, describing them not only as "bitchy," but also as "castrating," "Iron Maiden," "Dragon Lady," "abrasive," and "unfeminine." The behaviors for which men are rewarded—speaking forcefully, taking a strong stand, actively participating—may be penalized when women engage in them.

No matter what style of communication a woman uses, whether assertive speech or the softer speech typically associated with women, it is likely to be devalued. Indeed, women who speak in the more "typical female" manner may be considered less knowledgeable, less confident, less able.

In the 1970s and 1980s, white women particularly were encouraged to change their speech by learning to speak "assertively," the assumption implicit in this recommendation is that the difficulties women faced were *within themselves*—characteristics to be remediated and changed. It is now apparent that institutions must also change, that women's ways of talking have value, and that *everyone* needs to know and be comfortable with various styles of speech and to choose a style to suit a particular situation.

Though often unnoticed, women's speech, like men's, has a value of its own. Women's behavioral style—listening, clarifying, and providing affirmative verbal and nonverbal feedback such as nodding—encourages others to speak and participate. Indeed there is a trend in management training to help supervisors engage in more collaborative and accommodating speech patterns, although the fact that women often speak this way is generally ignored in such discussions.

The Responsive Reader

1   Do any of the *generalizations* in this summary article have a special meaning for you? Identify three or four that make you say "This I have observed myself" or "This goes counter to my own experience." Provide examples or testimonies pro or con from your own experience or reading. For instance, in your experience has women's speech been generally more apologetic and hesitant? Do men maneuver conversations to topics they are interested in or concerned about?

2   Can you give *supporting examples* for the role of sports lingo and military talk in the way men talk? (Can you explain what a "Hail Mary play" is or what a "hat trick" is?) Do you think the male familiarity with sports talk and military talk hinders communication between the genders? Is it keeping women from becoming "part of the team" in business or other fields?

3   How would you sum up the basic gender gap in communication treated here in a short *capsule summary*? One student reader summarized the findings in this guide as follows: Females use communication skills for linking with each other and finding connections, whereas males use

communication for achieving higher personal rank. Men's speech is more "interruptive, assertive, and controlling." What would you highlight in your own capsule summary?

4 Instead of advising women to imitate men, recent studies have pointed to the *advantages* women have in interpersonal communication. Current statistics support claims that now more women hold intermediate management positions than men. Are women more likely than men to have the social skills and language skills required in working with people? Where does this summary report address this question? What experience or evidence can you cite to support or challenge these claims?

Talking, Listening, Writing

5 Promoters of assertiveness training for women encouraged them to speak more assertively in order to hold their own. Others countered that what was really needed was sensitivity training for men to make their communication styles less domineering. Still others stressed that what needs to change are the traditional patterns of talking and interacting in our institutions. Which of these three approaches do you think is most necessary or promising? How do you support your choice?

6 The article from the Women's Webpage at a California campus with a technology emphasis was intended to alert future teachers to "gender differentials" in language use. Do you think future teachers should be provided with this kind of guide? Do you think new students would profit from studying this guide during orientation to college life and college work?

Collaborative Projects

7 Students of group dynamics have often developed techniques for tracking and charting patterns of human interaction. You may want to work with a group of students charting patterns of language use in college classes, with permission of the instructors.

CULTURAL ETIQUETTE: A GUIDE

Amoja Three Rivers

"Cultural etiquette is intended for people of all 'races,' not necessarily just 'white' people, because no one living in Western society is exempt from the influences of racism, racial stereotypes, race and cultural prejudices."

The following guide to language etiquette first appeared in the fall of 1991, at a time of growing concern with the role of demeaning or hateful language in perpetuating prejudice and inciting violence. Media organizations, educational institutions, and government agencies were beginning to publish guidelines for avoiding racist and sexist language. In the years since, colleges, government agencies, and corporations have tried initiatives ranging from speech codes to sensitivity training to discourage hate speech or abusive and demeaning verbal behavior. At the same time, a backlash against "political correctness" or the "language police" was gathering momentum. Today, the aggressive, abrasive, or polemical style of the author of this guide to linguistic etiquette still raises the hackles of those who feel targeted by her charges and admonitions.

Ms. magazine published the article as part of a series on race and women. The editors called it a "creative attempt to shed some light—and levity—on the serious task of dispelling racial myths and stereotypes." The author is a co-founder of the Accessible African Herstory Project and was described by the editors of Ms. *as a "lecturer, herstorian, and craftswoman." Much of the article focuses on how language—ready-made phrases, loaded words—channel or distort our thinking. The article provides a guide to words that can short-circuit communication—make people see red. This article should make you think about the power of words to shape our thinking and our views of other people.*

Thought Starters: Whatever the color of their skin, people tend to be thin-skinned when they encounter words that they perceive to be slurs on their group, religion, or background. Do you encounter ways of talking about a group with which you identify that you find embarrassing or offensive?

Cultural Etiquette is intended for people of all "races," nationalities, and creeds, not necessarily just "white" people, because no one living in Western society is exempt from the influences of racism, racial stereotypes, race and cultural prejudices, and anti-Semitism. I include anti-Semitism in the discussion of racism because it is simply another manifestation of cultural and racial bigotry. 1

All people are people. It is ethnocentric to use a generic term such as "people" to refer only to white people and then racially label everyone else. This creates and reinforces the assumption that whites are the norm, the real people, and that all others are aberrations.

"Exotic," when applied to human beings, is ethnocentric and racist.

While it is true that most citizens of the U.S.A. are white, at least four fifths of the world's population consists of people of color. Therefore, it is statistically incorrect as well as ethnocentric to refer to us as minorities. The term "minority" is used to reinforce the idea of people of color as "other."

A cult is a particular system of religious worship. If the religious prac-   5
tices of the Yorubas constitute a cult, then so do those of the Methodists, Catholics, Episcopalians, and so forth.

A large radio/tape player is a boom-box, or a stereo or a box or a large metallic ham sandwich with speakers. It is not a "ghetto blaster."

Everybody can blush. Everybody can bruise. Everybody can tan and get sunburned. Everybody.

Judaism is no more patriarchal than any other patriarchal religion.

Koreans are not taking over. Neither are Jews. Neither are the Japanese. Neither are the West Indians. These are myths put out and maintained by the ones who really have.

All hair is "good" hair. Dreadlocks, locks, dreads, natty dreads, et   10
cetera, is an ancient traditional way that African people sometimes wear their hair. It is not braided, it is "locked." Locking is the natural tendency of African hair to knit and bond to itself. It locks by itself, we don't have to do anything to it to make it lock. It is permanent; once locked, it cannot come undone. It gets washed just as regularly as anyone else's hair. No, you may not touch it, don't ask.

One of the most effective and insidious aspects of racism is cultural genocide. Not only have African Americans been cut off from our African tribal roots, but because of generations of whites pitting African against Indian, and Indian against African, we have been cut off from our Native American roots as well. Consequently, most African Native Americans no longer have tribal affiliations, or know for certain what people they are from.

Columbus didn't discover diddly-squat.

Slavery is not a condition unique to African people. In fact, the word "slave" comes from the Slav people of Eastern Europe. Because so many Slavs were enslaved by other people (including Africans), their very name came to be synonymous with the condition.

Native Americans were also enslaved by Europeans. Because it is almost impossible to successfully enslave large numbers of people in their own land, most enslaved Native Americans from the continental U.S. were shipped to Bermuda, and the West Indies, where many intermarried with the Africans.

People do not have a hard time because of their race or cultural back-   15
ground. No one is attacked, abused, oppressed, pogromed, or enslaved be-

cause of their race, creed, or cultural background. People are attacked, abused, oppressed, pogromed, or enslaved because of racism and anti-Semitism. There is a subtle but important difference in the focus here. The first implies some inherent fault or shortcoming within the oppressed person or group. The second redirects the responsibility back to the real source of the problem.

Asians are not "mysterious," "fatalistic," or "inscrutable."

Native Americans are not stoic, mystical, or vanishing.

Latin people are no more hot-tempered, hot-blooded, or emotional than anyone else. We do not have flashing eyes, teeth, or daggers. We are lovers pretty much like other people. Very few of us deal with any kind of drugs.

Middle Easterners are not fanatics, terrorists, or all oil-rich.

Jewish people are not particularly rich, clannish, or expert in money   *20* matters.

Not all African Americans are poor, athletic, or ghetto-dwellers.

Most Asians in the U.S. are not scientists, mathematicians, geniuses, or wealthy.

Southerners are no less intelligent than anybody else.

It is not a compliment to tell someone: "I don't think of you as Jewish / Black / Asian / Latina / Middle Eastern / Native American." Or "I think of you as white."

Do not use a Jewish person or person of color to hear your confession   *25* of past racist transgressions. If you have offended a particular person, then apologize directly to that person.

Also don't assume that Jews and people of color necessarily want to hear about how prejudiced your Uncle Fred is, no matter how terrible you think he is.

If you are white and/or gentile, do not assume that the next Jewish person or person of color you see will feel like discussing this guide with you. Sometimes we get tired of teaching this subject.

If you are white, don't brag to a person of color about your overseas trip to our homeland. Especially when we cannot afford such a trip. Similarly, don't assume that we are overjoyed to see the expensive artifacts you bought.

Words like "gestapo," "concentration camp" and "Hitler" are only appropriate when used in reference to the Holocaust.

"Full-blood," "half-breed," "quarter-blood." Any inference that a   *30* person's "race" depends on blood is racist. Natives are singled out for this form of bigotry and are denied rights on that basis.*

"Scalping": a custom also practiced by the French, the Dutch, and the English.*

* Reprinted with permission from *The Pathfinder Directory*, by Amylee, Native American Indian Resource Center. [Author's note]

Do you have friends or acquaintances who are terrific except they're really racist? If you quietly accept that part of them, you are giving their racism tacit approval.

As an exercise, pretend you are from another planet and you want an example of a typical human being for your photo album. Having never heard of racism, you'd probably pick someone who represents the majority of the people on the planet—an Asian person.

How many is too many? We have heard well-meaning liberals say things like "This event is too white. We need more people of color." Well, how many do you need? Fifty? A hundred? Just what is your standard for personal racial comfort?

People of color and Jewish people have been so all their lives. Further, 35 if we have been raised in a place where white gentiles predominate, then we have been subjected to racism/anti-Semitism all our lives. We are therefore experts on our own lives and conditions. If you do not understand or believe or agree with what someone is saying about their own oppression, do not automatically assume that they are wrong or paranoid or oversensitive.

It is not "racism in reverse" or "segregation" for Jews or people of color to come together in affinity groups for mutual support. Sometimes we need some time and space apart from the dominant group just to relax and be ourselves. If people coming together for group support makes you feel excluded, perhaps there's something missing in your own life or cultural connections.

The various cultures of people of color often seem very attractive to white people. (Yes, we are wonderful, we can't deny it.) But white people should not make a playground out of other people's cultures. We are not quaint. We are not exotic. We are not cool.

Don't forget that every white person alive today is also descended from tribal peoples. If you are white, don't neglect your own ancient traditions. They are as valid as anybody else's, and the ways of your own ancestors need to be honored and remembered.

"Race" is an arbitrary and meaningless concept. Races among humans don't exist. If there ever was any such thing as race, there has been so much constant crisscrossing of genes for the last 500,000 years that it would have lost all meaning anyway. There are no real divisions between us, only a continuum of variations that constantly change, as we come together and separate according to the movement of human populations.

Anyone who functions in what is referred to as the "civilized" world 40 is a carrier of the disease of racism.

Does reading this guide make you uncomfortable? Angry? Confused? Are you taking it personally? Well, not to fret. Racism has created a big horrible mess, and racial healing can sometimes be painful. Just remember that Jews and people of color do not want or need anybody's guilt. We just want people to accept responsibility when it is appropriate, and actively work for change.

The Responsive Reader

1   The writer attacks stereotypes about "hot-blooded" Latins, "inscrutable" Asians, athletic blacks, rich Jews, Middle Eastern terrorists, and others. Which of these stereotypes have you encountered—where and how? Have they shaped your own thinking?
2   What are the author's objections to the terms *minority, exotic, cult, halfbreed, racism in reverse,* and *race* itself? What other uses of language does she ask you to reconsider? How serious or valid do her objections seem to you?
3   When conversations turn on sensitive subjects, it is easy to say the wrong thing. What advice does this guide to etiquette give for conversations with people from different ethnic or cultural backgrounds? What pitfalls does Three Rivers warn against? How helpful or valid are her warnings?
4   The author uses weighty words like *ethnocentric, anti-Semitism, bigotry, genocide.* What do these words mean to you? How does the author use them?
5   The writer defends herself against the charge of being oversensitive—do you think she is?

Talking, Listening, Writing

6   The author says that "no one living in Western society is exempt from the influences of racism." Do you agree?
7   At the end, Three Rivers asks, "Does reading this guide make you uncomfortable? Angry? Confused? Are you taking it personally?" What are your answers to these questions?
8   What has been your own experience with the power of language to hurt people, to divide them, or to hold them back?

Collaborative Projects

9   Many colleges have considered speech codes aimed at hate speech or offensive language. Working with a group, investigate the history and the pros and cons of such initiatives.

A BATTLE OVER A NAME IN THE LAND OF THE SIOUX

Andrew Brownstein

> **"Onlookers at a homecoming parade performed the Atlanta Braves' 'tomahawk chop' as dancing American Indian children passed on a float, and then yelled at them to 'go back to the reservation.'"**

First published in February 2001, the following article asked teachers, alumni, and sports fans: What's in a name? In the seventies, the Stanford University football team ceased to be the Stanford Indians and became the Stanford Cardinals. A student vote had agreed that the Indian label brought negative stereotypes into play. Professional football teams still call themselves the Redskins or the Braves, although there is no team calling itself the Palefaces. One team still calls itself the Buffalo Bills, after a notorious killer of Native Americans.

The following article is a shortened version of an article in The Chronicle of Higher Education, *a professional journal for educators that examines issues affecting colleges and faculties in carefully researched and documented articles. As the author says, "mascot controversies come and go" in the academic world, but some are more costly, long-drawn-out, and divisive than others.*

Thought Starters: How important are sports teams to the image of a college or university? What would Notre Dame be without its football team? Do any traditional names, logos, or mascots of college teams have a special meaning for you? Do you know of any that have been changed in response to pressure or criticism?

GRAND FORKS, N.D.

The message came in March, when winter lingers and the frost still covers the silent prairie that surrounds the University of North Dakota.

The sender was anonymous. The recipient was Ira Taken Alive, a former student at the university who is a Lakota Sioux and the son of a tribal elder at the Standing Rock Indian Reservation.

"I assume this is the guy who wants to change the Fighting Sioux name," the e-mail message began. Mr. Taken Alive, a junior in 1999, when he received the message, had challenged the name of the university's sports teams, which he felt demeaned his people and stood as a barrier to the progress of American Indians in general.

As he sat in front of his computer, he read on: "There are many people who want your head, no joking. I am not one of those people, but I have heard some nasty talk by people about doing stuff to you. So take this from me, a concerned human being, watch out for your life."

University officials were never able to trace the source. But Mr. Taken   5
Alive says he had had enough—of the endless debates, the taunts, the vandalism to his car—that came from fighting the Fighting Sioux. In the fall, he transferred to another university; he returned quietly last summer to finish his degree.

Withdrawing a Huge Gift

Mascot controversies come and go in academe. But words can be costly in the ancestral home of Crazy Horse and Sitting Bull, on a campus where American Indians are the largest minority group.

This past December, it looked like the name debate might exact a very specific price: $100-million. That was the amount that Ralph Engelstad, a Las Vegas casino owner, had promised to his alma mater, largely to build a luxurious new hockey arena that would bear his name. In a sharply worded letter addressed to the university's president, he threatened to abandon the half-completed project, which he was personally overseeing, if the university dropped the Fighting Sioux name.

President Charles E. Kupchella, following protests by students and tribal leaders, had formed a commission that had been investigating the naming controversy for five months. He planned to announce his decision after New Year's. But a day after he and members of the State Board of Higher Education received the letter, the board launched a pre-emptive strike, voting 8-0 to keep the name.

It has not helped public relations at the university that its benefactor has a troubled past in the area of racial sensitivity. In 1988, Nevada authorities discovered that Mr. Engelstad had held two parties on Hitler's birthday, and kept a trove of Nazi paraphernalia at his Imperial Palace hotel and casino. He was fined $1.5-million for damaging the reputation of the State of Nevada.

That the episode has turned surreal is a fact that not even the univer-   10
sity's seasoned flacks try to conceal. "Oh, it's strange," says Peter B. Johnson, the college's spokesman. "It could be a movie script."

Where Two Worlds Converge

Grand Forks, population 49,000, sits where the Red Lake River meets the Red River of the North. But the university here may as well be the convergence of two worlds.

For most of the athletes and fans on this campus of 11,000, the Fighting Sioux name is a source of pride and honor. The powerhouse men's hockey team won Division I's "Frozen Four" championship last year; over the decades, the team has sent 54 players to the National Hockey League.

The university can also lay claim to being one of the top institutions for American Indians in the country. It houses 25 American Indian programs—mostly financed with federal grants—including *Native Directions,* a quarterly student magazine of American Indian life and culture; an Indian studies major; and the Indians Into Medicine program, which credits itself with training a fifth of the Native American doctors in the country.

Yet, there is a disconnect. Many of the 350 American Indian students at North Dakota say that beneath the campus's Main Street friendliness lies a dark current of racism, a facet of university life that the name controversy has brought uncomfortably to the surface.

"They say they keep the name to honor and respect us, but those 15 words have lost all meaning," says Alva Irwin, a Hidatsa Indian and senior majoring in social work and Indian studies. "How can they honor us by keeping something we clearly don't want?"

Once known as the Flickertails, the university's intercollegiate sports teams have been called the Sioux since 1930, when the name was changed to strike fear into the hearts of the Bison at rival North Dakota State University, in Fargo. There were no protests at the time, because there were virtually no American Indian students here. Native Americans didn't start attending the university in large numbers until the 1960's.

Ugly Incidents

Once on campus, they saw that the use of the name extended far beyond athletics. In 1972, fraternity members at the now-defunct King Kold Karnival created a lurid sculpture of a naked Indian woman, with a sign reading "Lick 'em Sioux"; an American Indian student was briefly jailed after he got into a fight over the sculpture with fraternity members, sending three of them to the hospital.

Tensions ran high again in 1992, when onlookers at a homecoming parade performed the Atlanta Braves' "tomahawk chop" as dancing American Indian children passed on a float, and then yelled at them to "go back to the reservation."

As recently as this past fall, says one student, Michael Grant, fraternity members dressed as cowboys and Indians flashed a cap gun at his wife and infant daughter. "Do you realize what would have happened if I had been there?" says Mr. Grant, an Omaha Indian and a sophomore majoring in Indian studies. "I wouldn't be here, man. I'd be in jail."

The name always takes center stage whenever the Bison come to 20 town. In the 1990's, North Dakota State fans started chanting "Sioux suck" during games, and, over the years, the slogan has taken on ever more inventive permutations.

For years, it was impossible to drive down Interstate 29 from Grand Forks to Fargo without seeing the abandoned barn with the giant slogan painted on it. And then there's the T-shirt worn by North Dakota State fans. It shows a stereotypical American Indian suggestively between the legs of a bison. A caption reads, "We saw. They sucked. We came."

"It's like we're not even human," says Anjanette Parisien, a Chippewa senior majoring in biology and Indian studies.

"This Is Sioux Territory"

Earl Strinden doesn't see it that way. The semi-retired chief executive officer of the university's alumni association and Mr. Engelstad's friend for 40 years, Mr. Strinden helped clinch the 1998 deal that culminated in the $100-million pledge.

Wearing a sports coat in the school's signature green, he marches over to a framed map of the Dakota territories that graces a wall in his campus office. He points to faded print marking what was once the Great Sioux Nation. "This is Sioux territory, for crying out loud!" he says.

The point is made again and again by alumni: The Sioux are indeli-   *25* bly etched into the state's lore and culture. To rid the campus of the name would be to rob the state of one of its great traditions and to further isolate American Indians.

"When the hockey team plays in Boston, the people will think, 'Fighting Sioux, what's that?'" Mr. Strinden says. "They'll want to find out about the Sioux. There are those on this campus who want to make sure that Native Americans are always victims."

During the interview, two American Indian students in his office nod vigorously, as if the notion of hockey as export of Indian culture is self-evident.

"If we lose the name, it's going to help erase our culture," says Greg Holy Bull, a Lakota Sioux and a graduate student in fine arts.

A "Deplorable" Name

At the *Dakota Student,* the semi-weekly student newspaper, the subject of Mr. Engelstad and the name is something of a newsroom obsession. One Sunday, staff members vowed not to talk about the issue all day. The silence lasted until 3 p.m.

When Evan Nelson, the sports editor, first came to the university, he   *30* thought "the whole issue was garbage." But after working the sports beat for a year and a half, he came to view the name as "deplorable."

"It was hearing all those ignorant bastards—the alumni, the athletes, the fans—talking about Indians that did it for me," says Mr. Nelson, a junior and a communications major from Sioux Falls, S.D.

He raised eyebrows among his sources with a recent column, in which he wrote that the state board's decision on the Fighting Sioux name was "an act of malice and contempt." The racism behind the name is subtle, Mr. Nelson says. "There are no hate crimes. It's not like the Deep South in the 60's, where police were brushing crowds with fire hoses." It's the "Injun" jokes and terms like "prairie nigger." It's in the oft-repeated comments that Indians are all drunks or are going to college on the government dole. It's the person who will wear a jacket with the mascot of an Indian, but won't talk to one.

"My grandparents have been telling me since I was 2 years old that the Indians are stealing from us," he says. "This is a very white-bread part of the world."

To the majority of students—82 percent, according to a recent poll—the issue has nothing to do with racism. It's just the name of a sports team. Kim Srock, a sophomore discussing the debate in Jim McKenzie's advanced-composition class, expresses annoyance that so much is being made of a five-letter word.

"It's like, get a life," she says. "This is a game—it's not about Indians. 35 They're like a bunch of crybabies. Get over it."

If the subject of race is the university's most divisive issue, hockey is its No. 1 passion. So it makes sense that the biggest controversy in recent years would be a combination of both.

The joke in this corner of the world is that children learn to skate before they can walk. The enthusiasm for the sport is hard to miss. On game day against the rival Golden Gophers of the University of Minnesota, ticket lines will start forming around noon, even in the sub-zero chill. Local merchants sell coffee and barbecued ribs as tailgaters, often in green and white face paint, warm themselves near bonfires.

They come to see players like Jeff Panzer, the center and a Grand Forks native, who is Division I's top scorer and a leading candidate for the Hobey Baker trophy, college hockey's equivalent of the Heisman.

The new arena, now estimated at over $85-million, promises to be an even bigger draw. Billed as one of the finest hockey stadiums in the nation, the complex will house 11,400 fans, 48 luxury skyboxes, and a second ice rink for Olympic-style play.

The Responsive Reader

1 How does Brownstein's *introduction* use the anonymous e-mail message to Ira Taken Alive to dramatize the issue? How would you have reacted to the message? How would you have reacted to the anonymous correspondent identifying himself as a "concerned human being"? How does the introduction sum up the basic issue?

2 How much do you learn here about the *history* or various stages of the controversy and the major players involved? Are you surprised by the action or actions of the university president? Are you surprised by the action of the State Board of Education? Are you surprised by the stance taken by the multimillion-dollar benefactor?

3 As you would expect in a professional journal, Brownstein tries to present *both sides* of the controversy. What evidence does he cite that for

many athletes and fans "the Fighting Sioux name is a source of pride and honor"? What evidence does he cite that the university is "one of the top institutions" for Native Americans in this country?

4   On the other hand, what evidence does Brownstein cite of the "*dark current of racism*" beneath the surface friendliness of the campus? What seems to have been the special role of fraternity members? (Do you think it is fair that fraternities are often mentioned in this kind of context?) Why was the benefactor's "troubled past" a special problem for the university? (The benefactor went on record saying that he despises everything Hitler stood for, that many other collectors collect Nazi memorabilia, and that the Hitler's birthday party was a joke.)

5   Some of the uglier details and incidents Brownstein describes relate to the *taunting* and juvenile rivalry between fans of competing teams. To you, do they seem more serious than that? Did they bring an ugly undercurrent of racism into play? Why or why not?

6   To judge from this article, do the protesters *speak for themselves* or for all or most Native American students on the campus? Do the students showing racist attitudes seem to represent a sizable portion or a majority of the student body? When you try to decide who is right and who is wrong, does it matter how strong or widespread support is on either side?

Talking, Listening, Writing

7   What images and associations do you and members of your generation associate with names like the Sioux, Chief Crazy Horse, and Sitting Bull? What do you think of the argument that keeping the team name will help honor the Native American past and keep the history of a proud people alive?

8   If you were of Irish American descent, would you object to a college team being named the "Fighting Irish"? Why or why not? Would this be a different matter from calling a college team the "Fighting Sioux"?

9   Have you seen instances of people protesting against prejudice or injustice being accused of perpetuating a "victim mentality"?

BILINGUALISM: ASSIMILATION IS MORE THAN ABCs

Jorge R. Mancillas

"This is a priceless resource: a new generation of Americans committed to preserving and strengthening a democratic and pluralistic U.S. society, but also having a birthright familiarity with Latin American, Asian, or Middle Eastern societies."

Like millions of immigrants and children of immigrants, Jorge R. Mancillas speaks English as a second language. He came to this country from Ensenada in Mexico and wrote the following article in 1993 while an assistant professor of anatomy and cell biology at the UCLA School of Medicine. He takes a stand on an issue of special concern in areas with large Spanish-speaking school populations, such as New York City, Miami, Texas, and California.

What should the schools do for students whose proficiency in English is limited or nonexistent? The traditional policy had been immersion (or, more informally, sink or swim). Everyone was taught all subjects in English, and the use of any other language even during recess was discouraged or banned outright. This policy was once credited with turning the children of Jewish, Polish, German, Armenian, and Czech immigrants into Americans after a few years of schooling.

In the seventies and eighties, with high dropout rates for ESL (English as a second language) students, a different policy was mandated by the federal government. Bilingual education provides instruction in subjects like reading, math, geography, and history in the students' original language, to keep them from falling behind while they are still learning English. Bilingual education has come in for much criticism: It has been charged with perpetuating the linguistic and cultural separation of immigrant children. It has had to grapple with inadequate funding, a shortage of bilingual teachers, and the proliferation of foreign languages among our school populations, ranging from Spanish to Vietnamese, Chinese, Tagalog, Lebanese, and Russian.

Thought Starters: Do you know people who are bilingual? How many of your classmates are bilingual? What is meant by "bilingual education"?

Imagine going from a working-class neighborhood in Ensenada to the University of California at Berkeley. Having graduated from high school with the Mexican equivalent of a 4.0 GPA, having studied English and worked in my hometown's tourist industry, and having passed the TOEFL

5

(Test of English as a Foreign Language) without difficulties, I sat in my first lecture at Berkeley full of confidence and excitement.

I had just been exposed to the United States' dual immigration policy. For the first time in my life, I had been treated courteously by immigration officials: With a letter of acceptance from one of the world's most prestigious universities, my expected contribution to Mexico's brain drain was greeted with the prompt dispensation of a student visa. Now, sitting in the front row of a large lecture hall, I opened my notebook as the professor began to speak. A few minutes later, I was devastated.

Engaging in conversation with tourists at a hotel desk and passing the TOEFL were quite different from trying to grasp complex concepts in psychology delivered at the pace required by 10-week quarter terms. I was lost. Trying to absorb the material from the 600-page psychology textbook was no easier.

Still, that was the easiest part. I also had to fulfill the English 1A requirement, for which we had to read a text and write a report at the end of each week. Assigned reading for the first two weeks: Theodore Roszak's "The Making of the Counter-Culture" and Norman Mailer's "Miami and the Siege of Chicago." Quite a tall order for a boy who had grown up in Ensenada. It was more than the language that I was "deficient" in; it was the implied understanding of the culture and politics.

Sitting in the back of the classroom, I struggled for two quarters as I 　10 had never struggled before in my life, and I barely managed to maintain a C average. My self-esteem was shattered. I forged ahead, however, understanding very well what the educational opportunity that I had before me meant to my future prospects. By the time I graduated, my grade average was up to an A, although my overall average was much lower due to the impact of the first quarters.

Years later, I find myself part of the faculty at the UCLA School of Medicine and the director of a research laboratory affiliated with UCLA's Brain Research Institute. Had I not been able to overcome the hurdles of my first few months at Berkeley, emotional as well as practical—and I almost didn't—my life and any contribution I may be able to make to society would have been very different.

This experience comes to mind when I hear arguments about bilingual education for the substantial proportion of children with limited English proficiency in the Los Angeles Unified School District. It is easy for me to understand the experience of children finding themselves in a new culture, wanting and struggling to master the English language but lagging behind in other subjects while they do. By the time they learn English— and almost invariably they do—they are behind academically; they are left with gaps in their academic development. Even worse, their self-esteem has suffered considerably, for at that tender age, their sense of self-worth is shaped to a large degree by their perception of how they measure up in comparison to, and in the eyes of, their peers.

Why would we want to academically disable and emotionally impair thousands of children instead of providing them with the mechanisms that allow for a healthy transition to their adopted culture?

The Mexican government's recent contribution of school texts and bilingual teachers to the LAUSD was born of compassion for Spanish-speaking children. It also was influenced by the government's intelligent understanding of Mexico's need to respond to ongoing changes in contemporary society; the Mexican educators who will be exposed to the U.S. educational system and culture will be a valuable resource upon returning to their country.

Children with limited English proficiency must be seen, like other 15 children, as a valuable resource, not as a hindrance or a burden. If we help them to integrate successfully into the mainstream while preserving their original language and cultural skills, they will be the bridge-builders this country needs to succeed in the global community.

This is a priceless resource: a new generation of Americans committed to preserving and strengthening a democratic and pluralistic U.S. society, but also having a birthright familiarity with Latin American, Asian or Middle Eastern societies. Think of what these children might contribute in an age of revolutions in communications and development that we, today, can hardly imagine.

Against this possibility, the alternative is ludicrous: to create a large population of school dropouts, hostile to the mythical "mainstream American culture" to which, they are made to feel, they have nothing to contribute because they are culturally and linguistically deficient.

Those who oppose bilingual education are propelled more by fear of others and insecurity about their own capabilities, identity, and culture. To follow them is to go against the current of history and embark on a futile attempt to become culturally insular and ethnically "clean." Our only other choice is to embrace change and learn the value of diverse expressions of the human experience as a strong basis for our place in the global society of the 21st Century. From that perspective, the monetary cost of bilingual education is trivial and a sound investment in the future.

The Responsive Reader

1 Advocates of bilingual education stress the *adverse effect* that English-only instruction has on students' overall academic performance and on their self-image or self-esteem. What light does Mancillas's experience throw on this issue?

2 What for Mancillas are the *social costs* of failure to integrate second-language students "successfully into the mainstream"?

3 A much–debated question is whether bilingual education should be a *transition* to full English proficiency or whether students should at the

same time "maintain" their first language and culture. What is Mancillas's answer to this question? What are the reasons for the stand he takes?

Talking, Listening, Reading

4 What has been your own experience or what has shaped your own views on the issue of bilingualism? Is it an issue in schools you know?
5 Mancillas uses or alludes to buzzwords that have played a prominent role in public discourse in recent years: *ethnic cleansing, pluralism, diversity, a global perspective*. Why and where does he use them and with what effect?

FIND IT ON THE WEB

During strong English-only agitation in the late nineties, the controversy over bilingual education escalated. Various legislative initiatives were aimed at ending bilingual education, and voters in California passed an antibilingual referendum. Arguments of those who declared bilingual education "a failure" were forcing school districts to abandon their bilingual programs. You may want to do a quick-search on the Internet to find news on recent developments or initiatives.

POWER OF WORDS IN WARTIME

Robin Tolmach Lakoff

**"Bullets and bombs are not the only tools of war.
Words, too, play their part."**

*A shared language provides a powerful bond. At the same time, language
often serves to outgroup "the other" or to label others as "sunshine patriots"
or "fair-weather" friends. The names we call people show if we think of them
as one of "us" or one of "them." The labels we attach to people show if we
think of them as potential allies or potential enemies.*

*Lakoff is a linguist, a professional student of language, at the University of
California at Berkeley who authored* The Language of War. *She published the
following essay on the language of war in the* New York Times *in May 2004.*

*Like other linguists, she knows that language plays a major role in prepar-
ing people to choose sides in fateful conflicts. Sociolinguistics studies the role
language plays in making people become identified with a group, a political ideology, a religion, or a national agenda. What role does language play in persuading nations to go to war? What role does it play in justifying the casualties and suffering on both sides?*

Thought Starters: What war movies or historical documentaries have you
seen where the enemy was depicted as evil or subhuman? What war movies
or historical documentaries have you seen where the enemy became fellow
humans?

An American soldier refers to an Iraqi prisoner as "it." A general   *1*
speaks not of "Iraqi fighters" but of "the enemy." A weapons manufacturer
doesn't talk about people but about "targets."

Bullets and bombs are not the only tools of war. Words, too, play their
part.

Human beings are social animals, genetically hard-wired to feel compassion toward others. Under normal conditions, most people find it very
difficult to kill.

But in war, military recruits must be persuaded that killing other
people is not only acceptable but even honorable.

The language of war is intended to bring about that change, and not   *5*
only for soldiers in the field. In wartime, language must be created to enable combatants and noncombatants alike to see the other side as killable, to
overcome the innate queasiness over the taking of human life. Soldiers, and
those who remain at home, learn to call their enemies by names that make
them seem not quite human—inferior, contemptible and not like "us."

The specific worlds change from culture to culture and war to war. The names need not be obviously demeaning. Just the fact that we can name them gives us a sense of superiority and control. If, in addition, we give them nicknames, we can see them as smaller, weaker and childlike — not worth taking seriously as fully human.

The Greeks and Romans referred to everyone else as "barbarians"— etymologically those who only babble, only go "bar-bar." During the American Revolution, the British called the colonists "Yankees," a term with a history that is still in dispute. While the British intended it disparagingly, the Americans, in perhaps the first historical instance of reclamation, made the word their own and gave it a positive spin, turning the derisive song "Yankee Doodle" into our first, if unofficial, national anthem.

In World War I, the British gave the Germans the nickname "Jerries," from the first syllable of German. In World War II, Americans referred to the Japanese as "Japs."

The names may refer to real or imagined cultural and physical differences that emphasize the ridiculous or the repugnant. So in various wars, the British called the French "Frogs." Germans have been called "Krauts," a reference to weird and smelly food. The Vietnamese were called "slopes" and "slants." The Koreans were referred to simply as "gooks."

The war in Iraq has added new examples. Some American soldiers refer to the Iraqis as "hadjis," used in a derogatory way, apparently unaware that the word, which comes from the Arabic term for a pilgrimage to Mecca, is used as a term of respect for older Muslim men.   10

The Austrian ethologist Konrad Lorenz suggested that the more clearly we see other members of our own species as individuals, the harder we find it to kill them.

So some terms of war are collective nouns, encouraging us to see the enemy as an undifferentiated mass, rather than as individuals capable of suffering. Crusaders called their enemy "the Saracen," and in World War I, the British called Germans "the Hun."

American soldiers are trained to call those they are fighting against "the enemy." It is easier to kill an enemy than an Iraqi.

The word "enemy" itself provides the facelessness of a collective noun. Its non-specificity also has a fear-inducing connotation; enemy means simply "those we are fighting," without reference to their identity.

The terrors and uncertainties of war make learning this kind of language especially compelling for soldiers on the front. But civilians back home also need to believe that what their country is doing is just and necessary, and that the killing they are supporting is in some way different from the killing in civilian life that is rightly punished by the criminal justice system. The use of the language developed for military purposes by civilians reassures them that war is not murder.   15

The linguistic habits that soldiers must absorb in order to fight make atrocities like those at Abu Ghraib virtually inevitable. The same language that creates a psychological chasm between "us" and "them" and enables

American troops to kill in battle, makes enemy soldiers fit subjects for torture and humiliation. The reasoning is: They are not really human, so they will not feel the pain.

The Responsive Reader

1 According to Lakoff, what role does language play in creating the wartime *psychology?* How does Lakoff trace the change from "Thou shalt not kill" to the killing of the enemy in wartime? What role does language play? (According to Lakoff, what is the role of language in making possible wartime atrocities?)

2 What does Lakoff say about labels like *barbarian, frog, Hun, kraut,* or *Yankee?* What is the *etymology* or word history of these words in your dictionary? What do the dictionary etymologies add to the references or explanations by Lakoff?

3 How much *demeaning* outgrouping language survives from periods of bloody conflict? To judge from your personal observation or role as a media watcher, are there still Southerners thinking of Northerners as "Yankees"? Are there still people who to refer to Japanese or Japanese Americans as "Japs"? Are there people who refer to South East Asians as "gooks"? How divisive or damaging are such labels? Do you agree with Lakoff that labels like this "need not be obviously demeaning"?

4 Have you seen examples of groups adopting a label that was long an insult (like the N-word or the *queer* label) and defiantly using it instead as a badge of pride?

Talking, Listening, Writing

5 In ancient Greek tragedy, a true tragic conflict opposed the hero or heroine to a worthy antagonist or formidable challenger. In some later literature, the warrior or fighter took pride in having battled against a worthy opponent or "noble foe." As a reader, spectator, or student of history, have you encountered examples of either tradition? Is the idea of the "worthy antagonist" or the "noble foe" dead in today's world?

6 In a Bible story, survivors fleeing from defeat in battle were asked to pronounce the word *shibboleth.* People from the enemy tribe could not hear or pronounce the *sh* sound and said *sibboleth* instead. They were killed. Can you identify words or expressions that serve as a less lethal but still outgrouping shibboleth in our society today? Can you point to words or expressions likely to make people undesirable in a group or circle of friends? Can you warn job applicants of words that may make them seem unacceptable in a job interview or in a teaching institution?

A GATHERING OF DEAFS

John Heaviside

A student poet marvels at the supple rich sign language of the hearing-impaired.

Researchers like Oliver Sacks have written about the heightened sensitivity, or acuteness of other senses, that people who are color-blind or have other impairments may develop to compensate for what we normally see as deficiencies. Authors writing about the deaf community have written about the hearing-impaired not as medical cases or people with disabilities but as people who share a rich culture, historically conditioned and transmitted across generations. In that culture, signed languages (sign languages or gesture languages) play a central role.

Authors writing about the structure and uses of American Sign Language (ASL) have stressed the "linguistic richness" of the languages of the deaf, describing them as "rich systems with complex structures that reflect their long histories." John Heaviside wrote the following poem about the deaf as a student in 1989 and published it in the Olivetree Review, *a publication devoted to student work at Hunter College of the City University of New York.*

Thought Starters: What do you know about or what experience have you had with alternative language or writing systems like braille or ASL?

A Gathering of Deafs

By the turnstiles	*1*
in the station	
where the L train greets	
the downtown six	
a congregation of deafs	*5*
passes forth	
jive wild	
and purely physical	
in a world dislocated	
from the subway howling	*10*
hard sole shoe stampede	
punk rock blasted radio	
screaming, pounding, honking	
they gather in community	
engaging	*15*
in a dexterous conversation	

An old woman
of her dead husband tells
caressing the air
wrinkled fingers   *20*
tell the story
delicate, mellifluous motion
she places gentle configurations
before the faces of the group

A young Puerto Rican   *25*
describes a fight with his mother
emphasizing each word
abrupt, staccato movements
jerking his elbows
and twisting his wrists   *30*
teeth clenched
lips pressed
the story concluded
a fist into his palm

By the news stand   *35*
two lovers
stroke the air
syllables
graceful and slow
their joining   *40*
the flow
of fingertips

The Responsive Reader

1 How does the world of sound acquire negative connotations in this
   poem? How does it set the scene for the contrasting world of the deaf?
2 What do you learn from this poem about the signed language of the deaf
   as a language? What are key features it shares with spoken language?
   How is it different?
3 What are the usual meanings of *serene, dexterous, mellifluous, staccato, congregation*? How does the poet transpose these words to the culture of
   the deaf?
4 Why or how did the poet select the "speakers" that he asks us to focus
   on in this poem?

Talking, Listening, Writing

5 What has been your experience with people with impaired sight, hearing, or mobility? How much do you know from firsthand experience or
   observation? How much is hearsay or stereotype?

6 What is the reaction of people in our society to the hearing-impaired? How are attitudes in our society changing toward people with disabilities? How much progress has society made toward recognizing the needs and rights of the disabled?

Collaborative Projects

7 Many colleges now employ interpreters who translate oral instruction into signed language. If you can, arrange for such a person to come and speak to your class about the language of the deaf.

FORUM: *Language and Social Class*

The way we talk enables people to put us into mental bins. They stereotype us as "one of us" or "one of them." They mentally earmark us as middle class or lower class, educated or uneducated, Southerner or Yankee, American-born or immigrant. In many other countries, language differences are even more conspicuous as telltale signs of social class or regional identity than in ours. In London, bankers speak a kind of BBC English that sounds snooty to most Americans, while cab drivers speak a Cockney dialect that is nearly unintelligible to the visitor.

In this country language differences are less obvious than in countries where people in isolated rural areas speak a local dialect hardly understood by their city cousins. The way Americans move and mingle has prevented the development of regional differences that could become true barriers. In addition, first the movies and radio and then television have had a leveling effect. Nevertheless, language differences continue to play a huge but often unexamined role as markers of social class and of ethnic or regional origin.

Millions of Americans have always been bilingual. They learned American English as a second language, allowing them to function and do business beyond the circle of their family and friends or tightly knit ethnic group. Their English showed traces of the Italian, Polish, Chinese, or Yiddish they brought from across the sea—or of the Spanish their ancestors spoke in what was once part of Mexico. Other millions of Americans have always been bidialectal. They grew up with a variety of English different from school English and media English. They spoke a rural dialect or downhome variety of English at home, in the neighborhood, and with their friends. They learned to speak and write standard English as the language of school and office, of the media and public life.

Since our accents or dialects serve others as a class marker or as a means of outgrouping and ingrouping, many have always worked at "crossing over" to a prestige dialect. They have tried hard to move from country talk to city talk, from a heavy Irish brogue to refined Harvard English, from a Yiddish-tinged New Yorkerese to something less ethnic. School systems have often held out the promise of linguistic assimilation. If minority students learned to "talk white," then society—teachers, employers—would treat them as if they were white. Today this program of linguistic upgrading or language assimilation works for some, but it fails to work for many others. Why?

SMALL TAWK

Mark Francis Cohen

"Brooklynese is more than a local thing. It is perhaps the most recognizable regionalism in the world, thanks mainly to movies and television, which have transformed it into an emblem of class as much as of place."

Outside your family or group of friends, do you "watch your language"? The novelist Tom Wolfe, noted for his flashy, flamboyant style, said that in the South it is "considered very good form, and very macho" for successful or upper-class males to speak with "downhome accents." He said that this would never happen in New York—successful people or wannabe sophisticates would never slip "into a Brooklyn street accent." Other observers have noticed people from Texas or the Midwest changing their way of talking: The world-renowned American poet T. S. Eliot, from St. Louis, moved to England and spoke with an acquired Oxford accent. The widely syndicated pundit George Will name-drops Harvard and Oxford and hardly ever mentions that he is a homeboy from a small burg in Illinois.

The following article looks at both the funny side and the serious side of a basic fact of American life: The natural way of talking of many working-class Americans in our big cities is different from what English teachers and media pundits consider good English. Mark Francis Cohen is a New York—based freelance journalist who used to cover Brooklyn for the staid New York Times. *He wrote this article for the* New Republic *in 1996.*

Thought Starters: Do you adjust the way you talk for different groups, different contexts, different situations? Where and how?

Sitting in his cluttered Manhattan office, Sam Chwat, accent coach to the stars, is holding court with one of his not-so-famous clients in what amounts to a public flogging. The subject of the flogging is an upwardly mobile woman with short, chestnut-colored hair and a knit sweater wrapped around her shoulders, who has come here to eliminate her cumbersome Brooklyn accent. Every session costs $185, but it's worth it, she says, for a chance to learn from the man who once tutored—and cured—Tony Danza.

Chwat (whose name, he tells me, is pronounced Sh-wah but is usually mispronounced by New Yorkers as Sh-whaat?) implores the woman to begin chatting about her children just so he can pounce on every offensive sound she emits. Soon, in the middle of her sixth attempt to say "six-yeehs-huld" like a Midwesterner, Chwat erupts: "Wai, wai, wait! You're screwing it up. If you pucker, it's going to screw it up. A puckered 's' is going to give you a 'sh.' Like 'In the office she . . .' try *that*—without puckering."

"In-thuh-aw-fish-she," she gurgles.

"I need an 's,'" he chimes.

"In the aw-fis-she."

"That's it! And—" 5

"Six-yeers-old."

"You got it, and she had a list of what?"

"She hadda lish ah . . ."

"Don't pucker!" 10

"She hadda lish ah quesh-chuns."

"You blew it!"

Slowly, she says: "She had a list of quest-chuns."

"You're right!" Later, Chwat declares: "It's important to note she doesn't have a lisp. This is just a local thing."

Of course, Brooklynese is more than a local thing. It is perhaps the 15 most recognizable regionalism in the world, thanks mainly to movies and television, which have transformed it into an emblem of class as much as of place. Yet, in the borough of Brooklyn, of all places, Brooklynese is suddenly on the brink of extinction or at least some serious evolution—thanks to the old ethnic Brooklynites, who no longer want to speak it, and to the new ethnic Brooklynites, who are changing it beyond recognition.

Of course, it was ethnic groups that created Brooklynese in the first place. First it was the early Dutch and French settlers, trying to learn English after the British captured Brooklyn in 1664. These groups, which already had trouble pronouncing the King's "th"s, assumed the Cockney sounds around them—and that meant eliminating the final "r" in many words, just like the colonists. And so the ancestors of Brooklyn's mudduhs were born.

In the 1840s, Irish immigrants added a muscularity to the dialect. The Irish tongue made "th"s into hard "t"s and "ir"s into "oi"s—thirty-third became "toity-tird." Turn-of-the-century Italian immigrants found the Brooklyn tone flat and flavorless, devoid of rhythm, and so they imbued the vowels with a sing-songy passion. Thus, "mayyn." But—whoops!—they robbed some words of their consonants. Ergo, "tawwk." Meanwhile, Jews speaking Yiddish were arriving in droves, striking new intonation riffs as well as word substitutions. Declarative sentences sounded like questions? Wordsrantogether, and "v"s replaced "w"s. Ultimately, on a steamy summer day, as kids played stickball and fire hydrants sprayed water on the streets below, it was not uncommon to hear an apartment dweller produce a hands-in-the-air wail of "Oh-pin-duh-vinda-awe-red-de!"

By 1950, Brooklynese had become nationally recognized—and derided. According to Margaret Mannix Flynn, a former professor of speech at Brooklyn College who is generally considered the doyenne of Brooklynese, the advent of radio, movies and television would, oddly enough, diminish its real use. For one thing, whenever a movie character invoked the

Brooklyn warble, Flynn observes, "he was always the poor schlump. And he spoke the language that the average guy and gal could identify with." Meanwhile, radio and television broadcasts were entering more homes. To the extent that news segments were suddenly being heard and seen all over, announcers had to be starkly accentless and regionally unspecific. With this need for crushing universality, a standard American English was born—the so-called newscaster's speech. Whereas Brooklynites once took pride in the fraternity of the accent, people now understood it to be a feature of the working class, an association that sticks to this day. As the borough's aspiring eggheads and social climbers became conscious of the accent's symbolism, they decide to rid themselves—and their children—of it. In the ensuing years, as the aspiring middle class fled to the suburbs of Long Island and New Jersey, a new wave of Southern blacks and Puerto Ricans took their place and made their own mark. Spanish, for example, has pushed the accent in a different direction—providing us with the quick, guttural sounds we have today.

Not that Brooklynese has lost all of its familiar features: it's still blind to things like final "r"s and, in some of the neighborhoods, still home to "youse," as in "youse guyz." Yet, given the dizzying variety of Brooklyn's new immigrants—remember, it's not just Hispanics, but Russians, Chinese, Dominicans, Jamaicans, and Haitians, too—most linguistic experts predict it's only a matter of time before traditional Brooklynese morphs into something wholly different. "It's dying," announces William Stewart, a linguist at the CUNY Graduate Center. "Any place you have immigration, differences are created; and, as children interact, these differences get leveled off, and a new variety is formed."

A week has passed since the session in Sam Chwat's office. Alan   20
Rodin, a speech pathologist who teaches accent elimination, is giving me a tour of Brighton Beach, which is now predominantly Russian. He's conducting an informal survey of how young people speak, and at one point near the boardwalk he approaches an eleven-year-old boy who has brown hair, deeply set blue eyes, and a down-to-his-knees black T-shirt. When the boy confirms his Russian origins, Rodin flashes a clipboard and asks, "Would you read these words for me?"

"Sure," the boy says in a formal-sounding English, as he glances up at the page and ticks off the answers. "Three. Dog. Soda. Water. Give me this."

"Have you ever heard someone say 'dis' instead of 'this'?" Rodin asks.

"Well, sure," he says. "You know—dis! Don't 'dis' me."

"Oh boy," Rodin says, shaking his head. "There's not going to be a Brooklynese for long."

The Responsive Reader

1   Which of the language features treated in this article do you recognize? Which can you demonstrate or explain to classmates who might have less of an ear for language differences than you do?

2 What do you think is the major purpose of this article, or what are its major effects on the reader? Do you tend to think of the language differences treated here as a source of amusement, or of embarrassment, or of important pointers for human interaction?

Talking, Listening, Writing

3 What is the difference between a language and a dialect? One language scholar said jokingly that a dialect is a language that has an army and a navy. You might want to check out the treatment of "dialect" in a major online encyclopedia or other authoritative source.

4 Have you known or observed people who consciously or deliberately speak a regional or "downhome" kind of speech? Have you known or observed others who have tried hard to change speech patterns that might reveal their ethnic, social, or regional origins? How successful were they?

5 Much ethnic humor is dialect humor or foreign-accent humor. Can you imitate the speech patterns of others? Can you give your classmates a sample? Is dialect humor always mean-spirited or condescending, or can it be nonoffensive?

Collaborative Projects

6 Both in this country and in Europe, there has been a revival of interest in dialects as a rich source of nostalgia and regional pride. You may want to team up with classmates to stage a festival of American dialects with stories, poetry, or humor from dialect sources—including perhaps Minnesota-Scandinavian, Cajun, Yiddish-tinged American, deep South, Irish American, Mexican American, Puerto Rican American, Hawaii pidgin, and others.

EBONICS: OPENING PANDORA'S BOX

Toni Cook

"Everyone in my family, whether it was Mom or Dad, they were always crusaders. You never earned the right to snub your nose at anybody based on speech patterns."

The school board in the predominantly African American city of Oakland in California caused a huge media flap when it called the Black English spoken by many of its students "Ebonics" and said that it should be recognized as a separate language showing the influence of African roots. Soon amended or "clarified," the school board's resolution called for "maintaining the richness and legitimacy" of the students' "primary language" while teaching them standard English.

The Oakland initiative caused an outpouring of criticism and of vicious racist humor on the Internet, with the voices of scholars and teachers concerned about the failure of traditional methods at first largely drowned out. Linguists, or language scholars, say that calling the Spanish, the rural dialect, or Black English that students bring to school inferior or illiterate is counterproductive. In the past, it has not produced large numbers of well-educated students with perfect accents but instead has created large numbers of hostile dropouts.

Dialect features like the double negative, from Chaucer's "He never yet no villainy ne said" to the blues singer's "I ain't got nobody," have been part of English for centuries. Slaves brought to the New World from Africa developed various kinds of Creole or Creolized languages with vocabulary items (like gumbo) and speech patterns indebted to African languages. Gullah, spoken in the isolated islands off the shore of Georgia and South Carolina, has been described as the African American dialect closest to becoming a separate language.

In the following interview, Toni Cook, a member of the Oakland school board, talks about the thinking that went into the board's resolution. Cook has B.A. and M.A. degrees with honors from UCLA. She served as associate dean at Howard University and as national director of advance for Jesse Jackson's presidential campaign in 1984.

Thought Starters: Are people you know well bilingual? Are any bidialectal? When and how do they shift from one language or one dialect to another?

Q: Other than making a lot of people mad, what have you done here?   1

A: I've sounded a bell that everyone is talking about. We got a call from Amsterdam, and another one from South Africa. I'm finding that more people are becoming anywhere from supportive to understanding about this.

Q: Has anyone given you serious trouble?

A: Someone called from a radio talk show and played real raw, racist stuff live and on air. My reaction to the first flood of phone calls (on my answering machine) was to deep-six every call.

Q: Why?   5

A: I was broadsided by the controversy. I didn't get home (from the board meeting) until 2 A.M. and I didn't listen to any news the next day because I didn't think anything we did was newsworthy. I'm just thinking, "I can't function." So I get up and make the call (to my job at the San Francisco Housing Authority): "I'm not coming." Then Edgar, our board's assistant, calls and says, "Can you come over?" I said, "Edgar, I'm trying to put a lie together about why I'm not going to work." He said, "All hell has broken loose on the resolution." I said, "What resolution?" He said, "The one put out by the African American task force. The mayor's on a rampage."

Q: Why was [Mayor] Elihu Harris so mad?

A: I used to work for Elihu. He could be mad at anything! And when I got there, he had already gone off to [Superintendent] Carolyn Getridge. And he asked me, "Do you know what you have done? I'm getting calls from everybody in the world! This is embarrassing to Oakland! You all have adopted a policy that's going to teach black English!"

I said "Elihu, I know you're cheap, but do you have television? Did you watch the school board meeting last night? We meant you no ill will in terms of your challenges with the city. But our kids are being ridiculed if they speak standard English—'Ugh, you talk like a white girl!' So this is the problem we're faced with, and this is how we're going to deal with it." Elihu kind of calmed down a little and began to focus on why we did it like we did it.

Q: What did you do and why did you do it?   10

A: I asked the superintendent to form a task force to look at the performance of African American kids. Since I've been on the board, drop-out rates, suspensions, expulsions, truancy—all have gone up for African American kids. But enrollment in the gifted and talented program and presence in college-bound, honors and advanced-placement classes were not proportionate to black enrollment, which is 53 percent.

Q: What about special education?

A: Of 5,000 kids in that, 71 percent are African American. And they were in there for "causing disruption."

Q: Aren't special education classes supposed to be for students who are disabled or have learning disabilities?

A: Yes. And you have to have a referral to be placed in the program.   15 The referrals disproportionately were because of a "language deficiency."

Q: What's that?

A: When you really dug down, it's that they weren't writing or speaking standard English. We found there were white and black teachers making referrals. And white and black principals—disproportionately black—saying yes. So when the task force began to talk with teachers, it was like, "Well, we don't have any strategies for these kids." The only one they had was the [state's] Standard English Proficiency Program for a few teachers who got that training.

Q: So what did you do?

A: You know, there's an old guy who comes to the board meetings named Oscar Wright. He came to every board meeting until his wife died about a year ago. And he would stand with those trembling hands and talk about the performance of African American kids—test scores, truancy— and he said, "I see having four black board members has made no difference in what these kids are doing."

And we hung our heads, because it was true! We had a crisis situation   20
and we kept coming up with old ways. Or ways that were so homogenized
they didn't really wake anybody up.

Q: You're saying that test scores will go up as African American students begin speaking standard English?

A: Yes. Which ultimately means—more critically—that they can go
from high school to college if that's their choice. You can no longer drop
your kid off in kindergarten and expect to pick him up in the 12th grade
with a diploma that means he's ready for college. We should quit making
these promises that we're going to do that by adding health programs, and
all those other kinds of things. That is not about education. I know they
need all that, but there isn't any education strategy here. When it's directed
to African American kids, it's basically the assumption that we have to control them before we can educate them.

Q: You don't feel that way?

A: No.

Q: How can you teach a kid who's out of control—whether threat-   25
ening a teacher or just making noise?

A: Teachers need the teaching and learning tools to know how to
communicate with these youngsters to capture their attention. We have
some kids with a proven record of suspension in the third grade, and they're
going like this [waves wildly] in the math class! I've seen that at some of our
schools in the deepest parts of the flatlands.

Q: Are you saying their teachers caught their attention because they
spoke ebonics?

A: What they knew was how to hear the child, listen to the child,
correct the child, and make the child feel good about being corrected.
These are teachers who have been through our Standard English Proficiency Program.

Q: Give me an example.

A: Well, I go to classes to read to the kids. Everybody knows   30
Dr. Seuss, so I made the presumption that I could read a page and the child
would read a page. I found two things: Either the kids could not read, or
they could read, but the words they pronounced were definitely not on that
piece of paper.

Q: What were they saying?

A: -*ing's* left off of words, consonants left off words, and you begin to
think: "Does this kid have dyslexia? Half the word is falling off." And then
I went to Prescott Elementary, and I noticed that in [teacher] Carrie Secret's class, where most of the kids are from the housing projects, they were
excited about learning. They could read, and tell you what they had read,
had great diction, good reasoning skills. And this was the third grade.

Q: You're saying that the kids in this class had better diction than kids
in other classes with the same background?

A: Yes. And I began to ask Carrie Secret, "What are you doing differently?" She told me about the Standard English Proficiency Program. So

when a kid did not make the -*ing* sound, or left off a consonant or made a word singular when it should be plural, or plural when it should be singular, Carrie would repeat back to the young people until they began to hear the correct word.

Q: How did she do it?

A: The child says, "I'm going wif my mother." Or, "I'm goin 35 home." She says, "Where?" And the child says, "I'm going to go home."

Q: When you heard children speaking standard English, you were thrilled. You're sounding like the critics of your own ebonics resolution.

A: Standard English is (necessary) to go to a four-year college, to being accepted in an apprenticeship program, to understanding the world of technology, to communicating. We owe it to our kids to give them the best that we've got.

Q: There's great disagreement over black English as a language, language "pattern" or just street slang. What is black English?

A: All I know is that it's not slang. The linguists call that "lazy En- 40 glish." But our children come to school with this language pattern. Go back to what they call the Negro spiritual: "I'm going to lay my 'ligion down." That was the code song that got you your ticket on the Underground Railroad. It's the way the words were used. So they might have thought we were old dumb slaves, but it served a purpose. It was communication.

Q: Do some parents and children resist speaking standard English because they really see it as white English?

A: I don't think they consciously resist. My youngest daughter has had that criticism: "You talk like a white girl." It's another way of saying, "How come you don't sound like us?" It hurts to be accused of that. When I was a girl, it was a goal to speak standard English, not a ridicule. I have no idea how that changed.

Q: Why don't children automatically know standard English, since they hear it all the time on television and at school?

A: Two things. African Americans whose economic status and exposure is closer to that of the Huxtables have the exposure to work with the youngsters, and teach them about the "two-ness" of the world they're involved in. But some schools are located in very depressed areas, have a primary population of African Americans on a fixed income. They see very little, the young people are exposed to very little, and there isn't a whole lot of reason in the home—this is just my guess—to adopt the behavior of duality.

Q: Do you believe that the language pattern of black English is 45 genetic?

A: It's ancestral. "Genetic" doesn't say "in your blood, in your biology." It says, "in the beginning!"

Q: Following that logic, why don't other ethnic groups use the grammar of their immigrant ancestors?

A: No other group in America, outside the Native American, ever had to grope (as we did) with the new language. If you didn't get off the

Good Ship Lollypop speaking English, learning it was exacerbated by the fact that you had to sneak to teach yourself. Then if you stay together in an isolated, segregated environment, the language pattern persists over time.

Q: And yet there are millions of African Americans who speak with no trace of ebonics.

A: And there are an awful lot of second- and third-generation Chinese who speak perfect English, but when they go home to grandmother, they make the switch.

Q: And many African Americans don't. Is this an issue of class?

A: In some instances, it is class. You know, having come from a family of educators, it was a symbol of your ability to speak the King's English. I remember my mother telling me the tragedy is that as those kids became comfortable with the tools of the middle class, one of which was language, they began to turn their backs on their parents. They were embarrassed about their language style.

Q: This is the traditional immigrant experience. What's unusual is for children to cling to the language patterns of their elders.

A: Here is where it's confusing to some, but to others, I think they have ulterior motives.

Q: What's the ulterior motive?

A: The English Only campaign. We talked informally among the school board members. Be careful, don't get caught up in the English Only campaign.

Q: And the ulterior motive is the anti–affirmative action movement?

A: The funding is from the same platform. Right-wing America. It used to be that we'd just simply say it was racism. But now they are so sophisticated that it's about being anti-black, anti-Jewish, anti-immigrant, anti anything that's not Christian. Anti-urban, anti-female, I mean they just kind of took everybody and just threw us all over there together. We have no allies over there. None whatsoever.

Q: If nothing else, you've gotten them to add anti-ebonics to the list. But you've also gotten many people on your side, haven't you?

A: I'd love to be able to tell you how we plotted and planned to become the topic of everybody's conversation in the world. That's dishonest. It took me by surprise.

Q: You had been very opposed to changing any of the controversial wording in you resolution—that ebonics is "genetically based," for instance, and that students will be taught "in ebonics." Yet you changed your mind. What happened?

A: Sometimes you have to look: Are you winning the battle but losing the war? The African American Task Force met (for about 10 hours) last week and got no closure on the word "genetics." Then Oscar Wright, the old man of the group, said, "If removal of this word will heal the pain of the African American community, then remove the word." When that old man gave the word, we moved on. I felt fine about that. I would have stayed on course, but the village said to do things differently.

Q: Did you grow up speaking ebonics?

A: No, but I heard it. You've got to think about coming up in a seg-regated time. In 1954, when the school desegregation decision came, I was 10. But the more I think about it, the more I think about how blessed I've been. Both of my parents had graduate degrees. My dad was a dentist. My mom was a linguist with the National Security Agency. We were never quite sure what she really did. We knew she spoke perfect Russian. We used to say Mom was a spy for the FBI. And we always thought that Mommy was the smartest thing we ever saw.

Q: So language and politics were always entwined in your family? 65

A: Everyone in my family, whether it was Mom or Dad, they were always crusaders. You never earned the right to snub your nose at anybody based on speech patterns. I remember a time we went down the street, and a drunk said something to my sister Twink, and she laughed. Mom gave her a backhand, and said, "That man meant nothing but to be kind. Go back and say: 'How do you do, sir?'" She was serious. My mother was 4-foot-9, and 89 pounds, boy. And she spoke perfect English.

Q: Did you send your own children to private schools?

A: Both (religious and public) schools. I have two girls. Arlene, 31, is teaching in San Francisco. Leslie will be 33 this year. They got exposed to some things in all environments. But only in California was the diversity. Here they've got everybody. I like that. This is real.

Q: California's diversity is unusual even in America, isn't it?

A: But that's the advantage. That's the gift. If we are really taking 70 pride in the diversity, is it not important that we know something about everything that makes us Americans? Because the tragedy is that really, multicultural curricula in our schools are predicated in the philosophy of, "Can't we all get along?" I don't care whether we all get along. I care whether you respect me and know something about me.

Q: Why is that the job of teachers? Why isn't that the job of parents and neighbors and friends?

A: It's all of our jobs. But I think what this (ebonics issue) does is show we are a long way from being a multicultural society. Somehow, talk-ing about anything African American makes people very tight-lipped and angry, and wondering, "Am I being politically correct?" Our prejudice comes out.

Q: Or our ignorance?

A: Yeah. If you ever want to see how segregated our schools are, go to the teachers' lounge. Very segregated. We are all operating from a state 75 of ignorance.

Q: How will the Oakland school board pay for expanding this pro-gram to teach standard English?

A: The program is now paid for by federal Title I money. So we'll move money from other Title I programs that are less effective, and into this one, which makes more sense. And we'll evaluate how well it's going.

Q: In Los Angeles, school board member Barbara Boudreaux said she will try to get federal funding if the board approves her ebonics resolution. Will Oakland do the same?

A: It's a useless fight. Those bilingual kids don't get enough money already. Besides, those are federally mandated funds. When you start using those funds for other than what the law mandates, you get into a very dangerous zone called "supplanting." That is not our goal.

Q: And that's illegal?   80

A: Hell, yes.

Q: Was your resolution a trial balloon for bilingual funds that Riley did not go for?

A: No. There was never any intent on the part of the board to ask for bilingual funds. No. The intent is to expand the Standard English Proficiency Program.

Q: Why did you and the board make it so difficult for the public to get copies of your resolution? The board seemed to be hiding it.

A: I know, I looked for it on the Web site and I didn't see it, either.   85 I don't understand why.

Q: Is it because the resolution didn't stand on its own until the board prepared to change its controversial wording on Wednesday?

A: For me it always stood on its own. But it was getting to be ugly — which black leader can we find to kick y'all in the butt now? They were not focusing on the problems of kids that brought us to this point.

While Rome is burning, we're trying to figure out whether the song we're singing is politically correct. But now that we've gotten past the wordsmithing, it's time to roll up our sleeves and do the work. We've got a class that is getting ready to graduate and may not even have a grade-point average of 1.8! Rome is burning, folks. It's burning! I don't know how much more pitiful we've got to get.

The Responsive Reader

1 How does Cook sketch out the concerns that led the school board to adopt the controversial resolution? What were typical student attitudes toward language in her district? What were typical attitudes of teachers and administrators? What is Cook's view of the connection between poor academic performance on the one hand and students' and teachers' attitudes toward language on the other?

2 Some of the critics of the Oakland resolution called Black English "slang." What is Cook's answer? What is your own definition of slang, and what to you are typical current examples?

3 What does Cook mean by the "two-ness" of the world of her students? What does she mean by the "behavior of duality"? Why do some African American students learn it while others don't?

4 How would you describe Cook's basic attitude toward standard English? What was her own experience with standard English? What did her par-

ents teach her about language? How were language and politics entwined in her upbringing?

5   According to Cook, what makes the relationship of African Americans
    to the English language different from that of immigrant groups from
    non–English-language backgrounds? Why does she think, for instance,
    that language issues are different for the many Asian students in her area
    of California?

6   Charges of racism started flying both ways in the Ebonics controversy.
    What "ulterior motives" does Cook identify or suspect on the part of
    people who attacked the initiative? How does she think the politics of
    racism have changed from earlier days of crude, overt antiblack preju-
    dice? (What do you know about the English Only movement?)

Talking, Listening, Writing

7   Do you know people who are or were embarrassed by the language of
    their parents, family, or neighborhood? Are you?

EBONICS PLAN IS WORTH A LISTEN

Angelo Figueroa

**"This fact remains: Black kids who grow up in the
inner-city speak in a distinct dialect that makes
learning standard English a major challenge."**

*Many of those vocal in the Ebonics controversy were people never seen vis-
iting inner-city schools or drumming up funds for the improved recruitment and
training of minority teachers. In the words of one African American commentator, for a while "it was hard to sort everything out, what with all the hollering and the blood and the hum of the chainsaws." Finally people talking about
their own experiences with becoming bilingual or bidialectal or with teaching
bilingual or bidialectal students were beginning to be heard.*

*Angelo Figueroa is a Latino columnist who went to school in a predomi-
nantly black neighborhood in Detroit. When he wrote this article in 1996, he
was working for a newspaper in San Jose, another city with a large minority
population. The ethnic mix in the area includes Mexican Americans, Fil-
ipinos, Vietnamese, and Koreans, among others.*

Thought Starters: In a widely publicized sensational court case, a prominent African American lawyer criticized a witness for saying he heard "a

black voice." Do you think you can tell whether a person calling you on the telephone is black, or from a Spanish-speaking background, or from some other distinct linguistic group? Why or why not? How can you be sure?

_____

If you're like me, you probably never heard of the word Ebonics.   1

Well, the word will probably become part of our collective lexicon.

Ebonics, as I understand it, is a word to describe black vernacular or more simply, the way some black people talk. The term derives from the words ebony and phonics.

Oakland public school officials made national headlines when they declared that Ebonics is so radically different from English that it merits special recognition. The district wants to train Oakland teachers to understand Ebonics so they can use it as a springboard to teach black students standard English.

Now, I suspect that many of you—or at least the guy who called me   5
Friday to rant about the issue—believe that this is insane.

Why should tax dollars be used to teach teachers how to use a fractured form of English?

I can understand the stick-to-the-basics sentiment, but don't agree with it.

How, for example, is our average school teacher supposed to translate something like this if they don't understand it:

> *Yo, what up, dog? What it be like? I's fixin' to scoop you in my hoopty so we can jet to Jerome's crib and kick it. I likes to listen to some mad tunes, if Jerome's moms don't be trippin, all-ight?*

While this may be a hack's example of Ebonics and common street slang, this fact remains: Black kids who grow up in the inner-city speak in a distinct dialect that makes learning standard English a major challenge.

I grew up in a predominantly black neighborhood in Detroit. I   10
learned the street slang and sentence structure that everyone else around me employed.

Spanish was my first language, adding to my language confusion.

Fortunately, I've always loved to read and learned standard English more from books than grammar classes. Otherwise, I wouldn't be writing this column.

For many kids, the language barrier created by a mixture of slang and Ebonics places them at a disadvantage when they have to work or study outside their communities. Many are so intimidated, in fact, that they simply drop out—out of school and the mainstream.

That's why I applaud the Oakland school system if the goal is to make teachers aware of Ebonics so that they can help students overcome its potentially crippling impact.

Some may counter that it would be better if the black community 15 simply abandoned black English. But that's like expecting Latinos to stop speaking Spanish because a law making English the official language is passed.

It's not realistic.

Black folks have been speaking a different dialect and using different phrasing to express themselves since the days of slavery. There's nothing wrong with that. If there were, Texans and New Yorkers would have been forced to take diction classes long ago.

Language isn't static. It's constantly evolving. Ebonics and street slang add spice to our language and give its speakers a sense of cultural identity they can be proud of.

But let's be clear about one thing: Ebonics and slang don't play in the boardroom. In other words, it doesn't work in a marketplace where standard English rules.

Both blacks and Latinos must recognize that mastering English is vi- 20 tal to their success in the United States.

That's the way it be's whether we likes it or not.

The Responsive Reader

1   How does Figueroa's own experience give him a special insider's perspective on the controversy? A major issue was whether or not the challenges facing Spanish-speaking students and students with Black English are similar.

2   What do you think is Figueroa's answer? How would you sum up his position on the relation between "dialects," or "vernaculars," and standard English? What should be the teachers' goals? What methods might work?

Talking, Listening, Writing

3   Do both sides in the controversy accuse each other of "stigmatizing" the students? Why or how? Why would the students be stigmatized, and what could or should be done about it?

4   Some Americans retain a first language or downhome dialect. Others seem to leave it behind at least in part more quickly than others. And some rediscover a first language or dialect as they go back to their roots. To judge from your own experience or observation, what makes the difference? Do you think of a first language or downhome dialect as a liability or as an asset?

5   The playwright Imamu Amiri Baraka once said, "I heard an old Negro street singer, Reverend Pearly Brown, singing, 'God don't never change!' This is a precise thing he is singing. He does not mean 'God does not ever change!' He means 'God don't never change!'" What is the difference? What is Baraka talking about?

WRITING
WORKSHOP 9

Writing to Define

Define important terms to make sure they have the same meaning for you and your readers.
As a writer, you have to be prepared for a key question: "What do you mean?" Definition stakes out the territory a term covers. To define means to draw the line.

- We hear much today about dysfunctional families. When does a family qualify for the label *dysfunctional?*

- Who is poor in our society? It depends on where we draw the *poverty line.* Poor people live the realities of poverty every day. However, in legislation and in assistance programs, poverty is a matter of definition. How far below the living standard of average Americans does a family have to be to before it is officially classified as poor?

- Who is a *qualified applicant* for a job or a promotion? It depends on the criteria of the people who do the hiring. What qualifications are they looking for? Do they require a high school diploma or a college degree? Do they require previous experience? Do they require a high score on a psychological aptitude test?

Definition makes sure that words do not remain "just words." Careful definition prevents misinterpretation or misreading. It can clear up confusion for your readers. It can alert them to slow shifts in the meaning and uses of important words.

Triggering

Identify important terms that may confuse, mislead, or deceive your readers.

When does definition become an issue? When may a reader say: "What exactly do we mean by this word?" Here are situations that may make you decide to define a key term:

▪ *You help readers see why a current buzzword pinpoints an issue.* Why did terms like the following start to come up again and again in headline news and on the business pages of newspapers?

OUTSOURCING Companies farm out work previously performed by their own fulltime employees to middleman organizations to secure substantial savings when the work is performed by temporaries without union protection, pension rights, or health plans. Also, the quasi-anonymous middleman employers are less subject to media scrutiny or litigation than prominent national corporations.

OFFSHORING Instant computer hookups make it possible for companies and government agencies to outsource much white-collar and high-tech work to countries like India and China. Corporations realize big savings by laying off American workers and using highly skilled, English-proficient overseas personnel for functions including accounting services, credit card billing, and software development.

▪ *You explain a difficult word or technical term.* A brief definition may be needed to fill in a blank in your reader's mind. Will your readers know that the term *recidivism* refers to repeat offenders? You may need to explain briefly the pattern of released convicts becoming repeat offenders and returning to prison as if through a revolving door. A brief example showing the word used in context usually helps.

A recent study indicates that the **recidivism** rate—the rate of released inmates returning to jail as *repeat offenders*—may be as high as 79 percent.

▪ *You narrow the meaning of a general label.* Often definition is needed to give exact meaning to **umbrella terms** that cover much ground. What for you is the core meaning of a *conservative?* What values would you expect a "true conservative" to uphold in areas like foreign relations, the environment, or government services? What would you include in a capsule definition of a *liberal agenda?* How militant or progressive does a publication or program have to before you label it *radical?*

▪ *You redefine important categories.* The boxes you are expected to check on a questionnaire may make you ask: "What do you mean?" Is a person with two French and two Hawaiian grandparents of "European descent"? Is a person with an Irish father and an African American mother white or black? Who is Jewish in our society is a matter of definition. Is it a matter mainly of culture? religion? family tradition? race?

■ *You examine emotionally charged words and labels.* You may have to alert your readers to the **connotations**—the emotional or judgmental overtones—of offensive words, of fighting words, of words perceived as condescending or insulting. Why are terms like *race* or *minority* under attack today? (Is it because they are often used to identify *someone else's* race or to label someone *outside* the mainstream as a minority?)

Gathering

Gather evidence of how an important term is used in the real world.

How do you gather material for a definition paper? When you explore the meanings of important words, you become a word watcher. Your note-taking and file-building will collect material to help you answer questions like the following:

- What does a key word mean in practice?
- Who uses the word? in what situations? for what purpose?
- Are there several main uses or related meanings?
- Have there been important changes in the meaning or use of the word?

You may know the word *anecdote* as a term for a short and often amusing story that had some personal meaning for the person telling it. However, when you check out research material, you may find a more technical important use of the term used in evaluations of research material. You may read passages like the following:

> The love of the media for human interest-stories may actually keep them from analyzing the social issues they raise. Coverage based on **anecdotes** has a way of blaming the individuals directly or indirectly for hardships instead of probing the responsibility of government or society.
>
> The dominant media approach is an **anecdotal** story that focuses on individuals and their problems but is short on social context or discussion of the underlying issues.

Evidence such as this shows that the labels *anecdote* and *anecdotal* are used by researchers who warn against exclusive reliance on limited personal observation and testimony. Will vivid human interest stories be truly representative? Should they be checked against more objective research techniques tracking and verifying larger patterns?

An **extended definition** is a definition in depth of a much-used important term. Early in gathering material for an extended definition you may set up slots for different kinds of supporting information. Such categories become a **discovery frame,** serving to program a systematic stock-taking of promising material.

Here are categories you may set up as you collect material for a definition of the term *Latino*.

Latinos—Stand Up!

PERSONAL EXPERIENCE   Where did you become aware of the term *Latino?* Where did you hear or see it used—in school, on the news, in political discussion? Who used it and for what purposes? Did you become aware of it as an Anglo or other outside observer? Or were you a member of a group that identified with the term?

CORE MEANING   What is the current core meaning of the term *Latino?* Is there a common denominator?

Latinos (*Latino* for a male, *Latina* for a female) are people speaking one of the Latin-derived languages of Central and South America—Spanish or Portuguese. They speak one of the languages of Latin America, or they may still know it after acquiring English as a second language. They may maintain cultural ties with the traditions or religion of Spanish-speaking people of the Americas.

HISTORY   What is the origin or historical background of the term? Were there major stages in its development?

Latin was the language of the ancient Roman empire. Spanish and Portuguese developed as local varieties of Latin in Roman imperial territories that are now Spain and Portugal. The Spanish and Portuguese invaders or conquistadores brought these Latin languages to the New World, where they became the dominant languages of Latin America. Only remnants of the indigenous original native languages are still spoken, for instance, among the Maya of Guatemala

RELATED OR CONTRASTING TERMS   What related terms cluster around the term? What other choices or alternative terms are often used?

The terms *Latino* and *Hispanic* are often used interchangeably in political discussion or news reports. However, *Hispanic* is a more limited term. Literally interpreted, it would leave out immigrants from Portuguese-speaking Brazil. Also, advocates asserting pride in the indigenous populations of the Americas before the Spanish conquest may reject the associations of the term with a history of conquest and persecution. Many consider *Hispanic* mainly a government classification. In the American Southwest, the term *Chicano* (female *Chicana*) became widely used by politically active Mexican Americans identifying strongly with their Mexican past. Writers and artists have started to use the term *Americanos* to refer to Americans with strong ties to Latino culture.

POPULAR OR MEDIA STEREOTYPES   What popular misunderstandings cluster around the term?

Popular journalism and government agencies use the term *brown* when actually Latinos show a whole range of physical characteristics and skin color attesting to their multiracial ancestry. They are many black Latinos of African ancestry, many fair-skinned Latinos of European ancestry, and many shades of skin color for Latinos of indigenous ancestry.

CHANGING CONNOTATIONS   Have the media by and large left offensive stereotypes behind? How do the media reflect changing perceptions and associations?

Gradually the media have moved beyond the stereotypes of low-income or undocumented Latinos to recognize those successful in business, in education, and politics, with Latino voters becoming a major political force. Latino performers like Linda Ronstadt and Marc Antony have reached large audiences. At the same time, the media and the political establishment increasingly recognize the contribution of Spanish-speaking immigrants who do much of the nation's work.

Shaping

Structure an extended definition to highlight major issues, major dimensions of the term, or major stages in its history.
What are effective organizing strategies for presenting an extended definition? Here are some strategies you may choose or adapt in organizing a definition paper:

- *Aim at establishing a core meaning for a much debated term.* For example, you may examine several real-life examples of *affirmative action,* to find what they have in common. Examples may include requirements for reserving a share of government contracts for minority-owned or minority-operated firms. They may include aggressive programs for bringing students from inner city schools to a leading university. They may include programs for helping women to break through the "glass ceiling" and advance to top-level management. How are these requirements and initiatives related? What do you think is the prevailing or most useful meaning of the term? Is there a common denominator that you can present as your thesis early in your paper?

- *Focus on a misunderstanding of a term and try to correct it.* You lead from the misleading or counterproductive use of the term to what you consider its true meaning. For instance, affirmative action is often defined in terms of compensatory justice — compensating or making amends for injustices of the past. Other advocates of affirmative action initiatives focus on the present—stressing the need to level the playing field in a society promising that all are "created equal." However, still others look toward the future and stress the common-good argument: They do not want the next generation to inherit a society where poverty and neglect have led to spiraling crime and violence.

Leveling the Playing Field

THESIS: Affirmative action benefits society as a whole.

- Compensatory justice appeals to a sense of white guilt and asks society to make amends for past injustice.
- Leveling the playing field requires action to make up for present inequalities in educational and economic opportunity.
- The common-good argument asks for affirmative action to prevent escalating crime and violence in the society of the future.

- *Focus on establishing a historical perspective.* For instance, what do people mean by *grassroots democracy?* You decide to trace key stages in the meaning of the term *democracy* from its original Greek meaning—"rule by the people"—to modern times. You move from the *direct* democracy of ancient Greece (with a whole electorate of eligible citizens voting on major decisions) to the *representative* democracy of modern times (voting on major issues by proxy through elected representatives or delegates of the people). From there, you move to the participatory, town-meeting democracy advocated by those who claim that democratic institutions have become too isolated from the people.

The Voice of the People

THESIS: True democracy means giving the people a real voice in shaping their destiny.

- DIRECT DEMOCRACY—All qualified citizens vote.
- REPRESENTATIVE DEMOCRACY—Elected representatives vote as delegates.
- PARTICIPATORY DEMOCRACY—Citizens participate in decision making at the grassroots level.

Revising

Revise your definition to sharpen it and back it up with convincing examples.

How much are you going to profit from suggestions and criticism from instructor's feedback or peer reviewers?

- *You may need to draw a clearer line.* When does flirtation become sexual harassment? When does criticism of the government become unpatriotic?

- *You may need to add convincing real-life examples.* Hypothetical or made-up examples carry little weight. They are easy to write and easy to slant in order to prove a desired point.

- *You may need to strengthen your paper with a detailed case history.* For a paper on racial balance in the schools, you may decide to trace a school desegregation case from original petitions and actual legal opinions through successes and reverses.

- *You may need to acknowledge damaging negative connotations.* For many readers, the term *gun control* evokes fears of goverment control and bureaucratic meddling. Shifting the emphasis to *gun safety* may broaden the base of support for efforts to reduce gun violence.

EDITOR'S TIP!   *Avoid bland or obvious dictionary definitions.* Try not to start a paper by saying "Webster's Dictionary defines *equity* as the practice of being fair and equal." (Note that Noah Webster is long dead, and several publishers of dictionaries have appropriated his name to help promote their books.) Use a dictionary definition only when it will help readers rethink vague or fuzzy uses of a weighty term like *genocide* or *cooptation*.

A Paper for Peer Review

What is the overall plan in the following student paper? What problems of definition does the writer recognize? What is the core definition that emerges from the paper?

Dem's Fightin' Words!

When does ordinary name-calling turn into offensive slurs?
Where do we draw the line when people use racial epithets or demeaning language directed at other groups? What do we do about it? **Drawing the line between offensive speech and legitimate expression is not easy.**
————————>>>>>>>>>>>>>>>>>>>

(The **introduction** raises the issue and leads into a cautiously worded **thesis**.)

"Faggot! Hope you die of AIDS! Can't wait till you die!" These words were shouted, not by an ignorant twelve-year-old, but by Keith R., a law student at Stanford University. Weeks later, when confronted, he said he had used offensive language on purpose in order to test the limits of freedom of speech at Stanford. Others doubt that his use of language was an experiment; they say it closely coincided with opinions he had expressed in *The Stanford Review*.
————————>>>>>>>>>>>>>>>>>>>>>>>>>>>>>>>>>>

(After the very general introduction, this paragraph brings the issue to life by bringing in a provocative test case.)

When dealing with abusive individuals like R., the natural impulse is to legislate, to pass ordinances, to enforce guidelines. If we could only ban offensive language, expel the offender, or shut down an offending magazine, we would get rid of the problem. Many colleges have tried this tack by instituting "Fighting Words" rules. Responding to the pain felt by the victims of racism, sexism, and homophobia, these schools have as necessary amended their constitutions to forbid certain offensive expressions. Violators may be reprimanded or even expelled. At Dartmouth, for instance, a student was called on the carpet for asking in class whether it was possible to "cure" homosexuals.

————————————>>>>>>>>>>>>>>>>>

(This paragraph provides a sympathetic account of a **proposed solution** to the problems that was widely tried.)

The objection to such rules is that they inevitably have what lawyers call "a chilling effect" on the free expression of ideas. These rules inevitably pose a problem of definition: Where do we draw the line? Who decides what is offensive, and to whom? Standford's "Speech Code" made a brave attempt to minimize the problem by being very specific. It read in part: "Speech or other expression constitutes harassment or personal vilification if it: (1) intends to insult or stigmatize an individual or group of individuals on the basis of sex, race, color, handicap, religion, sexual orientation, or national or ethnic origin; (2) is addressed directly to the individual; (3) makes use of insulting or fighting words or gestures."

How would this rule apply to the speeches of Malcolm X, who for a time referred to whites as "white devils"? On the other hand, what set of rules could stop a person like Keith R. from being personally offensive? He could have expressed his hostility by gestures instead of words—a wink, a leer, a walk, humming a few bars of "Here Comes the Bride."

————————————>>>>>>>>>>>>>>>>>

(This paragraph presents one strong **objection** to the solution proposed earlier.)

The British writer Christopher Isherwood (who often referred to himself as Christopher Swisherwood) insisted on using words like *faggot* and *queer*. He said that by using them and making them ordinary, he could help take away their power to insult and to hurt. Would Mr. Isherwood be censored today on Stanford's green and pleasant lawn? No, say supporters of the Speech Code, because his use of language was not intended to offend. **But this puts the censors into the business of judging the intent of an expression—looking into people's heads to judge what made them say what they said.** Who is going to say if an expression was used insultingly, kiddingly, or ignorantly?

————————————>>>>>>>>>>>>>>>>>

(This paragraph has presented an **additional objection** to the proposed solution aimed at controlling offensive language.)

(PROPOSED ALTERNATIVE SOLUTION)
At Stanford, the reaction to the incident was a petition condemning R.'s behavior, signed by almost five hundred students and faculty members. At the law school, a large poster read: "Exercise your right of free speech. Tell this law student what you think of his behavior. It may be legal, but it isn't right." **This has to be the definition of offensive language in a free society: What bigots and racists say may be offensive, but they have the right to say it, and we have the right and duty to talk back to them.** That is what free speech is all about.
If you take away the bigot's right to shout "Faggot!" you may also be taking away my right to say: "Shut up, you creep!" You may be taking away my right to call a religious fanatic a bigot or my gun-toting neighbor a redneck. Bad ideas and bad language cannot be legislated against; they must be driven out by better ideas.

(The conclusion strongly presents the writer's own **alternative solution** to the probem of offensive language: talking back!)

YOUR TURN:

1 Have you observed recent examples of people insulted or stigmatized "on the basis of sex, race, color, handicap, religion, sexual orientation, or national or ethnic origin"? What happened? How did you or others react? Were there any repercussions or consequences?

2 Do you think some kinds of hateful speech should be suppressed? Where would you draw the line?

3 Do you think violent speech needs to be stopped before it leads to violent acts? Why or why not?

Writing Options 9: Defining Your Terms

1 Where do you draw the line between ordinary abusive language and hate speech? To judge from your own observation, how serious a problem is hate speech on campus or in the larger society? Can or should it be counteracted? Are speech codes the answer?

2 For a time, voters and court decisions seemed to spell the end of affirmative action. Public opinion turned against quotas and "racial preferences." Then a Supreme Court decision and major initiatives by colleges and universities reopened the debate over affirmative action. What does the term *affirmative action* mean today?

3 What does the term *minority* mean? What kind of group qualifies as a minority? Who decides? For instance, do Polish Americans count as a minority group? Are Jews a minority group? Are there different kinds of minorities—ethnic, cultural, racial, or religious?

4 Which Americans are white? Who decides? Are Mexican Americans white? What test cases might you examine? Are possible descendants of Thomas Jefferson and a half-white woman who was one of his slaves and a half-sister of his deceased wife white or black?

5 What does *macho* mean? Are the term and the machismo it labels a thing of the past? Who uses the term and why? How do you react to it?

6 Public figures and religious leaders praising traditional values are defending traditional marriage. How would you define the traditional marriage? Where or how widely does or did it exist in real life? Some critics claim that it exists mostly in reruns of old movies and fifties television programs. Are they right, or are they wrong?

7 Are young women today reluctant to identify themselves as feminists? Why or why not? Is it true that many take advances or progress for granted but resist the label?

8 Current surveys show that fewer young Americans identify with organized religion, but at the same time there is much search for a spiritual dimension in life. How do you define spirituality?

9 What is "compassionate conservatism"? Who uses the term? Who objects to it and why?

10 Is there such a thing as reverse racism or reverse dicrimination?

10

VIOLENCE
Living at Risk

Khalid al-Mihdhar passes through a security checkpoint at Dulles airport in Washington.

Brothers Nawaf (left) and Salem al-Hazmi leave checkpoint on their way to the plane.

Hijackers were searched at D.C. airport on 9/11

Hani Hanjour believed to have piloted the flight, passes a checkpoint without incident.

Nawaf al-Hazmi is examined by an airport security official before boarding American Airlines Flight 77 on the morning of Sept. 11, 2001.

Photo by Associated Press

Report out Today   Video shows 4 pulled aside before boarding flight

VISUAL LITERACY 10
SURVEILLANCE CAMERA: THE FACE OF TERROR

Traditional war photography and film making showed the faces of a country's own and also often the faces of the enemy. In modern wars, the people killed or maimed in bombings or terror attacks have increasingly never seen the faces of their enemy. Sometimes viewers unexpectedly get a glimpse from nonconventional sources: A surveillance camera at an East Coast airport watched terrorists being screened or even searched without arousing suspicion before boarding a plane on their suicide mission. The passengers shown here were part of the September 11 terrorist attack on the World Trade Center and targets in the nation's capital. Finally released to news sources and the general public, these fuzzy surveillance camera pictures show several of the hijackers taking their carry-on luggage with them onto the doomed planes.

Reading the Image

1   Developing and installing of *security equipment* has become a major industry. Surveillance cameras are widely used in banks and airports. Where else have you seen them? What purposes do they serve? How do they work? Are you surprised there was archived footage of the suicide terrorists before they highjacked the plane they crashed into the Pentagon?

2   Do the media create or perpetuate *stereotypical images* of supposedly typical terrorists? What is your mental image of a terrorist? What do you expect terrorists to look like? Do the people shown in these pictures look like terrorists to you? Why or why not? What do they look like to you? (Some of them are wearing slacks and Oxford shirts.)

3   Has the war on terror caused or heightened *anti-foreign feelings* or antagonism toward foreigners? Are you or people you know suspicious of foreign-looking fellow passengers or fellow customers in a bank? Are there kinds of foreigners that make you suspicious or uneasy? Are there others you "feel comfortable with"?

4   Have you or people you know well gone through stepped-up *airport security* recently? The 9/11 surveillance videos were obtained by lawyers representing families of the victims. The lawyers charged that security screeners failed to examine the hijackers' carry-on baggage as required by federal regulations and airline standards and failed to discover the hijackers' weapons. Do you think current security procedures would foil the plans of a new generation of terrorists? Why or why not?

5   Airport screening personnel and security personnel are often given a *terrorist profile* of potential or suspected hijackers. Working alone or with a group, what profile of a potential terrorist would you provide to security personnel after studying these surveillance camera pictures?

10

VIOLENCE
Living at Risk

"As a crime victim and a citizen, what I want is the reality of a safe community—not a politician's fantasyland of restitution and revenge."

—BRUCE SHAPIRO

Is violence as American as apple pie? Drive-by shootings, youth gang killings, drug vendettas, serial killers, and celebrity murders provide a steady diet of crime news for the American public. Only the most horrible violent incidents, like the Columbine massacre of high school students by two suicidal fellow students who videotaped their goodbyes, merit extensive media coverage and soul-searching after the fact.

The media mirror a society in which violence is out of control and a major source of entertainment. Movies and television programs featuring Godfather mafiosi or Sopranos goons go on to top-of-the-charts sequels and reruns and win awards. Schwarzenegger movies featuring Terminator killers travel around the globe, advertising what a French journalist called the "culture of brutality."

Violence is an integral part of our historical and cultural legacy. The greatly improved firepower of early modern rifles made the American war of secession the most murderous war in American history. The twentieth century brought wars deploying an unprecedented technology of mass destruction. A generation of young men on both sides of the conflict was killed by machine guns and massive artillery bombardment in the trench warfare of World War I. In World War II, civilian casualties from saturation bombings, scorched earth policies, and campaigns of extermination rivaled the numbers of those killed in combat.

Many Americans came here as refugees with the physical and psychological scars of repression, starvation, and genocide. Today, American cities have rates of violent crime and random murder unprecedented in the developed countries of the West. Many Americans live in fear of violence. What is the answer? Will affluent Americans living in sheltered communities continue to vote for law and order candidates? Will the war on drugs continue to put large numbers of Americans from low-income or minority backgrounds behind bars?

FRIENDS KNEW ALLEGED GUNMAN'S PLANS

Ben Fox

"While staying overnight Saturday with his friend Joshua Stevens, 15, Williams spoke specifically about shooting up the school."

In the nineties, a spate of bloody school shootouts shook up parents and students long used to murderous gunplay as entertainment on the television and movie screen. Parents who said they bought guns to protect their families and homes discovered that they had not protected their children and their teachers when they attended school. While relatives of the dead and of maimed survivors often reacted with stunned disbelief, media commentators and an outpouring of online popular comment tried to fix blame. One psychologist blamed a lack of "impulse control" on the part of immature young people— in a society where most of the murderers killing family, ex-lovers, coworkers, or other targets of gun violence are adults.

How much of the following Associated Press report reprinted from American Online News *in 2001 is "just the facts, please"? How much is interpretation, editorializing, finger-pointing, or attributing blame?*

Thought Starters: How close have you been to gun violence? Do you know anyone who has been shot, or do you remember a report of a shooting that made a special impression on you? What was the person's story? Who did what? What led up to what? What was the aftermath of the shooting? Who was blamed? How could what happened have been prevented or avoided?

SANTEE, Calif. (March 6)—A 15-year-old boy fired randomly at fellow students and had eight bullets left in his gun when police cornered him in a bathroom after he killed two teen-agers at school, investigators said Tuesday.

Friends said the scrawny freshman accused in the nation's latest high school bloodbath talked about his plans over the weekend, and they took him seriously enough to pat him down before school started Monday.

One adult even warned Charles Andrew "Andy" Williams not to commit "a Columbine," and tried to call the boy's father but didn't follow through. But no one is known to have reported the threats that preceded Monday's attack that also wounded 13.

During a news conference, authorities said the carnage could have been much worse if not for the swift actions of a sheriff's deputy and an off-duty police officer who was on campus.

When the boy surrendered, his gun, a .22-caliber long rifle revolver, 5 was fully loaded with eight rounds of ammunition, its hammer cocked, investigators said.

"I do believe that if it had not been for the conduct of the people involved . . . it would have been even worse," Sheriff Bill Kolender said.

The gunman appeared to be firing indiscriminately, sheriff's Lt. Jerry Lewis said. Most of the students who were hit were struck as they fled down a hallway between the school's library and administration office.

"The information we have from the evidence and the witnesses (is) the suspect was firing randomly at anybody who was going by," Lewis said. "Any student who was going by he was shooting at."

Although Santana High closed Tuesday, students, parents and others gathered outside to place flowers at a makeshift memorial site and share their grief. Some expressed anger that acquaintances of Williams heard him make threats in recent days but failed to warn authorities.

"I think they're to blame, too," said Helen Howard, a 10-year resident 10 of the community who came to the high school with her husband. "I just can't understand why they didn't say anything."

During a morning counseling session at a church, an American Red Cross representative asked for a show of hands of people who had trouble sleeping the previous night. About a third of the 200 people who attended indicated they did.

"You may just feel like your heart is beating all the time and you can't calm down," Robert Bray, a Red Cross disaster mental health worker, told the audience. "I want to reassure you that people do get through this."

Teachers were told to report to school district headquarters.

As authorities dug into the case, the first question for many was: How could so many people see the warning signs and fail to act?

"That's going to be haunting me for a long time," said Chris Reynolds, 15 29, who heard the threats and didn't report them.

Williams, held in a juvenile facility Tuesday, will be charged as an adult with murder, assault with a deadly weapon and gun possession, District Attorney Paul Pfingst said. The adult prosecution is mandatory under a ballot measure approved last year, and the boy could face multiple life terms. Arraignment was set for Wednesday.

Pfingst said the gun belonged to Williams' father, Charles, a lab technician at the Naval Medical Center–San Diego, since July. It had been stored in a locked cabinet, investigators said. Sheriff's and FBI officials Monday night searched the Williams' apartment and said they removed seven rifles, a computer, a plastic crate filled with papers and files, and about a half dozen bags filled with evidence.

Bryan Zuckor, 14, and 17-year-old Randy Gordon were killed; 11 other students and two adults—a student teacher and a campus security worker—were wounded. The adults and four students remained hospitalized in good or fair condition.

The shooting happened Monday morning in this overwhelmingly white, middle-class suburb of San Diego, a town that prides itself on its country atmosphere and low crime rate.

Youngsters were out and about as one "block" of students who start   20
early in the day headed to their next classes and another group—Williams' "block"—arrived for their first classes.

The boy shot two people in a restroom, then walked into a quad and fired randomly, sheriff's Lt. Jerry Lewis said. He stopped to reload as many as four times, getting off 30 or more shots, Lewis said.

"It was total chaos. People were trying to take cover," said student John Schardt, 17, who was in a nearby classroom when the shooting started. He said the shooter had a smile on his face.

"Pop, pop, pop and everyone started ducking," recalled student Nika Ocen-Odoge.

Barry Gibson, 18, said he ran at the sound, then returned with two others when they saw a friend fall to the ground. The friend rolled onto his side, spitting up blood.

"We were asking him, 'Are you OK?'" Gibson told the *Los Angeles*   25
Times. Amid another burst of fire, Gibson ran. "I got hit in the leg," he said. "It went numb."

Authorities have said little about a motive for the rampage, but the suspect's life abounds in warning signs that have become as familiar as the TV images of frightened students being herded to safety from the presumed safe harbor of a suburban school.

Williams, whose parents are divorced, occasionally visited his mother, Linda Wells, in North Augusta, S.C. He and his father moved to California from Frederick County, Md., last year.

He's skinny kid, a skateboarder "wannabe" friends said. There's talk of recent scrapes with booze and a girl, a breakup, and a beating by another teen-ager at the skateboard park where he hung out. His skateboard was stolen twice, one friend recalled.

"He was picked on all the time," student Jessica Moore said. "He was picked on because he was one of the scrawniest guys. People called him freak, dork, nerd, stuff like that."

While staying overnight Saturday with his friend Joshua Stevens, 15,   30
Williams spoke specifically about shooting up the school, according to Stevens and Reynolds, who is dating Stevens' mother.

Both moved tentatively to head off trouble, but failed.

"My friend A.J. patted him down this morning for guns, but he said he was joking," Stevens told *The San Diego Union-Tribune*. "I guess he had (the gun) by his crotch."

Alex Ripple, a 14-year-old who was present, said they searched Williams' body but not his backpack.

Reynolds said he warned Williams: "I even mentioned Columbine to him. I said I don't want a Columbine here at Santana. But he said, 'No, nothing will happen, I'm just joking,'" Reynolds told the AP.

Reynolds tried to call Williams' father on Sunday, but gave up after 35 getting no answer and then a busy signal, the *Los Angeles Times* reported.

There have been signs since the 1999 Columbine High massacre that left 15 dead in Colorado that teens and those around them have become more willing to report threatening behavior. At least four times around the country in recent months students reported threats and possibly averted violent episodes at school.

The Responsive Reader

1 How many press reports or television news accounts like this Associated Press story have you read or watched? Can you construct a "generic" or archetypal *news report* of a school shooting that would include most of the common or recurrent elements? What "bottom-line" details would you include that most of the time seem to be part of the story? Compare your "Profile of a School Shooting" with those prepared by your fellow students. What did they include that you left out?

2 Most groups have a code of honor about not informing, or "snitching," on their friends. Do you think the *friends* in this instance did not care enough? What precautions did they take, and do you think these were insufficient? What would you have done that they did not do? Should the adults have done more?

3 An explanation surfacing often in this and similar accounts is the bullying and *outgrouping* that unpopular kids undergo in school. What form did it take in this case? Does what happened seem familiar or unusual to you? How common or widespread is this kind of thing? How serious is it? Does anyone have an answer to the problem? What can or should be done?

4 Although the familiar slogan says that guns do not kill people, two young people in this incident were killed by shots fired from a gun that was still "fully loaded," with plenty of ammunition to kill many additional people. In this long press report, how many lines are devoted to the *gun?* What kind was it? Where did it it come from? Why did the boy have it? Why do you think the father had seven guns?

Talking, Listening, Writing

5 This report says that after the "bloodbath" the first question many asked was: "How could so many people see the warning signs and fail to act?" What would have been your first question?

Collaborative Projects

6   After a tragedy such as this, are the victims often briefly mourned and
    then forgotten? How much attention is devoted to the victims? Work-
    ing with a group, you may want to explore the aftermath of a school
    shooting or prepare a tribute to a victim or victims of gun violence you
    knew or read about and especially cared about.

A PEACEFUL WOMAN EXPLAINS WHY SHE CARRIES A GUN

Linda M. Hasselstrom

"I am a peace-loving woman. But events in the past 10 years have convinced me I am safer when I carry a pistol."

For a time it seemed that the argument over gun control had divided the American public into two camps. Debate seemed polarized: Liberals were asking citizens to hand in their guns as a first step toward a safer, saner world. Conservatives seemed to be defending the constitutional right of citizens to assemble arsenals of lethal weapons for armed resistance against an evil government.

In recent years, however, women especially have been rethinking their attitude toward guns as the symbol of a violence-prone civilization. Increasingly, law enforcement seemed incompetent to protect women from battering abuse and homicidal violence. Linda M. Hasselstrom originally wrote the following widely read call for women's self-reliance and self-defense in 1991 for the High Country News, *a regional Rocky Mountain publication. She is from the grasslands of western South Dakota near the Black Hills. Her family had homesteaded in the late 1800s in the "vast emptiness" of the South Dakota prairie along with other Swedes and Norwegians. She has worked as a cattle rancher, saying that "someone who pays attention to the messages the natural world sends can bring cattle home the day* before *a blizzard nine times out of ten." A poet and environmental activist, she for years operated her own small press, named Lame Johnny after a horse thief.*

Thought Starters: What advice does law enforcement give to women concerned about safety? Is it helpful? Is it useless? Does it reflect a male point of view?

I am a peace-loving woman. But several events in the past 10 years   *1*
have convinced me I'm safer when I carry a pistol. This was a personal decision, but because handgun possession is a controversial subject, perhaps my reasoning will interest others.

I live in western South Dakota on a ranch 25 miles from the nearest town: for several years I spent winters alone here. As a free-lance writer, I travel alone a lot more than 100,000 miles by car in the last four years. With women freer than ever before to travel alone, the odds of our encountering trouble seem to have risen. Distances are great, roads are deserted, and the terrain is often too exposed to offer hiding places.

A woman who travels alone is advised, usually by men, to protect herself by avoiding bars and other "dangerous situations," by approaching her car like an Indian scout, by locking doors and windows. But these precautions aren't always enough. I spent years following them and still found myself in dangerous situations. I began to resent the idea that just because I am female, I have to be extra careful.

A few years ago, with another woman, I camped for several weeks in the West. We discussed self-defense, but neither of us had taken a course in it. She was against firearms, and local police told us Mace was illegal. So we armed ourselves with spray cans of deodorant tucked into our sleeping bags. We never used our improvised Mace because we were lucky enough to camp beside people who came to our aid when men harassed us. But on one occasion we visited a national park where our assigned space was less than 15 feet from other campers. When we returned from a walk, we found our closest neighbors were two young men. As we gathered our cooking gear, they drank beer and loudly discussed what they would do to us after dark. Nearby campers, even families, ignored them: rangers strolled past, unconcerned. When we asked the rangers point-blank if they would protect us, one of them patted my shoulder and said, "Don't worry, girls. They're just kidding." At dusk we drove out of the park and hid our camp in the woods a few miles away. The illegal spot was lovely, but our enjoyment of that park was ruined. I returned from the trip determined to reconsider the options available for protecting myself.

At that time, I lived alone on the ranch and taught night classes in town. Along a city street I often traveled, a woman had a flat tire, called for help on her CB radio, and got a rapist who left her beaten. She was afraid to call for help again and stayed in her car until morning. For that reason, as well as because CBs work best along line-of-sight, which wouldn't help much in the rolling hills where I live, I ruled out a CB.

As I drove home one night, a car followed me. It passed me on a narrow bridge while a passenger flashed a blinding spotlight in my face. I braked sharply. The car stopped, angled across the bridge, and four men jumped out. I realized the locked doors were useless if they broke the windows of my pickup. I started forward, hoping to knock their car aside so I could pass. Just then another car appeared, and the men hastily got back in their car. They continued to follow me, passing and repassing. I dared not go home because no one else was there. I passed no lighted houses. Finally they pulled over to the roadside, and I decided to use their tactic: fear. Speeding, the pickup horn blaring, I swerved as close to them as I dared as I roared past. It worked: they turned off the highway. But I was frightened and angry. Even in my vehicle I was too vulnerable.

Other incidents occurred over the years. One day I glanced out a field below my house and saw a man with a shotgun walking toward a pond full

5

of ducks. I drove down and explained that the land was posted. I politely asked him to leave. He stared at me, and the muzzle of the shotgun began to rise. In a moment of utter clarity I realized that I was alone on the ranch, and that he could shoot me and simply drive away. The moment passed: the man left.

One night, I returned home from teaching a class to find deep tire ruts in the wet ground of my yard, garbage in the driveway, and a large gas tank empty. A light shone in the house: I couldn't remember leaving it on. I was too embarrassed to drive to a neighboring ranch and wake someone up. An hour of cautious exploration convinced me the house was safe, but once inside, with the doors locked, I was still afraid. I kept thinking of how vulnerable I felt, prowling around my own house in the dark.

My first positive step was to take a kung fu class, which teaches evasive or protective action when someone enters your space without permission. I learned to move confidently, scanning for possible attackers. I learned how to assess danger and techniques for avoiding it without combat.

I also learned that one must practice several hours every day to be   10 good at kung fu. By that time I had married George: when I practiced with him, I learned how *close* you must be to your attacker to use martial arts, and decided a 120-pound woman dare not let a six-foot, 220-pound attacker get that close unless she is very, very good at self-defense. I have since read articles by several women who were extremely well trained in the martial arts, but were raped and beaten anyway.

I thought back over the times in my life when I had been attacked or threatened and tried to be realistic about my own behavior, searching for anything that had allowed me to become a victim. Overall, I was convinced that I had not been at fault. I don't believe myself to be either paranoid or a risk-taker, but I wanted more protection.

With some reluctance I decided to try carrying a pistol. George had always carried one, despite his size and his training in martial arts. I practiced shooting until I was sure I could hit an attacker who moved close enough to endanger me. Then I bought a license from the county sheriff, making it legal for me to carry the gun concealed.

But I was not yet ready to defend myself. George taught me that the most important preparation was mental: convincing myself I could actually *shoot a person*. Few of us wish to hurt or kill another human being. But there is no point in having a gun—in fact, gun possession might increase your danger—unless you know you can use it. I got in the habit of rehearsing, as I drove or walked, the precise conditions that would be required before I would shoot someone.

People who have not grown up with the idea that they are capable of protecting themselves—in other words, most women—might have to work hard to convince themselves of their ability, and of the necessity. Handgun ownership need not turn us into gunslingers, but it can be part of believing in, and relying on, *ourselves* for protection.

To be useful, a pistol has to be available. In my car, it's within instant   *15*
reach. When I enter a deserted rest stop at night, it's in my purse, with my
hand on the grip. When I walk from a dark parking lot into a motel, it's in
my hand, under a coat. At home, it's on the headboard. In short, I take it
with me almost everywhere I go alone.

Just carrying a pistol is not protection; avoidance is still the best approach to trouble. Subconsciously watching for signs of danger, I believe
I've become more alert. Handgun use, not unlike driving, becomes instinctive. Each time I've drawn my gun—I have never fired it at another
human being—I've simply found it in my hand.

I was driving the half-mile to the highway mailbox one day when I
saw a vehicle parked about midway down the road. Several men were standing in the ditch, relieving themselves. I have no objection to emergency
urination, but I noticed they'd dumped several dozen beer cans in the road.
Besides being ugly, cans can slash a cow's feet or stomach.

The men noticed me before they finished and made quite a performance out of zipping their trousers while walking toward me. All four of
them gathered around my small foreign car, and one of them demanded
what the hell I wanted.

"This is private land. I'd appreciate it if you'd pick up the beer cans."

"What beer cans?" said the belligerent one, putting both hands on the   *20*
car door and leaning in my window. His face was inches from mine, and
the beer fumes were strong. The others laughed. One tried the passenger
door, locked; another put his foot on the hood and rocked the car. They
circled, lightly thumping the roof, discussing my good fortune in meeting
them and the benefits they were likely to bestow upon me. I felt very small
and very trapped and they knew it.

"The ones you just threw out," I said politely.

"I don't see no beer cans. Why don't you get out here and show them
to me, honey?" said the belligerent one, reaching for the handle inside
the door.

"Right over there," I said, still being polite. "—there, and over
there." I pointed with the pistol, which I'd slipped under my thigh. Within
one minute the cans and the men were back in the car and headed down
the road.

I believe this incident illustrates several important principles. The men
were trespassing and knew it: their judgment may have been impaired by al-
cohol. Their response to the polite request of a woman alone was to use
their size, numbers, and sex to inspire fear. The pistol was a response in the
same language. Politeness didn't work: I couldn't match them in size or
number. Out of the car, I'd have been more vulnerable. The pistol just
changed the balance of power. It worked again recently when I was driving
in a desolate part of Wyoming. A man played cat-and-mouse with me for
30 miles, ultimately trying to run me off the road. When his car passed mine
with only two inches to spare, I showed him my pistol, and he disappeared.

When I got my pistol, I told my husband, revising the old Colt slo- 25
gan, "God made men *and women*, but Sam Colt made them equal." Recently I have seen a gunmaker's ad with a similar sentiment. Perhaps this is
an idea whose time has come, though the pacifist inside me will be saddened if the only way women can achieve equality is by carrying weapons.

We must treat a firearm's power with caution. "Power tends to corrupt, and absolute power corrupts absolutely," as a man (Lord Acton) once
said. A pistol is not the only way to avoid being raped or murdered in today's world, but, intelligently wielded, it can shift the balance of power and
provide a measure of safety.

The Responsive Reader

1 Why was Hasselstrom dissatisfied with the advice she was given about
   how to avoid danger? What *alternatives* did she check out before she
   turned to guns? What were her conclusions?
2 What about where and how she lived put Hasselstrom especially *at risk?*
   What are the key points she is trying to make about the incidents she
   describes? Do you think these are "isolated incidents" or parts of a familiar pattern of male behavior?
3 How concerned is Hasselstrom about the "intelligent" use of guns?
   What does she think it takes for women to use guns successfully for protection? What *warnings* or advice does she have for other women?

Talking, Listening, Writing

4 The incidents that Hasselstrom reports took place in an isolated rural setting. Do you think her arguments could apply equally in a crowded urban environment? Why or why not?
5 Do you think that safeguards or precautions could be developed to limit
   the use of guns to self-defense or to make them safer for their owners
   and their families?
6 Are there still men who think that female victims of rape or male violence probably "asked for it"?

BEYOND THE FINGER POINTING

Fred Barbasch

> **"Might those Americans who genuinely believe in a constitutional right to bear arms accept a revision of the amendment to suit the era of automatic weapons?"**

After a shootout at a Colorado high school, a columnist for the Washington Post *said that "handgun shootings are a bloody way of life across America." On April 20, 1999, Hitler's birthday, two students at Columbine High School who wore black trenchcoats and exchanged Nazi salutes gunned down thirteen students and one teacher, killing themselves and maiming other students for life. Their weapons included handguns and a sawed-off shotgun. One of the dead was an African American student whom the killers singled out using a racist epithet and whose parents had complained without effect about an earlier death threat aimed at their son. In a video that had been seen by others, the two students had staged a homicidal fantasy, killing fellow students.*

Like other shootouts, the event produced a feeding frenzy on the part of the media and a temporary clamor for gun control. The leadership of the National Rifle Association took the stand that "it's not a gun control problem; it's a culture control problem." The author of the following article was the business editor of the Washington Post. *He was the newspaper's London correspondent from 1994 to 1997. Barbash tries to take his readers beyond the immediate aftermath of the Columbine incident when, in the words of another writer for the* Washington Post, *"commentators, politicians, and all manner of experts were on television attacking their favorite scapegoats." Barbash tries to put the Columbine tragedy in a larger context.*

Thought Starters: Would you describe the high school or high schools you attended as a "safe environment"? Why or why not?

In March 1996, a demented gun enthusiast wielding four perfectly legal weapons walked into a primary school in Dunblane, Scotland, and mowed down a teacher and 16 children, ages 5 and 6, before killing himself. I arrived at the school a few hours later to cover the story and left the town after several wrenching days thinking about my own children and whether there was any possibility that the British would seize the moment to attack their gun problem, lest they wind up like the United States.

To my amazement, the shootings did provoke a serious nationwide deliberation, which included public hearings before a government-appointed commission about the way the perpetrator got his guns, the

1

warning signs that might have been heeded but weren't, and the effectiveness of existing gun laws. The commission also considered the extent to which any new and restrictive legislation might affect the thousands of target shooters and gun clubs (including one composed of members of the House of Commons) and whether a change in the law could be structured to preserve their sport while also protecting the public.

The testimony at the hearings replayed in excruciatingly slow motion the methodical slaughter of the Dunblane children, which regalvanized the public's anger. By the time legislation reached the floor of the Commons, the politicians knew they were being watched closely by their constituents, who were mobilized by lasting rage and by a grass-roots organization called Snowdrop. Over the considerable opposition of Britain's gun clubs and shooting enthusiasts—which have been an important force and an established part of British tradition—the Parliament soon enacted a ban on private possession of all large-caliber handguns. That was the work of a Conservative government. In June 1997, the newly elected Labor government tightened what was already one of the world's tightest gun laws by banning all handguns, regardless of caliber.

It was a "national conversation," something we often talk about here in the United States but rarely have—and have never really had on the subject of guns. The closest we've come to one was after the 1981 shooting of President Reagan and his press secretary, James Brady, a reaction that ultimately produced the 1993 Brady Act requiring federal background checks on gun purchasers.

So when a 14-year-old opened fire on his West Paducah, Ky., high school classmates in December 1997, killing three and wounding five, I thought that this would move us beyond the paralyzed and polarized debate that now characterizes our discussion about the right to keep and bear arms. It didn't happen. I thought the same thing after the shootings in Jonesboro, Ark., where two middle schoolers killed four girls and a teacher and wounded 10 others in March 1998. Then came Edinboro, Pa., (April 1998, one dead) and Springfield, Ore. (May 1998, two killed, more than 20 hurt). Four in six months, and still there was no reaction to compare with what I saw in Britain after Dunblane. The American response was more of the same—incantations from the extremes; silence from the middle, and prayers and pieties from the top.

Perhaps the massacre at Columbine High School in Littleton, Colo., will be the one that rouses us. We'll see. The first signs have been discouraging.

The president, in his public comments immediately after the shootings in Colorado, said that something should be done. But for the life of him, he couldn't bring himself to mention anything specific. "Well, I think on this case it's very, very important that we have the facts, in so far as we can find them out. You know, we had the conference here last fall. The attorney general and the secretary of Education prepared the handbook for all the schools that we asked to be widely used. And we do have, from bitter and sad experience, a great cadre of very good, effective grief counselors. . . . I think after a little time has passed, we need to have a candid assessment about what more we can do to try to prevent these things from happening."

His wording—"after a little time has passed"—suggests that it would somehow be reckless or in bad taste to discuss remedies in our current state of grief. However, the administration signaled that it understood that something beyond prayers was called for. It announced that it would send Congress a series of gun control measures, including one aimed at adults who, through negligence, allow guns to fall into the hands of children. Hillary Rodham Clinton spoke out as well and Attorney General Janet Reno said, "We've got to get the guns out of the hands of young people"—which sounds good until you think about it. (Why only young people? The Dunblane massacre was the work of an adult.)

Meanwhile, the so-called gun "lobby"—the shorthand by which the media often describe the National Rifle Association and its supporters— conveyed that it understood the potentially explosive nature of this moment perhaps better than the president. Colorado sponsors of legislation to permit the carrying of concealed weapons and limit the ability of municipalities to restrict guns were busy withdrawing their bills. "Nobody's going to be able to discuss it rationally," Bill Dietrick, an NRA lobbyist in Colorado, told the *Denver Post.*

On the same day, the NRA itself said that it was canceling most of the events planned for its annual convention (which just happened to be set for Denver) to "show our profound sympathy and respect for the families and communities in the Denver area in their time of great loss."   *10*

I have no reason to doubt the NRA's sympathy. But I suspect what it really respects is the power that comes from an enraged populace, particularly from those who heretofore have remained uninvolved.

Acting While Enraged has moved this nation mightily in the past. A novel, "Uncle Tom's Cabin," galvanized abolitionist sentiment in the North before the Civil War. Another novel, Upton Sinclair's "The Jungle" (1906), helped give us our food safety laws. A horrible fire at the Triangle Shirtwaist Factory in 1911, in which 146 mostly immigrant female workers died because they had no way out, inspired the enactment of workplace health and safety laws. The Selma-to-Montgomery march helped inspire the civil rights revolution. Footage of men in barbed-wire camps moved us to involvement in Bosnia. Descriptions of small children laboring overseas to make our expensive running shoes is changing industrial practice. The list is as long as our history.

I sense great shock over these repeated outbreaks of violence at schools. But I do not yet sense outrage. Is it that school shootings are somehow seen as isolated acts with little or nothing in common? Or by accepting, as I certainly do, that there is a strong cultural aspect to such violence, do we somehow foreclose discussion of remedies that might only get at part of the problem rather than the whole?

We will, some experts tell us, never be able to fully explain the reasons for acts as heinous as those at Columbine High School. I accept that. But it's not the American way to conclude that nothing, therefore, can be done to stop those inclined to such violence.

Similar arguments against a proposed course of action—it won't solve 15 the whole problem, it might not work at all, the criminals will just ignore it—have been made against almost every piece of important social legislation in U.S. history. They've been made and generally rejected on the theory that in the absence of all the answers, we should go with the ones we have.

Why the stalemate? We let ourselves off too easily by blaming "the gun lobby." The gun lobby is powerful only insofar as the rest of America stays out of the debate. This is the classic situation of the funded and boisterous minority wielding outsized power thanks to the quiescence of everyone else.

The Second Amendment argument—at least in its current form—is a political one, deployed as a conversation stopper. Whatever the actual meaning of the Second Amendment to the Constitution ("A well regulated Militia, being necessary to the security of a free State, the right of the people to keep and bear Arms, shall not be infringed."), it is no bar to a vigorous debate over the pros and cons of banishing assault weapons or automatic weapons or semi-automatic weapons or any other high-powered weaponry. Because the Supreme Court has never defined how this flintlock-era part of the Bill of Rights applies to individual ownership of weapons of massive destruction, I (and more importantly, most legal scholars) see no constitutional obstacle to legislation.

Might those Americans who genuinely believe in a constitutional right to bear arms accept a revision of the amendment to suit the era of automatic weapons? By now, I suspect, most Americans believe that violence in the schools and in the country generally is both a gun problem and a culture problem. More importantly, I believe that most Americans would say that addressing the availability of high-powered guns somehow precludes tackling cultural issues. And it would be my estimate that most Americans, rather than regarding a gun control initiative as bad taste at this point or as disrespectful to the families of Littleton, would consider it part of an appropriate response to the deaths in Colorado.

The problem so far is that "most Americans" have been disinclined to join this controversy, as was the case with most Britons until the Dunblane killings. In my view, the greatest insult to the friends and families in Dunblane, West Paducah, Jonesboro, Edinboro, Springfield, Littleton and indeed to ourselves, would be silence.

The Responsive Reader

1   Do you think the Dunblane and the Columbine shootings can be use-fully *compared?* What is similar, and what is different? Are the two coun-tries too different to make the comparison useful, or is there a similar lesson to be learned from both events?

2   Barbasch directs his *criticism* at both the general public and the political leadership of the country. What does he fault them for? What does he say about the role of the gun lobby? What is his attitude toward the NRA?

3   What examples does Barbasch cite of other issues in our history where aroused *public opinion* brought about important changes in attitudes and legislation? Which of these to you seem most and which least relevant or convincing?

4   After he became president of the NRA, Charlton Heston said that the *Second Amendment* was the "most vital" of all the amendments and "more essential" than the First Amendment. Often disagreements about the amendment focus on its reference to a militia. Why does the refer-ence matter? How does Barbasch seem to go beyond familiar arguments?

Talking, Listening, Writing

5   President Clinton has said that he went hunting as a boy and that he un-derstands the gun culture of his Southern home state. What has been your experience with or observation of the "gun culture"? Can you contribute anything to the current dialogue about gun control from your experience?

6   NRA spokespersons stress the failure of society to enforce laws aimed at controlling gun-toting criminals or felons. Would more stringent con-trols on criminals have affected the incidents Barbasch discusses?

7   Media critics charge that the media exploit the sensational thrill of vio-lent events like the Columbine shootings but do not follow up by show-ing the true cost in human suffering. Check media coverage of the Columbine event: How much follow-up coverage has there been of the shattered lives of the victims' families or of the years-long odyssey of wounded and maimed shooting victims?

8   To do something about murderous drunken-driving accidents after proms or graduation parties, some schools require that all students at-tending such events arrive by bus rather than private car. Do you think schools and parents could develop any similar initiatives, programs, or precautions to help stem gun violence in schools? (As a parent, would you be fatalistic about gun violence in the schools?)

FIND IT ON THE WEB

For background on current gun-control initiatives and recent developments on the gun-control issue, one student researcher went to websites like the ones described below:

- The official homepage of the National Rifle Association (www.nra.org) guides the researcher to speeches by prominent NRA officials, videos, and archives providing facts, statistics, and information about gun-related legislation.

- The website for the Anti-Gun Coalition of America (www.agca.com) provides information on people, organizations, and businesses that favor strong anti-gun legislation. It provides helpful links to other sites.

- While the NRA has moved toward possible compromise on issues like gun safety training, the Gun Owners group (www.gunownersca.com) is known as one of the more uncompromising pro-gun groups. Following up the Gun Owners logo may lead the researcher to "fact sheets" and other publications by the Gun Owners Foundation Online.

WHITE MAN

Tobias Wolff

"I was the tallest man out there by at least a head, and I had to stay right next to the radio operator, who had this big squawking box on his back and a long antenna whipping back and forth over his helmet. And of course I was white."

Tobias Wolff became known for his autobiographical This Boy's Life, *which has been called "an unforgettable memoir of an American childhood."*

Like other young Americans of his generation, Wolff found himself in the army in Vietnam—in a nightmarish losing war, in a disorienting different culture, and in alien natural surroundings. After World War II, the French had lost a disastrous colonial war to reestablish their rule over their Indochinese territories. The independence movement in the former Indochina was led by the communist Vietminh in Vietnam and the Khmer Rouge in Cambodia, and the United States joined in the fight to defend Western-sponsored local governments in the name of the Cold War struggle against communist aggression. The Vietcong, the southern arm of the North Vietnamese liberation movement, led a classic guerilla war against conventionally trained American troops.

In his In Pharaoh's Army: Memories of the Lost War *(1994), Wolff wrote a searingly honest eyewitness account from the point of view not of the generals, the propagandists, or the political commentators but of the unknown ordinary soldiers sent out to fight, to die, or to return shell-shocked and traumatized to society.*

Thought Starters: Is the Vietnam War ancient history for you or others of your generation? Do you know anyone who, like Wolff, is still close to the traumas and controversies of the lost war? Has the war and its aftermath disappeared from the news?

A week or so after Sergeant Benet and I made our Thanksgiving raid on Dong Tam, the division was ordered into the field. The plan called for our howitzers and men to be carried by helicopter to a position in the countryside. I was sent ahead with the security force responsible for preparing the ground and making sure it was safe to land. My job was to call in American gunships and medevacs if any were needed. I could even get F-4 Phantom jets if we ran into serious trouble, or trouble that I might consider serious, which would be any kind of trouble at all.

The designated position turned out to be a mudfield. We were ordered to secure another site some four or five kilometers away. Our march took us through a couple of deserted villages along a canal. This was a free-fire zone. The people who'd lived around here had been moved to a detention camp, and their home ground declared open to random shelling and bombing. Harassment and interdiction, it was called, H and I. The earth was churned up by artillery and pocked with huge, water-filled craters from B-52 strikes. Pieces of shrapnel, iridescent with heat scars, glittered underfoot. The dikes had been breached. The paddies were full of brackish water covered by green, undulant slime, broken here and there by clumps of saw grass. The silence was unnatural, expectant. It magnified the sound of our voices, the clank of mess kits and weapons, the rushing static of the radio. Our progress was not stealthy.

The villes were empty, the hooches in shreds, but you could see that people had been in the area. We kept coming across their garbage and cooking fires. Cooking fires—just like a Western. In the second village we found a white puppy. Someone had left him a heap of vegetable slops with some meat and bones mixed in. It looked rotten, but he seemed to be doing okay, the little chub. One of the soldiers tied a rope around his neck and brought him along.

Because the paddies were flooded and most of the dikes broken or collapsed, we had only a few possible routes of march, unless we moved off the trail; but mucking through the paddies was a drag, and our boys wouldn't dream of it. Though I knew better I didn't blame them. Instead we kept to what little remained of dry land, which meant a good chance of booby traps and maybe a sniper. There were several troops ahead of me in the column and I figured they'd either discover or get blown up by anything left on the trail, but the idea of a sniper had me on edge. I was the tallest man out here by at least a head, and I had to stay right next to the radio operator, who had this big squawking box on his back and a long antenna whipping back and forth over his helmet. And of course I was white. A perfect target. And that was how I saw myself, as a target, a long white face quartered by crosshairs.

I was dead sure somebody had me in his sights. I kept scanning the 5 tree lines for his position, feeling him track me. I adopted an erratic walk, slowing down and speeding up, ducking my head, weaving from side to side. We were in pretty loose order anyway so nobody seemed to notice except the radio operator, who watched me curiously at first and then went back to his own thoughts. I prepared a face for the sniper to judge, not a brave or confident face but not a fearful one either. What I tried to do was look well-meaning and slightly apologetic, like a very nice person who has been swept up by forces beyond his control and set down in a place where he knows he doesn't belong and that he intends to vacate the first chance he gets.

But at the same time I knew the sniper wouldn't notice any of that, would notice nothing but my size and my whiteness. I didn't fit here. I was out of proportion not only to the men around me but to everything else—

the huts, the villages, even the fields. All was shaped and scaled to the people whose place this was. Time had made it so. I was oafish here, just as the Vietnamese seemed oddly dainty on the wide Frenchified boulevards of Saigon.

And man, was I white! I could feel my whiteness shooting out like sparks. This wasn't just paranoia, it was what the Vietnamese saw when they looked at me, as I had cause to know. One instance: I was coming out of a bar in My Tho some months back, about to head home for the night, when I found myself surrounded by a crowd of Vietnamese soldiers from another battalion. They pressed up close, yelling and pushing me back and forth. Some of them had bamboo sticks. They were mad about something but I couldn't figure out what, they were shouting too fast and all at once. *Tai sao?* I kept asking—Why? Why? I saw that the question infuriated them, as if I were denying some outrage that everyone there had personally seen me commit. I understood that this was a ridiculous misunderstanding, that they had me confused with another man, another American.

"I'm the wrong man," I said. "The wrong man!"

They became apoplectic. I couldn't get anywhere with them, and I soon wearied of trying. As I pushed my way toward the jeep one of them slashed me across the face with his stick and then the rest of them started swinging too, shoving for position, everyone trying to get his licks in. I fought back but couldn't hold them off. Because of my height I took most of the punishment on my shoulders and neck, but they managed to hit me a few more times in the face, not heavy blows but sharp and burning, as from a whip. Blood started running into my eyes. They were swinging and screaming, totally berserk, and then they stopped. There was no sound but the feral rasp and pant of our breathing. Everyone was looking at the bar, where an American lieutenant named Polk stood in the doorway. He was the one they were after, that was clear from his expression and from theirs.

With an unhurried movement Polk unsnapped his holster and took 10 out his .45 and cocked it. He slowly aimed the pistol just above their heads, and in the same dream time they stepped back into the street and walked silently away.

Polk lowered the pistol. He asked if I was all right.

"I guess," I said. "What was that all about, anyway?"

He didn't tell me.

I was halfway home before it occurred to me that I could have saved myself a lot of trouble by pulling my own pistol. I'd forgotten I had it on.

Sergeant Benet cleaned my wounds—a few shallow cuts on my fore- 15 head. He had a touch as gentle as a woman's, and feeling him take me so tenderly in hand, dabbing and clucking, wincing at my pain as if it were his own, I started to feel sorry for myself. "I don't get it," I said. "Polk doesn't look anything like me. He's almost as big as you are. He doesn't have a moustache. He's got these piggy little eyes and this big moon face. We don't look *anything* alike!"

* * *

We found the second position to be satisfactory and set up camp for the night. Though the troops weren't supposed to build fires, they did, as always. They dropped their weapons any old place and took off their boots and readied their pans for the fish they'd collected earlier that day by tossing hand grenades into the local ponds. While they cooked they called back and forth to each other and sang along with sad nasal ballads on their radios. The perimeter guards wouldn't stay in position; they kept drifting in to visit friends and check on the progress of the food.

Nights in the field were always bad for me. I had a case of the runs. My skin felt crawly. My right eye twitched, and I kept flinching uncontrollably. I plotted our coordinates and called them in to the firebase and the air support people, along with the coordinates of the surrounding tree lines and all possible avenues of attack. If we got hit I intended to call down destruction on everything around me — the whole world, if necessary. The puppy ran past, squealing like a pig, as two soldiers chased after him. He tumbled over himself and one of the troops jumped for him and caught him by a hind leg. He lifted him that way and gave him a nasty shake, the way you'd snap a towel, then walked off swinging the puppy's nose just above the ground. After I finished my calls I followed them over to one of the fires. They had tied the puppy to a tree. He was all curled in on himself, watching them with one wild eye. His sides were heaving.

I greeted the two soldiers and hunkered down at their fire. They were sitting face-to-face with their legs dovetailed, massaging each other's feet. The arrangement looked timeless and profoundly corporeal, like two horses standing back to front, whisking flies from one another's eyes. Seeing them this way, whipped and sore, mired in their bodies, emptied me of anger. I shared my cigarettes. We agreed that Marlboros were number one.

The Responsive Reader

1 What was Wolff's assignment or role in the military dimension of the conflict? What early in his story can be read as if it were part of a straightforward bulletin from the front? Where does his account first become colored by the surreal or nightmarish quality that many participants came to associate with the Vietnam war?

2 White Americans are used to being lectured about using or abusing their race as a badge of privilege. How does Wolff's account turn the tables on this assumption of white superiority and privilege? What details and what incidents dramatize the traumatizing changed perspective that makes the white man see himself as target, as enemy, and as resented alien intruder? How did Wolff cope with his role as the designated target and enemy?

3 What do you learn from Wolff's account about the ordinary unglamorous, unheroic day-to-day reality of war for the foot soldiers between

murderous combat encounters? How serious or how casual are they about their assigned duties? What occupies their time? What signs are there of the camaraderie of the doomed?

4   Volumes have been written and countless documentaries produced about the motives, war aims, political movements, strategies, and changing fortunes of the Vietnam war. What is Wolff's perspective, attitude, or involvement concerning the war?

5   Racism became a poisonous undercurrent during the Vietnam war. Does it play a role in this account?

Talking, Listening, Writing

6   What war movies about Vietnam have you watched? How does Wolff's account compare with the picture they present of the war? What is similar, and what is different?

Collaborative Projects

7   Among books honoring the grunt or the high-risk FNG (f— new guy), Tobias Wolff's *In Pharaoh's Army*, Larry Heinemann's *Close Quarters*, and Tim O'Brien's *Going after Cacciato* stand out. Working with a group, you may want to organize a reading and discussion of selections from these and other survivors' testimonies. Denise Levertov's "What Were They Like?," Alberto Rios's "Vietnam Wall," and Jeffrey Harrison's "Reflection of the Vietnam Memorial" are among poems you may want to include in a reading paying tribute to the Vietnam war dead and victims of war.

THE BOY DIED IN MY ALLEY

Gwendolyn Brooks

An eloquent African American poet voices her overwhelming grief and helpless bystander's guilt as a witness to the senseless destruction of youth in her community.

The following poem is part of a life's work of powerful poems about the African American community by a woman who was a major force in the movement toward defining black identity and fostering black pride. From her early poems she published as high school student to her death in 2000, Gwendolyn Brooks wrote poems that became classics of American literature, including "Piano After War," "The Chicago Defender *Sends a Man to Little Rock," "Hunchback Girl: She Thinks of Heaven," and "The Chicago Picasso."*

Brooks wrote eloquent, challenging poems expressing her loyalty to people trapped in a web of poverty and racism. She populated the imaginary community of Bronzeville with a haunting array of the human beings behind the stereotypes and statistics. Her widely known poem "We Real Cool" has been called an anthem for doomed youth—who act "cool" and defiant as a defensive armor, who have dropped out and find themselves in the slow lane to a dead end.

Brooks grew up in a home filled with poetry, story, and song. "No child abuse, no prostitution, no mafia membership," she later said about her close-knit, loving family. She came to Chicago from Kansas and was honored as poet laureate of the state of Illinois. She was the first African American woman to receive a Pulitzer Prize for poetry. Brooks spent much time working with young people in colleges and schools and promoting workshops and awards for young poets.

Thought Starters: How do people in a community learn of incidents of violence in their neighborhood? Who are the witnesses? Who are the messengers? Who are the observers? What are their feelings and reactions?

Without my having known.   1
Policeman said, next morning,
"Apparently died Alone."
"You heard a shot?" Policeman said.
Shots I hear and Shots I hear.   5
I never see the dead.

The Shot that killed him yes I heard
as I heard the Thousand shots before;
careening tinnily down the nights
across my years and arteries.   10

Policeman pounded on my door.
"Who is it?" "POLICE!" Policeman yelled.
"A boy was dying in your alley.
A boy is dead, and in your alley.
And have you known this Boy before?"   15

I have known this Boy before.
I have known this Boy before, who
ornaments my alley.
I never saw his face at all.   20
I never saw his futurefall.
But I have known this Boy.

I have always heard him deal with death.
I have always heard the shout, the volley.
I have closed my heart-ears late and early.
And I have killed him ever.   25

I joined the Wild and killed him
with knowledgeable unknowing.
I saw where he was going.
I saw him Crossed. And seeing,
I did not take him down.   30

He cried not only "Father!"
but "Mother!
Sister!
Brother!"
The cry climbed up the alley.   35

It went up to the wind.
It hung upon the heaven
for a long
stretch-strain of Moment.

The red floor of my alley   40
is a special speech to me.

The Responsive Reader

1   We usually learn about deadly violence from our newspapers or television news. How does it change our perspective that we learn about the murder in this poem from the police officer yelling and pounding on the door? How does the poet feel about the police officer? Is he just a harbinger of bad tidings—a messenger bringing bad news? Is he just "doing his job?" What is his role in the poem?

2   Did the poet or the person speaking in the poem know the dead boy, or didn't she? If the poet "never saw his face at all," how can she say, "I have known this Boy before"?

3   How did the poet see the boy "Crossed"? What makes her say "I did not take him down"? How is the religious analogy or allusion carried through into the last words that the poet hears the boy cry out in her mind?

4   How can the poet say "I have killed him ever"? How can a person be both "knowledgeable" and "unknowing"?

5   Is there any hint or suspicion in the poem of who actually killed the boy? Is it strange that there is no speculation about an actual suspect? Why do you think the poet never asks the question?

6   How would you sum up the "special speech" that the blood-stained floor of the alley has for the poet?

Talking, Listening, Writing

7   Why does so much of what we respond to in this poem come to us as sounds—sounds heard, remembered, or imagined? How does the poet use language to make sure we hear the sounds with our mind's ear? What are striking examples?

8   Are you one of the people who hear the shots but "never see the dead"? Have you closed your own "heart-ears late and early"?

9   Brooks once said, "I am absolutely free of what any white critic might say" about her poetry—because it would be amazing if a white person could enter into the reality of the experience of African Americans in this country. Do you think a reader would have to be African American or a member of a minority group to understand this poem and respond fully to its message? Why or why not?

Collaborative Projects

10   In one of her poems, Brooks wrote: "Art hurts. Art urges voyages—and it is easier to stay at home/the nice beer at the ready." Working with a group, you may want to organize a poetry reading to honor Gwendolyn Brooks and her work.

FORUM: *Tough on Crime*

The fear of crime became a major theme in American politics. In the attack ads that political candidates use to make an opponent look bad, the charge of being "soft on crime" plays a major role. An incumbent is blamed when a convicted killer is paroled and kills again. Legislators are blamed when a child molester returns to a community without warnings going to parents. Law-and-order candidates promise voters to put career criminals in jail and "throw the key away."

Are tough sentences serving as a deterrent to crime? Do they express society's thirst for retribution or vengeance? Are they counter-productive, producing large numbers of embittered antisocial ex-offenders with no hope of reintegrating into society?

THE BROKEN WINDOW THEORY

Nathan Glazer

"New York City alone, with 3 percent of the American population, accounted for a large part of the national plunge in crime."

With crime rates in the United States unparalleled by rates in other developed countries, law enforcement in this country has come in for much public scrutiny. One section of public opinion accuses police and crime-fighting agencies of being too permissive—too lax in dealing with drug dealers, muggings, violent behavior at sports events, and molestation of citizens using public transport. Another section of public opinion accuses police of being too aggressive and insensitive, with many incidents of harassment of or police brutality toward members of minority groups.

A major drop in official crime rates was at first greeted with skepticism by experienced observers of the crime scene. Were citizens accepting petty crime as a fact of life, no longer reporting it because they expected little assistance from the police? Did city authorities downplay crime statistics in order not to scare away businesses or tourists? Nathan Glazer is a widely published journalist who wrote the following article for the "Hard Questions" column of the New Republic *in 1997, when the "Broken Window Theory" was widely touted and scrutinized.*

Thought Starters: Is crime a concern in your neighborhood or on your campus? What kind of crime is most common or most serious? What crime prevention initiatives have you observed? What steps have you taken to protect yourself?

Good news is always welcome, but it is also somewhat unsettling   1
when one has no idea why the news is good. New York City . . . recorded less than 1,000 murders in a year for the first time in over two decades, as part of the persisting and sharp drop in crime. Reported crime has fallen more than 43 percent in the city in . . . four years, and it has been noted that New York City alone, with 3 percent of the American population, accounts for a large part of the national plunge in crime. And, while New Yorkers may not fear murder on a day-to-day basis, something they do constantly fear—car theft—[showed] an equally astonishing drop, from 147,000 in 1990 to 60,000.

There has also been a decline in infant deaths in New York City to fewer than 1,000. . . . Though not as sharp as the drop in crime, the infant mortality rate fell from 21.6 per 1,000 births in 1970 to about 8 in 1996. It takes a long time for social policy analysts to examine all the figures and to accurately explain them. At the moment, even the experts appear to be guessing. One authority quoted in *The New York Times* attributed the reduction in crime to three forces: the decline of crack, the economic upturn and more aggressive policing strategies. One of the causes—the [economy]—seems dubious: there has been little correlation between crime and economic surges (or recessions) in the past. Moreover, there [wasn't] much of an economic upturn in New York City for the unskilled and less educated who contribute most to crime; indeed, the city's unemployment rates have remained persistently high, much higher than the national average.

The other two explanations—the decline of crack and more aggressive policing—seem more convincing to me. And they underscore a fundamental divide in how we explain changes in social statistics: Are they due to some . . . change in society and individual behavior, or is there some change in government that directly affects how people behave?

Certainly government will take the credit for these welcome results. The strongest thing going for Mayor Rudolph W. Giuliani [was] the remarkable decline in crime during his tenure. But does government really deserve the credit? And, if so, what change in government caused the transformation?

George Kelling, now a criminologist at Rutgers University, has been 5 the leading advocate of the "broken windows" theory, named after a 1982 article he wrote with the political scientist James Q. Wilson. Kelling argues that when the environment deteriorates because the police ignore relatively minor transgressions of civility and decent public behavior, not only do these transgressions increase, but more serious crimes do as well. Get the police out of the police cars, he says. Let them walk the beat again, talk to the people in the community, stop kids from breaking windows even in abandoned buildings, pay some attention to the mild transgressions rather than focus exclusively on the worst. His views have been persuasive. There has been a shift nationwide to more community policing. It is certainly an attractive theory. Even if it does not reduce serious crime, it contributes to a better environment.

But there have been other changes in policing and crime control that make it difficult to pinpoint one cause for the lower crime rates. According to *The New York Times*, in one neighborhood that has seen such a decline, "Federal, state, and local law enforcement agencies are working to drive out drug dealers with aggressive policing tactics." In another New York neighborhood, a pilot program has consolidated the various divisions of the police—housing, narcotics and others—under the control of a locally based commander, making it easier to coordinate investigations and capture drug peddlers.

And there are other potential causes for the abrupt decline in crime. A TV program, reporting on an equally sharp drop in teenage murders in

Boston, claims the fall is due to more aggressive control of teenagers on probation as probation officers work more closely with the police. A story in *The American Lawyer* attributes much of the reduction in New York City's murder rate to an aggressive young prosecutor using the Federal Racketeering Control Law to put away gang leaders for longer prison terms, and indeed, in the areas where the gang leaders have been prosecuted and incarcerated, there has been a sharp drop in homicides.

But there have also been other changes, owing nothing to government. More people now protect their cars against theft with wheel locks and car alarms (which unfortunately contribute to the din of the city). And more people install better door and window locks. Here people are acting on their own, regardless of what government does or doesn't do.

The steady fall in the infant mortality rate has received less attention in the press. But there do not appear to be any major new government interventions that might be responsible for it. Most programs directed at expectant mothers and infants have existed for twenty to thirty years, and in the last decade we have heard more about efforts to cut these programs than expand them. So we are back to the same question: Is government doing something right, or are more people simply doing something right?

We have become more skeptical about what government can do, but these positive changes, at least in crime, suggest that we have perhaps become too skeptical. The issue is not simply that government is doing something, but what it does and how it does it. Yet the changes we are seeing go beyond any governmental action. I do not think any expert would have predicted that the various reforms in policing and prosecuting would cause the recent plunge in crime. Nor do I think any expert looking at social conditions and government programs in New York City in 1980 could have predicted that the infant mortality rate would fall by 50 percent. 10

Perhaps government has been working less on social theory and more on resolving urgent problems through direct action. For example, New York City was afflicted for many years by the infamous squeegee men, who manned every major automobile entry into the city, cleaning windshields, often forcibly, in exchange for a tip. If upon taking office Mayor Giuliani had consulted sociologists, few would have predicted that having police simply get rid of the squeegee men would have much impact. But that is what the mayor did—and, strangely enough, the squeegee men did not return; nor was there any discernible increase in some other form of uncivil behavior or street extortion. So government can become more sensible even as it becomes smaller. But these statistics suggest that we are seeing changes in people's behavior that cannot simply be explained by what government is doing.

The Responsive Reader

1   What *statistics does* Glazer cite to support the widely believed conclusion that New York City did indeed experience a major drop in crime in the

nineties? What areas of city life or what branches of crime were affected? What makes the statistics "astonishing"?

2   What is the *broken windows* theory? How did it change law enforcement and police practices? How much credit does Glazer give to this explanation for the decline in crime in New York City in the 1990s? What changes in citizens' behavior and attitudes may have played a role? How are statistics for infant mortality related to the issue of crime rates?

Talking, Listening, Writing

3   Do you think that police should devote more time and effort to the so-called quality-of-life issues—preventing vandalism, fare-beating on public transportation, and other petty crimes? Why or why not? Do you agree with Glazer that such police work "contributes to a better environment"? Or do you think police work should focus on more serious violations of the law?

4   Official crime rates dropped nationwide in the 1990s, but local news broadcasts around the country have continued to devote a large percentage of their air time to coverage of local crime. If you watch television news, do you see much crime coverage? Do you think that news broadcasts about crimes make people more alert and careful? Or do you think they make viewers feel less secure by covering crime? Why or why not? What kind of crimes seem to get the most attention?

Collaborative Projects

5   Have charges of overly aggressive or insensitive police work been an issue in your area or community? Working with a group, you may want to track newspaper coverage of citizens' complaints, reports of police commissions, or other indicators of problems related to law enforcement practices or police tactics. What groups or organizations play a role in police-related controversies? Is there a pattern or common thread in the charges or the issues raised? What has been the outcome in key cases?

EMOTIONS CLOUDING RATIONAL DECISIONS

Steven Musil

> **"Many of us who were working at Chili's at the time of the murder were hoping for the death sentence. We wanted to see him die in the gas chamber for what he did to you."**

College campuses are no longer refuges from a violent outside world. Emergency phones and escort services are an attempt to provide some minimal security after spates of rapes in dorms or assaults in parking lots. Students working a few blocks from college campuses witness shootouts in fast-food restaurants or convenience stores.

Steven Musil was an editor for a student newspaper in 1998 when he wrote the following editorial about the loss of a friend. He writes as a witness—someone who took in and cared about something that for many newspaper readers was just a statistic. Musil asks a central question that for many remains unresolved: In a case like this, how do we make the punishment fit the crime? How do we respond to the cry for retribution or for vengeance?

Thought Starters: Do you think of your school or campus as a safe place? Are you aware of safety precautions? Do you take precautions yourself?

> **"An eye for an eye and the whole world goes blind."**
>
> —GANDHI

The following is an open letter to a lost friend.

Dear Dennis,

It has been two-and-a-half years since we last spoke. I'm sorry that I 1
haven't written to you before but I wasn't sure where to send this. I haven't seen you since two days before your funeral and I'm sure you must have many questions. First off, you probably know by now that Tony was your killer. Last week, a jury found him guilty and sentenced him to life in prison without the possibility of parole.

All the articles in the newspaper got me thinking about the whole mess again. I watched some of the trial downtown and a couple days ago I visited your memorial in front of Chili's. It has been hard to forget lately.

Many of us who were working at Chili's at the time of the murder were hoping for the death sentence. We wanted to see him die in the gas chamber for what he did to you. Some of us even felt sorry for him before we realized that he murdered you. The autopsy reported that you were shot once in the back of the head with a sawed-off .22-caliber rifle and then twice in the face after you fell to the floor.

The coroner said that you probably didn't know what was happening and you died instantly without suffering. Is that true? The sheriff found the rifle and about $1,600 in cash in his apartment on the day of your funeral. I was one of the last to be told.

The jury "let him off" because he had "no prior convictions of vio-   5
lent crimes or anything of that sort," according to the jury foreman.

Everyone at Chili's liked you Dennis. Even Tony. He testified that he was in a confused, cocaine-induced trance and needed the money to cover some debts. He said that he knew he would have to kill whoever was in the restaurant at the time. You weren't even scheduled to work that day, but were doing another manager a favor. I'm thankful no one else was there.

It just seemed so unfair. You were so young. So nice, so gentle. I regret the hard time we gave you at the Fourth of July party the night before. Do you remember? We were kidding you because you were the only married manager without children. The night before you died you said that it was time to have a child.

They closed the store for a couple of days for the investigation and to clean up. With all the extra time, some of the cooks decided to go camping, stay together. We had a real hard time dealing with it so we just took off. We ended up on a beach south of Santa Cruz. We bought a couple cases of beer, built a bonfire and toasted your memory all night until the sun came up the next day.

That night we made a pact to visit the campsite every year in your honor. A year later, I was the only one that returned. Many of those people don't work at Chili's anymore and are hard to get a hold of. I'm sure they haven't forgotten you.

It touched some people so that they revised their personal stance on   10
capital punishment. After your murder there were people stating that they had rethought the issue and now supported the death penalty, gun control, and assorted other related causes. I admit that I too made my gun control decision based on the emotional aftershock. I'm not sure if someone can make a rational decision of such importance based on an emotionally traumatic event.

Anyway, I don't have a lot of room to write to you. I have to tell you that I'm putting this behind me and you probably won't hear from me again. Know that we haven't forgotten you just because we are going on with our lives. Somehow I think you would have wanted it that way. Take care of yourself.

Your friend,
Steven

The Responsive Reader

1   What are the bare facts in this case? What are allegations, theories, or excuses?
2   What does this "letter to a lost friend" accomplish? What did it do for the writer? What does it do for the reader?

Talking, Listening, Writing

3   Who or what is to blame? What, if anything, can be done to help prevent a similar tragedy? Does this editorial make you rethink your position regarding "death penalty, gun control, and assorted other related causes"?
4   Musil says, "I'm not sure if someone can make a rational decision . . . based on an emotionally traumatic event." Don't we have a right to be emotional about events like the one that is the occasion for this editorial? Shouldn't we be emotional? What would a "rational" reaction be to what happened in this case?
5   A tired joke has it that when the students at one college were asked whether they were concerned about apathy concerning social issues, 87% responded: "I don't care." Do you think students of your generation or on your campus are guilty of apathy?
6   Write your personal response to the author of this "letter to a lost friend."

A THREAT TO JUSTICE

Families to Amend Three Strikes

"The state has built 19 prisons and only two universities in the last ten years."

Family members, friends, and sympathizers who maintain year-long vigils outside jails both in this country and in other countries in the world usually do not have the benefit of well-funded publicity campaigns or high-priced legal talent.

The following text is from leaflets passed out in front of a county jail by members of prisoners' families. They claimed that a three-strikes law that had been advertised as getting repeat offenders off the streets was in fact putting many nonviolent offenders away for life, destroying not only their lives but the lives of their families. A long list of supporting organizations included the Los Angeles Times Editorial Board, the Bakersfield chapter of the American Legion, the American Civil Liberties Union, the California Association of Black Lawyers, the Archdiocese of Los Angeles, the National Lawyers Guild, la Gente de Aztlan, and Amnesty International.

Thought Starters: Suppose you are passing outside a court of law or local jail. Relatives of inmates approach you with leaflets and ask you to sign a petition. The governor has just vetoed changes to a three-strikes law that is putting family members away for life. Many of the family members whose pictures you are shown are in jail for nonviolent crimes. What would you say to the petitioners? Would you sign? Why or why not?

TAXPAYERS HAVE BECOME VICTIMS OF THREE STRIKES Nonviolent offenders are being locked up in maximum housing units costing the taxpayer $27,000 per inmate per year. There are approximately 165,000 inmates in California prisons. A prison housing 4,000 inmates costs $300 million to build and $100 million a year to run. Three Strikes will add tens of thousands of prisoners to the state system. The state has built 19 prisons and only two universities in the last ten years. Prisons go up while schools fall down. Three Strikes does not make our street safer. It is about a prison industry complex. We need prevention, not detention. Let the time fit the crime. Put our money back into our education, environmental, social, elderly, youth, and other community programs.

SOCIETY HAS BECOME A VICTIM OF THREE STRIKES 80% of law enforcement time and money is spent prosecuting minor offenders, not violent criminals. The Justice Policy Institute states that "states that have not enacted harsher prison sentences for repeated felons have actually experienced a greater drop in crime than states that do have such laws." California has one of the highest incarceration rates in the world. Prisons are big business and people are the commodity.

FAMILIES HAVE BECOME VICTIMS OF THREE STRIKES The Three Strikes Law has led to unduly harsh sentences for people with no history of violence, or people who have been convicted of relatively minor crimes. People with drug addictions are being "rehabilitated" with life sentences. Thousands of families have been affected. Many families have lost their families, friends, jobs, homes, and now live in poverty, again at the taxpayer's expense.

CONSIDER THIS 70–80% of Second and Third Strike convictions involve NONVIOLENT or NONSERIOUS OFFENSES. Nonviolent crimes and minor offenses (property crimes) such as possession of less than a gram of cocaine, forgery, or stealing a pair of jeans, result in a Strike. Multiple counts during one act count for multiple Strikes. The law is being retroactively applied, meaning crimes committed back in the 60s or 70s can count as Strikes. The Three Strikes Law is applied to juvenile crimes—going back to 16 years of age.

Our organization started in Orange Country in 1996. It was started by family members and friends of people who have been sentenced under the Three Strikes Law. We do not provide legal services. However, we keep current on any legal changes in the law. Our goal is to get Three Strikes back on the ballot, AMENDED. We believe the voters of California did not understand the Proposition they voted for. Three Strikes was publicized as aimed at violent offenders. However, 70–80% of offenders sentenced under the Three Strikes Law are NOT violent offenders. In fact, you do not have to commit a violent crime to go to prison for the rest of your life.

This law is an injustice to every person in California. Martin Luther King Jr. said, "an injustice anywhere is a threat to justice everywhere."

The Responsive Reader

1 How would questions like the following affect the way you react to the petition: How important to you is the distinction between "violent" and "nonviolent" crimes? Should new sentencing laws be retroactively applied to offenses dating back many years? Should they be applied to juvenile crimes from age sixteen?

2 Is cost to the taxpayer of lifelong incarceration a major consideration for you? Why or why not?

Talking, Listening, Writing

3 Teachers come to jails without pay to teach courses for inmates. After one of her students had been arrested, one teacher visited the prison late at night to bring a midterm exam for the student to take in case he was released and had a chance to rejoin the class. Do you think this kind of personal initiative does any good? Why or why not?

4 How do you explain the gap between the legislators and the range of organizations supporting the families' initiative?

OTHER VOICES

Amending the Three-Strikes Law

In 2004, a public opinion poll in California showed a big margin of public support for a measure requiring that the third and final of all three "strikes" must be a serious, violent felony to make a defendant eligible for 25 year-to-life sentences. Under the original law, only two of the three strikes had to be a violent or serious felony to make a repeat offender eligible for three-strikes sentencing. According to the poll, only 14 percent of the voters were opposed to amending the original law. An aggressive public relations effort by a governor installed as the result of a well-funded recall election in the end defeated attempts to amend the law.

Comment on the poll results ranged from support from backers of the new measure to voices warning that the change would release violent felons back into California.

> The backers of the revised three-strikes measure, Citizens against Violent Crime, say that the state has wasted $6 billion in the last 10 years incarcerating minor offenders under the sentencing structure by counting nonviolent offenses toward the three strikes. The ballot measure, they argue, would save California $750 million per year by requiring only violent offenses to be considered for the strikes. . . . The measure is opposed, however, by powerful political groups, including the California Correctional Peace Officers Association, dozens of district attorneys, sheriffs, lawmakers, and victims' rights groups.
>
> Christian Berthelsen, "3 Strikes Too Harsh, Poll Says," *San Jose Mercury News*

1 The original law had been passed during a time of public outrage over the kidnap and murder of a 12-year-old by a repeat offender out on parole. Do you think there should be a cooling off period before harsh punitive laws are passed after a heinous crime?

2 Results of the poll were based on telephone interviews conducted in English and Spanish with 647 people likely to vote in a November statewide election. Do you think such a poll truly represents public opinion?

FRUITLESS PUNISHMENT

San Francisco Chronicle *Editorial*

According to a Justice Department report, 2,078,570 Americans were in prison in early 2004. When people on probation or parole were added to the "correctional population," a record 6.9 million Americans were under the control of the criminal justice system.

What is the purpose of incarceration—of keeping millions of Americans in overcrowded jails? Is the purpose to keep criminals off the streets and making neighborhoods safer? (But is it true that most convicts are eventually released—some earlier than expected because of severe overcrowding in the nation's jails?) Is the purpose to deter criminals by harsh punishment? (But is it true that the number of Americans in jail vastly increased in recent years?) Is the purpose to educate and rehabilitate criminals so that they re-enter society as productive citizens? (But is it true that training and education programs were for a time largely abandoned?)

Sources like the following 2004 newspaper editorial claim that the rate of recidivism—of ex-convicts convicted of repeat offenses after their release—recently reached a staggering 79 percent. The editorial writer blames "confounding public policies"—thoughtless, counterproductive policies that make us shake our heads.

Thought Starters: Does rehabilitation seem like an old-fashioned or obsolete concept to you? Why or why not? Do you use terms like *hardened criminals* or *career criminals*? Why or why not?

Each year, 125,000 inmates are paroled from California prisons with $200 in their pockets and a figurative pat on the back. They are freed because they've paid their debt to society and served their time. So why do we keep punishing them with barriers that hinder their chance for legitimate recovery?

Under confounding public policies, ex-inmates are denied opportunities that most of us take for granted.

For example, people with felony drug convictions are denied welfare and food stamps *for life.* Since 1996, more than 37,000 former female inmates have been deemed ineligible for welfare.

Former inmates can't apply for student loans or public housing. They often are denied custody of their children, access to public-sector jobs, or the right to acquire any of more than 30 licenses for vocations such as acupuncture and real estate.

Instead of producing self-supporting citizens and more secure communities, the policies create a perpetual class of increasingly marginalized people.

The Little Hoover Commission reports that 70 to 90 percent of parolees are unemployed—a figure with alarming implications for public safety. Nearly all of the 6,900 parolees remanded to Oakland are jobless and, police say, disproportionately responsible for the city's violent crimes.

"How do you eat if you can't get a job (or) food stamps?" asks Linda Evans of All of Us or None, an advocacy group for ex-inmates. The answer is apparent, given the state's $5 billion prison budget and 79 percent recidivism rate.

To close the revolving door, state and local governments need to work with business to hire former inmates. State prisons need to prepare inmates to re-enter communities. But mostly, the Legislature must repeal statutes that senselessly inhibit inmates from becoming productive citizens and, in the process, cost us dearly in taxes and community security.

The Responsive Reader

1 Prepare a list of key *facts* about the legal status and limitations of a released inmate that emerge from this editorial. Which seem most predictable or reasonable? Which to you seem unexpected or surprising?

2 What is the *thesis* stated or implied of the editorial? How would you sum up the editorial position presented in this editorial? What phrases or sentences most directly echo or repeat the key idea or ideas?

3 To judge from this editorial, what would be a typical *scenario* for the return of a prisoner to society? What do you think legislators or judges expect inmates to do after their release from prison? What happens in the real world between the person's release from and return to prison? How are the ex-convicts expected to survive?

Talking, Listening, Writing

4 As a voter or concerned citizen of a community, would it be your position that people convicted of a felony

- should serve their sentence and then be considered to have "paid their debt to society"?
- should be excluded from rights and benefits for life and barred from access to education and many kinds of employment?
- should participate in prison programs providing education and rehabilitation?
- should be required to participate in supervised post-release follow-up programs facilitating their return to society?

Explain and defend your choice.

5 Do you think ex-felons should be denied the right to vote? Does denying them the vote create a disenfranchised underclass?

Writing to Persuade

If you want to persuade your reader, know your audience.

The goal of persuasion is change. Your task is to change attitudes, beliefs, or behaviors. Persuasive writing aims at a result: a vote, a sale, or support for a cause. The first rule of persuasive writing therefore is: Know your audience. Who are they? What are their needs? What are their attitudes or traditions? What is their age group, their religion, or social class? How are you going to relate to their allegiances and commitments? Are you going to find common ground? Are you going to be able to appeal to shared values?

In discussing current issues or in charting promotional campaigns, consultants and strategists focus on defining their **target audiences.**

- Campaign strategists divide the country into conservative-leaning heartland states and liberal-leading states on the two coasts.

- Advertisers direct their sale campaigns at target audiences like teenagers with spending money, career women, homemakers, or upwardly mobile males.

What is going to be your own target audience?

THE RECEPTIVE AUDIENCE   Persuasive writing is a moral booster when you write for an audience ready to cheer you on. On debated issues, are you going to appeal mainly to a **sympathetic audience**—readers already largely on your side? Are you writing to strengthen their resolve, urging them to persevere in the struggle? Are your writing to show them how to deal with obstacles or objections?

The Audience Profile

Political candidates and advertisers increasingly direct their messages at voting blocks like Latino or Hispanic Americans. What is the makeup of their target audience? The following might be an audience profile compiled from *Hispanic Magazine* (at Hispanic Magazine.com) and other sources:

According to recent estimates, Latinos account for 13 percent of the population, making up the fastest growing ethnic group. Large areas of the country have Spanish-language radio, television, and print media advertising. With hugely successful bilingual entertainers like Ricky Martin and Jennifer López, many Latinos saw "Hispanic culture explode." Many Latinos have multiethnic or multiracial roots. A person may be of mixed Puerto Rican, Cuban, and black ancestry. Another person may have Mexican, Irish American, and Native American roots. The president of a Hispanic think tank claims: "Latinos are integrating into American society at a very rapid pace that people do not realize." Interethnic dating and intermarriage with non-Latinos is a growing trend. Many Americans of partially Latino ancestry no longer have Hispanic surnames, which used to serve the Census Bureau and other agencies as a rough indication of Latino or Hispanic ancestry.

Your Turn: Write a similar audience profile for an ethnic group, regional group, religious group, age group, social class, or other target audience that you know well.

THE HOSTILE AUDIENCE   Persuasive writers respond to a special challenge when they promote an unpopular view. On issues like amnesties for illegal immigrants or legalizing gay marriage, is there a point in taking on a **resistant audience?** What will it take to make them listen to "the other side"? Is there a way to find common ground?

THE UNDECIDED AUDIENCE   Persuasive writing can truly make a difference when it aims at an audience open-minded enough to listen to reason. Is there still a **general audience** that will respond to appeals on public issues that matter to concerned citizens? Can activists mobilize a consensus on issues affecting the community regardless of political affiliation.

Triggering

Persuasive writing aims to send a message or to sway the reader.

Persuasive writers have an agenda. The agenda may be to protect endangered neighborhood mom-and-pop businesses. Or it may be to protect the few remaining habitats of the monarch butterflies of the Pacific coast. Or it may be to keep student loans available and affordable for working class students.

■ *Much persuasive writing asks for support on basic economic issues.* A writer may ask us to support efforts to raise the minimum wage to bring it closer to "living wage" policies in major American cities. Hotel maids, dishwashers, parking attendants, and other support personnel may be on strike against chains operating posh convention hotels. Who is going to support their efforts to have labor union representation? Who will help them preserve their health benefits?

■ *Much persuasive writing asks for the readers' support on community issues.* A writer may ask us to help preserve public access to beaches as "big pockets" developers move in on remaining coastline and seabird habitat to build condos, golf courses, and luxury resorts.

■ *Much persuasive writing pleads with the reader to support an embattled cause.* A writer's powers of persuasion are tested when a cause seems embattled or when past progress is in danger of being reversed. The writer may be sounding the alarm when cuts in funding for mental health or drug rehabilitation programs defeat the efforts of dedicated professionals and support groups to help at-risk populations.

Gathering

Gather supporting material that will carry special weight with your audience.
What kind of material will have a persuasive effect on your readers?

■ *Draw on widely recognized or respected sources.* For instance, on public health issues, readers are likely to accept as authorities professionals who publish in *JAMA (Journal of the American Medical Association)* or the prestigious *New England Journal of Medicine.* When you try to counteract charges of widespread anti-Americanism in Europe, your readers may be swayed by the testimony of witnesses who have long worked overseas as journalists, teachers, or employees of multinational corporations.

■ *Listen to the people involved.* Make their voices heard. Listen to the stories of people whose lives have been affected. Establish them as authorities. When you support current efforts to strengthen drunk-driving laws or gun-control legislation, use **case histories** of individuals or families still living years after with the aftermath of a traumatic event.

■ *Make effective use of insiders' information.* Pay close attention when your sources cite internal memos, company e-mail, or confidential reports rather than official press releases. Listen to people recalling informal conversations rather than public relations handouts prepared for a public meeting.

- *Pay special attention to candid interviews.* Listen when people who feel misrepresented or slighted tell their side of the story.

Shaping

Stress points that will have an impact on your target audience.
Persuasive writers plan their strategy. What pleas or appeals will address the needs of the audience? What will promise solutions to their problems? What will reassure them about threats to their well-being? What will help defuse damaging accusations or counteract scare tactics of the opposing side? Much strong persuasive writing is an effective mix of positive reinforcement and of warding off possible objections or counterarguments.

Persuasive writers identify major points that will get the attention of their intended readers:

- They emphasize points that will find a receptive audience.
- They may decide to concentrate on arguments that will cause an undecided audience to rethink previous positions or attitudes.
- They arrange them in the order that will best build their case.

The following is one writer's plotting of a strategy to build support for local initiatives heading off large impersonal outside forces. Citizens groups and elected officials in communities around the country have in recent years fought large chains and megacorporations driving out small local business, depressing wages, and lowering the living standard of workers and their families.

Walmartization: A High Price to Pay

THESIS: The billion-dollar Walmart retail organization had to launch a million-dollar public relations campaign to refute charges that it was harming workers and communities.

1. PROTECTING THE COMMUNITY   A grown community has a web of small businesses run by people who know and trust their customers and vice versa. They pay local taxes and support local schools and law enforcement. Huge chains that run out local business are run by anonymous impersonal out-of-state forces with no roots or loyalties in the community.

2. PROTECTING EARNING POWER   Although the corporation may claim it pays "competitive" wages, the income of many temporaries and part-time employees is close to or below government poverty guidelines.

3. PROTECTING HEALTH CARE   Critics of corporate policies claim that many employees with no or inadequate health benefits have to turn to already overburdened public health facilities at an added cost to the taxpayer, thus forcing the taxpayer to subsidize the corporation.

4 PROTECTING WORKERS' RIGHTS TO ORGANIZE As isolated individuals, workers are powerless when facing the vast financial and legal resources of a megacorporation. The corporation may actively discourage or undercut labor union representation, banning organizing activities and harassing or firing employees suspected of participating in union activities. The corporation is strongest in nonunion states or territories.

5 PROTECTING WOMEN'S PROGRESS TOWARD EQUALITY Critical articles and lawsuits claim that earnings of female employees are consistently lower than those of males. Lawsuits allege that women managers hit a "glass ceiling."

Revising

Profit from feedback to make your writing more persuasive for your intended audience.

In today's media world, much commercial and political promotion has already been test-run and fine-tuned with input from focus groups and experts on audience psychology. What input may help you to make your writing more persuasive? What feedback can make you more audience-conscious?

WEIGHING READER RESPONSE The feedback you receive for your paper from peer reviewers or from your instructor is likely to focus on how effectively your paper reaches its intended audience. The facing page shows a **running commentary** by an instructor on a paper investigating health insurance for mental illness. To judge from this commentary, what were the strengths of the paper? What needed work?

THE LIMITS OF PERSUASION Revision gives you a chance to rewrite your paper to sidestep familiar pitfalls. An aggressive or polemical style—name-calling, personal attacks, sweeping charges or accusations—is a double-edged weapon. It may cause the audience to ask not what is wrong with your target but instead what is wrong with you—the writer.

- *Give facts and believable testimony to show you respect your readers' intelligence.* Make statistics believable by not just citing a major provocative figure but by giving detailed numbers and identifying the source,

- *Check the credibility of your sources.* Be wary of clearly biased or partisan testimony. Readers may not be convinced by a spokesperson's defense of agency policy. Show your awareness of likely bias in a fired employee's disgruntled remarks—or in a CEO's defending the company's questioned accounting practices.

- *Guard against slanting the evidence.* If you filter out all doubt or disagreement, your readers may discount your tract as one-sided propaganda. Take on and try to rebut major objections likely to arise in the your read-

INSTRUCTOR FEEDBACK

1   INTRODUCTION: Your opening statistics should wake up the apathetic
    reader. However, they need to be attributed to somebody. Who said this?
    What is the credibility of the source?

2   THESIS: The point that a "huge step" has been taken toward equal treat-
    ment of physical and mental illness, in spite of the resistance of the insur-
    ance companies, comes through very clearly. The rest of your paper fol-
    lows up your thesis extremely well.

3   FOLLOW-UP: Explanation of the traditional "stigma" attached to mental
    illness and contrasting medical definitions of mental illness really back up
    your thesis. Good backup from sources here. (However I would leave out
    the dictionary definition, which seems routine or predictable and has no
    real punch.)

4   ORGANIZATION: The key point that mental illness is "treatable" leads you
    naturally to a look at current new medications. However you seem to take
    a detour when talking mostly about problems with the new drugs. Make it
    clearer that you basically *endorse* the hopeful new developments, but that
    you are also sounding a warning that the drug-happy American public
    might expect too much from miracle drugs?

5   COUNTER-TRENDS: The part of your paper examining the restriction and
    denial of medical treatment as the result of a for-profit health care system
    is strong. You make good use of a local authority at your own college. You
    explain well the economics of the shift from fee-for-service to managed
    care. Some of your audience might need more explanation of "managed
    care."

6   CONCLUSION: Good circling back to the story of your friend's brother.
    Good and memorable punchline—many readers are likely to remember it.

ers' minds. For instance, make sure you cite both management and workers when investigating a labor dispute.

   ▪ *Remember that name-calling may backfire with fair-minded readers.* Some
writers keep up a drumfire of labels like *inexcusable, self-interested, incompetent, maniacal, thought control, greedy for profits,* and *using political ploys.* Save
weighty words and serious charges for places where you have clearly earned
the right to use them. Support them by careful presentation of evidence.

An Editorial for Review

   In times of war or national emergency, foreigners have often been
scapegoats. They have experienced antagonism or persecution by a traumatized public that associates them with the enemy. Will the author of the following excerpted editorial succeed in persuading fair-minded readers not to

penalize the foreigner in our midst? Will readers reconsider their image of immigrants, foreign residents, and visitors guilty by association—suspected of sympathizing with or assisting the enemy because of race, national origin, or religion?

The people defended in the following editorial were educated or working in the U.S. They were often friends of America and admirers of American values, best qualified to serve as ambassadors of goodwill counteracting a rising tide of anti-Americanism abroad.

Convenient Targets

Immigrants have gotten a bad rap since 9/11. **Suffering racial profiling, hate crimes, job loss, arbitrary detention, deportation, and denial of due process, they have become convenient scapegoats after the tragedy.**

(The opening paragraph strongly states the **thesis,** appealing to *shared values* Americans traditionally believe in—protection against arbitrary government action and belief in due process. It assumes a strong shared rejection of racial profiling and hate crimes.) —————————>>>>>>>>>>>>>

The dust had barely settled on the rubble of the World Trade Center when the Justice Department arrested and detained over 1,200 Arab, Muslim, and South Asian immigrants who were not even suspected of criminal activity. For months they were held without charges and denied access to counsel.

(This **follow-up** appeals to the *traditional belief* in the rule of law. It uses the phrases "not even suspected of criminal activity," "held without charges," and "denied access to a counsel.")
—————————>>>>>>>>>>>>>

While the country was still reeling from the shock of the attacks, and engulfed in patriotic fervor, the Congress hastily passed the USA Patriot Act with little public debate. The law accords broad powers to investigative agencies like the FBI to spy on immigrants and citizens. While the Patriot Act threatens the privacy of citizens also, its most ominous provisions strip the basic civil liberties of non-citizens. It permits detention and deportation of non-citizens who provide assistance even for lawful activities of a group the government claims is a terrorist organization. . . .

(The writer here continues to use **connotative language** carrying strong *value judgments:* "spy on immigrants and citizens," "threatens the privacy," "most ominous provisions," "even for lawful activities.")
—————————>>>>>>>>>>>>>

It is time to turn the tide. We need to remind our elected representatives that immigrants have always formed the bedrock of American economy and culture. They do much of the research in our universities, provide health care in remote areas, build our homes, harvest our crops, and drive technical innovation. They are part of our families. It is time to move beyond fear and repeal shortsighted laws that unfairly target immigrants.

(This strongly worded **conclusion** appeals to the traditional pride in the immigrants that built this country. It invokes the work ethic (from work in the fields to high-tech research "technical innovation"), and public service ("health care in remote areas").)

editorial in *India Currents*, November 2, 2003

YOUR TURN:

1 Do you think appeals like this can counteract forces of xenophobia—"fear of foreigners"? Why or why not?

2 Do you think Americans need to be reminded of their many ties with people from other countries through intermarriage?

3 In ancient Greek tradition, it was an injunction of the gods to welcome the stranger coming to your door or to honor the foreigner in your midst. Were you taught this kind of tradition of welcoming the stranger?

Writing Options 10: Persuading Your Readers

1 Are you a booster, an activist, or a supporter of good causes? Write a fundraising letter asking readers to support a cause or initiative to which you are committed.

2 Do you care about unacceptable drop-out rates for students from minority or low-income families? Write a letter to at-risk students in high school or college to persuade them to resist becoming dropouts or being pushed out.

3 Do you care about the down and out? Write a letter to members of the affluent majority asking them to rethink their attitude toward a "lost cause": the homeless, drug addicts, or other Americans written off by society.

4 When is a young American old enough to vote, to drink, or to die in a war? Write a letter-to-the-editor advocating a change (or resisting a change) in the voting age, the drinking age, or other age-specific qualification.

5 Do gay and lesbian Americans have equal rights? Write a letter to your local newspaper in support of gay marriage or in defense of traditional marriage.

6 Is your community supporting struggling artists, an art museum, an orchestra, or a ballet or opera company? Write a letter-to-the-editor to a

local newspaper pleading for continuing or strengthened community support for the arts. Or defend those who say the arts should be financed by art lovers and not the taxpaying public.

7   Do you read news stories about hardship cases involving immigration issues? Write a letter to your congressional representative or a responsible official. Criticize or support a disputed decision by the immigration authorities concerning amnesty, asylum, or deportation.

8   Write a letter-to-the-editor to join in a dialog about how we honor our past or our roots. Support or reject a proposed or challenged memorial, special holiday, or commemorative event.

9   How should schools deal with teenage pregnancy? For instance, should they bar pregnant students from attending classes or from graduation ceremonies?

10   Write a letter trying to change "hearts and minds" on a current controversial medical issue like stem-cell research, the morning-after pill, or medical marijuana.

11

ENVIRONMENT
Saving the Planet

NATURE PHOTOGRAPHY: THE RETURN OF THE CONDOR

Nature lovers are fascinated by photographic records of endangered wild-life brought back from near extinction. They marvel at pictures of the still-surving bald eagle or the endangered whooping crane. Many have followed the saga of the condor, one of the largest and rarest birds in North America, soaring over the forests and canyons of the West with a 10-foot wingspan at up to 55 miles an hour. The large birds became nearly extinct in the 20th century, in part because of lead poisoning caused by their feeding on carrion containing bullet fragments. After they were reduced to a population of just nine birds in the wild in the early eighties, a breeding program raised the number of birds in captivity to more than 160. Scientists began releasing condors into the wild in the early eighties, and ten years later more than 50 of the birds soared over the Grand Canyon and California.

Reading the Image

1   Are you or your friends nature lovers? *Bird watchers* pursue their activities with a special dedication and emotional satisfaction. What feelings did the photographer hope to stir in the viewer by capturing this bird in full flight? Does the size of the bird matter? What special feelings might a viewer experience watching so large a bird?

2   Naturalists are professionals or amateurs who combine detailed accurate *observation* of the natural world with a strong loyalty to the surviving wildlife of the planet. How accurate an observer are you? How would you describe what you see here to someone who has not seen the bird or pictures of the bird? What features would a trained observer point out that might help hikers recognize the bird and tell it apart from other large birds of prey?

3   How large is the *audience* for appeals to save endangered wildlife? Would you pay taxes to support wildlife refuges, protect wetlands, or fund programs to endangered species? Why or why not?

4   The *language* we use about the natural world often reveals basic attitudes. Would you call the interest in nature to which this image appeals a hobby? Would you call it a luxury? Would you call it a communion with nature? Would you call it a tribute to fellow creatures?

5   Publications from *National Geographic* to *Audubon* magazine cater to bird lovers and especially admirers of the endangered big birds. A range of publications publishes startling beautiful examples of *nature photography* focused on the surviving examples of the once incredibly rich bird populations of the North American continent. You may want to collaborate on a project creating a classroom display or campus exhibit of nature photography focused on the big birds.

11

ENVIRONMENT
Saving the Planet

**Once we live no longer beneath our mothers' hearts,
it is the earth with which we form the same dependent
relationship, relying complete on its cycles and
elements, helpless without its protective embrace.**

—LOUISE ERDRICH

A science fiction poem reported the journey of a space traveler from a distant civilization who checked out Planet Earth and found that after a great final ecological catastrophe it had become "uninhabitable." Will our current exploitation of natural resources, our poisoning the oceans and heating up the atmosphere, and our destruction of the remaining wildlife endanger life on this planet? Is it true that Western industrial civilization is at war with nature and is bound to destroy our natural environment? Is it possible for people in the modern world to live in harmony with nature?

A central goal of Western civilization has long been to tame and control nature. Progress meant advances in freeing humanity from hunger and disease. It meant release from back-breaking toil in the fields to wrest meager crops from the earth. Without technology, one of its defenders has said, a human being would be a naked ape—at the mercy of droughts, floods, blights, and epidemics. Cities would cease to exist, with bands of survivors roaming the countryside and plundering and scrounging for food.

In recent times, however, many observers have voiced second thoughts about the blessings of our technological civilization. Our technology, our modern lifestyle, has increasingly isolated us from contact with the natural world. Air-conditioned buildings isolate us from the changing winds and the fresh air. We walk on asphalt and concrete rather than on sand or grass. We fly over prairies and rivers and mountains with the windows closed, watching a Hollywood movie. The toxic byproducts of our technological civilization are poisoning the rivers, the oceans, the air. Manipulations of the genetic heritage that evolved over millions of years take place with little knowledge of short-range risks and long-range effects.

Many have turned to other cultural traditions to search for a different sense of the relationship between humanity and nature. Other cultures have envisioned a more organic relation between human civilization and the natural world. They have or had a better sense of the interdependence of creatures. Some cultures have taught human beings to look at all living things with reverence. Their myths or religious traditions kept people in touch with their roots in the natural world.

An active ecological movement has fought to reverse the trend toward the exploitation and destruction of our natural environment. Environmental activists have tried to block floating factories that were decimating fish populations. Tree sitters in the forests and environmental organizations in the courts have battled to stop logging companies that were clear-cutting ancient forests. Politicians and business leaders began to reckon with those agitating to preserve the wilderness or crusading for clean water and clean air. Concerned scientists joined in an international effort supporting laws and treaties designed to stop or slow down the trend toward global warming.

THE LAST OF THE WILD SALMON

Marie de Santis

In a classic essay, the wild salmon's struggle to return to its spawning grounds becomes a symbol of the secret of life.

We tend to be armchair ecologists who know the threatened wildlife of our planet mostly from television specials. The author of the following article knows the life of the oceans and rivers from close personal observation. De Santis worked for eight years as a commercial fisherwoman and the captain of her own boat. She told her story of the lure of the sea and of the hard work and dangers faced by those who make a living from the sea in her book Neptune's Apprentice *(1984).*

In the following excerpt from her book California Currents *(1985), she pays tribute to the wild salmon who are endangered by the destruction of their spawning grounds and the obstacles that dams and polluted or diverted rivers present to their age-old journey upstream. She hated to see the wild salmon replaced by artificially bred fish "no more suited to the stream than a poodle is to the woods." She addressed her book to those who "wish to continue living in a world with real animals" and who want future generations to "see more than the broken spirits of the animals of the zoo."*

Thought Starters: What animal would you choose as the best symbol of the threatened life on our endangered planet?

In a stream so shallow that its full body is no longer submerged in the water, the salmon twists on its side to get a better grip with its tail. Its gillplate is torn, big hunks of skin hang off its sides from collisions with rocks, there are deep gouges in its body, and all around for miles to go there is only the cruelty of more jagged rocks and less and less water to sustain the swim. Surely the animal is dying!

And then the salmon leaps like an arrow shot from a bow; some urge and will and passion ignores the animal body and focuses on the stream.

Of all the extremes of adaptation to the ocean's awful toll on the young, none is more mythic in proportion than the salmon's mighty journey to the mountain streams: a journey that brings life to meet death at a point on a perfect circle, a return through miles of narrowing waters to the exact gravel-bedded streamlet of its birth. A journey to spawning and death, so clear in its resemblance to the migrations of the sperm to the egg as to entwine their meanings in a single reflection.

On every continent of the northern hemisphere, from the temperate zone to the arctic, there is hardly a river that hasn't teemed with the salmon's spawn: the Thames, the Rhine, the rivers of France and Spain, Kamchatka and Siberia, Japan (which alone has more than 200 salmon rivers) and the arctic streams of Greenland. From the Aleutians to Monterey Bay, through the broadest byways to the most rugged and narrow gorge, the salmon have made their way home. There are many journeys for which the salmon endure more than 1000 miles.

As soon as the ice melts on the Yukon, the king salmon enter the   5
river's mouth, and for a month, the fish swim against the current, 50 miles a day for a total of 1500. And like every other salmon on its run, the king salmon fasts completely along the way. In other rivers, salmon scale vertical rocks up to 60 feet high, against hurtling waterfalls.

The salmon gets to spawn once in life, and maybe that's reason enough. The salmon's instinct to return to the place of its birth is so unmodifiable and of such purity as to have inspired hundreds of spiritual rites in as many societies of human beings.

The salmon arrives battered and starved, with a mate chosen along the way, and never has passion seemed less likely from two more wretched-looking beings. But, there in the gravel of the streamlet, the female fans out a nest with the sweep of her powerful tail and the male fends off intruders. The nest done, the two fish lie next to each other suspended in the water over the nest; their bodies quiver with intense vibrations, and simultaneously they throw the eggs and the sperm. Compared with the millions of eggs thrown by a cod in a stream, the salmon need throw only 2000 to 5000. Despite the predators and other hazards of the stream, these cold mountain waters are a sanctuary compared with the sea. For the next two or three days, the pair continue nesting and spawning until all the eggs are laid. Then the salmon, whose journey has spanned the ocean and the stream, lies by the nest and dies.

Soon the banks of the streams are stacked with ragged carcasses, and the animals of the woods come down for a feast. The stream lies quiet in the winter's deepening cold. But within a month two black eyes appear through the skin of each egg. And two weeks later, the water is again alive with the pulsing of millions of small fish feeling the first clumsy kicks of their tails. The fingerlings stay for a while, growing on the insects and larvae that have been nurtured by the forest. Then, one day, they realize what that tail is for and begin their descent to the sea, a journey mapped in their genes by the parents they left behind.

The young salmon arrive in the estuary facing the sea, where they linger again and learn to feed on shrimp, small crustaceans and other creatures of the brine. Here, also, their bodies complete an upheaval of internal and external changes that allow them to move on to the saltier sea. These adaptations require such extraordinary body transformations that when the same events occur on the stage of evolution they take millions and millions of years. In the life of the salmon, the changes take place in only a matter of months. One of life's most prohibitive barriers—that between fresh and salt water—is crossed, and the salmon swim back and forth, in and out of the sea, trying it on for size.

Then one day, the youngsters do not return. The stream is only a dis-   10
tant memory drifting further and further back in the wake of time, only different—a memory that will resurrect and demand that its path be retraced.

So accessible is the salmon's life in the stream that more is known
about the reproduction of this fish than any other ocean animal. With the
ease of placing cameras underwater, there isn't any aspect of this dramatic
cycle that hasn't been captured in full color in some of the most spectacular
film footage ever made.

But once the salmon enters the sea, the story of its life is a secret as
deep and dark as the farthest reaches of the ocean it roams. The human eye
with its most sophisticated aids, from satellite to sonar, has never caught
more than a glance of the salmon at sea. Extensive tagging programs have
been carried out, but they tell us little more than that the salmon is likely
to be found anywhere within thousands of miles of its origins, and even this
is only a sliver of the picture because the tags are recovered only when the
salmon is caught by fishermen, who work solely within the narrow coastal
zone. Along with a few other pelagic fishes, like the tuna, that claim vast
stretches of sea for their pasture, the salmon's life remains one of the most
mysterious on earth.

The Responsive Reader

1   What makes the stage of the salmon's life cycle that she describes at the
    beginning the symbolic *high point* for the author?
2   What are the *major stages* of the salmon's life journey? What are key
    events or striking details at each stage?

Talking, Listening, Writing

3   For you, does the salmon's life cycle make a good symbolic representa-
    tion of life on this planet? Why or why not?
4   What plant or animal with an especially rich or varied life cycle have you
    studied or do you know well? Trace it in rich authentic detail, empha-
    sizing major stages.
5   Do people, institutions, or ideas have life cycles similar to those de San-
    tis observed in the natural world? Focus on one central example, and
    bring it to life for your reader.

Collaborative Projects

6   How successful is the struggle to restore life to lakes and streams poi-
    soned by pollution? What have been notable successes and notable fail-
    ures? What in particular is the current status of attempts to save the wild
    salmon? For a possible research project, work with a group to collect and
    collate data from authoritative sources.

THE BOOK OF THE TREE-SITTERS

Jack Hill

"You can't replant a thousand-year-old forest. We're destroying something we don't understand."

Jack Hill is a trend watcher who looks in the day's news for evidence of the larger patterns that shape our future. The following article is part of a series he published in Harper's magazine in 2003, studying trends like the revival of religious zeal in contemporary Christianity, Judaism, and Islam.

In tracing the growth of environmental awareness, he writes about his own experiments with a composting process that turns clippings, discarded potato peels, and other refuse into rich earth. He listens to people who live "off the grid"—disconnected from public utilities, growing their own food. He goes to schools where environmental awareness (and learning activities like composting) are part of the curriculum. He studies the world view and psychology of early Christian ascetics who seceded from the urban living and creature comforts of their time.

Hill sees evidence that new ecological ideas about our relation to the land and to the planet are spreading everywhere. Will a new "eco-faith" eventually connect people in many parts of the world?

Thought Starters: For some people, trees, like much else in our world, are a matter of economics. They are commodity—a resource that can be bought and sold. They are subject to property rights and laws of supply and demand. For you or members of your generation, is a tree just a tree? Or does it have a vital or spiritual significance?

On October 4, 2001, a radical environmentalist who had taken the forest name Tre Arrow shimmied up a tree as a crew of loggers arrived to cut timber on a parcel of Oregon public land called God's Valley. Then Tre Arrow fell, breaking his sixty-foot plunge by slamming into some limbs before crashing to the ground, his head split open, a lung punctured, bones broken.

The news coverage was interesting. The Associated Press simply reported that he "tumbled 60 feet from a treetop perch in the Tillamook State Forest and suffered multiple broken bones." What none of the stories reported was that the loggers chased this radical higher and higher up the tree, lopping off all the lower branches. When the chain saw got close, Tre Arrow leapt into another tree, so they sheared the bottom limbs off that one too. With no way out, Tre Arrow sat in the tree with no water or food. The loggers and law-enforcement officials below shouted insults, shone lights, and blared music at him throughout the night. The jeering and mockery at this guy lasted for forty-eight hours. It only ended when the object of their hatred passed out right in front of their eyes and plummeted to the ground. The state forestry spokesman, Jeff Foreman, told a newspaper: "That was unfortunate and obviously something we hoped would not happen."

Or precisely what we hoped might happen. You know, depending.

Tree-sitting dates only to the late nineties as a form of protest. The practice became popular in 1998 after a young woman named Julia Hill climbed up a giant redwood tree in California and stayed there for two years. She took a forest name, Butterfly, and gave her tree a name, Luna. She later wrote a book about her experience at defeating a timber company's intention to cut down thousand-year-old redwoods. On some websites, the denunciations of "dreadlocked bongo-playing hippies" and rage at their "stupidity" are commonplace. Tree-sitters tend toward odd language, like calling their trees "ancient ones," one of those crypto-aboriginal terms that drive opponents berserk. In terms of private property, tree-sitters are obvious trespassers. The timber companies have legal permits. Often they are cutting trees on land they *own*. As a matter of law, tree-sitters are completely wrong. As a matter of logic, they don't make any sense; saving one tree, as often happens, would appear to accomplish nothing.

"We climb the trees so people will look at them differently," said a   5
tree-sitter named Spindle whom I contacted by cell phone. "These trees want to survive. They are not just lumber to be milled. We want people to see that they are homes to dozens of animals, they hold the soil, and they are there because they want to be."

Beginning in 2000, the citizens of a town in Oregon called Cottage Grove grew concerned that a stand of ancient Douglas firs that they had all grown up near was going to be timbered. They protested to the state and federal governments but were rebuffed. So a few of the locals joined with Janine Nilsen, who runs a horse stable outside of town, and contacted some tree-sitters. Under cover of darkness, they slipped onto this publicly owned land and erected a platform 130 feet up a Douglas fir to support three newly baptized dryads—Talcon, Savage, and Kiwi. The cut has been postponed as the owner tries to find out what his legal options are.

"It's more than just the tree-sit," Nilsen said. "We need to take a look at our forest. We're letting our natural resources go. But we are part of it, and we can't lose that part of ourselves. It's hard to put into words. It's a feeling. Language is so limited. It's something we need desperately. We have a misapprehension of nature. We're trying to make the world live by our standard instead of understanding how the world works."

Now many in Cottage Grove support the bongo-playing hippies. It might not have happened only a few years ago, but, according to Nilsen, there is mainstream support as folks bring water and provisions to supply the dryads in the trees.

"I think it's very dangerous the way we're cutting trees," Nilsen said. "I think that's the message of the tree-sitters. You can't replant a thousand-year-old forest. We're destroying something we don't understand."

The middle-class acceptance of tree-sitting broke new ground last fall   10 when a man climbed a tree in northern California. This single old tree was scheduled to be cut to make it possible to widen a road. Public support gathered regularly near the tree. In the end, the police got him down with a court order, but only after the developers agreed to hire a company that specializes in the moving of giant ancient trees.

Since Julia Hill's debut, dozens of tree-sitters have popped up in California and Oregon. Right now, to the best of my research, I can find five active tree-sits, three in Oregon and two in California. In each case, the trees have been given names. A giant 800-year-old Douglas fir named Monteverde is currently being occupied to prevent the Zip-O Lumber Company from clearing out its stand. Down the road, Happy is being occupied by two sitters, Life and Glisten. The names can get funky. One tree-sitter who went by the name Dirt inspired classrooms of children to write him letters. Their thoughts aren't all that different from my own: "Why is your name Dirt? Is it because trees don't have showers? Maybe it's because you love dirt."

What's truly peculiar about tree-sitting is that its inherent danger hasn't stopped the flow of volunteers. Two people have died. One was a twenty-two-year-old girl who accidentally met her end, as local reports noted, "falling from a tree that the logging protesters called Truth."

The Responsive Reader

1   Can you compile a *factual summary* of the events Hill highlights in his account? The struggle between the tree sitters and the logging interests became a highly emotionally charged issue. In what Hill tells his readers, what details seem most impartially factual? Where does his account most strongly stir the reader's emotions?

2   According to Hill, what is the *legal situation* that many protesters confront? Many lawsuits and legal challenges have swirled around contested plans for logging in both private and national forests. As far as the law is concerned, are the loggers in their legal rights? If so, does that settle the matter?

3   What do you think of the tree sitters giving trees *poetic names?* Why are they shedding their own duly registered "bourgeois" names? Is there any pattern in the new names they choose? Have you seen other individuals or groups go through a "renaming" phase?

Talking, Listening, Writing

4   Do you sympathize with the goals of the *environmental movement?* According to Hill, the people sometimes called "nature freaks" in the media prefer to "eat simple food grown in the backyard in order to avoid

fast foods, processed foods, and environmentally luxurious foods (such as winter strawberries flown in from New Zealand." Many people who sympathize with the environmental movement support some of its goals—but they travel with it only part of a way. How far would you identify with the environmental movement as Hill describes it:

- part of the way?
- all the way?
- not at all?

Talking, Listening, Writing

5 Hill has claimed that many people who consider themselves solidly middle-class, conservative in outlook, have nevertheless absorbed much of today's environmental perspective. Do you think this is true? Can you cite examples for or against?

Collaborative Projects

6 Early American poets sang the glories of the "primeval forest." Much recent controversy has centered on efforts to save the remaining "old-growth" forests. Working alone or with a group, can you collect and interpret basic facts? How old are these old-growth forests? How much area of old-growth forests still exists in this country? How are they threatened, or how well protected are they?

FIND IT ON THE WEB

Among environmental organizations much in the news, the Sierra Club is one of the most prominent and well-funded. What can you find out about their aims and track record on environmental issues?

CALIFORNIA CONDOR'S COMEBACK

Jane Kay

"For at least a while longer—and we most prayerfully hope, for thousands of years to come—the California condor is again a free-living species."

Jane Kay wrote the following interim report on the efforts to reintroduce the endangered California condors into the wild as an environment writer for a leading West Coast newspaper. Since she published her report in 2002, nature lovers have continued to track the successes and setbacks of the effort to have the big birds again hatch, breed, and forage in their original wild habitat, outside the zoos where the surviving specimens had been sheltered.

Part of the price Americans paid for the settlement of the American continent was the extinction or near extinction of the fantastic wildlife that flourished here before the arrival of the Europeans. The vanished flocks of passenger pigeons were estimated to number in the millions. Huge herds of buffalo had roamed the prairies, and their extinction took with them the livelihood and the lifestyle of the Native Americans of the plains. Early American naturalists painted huge swarms of flamingos circling in the skies and nesting in the swamps.

In the final decades of the twentieth century, environmentalists, naturalists, and researchers mounted a dedicated effort to save remaining endangered wildlife from extinction. Special efforts concentrated on saving the big birds: the bald eagle, the crane, the condor.

Thought Starters: What is the special fascination that birds have for bird watchers and ornithologists? What do you know about Audubon and the Audubon Society? What kinds of birds do you know by name and by sight? Do any have a special meaning for you?

When eminent naturalist Roger Tory Peterson published the third edition of "Western Birds" a dozen years ago, he grimly noted that the 40 surviving California condors in the world lived in zoos. *1*

Scientists had captured the last wild condors as part of an unprecedented attempt to save an endangered species. They would breed them, hatch the eggs and raise the young in cages. The goal: Return the largest flying birds in North America to nature.

Today, 10 years after biologists freed the first of those captive condors, no one is claiming that the giant scavenger is exactly flourishing. But after years of setbacks and missteps, the signs are encouraging.

Condors are increasing in numbers, surviving to maturity in the wild and acting more like real wild condors. There are 183 California condors alive today. Fifty-eight live free—33 in California and 25 in Arizona and Utah—and the remaining 125 are in breeding programs.

A huge leap forward came last year when three condors laid eggs in the wild, the first in 15 years.

Condor biologists are upbeat about the bird's prospects.

"This magnificent bird was on the brink of extinction. And now people can see condors in the wild," said Bruce Palmer, California condor recovery coordinator for the U.S. Fish and Wildlife Service.

"A bird like this can never be remade. When they soar over your head, you can hear the wind through their feathers. It sends shivers up my spine," Palmer said.

Just as the peregrine falcon's removal from the federal endangered species list inspired other programs to save species, the condor is giving impetus to efforts to save the whooping crane, the bald eagle and the wolves.

The condor dates back hundreds of thousands of years. In the Pleistocene era, it fed on carrion of mammoths and later elk, antelope, seals and whales. As those mammals declined in numbers, the condor turned to cattle and sheep carcasses.

In prehistoric times, the condor lived as far south as Florida and along the Eastern Seaboard to New York. On the West Coast, it ranged from British Columbia to Baja California. In recent times, the condor lived in coastal mountains from California to Oregon and in the Sierra Nevada. It scavenged in grasslands, forests and canyons.

No one could miss the giant birds, with their 9 1/2-foot wingspans. Their distinctive, naked red-orange heads, spiked with feathers and rimmed by black ruffs, change color with mood. Their black wings are lined with white.

The population dropped with the arrival of modern settlers, who hunted the birds. During the Gold Rush, miners stored gold dust in their quills. The condors also died from eating poisoned rodents and coyotes and carrion peppered with lead bullet fragments. They got tangled in power lines and soaked in oil spills.

By the 1940s, they bred only in the Sierra and the coastal range of California from Los Angeles to Monterey. They were sighted in Arizona.

Fearing the end of the species, the U.S. government listed condors among the first animals to win special protections for endangered species. After years of debate, the scheme was devised to preserve the species by breeding them in captivity. And in 1987, resource managers caught the last 27 condors and put them in the San Diego and Los Angeles zoos.

From the earliest days, the program faced emotional opposition. At the crux of the debate was whether humans should intervene to save a species that some experts believed was heading toward the evolutionary abyss no matter what was done.

The late conservationist David Brower stood against capturing the condors, saying it was a greater evil than letting the species "disappear with dignity."

Some critics questioned the wisdom of spending millions of dollars on the condor—the figure stands at $40 million so far, two-thirds from private donations—when it might be better spent on other endangered species.

Others debated the philosophies for managing the birds and for ensuring that their habitats were safe.

But the federal program forged ahead, and on Jan. 14, 1992, scientists released the first pair of captive condors in Los Padres National Forest, 50 miles northwest of Los Angeles. The young female, Xewe, was shot at and survived. But her partner, Chocuyens, was found dead nine months after release, poisoned by ethylene glycol, possibly from antifreeze. *20*

Since then, of the 128 birds released, 45 died from various causes, 25 have been returned to captivity and 58 remain free.

The releases have occurred every year in three locales: in Los Padres, north of Ventura; near the Vermilion Cliffs, 30 miles north of Grand Canyon National Park; and within the Ventana Wilderness in Big Sur.

Life is hard for wild condors raised in captivity. Although caretakers try to minimize human contact, condors are a naturally inquisitive species and often seek out populated areas where they can get into trouble. Many have had to be recaptured for their own protection. In recent years, breeders have placed them with parents or mentor birds for socialization.

But the biggest cause of death is lead poisoning, affecting 20 or more birds.

A big break came in March. After 15 years without a single egg in the wild, a condor released in the Grand Canyon laid an egg hidden away in a cave, just as its ancestors had done. The egg was cracked, quite common among inexperienced birds, scientists said. *25*

In June, north of Ventura, two females each laid an egg in the same cave. They were taking turns sitting on one of the two eggs. "We figured these eggs were never going to make it on their own," said Fish and Wildlife biologist Greg Austin.

The team rappelled down and grabbed both the eggs, replacing them with one dummy egg. One of their eggs was dead, but one was alive. They rushed the live one to the Los Angeles Zoo, where it hatched. Austin and others took an egg about to hatch from the zoo back to the nest. Two days later, it hatched. Three days later, the hatchling was found dead outside the cave.

"We really wouldn't expect for them to be successful in their first breeding attempt ever," Austin said. "The way we look at it, it's a benefit to those birds. We don't think they know what to do until they see it. They live for so long, they're going to figure it out."

Harvard evolutionary biologist Edward O. Wilson, in his new book, "The Future of Life," says "11th-hour rescues from obliteration," such as the work done for the condor, "have confirmed the generally innate resilience of endangered species.

"Given protection and uncontaminated food, the combined group flourished," Wilson wrote. "For at least a while longer—and we most *30* prayerfully hope, for thousands of years to come—the California condor is again a free-living species."

The Responsive Reader

1 What *factual information* does this article give you about the condor and its history? How would you describe the bird and its existence in the wild?
2 What do you learn about the aspects of *human civilization* that threatened the survival of the birds? What do you learn about the dangers they still encounter from humans today?
3 What was the situation at the beginning of the rescue efforts? What is the rationale for the current rescue effort—how is it supposed to work? How is it working out? What would you include in an *interim report?* How does the writer sum up the prospects for eventual success?
4 This article includes much factual information about the rescue initiatives. Where does the excitement, the fascination, or the *enthusiasm* that motivates those involved shine through? Do you think you could share in it? Why or why not?

Talking, Listening, Writing

5 Do you think the estimated $40 million spent on the effort to save the condors is well spent? Why or why not? Do you think the money should have been spent on more urgent needs? Do you think the condors should have been allowed to die "with dignity"?

Collaborative Projects

6 Working with a group, you may want to compile a status report on efforts to protect or bring back another species of the endangered big birds, such as the bald eagles or the sandhill cranes.

DREAMS OF THE ANIMALS

Margaret Atwood

**A sharp-eyed critic of our callous modern civilization
indicts our abuse of our fellow creatures and the denial
of our kinship with the animal world.**

The environmental movement and the Green parties of Europe have rekindled our sense of kinship with the animal kingdom of which we are a part. Animal rights activists have protested the wretched unnatural conditions of the caged animals in traditional zoos. They started crusades to save animals once marked for extinction as predators or vermin.

Margaret Atwood may be the Canadian author best known by American readers. She published several volumes of poetry, and she has written about survival in harsh natural surroundings as a central theme in Canadian literature. Her novel The Handmaiden's Tale *(1985) was made into a chilling future fiction movie envisioning an anti-Utopian, dystopian society of the future in which sexism has run amok. She has said that she confronted "issues related to growing up female and sex-role changes long before they were popularized by the women's movement."*

The following widely reprinted poem was included in her Selected Poems
1965 – 1975.

Thought Starters: Do you like zoos? Do you like circuses? Do you like
dog shows? Why do activists object to them?

Mostly the animals dream   1
of other animals   each
according to its kind

      (though certain mice and small rodents
      have nightmares of a huge pink   5
      shape with five claws descending)

:moles dream of darkness and delicate
mole smells

frogs dream of green and golden
frogs   10

sparkling like wet suns
among the lilies

red and black
striped fish, their eyes open
have red and black striped
dreams   defense, attack, meaningful   15
patterns

birds dream of territories
enclosed by singing.

Sometimes the animals dream of evil   20
in the form of soap and metal
but mostly the animals dream
of other animals.

There are exceptions:

    the silver fox in the roadside zoo   25
    dreams of digging out
    and of baby foxes, their necks bitten

    the caged armadillo
    near the train   30
    station, which runs
    all day in figure eights
    its piglet feet pattering,
    no longer dreams
    but is insane when waking;

    the iguana   35
    in the petshop window on St. Catherine Street
    crested, royal-eyed, ruling
    its kingdom of water-dish and sawdust

    dreams of sawdust

The Responsive Reader

1   In the first half of the poem, why did Atwood choose the animals she
includes? Why didn't she choose stereotypically beautiful, graceful, or
cuddly animals to enlist the sympathies of the reader? Which of these animals would you usually find ugly or repulsive? (How do you feel about
frogs, moles, or rodents?) How does the poet take you into the animals'
world? How does she change or go counter to the *usual associations* the
animals bring to mind?

2   What is the *key difference* between the animals in the wild and the animals we see in the second half of the poem? What are striking or telling

contrasts? The poem does not editorialize or spell out the poet's message. What for you is the message carried by the images the poem calls up in the reader's mind?

3 What is the difference between the evil or nightmarish threats the animals encounter in the wild and the evil represented by *humans?* Is there a difference?

Talking, Listening, Writing

4 What do you know about initiatives to create more natural habitats for zoo animals? Have you visited or heard about enlightened modern model zoos? Do you think they would meet the objections of activists criticizing the traditional zoo mentality?

5 Pet owners, animal trainers, and other people working with animals are often accused of reading human or near-human thoughts and emotions into what they observe in animals. They see evidence of loyalty, fear of abandonment, anger, hostility, confusion, and other familiar human mental states. Are they going too far in projecting human thoughts and feelings onto animals? Have you been around animals enough to form an opinion on this question?

6 A whimsical cartoonist turned the tables on zoo visitors by imagining a people zoo where visiting animals could gawk at different specimens of the human species. You may want to write about an imaginary visit to a people zoo as a representative of the animal world.

FIND IT ON THE WEB

Look at the website of a group such as People for the Ethical Treatment of Animals (PETA). What are their beliefs about animal rights? Do you agree with some or all of their positions? Can you find statements by animal trainers or zoo officials who present a different view?

FORUM: *The Endangered Ecosphere*

It took hundreds of millions of years to produce the life that now inhabits the earth.

—RACHEL CARSON

Concerned scientists and political activists warn us that humanity has developed the know-how to poison our planet or to kill all life on it several times over. Believers in progress had long celebrated science and technology as the means of liberating humanity from its ancient scourges: backbreaking toil, the threat of mass starvation, and uncontrolled diseases decimating humankind. However, science, long advertised as the fairy godmother of comfort and prosperity, has come to be seen by many as a mixed blessing, with our modern industrial lifestyle threatening to pollute our environment and make it uninhabitable for future generations.

Ordinary citizens and newspaper readers often find themselves caught between two camps: Environmentalists see themselves as watchdogs and whistleblowers and warn of ecological disaster. Conservatives advertise themselves as voices of realism and common sense and label the other side doomsayers and alarmists. Do you incline to one side or the other? Do you follow news reports on environmental issues?

DON'T MENTION GLOBAL WARMING

Molly Ivins

"We continue to report global warming as though it were a 'debate' among scientists. It is not."

As the result of the warming of the earth's atmosphere, the polar icecaps are melting. Age-old glaciers are receding. In 2004, in a single year, centennial hurricanes and other climate changes devastated Caribbean islands and the American Southeast. Killer storms and unprecedented flooding were hitting countries like France and Germany. In the following column first published in the Forth Worth Star *in August 1998, Molly Ivins was one of the early voices asking Americans not to dismiss scientists' warnings about global warming as "uncertain science."*

Ivins is a nationally syndicated Texas columnist who has served as a gadfly critic of politicians both in Texas and nationally who are part of an "old-boy" network and who serve the corporate interests that finance their campaigns. She wrote this column when unprecedented heat and drought were devastating the American Southwest. The death toll and record-breaking heat wave made many readers take a second look at the global warming theory.

Emissions from "greenhouse" gases resulting from our industrialized modern lifestyle are heating up the earth's atmosphere. The melting of the polar ice will inundatate large coastal areas and swamp coastal cities. Catastrophic climatic changes will turn large agricultural areas into deserts. An international treaty signed in Kyoto, Japan, set goals for changing the behavior of both industrialized and developing countries. Much foot-dragging by major polluting countries like the U.S. and Russia delayed implementation of the urgent recommendations.

Thought Starters: Global warming and the destruction of the ozone layer became highly charged political issues. How much do you know about the scientific issues underlying the controversy? Can you fill in your classmates on what is involved?

AUSTIN, Texas—As Texas endures the slow, agonizing death of our entire agricultural sector by drought, a check of our media and political leaders shows we are also suffering from a bizarre silence on a topic that could be described as "the cause that dare not speak its name."

Local newspapers have responded heroically to the heat wave that has now killed more than 120 Texans, unleashing a torrent of efforts to help those most in peril. The one topic they have not addressed is: Why is this happening?

Of the few articles on the subject, all are limited to the answer "El Niño," which is half right. According to climatologists, this is an El Niño drought: El Niño shifted the jet stream just enough to hold the high that normally sits over the Rockies in the summertime east over Texas, so we are not getting the clouds and cooling that normally give us some relief. But the other half of the answer, global warming, has gotten little or no attention.

A recent *Dallas Morning News* article gives the flavor of what little coverage global warming has gotten: "What did skies over Texas and a Washington debate about global warming share this week? An unusual amount of hot air, say experts on both meteorology and politics." Heh-heh.

The media are doing so poorly on this issue that it's an embarrassment   5
to the profession, and we are being hoist partly by the petard of our infamous "objectivity." We continue to report global warming as though it were a "debate" among scientists. It is not.

What we mistake for a "debate" is actually a public relations campaign by the American Petroleum Institute, which has recruited and funded a few scientists who question the entire phenomenon. They, in turn, are given equal weight by the media, as though they were precisely as objective as the 2,500 scientists who work with the United Nations' Intergovernmental Panel on Climate Change.

According to USA Today, when 14 energy industry lobbyists gathered in April to work out the details of a $6 million lobbying plan on global warming, they targeted Congress, the news media, the public and . . . schoolchildren. "Informing teacher/students about uncertainties in climate science will begin to erect a barrier against further efforts to impose Kyoto-like measures in the future," says a memo obtained by the National Environmental Trust.

The notion that the IPCC is some group of fear-mongering enviros is easily disproved by study of any of its cautious work or the testimony of its chairman, Robert T. Watson. On the other hand, the API's notorious PR campaign is designed, in the words of its own strategy documents, to "reposition global warming as theory rather than fact."

In addition, a number of conservative think tanks have been churning out dubious studies allegedly proving that doing much of anything about global warming will cost each and every citizen a small fortune and "radically" affect all our lives. These studies have been given solemn coverage by the press.

Among the most important developments this year is the formation of   10
a coalition of major companies—including Sun Co., 3M, British Petroleum, Lockheed, Maytag, United Technologies, Boeing, etc.—that not only accept climate change as a serious threat but also believe that action is necessary and can be taken without economic damage.

Meanwhile, the Republican Party of Texas has adopted the flat statement: "We oppose the theory of global warming and the Kyoto Agreement." That certainly takes care of that, as far as Texas Republicans are concerned.

The Responsive Reader

1   Many newspaper readers came to think of the global warming issue as a topic of *controversy* or a debate. Ivins claims the controversy is not a "debate." What is her point? What evidence does she have to back up her claim?
2   How does the *bottom line* enter into the controversy about global warming?
3   Ivins pins her charges and assertions to an array of carefully selected quotes, both pro and con. What *sources* does she use in this column, and how does she use them?

Talking, Listening, Writing

4   Ivins is sarcastic about the "objectivity" of the media. Why or how?
5   Do you consider Ivins herself objective or biased? She is the kind of assertive, aggressive writer who attracts loyal fans while alienating other readers. With which camp do you tend to identify? Why?
6   According to Ivins, a public relations campaign is aimed at making teachers and students think of global warming "as theory rather than fact." What is the point of insisting that scientific theories be identified as theories?

FIND IT ON THE WEB

How familiar are you with the ideas of environmentalists? What do you know about Greenpeace and the Green parties of other countries? Green parties or politically organized environmentalists are on the march in Europe and are beginning to play a role in state-level politics in the United States. You may want to look for articles on the Green parties of Europe in publications like the British *Guardian* or the *Economist*.

SAVING NATURE, BUT ONLY FOR MAN

Charles Krauthammer

"A sane environmentalism, the only kind of environmentalism that will win universal public support, begins by unashamedly declaring that nature is here to serve man."

Charles Krauthammer is a Washington Post *columnist who has long been a strong voice of a conservative political agenda. He has been a vocal critic of American liberals, attacking their "sentimental" Romanticizing of the indigenous peoples of the Americas on occasions like the contested celebrations of the 500th anniversary of the voyage of Columbus to the New World. A frequent contributor to the glossy advertising-heavy* Time *magazine, Krauthammer has in recent years become an aggressive advocate of a "get-tough" stance toward America's enemies and of a go-it-alone foreign policy agenda leaving behind faint-hearted former allies.*

In this Time *magazine essay first published in June 1991, he sounded a warning much repeated since by business interests and the political right: the "job-destroying" economic cost of environmental or ecological initiatives designed to protect our natural environment and honor our kinship with nature.*

Thought Starters: Has the environmental movement made a difference? Has it created a backlash?

Environmental sensitivity is now as required an attitude in polite society as is, say, belief in democracy or aversion to polyester. But now that everyone from Ted Turner to George Bush, Dow to Exxon has professed love for Mother Earth, how are we to choose among the dozens of conflicting proposals, restrictions, projects, regulations and laws advanced in the name of the environment? Clearly not everything with an environmental claim is worth doing. How to choose?

There is a simple way. First, distinguish between environmental luxuries and environmental necessities. Luxuries are those things it would be nice to have if costless. Necessities are those things we must have regardless. Then apply a rule. Call it the fundamental axiom of sane environmentalism: Combatting ecological change that directly threatens the health and safety of people is an environmental necessity. All else is luxury.

For example: preserving the atmosphere—stopping ozone depletion and the greenhouse effect—is an environmental necessity. In April scientists reported that ozone damage is far worse than previously thought.

Ozone depletion not only causes skin cancer and eye cataracts, it also destroys plankton, the beginning of the food chain atop which we humans sit.

The reality of the greenhouse effect is more speculative, though its possible consequences are far deadlier: melting ice caps, flooded coastlines, disrupted climate, parched plains and, ultimately, empty breadbaskets. The American Midwest feeds the world. Are we prepared to see Iowa acquire New Mexico's desert climate? And Siberia acquire Iowa's?

Ozone depletion and the greenhouse effect are human disasters. They   5
happen to occur in the environment. But they are urgent because they directly threaten man. A sane environmentalism, the only kind of environmentalism that will win universal public support, begins by unashamedly declaring that nature is here to serve man. A sane environmentalism is entirely anthropocentric: it enjoins man to preserve nature, but on the grounds of self-preservation.

A sane environmentalism does not sentimentalize the earth. It does not ask people to sacrifice in the name of other creatures. After all, it is hard enough to ask people to sacrifice in the name of other humans. (Think of the chronic public resistance to foreign aid and welfare.) Ask hardworking voters to sacrifice in the name of the snail darter, and, if they are feeling polite, they will give you a shrug.

Of course, this anthropocentrism runs against the grain of a contemporary environmentalism that indulges in earth worship to the point of idolatry. One scientific theory—Gaia theory—actually claims that Earth is a living organism. This kind of environmentalism likes to consider itself spiritual. It is nothing more than sentimental. It takes, for example, a highly selective view of the benignity of nature. My nature worship stops with the April twister that came through Kansas or the May cyclone that killed more than 125,000 Bengalis and left 10 million (!) homeless.

A nonsentimental environmentalism is one founded on Protagoras' maxim that "Man is the measure of all things." Such a principle helps us through the thicket of environmental argument. Take the current debate raging over oil drilling in a corner of the Alaska National Wildlife Refuge. Environmentalists, mobilizing against a bill working its way through the U.S. Congress to permit such exploration, argue that Americans should be conserving energy instead of drilling for it. This is a false either/or proposition. The U.S. does need a sizable energy tax to reduce consumption. But it needs more production too. Government estimates indicate a nearly fifty-fifty chance that under the ANWR lies one of the five largest oil fields ever discovered in America.

The U.S. has just come through a war fought in part over oil. Energy dependence costs Americans not just dollars but lives. It is a bizarre sentimentalism that would deny oil that is peacefully attainable because it risks disrupting the calving grounds of Arctic caribou.

I like the caribou as much as the next man. And I would be rather   10
sorry if their mating patterns are disturbed. But you can't have everything. And if the choice is between the welfare of caribou and reducing an oil

dependency that gets people killed in wars, I choose man over caribou every time.

Similarly the spotted owl in Oregon. I am no enemy of the owl. If it could be preserved at no or little cost, I would agree: the variety of nature is a good, a high aesthetic good. But it is no more than that. And sometimes aesthetic goods have to be sacrificed to the more fundamental ones. If the cost of preserving the spotted owl is the loss of livelihood for 30,000 logging families, I choose family over owl.

The important distinction is between those environmental goods that are fundamental and those that are merely aesthetic. Nature is our ward. It is not our master. It is to be respected and even cultivated. But it is man's world. And when man has to choose between his well-being and that of nature, nature will have to accommodate.

Man should accommodate only when his fate and that of nature are inextricably bound up. The most urgent accommodation must be made when the very integrity of man's habitat—e.g., atmospheric ozone—is threatened. When the threat to man is of a lesser order (say, the pollutants from coal- and oil-fired generators that cause death from disease but not fatal damage to the ecosystem), a more modulated accommodation that balances economic against health concerns is in order. But in either case the principle is the same: protect the environment—because it is man's environment.

The sentimental environmentalists will call this saving nature with a totally wrong frame of mind. Exactly. A sane—a humanistic—environmentalism does it not for nature's sake but for our own.

The Responsive Reader

1   What is the essence of Krauthammer's "sane environmentalism"? What are the *test cases* that help him expound his thesis? (What does he mean by "anthropocentrism"?)
2   What is Krauthammer's basic *philosophical difference* with what he calls "sentimental" environmentalism?

Talking, Listening, Writing

3   Prepare an oral presentation or write an essay to support or rebut Krauthammer's position. Support your point of view with detailed examples or cases in point.

Collaborative Projects

4   Krauthammer's allies on the political right have attacked warnings concerning global warming as based on uncertain or "faulty science." What are recent estimates from the scientific community? How widely accepted are they?

FEEDING TEN BILLION PEOPLE

Mark Sagoff

Biotechnology introduces "an entirely new stage in humankind's attempts to produce more crops and plants."

Sagoff's reassuring optimistic assessment of the planet's capacity for feeding its exploding human population was first published in the conservative Atlantic Monthly *in 1997.*

In the seventies and eighties, warning voices had said that the population explosion was straining the ability of the planet to feed the human race. We were burning up irreplaceable natural resources at a disastrous rate, in the process polluting the earth, the air, the rivers, and the oceans. We were heedlessly using up the limited resources of Spaceship Earth. The nineties saw a strong countermovement attacking pessimistic environmentalists as alarmists and naysayers.

In the debate between the ecological doomsayers and the ecological pollyannas, Mark Sagoff is on the side of the optimists. He cites experts who claim that known reserves of oil and natural gas will last seventy to a hundred years. In the future, theoretically feasible drilling technology could tap geothermal energy—the heat of the earth's core—in amounts far exceeding our needs. Tidal energy and solar power are other largely untapped nonpolluting natural resources. In the following section from a larger article, Sagoff sets out to refute the theory that catastrophic food shortages will result if the planet's population continues to grow at projected rates.

Thought Starters: Have you encountered warnings about overpopulation and ecological catastrophe? Where or in what context? What was your reaction?

The United Nations projects that the global population, currently 5.7 billion, will peak at about 10 billion in the next century and then stabilize or even decline. Can the earth feed that many people? Even if food crops increase sufficiently, other renewable resources, including many fisheries and forests, are already under pressure. Should we expect fish stocks to collapse or forests to disappear?

The world already produces enough cereals and oilseeds to feed 10 billion people a vegetarian diet adequate in protein and calories. If, however, the idea is to feed 10 billion people not healthful vegetarian diets but the kind of meat-laden meals that Americans eat, the production of grains and oilseeds may have to triple—primarily to feed livestock. Is anything like this kind of productivity in the cards?

Maybe. From 1961 to 1994 global production of food doubled. Global output of grain rose from about 630 million tons in 1950 to about 1.8 billion tons in 1992, largely as a result of greater yields. Developing countries from 1974 to 1994 increased wheat yields per acre by almost 100 percent, corn yields by 72 percent, and rice yields by 52 percent. "The generation of farmers on the land in 1950 was the first in history to double the production of food," the Worldwatch Institute has reported. "By 1984, they had outstripped population growth enough to raise per capita grain output an unprecedented 40 percent." From a two-year period ending in 1981 to a two-year period ending in 1990 the real prices of basic foods fell 38 percent on world markets, according to a 1992 United Nations report. Prices for food have continually decreased since the end of the eighteenth century, when Thomas Malthus argued that rapid population growth must lead to mass starvation by exceeding the carrying capacity of the earth.

Farmers worldwide could double the acreage in production, but this should not be necessary. Better seeds, more irrigation, multi-cropping, and additional use of fertilizer could greatly increase agricultural yields in the developing world, which are now generally only half those in the industrialized countries. It is biologically possible to raise yields of rice to about seven tons per acre—about four times the current average in the developing world. Super strains of cassava, a potato-like root crop eaten by millions of Africans, promise to increase yields tenfold. American farmers can also do better. In a good year, such as 1994, Iowa corn growers average about 3.5 tons per acre, but farmers more than double that yield in National Corn Growers Association competitions.

In drier parts of the world the scarcity of fresh water presents the greatest challenge to agriculture. But the problem is regional, not global. Fortunately, as Lester Brown, of the Worldwatch Institute, points out, "there are vast opportunities for increasing water efficiency" in arid regions, ranging from installing better water-delivery systems to planting drought-resistant crops. He adds, "Scientists can help push back the physical frontiers of cropping by developing varieties that are more drought resistant, salt tolerant, and early maturing. The payoff on the first two could be particularly high."

As if in response, Novartis Seeds has announced a program to develop water-efficient and salt-tolerant crops, including genetically engineered varieties of wheat. Researchers in Mexico have announced the development of drought-resistant corn that can boost yields by a third. Biotechnologists are converting annual crops into perennial ones, eliminating the need for yearly planting. They also hope to enable cereal crops to fix their own nitrogen, as legumes do, minimizing the need for fertilizer (genetically engineered nitrogen-fixing bacteria have already been test-marketed to farmers). Commercial varieties of crops such as corn, tomatoes, and potatoes which have been genetically engineered to be resistant to pests and diseases have been approved for field testing in the United States; several are now being sold and planted. A new breed of rice, 25 percent more productive than any currently in use, suggests that the Gene Revolution can take over where the Green Revolution left off. Biotechnology, as the historian Paul Kennedy has written, introduces "an entirely new stage in humankind's attempts to produce more crops and plants."

Biotechnology cannot, however, address the major causes of famine: poverty, trade barriers, corruption, mismanagement, ethnic antagonism, anarchy, war, and male-dominated societies that deprive women of food. Local land depletion, itself a consequence of poverty and institutional failure, is also a factor. Those who are too poor to use sound farming practices are compelled to overexploit the resources on which they depend. As the economist Partha Dasgupta has written, "Population growth, poverty and degradation of local resources often fuel one another." The amount of food in world trade is constrained less by the resource base than by the maldistribution of wealth.

Analysts who believe that the world is running out of resources often argue that famines occur not as a result of political or economic conditions but because there are "too many people." Unfortunately, as the economist Amartya Sen has pointed out, public officials who think in Malthusian terms assume that when absolute levels of food supplies are adequate, famine will not occur. This conviction diverts attention from the actual causes of famine, which has occurred in places where food output kept pace with population growth but people were too destitute to buy it.

We would have run out of food long ago had we tried to supply ourselves entirely by hunting and gathering. Likewise, if we depend on nature's gifts, we will exhaust many of the world's important fisheries. Fortunately, we are learning to cultivate fish as we do other crops. Genetic engineers have designed fish for better flavor and color as well as for faster growth, improved disease resistance, and other traits. Two farmed species—silver carp and grass carp—already rank among the ten most-consumed fish worldwide. A specialty bred tilapia, known as the "aquatic chicken," takes six months to grow to a harvestable size of about one and a half pounds.

Aquaculture produced more than 16 million tons of fish in 1993; capacity has expanded over the past decade at an annual rate of 10 percent by quantity and 14 percent by value. In 1993 fish farms produced 22 percent of all food fish consumed in the world and 90 percent of all oysters sold. The World Bank reports that aquaculture could provide 40 percent of all fish consumed and more than half the value of fish harvested within the next fifteen years.

10

Salmon ranching and farming provide examples of the growing efficiency of aquacultural production. Norwegian salmon farms alone produce 400 million pounds a year. A biotech firm in Waltham, Massachusetts, has applied for government approval to commercialize salmon genetically engineered to grow four to six times as fast as their naturally occurring cousins. As a 1994 article in *Sierra* magazine noted, "There is so much salmon currently available that the supply exceeds demand, and prices to fishermen have fallen dramatically."

For those who lament the decline of natural fisheries and the human communities that grew up with them, the successes of aquaculture may offer no consolation. In the Pacific Northwest, for example, overfishing in combination with dams and habitat destruction has reduced the wild salmon population by 80 percent. Wild salmon—but not their bio-engineered aquacultural cousins—contribute to the cultural identity and sense of place of the Northwest. When wild salmon disappear, so will some of the region's history, character, and pride. What is true of wild salmon is also true of whales, dolphins, and other magnificent creatures—as they lose their economic importance, their aesthetic and moral worth becomes all the more evident. Economic considerations pull in one direction, moral considerations in the other. This conflict colors all our battles over the environment.

The transition from hunting and gathering to farming, which is changing the fishing industry, has taken place more slowly in forestry. Still there is no sign of a timber famine. In the United States forests now provide the largest harvests in history, and there is more forested U.S. area today than there was in 1920. Bill McKibben has observed . . . that the eastern United States, which loggers and farmers in the eighteenth and nineteenth centuries nearly denuded of trees, has become reforested during this century (see "An Explosion of Green," April, 1995, *Atlantic*). One reason is that farms reverted to woods. Another is that machinery replaced animals; each draft animal required two or three cleared acres for pasture.

Natural reforestation is likely to continue as biotechnology makes areas used for logging more productive. According to Roger Sedjo, a respected forestry expert, advances in tree farming, if implemented widely, would permit the world to meet its entire demand for industrial wood using just 200 million acres of plantations—an area equal to only five percent of current forest land. As less land is required for commercial tree production, more natural forests may be protected—as they should be, for aesthetic, ethical, and spiritual reasons.

The expansion of fish and tree farming confirms the belief held by Peter Drucker and other management experts that our economy depends far more on the progress of technology than on the exploitation of nature. Although raw materials will always be necessary, knowledge has become the essential factor in the production of goods and services. "Where there is effective management," Drucker has written, "that is, application of knowledge to knowledge, we can always obtain the other resources." If we assume, along with Drucker and others, that resource scarcities do not exist or are easily averted, it is hard to see how economic theory, which after all concerns scarcity, provides the conceptual basis for valuing the environment. The reasons to preserve nature are ethical more often than they are economic.

The Responsive Reader

1   At the beginning, what are the key questions Sagoff asks about the ability of the planet to feed the multiplying human race? Where at the end does he finally give a definitive answer to these questions? What is it?

2   Sagoff charts the history of increases in food production in recent decades, using the formidable array of statistics that is his trademark. What are key numbers? Where do they come from, and what do they show?

3   What are key data in Sagoff's optimistic account of future possibilities and prospects? What are major developments pointing toward an "entirely new stage" in food production? What is aquaculture?

4   Deforestation and logging of old-growth forests have long been targets of environmental activists. What account does Sagoff give of tree farming? Do you think it will defuse the controversies about the destruction of the world's forests?

5   In talking about the specter of famine, Sagoff shifts the emphasis away from limited natural resources in order to focus on other sources of scarcity and starvation. What are they? How much do you know about them?

Talking, Listening, Writing

6   What is new to you in Sagoff's arguments? What is familiar? Does he change your mind on any important issues?

7   Sagoff says that the reasons for protecting nature are moral or aesthetic rather than economic. Ethical, aesthetic, and spiritual considerations will have to provide the conceptual basis for valuing the environment. What does he mean? How would this emphasis change current attitudes about the environment?

8   Have you ever been concerned about hungry fellow Americans? Have you ever been concerned about world hunger? Do you know of any promising initiatives to combat hunger and malnutrition?

9   If you tend to agree with people like Sagoff, you may want to write an open letter to activists who predict ecological catastrophe. If you tend to disagree with Sagoff, you may want to write an open letter responding to his arguments.

FIND IT ON THE WEB

Recent years have seen many studies evaluating for a general audience current studies of population growth and of the ability of the planet to feed its burgeoning human population. An early example bringing together much detailed information from authoritative sources was Bill McKibben, "The Future of Population: A Special Moment in History" (*Atlantic*, May 1998). McKibben was the author of several books about the environment, including *The End of Nature* (1989) and *Hope, Human and Wild* (1995). Working with a group, you may want to track more recent statistics on population growth or world hunger.

Arguing Your Case

Present a structured argument to help fair-minded readers think the subject through.

A logical argument moves the discussion of an issue beyond personal preference, beyond personal likes and dislikes. It asks readers to approach a subject with an open mind. It asks readers to look at evidence objectively—unswayed by bias, prejudice, or ulterior motive. When you present a reasoned argument to your readers, you act on your faith that they will listen to reason. You trust them to use their own minds and draw their own logical conclusions. They may not agree with you, but you may at least lead them to reexamine their own thinking.

Current discussions of argument map out three requirements: First, you need to formulate your *claim* clearly in your own mind: What point are you trying to prove? Second, you need to have ready the data or the evidence that you have gathered to *support* your claim. Third, you prepare to take your reader through the logical steps that connect your claim and your data and thus *warrant* your conclusions.

Three major reasoning patterns help you structure papers that present a strong argument:

INDUCTIVE REASONING   *Inductive reasoning formulates general conclusions after studying carefully observed examples.* **Inductive,** generalizing reasoning is the most easily demonstrated procedure that our minds use to process information. Induction moves from careful observation of specifics toward cautiously formulated general points. Trend watchers and media watchers collect similar or related examples to show a general tendency or

658

direction in current events. They track occurrences of what they see as a general pattern. At the same time, they try to account for apparent exceptions or to meet objections from unconvinced readers. They need to convince the reader that their examples are authentic and representative and justify the general conclusions they have reached.

The inductive think scheme moves from observation to inference— from fact to theory. It has for centuries been the model for Western science. Early scientists stressed firsthand observation and then used inductive reasoning to formulate physical laws.

OBSERVATION 1   Objects we drop fall to the floor and not to the ceiling.

OBSERVATION 2   Apples drop to the ground instead of flying off toward the sky.

OBSERVATION 3   The moon is kept in orbit around the earth instead of hurling off into space.

OBSERVATION 4   The earth is kept in orbit around the sun instead of floating out of our solar system.

——————————————————>>>>>>>>>>>>>>>>>>>>>>>>

GENERAL CONCLUSION: **An all-pervading physical force—gravity— pulls material objects toward one another, with the massive gravitational pull of the earth and the sun overcoming all opposed forces.**

PRO-AND-CON REASONING   *Much productive reasoning balances off opposing points of view.* Playing off **pro and con** mirrors the way a public consensus takes shape on many debatable issues. By listening to both sides, we can hope to weed out what is clearly self-serving, partisan, or extreme in order to find common ground. Ideally, we move from statement to counterstatement and on to a balanced conclusion acceptable to many readers.

STATEMENT: To protect minors, we need laws to keep violent and offensive material off the big and small screen.

COUNTERSTATEMENT: Many viewers are not minors but mature adults who have the right to make their own decisions.

——————————————————>>>>>>>>>>>>>>>>>>>>>>>>>>>>>>

BALANCED: **Rating systems and optional filtering software make possible parental control.**

Scholarly studies of this kind of thinking still use technical terms from early Greek inquiries into the workings of the human mind:

THESIS: In a democracy, the people as a whole make the most important decisions.

ANTITHESIS: It takes an educated elite to make informed decisions on key issues.

———————————————— >>>>>>>>>>>>>>>>>>>>>>>>>>>>>>>>>

SYNTHESIS: **It takes an educated citizenry to make informed decisions.**

DEDUCTIVE REASONING   *Much of our reasoning follows the opposite of the inductive procedure.* **Deduction,** or deductive reasoning, spells out something that we believe. We expect our readers to accept it as true. We then show how the general principle applies to a specific situation. Deductive reasoning moves from the general to the specific. It invokes principles that we expect the reader to share. It then applies these to the situation in question.

Inductive and deductive reasoning work together if we first develop general physical laws or patterns of behavior. We then use them to predict behavior in a specific situation. For instance, if the law of gravity holds true, a space module passing Venus or Mars should be pulled toward the planet or deflected into an orbit around the planet.

Many arguments concerning values or behavior follow a deductive IF-THEN pattern:

IF: All human beings, regardless of race, are created equal.

THEN: **Slavery is evil.**

IF: Citizens of different religions have equal rights in American courts.

THEN: **A judge may not display the biblical Ten Commandments in his court.**

IF: The foundation of democracy is an educated citizenry.

THEN: **Providing universal public education is a civic duty.**

Deductive arguments hinge on the initial *if*—the initial assumption, or **premise.** If the premise does not hold true, the argument does not convince. If it is true that many ordinary people are not really intelligent enough to make informed political decisions, we are relieved of our obligation to provide free universal public education. We may then decide to train an elite to guide the nation and settle for minimal vocational training for those who only need basic skills and the ability to follow instructions.

Deductive reasoning is often charted as a three-step pattern: "If A is true, and if B is true, then C must also be true."

IF: The U.S. Constitution separates church and state, religion and government.

AND IF: The nativity scene is a religious symbol.

THEN: **The nativity scene should not be displayed at city hall.**

The shared assumptions are your **premises**—they provide the foundation on which the argument rests. A successful argument takes the reader from accepted premises through a chain of reasoning to a valid conclusion. A three-step argument, moving from two accepted premises to a justified conclusion, is called a **syllogism:**

FIRST PREMISE: All full-time students are eligible for the loan program.

SECOND PREMISE: You are a full-time student.

CONCLUSION: **Therefore, you are eligible.**

FIRST PREMISE: No undocumented aliens will be hired.

SECOND PREMISE: I am an undocumented alien.

CONCLUSION: **Therefore, I need not apply.**

FIRST PREMISE: No one with an arrest record will be hired.

SECOND PREMISE: I do not have an arrest record.

CONCLUSION: **Therefore, I am eligible.**

In each of these arguments, the first premise specifies what it includes or rules out. The conclusion necessarily follows because the premise includes or rules out *all* members of a group. We cannot argue with the *therefore* that takes us of the logical conclusion.

CHECKING YOUR LOGIC   As you structure a logical argument, prepare for challenges from readers who remain unconvinced:

▪ *In practice, many arguments are not true syllogisms.* Arguments that use *some* or *many* instead of *all* or *no* in the first premise are less airtight.

They lead to a conclusion that is not certain but only *probable:*

IF: Most members of the Achievement Club are business majors.

AND IF: Maria is a member of the Achievement Club.

THEN: **Maria is likely to be a business major.**

▪ *An argument may rest on doubtful assumptions.* Check for **questionable premises.** When you present an argument like the following, your readers may challenge your premises rather than your conclusions:

IF: Students learn best in a relaxed, supportive atmosphere.

AND IF: The present system of exams causes tension and anxiety.

THEN: Exams work against true learning.

(But do not at least some students perform better under pressure?)

■ *Your readers may refuse to go along with your argument because of un-stated assumptions.* Check for **hidden premises.** When you bring these out into the open, you have a chance to reexamine them and revise them if necessary.

PREMISE:	My economics teacher is from a middle-class background.
CONCLUSION:	**She cannot be expected to sympathize with the poor.**
HIDDEN PREMISE:	(People cannot sympathize with someone from a different class?)

■ *An argument may look logical and yet produce the wrong result.* For in-stance, the first premise may start with the **nonexclusive *all.*** It is then easy to draw a wrong conclusion. The word *all* includes everyone in a group—but it does not *exclude* others. It often means "all of the above—and maybe others."

FIRST PREMISE:	All Marxists quote Karl Marx.
SECOND PREMISE:	Professor Darien quotes Karl Marx.
WRONG:	**Therefore, Professor Darien must be a Marxist.**

(Like other non-Marxists, she may quote Marx on key issues but dis-agree with many of his conclusions.)

FIRST PREMISE:	All pigeons have feathers.
SECOND PREMISE:	My canary has feathers.
WRONG:	**Therefore, my canary is a pigeon.**

Triggering

Recall your readers to basic principles that may have been ne-glected or ignored.

We feel the need to appeal to shared basic values when public opin-ion or official policy seems to move in the wrong direction. We remind readers of basic principles when an issue is too important to be decided on the basis what will be an acceptable compromise or what will "make every-one happy." We appeal to principle when we decide it is time to take a stand. We may invoke basic principles when defending our position on public education, drunken driving laws, Christmas displays on public prop-erty, welfare reform, military service, or capital punishment.

Writing about an important issue, you will often take your stand on assumptions that you expect your intended readers to accept:

All young Americans are entitled to a quality education.

Money should not be the deciding factor in finding a defendant innocent or guilty.

The U.S. Constitution guarantees citizens the right to bear arms.

You then apply these principles to a specific situation. You show how the principle applies to a new proposal for funding schools, or a widely publicized court case, or a proposed gun control ordinance. When building an argument on such shared assumptions, you face two basic tasks. First, you need to state your basic assumptions carefully and convincingly enough so that they will put your readers in an assenting mood. You then need to build an argument on these assumptions that has the force of logic.

Gathering

Gather material to show that the values you appeal to are widely shared or are rooted in our common history. What will remind your readers of basic values or commitments at stake in a currently debated issue?

TRADITIONAL VALUES *Show that values you appeal to are widely shared traditional convictions or commitments.* On our obligation to the poor, you may decide to quote an eloquent statement by a widely respected leader. Or you may present a modern rereading of a parable from the New Testament. Who was the Good Samaritan? In our modern society, who are the Good Samaritans? Who were the people who crossed to the other side of the street to avoid helping the traveler "fell among thieves"? Who are the people in our modern world who are crossing to "the other side of the street"? Who in our modern world are the people who rescue and befriend those in need of help?

HISTORICAL PRECEDENTS *Show that major principles or rights are rooted in our shared history.* For instance, what is the history of our protections for freedom of speech? Why were printers and journalists in the colonies concerned about their freedom to print? How did they use the power of the pen to mobilize the American rebellion against the superior might of the British empire? What are the roots of First Amendment rights in earlier British history? Where in modern times have censorship forces been especially strong and repressive?

CURRENT TESTIMONY *Bring in support from public opinion and eloquent current testimony.* Perhaps you want to appeal to the principle of compassion in arguing against "heroic" medical procedures that prolong the suffering of the terminally ill. Your **reading notes** for your paper might include entries like the following:

DEATH WITH DIGNITY

- -

Public opinion polls show that most Americans oppose the use of "heroic measures" to keep patients alive when there is no hope of recovery. A Louis Harris poll found that 82% supported the idea of withdrawing feeding tubes if it was the patient's wish.

In many cases, the family and the staff agree that the patient in question "derives no comfort, no improvement, and no hope of improvement" from further medical treatment. Many Americans linger in a hopeless twilight zone between life and imminent death.

Recent studies show the tremendous financial burden and the anguish suffered by their families.

Shaping

Plan your strategy so that your argument will move the reader along.

Effective argument changes minds or compels belief. It moves or pushes the reader along—even if the reader was used to a different line of thinking. What will be your best strategy when you try to move your reader along? Study different styles and models of argument:

ARGUING FROM PRINCIPLE *Establish a key principle and then apply it to a current test case.* You first dramatize the current situation that raised the issue. You then single out the principle (or principles) involved, presenting them in such a way that the argument will speak strongly to the shared values of the intended audience. Then you apply the principle (or principles) to a current issue or specific authentic examples.

CLAIM AND SUPPORT *A traditional style of argument starts with a strong assertive claim.* Perhaps you support liberalized immigration regulations allowing highly qualified foreigners to come into the country. You start with a strongly worded plea. Then you document case after case where highly skilled immigrants have proved an asset in areas like computer programing and medicine. In fact, the countries of origin of such highly skilled newcomers often complain about a "brain drain."

You might chart your strategy as follows:

The Brain Drain: Boon for the U.S.

STRONG CLAIM:	**Rather than taking jobs from Americans, highly qualified immigrants fill serious gaps and help the U.S. stay competitive in the modern world.**
REASON ONE:	With science education in the U.S. lagging, highly trained immigrants can help us prevent countries like India and China from overtaking us in high-tech fields.

REASON TWO:	Skilled medical practitioners provide much-needed backup at a time when emergency rooms are often badly understaffed.
REASON THREE:	Teachers from foreign countries expose today's college students to a broader international perspective and prepare them to compete successfully in tomorrow's global world.

THE *YES, BUT* ARGUMENT   *A modern style of argument first establishes common ground.* Before you come on strong, you ask yourself: What are the people on the other side thinking? How about first showing them that you respect their right to their own opinion and that you honor their commitments? Then, once you have shown you are sensitive to their concerns, you ask them to listen to yours.

The result may be a "**Yes, but**" style of argument, with a pattern like the following. Transitions like *it is true or granted that* signal that you are honoring commitments or concerns of your audience:

The Brain Drain: Boon or Bane?

People opposed to a stepped-up importation of highly skilled newcomers **express important reservations.** . . .

It is true that exemptions to immigration laws for special interest groups tend to set a bad precedent. . . .

Granted, free access for foreign graduates may lead Americans to neglect building up their own graduate schools and funding of high-tech research. . . .

Nevertheless, the fact remains that highly skilled immigrants can be an important asset in the fiercely competitive global struggle. . . .

Revising

Revise to make sure your argument will stand on its merits.
When we write with special conviction, we are likely to come on strong. We may use emotional language. We may be impatient with the opposition. We may sound very sure of ourselves. Give yourself time to reread a paper that you wrote in an angry mood or in the heat of passion. Rereading the paper later in the sober light of day, you have a chance to take some of the heat or steam out of the argument.

In revising your paper, listen to feedback like the following:

■ *Try not to invoke large abstractions like Science or History or Common Sense.* "Science says . . . is a weak argument, because specific scientists make limited assertions. Scientists disagree among themselves and revise the "received wisdom" in the light of new findings and challenges to traditional theories. Quote specific scientists, and try to show that they are recognized authorities or people in the mainstream of current scientific opinion.

- *Try not to dismiss or brush off opposing points of view.* People who feel insulted or ignored are not likely to listen attentively. You are then not likely to change their minds. (For example, not everyone who endorses tighter background checks for foreign students from Middle Eastern countries is a racist.)

- *Tone down passages that make you sound bigoted or prejudiced.* ("The average criminal is a brutal individual who deserves exactly what he got.")

- *Strengthen logical links.* Signal turns in the argument. Use the **transitions** that are needed to hold an argument together. Insert a strategic *therefore* or *consequently* to signal that you are drawing a logical conclusion. Use *however* or *nevertheless* to signal that you are raising a major objection. Use links like *on the one hand* and *on the other hand* to show that you are playing off the pro and con.

- *Avoid familiar kinds of shortcut thinking.* Advocates of straight thinking warn against familiar **logical fallacies**—predictable ways of reaching the wrong conclusion.

THINKING STRAIGHT

A Checklist of Logical Fallacies

Guides to straight thinking warn against shortcut reasoning like the following:

1 **hasty generalization.** Beware of sweeping generalizations about "what the American people want" or "the worldview of the younger generation" after talking to only friends and family. Try not to generalize about "how Asians think" after knowing only a few Vietnamese or Filipino students.

2 **unrepresentative sample.** You cannot determine student sentiment on current campus issues by talking only to students in your own living quarters. You may have to listen as well to co-op dwellers, people living off campus, and commuters. You should probably talk to re-entry students, minority students, and part-time students.

3 **false analogy.** An analogy is a detailed, systematic comparison between two things that are similar in several ways. A false analogy stretches the similarities between two things too far. Is our nation like a lifeboat—with only so many spaces? Would it be swamped if we allowed a large number of the people to climb aboard? No nation has unlimited resources, and absorbing too many immigrants might "swamp" institutions. However, sooner or later the analogy breaks down. Immigrants have often brought new talents and developed new resources (which newcomers to a lifeboat cannot do).

4 **scapegoating.** Political candidates may blame an unpopular group for loss of jobs or a lost war. Factory workers may blame immigrants or "affirmative action hires" rather than automation or foreign competition for the loss of highly paid factory jobs.

5 **ad hominem.** *Ad hominem* arguments aim "at the person" instead of the issue. Rather than discussing a candidate's proposals regarding school vouchers or health care, an opponent might call attention to a divorce, an alcoholic relative, visits to a psychiatrist, or sexual orientation.

6 **false dilemma.** A true dilemma puts us in a tight spot and leaves us only two ways out—both bad. A true dilemma may face medical researchers conducting animal experiments. Should they abandon experiments that torture animals? Or should they continue experiments that benefit suffering human beings? A *false* dilemma narrows your choices to two—so that you will shun the obviously bad one and opt for the one favored by the writer. A false dilemma sets up an either-or choice: Either let a downtown area deteriorate, or raze the area and rebuild. A third alternative, hidden from view here, might be to restore and renovate.

7 **rationalization.** When you rationalize, you choose explanations that make you look good or feel good. When a supervisor treats you poorly, the reason may be that the supervisor is prejudiced against your group. However, the reason may also be that your job performance is inadequate, regardless of what group you represent.

8 **slanting.** Interested parties tend to slant data or suppress damaging evidence. They may exaggerate everything that favors their cause and leave out contrary testimony. Skeptical readers ask: Who on this issue has an axe to grind? Who has an interest in tampering with the evidence?

9 **bandwagon.** Advertisers and public relations experts try to sway us by letting us know that "everybody does it" or "everyone thinks so."

10 **reductio ad absurdum.** To push the position of the opposing sides to an absurd extreme, propagandists may seize on the silliest or most ridiculous example of what they claim the opposition stands for, like barring Santa Claus from the city's Christmas parade in the name of the separation of church and state.

A Paper for Peer Review

In your own words, what are the principles invoked and boldfaced in the following reprinting of a student paper? Can you chart the student writer's arguments according to the *if–then* pattern? Are you prepared to follow the argument from the principles stated to the logical conclusion?

Justice Denied

"On the subject of crime, all politicians are demagogues," says a columnist in a recent issue of the *New Republic*. Playing to the public fear of violent crime, legislators everywhere are advocating stiffer sentencing laws and more and bigger prisons. The death penalty, which was in abeyance in the seventies and eighties, has made a comeback. The courts are shortening the appeals process that has kept many convicted criminals on death row for ten, twelve, or fourteen years. However, in spite of the strong grass roots support for the revival of the death penalty, capital punishment violates basic principles underlying the American system of justice.

The weakness of passionate last-minute appeals for clemency is that they tend to focus on the special circumstances of the individual case. A murderer was the victim of child abuse. A rapist suffered brain damage. By focusing on the individual histories of those waiting on death row, we run the danger of losing sight of the principles at stake when a civilized society reinstitutes capital punishment.

Most basic to our legal system is the commitment to even-handed justice. **We believe that equal crimes should receive equal punishment.** However, the death penalty has always been notorious for its "freakish unfairness." In the words of one study, "judicial safeguards for preventing the arbitrary administration of capital punishment are not working." Some murderers walk the streets again after three or five or seven years, whereas others—because of ineffectual legal counsel, an ambitious prosecutor, or a hanging judge—join the inmates waiting out their appeals of death row. Judges and juries apply widely different standards. In one celebrated case, two partners in crime were convicted of the same capital crime on identical charges. One was executed; the other is in prison and will soon be eligible for parole.

We believe that all citizens are equal before the law. Justice should be blind to wealth, race, or ethnic origin. However, poor defendants are many times more likely to receive the death penalty than wealthy ones. Rich defendants are protected by highly paid teams of lawyers whose maneuvers stymie the prosecution. Defendants with millions to spend bring in an array of experts who baffle the jury. Minority defendants convicted of capital crimes have a much higher statistical chance of being executed than white defendants. . . .

Finally, fairness demands that the judicial system correct its own mistakes. If someone has been unjustly convicted there should be a mechanism for reversing the verdict and setting the person free. No one doubts that there are miscarriages of justice. Witnesses admit to mistaken identification of suspects. A convict confesses on his deathbed to a crime for which someone else was convicted. A woman withdraws a rape charge years after the accused was sent to prison. However, in the case of the death penalty, any such correction of error is aborted. The judicial system buries its mistakes. We are left with futile regrets, like the prosecutor who said: "Horrible as it is to contemplate, we may have executed the wrong man."

YOUR TURN:

1 Do you agree with the premises on which the arguments in this paper is based? Do you agree with them all, in part, or not at all?

2 Do you think the principles will command the assent or at least the respect of the intended readers?

3 How authentic or convincing do the test cases or key examples seem to you?

4 Current opinion polls show that a majority of Americans support the death penalty. What do you think are key arguments they would present in support? How would they refute the arguments of the student writer?

Writing Options 11: Arguing from Principle

1 Should a college assure parity in funding for men's and women's sports? Why or why not? If you answer in the affirmative, how would parity be achieved?

2 Should women receive equal pay not only for the same jobs but also for jobs of "comparable worth"? How would you measure comparable worth? What principles are involved?

3 Should employers have the right to ban romantic relationships in the workplace? On what grounds? Should they have the right to rule out dating or romantic relationships among employees? among managers?

4 Do widely used tests or qualifying exams work against equal opportunity for candidates from other than conventional white middle class backgrounds? What principles are at stake?

5 In the past, the "children of divorce" often stayed with the mother. In awarding custody of children in divorce cases, should the courts continue to give preference to the mother? Why or why not?

6 Should employers or government agencies have the right to regulate appearance—for instance, banning facial hair (like beards for police officers), veils for women (required by the woman's religion), or turbans for men?

7 Should the military have the right to ban or expel gays and lesbians? What principle is involved or violated in recent "Don't ask, don't tell" policies?

8 Should the United States do more to help fight AIDS in Africa or in other third-world areas?

9 World leaders have presented proposals for an international tax raised in wealthy nations to help poorer countries. Do you support such proposals? Should the United States and other developed countries do more to alleviate poverty around the world? Why or why not?

10 Who should decide if life support systems of terminally ill patients can be disconnected—the patient? the family? a doctor? the courts?

12

TOMORROWS
Imagining the Future

VISUAL LITERACY 12:
COMPUTER GRAPHICS: THE ANDROID FUTURE

Committed fans of information technology are fascinated by the next steps in robotics. Will the future bring increasingly humanlike androids? Will they no longer be just robots performing simple tasks? Will they still obey commands like well-trained pets? Or will the androids of the future learn to make their own decisions and manufacture their own replacements? Will they evolve the capacity to feel human emotions? Will they evolve the capacity to rebel against and declare independence from their human masters? Do these questions interest you, excite you, or disturb you?

Reading the Image

1   How does this image get the viewer's *attention?* What is eye-catching about this image? Would you have stopped to look at this image while browsing through a magazine? Why or why not?

2   *Computer graphics* are greatly extending the graphic artist's resources for manipulating reality. Do you think the underlying photograph of a human figure was originally an actual photograph of a human being? What is the overlay of lines and dots over the face? Where does it come from? What does it suggest? How does the background lighting suggest future rather than past?

3   Who would be the ideal *target audience* for this image? Do images like this fascinate you? Do they alienate you? Is this image frightening to you? Why or why not?

4   Science fiction writers long wrote utopias. They envisioned ideal or highly advanced future societies. Modern technology had erased poverty, disease, or cutthroat competition for resources. Gradually, others started to write dystopias. They envisioned future societies where modern technology or media of communication were used as instruments of repression and thought control. Working with a group, you may want to develop a questionnaire for a *survey* of fellow students. Do they look toward the future with hope or with fear?

12

TOMORROWS

Imagining the Future

I guess so many things are happening today that we're too busy to do anything but look, talk, and think about all of it. We don't have time to remember the past, and we don't have the energy to imagine the future.

—ANDY WARHOL

What is our destiny on this planet? When modern art and literature have asked this existential question, they have often encouraged us to imagine humankind as a race finding itself on an alien planet. Without clear signposts or a clear road map, humankind had to create societies, build cities and institutions, and forge bonds of loyalty and devotion.

The utopias of early science fiction envisioned a future when human beings had succeeded in the task of transforming the world into a habitat hospitable to human life. Literally, a utopia is a place that exists "nowhere"—only in our dreams. Often these utopias were imaginary commonwealths where human beings had outgrown their tendencies toward selfishness, conflict, and war. They had learned to live in harmony, to share the wealth, to marry sagely and raise their children without traumas. They had learned to follow wise leaders—or to do without leaders altogether.

However, gradually apprehension and disillusionment seeped in: Writers wrote *dys*topias—the opposite of books projecting an ideal future state. Dystopias took readers to nightmare worlds where people were faceless nobodies in beehive societies. All pleasure or satisfaction came from artificial stimulants. Books were likely to be banned, and their owners persecuted. Big Brother (or the big master computer) did the thinking for everybody. A ghastly newspeak channeled everyone's language into officially approved ways to talk.

Aldous Huxley's novel *Brave New World* (1932) was read by millions of readers as one of the first great modern dystopias—in which the perennial human dream of a perfect utopian future had been turned inside out. His society of the future was populated by happy zombies manipulated by the all-pervasive media. Giving up on the utopian dream of a society in which all are created equal, Huxley's *Brave New World* featured an elaborate caste structure with the alphas at the top and the epsilons at the bottom.

Stoned on a synthetic happiness drug, the people at the lower levels of the social heap accepted their lot.

How optimistic or pessimistic are Americans today about the trends shaping the society of the future? What kind of world are we leaving for the next generation?

WORKERS WHOSE JOBS GO OVERSEAS LOOK FOR HELP

T. A. Badger

"It could be you tomorrow."

Who will have jobs in the global economy? Years ago, automobile workers saw their jobs go from the car factories in Detroit or Flint in Michigan to factories south of the border. American textile workers saw their jobs migrate first to Mexico and then from there to China. A New Yorker article in 2004 told the story of textile workers in Texas laid off by the Fruit of the Loom company who were sent to retraining programs for jobs that did not materialize.

After years of an eroding manufacturing base in rust belt states, not only blue-collar workers but also white-collar workers in insurance work, accounting work, and customer service began to see their jobs outsourced to low-wage countries. A latest wave of offshoring was gathering momentum as high-tech and engineering jobs were shifted abroad by companies from Hewlett-Packard to IBM. A range of establishment sources including the chairman of the Federal Reserve Board projected a migration of jobs from the high-tech sector of three million or more during the next few years.

The following Associated Press release from June 2004 was part of the extensive media coverage of the growing offshoring trend. The sources quoted urge workers to unionize and use collective bargaining agreements to protect jobs and secure their employment rights.

Thought Starters: Privatizing, downsizing, outsourcing, and temp jobs became watchwords for the American economy of the new century. Where have you seen these trends in action? What do they mean in practice? How do they shape the lives of the people affected?

During his 15 years with the Boeing Co., Stephen Gentry never pictured himself wearing the union label.

Then the computer programmer from Auburn, Wash, was laid off last summer after training his replacement, a high-tech worker in India.

Now Gentry, who hasn't worked since, is among those convinced that America's white-collar workers have to band together to keep their futures from being exported to places where skilled labor comes cheap.

"I don't see any other options," said Gentry, 52, who's joined a Seattle union trying to organize tech workers around the country. "There's no loyalty anymore. I feel my job was taken by corporate greed."

For some unions, the growing concerns about offshoring are an op-   *5*
portunity to recruit more workers like Gentry.

"I get a call last week from Intel; I get a call from Microsoft; I get calls
from places we never used to get calls from," said Andy Banks, organizing
director for the International Federation of Professional and Technical Engineers in Silver Spring, Md. "People are realizing that labor unions are the
best-kept secret in America. You have no employment rights at work unless you have a collective bargaining agreement."

The issue's potency, particularly during a jobless economic recovery,
was proven when the Communications Workers of America negotiated a
new contract with SBC Communications Inc. after a four-day strike. As
part of the deal, the San Antonio phone company agreed to work with the
union to return an estimated 3,000 company jobs in India and the Philip-
pines to the United States.

During the strike by CWA's 102,000 SBC workers, thousands of
picketers around the country hoisted anti-offshoring signs saying "SBC
Unpatriotic" and "Keep Jobs in America."

"There is something to be said for shaming a company if you say, 'This
company will outsource good jobs from our community,'" said Christian
Weller, a researcher at the Center for American Progress, a Washington
think tank. "In the current environment, it's a land mine for the company.
There's a real receptive audience for this."

That connection was important for CWA, given that for decades la-   *10*
bor unions have been losing bargaining clout and public prestige.

Fewer than 10 percent of the nation's private-sector workers are
unionized, down from a peak of 37 percent in 1960, according to federal
statistics.

"This is a kind of lever to convince the public that labor is under pressure more than people realize it is, that it could be you tomorrow," said
Alex Colvin, a labor professor at Pennsylvania State University.

But another labor organizer said the foreign outsourcing issue can cut
both ways.

"They're afraid that their job is not secure, and therefore they want a
union to protect them," Kevin Kistler of the Office and Professional Employees International in New York, said of workers. "But they're also afraid
to stick their head up and try to help form the union because their job is so
tenuous."

The number of U.S. high-tech and service jobs that have been moved   *15*
overseas so far is relatively small, but a report last month said the pace is
quickening.

Forrester Research estimates that about 830,000 such positions will be
relocated to India, Russia and other low-wage nations by the end of 2005
and that 3.4 million jobs representing $136 billion in U.S. wages will be lost
by 2015.

Labor organizer Banks said the CWA's success with SBC is an impor-   10
tant lesson for other unions.

"If we have enough examples where people are winning the outsourcing issue, why wouldn't people turn to unions?" he said. "It can be the
one issue that can revitalize the labor movement."

Banks said offshoring work was a key issue that helped his union recently organize 250 engineers and architects employed by the city of San
Jose. He said a drive to organize engineers will start soon in Seattle.

The Responsive Reader

1 Like many other news reports, this report starts with a *human interest*
story. What makes the story unsual or attention-getting? What is the
message it conveys? How effective is it?

2 What are the *facts* and estimates about offshoring provided in this report?
Have you seen similar estimates? How serious do they seem to you?

3 Observers tracking long-range *trends* remind readers of a time when labor unions were a powerful political force. Where or how does this news
report remind readers of the decline of the American labor movement?
On the other hand, what evidence does the article cite of a potential revival of union strength in today's economic climate? What are the factors cited?

4 Who is the *audience* for this news report? Do you think this news report
would appeal to a limited audience only? Would the ideal reader feel
worried about a threatened job or be bitter about a job lost? Do you
yourself make a good audience for this article?

5 Much current writing strongly supports a political or economic *agenda*.
Do you think this article as a whole makes an effective plea for action?

Talking, Listening, Writing

6 If you were asked to train a low-wage high-tech worker abroad to replace you, would you agree or refuse? How would you defend your
decision?

7 If your municipality or state used taxpapers' money to outsource ad-
ministrative work to foreign locations, would you support a movement
to ban the practice? Why or why not?

8 When you see references to labor unions, is the image of a factory
worker or truck driver the first picture that comes to mind? Why or why
not? What do you know about union organizing or union representation for nurses or members of other professions?

OTHER VOICES

Exporting High-Level Jobs

Highly skilled work in in the high-tech sector was long considered least vulnerable to outsourcing or offshoring to low-wage countries. The following excerpts from a *New York Times* article track arrangements between outsourcing companies from India and American high-tech companies that in the end lead to top-level work developing sophisticated new software projects and large-scale innovations being offshored to India.

Software architects are highly skilled workers who often earn six-figure salaries in the United States. Microsoft contracts with Infosys and Satyam show that the work of software architects, senior software developers and software developers was being done by employees of the Indian companies working at Microsoft facilities in the United States.

Their work did not come cheap for Microsoft, which was billed $90 an hour for software architects, or at a yearly rate of more than $180,000. Senior software developers were billed at $72 an hour and software developers $60 an hour.

The on-site work, said Hira, an expert on offshore outsourcing, is usually done by Indian software engineers who come to the United States on H-IB visas, which allow foreign workers to be employed in the United States for up to six years.

The Indian workers are paid a fraction of what their employers collect. The top annual salaries paid by Indian outsourcing companies to Indian software experts are $40,000 or so, Hira said. Critics of the outsourcing trend regard such agreements with Indian contractors, both in the United States and in India, as a step toward shifting more skilled technology jobs overseas.

"Microsoft has hired vendors whose whole reason for being is to transfer work offshore," said Marcus Courtney, president of Wash-Tech, an affiliate of the Communications Workers of America.

Steve Lohr, "Exporting High-Level Jobs to India," *New York Times*

1 Are you surprised that technology workers are joining labor unions like the Communication Workers of America?

2 Would the outsourcing practices of a company like Microsoft or Hewlett-Packard influence your decisions to buy or not to buy their products? Why or why not?

3 Critics of downsizing and outsourcing practices claim that they hurt American workers while offering large rewards to the middleman—the independent entrepreneurs and organizers who help companies turn good jobs into temp work or ship the work abroad. Using the figures in this article, can you do the math on who profits from the exporting of high-level jobs?

OUTSOURCING MYTH UNDERCUTS THE U.S.

Ruben Navarette

Americans "have nothing to be afraid of . . . they can compete with Indians or anyone else."

Ruben Navarette is an outspoken conservative syndicated Texas columnist, who strongly identifies with his home state. He first published the following column in the Dallas Morning News *during the heat of the presidential election campaign in the fall of 2004. Like other strong conservative voices, Navarette invokes "core principles" and calls for courage in implementing them in the "real world." He does not hesitate to criticize those who share his goals and his values when they seem to falter in getting the message out. In a state with large second-language and immigrant populations, he departs from the anti-immigration stance of some fellow conservatives. He credits today's new immigrants with a renewal of the spirit of enterprise and optimism that animated previous immigrant populations in America.*

In the following column, Navarette joins forces with the free-traders and free-enterprise advocates who oppose legislation and other initiatives to limit or reverse the trend toward offshoring high-tech jobs. He sees the attempts to limit offshoring as a weak retreat from the spirit of aggressive competition that the country will need to survive in the global economy of the future.

Thought Starters: Have you heard lectures or read articles by advocates of free trade? Have you heard free-enterprise arguments in favor of lowering or abolishing trade barriers such as tariffs? On the other hand, have you seen evidence of protectionism—efforts to save American jobs or campaigns urging us to "buy American"?

The myth endures that the outsourcing of American jobs is tantamount to treason. But what's really unpatriotic is the movement to stop it.

You see it everywhere. You've got John Kerry, the Democratic presidential nominee, calling corporate executives who ship jobs overseas "Benedict Arnolds" in a bid to get organized labor excited about his candidacy.

You've got CNN's Lou Dobbs bemoaning the "Exporting of America" by listing the names of American companies that send jobs offshore, branding them with the 21st century's version of the Scarlet Letter—a big "O" for outsourcer.

But, as I travel the country, I've decided that what makes me angriest about this debate is that it offends my sensibilities as an American. The line advanced by the panderers and the protectionists goes against everything I was ever taught and believe about how Americans never run from a fight, never duck the competition, never cower in fear and never, ever surrender.

Understand this much. That's the extent of what the protectionists are   *5* peddling—surrender. By campaigning so vigorously, and so loudly, to try to prevent companies from sending jobs abroad in a changing economy, they're advertising the fact that they have absolutely no confidence in the ability of Americans to adapt to these changes.

Instead of pumping up their countrymen and telling us that we can and will succeed on the global stage, they'd rather convince Americans that we don't have a prayer of competing and shouldn't even bother trying.

How depressing. And how tragic that the line is catching on.

Case in point: A college student tells an interviewer for the Lou Dobbs program that he has decided to give up his pursuit of a career as a computer programmer because he is afraid the job he is going after is headed to India, where someone will do it for a fraction of the salary he believes he deserves.

Rather than lower his asking price or acquire more schooling or take on a new set of computer skills that might allow him to compete with Indian workers, the young man has opted to throw in the towel and abandon his dream of becoming a programmer:

Instead, he has decided to become—gasp—a lawyer.   *10*

Let's think about our young friend. Here he is changing careers at about the age that one is able to legally buy a drink in a bar. He could have been a bit more honest and acknowledged that at least part of his hesitance in competing with people from countries such as India or China isn't just that they work for less. It could be that they work harder. Or study more.

Who could blame the young man for not wanting to compete for jobs with people like that? But he prefers to couch the argument in terms of foreign competitors being willing to work for less than Americans demand.

Say, this kid might make a good lawyer after all.

On a recent trip to New Delhi, Secretary of State Colin Powell offered reassurances that the Bush administration would not try to halt the outsourcing of high-tech jobs to India.

Great. But what the administration needs to do next is to begin a na-   *15* tional campaign, perhaps run through the Labor Department, to convince Americans they have nothing to be afraid of, that they can compete with Indians or anyone else if they will only tap into the things that Americans have and have always had in abundance: Ingenuity. Confidence. Fearlessness. Optimism. The belief that any product can be improved upon and the next great idea is just around the corner.

Americans used to have all that in their personal arsenals. If they no longer do, then, well, the fact that jobs are going overseas is the least of our worries.

The Responsive Reader

1 Navarette uses an aggressive *polemical* style of argument—strong verbal putdowns and personal attacks, and sweeping charges or accusations. How do you react to highly charged emotional or abusive language like *panderer, peddling, cower in fear,* and *surrender?* Can you find additional examples in his column? (Do you think he was provoked by "the other side"?)

2 *Hyperbole*—extreme exaggeration—is a standard method of aggressive argument: "absolutely no confidence" or "don't have a prayer." Can you find other examples in this column? Do you think these extreme charges will "pump up readers"? Why or why not?

3 How does Navarette use the *case history* of the student he calls "our young friend"? Do you think his account of the person is fair (or is it personally insulting)? Do you think the advice Navarette gives the student is valid or helpful? What advice would you have given the student?

4 Ingenuity, confidence, fearlessness, and optimism are *abstractions* that serve as large umbrella labels for attitudes in a person's "personal arsenal." Abstractions "pull us away" from the specific examples and real-life situations that they bundle together. Can you fill in some current or recent convincing real-life examples under one of these headings—such as ingenuity or confidence or the "next great idea"?

Talking, Listening, Writing

5 Several student readers who responded to this column quoted Winston Churchill, British statesman and wartime leader in World War II, as saying: "A pessimist sees the difficulty in every opportunity; an optimist sees the opportunity in every difficulty." Do you think these are good contrasting definitions of the pessimist and the optimist? Or would you change or revise them? To which side do you personally incline? Do you or people you know well incline to being a "realist" as a third choice? How would you define the realist?

FOR MANY, GOOD HEALTH CARE BARELY EXISTS

Steven Findlay

"57,000 Americans—insured and uninsured—die needlessly each year because they do not receive the best care."

Modern medicine is a success story of human intelligence put in the service of humankind. Killer diseases like polio, tuberculosis, or typhoid have been tamed and flare up only when health systems or services break down. The media highlight promising research into the causes and prevention of diabetes, breast cancer, and Alzheimer's or Parkinson's disease. Advances in the study of the biochemistry of the brain have produced silver bullet treatments that can restore Americans with mental illnesses to useful productive lives. However, many have no access to treatment and are left to roam the streets homeless.

The Washington-based health care analyst who wrote the following article published it in USA Today *in October 2003 at a time when spiraling health care costs and unaffordable health insurance were much in the news. The author acknowledges the successes of the American health care system but alerts his readers to the "dark side." Many millions of Americans have no health insurance coverage at all. According to current news reports, in many areas underfunded public hospitals or emergency rooms are shutting down. Have advances in medical care and medical technology outpaced the willingness of Americans to pay for them? The cost of health care looms large in labor disputes and election campaigns. In a recent presidential campaign, both major candidates promised to promote programs to reduce the numbers of the uninsured— one by an estimated one-fifth and another by a more ambitious one-half.*

Thought Starters: Have you or people close to you witnessed examples of advanced modern health care making a major difference? Or can you report instances where a breakdown in medical care or medical services has hurt the people involved?

You have a heart attack. Your spouse gets you to a major teaching hospital in 15 minutes. Within another 30 minutes, doctors thread a tiny device into the clogged artery that caused the attack—and reopen it (a procedure called angioplasty). You leave the hospital the next day with a handful of prescriptions and lifestyle advice that will sharply lower your risk of a second attack. You are back at work in a week.

After a heart attack in 1965, you would have been in the hospital a week or more and had a 28% chance of dying there. Today, that chance is only one in 10.

A routine mammogram shows a suspicious lump. A breast cancer specialty center at a leading hospital gives you the bad news: It's cancer, but caught early. Within a week, surgeons excise the lump, and follow-up chemotherapy eradicates the cancer.

Your life hangs by a thread after a bad car accident. Within minutes, a helicopter arrives. You are stabilized and whisked to a trauma hospital, where a surgical team of doctors and nurses labors for hours, skillfully putting you back together.

Such success stories are a testament to modern medicine's enormous scientific progress, improved knowledge and innovation. Unfortunately, there's also a dark side to our medicine and health care: unequal access, substandard care, woeful disorganization and inefficiency and outdated computer systems—all routinely harming people.

A slew of recent studies has further illuminated the problems and underscored the urgent need for major reforms in how we organize, pay for and deliver medical care in the United States.

Start with the Census statistics released Monday. Another 2.4 million Americans last year joined the ranks of those without health insurance. That brings to 43.6 million the number at a higher risk of not getting necessary care. In 2001, more than half—54%—of the uninsured ages 19 to 64 failed to get needed care, compared with 21% of people with insurance. The Institute of Medicine estimates 18,000 die unnecessarily every year as a result.

Or take heart attacks. Despite the gains, 40% of those eligible for angioplasty from July 2002 to this past June didn't get it. The main reason: Most hospitals don't have the right technology or trained personnel.

What about exemplary emergency care? An investigation by USA TODAY, published in July, found that paramedics revive fewer than 10% of people with sudden cardiac arrest who could be saved. Emergency medical systems in most of the 50 largest U.S. cities are "fragmented, inconsistent and slow." A related study published in August in the *Annals of Emergency Medicine* found emergency rooms nationwide were short of beds and staff, with 59% reporting the routine use of hallways for treatment.

Nursing homes are no better. A July report by Congress' General Accounting Office found that a fifth of nursing homes have serious deficiencies that caused residents actual harm or placed them in immediate jeopardy.

Mental health care? A presidential commission in July called for "fundamental transformation" of the "patchwork relic" of disjointed federal and state programs that often impedes access to care. The study also called for equal insurance coverage of mental illnesses.

A fragmented system begets substandard care. A landmark study published in June in *The New England Journal of Medicine* found that, overall,

Americans receive the clinical care they should get—that is, the optimal, recommended, "best," scientifically based care—55% of the time. And the National Committee for Quality Assurance, an independent group that tracks the quality of heath care, estimates that 57,000 Americans—insured and uninsured—die needlessly each year because they do not receive the best care.

While there are no blackouts, the U.S. health system is as shaky and vulnerable as our electrical grid. Its thousands of daily failures—a missed diagnosis here, an unnecessary surgery there—come drip by drip. The prestigious, non-profit Institute of Medicine said as much several years ago, when it catalogued the toll taken by medical errors: 44,000 to 98,000 deaths a year, with far more non-fatal mistakes.

The good news: The reports and research have spurred action. More hospitals and doctors are working to reduce medical errors. Employers and insurers are beginning to insist that providers measure and improve the quality of care, and then prove it. The government is committing more resources.

Yet progress is still too slow, given the costs in lives and money. Inertia and resistance to change are partly to blame. But there are major issues that need action:

- Lawmakers have failed to expand health insurance coverage. It's a singular embarrassment that the U.S. remains the only developed nation that does not ensure all of its citizens access to coverage.

- Large employers, health plans and the government ought to rapidly compel doctors and hospitals to gather and publicly report data on the care they deliver and the outcomes of treatment.

- Health care lags behind in the use of information-technology tools. Doctors and hospitals should receive tax breaks for innovations that improve care, such as electronic medical records and handheld devices that help select treatments and medicines.

Yes, all this is expensive—tens of billions of dollars each year initially. But most experts agree the investment will more than pay off long term.

It's natural to want to believe in our doctors and the system when we are sick and vulnerable. Indeed, the darker side is harder to grasp and so anxiety provoking that we are in collective denial. That must end. Until consumers become engaged—even outraged—needed changes are unlikely to come quickly enough.

The Responsive Reader

1   Findley's article follows a classic three-part *plan:* He first pays tribute to significant achievement in a major area of public concern. He then focuses on major serious problems that remain unsolved. He finally sizes up current progress toward tackling the problems. Where is the *turning*

point or key transition taking the reader from each major segment of the article to the next? Where is the central claim or guiding thought of each segment most completely or directly spelled out?

2   What are the hard *data* that Findlay cites to support his claims? What specific detailed statistics shore up his claims? Which for you are familiar or amount to "old news"? Which are striking or alarming?

3   How much of Findlay's article draws for support on authoritative *sources?* Informed readers respect the *New England Journal of Medicine* as one of the most reliable and responsible scholarly publications in the field of medicine. What other sources does Finlay rely on? Do they seem partisan or nonpartisan? Do they seem professional?

Talking, Listening, Writing

4   Do critics of the health care system rely too much on isolated instances that are merely "anecdotal"? Do they concentrate on one area with special problems instead of looking at the "larger picture"? Do you think such charges could be brought against this writer?

5   Have you ever been in the emergency room of a public hospital? In a **journal entry** or in notes for a class presentation, tell the story.

6   Do you think most people are resigned to accepting the American health system as it is? Would it be fair to say that young people are bored by health care issues until tragedy strikes or serious health issues affect them or people close to them?

Collaborative Projects

7   What is a "single-payer" health care system? In recent political campaigns, candidates have presented competing plans for extending health care coverage to America's uninsured. How many uninsured Americans do they propose to benefit? What are the estimates of costs?

Who's Your Doctor?

Doctors were long at the top of the professional pecking order. How are their status and their role changing as the health care system evolves? The following capsule portrait is from a more general revision of familiar assumptions about members of professions including medical practice, engineering, and teaching. Are once independent professionals increasingly becoming part of "salaried labor"?

> Once an independent entrepreneur, the salaried physician or engineer—now characteristic of the medical, engineering, and legal professions—has been reduced to a well-paid worker with a huge education debt. Recent trends in corporate life, including healthcare institutions, have stripped these professionals of their most prized possession, autonomy. Increasingly subject to strict supervision, doctors have little discretion in describing treatment regimes, which has prompted some of them to organize into trade unions.
>   Stanley Aronowitz, "All in the Family?" *The Nation*

Your Turn:

1   Have you seen evidence that important decisions about a patient's health care may be made not by physicians but by insurance companies or health care organizations?

2   Are family doctors a thing of the past? Are independent general practitioners a thing of the past? Is personal choice of a physician a thing of the past?

FEDERAL FOOLISHNESS AND MARIJUANA

Jerome P. Kassirer

"I believe that a federal policy that prohibits physicians from alleviating suffering for seriously ill patients is misguided, heavy-handed and inhumane."

"Death with Dignity" became a watchword in the nineties. Surveys revealed that large numbers of terminal patients were kept alive by a depersonalized medical technology, often in severe pain, and against their own express wishes, against the wishes of family, and against the better judgment of the nursing staff most directly involved with dying patients. As part of the movement to honor the rights and needs of dying patients, states started to pass laws allowing the medical use of marijuana to alleviate the extreme retching nausea or severe discomfort many terminal patients are subjected to as the result of chemotherapy or other medical interventions.

Ample legal precedent exists: In two world wars, morphine was used to alleviate the hellish pain suffered by severely wounded veterans. The Virginia legislature passed a law in 1979 allowing doctors to prescribe marijuana to treat glaucoma and to help cancer patients cope with the side effects of chemotherapy. Nevertheless, politicians afraid of being labeled soft on drugs started a campaign to criminalize the patients and compassionate doctors or family.

In the following editorial first published in 1997, the editor-in-chief of the New England Journal of Medicine, *the most prestigious medical journal in the country, published since 1812 by the Massachusetts Medical Society, weighs in on the subject of medical marijuana. In the words of a newspaper editor, the* Journal's *"editorials and commentaries by medical specialists have long played a major role in debates over health policy controversies." Dr. Kassirer is a kidney specialist formerly on the faculty at Tufts University Medical Center in Boston.*

Thought Starters: From your reading or firsthand observation, what do you know about living wills, hospices, or organizations assisting the dying?

The advanced stages of many illnesses and their treatments are often   1
accompanied by intractable nausea, vomiting or pain. Thousands of patients with cancer, AIDS and other diseases report they have obtained striking relief from these devastating symptoms by smoking marijuana. The alleviation of distress can be so striking that some patients and their families have been willing to risk a jail term to obtain or grow the marijuana.

Despite the desperation of these patients, within weeks after voters in Arizona and California approved propositions allowing physicians in their states to prescribe marijuana for medical indications, federal officials, including the president, the secretary of health and human services, and the attorney general sprang into action. At a news conference, Health and Human Services Secretary Donna E. Shalala gave an organ recital of the parts of the body that she asserted could be harmed by marijuana and warned of the evils of its spreading use. Attorney General Janet Reno announced that physicians in any state who prescribed the drug could lose the privilege of writing prescriptions, be excluded from Medicare and Medicaid reimbursement, and even be prosecuted for a federal crime. General Barry R. McCaffrey, director of the Office of National Drug Control Policy, reiterated his agency's position that marijuana is a dangerous drug and implied that voters in Arizona and California had been duped into voting for these propositions. He indicated that it is always possible to study the effects of any drug, including marijuana, but that the use of marijuana by seriously ill patients would require, at the least, scientifically valid research.

I believe that a federal policy that prohibits physicians from alleviating suffering by prescribing marijuana for seriously ill patients is misguided, heavy-handed and inhumane. Marijuana may have long-term adverse effects and its use may presage serious addictions, but neither long-term side effects nor addiction is a relevant issue for such patients. It is also hypocritical to forbid physicians to prescribe marijuana while permitting them to use morphine and meperidine to relieve extreme dyspnea (difficulty breathing) and pain. With both these drugs, the difference between the dose that relieves symptoms and the dose that hastens death is very narrow; by contrast, there is no risk of death from smoking marijuana. To demand evidence of therapeutic efficacy is equally hypocritical. The noxious sensations that patients experience are extremely difficult to quantify in controlled experiments. What really counts for a therapy with this kind of safety margin is whether a seriously ill patient feels relief as a result of the intervention, not whether a controlled trial "proves" its efficacy.

Paradoxically, dronabinol, a drug that contains one of the active ingredients in marijuana (tetrahydrocannabinol), has been available by prescription for more than a decade. But it is difficult to titrate the therapeutic dose of this drug, and it is not widely prescribed. By contrast, smoking marijuana produces a rapid increase in the blood level of the active ingredients and is thus more likely to be therapeutic. Needless to say, new drugs such as those that inhibit the nausea associated with chemotherapy may well be more beneficial than smoking marijuana, but their comparative efficacy has never been studied. 5

Whatever their reasons, federal officials are out of step with the public. Dozens of states have passed laws that ease restrictions on the prescribing of marijuana by physicians, and polls consistently show that the public favors the use of marijuana for such purposes. Federal authorities should rescind their prohibition of the medicinal use of marijuana for seriously ill patients and allow physicians to decide which patients to treat. The government should change marijuana's status from that of a Schedule I drug (considered to be potentially addictive and with no current medical use) and regulate it accordingly. To ensure its proper distribution and use, the government could declare itself the only agency sanctioned to provide the marijuana. I believe that such a change in policy would have no adverse effects. The argument that it would be a signal to the young that "marijuana is OK" is, I believe, specious.

This proposal is not new. In 1986, after years of legal wrangling, the Drug Enforcement Administration (DEA) held extensive hearings on the transfer of marijuana to Schedule II. In 1988, the DEA's own administrative-law judge concluded: "It would be unreasonable, arbitrary, and capricious for DEA to continue to stand between those sufferers and the benefits of this substance in light of the evidence in this record." Nonetheless, the DEA overruled the judge's order to transfer marijuana to Schedule II, and in 1992, it issued a final rejection of all requests for reclassification.

Some physicians will have the courage to challenge the continued proscription of marijuana for the sick. Eventually, their actions will force the courts to adjudicate between the rights of those at death's door and the absolute power of bureaucrats whose decisions are based more on reflexive ideology and political correctness than on compassion.

The Responsive Reader

1   What are the *key points* in Kassirer's support for his thesis that "a federal policy that prohibits physicians from alleviating suffering by prescribing marijuana for seriously ill patients is misguided, heavy-handed and inhumane"? What is the problem with asking for more research? What is the problem with drugs providing alternative therapy? What are the key arguments in favor of using marijuana?
2   What, according to Kassirer, is the *history* of the "legal wrangling" over the issue?
3   As Kassirer sees it, what does the *future* hold? How does he sum up the choice that will confront the courts, politicians, and voters?

Talking, Listening, Writing

4   Do you think controversies like the ones about medical marijuana or assisted suicide tend to polarize the public along predictable liberal vs. conservative lines? Why or why not?
5   What would you say in a letter to the editor in response to Kassirer's editorial?

6   Would you risk a jail term to relieve the insufferable pain of a dying patient?

Collaborative Projects

7   Kübler-Ross was among the pioneers objecting to doctors playing God and using a runaway medical technology in indefinitely prolonging the death agonies of patients. Working with a group, you may want to investigate current thinking and current controversies on the subject of death with dignity.

FIND IT ON THE WEB

You may want to explore the treatment of the politics and ethics of health care in authoritative journals read by professionals and scientists including, among others, the *New England Journal of Medicine, JAMA (Journal of the American Medical Association)*, and *Nature* (a science journal published in Britain).

Do these journals have websites? Are they available online? Are recent copies available in your college library? You may want to look for material dealing with an issue like death with dignity, health care for profit, or the use of DNA in paternity cases.

AMERICA'S LAST HONEST PLACE

Marc Cooper

"Las Vegas is the most efficient machine ever designed to relieve the willing or the weak of their earthly fortunes, whether that weakness is gambling, sex, drink, spectacle, or consumption."

JOHN M. BRODER, *NEW YORK TIMES*

Las Vegas is the flagship of the expanding casino culture at a time when the virtual reality of the entertainment world absorbs ever growing amounts of time and money in American life. According to current estimates, Americans today devote only about 17 percent of their waking hours to work, down from 70 percent a century ago. An estimated 35 million visitors a year pass through Las Vegas, which has been called the "nation's adult amusement park" and is the site of a sprawling burgeoning multibillion-dollar gambling and entertainment complex. The glittering entertainment capital in the desert attracts a huge slice of America's convention business and visitors from around the world.

Critics of American popular culture keep alive memories of the mob era of the forties and after when organized crime ran casinos and when gangsters like Meyer Lansky and Bugsy Siegel became part of American folklore. Today huge "entertainment companies," supported by city and state politicians allied to the casino culture, have become symbols of the American worship of big money. When this article was first published in 2004, the entrepreneur who created the Bellagio as one of the first super hotel-casinos of the new era was already planning another 2,700-room hotel casino estimated to cost $2 billion. The glitz and glamor of the city's "resort industry" testifies to the nation's weakness for extravagance and garishness. Las Vegas lures people with ordinary lives to a fantasyland of recreations of glamorous distant times and places. There they can enjoy the thrill of feeling like a high-roller, although statistics show that in the end the client always loses; the casino always wins.

The author of the following excerpted article from the Nation *magazine explores a basic paradox or apparent contradiction: In a society that long ranked gambling as sinful, how can Las Vegas have become for many Americans "a beacon for the future"?*

Thought Starters: Do you know people who buy lottery tickets? Do you know people who gamble in casinos? Do they know what the odds are? What are they thinking?

In a city where the only currency is currency, there is a table-level democracy of luck. Las Vegas is perhaps the most color-blind, class-free place in America. As long as your cash or credit line holds out, no one gives a damn about your race, gender, national origin, sexual orientation, address, family lineage, voter registration or even your criminal arrest record. As long as you have chips on the table, Vegas deftly casts you as the star in an around-the-clock extravaganza. For all of America's manifold unfulfilled promises of upward mobility, Vegas is the only place guaranteed to come through—even if it's for a fleeting weekend. You may never, in fact, surpass the Joneses, but with the two-night, three-day special at the Sahara, buffet and show included, free valet parking and maybe a comped breakfast at the coffee shop, you can certainly live like them for seventy-two hours— while never having to as much as change out of your flip-flops, tank top or NASCAR cap.

"Las Vegas as America, America as Las Vegas. It's like what came first? The chicken or the egg?" says Vegas historian Michael Green. "Fresno, California, doesn't have a row of casinos, but you can be sure it has some part of town where you can go for vice even though it's supposed to be illegal. Here it's not necessarily vice in the first place, but it's certainly not illegal. We have the same sort of stuff and more. Except that unlike in most places, here it's just out in the open."

What extraordinary prescience social critic Neil Postman displayed when he wrote in his 1985 book *Amusing Ourselves to Death* that Las Vegas—where Wall Street corporations had replaced mafias and mobs— should be considered the "symbolic capital" of America. "At different times in our history," Postman wrote, "different cities have been the focal point of a radiating American spirit." In the era of the Revolutionary War, Boston embodied the ideals of freedom; in the mid-nineteenth century, "New York became the symbol of a melting-pot America." In the early twentieth century, the brawn and inventiveness of American industry and culture were captured in the energy of Chicago.

"Today," Postman concluded, "we must look to the city of Las Vegas, Nevada, as a metaphor of our national character and aspiration, its symbol a thirty-foot-high cardboard picture of a slot machine and a chorus girl. For Las Vegas is a city entirely devoted to the idea of entertainment, and as such proclaims the spirit of a culture in which all public discourse increasingly takes the form of entertainment. Our politics, our religion, news, athletics, education and commerce have been transformed into congenial adjuncts of show business, largely without protest or even much popular notice."

When Postman penned these words, little could he imagine that the Vegas he was writing about was the "old" Las Vegas and that Sin City was just a few years away from a radical makeover. Nor could Postman fully fathom that America itself was in the throes of a cataclysmic transformation. The more both places changed, the more they mirrored each other. In 1989

Steve Wynn—with junk-bond financing from Michael Milken—stunned the Strip with his $700 million Mirage Hotel and Casino and touched off a revolution. One after another, the old Rat Pack—era hotels were dynamited and in their place rose staggering Leviathans of modern, market-based entertainment: the biggest casino in the world, then the biggest hotel in the world, then the most expensive hotel in the world, the biggest man-made hotel lake in the world, the hotel with the biggest rooms in the world, and so on. . . .

Indeed, just as quickly as Las Vegas consumes and erases the past and scrambles the present, it now shines to many as an attractive beacon of the future. Unlike almost any other place in America, Las Vegas is one city where unskilled labor can still—thanks to vibrant unions and wealthy and efficient employers—earn middle-class wages. Vegas food servers, car parkers, cashiers, even maids, can still buy into the new American dream, purchasing a house and putting their kids through school. A high school grad can become a professional dealer for three hundred bucks' worth of tuition and a few weeks of practice pitching cards—and most likely get a job. Where else in America can you regularly find 60-year-old, bouffant-coiffed cocktail waitresses proudly wearing union buttons (those of the mighty Culinary Workers Local 226) and going home to peruse the statements of their fattening pension accounts?

Even though the terrorist attacks on the World Trade Center slowed (slightly) what has traditionally been the recession-proof Vegas economy, a steady stream of 5,000–6,000 domestic economic refugees a month still pour into and around the city. Only 6 percent of adults living in Vegas's Clark County were born here—the lowest such figure anywhere in America. And although water supplies are drying up, schools are strained and suicide and domestic violence rates are among the highest in the nation, they keep pouring in. Purchasers of new houses—at prices far below those of the two coasts—are wait-listed. Vegas's population doubled during the 1980s, and doubled again in the '90s. Vegas continues to be the fastest-growing metropolitan area in America.

This generation of immigrants, however, is different in many ways from the grifters, hustlers and outcasts who huddled here over the past century. Sure, there will always be a certain batch of trimmers, fugitives and shakedown artists looking to launder themselves in the Vegas sun. But most of those now crowding into Las Vegas are fleeing from an America where everyday life has become too much of a gamble—where either the Reagan recession of 1981, the Bush slump of 1990 or the burst bubble of a decade later has left them as devastated as a blackjack player who bet it all only to have his pair of tens get trounced by the dealer's Ace-King. The only risk they are interested in now is the off chance that Vegas can provide the normalcy, the security, the certainty, that once underpinned their lives, or at least their dreams.

What a turnaround it has been for once lowly Las Vegas—and for the nation around it. Barely fifteen years ago, the august Citicorp was queasy about publicly admitting that its major credit-card processing center had been relocated to an unincorporated suburb of Las Vegas. A deal with state authorities allowed the banking corporation to postmark and camouflage its mail as coming from "The Lakes, Nevada" instead of from sinful Vegas. Today, that same neighborhood sports several high-end casinos and luxury hotels. And Citicorp's own credibility, in the aftermath of the great Wall Street accounting scandals, ranks somewhere below that of a midtown three-card-monte hustler.

Nor could Neil Postman have known back in 1985 that casino gambling was about to be fully destigmatized within a decade—and delicately renamed "gaming." The resulting shift in public attitudes would not only definitively cleanse Vegas's image but also net it a growing bonanza. As recently as 1988, casino gambling was legal only in Nevada and in Atlantic City. But as American industry continued to wash up offshore and the commercial tax base atrophied, one strapped state and municipality after another turned its forlorn eyes toward the gaming tables and slot machines. Impoverished Indian tribes were more than willing to sign gambling compacts with state governments. The result: Now twenty-seven states have Nevada-style casinos, and forty-eight states have at least some form of legal gambling. With local budgets again being squeezed by burgeoning deficits, government itself is thinking about going into the casino business. In the spring of 2003, Chicago Mayor Richard Daley said he'd like to open a municipal casino. Before the 1989 opening of the Mirage unleashed the New Vegas revolution, only 15 percent of Americans had ever visited the city. By mid-decade that number had doubled. In its 1996 annual report, Circus Circus celebrated the news: "In an era when social attitudes toward play, and the means to afford it, have dramatically changed, so has the role of the casino."

The past seven years have shown an ever more dramatic shift toward the mainstreaming of gambling. A gambling-industry poll claimed that in the single year of 2001, 51 million Americans—more than a quarter of the population over age 21—visited a casino, chalking up a national total of almost 300 million visits. More than 430 commercial casinos nationwide brought in $26.5 billon in revenue—two and a half times what Americans spent on movie tickets, $5 billion more than they spent on DVDs and videos, and $3 billion more than on cosmetics and toiletries.

The explosion of legalized gambling nationwide has had little but positive impact on Las Vegas. "All it did was increase the average Joe's appetite for gambling," says a veteran Vegas Strip pit boss. "You know, it's like baseball. We see all those local Indian casinos and riverboat casinos and local slot parlors as our farm teams. They suck in a lot of average American types who never thought about gambling before. But once you play on the farm team, who doesn't want to play in the majors? And Las Vegas is the friggin' World

Series. It's kind of like, You build the casinos out there and they'll come. But eventually they'll come here."

The Responsive Reader

1 For *historical background,* Cooper quotes Neil Postman, who was widely published as an observer of American culture, as saying that Boston, New York, and Chicago at different times were symbols of the American national spirit. What did each stand for or represent? For what strand in American history was each a powerful symbol?

2 What was the *radical change* or "cataclysmic" transformation Cooper traces? For Postman, what were the familiar images or central metaphors that represented the Las Vegas of the "ratpack" past? What was the guiding principle of the new era? How did it illustrate what foreign obervers see as the American love of hyperbole or overstatement, of pushing things to extremes?

3 To judge from Cooper's article, what is the *target audience* for the lure of the casino capital? What would you include in a profile of the ideal customer? Are there different kinds of audiences for what the city offers?

4 Cooper shows the largely unknown *other side* of the city as a place to live and work. What does he say about employment opportunities, living standards, and schools? What makes the life of the real city a paradoxical, at first seemingly contradictory contrast with the familiar hype of the tourist mecca?

5 Cooper sees recent changes in the public image of Las Vegas as part of *national trends.* How did gambling (or "gaming") become accepted as part of the mainstream? What changes in cultural attitudes or moral standards were occurring? What economic developments were a major factor?

Talking, Listening, Writing

6 Is gambling an ingrained trait of the American national character? Is the bonanza mentality—striking it rich—more widespread than the work ethic?

7 What city would you nominate today to be a true symbol of the American national spirit? What city for you best represents the America of the future? How would you defend your choice?

FIND IT ON THE WEB

Entertainment Capital of the World

In the summer of 2004, the *New York Times* put "On the Web" a range of articles with titles like "The Pied Piper of Las Vegas Leads the Willing into Midnight and Beyond" and "When a City Discovers the Virtues of Vice. And Vice Versa." The material, including interviews with people featured in the series, was available at nytimes.com/lasvegas. What light do the articles and other materials shed on questions raised in the series:

- Is local and state government the "willing handmaiden" of the gambling industry?
- Are the ties with organized crime a thing of the past?
- Will mega-resorts drive out small-scale casino operators?
- Will the entertainment industry cultivate a family-friendly or a "naughty" image?

LIFE AND DEATH AMONG THE XEROX PEOPLE

Olga Cabral

"I wrote urgent xxxxxxxxxx's every day/to faces flat as paper"

The nineteenth-century gospel of progress promised a better future when the march of technology would free humanity from backbreaking toil and banish the specter of famine. Spectacular advances in transportation and communication bridged huge distances. During the twentieth century, skeptical voices began to voice second thoughts, warning of the negative side effects and unintended consequences of technological advances. They protested the congestion and pollution caused by the public's love affair with the automobile. They warned of nuclear disaster. A new generation of office workers found themselves working in the dehumanized modern office envisioned in the following poem.

Olga Cabral was born in Port of Spain in Trinidad. After coming to New York, she ran an art gallery, and she published juvenile fiction and several collections of poetry. She has written haunting, provocative poems on subjects like world hunger: "black child/brown child dying/on the naked roadsides/of HUNGER."

The following poem was included in her collection Voice/Over: Selected Poems *published in 1993 by a press in Albuquerque, New Mexico.*

Thought Starters: For how much of your ordinary day do you listen to synthesized voices, push buttons to communicate, or otherwise interact with automated or robotized devices? Do you miss the human contact that the new systems and devices have replaced, or do you welcome the convenience or efficiency of dealing with machines and automated systems?

It was the wrong office   *1*
    but I went in
not a soul knew me
    but they said: Sit Down
they showed me corridors of paper   *5*
    and said: Begin Here

They wheeled in a machine
    a miniature electric chair
sparks flew from the earplugs
    antennas sprang from my nostrils   *10*

they switched on the current
    the machine said: Marry Me

I had forgotten my numbers
    they said it could be serious
they showed me the paper cutter   *15*
    it sliced like a guillotine
my head fell bloodlessly
    into the waste basket

I mined my way through stockrooms
    I wrote urgent XXXXXXXXXX's every day   *20*
to faces flat as paper
    the telephones feared nothing human
the windows were mirages
    permanently nailed shut

They handed me a skin
    and said: Wear This   *25*
it was somebody else's life
    it didn't quite fit
so I left it lying there . . .
    that was a queer cemetery.   *30*

The Responsive Reader

1   What details from the *real world* of office work surface in this poem in a spooky, frightening form? For example, have you ever felt that you were being equipped with earplugs and antennas? In what kind of building would you feel that "the windows were mirages/permanently nailed shut"? What would make a user feel married to a piece of equipment or a machine?

2   The poet starts by saying that "it was the wrong office" and "not a soul knew me." She says toward the end, "it was somebody else's life." Have you ever experienced similar feelings at work, in school, or in another situation? How do people cope with such feelings of *alienation?*

Talking, Listening, Writing

3   Critics charge that current methods of supervision and monitoring have contributed to the depersonalizing and dehumanizing of office work. One student wrote, "Productivity was the paramount concern of the company; each and every second was counted, monitored, and evaluated by the master computer." Have you experienced or observed current corporate methods of scheduling and monitoring? How did you react or adjust?

4 What is ergonomics? What is repetitive motion syndrome or repetitive stress syndrome? Working conditions in the computerized workplace have given rise to new kinds of stress and injury that become the subject of protests or litigation. Working with a group, investigate current complaints, suggested remedies, or recent or proposed legislation.

FORUM: *Terror Invades America*

On September 11, 2001, for the first time since the Civil War, war came to the American homeland. As millions watched in horror, first one of the twin towers of the World Trade Center in lower Manhattan started belching flame and smoke after being hit by a hijacked American passenger plane. Then a second plane hit the second tower. Eventually both towers collapsed, burying over 3,000 people—workers and customers of the many national and international firms sharing the buildings. On an ordinary working day, as many as 50,000 people came to the trade center, and only a miracle of coordinated evacuation procedures allowed many people to reach safety. The dead included a large number of police officers and firefighters who had rushed to the disaster scene. A third plane, also hijacked by Muslim fundamentalists, crashed into the Pentagon, with hundreds of additional casualties. A fourth hijacked plane crashed in Pennsylvania, killing all aboard, after heroic passengers took on the terrorists.

The terrorist attack had not come without warning. An earlier attempt to blow up the World Trade Center using a car bomb had done limited damage, and the case against the terrorists implicated was still wending its way through the legal system. Horrendous bombings of two American embassies in Africa, staged by the same fundamentalist network that planned the September 11 attack, had killed and maimed hundreds of local workers and bystanders. Worried flight instructors had tried to warn the authorities about Middle Eastern nationals wanting to learn how to fly but not how to land a large commercial plane. However, these warnings were dimissed or misdirected, never reaching the FBI or the CIA or the Pentagon.

Earlier in 2001, the chair of a Harvard University institute studying international relations and the "Clash of Cultures" had congratulated Americans on the "vigilance" that he said had prevented further attacks from the terrorists. After September 11, political leaders and media voices said that what we had seen was America's "loss of innocence" and that "things would never be the same."

MANHATTAN DISPATCH

David Grann

**"His Polaroid had just come into focus and you could
see, through smoke, one of the towers still standing.
'You'll never see that again,' he said."**

*New York City is the financial and cultural capital of the United States,
and with its surrounding suburban areas it is the heart of American publishing. Many editors and journalists lived and worked within a few dozen blocks
of the twin towers targeted in the September 11 attack. Many lost or knew
people who lost cherished friends or relatives in the attack. Grann is one of several contributors to* New Republic *magazine who lived and worked in Manhattan or across the bridges in Brooklyn. He is writing as an eyewitness—
someone who can say: "I was there." He tells us what he saw, heard, and
felt—before the flood of explanations, interpretations, accusations, and calls to
arms the event would loosen.*

Thought Starters: Where were you on September 11? How did you learn
of the attacks? Do you remember what eyewitnesses saw or said? What went
through your mind as you watched the images or listened to the voices?

By the time I reached the roof of my apartment building on 21st   1
Street, one of the towers was already gone. All you could see was a plume
of smoke. An elderly tenant, who lives in the penthouse, was leaning over
her railing, blinking at it.

"Some fool flew right into it," she said.

The doorman, Miguel, pulled out a Polaroid camera and took a snapshot. "I saw the plane come right in and hit it," he told me. "It was too low."

We stood there for a while not sure what to do. More and more
people came up. One tenant said he saw the first plane flying so low he
thought it was going to land on the street; a woman, whom I occasionally
exchange glances with in the elevator, said we were "under siege" by terrorists. Then the second tower came down. Everyone waited for a thun-
derous crash—one man even crouched behind the wall—but there was
not a sound except for the wail of sirens and the tenant in apartment 5A,
who said, "This is war."

After a while I got back into the elevator with Miguel. His Polaroid   5
had just come into focus and you could see, through smoke, one of the
towers still standing. "You'll never see that again," he said.

The police had blocked off our street with an armored car. On the
roof of the police station next door I could see snipers, poking their rifles

through crevices, even though there didn't seem to be anything to point them at. By then all the roads and subways were closed off and, though I had gathered up my reporter pads and recorder, I had no way of getting anywhere. On my way upstairs again, I bumped into a volunteer police officer in 16D who was rushing to the scene; though I had never spoken to him before, I asked him if I could tag along. "I'll get you as close as I can," he said.

We got in his car and switched on the siren. Uncertain how to get there, we turned down one road, then another, until we wound up on Second Avenue, where the police had created an emergency lane. We were swept into a long line of ambulances and fire engines, many with men hanging off the sides, or piled on the tops, heading toward the smoke now spreading over the lower half of Manhattan. As we progressed downtown, past the Second Avenue Deli at 10th Street and through the East Village, we could see more and more people coming toward us, a mass of humanity. They moved in a steady, almost orderly march. Occasionally we slowed to let a bunch pass. "Look at that man," said the cop driving me. A figure in an impeccable suit and tie was crossing in front of us. He looked as if he had just stepped out of a board meeting, except that he was blackened by ashes from head to toe. Some people had taken off their shirts and wrapped them around their mouths to protect them from the smoke, even as they carried their brief cases or cell phones. One person carried an umbrella.

By Lafayette Street the police had created an armed perimeter around the entire area and we parked by the subway station. Volunteer EMTs and doctors had gathered, but no more victims were arriving, and the stretchers lay on the sidewalk. As we passed through the first of several police barriers, the cop with me flashed his badge. He was a short, stocky fellow with a boyish face. He said he volunteered as an officer in Long Island, but that he "had never seen anything like this before."

As we moved deeper inside the perimeter, the sun seemed to disappear. The smoke stung our eyes and a fireman gave us surgical masks to help us breathe; on the ground, a thick layer of soot covered everything. On one of the cars someone had written in the ashes with his finger TRIAGE HERE, with an arrow pointing into a building, now abandoned. The smaller streets, leading to the World Trade Center, were empty save for firemen. At one point we came across a car, still idling, left in the middle of the road. We also saw a deserted fruit stand. Finally there was an opening in the row of buildings through which we could see, only 100 or so yards away, where the tower once stood, nothing but a mass of rubble.

Police cars and ambulances that had arrived for what they believed was the beginning of the rescue now sat cracked in half, their interiors still in flames. Several workers tried to put them out, their hoses stirring up the soot so that the few people in the vicinity rushed backward. A policeman removed a gas mask and said into a radio, "Haven't been able to find John. I'm still looking for John. We're still looking for John."

10

"I can't find my company," another fireman said.

There were no wounded visible, nor even the sound of a human cry. A man came by on a bicycle carrying a bucket filled with bottles of Evian water and little boxes of Visine, which he passed out. Several firemen took the bottles of water, sipped from them, and then poured them over their heads. We stood there for a long time, watching, and then an older man stumbled out of the smoke. He didn't seem to know where he was. There were no intact ambulances in the area, and he wandered toward a car that was on fire. "I better help him," my cop said. He took the man's arm and led him down the street. I asked him where he had come from, but he didn't seem to know. "I have MS," he said. We led him toward the perimeter, where other officers then carried him away.

When we walked back toward the rubble, I noticed something on the sidewalk. It had been cordoned off by yellow tape, as if part of a crime scene, but the tape had broken, which is why I hadn't noticed it before. Inside the area was a thick, metallic object about the size of a desk. "It's the fuckin' engine from one of the planes," a police officer told us. The cop and I stared at it for a while. "It must have cut through there," he said, pointing at the sky, "and landed all the way over here."

Not far behind it was a building with the door blown out, and we went inside for shelter. It was a real estate agency for luxury suites. There was an art deco painting on the wall and travel magazines strewn in the lobby. A camera was sitting on the front desk, along with other valuables, and a piece of half-eaten fudge. A message taped to the wall said MAKE SOFIA'S JOB EASIER.

The phones were working, and the cop and I both tried to call our 15 families. I could hear him on the phone talking to his dad and then to his girlfriend. Afterward he asked me if my wife was OK, and when I told him she was, he seemed genuinely pleased. Another fireman came in and tried to call home as well, when suddenly someone yelled, "Building coming down, clear out," and there was a rush of people outside, firemen and police running past, and the three of us tried to get out. I slipped and fell on the wet floor, then got back up and ran after the cop. There was the sound of an explosion behind us, but the building didn't come down.

Neither of us had much interest in watching the fire burn any longer, and there didn't seem to be anybody to help. So we started to walk uptown, our clothes and hair by now covered in soot. All around us, on the ground or fluttering in the air, were thousands of pieces of paper. They had been blown out of the World Trade Center and were still swirling. I began to catch them in my hands, occasionally bending to pick some up. One said, "World Trade Center Master Options List Report: OPPENHEIMER-FUNDS Inc. . . . Building 2WTC . . . Floor 30." Another paper, typed partly in Chinese, said "American TCC International Group, Inc., One World Trade Center, Suite 4763."

There were e-mails ("thanks for your voice message today") and desk calendars and Post-it notes. I tried to stuff them in my pockets, but I couldn't get them all. The cop saw me and began to catch them too. By the time we got to the car we had such a large mound I had to put some in the back. I wasn't sure what to do with them, but when I got home I sat down and began to read. Most were too charred, but I could make out small clues, about some man named Andrew in suite 101 who received a FedEx package from Stamford on August 6 and another man, named Philip, who worked at Kidder Peabody and sent a package, also on August 6, to General Electric for $8.83. There was part of a novel with the initials "S.P." written on the inside flap; the reader had underlined a passage that said: "There was one thing she was sure of. She was going to become an editor." There was a man named David who wrote long e-mails with phrases like "segment specific retention/winback" and "deliverables were reprioritized," and a woman who had sent an e-mail that said only, "I'll see you at two. Love S." After reading through them, I put them in a neat pile and stored them in a box in the back of a closet. Then I went back upstairs to join the other tenants who had gathered on the roof to watch the empty sky.

The Responsive Reader

1   Grann takes his readers as close to Ground Zero as they are likely to get. He gives them snapshots and surreal images of the *disaster scene,* of witnesses, of rescuers, and of survivors. What images and impressions are likely to stay in your mind? Do they add up to any dominating or powerful general impression? Is there a connecting thread? What was different from what Grann might have expected? What is different from what you might have expected?

2   Grann weaves in glimpses or *reminders* of the lives and working days destroyed by the disaster. What form do they take? What kind of silent testimony do they provide? What effect do they have on you as the reader?

3   Grann's account stays close to the *unedited raw data* of what he took in at the time and on the scene. The media, putting their spin on the news, soon started to look for tales of heroism. Would you call Grann and the people he encountered heroes? Why or why not? What do you learn about ordinary people caught up in a horrifying disaster from his account?

Talking, Listening, Writing

4   A foreign consular official based in Manhattan commented on the overpowering wave of patriotism that swept over the city and the American nation in the wake of the September 11 attack. What forms did it take? What explains it? Do you think it will have a lasting effect on how Americans think about themselves and others? Why or why not?

BROOKLYN DISPATCH: UNDER THE BRIDGE

Paul Berman

"By late morning, huge parades of people from Manhattan had begun to make their way on foot across the bridges into Brooklyn and were dragging themselves along Atlantic Avenue."

In the first days after the September 11 events, government officials and media people began to warn against scapegoating obvious targets: Muslim Americans, Arab Americans, or anyone looking vaguely dark-complexioned and Middle Eastern. In World War I, popular anger and resentment had turned against German Americans. In World War II, it had turned against Japanese Americans.

In the first days after the attack, Berman was one of many voices telling Americans that militant Islamic fundamentalism is a radical movement that does not represent the whole Muslim religion or the Muslim world. Berman is the author of A Tale of Two Utopias: The Political Journey of the Generation of 1968.

Thought Starters: Xenophobia, or hatred of foreigners, is often the ugly underbelly of a revival of patriotic fervor. At first hand or in the media, have you seen evidence of anti-Arab or anti-Muslim sentiment and prejudice?

I am writing seven or eight hours after the attack, and, through my study window in Brooklyn, I see black plumes still billowing from lower Manhattan. In the morning, from my rooftop, I watched the first flames encircle the twin towers and the black cloud float over the harbor. The smoke seemed oddly speckled with glinting white spots, which I at first thought might have been gulls. But they were papers sucked out of the burning buildings. Some of the specks were also, I later learned, human body parts. A silvery necklace as wide as a building seemed to drop from one of the burning towers. I thought it might have been part of the façade, tearing away. It was not the façade. The smoke cleared for a brief second, and the tower was gone. Below me, on Brooklyn's Atlantic Avenue, fire engines began to scream, trying to push their way through traffic into Manhattan. 1

By late morning huge parades of people from Manhattan had begun to make their way on foot across the bridges into Brooklyn and were dragging themselves along Atlantic Avenue, some of them still wearing masks over their mouths and noses, a white soot on their clothes and shoes. I went out into the street. Lower Atlantic Avenue has been a largely Arab district for some 70 years, filled with storefronts adorned with Arabic letters and names. Here and there among the crowd, people were hurling curses at Arabs and at foreigners. A round-faced man declaimed, "Don't let any more of these foreign Arabs come into this country no more! They hate us!" I stopped at a store where I know a clerk from Morocco. He has told me he admires the moderate and tolerant views of the late king of Morocco and of the new, young king. Now the clerk was standing taciturn behind the counter, his face compressed. Outside, the round-faced man was shouting, "We gotta get rid of all these foreigners!"

At Smith Street a woman who said she worked near the World Trade Center stood on the sidewalk, dust on her clothes; she, too, spoke against the Arabs. "This is where all these hateful people live!" she said, gesturing up Atlantic Avenue. I asked her what she had seen. She said she had seen people hurl themselves to the ground from very high floors of the World Trade Center. "Where is Bush?" she said, exploding in anger. "Where was the Army?" She had seen a terrified old man on the Brooklyn Bridge, unable to walk any further because of his panic, clutching a pole.

I walked to the Brooklyn Bridge and tried to cross into Manhattan, but I was turned away by the police. I tried to cross on the Manhattan Bridge, and I got part of the way over the river before I was turned back again. So I joined the endless stream of people going the other way, into Brooklyn—the vast and varied crowd that resembled a crowd in almost no other place on Earth, faces that were African, Asian, Latin, European—the whole of mankind. A Hasid sped by on a roller scooter. Near Long Island University, the sidewalks were filled with students passing out water, as if to the runners in a marathon.

It was a gratifying scene of communal solidarity. But on Fulton Street, 5 as I headed back to my home, I saw that the storekeepers had pulled down their metal shutters and the street was empty. A cop told me that looters had begun to run up and down Fulton Street. In exchange for that information, I told him a rumor I had heard from one of his colleagues on the Manhattan Bridge: that large numbers of cops could not be accounted for and were probably buried under the twin towers. "Don't tell me that," he said.

The Responsive Reader

1   What are striking or hard-to-forget sights or *details* from Berman's eyewitness account? How does it compare with or what does it add to Grann's testimony?

2   How serious or widespread do you think are the *antiforeign* sentiments Berman records? Where does he see compensating signs of "communal solidarity"? What would you say to the people Berman heard expressing anti-Arab or antiforeign sentiments?

3   Why do you think Berman makes a point of the *diversity* of the "vast and varied crowd" he saw "that resembled a crowd in almost no other place on Earth"?

Talking, Listening, Writing

4 In Berman's account, the mass of humanity streaming across the bridges in flight from the flaming holocaust of lower Manhattan becomes a symbol for the martyred civilian populations who are the victims of war. In the current spate of war movies, how much focus is there on the civilian victims of war?

Collaborative Projects

5 According to some recent estimates, civilian casualties in recent wars have far exceeded military losses. Working with a group, you may want to investigate the huge increase in civilian losses in World War II, the Korean War, or the Vietnam War.

AMERICA'S WEALTH DRAWS HATRED

Ken Garcia

"Our leaders may be quick to portray suicidal zealots as madmen and extremists, but it doesn't explain why there may be thousands of people ready to do harm to the United States."

In the first hours and days after the horror of the attack on the twin towers, many ordinary Americans used words like senseless, crazy, *and* unimaginable *to describe what they had seen on the ground or on the screen. However, the rhetoric of the administration and the media soon started using the vocabulary of a moral crusade against unspeakable evil. The forces of truth and justice would be mobilized and would prevail. When Americans started to listen to the instigators of the attackers, they in turn heard voices proclaiming a holy war against evil, calling divine justice down on America as the agent of Satan.*

Columnists like Ken Garcia tried to probe the reasons for the fanatical sense of righteousness and divine sanction of the suicide hijackers and for their murderous hatred of America.

Thought Starters: What did you know about Islam and the Muslim world before the September 11 attack? Had you heard the term *Islamic fundamentalism?* Had you paid attention to earlier attacks directed against Americans or American interests? Had you heard voices of warning? What did you think of them at the time?

If you walk around the financial districts of San Francisco, Seattle, Los Angeles or Chicago, it might be easier to see why outsiders or religious fundamentalists living in $20 tents might view the nation as blatantly prosperous, greedy, self-centered and uncaring. Despite the record prosperity in recent years, America gives less to help the world's poorest countries than other industrialized nations. But we spend most generously on ourselves— with the determined view that we have rightfully earned it.

That does not make us heroes to the world outside our borders. Americans are generally, some might say happily, oblivious of our country's image to the rest of the world. Our leaders may be quick to portray suicidal zealots as madmen and extremists, but it doesn't explain why there may be thousands of people ready to do harm to the United States for what is often viewed as its general excess.

In fact, there are millions of people around the world who despise our country for its wealth, its power, its military might, its crass commercialism, its often hypocritical moral views and its seeming detachment from so many of the world's problems. The United States is frequently viewed as isolated, pompous, hostile and self-serving—and that's among our allies.

So how could it be that a country like Afghanistan would get locked into our gun sights—a nation that we aided in its struggle against an oppressive Soviet regime, a nation whose soldiers we helped train, including one very high profile commander named bin Laden?

It helps if you know that Afghanistan is dirt poor, beset by famine, depleted by drought, fraught with political turmoil and run by a group that sees holy war as its sole spiritual alternative. No one will ever accuse the leaders of the Taliban of being overly moved by acts of reason. But the Taliban's apparent willingness to take on the globe's reigning superpower over their unblinking resolve to aid the world's best known terrorist at least provides a glimpse into the level of hate America inspires in some countries— places that in the coming months we may get to know frighteningly well.

It's hard to gain perspective when you spend each day in the heart and luxury of America's executive suites.

The Responsive Reader

1 Americans have traditionally thought of themselves as a generous people, with a tradition of goodwill toward others. Have you encountered or seen evidence of *anti-American* feeling or resentment—at home or abroad? What seemed to motivate it? Have you heard people voice grievances, accusations, or hate?

2 Have you seen evidence firsthand of the American *worship of excess* that might make others see the nation as "blatantly prosperous, greedy, self-centered and uncaring"? In what areas of American life? Do you see yourself surrounded by "crass commercialism"?

3   As a columnist for the *San Francisco Chronicle* before its takeover by the Hearst corporation, Garcia castigated a new brand of top managers who secured fantastic bonuses by reducing loyal employees to temporary status and stripping them of their benefits and who finally walked away with "obscene" payouts after selling their institution "down the river." Do you think Americans will be inclined to be more critical of greed and ostentatious display after the events of September 11? Why or why not?

Talking, Listening, Writing

4   Do you think critics of the nation's untrammeled pursuit of material wealth are unpatriotic?

Collaborative Projects

5   Americans are often accused of isolating themselves from the rest of the world and ignoring the resentments and revindications of others. Working with a group, you may want to interview foreign students on your campus to study their attitudes toward America.

PRIME TARGET IS WOMEN

Ellen Goodman

"For more than a century, arguments about tradition and change have taken place over women's bodies and women's rights."

Afghanistan, bordered by Iran, Pakistan, and the former Soviet republic of Uzbekistan, was early identified as the home base—the host country and sanctuary—of the religious fundamentalist network that had planned the September 11 attacks on the World Trade Center as part of a jihad, or holy war, against the infidel West. Afghanistan had been devastated and impoverished by many years of superpower politics and civil war. The fundamentalist Taliban had emerged victorious from the struggle against the Soviet occupation and had instituted a rigid regime of religious austerity and repression.

The decision of the Western powers to strike at the Taliban helped focus attention on the disfranchisement and oppression of the women of Afghanistan under a fundamentalist regime. Before the military action against the Taliban regime, an organization of Afghan women had smuggled out of the country videos documenting the oppression of Afghan women—the floggings, stonings, and shootings in a former sports stadium converted to a killing ground. Ellen Goodman, star columnist for the Boston Globe, *long a widely admired commentator on current issues, published this column in 2001.*

Thought Starters: Before the media spotlight on Afghanistan and the Taliban regime, were you aware of or concerned with repressive treatment or disfranchisement of women in other countries? Were people you know aware or concerned? Why or why not?

From time to time, you see one cross the screen. A spectral heap of humanity covered from head to toe.

You've been told that there is a woman under the burka, but there is no way to know. There is, after all, no public face on the women of Afghanistan. Nor is there any public voice. Laughing out loud is illegal. Singing is a crime.

From the very beginning, when the Taliban victory was welcomed by some as a promise of stability, this was the prime target of their campaign against unbelievers, against modern life and against the "West." The fundamental enemy of their fundamentalism took the female form.

The victims of their harshest internal terrorism were women, forbidden to work, banned from school, beaten for an exposed ankle, stoned for a lark. The female half of the population was placed under virtual house arrest, or if you prefer, slavery.

Now we see the Islamic fundamentalist attitudes toward women in new forms. In the will that one terrorist left behind ordering that "women are to be neither present at the funeral nor appear themselves sometime later at my grave." In the promise that "martyrs" in this jihad will secure a place in heaven—with 72 virgins to serve them.

Is "misogyny" too weak a word?

For more than a century, arguments about tradition and change have taken place over women's bodies and women's rights. It has happened in Afghanistan since the 1920s, when the reformist Afghan King Amanullah called upon the queen to remove her veil before a meeting of tribal elders, helping unite a rebellion against him. It has happened there since the 1980s when educated Afghan women were demonized as Soviet stooges.

But it's not just Afghanistan and not just Islam that have seen women as the symbol of life spinning out of control. Lynn Freedman, a public health professor at Columbia, talks about a "family resemblance" between fundamentalisms. All of them.

If fundamentalism, she says, "can be seen as, in part, a reaction to a sense of dislocation and a sense that their own culture is under siege, often women become the symbol of that. Women out of control are a symbol of their own situation out of control."

Indeed, in every text and every tradition, from Baptist to Buddhist, we can pick and choose references to support women's equality or to prove their inferiority.

Right now there is, of course, nothing to rival the regime or the repression in Afghanistan. An Afghan women's rights group operating out of Pakistan puts it best on its Web site, *www.rawa.org:* "Thank you for visiting the home page of the most oppressed women in the world." It is a sorry, but accurate, distinction.

So today, America is finally staking out women's rights as part of the moral high ground in the struggle against terrorism. But internationally, we still tiptoe around the subject of subjugation.

In the first shaky weeks of this war, we are making friends with the enemy of our enemy. The Northern Alliance may allow its women to go to school and to shop in public, if they have permission. But need it be said that these men are to the Taliban as the benign slaveholder is to the vicious slaveholder?

From the day that terrorist planes hit their targets, and Americans asked why, the president answered: They hate freedom. He has said more than once that we are in a struggle for freedom.

Now, catching a glimpse of the dehumanized shapes crossing the TV 15 screen, we know that freedom includes the women who form a mute and invisible backdrop to their own history.

The Responsive Reader

1 How much do you know about the *restrictions* that Goodman reminds her readers of—restrictions on singing, laughing, music, women in the workplace, women appearing in public, and women showing their faces or any part of their bodies? Did you become aware of striking or especially disturbing examples of repressive practices or attitudes?

2 How does Goodman explain the psychological dynamics or *cultural roots* of the fundamentalists' misogyny? What is the connection between hatred of Western culture and negative attitudes toward women?

3 What news reports or other evidence have you seen of Afghan women cautiously returning to the *world of work*—as doctors, teachers, journalists, and members of other occupations? Why does Goodman adopt a "wait-and-see" attitude toward the emancipation or liberation of Afghan women?

Talking, Listening, Writing

4 Do you think Americans have the right to lecture people from other cultures about traditional or deeply rooted cultural practices? Do you agree that "internationally," the United States should cease to "tiptoe" around the subject of women's subjugation and women's rights?

5 What evidence have you seen that there is a "family resemblance" in the attitudes toward women shared by fundamentalists of other religions?

Collaborative Projects

6 Goodman says that "in every text and every tradition" there is a range of evidence supporting claims of women's equality or inferiority. Is there a range of different positions on women's rights and the role of women in a religious tradition you know well or with which you have special ties? For instance, is there a range of different views among Christian denominations, among branches of Judaism, or among moderate and traditionalist representatives of Islam? Working with a group, you may want to investigate current controversies and their historical roots.

THE NEW TERRORISM

David Kay

"We need to identify the root causes that are changing our national security posture today and changing the threats that we face in the world."

David Kay gave the talk excerpted here at the Commonwealth Club of California in 2004, at a time of heated political debate. Opposing voices across the political divide were accusing each other of addressing mainly a "hallelujah chorus of the like-minded" and of oversimplifying "complex issues of war and social justice." In the meantime, the Commonwealth Club was continuing its long-established policy of providing a public affairs forum for a wide range of voices—public figures, journalists, artists, and influential commentators.

David Kay had been a weapons inspector in Iraq before the war, checking on the country's compliance with United Nations mandates. After the war in Iraq opened a new front in the war on terror, a period of intense public debate eventually followed reports of the successes of American and coalition forces. Americans with long records of public service and extended experience in foreign affairs began to question the intelligence reports or the claims of government officials about the threat from Iraq that had preceded the war. Kay had been widely quoted as saying "we were almost all wrong" about Iraq.

Thought Starters: What is a terrorist? What would you include in a profile of a potential terrorist? When does someone fighting or ready to die for a political movement, faith, or group become a terrorist?

We're struggling with a national security challenge which says that the enemy may be within us. Too often in the U.S., this discussion has taken the form of worries about terrorism, about weapons of mass destruction, both of which are important but are actually tactics. We need to identify the root causes that are changing our national security posture today and changing the threats that we face in the world.

The first is vulnerable societies or failed states. There are 50 to 70; these cut across the world: North Korea, Zimbabwe, Pakistan. Iraq was, at the time of Operation Iraqi Freedom, a failed state. We didn't recognize that, and military action would have probably taken a different form if we had. Why these states fail is important to understand. Part of the issue is demography. In Western Europe and the U.S., roughly 17 percent of the population is under 15. In the Middle East, it's 50 percent; under 24, it's 62 percent. Take Yemen—a small state with virtually no economy (unless drug smuggling is an economy, which it is for some states): It will have, at mid-century, the largest population in the Middle East, about 105 million people, without ever having had a public education system, a public health system, any form of a recognized economy, and struggling with over half of its population being under 15. Is there any surprise that, as you go through the ranks of Al Qaeda and other terrorist groups, you find a large proportion of Yemenis?

There are other issues, some economic. Most of the 50 to 70 states have a single dependable source of income: a crop, raw material, natural resource. It's hard to manage an economy like that, threatened with huge cycles of income disparity. Some of these often go in ways we don't recognize. The best example is Saudi Arabia. Per capita income is one-half of what is was in 1972. Sons look at their fathers, uncles, elder brothers—they had a life that they know they will not have.

Other things take place in many failed states: failure of social integration as they confront the external world. As some countries where Islam is the dominant religion make the transition to a modern society, economy and a modern world—and others don't make the transition—their struggle of an internal civil war takes the form, very often because of government policy, of an external civil war against others. . .

Terrorism has been around a long time, but terrorism was a means for an objective. The IRA: *Get the British out of Northern Ireland.* That's not what terrorism is about now. Terrorism is about what I've called the culture of death. *I die, therefore I am.* The willingness for ultimate sacrifice in order to obtain some lofty goal, which is in the hereafter.

Our image of terrorists is of young, hopeless men. The 9/11 terrorists or those who carried out the Madrid bombing are mostly middle aged; often came to where they are in life with fellowships, studied at good universities. Atta could have been an urban planner in Germany. They have capabilities that terrorists have never been able to have. The military is not the target. The terrorists are seeking symbolic targets, large numbers of casualties.

We face a situation where the intelligence apparatus that helped us win the Cold War is completely inadequate. The challenge is redesigning intelligence capability to have a national security strategy adequate for dealing with threats that we face. Anyone who believes the Department of Defense is the appropriate mechanism to deal with failed states has neither seen the Department of Defense nor a failed state.

We have tremendous comparative advantages. Take almost any country that has an education system that is practically nonexistent. An American model works very well: the community college system—a tremendous integrator of people from various economic and national stratas. The same thing is true of poverty, of social integration. We have so much to bring, and it is in the national security basket if we stop and think about it. We cannot do it if we only think about what the next war we are going to wage is, whether it is on terrorism, Islam, name your topic. We need an intelligence capability that helps us focus on where the problems are, and to think about a national security strategy that brings the full tools of America and our values and capabilities to bear to change the world—rather than simply worry about defending it after the attack.

The Responsive Reader

1   What for you is the key element or key criterion in Kay's *definition* of the New Terrorism? What elements in his discussion of terrorism are familiar? What elements are new or thought-provoking?

2   Americans have often been accused of being isolated from the rest of the world. Drawing on Kay's speech, what would you include in a *briefing* on key issues and key features of countries that Americans urgently need to know better?

3   In recent years, Americans have lived with warnings of impending threats. Do you see in the speaker's remarks sources of *positive* encouragement? What does he say about America's assets and capabilities? What does he say about our need to face the challenges of the future?

4   Does Kay mention the role of *religion* in the rise of terror? When Kay spoke, a terrorist attack had killed and maimed hundreds of passengers using commuter trains in Madrid in Spain. Many observers of spreading terror stressed the role of a growing *Jihad* holy war mentality. What seems to be Kay's attitude or explanation? Do you think he downplays or underestimates the role of religion in the "new terrorism"?

Talking, Listening, Writing

5   After the September 11 attack, the Russian poet Yevtushenko, who had been a Cold War dissident, pleaded with people in the West not to respond to hate with hate. Have you seen evidence that such a response is a strong temptation or threat? Have you seen signs of escalating mutual hatred? Have you seen evidence of attempts to counteract hate or find alternatives?

Research-Based Writing

In research-based writing, study a significant subject in depth, using and acknowledging the best available sources.

In research-based writing, you help your audience become informed or reach a responsible opinion after you sift a range of source material, looking for the best available or most trustworthy evidence. Your research assignment gives you a chance to explore a question that is on the minds of concerned readers but that has no easy or simple answer. Your research will help your readers go beyond what "everybody knows"—but has not really checked out.

The material you draw on may include

- "facts and figures"—such as statistical studies or survey data
- research studies from private or institutional sources
- testimony by qualified observers or firsthand witnesses
- commentary from experts or insiders
- official documents such as court decisions or agency reports
- material from personal contacts or interviews

You will have to sift and evaluate promising material from a range of sources. You may have to weigh conflicting testimony and try to resolve disagreements among experts. You will be asked for full **documentation**—a detailed complete record of source information and access information, so you can give full credit to your sources of information and ideas.

Respecting Intellectual Property

Plagiarism is the unacknowledged appropriation of someone else's intellectual property. Institutions impose serious penalties on writers who abuse the reader's trust. Today's sophisticated fraud detection software can track unacknowledged borrowed material from a staggering mass of source material. Develop your own potential, and respect the work of others.

Take pride in your own work. Remember these basic warnings from teachers and editors:

- Enclose all words and phrases you copy verbatim—word for word—in quotation marks.

- Whenever you copy and file sentences or passages, mark them clearly as copied material, taken over from the original source.

- When you take over ideas, original approaches, or conclusions from someone else, acknowledge your debt.

- Never pass off whole borrowed passages or complete pages as your own original effort.

Triggering

Choose a research question that will hold the attention and satisfy the curiosity of both you and your readers.

What current question or unresolved issue would motivate you to look for solidly based answers? What development in environmental science, medicine, or genetics raises challenging questions? What current controversy would motivate you to help readers move beyond stereotypes or partisan claims?

Here is a sampling of questions focused on current issues that you could use or adapt as a **research question** for a research-based paper:

AREA ONE: EDUCATION

1 Is testing the answer to the needs of underperforming schools or "failing schools"? How much testing is going on in schools in your community, in your larger area, or in the nation's schools? Who are the key players—educators, testing organizations, parents, politicians? What is the effect on low-income or second-language students?

2 What can be done to reduce current unacceptable dropout rates for students not finishing school? Can schools help minority

students or students from low-income backgrounds develop feelings of self-worth or self-esteem? What kind of motivation or incentives work?

3   Has the movement toward gender parity in college sports slowed down? Has it been reversed? Can you sort out conflicting claims about gains and losses in key areas of college sports?

4   Is there a movement to ensure that football players and other college athletes receive a true college education? Will student athletes have to meet minimum academic standards? Is there a movement to ensure higher graduation rates?

5   Have city schools in your area or state been resegregated? Has the movement to integrate public schools been abandoned or reversed?

AREA TWO: COMMUNITY ISSUES

6   Are big national chains endangering small local businesses or neighborhood stores? Will we be a Wal-Mart or a Starbucks nation?

7   Are youth gangs on the rise in your area or community? What is the story behind the media reports? What do educators, law enforcement officers, counselors, judges, or parents say?

8   Are gun control initiatives like an assault-weapons ban doomed? Will gun violence remain a threat in our communities or in our schools?

9   Are local law enforcement authorities hostile to teenagers?

AREA THREE: LANGUAGE

10   Will English-only initiatives help unite or divide Americans—in your state or nationwide?

11   Should schools do more to teach foreign languages? Should they do more to help young Americans be bilingual in tomorrow's global world?

AREA FOUR: ENVIRONMENT

12   Are efforts to bring back the wolves or other predators misguided? How do the programs operate? Who initiated them? Who opposes them?

13   Are our oceans going to be fished out? Are efforts to save depleted fisheries by moratorium or other government intervention proving successful?

14   Are "Save the Forests" initiatives defeated by economic and political realities? Is the battle to save our forests and fight defor-

estation a lost cause? What are the forces aligned on different sides of the issue?

15 Are we backsliding in the effort to create a cleaner environment? Is progress toward cleaner water and cleaner air being reversed? In your community or larger area, is the prospect for less pollution or more pollution?

16 Does the theory of global warming represent a consensus of concerned scientists? Or is it doubtful science? Is there an international consensus of scientists? Are people pointing to alleged disastrous results already occurring alarmists?

AREA FIVE: SEXUAL ORIENTATION

17 How is recognizing civil unions or domestic partnerships different from legalizing same-sex marriage? What are key differences in rights, obligations, or legal status? What is the long-range trend?

18 Articles and books with titles like *Same-Sex Marriage and the Constitution,* and conflicting court decisions have been examining whether an equal protection clause of a state or the federal constitution makes legislation banning same-sex marriages unconstitutional. What may be the answer?

Gathering

Draw on the full range of research sources and facilities available to you.

As a researcher today, you have unprecedented access to a wealth of research resources. The Internet carries current data, background information, research results, and informed opinion on a vast range of current topics. You may be using material from sources first published in hard copy and also available online but also material originally published online. College and community libraries welcome book lovers, scholars, and researchers. Budget cuts for library acquisitions and library hours are counterbalanced in part by interlibrary loans and ambitious new library projects in public-spirited communities. Newsstands and large-chain bookstores bulge with an incredible range of print publications, from the classics of world literature and magnificent annotated historical atlases to recently published material catering to every possible special interest.

The Internet offers you a range of pathways to its vast resources of information, scholarship, research, and opinion. Your Internet search may take you to a **citation** index. The citation index lists sources that may prove relevant to your project and shows you where to find them. Listings may include brief **annotation**—a brief description of the material indexed. Others may include an **abstract**—a somewhat longer summary of contents.

Source: hispanicmagazine.com, April 2005 issue. Reprinted with permission from Hispanic Publishing Associates.

Full-text databases allow you to read or download complete texts of articles or reports—some available free of charge and others available to individual subscribers or through your college library. Watch for indications that a text or document has been abridged, excerpted, adapted, or otherwise modified.

Listing of an Article with Brief Annotation

Data include publishing date, numbers of volume and of issue, and page number:

ADWEEK Southeast, Oct. 7, 2002 v23 i40 p33(1)

An informed intolerance? (Anti-Islamic Sentiment). (poll asked people about efforts to learn about Islam) (Brief Article) *Mark Dolliver.*

Instructors and librarians will urge you to go beyond the first quick results of a search on the most popular search engines. If they are available to you at your college, sign up for library tours and pick up brochures on new or expanded resources. Read articles or promotional material on new incentives for users of rival search engines like Google and Yahoo!. Here is a preview of the range of resources:

JOURNALISTIC SOURCES   *Major newspapers, newsmagazines, magazines of opinion, and popular science magazines cover current issues for the general reader.* These publications are available on newsstands and in periodical rooms of many college libraries. They are increasingly available online, often with access to back issues in online **archives.** Readers can today compare different versions of events and developments in a range of national and international sources.

> EXAMPLES: Broad, William J., and Andrew C. Revkin. "Has the Sea
> Given Up Its Bounty?" *New York Times.* National Edition.
> 29 July 2003: A12.
> Holy, Norman. "Tangled in the Food Web." *Earth Island
> Journal* Jan. 2004: 25.

PROFESSIONAL AND SCHOLARLY PERIODICALS   *College libraries subscribe to a selection of scientific and scholarly journals.* Many of these are increasingly available online, although access may be subject to subscription fees or fees per use. These publications range in difficulty from material accessible to the educated layperson to technical material for the specialist.

> EXAMPLES: Withgott, Jay. "Sea Change for Oceans Policy?" *Science Now*
> 15 Feb. 2004: 1.
> Palumbi, Stephen R., and Joe Roman. "Counting Whales in
> the North Atlantic." *Science* 2 Jan. 2004: 39.

ON–SITE PRINT RESOURCES   *Today's computerized library catalogs lead you to the full range of holdings of a college library.* The shelves of your college library are likely to hold books providing essential background or updating of earlier coverage on your selected topic. They will hold both classics and recent publications in areas like biographies of leading figures in American history, breakthroughs in the history of science, or in-depth studies of threats to the environment. The following is an example of a book published by a university press:

> EXAMPLE: Miles, Edward, ed. *Management of World Fisheries: Implications of Extended Coastal State Jurisdiction.* Seattle: U of
> Washington P, 1989.

DATABASES   *Specialized databases cater to investigators for every major area of research.* Your instructor or librarian may direct you to specialized **databases** for areas like education, psychology, biology, business, or imaginative literature. These will guide you to expert technical or scholarly sources for an academic specialty or field of study. In addition, by subscribing to an electronic mailing list or listserver like *Fish Ecology Listserver,* you can tap into up-to-date information and join in a lively forum for discussion of issues related to your topic.

ACCESSING A DATABASE

Extending Your Range

The following are sample entries prepared by a college librarian encouraging students to tap into databases in areas like government, biography, business, or other cultures. The name of the database (like *WilsonWeb* or *Congressional Universe*) appears after the publishing data for the entry. It is usually followed by identification of the publisher of the database, such as Gale Group or LEXIS-NEXIS.

DuVall, J. "Liberation Without War." *Sojourners* Feb. 2004:20–3. *WilsonWeb.* H. W. Wilson Company. 31 March 2004 <http://vnweb.hwwilsonweb>.

"Tribute to the Late Honorable Barbara Jordan." *Congressional Record* 24 Jan. 1996. *Congressional Universe.* Congressional Information Service. 19 Nov. 2003 <http.//web.lexis-nexis.com/cong-comp/>.

"Barbara Jordan." *Notable Black American Women. Book I* Farmington Hills, MI: Gale Research, 1992. *Biography Resource Center.* The Gale Group. 22 Nov. 2003 <http://www.galenet com/servlet/BioRC>.

Mergent FIS. *Company Data Report: Borders Group. Inc.* 24 Jan. 1999. *Thomson Research.* Thomson Corporation. 19 Nov. 2003 <http://www.fisonline.com>.

"Afganistan: Leader of Shi'i Faction Elaborates on the Position of Women." *Voice of the Islamic Republic of Iran External Service* 22 June 1997. *Global Newsbank.* NevsBank Inc. 19 Nov. 2002 <http.//infoweb.newsbank.com>.

WEBSITES   *Institutions, organizations, and individuals create websites offering services and promoting agendas.* A website often has live **links** to a large range of supporting material. Numerous ecology-oriented websites keep users posted on conservation efforts to save endangered marine life or endangered bird species.

> EXAMPLE: The Ornithology Website
>
> <http://www.mgfx. com/bird/resource/index.html>

REFERENCE WORKS   *Reference books in weighty volumes in a reference library or online provide extensive background for your exploration of current questions.* Reference books like the *Encyclopedia Britannica* or the *Encarta* encyclopedia are available online or on CD-ROM. They allow you to call up an article by typing in a key word or a string of key words—or allow you to type in a question and click for the answer. Expert and well-written articles have multiple links to further information and background of a full range of subtopics. The following is an example of an entry from the *Encarta Online Encyclopedia:*

> EXAMPLE: Bird: Endangered Birds<http://encarta.msn.com>

EDITOR'S TIP!   When drawing on Internet sources, you need to record the Internet address or access line (URL) that leads either to a specific item or to the service or archives where the material was available. Access information often includes the date the item was first posted and the date it was last accessed.

> EXAMPLE: Catalana, Robin. "A Fish Story of Dioxins and Food Safety."
>   28 Jan. 2004: 3 Sept. 2004. <http:/www.epnet.com/>.

EVALUATING YOUR SOURCES   *Convince your readers that you have consulted authoritative, reliable sources.* While the quantity of material available electronically has vastly increased, its credibility or usefulness varies tremendously. At one pole are **referred** journal articles—material evaluated and approved for publication by impartial outside reviewers. At the other pole, you may encounter "rants and raves" bypassing the traditional intermediate layer of editors and reviewers. What are the credentials of the sources you are quoting? What are their qualifications or affiliations? What is an author's credibility?

EVALUATING SOURCES

A Checklist

When sifting and evaluating promising sources, ask yourself questions like the following:

✔ *Is the source an authority on the subject?* What is the author's track record? Does the author draw on first-hand investigation? Has the author written or lectured on the subject? Is the author associated with a prestige institution or influential organization? Is the author quoted or consulted by others?

✔ *Is the work a thorough study of the subject?* Does it recognize previous work in the field? Does it look in depth at case histories, relevant experiments, or key examples? Does it examine and explain detailed statistics?

✔ *Does the author turn to primary sources?* Reliable authorities often settle important questions by tracking **primary sources.** They may consult legal documents, diaries and letters, or transcripts of speeches. They may turn to interviews with eye witnesses or reports on experiments.

✔ *Is the source up to date?* Does it recognize recent research or new facts? If it was first published ten or fifteen years ago, has the author updated the findings—in a later study or in a revised edition of a book?

✔ *Is the source impartial, or is it biased?* What are the commitments or loyalties of the authors? Are you going to recognize a pro-business commitment in material from the U.S. Chamber of Commerce? Are you going to make allowance for a pro-labor stance in material from the AFL–CIO or other labor organization? How credible is research on the health hazards of smoking if it was funded by a tobacco company?

✔ *For an online source, can you verify authorship and status?* Where did it originate? How reliable or authentic is it? Has it been shortened, adapted, pirated, circulated anonymously? How long is it likely to be available?

Searching for Articles

Look for promising current material in periodical publications.

Since colonial times, Americans have cherished the freedom to print. They have protected and extended the right to print and disseminate without government supervision or censorship a wide range of newspapers, newsmagazines, magazines of commentary and opinion, science publications, and journals of scholarship and research in a wide variety of fields. The Internet has vastly extended the potential and the reach of print material appearing regularly and aimed at both the casual reader and a constituency of faithful subscribers.

KNOWING PERIODICAL RESOURCES   *Explore the range of regularly published print materials.* Periodical publications range from daily newspapers and weekly newsmagazines to science magazines for the educated general reader and to scientific and technical journals for the specialist. Periodicals may appear on a daily, weekly, monthly, or quarterly basis.

■ For authoritative news coverage and informed opinion, you may turn to leading national newspapers. Widely quoted newspapers of record pride themselves on high journalistic standards, insisting on verifiable sources for news stories and sanctioning contributors submitting dubious or faked materials. In addition to late-breaking news, they provide in-depth background studies, detailed book reviews, and commentary on the art world and popular culture. Highly rated national and regional newspapers may include:

New York Times

Washington Post

Christian Science Monitor

Los Angeles Times

Chicago Tribune

Boston Globe

More aggressively one–sided nationally known newspapers include the *Washington Times,* the *New York Post,* and the *Wall Street Journal.* Most major newspapers are now available online (often with additional or supplementary material) and indexed in the National Newspaper Index.

■ Ranging from the conservative to progressive, newsmagazines and journals of opinion include *U.S. News & World Report, Time, Newsweek, Atlantic, Commentary, New Republic, Harper's, Mother Jones, Nation,* or *Ms.* magazine. Cutting-edge publications like *Wired* or *MicroTimes* print much material of special interest to students of computer science and electronic communication.

■ You may turn to experts, scholars, or scientists writing for the educated general public in publications like *Popular Science, Scientific American, Psychology Today, Discover* magazine, or *National Geographic.* Popularized science or research results made accessible to an educated public build the bridge from the knowledge of the specialist to applied science and the decision making of a responsible informed public.

■ You may be drawing on material in scientific, technical, or scholarly journals in areas like psychology, sociology, medicine, history, or art. For a study of trends in juvenile crime you may find relevant source material in a journal like *Crime and Delinquency.* For many readers, the most widely respected source or information and commentary on issues raised by advances in medical research has been the *New England Journal of Medicine,* For a paper on the implications of current brain research, your sources might include articles in journals like *New Scientist, Neurology, Nature,* or *British Journal of Educational Psychology.*

SEARCHING FOR BEST RESULTS   *Search both the most popular search engines and specialized databases for best results.* Instructors and librarians will encourage you to go beyond the first set of entries that come up during a Google or Yahoo! search. Computerized **databases** for areas like education, humanities, social science, or general sciences give you an instant listing of articles from hundreds of periodical publications in a field of study or area of research. Databases in areas like government policy or medical research will guide you to articles published by experts or professionals in specialized fields. For instance, for a paper on how schools have dealt with challenges to bilingual education, you may turn to the Education Full-Text database.

A student's search for entries under the key phrase "hate speech" in the Social Sciences Full-text database called up a range of entries, all from refereed education and social science journals. All showed the icon indicating that the material was peer reviewed—evaluated and approved for publication by outside impartial authorities in the relevant field.

By typing in **key words** or **retrieval codes,** you can call up lists of sources on subjects like speech codes, child abuse, wage parity, or illegal immigration. You can call up book reviews, articles by or about a person, or information about an institution or company.

When you are researching progress toward gender equity in college sports, for instance, the computer will call up articles whose titles or texts include the words you have typed in as key words or as possible subject headings. Depending on the focus and capability of your search engine, the search may call up sources with occurrences of the key word in the title only, in the title and an abstract, or in the title and the full text. Very general headings may generate large numbers of possible articles, so try combinations that will help you zero in on relevant material. Be similarly flexible and resourceful when a search yields only limited results. Writing about careers for women, a student found some of what she wanted under "Women—Employment." However, she found "a real bonanza" under more specific headings like "Women—television industry," "Women judges," and "Women lawyers."

REVIEWING THE BOOLEAN SYSTEM   *Study variations of the Boolean system to help you navigate the Internet.* Search engines or databases use somewhat different guidance systems to channel and maximize your search.

HELP pages or HELP files will give you directions and specify capabilities or limits.

- **Whole phrase** signals enclose whole phrases in quotation marks or in parentheses—so that the computer will not search separately for the words making up the combined phrase. Some search engines will assume that words you typed together (like *affirmative action*) should be searched for as the whole phrase.

"women's physical education"
(gender parity) in sports

- **Truncation**—most often signaled by a star or asterisk (★)—makes the computer search for not only a key word like *college* but also other forms from the same root, like *colleges* or *collegiate*. Some databases do not allow truncation within a whole phrase.

women and athlet*
women and colleg* sports

- **Wildcard** signals will allow for internal variations of a word, such as *woman* and *women:*

wom?n teams

★ **Operators** like AND, OR, NOT narrow or extend your search.

(gender parity) or (gender equity) and sports
funding and (college sports)
(women sports) not profession*

SORTING SEARCH RESULTS

The HELP page or HELP link of your search engine or database may tell you how to instruct the computer to arrange search results. In what order should the identified texts or documents be listed? Here are some possibilities:

MOST RECENT DATE	The latest or most recent published items will appear first.
RELEVANCE	The published items using your search terms or retrieval terms most frequently will appear first.
FREQUENT USE	The published items most often called up by other users will come first.
AUTHOR LISTING	Published items will be listed alphabetically by the name of the first identified author. (Unsigned or anonymous articles will be listed separately alphabetically by title.)
LISTING BY SOURCE	Articles appearing in the same journal or magazine may be grouped together, with the journals or magazines appearing in alphabetical order.

A student researcher obtained a range of leads like the following from the National Newspaper Index when looking for early newspaper coverage of women's progress toward equity in sports. Look at the format:

- After the title, this database often includes a brief parenthetical note on the focus or key point of the article.
- It then tracks the exact location of the item: publication, volume number, section and page, column (with length of article in column inches).
- It then gives the author's name and possible subject headings under which the item may be catalogued.

Database: National Newspaper Index

Subject: sports for women

The girls against the boys; women have played pro ball before. But never against men. Is this exploitation, or feminism . . . or both? (Coors Silver Bullets; the first women's professional baseball team)

The Washington Post, April 24, 1994 v117 pF1 col 3 (82 col in).

Author: Laura Blumenfeld

Subjects: Baseball (Professional)—Analysis Women athletes—Competitions

Features: illustration, photograph

AN: 15207085

Often source information includes an **abstract**—a summary of the findings or ideas developed in an article. The following printout from a sports-centered database includes an abstract that could help you decide whether the source is worth following up:

SilverPlatter 3.11   SPORT Discus 1975 – June 1999

TI: Sport and the maintenance of masculine hegemony

AU: Bryson, -L

JN: Womens-studies-international-forum-(Elmsford, -N.Y.); 10(4), 1987, 349–360 Refs: 37

PY: *1987*

AB: Discusses two fundamental dimensions of the support that sport provides for masculine hegemony: 1) it links maleness with highly valued and visible skills, and 2) it links maleness with the positively sanctioned use of aggression/force/*violence*. Examines four social processes through which *women* are effectively marginalized in their sport participation—definition, direct control, ignoring, and trivialization—using examples from the sports scene in Australia. Concludes that *women* need to challenge the definition of sport, take control of women's sports, persistently provide information and reject attempts to ignore women's sport, and attack the trivialization of *women* in sport.

AN: 213623

EDITOR'S TIP!   Check years covered by your database—it may have started comprehensive indexing only in the early 90s. For articles published before the 1990s, you may have to search the multivolume print indexes in your library. The *Readers' Guide to Periodical Literature* indexes magazines for the general reader, from *Time* and *Newsweek* to *Working Woman, Science Digest,* and *Technology Review.* Other guides to periodicals for the general reader include:

Applied Science and Technology Index

Biological and Agricultural Index

Business Periodicals Index

Humanities Index

Social Sciences Index

RECORDING PUBLICATION DATA   *Record complete publishing data for all your sources.* As you track promising sources, start a computer file or card file recording complete data for each item. Include complete name of author, complete title of articles, name of periodical, date, and complete or inclusive page numbers. Where appropriate, record the section of a newspaper or the volume number of a magazine. For Internet sources, include both the original posting date and the access date, which often shows how recently the material was available. Include brief **annotation** as a reminder of why the source seems promising or useful. Source records annotated by you might look like this:

Holy, Norman. "Tangled in the Food Web." *Earth Island Journal* Jan. 2004:25.

　　The author highlights the key issues concerning the loss of seabirds as a result of the reduction in fish populations. He provides statistics on what percentage of fish, sea birds, and biomass from the North Sea is removed by fishing each year. He explains how the ecosystem has eroded during the past forty years at an alarming rate. According to researchers at the University of British Columbia, only about one-sixth of fish species that existed in the early 1900s are left.

Searching for Books

Look for background material or in-depth studies in books.
　　A book you find exceptionally useful may be a standard treatment of a subject like the the law of supply and demand or the threat to the remaining rain forests. It may be a challenge to a strong current of public opinion, like the push to harsher treatment for juvenile offenders. You can search for a book by its author, by its title, or by its subject. Data given on computer listings and traditional index cards are similar, although they may be laid out differently.

- When you have heard of a promising book, you can look for it under the author's name or under the title. For instance, you would look under *Thurow* or under *Head to Head* for Lester Thurow's *Head to Head: The Coming Economic Battle Among Japan, Europe, and America.*
- When still looking for useful sources, you may check under subject headings. For instance, if you had not heard of Thurow's book you might be looking for books with a similar focus under subject headings like ECONOMIC FORECASTING, GLOBAL ECONOMY, INTERNATIONAL ECONOMIC RELATIONS, U.S. ECONOMIC POLICY, JAPAN—ECONOMIC POLICY, OR TRADE WARS—U.S. AND JAPAN.

Computer entries may look like the following **author card.** The **call number** will direct you or a librarian to the right section and the right shelf in the library.

Call #: LB 2343.32 F54 1991

Author: Figler, Stephen K.

Title: Going the distance: the college athlete's guide to excellence on the field and in the classroom/by Stephen K. Figler. Princeton, N.J.: Peterson's Guides, 1991. xi, 208 p.: illus; 23 cm.

Notes: Includes bibliography: pp. 203–208.

Subjects: College student orientation—United States

College athletes—United States.

Author: Figler, Howard E.

As with articles, prepare **source entries** or source cards giving the complete publishing data of a book for your record of promising sources:

HQ

1426 Wolf, Naomi. *Fire With Fire: The New Female*

W565 *Power and How It Will Change the 21st Century.* New York: Random, 1993.

CONSULTING REFERENCE WORKS Reference works, ranging from multivolume sets to compact manuals, provide detailed authoritative background information on a vast range of subjects. Many reference works are now available online. You will find specialized reference works in a guide like Eugene P. Sheehy's *Guide to Reference Books,* published by the American Library Association. The following reference works are often consulted:

- *The New Encyclopedia Britannica* (now an American publication), updated each year by the *Britannica Book of the Year*
- The *Encyclopedia Americana* with its annual supplement, the *Americana Annual*
- The Microsoft *Encarta Encyclopedia*
- *Who's Who in America,* a biographical dictionary with capsule biographies of outstanding living men and women
- *Who's Who of American Women*
- *The Dictionary of American Biography (DAB)*
- *American Universities and Colleges and American Junior Colleges*
- *The McGraw-Hill Encyclopedia of Science and Technology,* kept up to date by the *McGraw-Hill Yearbook of Science and Technology*
- *The Encyclopedia of Computer Science and Technology*
- The *Dictionary of American History* by J. T. Adams (in six volumes)
- The *International Encyclopedia of the Social Sciences*

Taking Notes

Take ample accurate notes, so that you can select and adapt what is most useful later.

To record the materials for a research-based paper, you enter or copy useful materials for your computer file. Many writers download promising material to be quoted from or excerpted later. In printed out or hard copy text, they highlight key passages for future use. They keyboard quotations and key data accurately so that they can later paste them into an early draft of a paper, adapting them and integrating them as needed. Some writers may still use handwritten note cards, which they can shuffle and organize in the order in which they will use them in their first draft. Many writers draw on their personal archives of newspaper clippings and photocopies of whole magazine articles or key pages.

To assure maximum usefulness of your notes, remember:

- *Start each entry with a tag or descriptor.* Show where the material tentatively fits into your paper. For a paper on pre-Columbian cultures, use headings like the following:

```
AZTECS—sacrificial rites
AZTECS—light-skinned gods
INCAS—tribal wars
```

- *Try to limit each entry to closely related information.* If you limit each entry to a key point, you can move the entry around and feed it into your project at the right spot—without having to break up an entry ranging over different points.

- *Mark all direct quotation with quotation marks.* Distinguish clearly between direct quotation (material you are quoting exactly word for word) and paraphrase (where you put less important material in your own words, often in condensed form).

- *Make sure each note shows the exact source.* Include all publishing information you will need later: full names, titles and subtitles, publishers or publications, as well as dates and places. Record exact page numbers: the specific page or pages for a quotation, but also the *complete* page numbers for an article.

Here are sample entries from a computer file. The student writer was investigating perspectives on the rise in juvenile crime, recording essential background: early statistics documenting the rise in youth crime; definition of a key concept (youth gangs redefined); comments on the failure of conventional approaches.

JUVENILE CRIME—EARLY STATS
In 1981, youths were charged with 53,240 violent crimes. Ten years later, the figure was 104,137.
Federal Bureau of Justice

JUVENILE JUSTICE
Trying juvenile offenders as adults and locking them up for long periods of time "looks tough but is shortsighted." Institutions for adult criminals are useless when it comes to crime prevention or rehabilitation. "Juveniles in adult institutions are five times more likely to be sexually assaulted, twice as likely to be beaten by staff, and 50 percent more likely to be attacked with a weapon than youths in a juvenile facility." "Three different studies conducted over a ten-year period . . . show significantly higher recidivism rates for youths tried in adult courts compared to those tried in juvenile courts."
Michael E. Saucier, national chair of the Coalition for Juvenile Justice, speech before Congress March 1994.

REDEFINING GANGS
"Despite conventional thinking, gangs are not anarchies. They can be highly structured, with codes of honor and discipline. For many members, the gang serves as family, as the only place where they can find fellowship, respect, a place to belong. You often hear the world *love* among gang members. Sometimes the gang is the only place where they can find it." (p. 58)
Luis J. Rodriguez, "Rekindling the Warrior," *Utne Reader* July/August 1994, pp. 58–59.

Organizing Research Materials

Develop a working outline and expand and revise it as you sort your material.

Few research projects proceed as an entirely open search. You are likely to bring questions and tentative answers to your project. Key issues and important terms will keep surfacing in materials related to your topic. What questions will guide you as you sort out promising material?

- *What is going to be your focus?* Is there a central question or debated problem that you will promise to explore or clarify? Are you narrowing your topic to a key area that you can explore in depth?

- *What will be the point of your paper as a whole?* Are you ready to sum it up in a trial thesis? Are you prepared to adjust or refine your thesis when added evidence raises new questions or makes you scale down tentative generalizations?

- *What will be your organizing strategy?* How will you lay out your material so that your readers can follow? What should come first? How much background or perspective will your readers need? Will you cover two sides of the issue? Will you lead up to an important proposal or change in attitude?

- *What are tentative major stages or parts of your paper?* Are you beginning to file the material you are collecting under major headings or subheadings?

Organizing Your Computer File

Early in your search, start organizing your material under major headings.

Are youth gangs on the rise in your area or in your community? Assume that making this question your research question, you have started gathering material from key sources and background information to build a computer file. You have been careful to track who said what. How are you beginning to group your material under tentative major headings?

Headings like the following can set up a discovery frame that helps you guide promising material into tentative slots or subdivisions of your paper.

Youth Gangs on the Rise

FACTS—What were the actual facts of key incidents played up in media accounts? What answers do you find to basic "journalist's questions" like who, when, where, why, and how? What are rock-bottom facts you would expect to see included in a police report?

THE GANG SCENE—What do media reports and police reports tell you about the youth gangs and the gang lifestyle? Are there relevant statistics? Who has compiled or updated them? According to the reports, what are the typical behavior and activities of gang members?

EXPERT OPINION—What experts are being widely quoted? Who are they—social scientists, neighborhood activists, community leaders? What do they say about the causes of gang violence? What do they say about the motivation of gang members or the appeal of gangs?

AUTHORITIES—What is the role of the police and the justice system in these reports? What do you learn about the workings of the police and the legal system?

ORGANIZATIONS—Who other than the police and the courts is involved or concerned with gang violence? What citizen initiatives or community programs are described? How successful are they?

ISSUES—What is the role of racial or ethnic labeling or identification in these reports? How much does race or ethnicity matter for this topic? What can you learn about race or ethnicity of the newspaper sources, police sources, institutional or organizational sources?

TENTATIVE CONCLUSIONS—What are root causes? What are misunderstandings or damaging stereotypes? What can be done? What works? What is the responsibility of the community?

From Files to Outline

Early in your project, develop a working outline.

Fit the material you have collected under major headings into a tentative overall scheme. What are questions or points in your material that seem to come up again and again?

A student who investigated juvenile crime found much evidence of a trend toward treating juvenile criminals as adults. The following might be a sampling of early notes. What key points are beginning to stand out?

Juveniles Tried as Adults

news reports with titles like "Teen Gets Life Term" and "Tougher Treatment for Juveniles"

juveniles tried in adult courts and sent to adult jails

candidates for office accuse judges and rival candidates of being "soft on crime"

strong trend toward harsher sentences

growing impatience with and lack of sympathy for the young criminal

disillusionment with programs for rehabilitation or giving young people in trouble a second chance

A first **scratch outline** might be jottings lining up tentative points. The student's first scratch outline might look like this:

SCRATCH OUTLINE:

current get-tough mentality

sensationalizing juvenile crime

failure of "liberal" approaches

trying juveniles as adults

At this stage, the material pointed to a general conclusion like the following that could be summed up in a **trial thesis:**

TRIAL THESIS: **As the public lost patience with crime, juvenile offenders were prime targets for harsher treatment.**

Trying to counteract the pessimism reflected in many sources, the student writer made an effort to look at the other side. Were there hopeful signs of more emphasis on prevention and rehabilitation? Were there newspaper reports about priests, teachers, or counselors trying to keep young people out of jail or out of gangs? Would a computer search yield articles with titles like "Jails or Jobs?" or "Alternatives to Hard Time"? Would members of the college faculty who have worked with troubled adolescents consent to be interviewed?

The following could be the revised and expanded **working outline.** The new, more positive emphasis would be reflected in a revised thesis:

WORKING OUTLINE

Getting Tough with Juveniles

THESIS: **Although juvenile offenders are prime targets of a "get-tough" approach to crime, the search continues for approaches promising prevention and rehabilitation.**

I   Conservative current climate
    current get-tough mentality
    sensationalizing juvenile crime
    perceived failure of liberal approaches

II Getting tough on juveniles
    trying juveniles as adults
    harsh sentencing

III Searching for alternatives
    emphasis on prevention
        education
        job training
    emphasis on rehabilitation
        counseling
        work camps

From Sources to Draft

Work material from your files or notes smoothly into your early draft.

How do you develop an early draft? As you follow your working outline, you feed in material from your note-taking and data-gathering. An effective paper weaves the material from your files or notes into your text to support your key points. It brings in the right kind of material to explain, illustrate, or defend the general points you present or the claims you make. For any point you make, imagine a reader who asks: "What made you think so? Where are the supporting data? Where are the witnesses, authorities, or concerned citizens who testify on this?"

Many writers start at the beginning and work their way through their tentative outline step by step. Other writers draft first the sections for which they feel best prepared or most confident. They then fill in the more difficult or more challenging sections later. Still other writers try to tackle the most challenging sections first, knowing that then the less difficult sections will be easier to complete.

USING YOUR SOURCES   *Make the best possible use of the fruits of your search.* As you report on the progress of your project to your instructor or your peers, can you explain where and how you are using your research materials? The following might be a fellow student's **progress report** showing the intended use of sources. The student is working on a detailed update of the issue of racial profiling—police sweeps or security checks singling out people pegged by color, race, ethnicity, or apparent foreign origin.

Racial Profiling and the Color Blind

1 A **case history** from a detailed current newspaper study dramatizes the issue and brings it into focus.

2 The introductory case history leads into the central thesis, buttressed by a **key quotation** from a defense attorney specializing in cases of false arrest and imprisonment without charges or access to counsel.

3 Two detailed **follow-up examples** of racial profiling from the Associated Press and another national news source help document the widespread use of the challenged practice.

4 The second of the follow-up examples leads into **"get-tough" commentary** from two aggressive law-and-order media sources—with a mix of direct quotation and paraphrase.

5 At the halfway point, the paper will reach its turning point: The constitutional issue will be presented and explained, with direct quotation from a **primary source:** the Fourth Amendment to the Constitution barring unreasonable "search and seizure." Two university-based **legal scholars** present careful and cautious statements examining implications and possible legal applications.

6 A statement from an active **civil rights organization** (ACLU—American Civil Liberties Union) makes the charge of racism overt and makes a strong point in the defense of civil liberties of those "hassled."

7 Statistics from **research reports**—one from a university-based institute and one from an independent think tank—back up the charges of
discrimination in police and Justice Department practices.

8 The conclusion tracks recent **court decisions** and leads up to the final
destination for many similar confrontations: the courts.

INTEGRATING YOUR SOURCE MATERIAL   *Know how to work
data and quoted material smoothly into your text.* Aim at the right mix of word-
for-word quotation and paraphrase. Know when to summarize and when
to zoom in on telling or revealing supporting detail.

In **direct quotation,** you copy material verbatim—word for word.
You put the author's exact words in quotation marks. You signal all omis-
sions—by an ellipsis of three spaced periods (four if it includes a sentence-
ending period). You signal your own added comments—by square brackets. In a **paraphrase,** you use *in*direct quotation. You put the author's ideas
and information into your own words—no quotation marks. Often words
like *that, why,* or *how* introduce indirect quotations:

DIRECT: The candidate for mayor said, "**If elected, I promise to make
the homeless people on our city streets my top priority.**"

INDIRECT: The candidate for mayor promised **that if elected she would
make the homeless on the city's streets her top priority.**

■ You will often use direct quotation for a key idea, a central thesis,
or an important claim. Use a sentence or more of direct quotation to highlight a strong personal statement. Quote at first hand a controversial idea
that might make a reader say: "Are you sure this is what the person said?"

DIRECT QUOTATION

Advocates of recovery groups claim that almost everyone is in some
sense a victim—mostly, of abusive parents. "**What we are hearing from the experts,**" John Bradshaw told an interviewer, "**is that approximately 96 percent
of the families in this country are dysfunctional to one degree or another.**"

■ When you paraphrase, you put what someone said or wrote into
your own words. Paraphrase gives you greater flexibility than direct quotation. You can shorten a long passage, highlighting key points. You can clarify technical information by translating it into accessible language. Even in
an extended paraphrase, you may include short quoted phrases for an authentic touch.

ALL PARAPHRASE

Sandra Benares, producer-director of documentaries, discussed the dilemmas of reproducing the language of the past in documentaries dealing with racial themes. **For Mark Twain's Huckleberry Finn, Huck's friend and fellow runaway, an escaped slave, is, in the language of the time, N—— Jim. Mark Twain did not mean the use of the N-word to brand Huck as a racist. Huck and Jim are best friends, on the run from a brutal society. Should a scriptwriter or director leave the N-word out?**

PARAPHRASE WITH PARTIAL QUOTE

As David Rieff says in a *Harper's* article on the recovery movement, Americans have always felt that they can make themselves over to become something new. The great American tales are about busting loose. Their heroes find a way **"of shucking off the bonds of family and tradition,"** striking out for new territories in order to achieve a new identity.

Review the way experienced writers *introduce* material from their sources. Who said this and where? Use the basic "Author X said . . . ," Remember that after a tag like "He says" or "the author states," a colon may replace the more usual comma before a long or especially weighty quotation. However, draw on the full range of other **credit tags,** or introductory phrases:

CREDIT TAGS

According to Julie Ayer, a violist with the Minnesota Orchestra, "Until the 1960s, if you were a woman who wanted to play in a major orchestra, your best chance was to take up the harp."

To quote psychologist Hilda Ignes, "Neurosis is the condition where an individual's emotional elevators go to top floor when least desired."

As Judith Guest says in *The Mythic Family*, "I have often been asked why it is that I only write about dysfunctional families. The answer that comes to mind is, what other kinds are there?"

In the words of journalist Ray Moynihan, writing in the *British Medical Journal*, researchers "with close ties to drug companies work with colleagues in the pharmaceutical industry to develop and define new categories of human illness."

Often you will include **credentials** of a source in your credit tag. What makes the quoted person credible or an authority worth listening to? What are the person's credentials?

AUTHOR CREDENTIALS

Ann Smith, director of a Pennsylvania family service clinic, wrote *Grandchildren of Alcoholics* to "bring this group of people out of hiding and into recovery."

Cynthia Tucker, editorial page editor for the the *Atlanta Journal-Constitution,* asked questions facing African Americans in the post-civil rights era: "How do we raise the academic achievement of black students? How do we curb black-on-black crimes?"

Review ways of weaving quoted material into your text. At some points in your paper, you may be using input from a *single source,* pulling from your notes the most important or relevant parts. Here is a sample paragraph, drawing extensively on an article by a *New York Times* reporter.

PARAGRAPH DRAWING ON ONE SOURCE

Individuals who work closely with juvenile criminals often support the idea of providing guidance and discipline. Being in close contact with young offenders, they come to know their motives and their needs. For instance, **Justice Michael A. Corriero, a member of the New York State Supreme Court in Manhattan,** tries to balance the need for punishment or deterrence with concern for the future life of the young offender. As Jan Hoffman of the *New York Times* reports, "**Judge Corriero** provides juvenile offenders hope for rehabilitation." **Corriero** gives juveniles the chance to earn a lighter sentence by placing them in "community-based intensive supervisory programs." **In the judge's view,** juveniles should not receive permanent felony conviction records—criminals convicted in adult courts have permanent records—since the juvenile "can't get a job with a felony conviction." And if the juvenile cannot contribute to society, **Judge Corriero asks,** "Have we really protected society?" ("Punishing Youths" B1).

Often, you will be pulling together related material from *several sources* to support a point. You will bring together or correlate input from a range of source material. The following sample paragraph integrates material from three different sources:

PARAGRAPH DRAWING ON SEVERAL SOURCES

The justice system is generally moving toward trying juvenile offenders in adult courts. Marvin Owens of Virginia Beach, Virginia, was sentenced to life imprisonment by **Circuit Judge Robert B. Cromwell Jr.** after a jury convicted Marvin of capital murder in the "execution-style slayings of his grandmother, a half-brother, and two cousins" ("Teen Gets Life" B7). Kevin Stanford was seventeen years old when he murdered Baerbel Poor in Jefferson County, Kentucky. After he had been transferred from juvenile court to adult court, the jury convicted Stanford of murder and sentenced him to death. When his case was appealed to the Supreme Court, **Justice Scalia,** in announcing the majority opinion, said that sentencing juvenile offenders to death did not violate the Eighth Amendment (*Stanford v. Kentucky* 316). **A survey of 250 judges conducted by Penn and Schoen Associates** and published in the *National Law Journal* found that "40 percent of the judges said the minimum age for facing murder charges should be 14 or 15, while 17 percent said it should be even lower, 12 or 13." ("Tougher Treatment" A16).

Use **block quotations** (four lines or more indented an inch or ten spaces, *no* quote marks) for special occasions. For instance, give an author a chance to state a key position with important ifs and buts or to record mixed feelings on a difficult subject:

BLOCK QUOTATION

Women have found it difficult to find affectionate or friendly terms that do not smack of traditional male condescension, like calling someone "sweetheart" or "honey." Kate Rounds, an editor at *Ms.* magazine, talks about the difficulty of finding a more friendly term than the formal *woman:*

> On a recent visit to a college campus, I was terrified by a big sign reading, "Women are not 'guys'!" For some time, I'd been using "guys" instead of "women," knowing I was offending the feminist language police. So I knew I'd have to watch my mouth during this visit. (96)

Revising

Budget time to revise early drafts in response to feedback or your own further investigation.

How much time will you have in your schedule for revising and rethinking?

BASIC REVISION STRATEGIES *Find time to address basic revision needs.* Some basic revision strategies are helpful when you revise a paper that has brought together a large amount of information. As you reread a draft, keep basic questions for revision in mind. Look at your writing through the eyes of a reader who has to take in a large body of material and follow your lead through several major stages:

- Have you done enough to define the central issue or bring your key question into focus?
- Have you adjusted your thesis to make it reflect what you learned later in your project? May it have changed your thinking?
- Have you done enough to set directions for your reader, creating expectations that your paper as a whole will meet?
- Have you done enough to show the connections between major sections of your paper?
- Have you done enough to introduce quotations and other supporting evidence? How do they fit in? What are they supposed to prove?

CHECKLIST FOR REVISION

Basic Revision Needs

✓ *Strengthen the overall framework.* Do not allow the reader to feel lost as facts, quotations, and details accumulate. Can you make major stages of your paper stand out more clearly? Can you signal the major steps in your argument more clearly to make them easier to follow?

✓ *Strengthen transitions.* Highlight connections between one part of the paper and the next. Insert a logical link like *however, on the other hand,* or *finally* at strategic points to clarify the connection between two ideas.

✓ *Revise for clear attribution.* Who said what? Who furnished statistics or background information? Repeat the name of a quoted author if a *he* or *she* might point to the wrong person.

✓ *Integrate undigested chunk quotations.* Check for a good mix of direct quotation, paraphrase for less important points, and summary of background information. If you have too many block quotations, break them up. Work partial quotations into your own text for a smoother flow.

✓ *Do a final check of documentation style.* Teachers and editors of research-based writing are sticklers for detail. Follow instructions for formatting the paper: running heads, indentation, spacing, capitals, colons, parentheses, quotations marks, and the like exactly as the style guide for your class or for your publication says.

REVISING AND RETHINKING *Consider major revision when appropriate.* To complete a major research effort, you may have to do more than strengthen and fine-tune your draft. You may be asked to build up a section you passed over too quickly, or you may need to address a major objection you overlooked. You may have to consider a change in strategy or a reordering of material.

By grouping material from sources under major headings, a writer will often already be setting up categories that may later become major sections of a paper. The outline of a finished draft may still reflect roughly the order in which the writer discovered promising material. Here is a search report on the controversy concerning Father Junipero Serra, a leading figure in the early missionary efforts designed to convert the Native Americans of California when the region was under Spanish rule.

SEARCH REPORT

Junipero Serra: The Controversy

RAISING THE ISSUE:

When Pope John Paul II in 1987 beatified Serra, this was the second of three steps necessary for the Church's awarding of formal sainthood.

OFFICIALLY APPROVED HISTORY:

The Online edition of the *Catholic Encyclopedia,* in an entry first prepared in 1912, praises Serra's "extraordinary fortitude," his "insatiable zeal, love of mortification, self-denial," and his executive abilities.

WEBSITES SHOWING VENERATION OF SERRA:

Recently accessed websites include home pages of churches named after Serra (one as recently as 1988) and range from the Serra Club of Bethlehem, Pennsylvania, to the Padre Serra Parish in Camarillo, California.

BALANCING PRO AND CON:

An entry on a PBS (Public Broadcasting System) website *New Perspectives on the West* summed up both the charges against Serra triggered by the papal initiatives and the arguments in his defense. Many Native Americans and academics condemned the initiatives, pointing to the harsh conditions of mission life and Serra's own justification of beatings and abuse. Defenders of Serra cited the context of his times, his personal sacrifices and religious zeal, and his opposition to punitive military expeditions against the Native Americans.

REEXAMINING THE MISSIONARY EFFORT

Descendants of the California tribes say that the missions were "labor camps" that destroyed a rich Native American culture "complex in its beliefs and traditions" and with an economic system ensuring "that even the poorest had access to resources." Father Serra "knew wherever the Spanish went, there would be death. He was not a demon, but he endorsed and administered a system that restrained people and executed people. He . . . believed that lives were less important than souls."

DEFENSE AGAINST CRITICISM

Defenders of the church position say that missionaries helped to improve the lives of the natives. They introduced the agricultural system of raising crops and livestock. "The Indians certainly faced terrible hardship" but "we must remember we are looking at it through a twentieth century viewpoint." We need to take into account "the societal norms towards unknown civilizations of the time" and that the missionaries saw themselves as responsible for the "care of the souls of the Natives for their salvation."

The outline for an early draft closely mirroring the search history for this project may have looked like this:

ORIGINAL OUTLINE

A Flawed Saint

- officially approved history
- evidence of current veneration of Serra
- balancing pro and con
- charges against Serra
- refutation of charges

Responding to feedback, the writer may decide on a revision effort responding to queries from readers. First of all, the revised version would highlight criticism of Serra from his own time, so that the current questions about Serra's role will not seem the hindsight of today's generation. They would not just seem to apply today's standards retroactively to the past. Furthermore, the revised and adjusted outline would keep the defenders of Serra from having the last word in a controversy that is still an open question in the minds of many readers. A reorganizing of key sections would allow the paper to conclude with a careful sizing up of the controversy by today's descendants of the Native American tribes that became part of the mission system:

REVISED OUTLINE

Junipero Serra: Updating the Controversy

THESIS: Father Junipero Serra is considered a saint by some, but to others he was a man who used brutal methods to advance a religion that was trying to survive in a new world.

- overview of the controversy
- background for Serra's life and work
- criticism of Serra from his own time
- defense of Serra from church sources
- testimony from descendants of the California tribes

Preparing the Documented Paper

Research-based writing requires you to follow an established format and provide full documentation.

From the start of your project, keep a complete record of where you found your research material. When you bring together the best current data and thinking on your subject, you may be asked to provide full **documentation.** You will need to have available complete source information and access information. Both you and your readers will need to be able to "return to the source"—to retrace your steps. Documentation is for readers who may want to check things out for themselves. They may want to see whether you have drawn on reliable and up-to-date sources. They should be able to verify the use you have made of your sources checking whether you have used them fairly and accurately.

Your files or notes should enable you to answer questions about your full range of sources:

PERIODICAL SOURCE *What will lead your reader to the right issue of a magazine or newspaper and the right page?* If a quotation came from a magazine article, what was the full name of the author? What was the exact title of the article or selection? What was the title of the publication where the article appeared? What was the date of the issue and the page number? What were the inclusive page numbers for a whole article? For a technical or professional journal, was there a special volume number (for a yearly set of issues) or a number for a specific issue? If you are quoting a newspaper story or editorial, is the journalist or columnist identified? What was the edition—for instance, morning or evening, national or regional? What was the section of the paper?

BOOK SOURCE *What will lead the reader to the right book and the right page?* In what book did you find the material or the information? Did it have one author or several authors? Who published it—where and when? Was the book assembled, edited, or translated by someone other than the author or authors? Is it an updated or revised edition? On what page (or pages) did this passage occur?

ONLINE SOURCE *If you found the material online, how much informa- tion do you have about its source?* Are authors or editors identified? Did the material first appear in print and was then republished online? What is the **Internet address** (URL) that will lead the reader to the online source? Is this material associated with an institution, agency, or organization? (Source lines ending in **.edu** or **.org** may point to an institution or organization rather than to a private or commercial "dot-com" source. A source line ending in **.gov** will point to a government or official agency source.)

Who created or maintained a website you visited? When was this ma- terial first posted and when did you last access it?

NONPRINT SOURCE *What is the source of your oral or visual material?* Input from nonprint sources may include material from interviews, radio and television programs, or lectures. Do you have the name and the date if you interviewed or consulted an expert, eyewitness, or insider? Can you give the names of director, sponsor, or key participants for material from a television program or series? Do you have the name of the speaker, spon- sor, and occasion for part of a lecture series? Do you have names of pho- tographers or artists, identity of sponsors, location, or dates for images?

Recognizing Documentation Styles

When writing a documented paper, pay special attention to format and style.

Documentation styles vary from one area of study to another. The source information you need to record is often similar or identical. How- ever, you format or package it differently for a different audience or acad- emic community. Areas across the curriculum use different systems of cod- ing information about sources.

- For papers in the humanities (English, philosophy), you will usually be asked to follow the documentation style of the Modern Lan- guage Association, outlined in the frequently updated *MLA Hand- book for Writers of Research Papers* (Sixth Edition, 2003).

- For papers in the social sciences—sociology, psychology, educa- tion—you will usually follow the APA style, outlined in the *Publi- cation Manual of the American Psychological Association* (Fifth Edition, 2001).

- For papers in the natural sciences, you may be required to follow the style of the Council of Biology Editors (CBE), the American Institute of Physics (AIP), or the American Chemical Society (ACS).

- For technical writing, you may be consulting a reference like the Microsoft *Manual of Style for Technical Publications*.

FIND IT ON THE WEB

Guides to Documentation Styles

For updates or finer points, you may check guides to documentation styles on the World Wide Web:

"Citation Style Guides/Citing Sources." American University Library <http://www.library.american.edu/e_ref/citation.html>

"Internet Citation Guides: Citing Electronic Sources in Research Papers and Bibliographies." University of Wisconsin-Madison. Memorial Library <http://www.memorial.library.wisc.edu/citing.htm>

Documenting Your Sources—MLA Style

Recognize basic features of the MLA style.
The MLA style provides specific guidelines for formatting your paper: No separate title page is necessary unless your instructor requires it. Use **double spacing** throughout, including in block quotations. Include **running heads** flush right at the top of every page, using your last name or short name followed by the page number: ***Caracolla 2.*** Continue consecutive numbering of running heads to the end, including pages for your source list or separate pages (headed "Notes") for special explanatory or background notes.

For documenting sources, the MLA style uses a two-track or two-tier system. It gives brief data (mostly page numbers) in parentheses in your text. It saves full publishing data for a final source list of "Works Cited" at the end.

- *In the paper itself, use parenthetical documentation.* In **parenthetical documentation,** you give exact page references in parentheses. You may also have to include quick abbreviated identification of sources where it is needed. However, leave complete identification of sources till the end. (No more footnotes, although footnotes may still be a part of other documentation styles.)

■ *At the end of your paper, furnish an alphabetic source list.* In your final source list, labeled **Works Cited,** you give complete information about your sources. Observe the rules for how to arrange the data and how to punctuate the entries. Study the way parentheses, quotation marks, underlining, colons, and other punctuation features are used in sample passages and sample entries. Double-checking details from the beginning will protect you from time-consuming and frustrating backtrackings later.

■ *Distinguish between complete publications and articles or other selections that are part of a larger whole.* Underline or italicize the titles of books and other complete publications: The Color Purple or *The Color Purple.* The *MLA Handbook* still requires **underlining** (underscoring) instead of italics for titles. Underlining tells a printer typesetting the material to italicize the underlined part. Your instructor may tell you whether to use underlining or italics in your paper. (Use italics for desktop publication or for camera-ready copy that goes directly to printing or photocopying.)

■ *Use underlining or italics for the whole and quotation marks for the part.* Put in quotation marks the titles of poems, articles, and other pieces that are parts of a publication: "A Woman by Any Other Name" (the title of magazine article); "Stopping by Woods" (a poem that is part of a larger collection).

■ *Follow current advice on how to credit electronic sources.* For online sources, include the **publication date**—the date the item was originally published or posted. Follow it with the **access date**—the date you accessed the source, downloading it or using it in your work. Put the **URL** or Internet address between **angled brackets.** Try to have the whole URL on the same line, or break it only after a period or a slash. Remember that URLs are like telephone numbers. They work only if every digit is exactly right.

Here is an entry for an item from news reports on foreign students and visitors caught in the 9/11 backlash:

Markelyn, Mary Beth. "Deadline Nears for Foreign Student Database." USA Today. 19 Jan. 2003. 12 May 2004.
<http://www.usatoday.com/news/nation/2003-01-19.htm>.

PARENTHETICAL DOCUMENTATION *Use parenthetical documentation mainly for page numbers but also for other information if needed.* Preferably, name author and publication in your running text. This way you make it clear who said what and who contributed what. You will then usually have to give only page numbers in parentheses. However, look at some of the other possibilities:

■ Use a simple *page reference* when you have identified the source: Octavio Paz has called the meeting of the Indian and the Spaniard the key to the Mexican national character (138).

- Give the *author's name* with the page reference when you have *not* identified the source:

A prominent Latin American writer has called the meeting of the Indian and the Spaniard the key to the Mexican national character (Paz 138).

- Identify *more than one author* if you have not mentioned them earlier:

Tests and more tests have often been a substitute for adequate funding for our schools (Hirsenrath and Briggers 198).

- Give an abbreviated title added when you quote more than one source *by the same author:*

Lin, who has called the homeless problem the result of "social engineering in reverse" ("Homeless" 34), examines current statistics in an indictment of official neglect (*On the Street* 78–81).

- Identify a source you found quoted by someone else:

Steinbeck said he admired "strong, independent, self-reliant women" (qtd. in Barnes 201).

- For a reference to a preface or other introductory material, give page numbers as lowercase roman numerals:

In his preface to *The Great Mother,* Neumann refers to the "onesidedly patriarchal development of the male intellectual consciousness" (xliii).

EDITOR'S TIP!   References to the Bible typically cite chapter and verse instead of page numbers (Luke 2.1). References to a Shakespeare play usually cite act, scene, and line (*Hamlet* 3.2.73–76). After block quotations, a parenthetical page reference *follows* a final period or other terminal mark. (See sample paper for examples.)

MODEL ENTRIES FOR WORKS CITED–MLA *Recognize features that set the MLA documentation style apart from styles for other areas of study.*

When you prepare your final list of Works Cited, you are following a distinctive required format. Indent the *second line* of an entry half an inch or five spaces. Leave only *one space* after periods marking off chunks of information. Abbreviate the *names of months* with more than four letters (Mar., Apr.) Abbreviate the names of publishers: "Houghton" for Houghton Mifflin; "Oxford UP" for Oxford University Press.

A CHECKLIST FOR

Works Cited—MLA Style

Know distinctive features of the MLA documentation style:

✓ first line of entry flush left, next line or lines indented

✓ author's last name first (Clinton, Hillary)

✓ full first names when used by authors—not just initials

✓ quotation marks for article or other part of a publication ("The Raven")

✓ underlining (or italics) for complete publication (Researching Online)

✓ normal use of capitals as in other titles (The Grapes of Wrath)

✓ no articles (*The, A,* or *An*) before names of publications (New York Times)

✓ months abbreviated if more than four letters (Jan., Mar., Sept.)

✓ names of publishers shortened (Houghton for Houghton Mifflin)

✓ complete page numbers for articles (do not use *p.* or *pp.*)

✓ Internet address or URL in angled brackets (<. . . . .>)

A   Entries for Periodicals—newspapers, magazines, journals

1 NEWSPAPER ARTICLE   For a signed article, include the author's name, with the last name first: **Berthelsen, Christian.** Put the the title of the article in quotation marks: "**Watchdog Agency Faces Budget Cuts.**" Underline or italicize the name of the newspaper: **Sacramento Bee.** Give the date and page numbers: **27 May 2004: 3.**

You may have to specify the section of the newspaper with the page number, such as **B3** or **D4.** You may have to identify a special edition: **Late ed.** or **National ed.** The + sign shows that an article is continued later in the same issue.

Ramirez, Pedro. "Drivers' Licenses for Illegal Immigrants." Central Valley
    Times 21 Mar. 2005: C11–12.

Ryan, Joan. "Race Divides Our English into Dialects." San Francisco Chronicle.
    Peninsula ed. 16 May. 2004: B1+.

2 UNSIGNED ARTICLE   Start with the title of the article. List it alphabetically by the first word of the title (not counting *The, A,* and *An*).

"City Lights Bookstore Becomes Landmark." San Francisco Chronicle 29 June
    2001: A22.

3 MAGAZINE ARTICLE   Include author (last name first), title of article, and name of publication. Give the date with complete page numbers.

Packer, George. "The Playing Field." New Yorker 30 Aug. 2004: 42–46.

Foote, Stephanie. "Our Bodies, Our Lives, Our Right to Decide." The Humanist
    July/August 1992: 2–8+.

4 ARTICLE WITH SUBTITLE   Include the subtitle after a colon.

Cox, Craig. "Corporate Playland: Mexico City's Adventure in Marketing to
    Niños and Niñas." Utne Reader Mar./Apr. 2001: 30.

5 ARTICLE WITH SEVERAL AUTHORS   Put last name first for only the first author listed. For more than three authors, you may decide to list all co-authors if the names seem important. Or you may decide to use et al. (no italics) for "and others."

McChesney, Robert W., and John Nichols. "Getting Serious about Media
    Reform." Nation 7 Jan. 2002: 11–17.

Martz, Larry, et al. "A Tide of Drug Killings." Newsweek 16 Jan. 1989: 44–45.

6 ARTICLE WITH VOLUME NUMBER   Include the volume number for a scholarly or technical periodical with continuous page numbering through a set of several issues—usually the issues for one year.

Steele, Shelby. "White Guilt." American Scholar 59 (1990): 497–506.

7 ARTICLE WITH VOLUME AND ISSUE   For a professional journal with separate page numbering for each issue of the same volume, give both the volume number and the number of the issue:

Winks, Robin W. "The Sinister Oriental Thriller: Fiction and the Asian Scene."
    Journal of Popular Culture 19.2 (1985): 49–61.

8 SIGNED AND UNSIGNED EDITORIAL   List a signed editorial under the editor's name. List an unsigned editorial under the first word of the title (not counting *The, A,* and *An*). Identify the entry as an editorial.

Kramer, Janet. "Focus on Magnet Schools." Editorial. Oakland News 12 Mar.
    2000: C3.

"Lemons in a Row." Editorial. New York Times National Ed. 13 July 2004:
    A18.

9 LETTER TO THE EDITOR Give the name of the letter writer. Include the title of the letter if available. Identify the entry as a letter.

Vandesi, Myrtle. "The Vanishing Monarch Habitats." Letter. <u>San Jose Mercury News</u> 25 Aug. 2004: C4.

10 BOOK REVIEW Start an unsigned review with the abbreviation Rev. for "review." For a signed review, include the reviewer's name and also any title for the review.

Rev. of <u>The Penguin Book of Women Poets</u>, ed. Carol Cosman, Joan Keefe, and Kathleen Weaver. <u>Arts and Books Forum</u> May 1990:17–19.

Lemann, Nicholas. "Lost in Post-Reality." Rev. of <u>Life the Movie: How Entertainment Conquered Reality</u> by Neal Gabler. <u>Atlantic</u> Jan. 1999: 97–101.

11 QUOTED MATERIAL IN TITLE If a title is enclosed in double quotations mark, use single quotation marks for quoted material within the title.

Will, George. "'Soft Money' Sheltered by Bill of Rights." <u>Washington Post</u> 3 Jan. 2001: 28.

B Entries for Books

12 STANDARD ENTRY FOR A BOOK Include basic publishing data: place of publication, publisher's name, and year. Use shortened or abbreviated names of publishers: *Prentice* for Prentice Hall, Inc., *Princeton UP* for Princeton University Press:

Tan, Amy. <u>The Kitchen God's Wife</u>. New York: Putnam's, 1991.

Hudson, Kathleen. <u>Telling Stories, Writing Songs</u>. Austin: U of Texas P, 2001.

13 BOOK WITH SUBTITLE Add subtitle after a colon.

Tyler-Graw, Marie. <u>At the Falls: Richmond, Virginia, and Its People</u>. Chapel Hill: U of North Carolina P, 1994.

Reed, Adolph, Jr. <u>Class Notes: Posing as Politics and Other Thoughts on the American Scene</u>. New York: New Press, 2000.

14 COAUTHORED BOOK For a coauthored article or book, put the last name first for the first author only. For more than three authors, you may decide to use *et al.* (not italics) for "and others." However, you may list all coauthors of an important work.

Fischer, Claude S., et al. <u>Inequality by Design: Cracking the Bell Curve Myth</u>.
Princeton: Princeton UP, 1996.

Fischer, Claude S., and Michael Hout, Martín Sánchez Jankowski, Samuel R.
Lucas, Ann Swidler, and Kim Voss. <u>Inequality by Design: Cracking the Bell
Curve Myth</u>. Princeton: Princeton UP, 1996.

15 WORKS BY SAME AUTHOR For an additional entry by the
same author, substitute three hyphens for the author's name:

Steinem, Gloria. <u>Outrageous Acts and Everyday Rebellions</u>. New York: Holt,
1983.

—. <u>Revolution from Within: A Book of Self-Esteem</u>. Boston: Little Brown,
1992.

16 EDITED BOOKS Name the editor (or editors) of material
edited or collected by someone other than the author or authors. Use the
abbreviation *ed.* or *eds.* For work by a single author, put an editor's name
after the title.

Shockley, Ann Allen, ed. <u>Afro-American Women Writers 1746–1933: An Anthology and Critical Guide</u>. Boston: G.K. Hall, 1988.

Barrett, Eileen and Mary Cullinan, eds. <u>American Women Writers: Diverse
Voices in Prose Since 1845</u>. New York: St. Martin's, 1992.

Dickinson, Emily. <u>The Complete Poems of Emily Dickinson</u>. Ed. Thomas H.
Johnson. Boston: Little, Brown, 1978.

17 TRANSLATED BOOK Name the translator for material translated from another language:

Freire, Paulo. <u>Pedagogy of the Oppressed</u>. Trans. Myra Bergman Ramos. New
York: Seabury, 1970.

18 NEW OR REVISED EDITION Add 2nd ed. or Rev. ed. for a
later edition of a book:

Guth, Hans P., and Gabriele L. Rico, eds. <u>Discovering Literature: Stories, Poems, Plays</u>. 3rd ed. Upper Saddle River, NJ: Prentice: 2003.

19 SPECIAL IMPRINT Identify a special imprint or special line of
books of a publisher, like the Vintage Books published by Random House.

Acosta, Oscar Zeta. <u>The Revolt of the Cockroach People</u>. New York: Vintage-
Random, 1989.

20 PART OF A COLLECTION Include complete page numbers for an article, poem, or other selection that is part of a *collection* or anthology:

Gutierrez, Irene. "A New Consciousness." <u>New Voices of the Southwest</u>. Ed.
　　Laura Fuentes. Santa Fe: Horizon, 1992. 123–34.

When you list several articles from the same collection, you may choose to list the whole collection as a separate entry in your Works Cited. You then also list the individual selections. You **cross–reference** them to the whole collection, giving simply the editor's name but also showing the complete page numbers. Items like the following would appear in appropriate alphabetical order in your Works Cited:

Aufderheide, Patricia, ed. <u>Beyond PC: Toward a Politics of Understanding</u>.
　　St. Paul, MN: Graywolf, 1992.
Boyte, Harry C. "The Politics of Innocence." Aufderheide 177–79.
D'Souza, Dinesh. "The Visigoths in Tweed." Aufderheide 11–22.

21 WORK IN SEVERAL VOLUMES Specify the volume if you have used only one. If you have used more than one, list the whole multivolume work.

Woolf, Virginia. <u>The Diary of Virginia Woolf</u>. Ed. Anne Olivier Bell. New York,
　　Harcourt, 1977. Vol. 1.
Churchill, Winston S. <u>The Age of Revolution</u>. New York: Dodd, 1957. Vol. 3
　　of <u>A History of the English-Speaking Peoples</u>. 4 vols. 1956–58.
Trevelyan, G.M. <u>History of England</u>. 3rd ed. 3 vols. Garden City: Anchor-
　　Doubleday, 1952.

22 INTRODUCTORY MATERIAL If you quote from introductory material written by someone other than the author, start with the contributor's name and add a label like *Introduction, Preface,* or *Foreword.* Include complete page numbers for the introductory material. These may be given as lowercase roman numerals. In the second sample entry, the roman numerals stand for 21–57.

Bellow, Saul. Foreword. <u>The Closing of the American Mind</u>. By Allan Bloom.
　　New York: Simon, 1987.11–18.
DeMott, Robert. Introduction. <u>The Grapes of Wrath</u>. By John Steinbeck.
　　Ed. Robert DeMott. New York: Viking, 1989. xxi-lvii.

23 ENCYCLOPEDIA ENTRY For entries appearing in alphabetical order in the best-known encyclopedias, omit publisher's name or page number. However, because of frequent updates or revisions, you may have to specify the edition.

"Aging." <u>Encyclopaedia Britannica: Macropaedia</u>. 1993 ed.

24 INSTITUTIONAL PUBLICATION Studies and reports often list an organization, commission, or institution as the author.

Task Force for Science Education. <u>Closing the Gender Gap in Science</u>. Houston:
    Doublefield, 2002.

25 PAMPHLET OR BROCHURE Informal locally published material may not identify authors or give full publishing information. Give as much information as is available. Use *n.d.* for "no date of publication."

Foothills Walking Club. <u>Saving the Green Spaces</u>. Fremont, CA. n.d.

26 REISSUED BOOK If an older book is being reissued unchanged, include the date of the original publication. If new material has been added (for instance, a new introduction), include that information.

Wharton, Edith. <u>The House of Mirth</u>. 1905. Introd. Cynthia Griffin Wolf. New
    York: Penguin, 1986.

27 PUBLISHED CORRESPONDENCE When you quote from a specific letter, show author, recipient, and date.

Hemingway, Ernest. "To Lillian Ross." 28 July 1948. <u>Ernest Hemingway:
    Selected Letters. 1917–1961</u>. Ed. Carlos Baker. New York: Scribner's,
    1981. 646–49.

28 BIBLE OR LITERARY CLASSIC Specify which of the many different Bible translations or editions of a Shakespeare play you have used. Put the editor's name first if you want to highlight the editor's contribution.

<u>The Holy Bible</u>. Revised Standard Version. 2nd ed. Nashville: Nelson, 1971.
Hubler, Edward, ed. <u>The Tragedy of Hamlet</u>. By William Shakespeare. New
    York: NAL, 1963.

29 TITLE WITHIN A TITLE An underlined (italicized) book title may include the name of another book. Shift back to roman (not underlined) for the title-within-a-title:

McNulty, Irene. <u>An Unauthorized Guide to Joyce's</u> Ulysses. Chicago: Wishbone,
    1997.

C   Entries for Electronic Sources—Online, CD ROM, e-mail

Guidelines for documenting electronic sources are being updated as new technology evolves and as users find new ways to make it serve their purposes. For most of your entries, start with as much of the usual publishing information as is available—including authors, titles, and dates. This way a reader may be able to locate the material even if an Internet address has changed or the material is no longer available online.

- Include the **posting date** or the date the material was last updated. Follow it with the **access date**—the date you visited the source or site. The access date can tell your reader how recently the material was available or how recently a link was a live link.

- For material from the Internet, include the **Internet address**— the **URL** (uniform resource locator). Put it between **angled brackets.** The electronic address will start with the access mode, usually <http:// . . . .>. (Other access modes include *telnet* and *ftp*.) The address will then go on to the relevant path and specific file names (often beginning with **www.** for the World Wide Web). If you can, have the whole URL on the same line. If not, have a break only after a period or slash. Doublecheck to make sure that dots, slashes, colons, capitals, and spacing are exactly right. Do not add hyphens, spaces, or final periods.

- For material from other electronic sources, specify the **medium,** such as CD-ROM, DVD, diskette, or magnetic tape.

30 NEWS SERVICE ONLINE   Include both publication date and access date:

Dellio, Michael. "A Wheelchair for the World." Wired News 27 July 2000.
    10 Jan. 2003. <http://www.wired.com/news/technology/
    0,1282,37795-2,00.html>

31 NEWSPAPER ONLINE   Include authors and original page numbers if available. The contents of major newspapers are often archived and kept available.

"Guiliani Vows an Even Shinier Polish on Big Apple." Washington Post online.
    2 Jan. 1998. A19+. 7 Jan. 2003. <http://search.washington post.com/
    wpsrv/Wplate/1998-01/02/1211-010298-idx.html>.

Coates, Steve. "A Dead Language Comes to Life on the Internet." New York
    Times on the Web 28 Oct. 1996. 7 Jan. 2004. <http://www.nytimes.com/
    web/doscroot/library/cyber/week/1028Latin.html>.

32 MAGAZINE ONLINE   Include reporters' names if available:

Neill, Monty. "Old Tests in New Clothes." Scholastic June 2003. 22 Apr. 2005.
    <http://teacher.scholastic.com/professional/assessment/oldtests/htm >.

33 ONLINE PUBLICATION ONLY   You will find material published only online, with no corresponding print publication:

People for Ethical Treatment of Animals. "Let's Visit Animal Research Labora-
    tories." 16 Sept. 1995. 2 Oct. 2002. <http://www.envirolink.org/
    arrs/peta/labvisit/office.html>.

34 ONLINE AND PRINT PUBLICATION   You will find books available both in print versions and online.

Barsky, Robert F. Noam Chomsky: A Life of Dissent. Cambridge: MIT Press,
    1997. 5 May 2001. <http://mitpress.mit.edu/chomsky/>

35 WEBSITE OF ORGANIZATION   Many organizations and special interest groups maintain websites, often with numerous **links** to material on special related topics.

Serra Club of Bethlehem, Pennsylvania. Blessed Junípero Serra. Updated 1
    Dec. 2000. 23 Jan. 2004.

36 REFERENCE BOOK ONLINE   If you can, give version number and date.

Britannica Online. Vers. 97.1.1. Mar. 1997. Encyclopaedia Britannica. 17 Sep.
    1999. <http://www.eb.com/>

37 CD-ROM   Give the name of the producer of the CD-ROM and production date if available. Since databases on CD-ROM are often updated, give date of the version you used if available.

Morring, Frank, Jr. "Russian Hardware Allows Earlier Space Station Experi-
    ments." Aviation Week and Space Technology 16 (May 1994): 57. Info-
    Trac: General Periodicals Index. CD-ROM. Information Access. Aug. 94.

38 PERSONAL E-MAIL   Give dates for e-mail to you or to others.

Shillings, Emily. E-mail to the author. 14 Feb. 2004.

Silva, Paul. "Re: Drug Tests for Athletes." E-mail to Joy Conroy. 17 Mar. 2005.

Nonprint Sources—Interviews, letters, talks, media sources

39 PERSONAL INTERVIEW   Keep a record of dates for interviews and other oral sources.

Whitehall, Jacob. Personal interview. 13 Feb. 2005.

Bouvier, Jacqueline. Telephone interview. 2 Feb. 2003.

40 PUBLISHED INTERVIEW Give the names of persons interviewed and persons doing the interviewing. Label the material as an interview.

Asimov, Isaac. Interview. <u>Scientists Talk About Science</u>. By Anne Harrison and Webster Freid. Los Angeles: Acme, 1987. 94–101.

41 PERSONAL LETTER For a letter to you, name the letter writer and label the material as a letter. Give the date.

O'Connor, Patricia. Letter to the author. 11 Aug. 2004.

42 SPEECH OR LECTURE Identify the speaker and give an appropriate label (Lecture, Keynote speech) along with such data as the occasion, the sponsor, the location, and the date. If you know the title of the talk, include it in quotation marks.

Rapoport, Hillel. "The Brain Drain: Curse or Blessing for Less Developed Countries?" Civil Society Lecture Series, Santa Clara. 16 Jan. 2003.

43 PRINTED SPEECH If you are quoting from to a print version of a speech, add full publishing data to the information about place, sponsor, and date. Use rpt. for "reprinted."

Malkowski, Vladimir. "Dissent and the End of the Soviet Empire." Public Affairs Forum, Albuqerque. 23 Aug. 1998. Rpt. <u>West Coast Review</u> Spring 1999: 76–82.

44 TELEVISION OR RADIO PROGRAM Underline (italicize) the title of a program. For an episode in a series, put the title of the specific episode in quotation marks, followed by the name of the series (with no italics or quotation marks). Identify network or station, and include location and date. Pull a name out in front to highlight a person's contribution.

<u>The Polish Americans</u>. Narr. Czeslaw Bialek. Writ. and prod. Vera Serstrom. KCSM, San Mateo. 17 Feb. 2005.

Serkoff, Earl. "Prokofieff." The Great Composers. KPFA, Berkeley. 6 July 2004.

SAMPLE RESEARCH PAPER–MLA STYLE

The following sample research paper was part of the movement to reexamine contested issues in American history. Study the strategy the writer developed to organize the search materials. Study the way the writer has used the material in the documented paper.

RESEARCH PAPER FORMAT—MLA   This sample student research paper observes the MLA guidelines for documentation. Study this paper as a model for the format of your own paper.

- *No* separate title page is necessary unless your instructor requires it.
- Use **double-spacing** throughout, including block quotations and Works Cited (no quadruple-spacing after title or before and after paragraphs).
- **Running heads** (*Richards 1* and so forth) start flush right at the top of page one and continue through the Works Cited page.
- The extra-wide indentation for a **block quotation** is roughly one inch or ten typewriter spaces on the left—no extra space on the right. (No quotation marks and no additional initial paragraph indentation.)

Sample Questions for Peer Review

✓   What did the student writer set out to do?

✓   Who would make a good audience for this paper?

✓   What organizing strategy did the writer work out for the paper?

✓   Where did the writer turn for material?

✓   What use did the writer make of material from the sources?

✓   How clear or helpful are attribution and documentation of the sources?

✓   How balanced or persuasive are the conclusions?

running head
flush right

Richards 1

Pat Richards

Professor Guth

double spacing
throughout

English 2

18 April 2004

Junipero Serra: Updating the Controversy

"Just as the Christian Jesus said, 'Forgive them, for they

know not what they do', we pray, 'Forgive them, Great Spirit, for

quotes within
quote

they know not what they do.'" These words were spoken by An-

thony Miranda, a Costanoan Native American in the basilica of the

Carmel Mission in California after its founder, Father Junipero

Serra, was being proposed for sainthood in Rome. His words drew

"shocked gasps and stares at what many of the worshipers consid-

ered a sacrilege." A man in the back of the basilica loudly called

out, "Why don't you take your pagan rites and get out of this

church?" The group of twenty Native Americans carrying ceremo-

nial rattles, feathers, and abalone shells filled with burning sage

retreated to the church cemetery. They assembled at the foot of a

crude wooden cross that marks the graves of "2,364 Christian In-

dians and 14 Spaniards," buried there between 1771 and 1833

author and page
number in

(O'Neill 17).

parentheses

When Pope John Paul II in 1987 beatified Serra, this was

the second of three steps necessary for the Church's awarding of

formal sainthood. Serra has been called "California's founding fa-

partial quotes

ther" and "the most overlooked man in American history" in one

of the leading religious magazines in the United States (Fay,

Gomez, and Wynn 71). In its entry on Junipero Serra, the PBS

Richards 2

(Public Broadcasting System) website <u>New Perspectives on the West</u> calls Serra "a virtual icon of the colonial era whose statue stands in San Francisco's Golden Gate Park and in the U.S. Capital." Current websites attest to the continued veneration of the Franciscan friar, including the home page of the Serra Club of Bethlehem, Pennsylvania. Several of these are home pages of churches named after Serra (one as recently as 1988), such as the Blessed Junipero Serra Catholic church or the church of the Padre Serra Parish in Camarillo, California. It has been said that Serra's devotion to his missionary work "was an inspiration to those who followed in his footsteps" (Krell and Johnson 310). After he died, we are told, his parishioners "flocked to the church where his body lay, bearing bouquets of flowers and weeping inconsolably" (Fink 48).

online references

However, Serra has also been accused of enslaving and torturing his converts, sending out search parties to hunt down the "fugitives" who escaped from his churches, and committing genocide. His proposed canonization (raising him to official recognition as a saint) provoked a storm of criticism from the American Indian Historical Society. According to an article in <u>U.S. News & World Report</u>. "records are replete with documentation of whippings and other harsh treatment" of the indigenous people under his jurisdiction ("Question" 24). Can both parties to this controversy be speaking of the same person?

quote marks for shortened title of unsigned article

According to Augusta Fink's <u>Monterey: The Presence of the Past</u>, Father Serra was born Miguel Joseph Serra in the humble town of Petra on the island of Majorca, Spain, in 1713. In 1749,

Richards 3

he realized his dream of becoming a missionary when he was sent

to Mexico to help convert the Native Americans to Christianity.

During the next twenty years, he founded and guided a mission

among the Pame tribe in northern Mexico and often preached in

Mexico City (4–8). At the Sierra Gordo Indian Missions, Serra

"learned the language of the Pame Indians and translated the cate-

chism into their language." In San Diego, he "founded the first of

the twenty-one California missions which accomplished the conver-

sions of all the natives on the coast as far as Sonoma in the

north" (Engelhardt). According to an article in *Life* magazine,

Serra arrived in California in 1769. "Unlike the Spanish military

and many of the clergy, he immediately made friends with the lo-

cal tribes." Serra died "cradled in the arms of some of his 6,000

Christian converts." According to the author of the article, "Serra

has been the unofficial state 'saint' for generations" (Fay, Gomez,

and Wynn 68–71).

Much recent work has painted a less saintly picture of the

Spanish priest. Alma Villanueva, a professor at the University of

California at Santa Cruz, spoke to me of "mass graves" of Indians

unearthed near several of the California missions and used the

term *genocide.* In the book The Missions of California: A Legacy of

Genocide, the American Indian Historical Society has circulated the

same charges. The book provides numerous documented reports of

the indigenous inhabitants being subjected to "forced conversion,"

"forced labor," and "physical punishment." It includes an account

of an early settler who wrote, "For the slightest things they re-

ceive heavy floggings, are shackled and put in stocks, and

inclusive page numbers for summary of information

credentials of oral source

Richards 4

treated with so much cruelty that they are kept whole days without a drink of water" (Costo and Costo 69).

In his book, The Ohlone Way; Indian Life in the San Francisco-
Monterey Bay Area, Malcolm Margolin quotes the explorer La Per-
ouse, who compared the missions in Father Serra's charge to slave
colonies he had seen in Santo Domingo:

> We declare with pain that the resemblance [to the Santo
> Domingo slave colonies] is so exact that we saw both the
> men and the women loaded with irons, while others had
> a log of wood on their legs. . . . Corporal punishment is
> inflicted on the Indians of both sexes who neglect their
> pious exercises. (162)

Margolin quotes a visitor to the mission at Santa Clara about
the confinement of young unmarried women by the padres "to assure the chastity of their wards":

> We were struck by the appearance of a large quadrangular
> building, which, having no windows on the outside, resem-
> bled a prison for state criminals. . . . The dungeons are
> opened two or three times a day, but only to allow the pris-
> oners to pass to and from the church. I have occasionally
> seen the poor girls rushing out eagerly to breathe the fresh
> air and driven immediately into the church like a flock
> of sheep, by an old ragged Spaniard with a stick. After
> mass, they are in the same manner hurried back into their
> prisons. (161)

double indent
for block quote
with bracketed
addition and
ellipsis for
omission

page numbers
only in
parentheses

Richards 5

A quote from one of Serra's fellow friars complains that the Native Americans "live well free but as soon as we reduce them to a Christian and community life . . . they fatten, sicken, and die" (PBS).

In response to protesters' charges, defenders of the church position have accused activists of spreading "wild opinion and speculation" and "a complete misrepresentation of the truth and the reality of this time period." In a detailed defense of Serra, Brian Grisin says, "there has never been one piece of historical documentation to prove any of their claims. . . . Expert, unbiased historians, after piecing through all the historical documentation and other evidence, have confirmed no abuses or mistreatment have occurred by Serra." The online edition of the <u>Catholic Ency-</u> <u>clopedia</u>, with a 1999 copyright, continues to use an entry on Junipero Serra first prepared by Zephryn Engelhardt for publication in 1912. The entry praises Serra's "extraordinary fortitude," his "insatiable zeal, love of mortification, self-denial," and his executive abilities. The extensive entry devotes half a dozen lines to the Native Americans at Serra's missions, with no comment on their treatment or their fate.

In a carefully argued rebuttal to the protesters' charges, Grisin stresses the benefits of the mission system to the Native Americans: The missionaries helped to improve the lives of the natives by introducing new and more reliable food—the agricultural system of raising crops and livestock. The natives "learned new trades, which later would become useful." Abuses are blamed on the Spanish soldiers: "The Indians certainly faced terrible hardship

online source

Richards 6

adjusting to this new way of life," but the military were to blame:
"They mainly suffered from abusive soldiers who were responsible
for the spreading of diseases, such as pox and syphilis, and the
mistreatment of Indians."

We must see the harshness of the system relative to its time.

mix of quotation
and paraphrase

"It is true when one looks at it from an anthropological view, the
mission system seems harsh. But we must remember we are looking at it through a twentieth century viewpoint." We need to take
into account "the societal norms towards unknown civilizations of
the time" and "what the Natives most likely would have endured
without a mission system." The missionaries saw themselves as
responsible for the "care of the souls of the Natives for their salvation." Then we can see that "the reasoning of Serra was for the
benefit of the Indians." As for the punishment of those resisting
conversion or trying to escape, "the claims by anti-Serra activists
of Indian whippings were really comparable to a slap on the wrist
(which was a common punishment in Spain)."

The goal of saving the souls of the natives was paramount:
"most importantly from the Catholic viewpoint, their souls were
saved (which was the only known way of achieving salvation from
the Catholic perspective of that time)."

Those defending Father Serra tend to play down or belittle the
hardships suffered by those in his care. Fink's book reports that
the last few years of Serra's life were "difficult ones." There were
"few new converts and many runaways among the Indians, and a
series of plagues, which were probably smallpox, had decimated
the small Christianized group that remained" (48). Margolin says

Richards 7

that "300 or more Indians out of a thousand might die during a severe epidemic year" (163).

To judge Father Serra's role in these events, we need to remember how badly the Spaniards and the Native Americans misunderstood each other. They represented two vastly different cultures. In the words of another book about the California missions,

> The California Indian has often been criticized because he lived a life of slothfulness, not stirring himself to raise crops, herd flocks, or practice other disciplined forms of food production characteristic of more advanced cultures. . . . Ironically, the civilized Spaniards, who looked down upon the childlike Indians, suffered famines after they first settled in the same environment when their imported foodstuffs failed to arrive on time. (Krell and Johnson 50)

author and page number after period ending block quotation

Serra probably never doubted the rightness of his actions. As Fink points out, the Native Americans "resisted conversion to the Christian faith, which required complete separation from the pagan community. Children presented for baptism had to live at the mission under the supervision of the padres" (43). It must be noted, however, that not even his countrymen always took his side. Governor Neve "refused to round up Indian fugitives from the missions, who, Serra felt, had broken the contract they made at baptism" (48).

Today, few of the five million visitors a year who come to the California missions remember the darker side of their history. Few

Richards 8

know the price the native tribes paid for the outposts of imperial Spain that the Spanish kings commissioned the Franciscan friars led by Fra Junipero Serra to establish along 600 miles of the Pacific coastline. Local newspapers describe the missions as "centers of commerce and communication" that promoted agriculture and trade and "served as the means to educate, convert, and civilize the various native tribes" ("Degrees" 2).

However, the historical evidence makes one thing clear: The methods employed by Serra and the Spanish missionaries were overzealous by twentieth-century standards. Some would argue that he was overzealous by anyone's and any time's standards. When we are faced with documented accounts of what happened to many indigenous inhabitants under his authority, it is hard to consider Father Serra worthy of being made a saint. In the words of Jack Norton, a Native American professor at Humboldt State University, a candidate for sainthood "should epitomize virtue and kindness" (qtd. in "Question" 24).

quoted at
second hand

Richards 9

Works Cited

Blessed Junipero Serra Catholic Church. Updated Jan. 2002.

23 Jan. 2004 <http://www.fatherserra.org/>

Costo, Rupert, and Jeanette H. Costo, eds. The Missions of Califor-

nia: A Legacy of Genocide. San Francisco: Indian Historical,

1987.

"Degrees of Separation." Visalia Times-Delta 6 Jan. 2004. 23 Jan.

2004. <http://www.visaliatimesdeltacom/news/stories/

20040106/opinion/1548639.html>

Donohue, John W. "California's Founding Father." America 11 May

1986: 306.

Engelhardt, Zephryn. "Junipero Serra." The Catholic Encyclopedia

Online Edition. 1999. 23 Jan 2004. <http://www.

newadvent.org./csthen/13730bhtm>

Fay, Martha, Linda Gomez, and Wilton Wynn. "So You Want to Be

a Saint." *Life* Sept. 1987: 68–71.

Fink, Augusta. Monterey: The Presence of the Past. San Francisco:

Chronicle Publishing, 1972.

Grisin, Brian. "Junipero Serra and the California Missions." 2001.

23 Jan. 2004. <http://www.geocities.com/Paris/Cathedral/

3300>.

Krell, Dorothy, and Paul C. Johnson, eds. The California Missions:

A Pictorial History. Menlo Park, CA: Lane, 1979.

Margolin, Malcolm. The Ohlone Way: Indian Life in the San

Francisco-Monterey Bay Area. Berkeley: Heyday, 1978.

O'Neill, Ann W. "Confrontation at the Mission." San Jose Mercury

News 26 Sept. 1987: B17–19.

first line of each
entry flush left,
additional lines
indented

URL of online
source

several authors

inclusive page
numbers

Richards 10

<u>Padre Serra Parish-Camarillo, CA</u>. 23 Jan. 2004. <http://www.
padreserra.org/index.htm>

PBS (Public Broadcasting System). "Junipero Serra." <u>New Perspec-</u>
<u>tives on the West</u>. 2001. 23 Jan. 2004. <http://www.pbs.
org/weta/thewest/people/s_z/serra.htm>

"A Question of Faith in California." <u>U.S. News & World Report</u>
11 May 1987: 24.

Serra Club of Bethlehem, Pennsylvania. <u>Blessed Junipero Serra</u>.
Updated 1 Dec. 2000. 23 Jan. 2004. <http://www.
catholic-church.org/serra-beth/serra-4.htm>

Villanueva, Alma. Personal interview. 2 Feb. 2004.

nonprint source

Documenting Your Sources—APA Style

Recognize basic features of the APA style.

Many publications in the social sciences follow the APA style of documentation, outlined in the *Publication Manual of the American Psychological Association* (Fifth Edition, 2001). You may be asked to follow this style in areas like psychology, linguistics, or education and also business, social work, nursing, and justice administration.

- For brief identification of sources in the text of a paper, the APA format uses the **author-and-date** method. When using this style, include year or date of publication after the author's name (Ortiz, 2002). Do not repeat the author's name between parentheses if you have already mentioned it in your text (2002).

- The APA style often gives a source and the publication date of research without a page reference. Interested readers are expected to become familiar with the relevant research literature and consider its findings in context. However, give an exact page reference with all direct quotation.

- For scholarly work, the APA prefers reliance on material from **refereed** professional publications. In refereed journals, the material has been reviewed and approved for publication by outside experts.

- The APA discourages the use of Internet material that may be available only for a limited time. Some material from online publications and also from special interest groups or newsgroups is preserved in web **archives.** You can access content from back issues of many major newspapers and other periodicals in their archives.

FIND IT ON THE WEB

Updating the APA Style

The APA-Style Helper 3.0 on CD-ROM is designed to help you format source information in the APA style. Check for updated information and current releases at http://www.apastyle.org/stylehelper.

Samples of Parenthetical Documentation

Study the following sample citations. Note distinctive features like the use of commas, the abbreviations *p.* or *pp.* for "page" or "pages," or the symbol & (the ampersand) for *and*.

I AUTHOR AND DATE ONLY:

Justice O'Connor affirmed memorably in the court's majority opinion that full participation by "all racial and ethnic groups" was essential if we are to realize the dream of one indivisible nation (Schevitz, 2003).

2 DATE ONLY —author's name in your own text:

Freeling tracked the new "care not cash" programs that city governments were promoting in their continuing efforts to get the homeless off the streets (2004).

3 PAGE REFERENCE —for direct quotation or specific reference:

For many writers today, race "is purely a social construction; it has no core reality outside a specific social and historical context" (Reed, 2000, p. 140).

4 WORK BY SEVERAL AUTHORS Name the several authors— up to six coauthors. Then add *et al.* (for "and others") instead of additional names. Name only the first of the authors and then put *et al.* in any later references.

Commercials tout crash diets that promise young women beauty and success (Mendoza, Phillips, & Watson, 2002).

The damaging effects of crash diets and appetite-suppressing drugs have been extensively documented (Simpson et al., 2003).

5 SAME AUTHOR For several publications in the same year, use a, b, c, and so on, in order of publication:

Paulson and her team have tracked the results of experimental treatments over a number of years (2002, 2004a, 2004b).

6 REFERENCE TO SEVERAL SOURCES List in alphabetical order, divided by semicolons:

Official statistics long underreported or underestimated the true extent of homelessness (Joel, 1999; Kramer & Swenson, 2002).

7 UNIDENTIFIED OR UNLISTED AUTHOR Identify source by shortened title:

Jury selection became the subject of study for self-styled "experts" ("Psyching out prospective jurors," 2002).

8 INSTITUTIONAL AUTHORSHIP In general, use **acronyms** (made up from initial letters) or abbreviations only in second or subsequent citation:

Many promising drugs or "silver bullets" proved to have disastrous side effects (National Institute of Mental Health [NIMH], 1999).

Research into the biochemistry of the brain has led to genuine breakthroughs in the treatment of emotional disorders (NIMH, 2000).

9 PERSONAL COMMUNICATIONS In the text of your paper, identify letters, memos, e-mail, or telephone interviews as personal communications. Include the date. Because they cannot be consulted or verified by the reader, omit personal communications in your list of References.

A professor of education at a local college called the extensive achievement testing of four-year-olds and five-year-olds "institutionalized academic child abuse." (Simon Perez, personal communication, November 3, 2004).

Sample Entries for References Directory—APA Style

Use the heading "References" for your final alphabetical listing of works quoted or consulted. Note the distinctive **author-and-date** sequence, with author identification followed by the date in parentheses:

Stefan, L. B. (1991). *Youth and the law: Getting tough on juvenile crime.*
     Boston: Benchmark Books.

- Start with the last name of the author, followed by *initials* (not full first names). Then put the date in parentheses. For dates of newspapers or periodicals, do not abbreviate months (2005, June 21). Indent the second line of each entry one half inch (or five typewriter spaces).

- Use *lowercase* letters in titles, except for words you would normally capitalize in your text. Do not put titles of articles in quotation marks. Italicize the name of a complete publication—newspaper, magazine, book. Use the full names of publishers, omitting tags like *Inc.* or *Co.:* Cambridge: Harvard University Press. Use *p.* or *pp.* for "page" or "pages."

A CHECKLIST FOR DOCUMENTATION

References—APA Style

The following are distinctive features of the APA documentation style:

✓ Start an entry in your list of References flush left; then indent next line or lines.

✓ For first names and middle names, use initials only.

✓ Put publication date in parentheses after authors' names.

✓ Use no quotation marks for titles of articles.

✓ Italicize titles of books and other whole publications.

✓ Use lowercase letters within titles.

✓ Show both date posted and date retrieved for Internet material.

✓ Use accurate URL or retrieval path for Internet sources.

A   Print Sources

1 STANDARD ENTRY FOR AN ARTICLE   Put the last name of the author first, followed by initials only (no first or middle names). Put the date in parentheses—do not abbreviate months: (2005, February 19). Do *not* put titles of articles in quotation marks. After the first word of title or subtitle, use lowercase letters except for words you would normally capitalize in your text. Italicize the name of the newspaper or magazine, and use normal capitalization for words in titles of publications. Keep the article *The* in the names of publications like *The Wall Street Journal* or *The New York Times.*

Include complete page numbers, using p. or pp. for "page" or "pages." If appropriate, specify the edition of the newspaper—early or late, east or west: *The Wall Street Journal,* eastern ed., p. A3.

Muschamp, H. (2001, May 6). Fitting into history's fabric. *The New York Times,* p. AR44.

Losos, J. B. (2001, March). Evolution: A lizard's tale. *Scientific American,* pp. 86–91.

If page numbers for the article are not continuous, use a comma to separate the numbers: pp. 7, 9–10.

Miller, G. (1969, December). On turning psychology over to the unwashed. *Psychology Today,* pp. 53–54, 66–74.

2 STANDARD ENTRY FOR A BOOK   Use initials only instead of an author's first name and middle name: Nader, R. Italicize the title and any subtitle of the book. Capitalize only the first word of title or subtitle, but capitalize proper names that are part of a title as you would in ordinary prose: *A life of Eleanor Roosevelt.*

Use the full names of publishers, omitting only tags like Inc. or Co.: Cambridge, MA: Harvard University Press.

Chomsky, N. (1994). *Secrets, lies and democracy.* Chicago, Odonian.

3 ARTICLE OR BOOK WITH SUBTITLE   Use a colon to separate title and subtitle.

Martin, R. (2002, February). Meltdown: Big steel in the borderless economy. *Wired,* pp. 88–93.

Reed, A. Jr. (2000). *Class notes: Posing as politics and other thoughts on the American scene.* New York: New Press.

4 ARTICLE OR BOOK BY SEVERAL AUTHORS   List the names of up to six coauthors, last names first. Put the *and*-sign, or ampersand (**&**),

before the last author's name. After six authors, put et al. (not italicized, for "and others") instead of additional authors' names.

Smith, D.V. & Margolske, R.F. (2001, March). Making sense of taste. *Scientific American,* pp. 32–39.

Minuchin, S., Rosman, B., & Baker, L. (1978). *Psychosomatic families: Anorexia, nervosa in context.* Cambridge, MA: Harvard University Press.

Boyer, P. S., Clark, C. E., Hawley, S. M., Kett, J. F., Salisbury, N., Sitkoff, H., & Woloch, N. (1995). *The enduring vision: A history of the American people.* Lexington: D. C. Heath.

Hale, P., Makgoba, M.W., Merson, M.H., Quinn, T., Richman, D.D., Vella, S. et al. (2001). Success hinges on support for treatment. *Nature, 412, 272.*

5 UNSIGNED OR ANONYMOUS PUBLICATION Start with the title and alphabetize by the first word of the title, not counting *The, A,* or *An.*

Assessing the Damage (2002, February 21). *Economist,* pp. 78–79.

6 JOURNAL ARTICLE WITH VOLUME NUMBER Italicize the volume number for a professional journal, with complete page numbers following after a comma: *6,* 152–169. Do not use p. or pp. after a volume number.

Harrison, R.G. (2001). Diverse origins of biodiversity. *Nature, 411,* 636–636.

7 VOLUME NUMBER AND ISSUE If needed, include both volume number and number of the issue. Put it in parentheses between the volume number and the page numbers: *6*(3), 152–169. The number of issue may be needed if page numbers are not continuous for the whole volume.

Steinhausen, H. & Glenville, K. (1983). Follow-up studies of anorexia nervosa: A review of research findings. *Psychological Medicine: Abstracts in English, 13*(2), 239–245.

8 SIGNED OR UNSIGNED EDITORIAL After the title, add the label Editorial in square brackets. If the editorial is unsigned, begin with the title.

Epstein, R. (2001, July/August). Physiologist Laura: She's not a psychologist, and we don't want her. [Editorial]. *Psychology Today,* p.5.

What is sacred? (1995, November/December). [Editorial.] *Mother Jones,* pp. 3–6.

9 LETTER TO THE EDITOR Add the label after the title, in square brackets.

Lafont, L. (2002, January 6). Retirement plans at risk. [Letter to the Editor.] *The Los Angeles Times* part II: 8.

10 BOOK REVIEW Start with author and title of a book review and include title of book reviewed in square brackets:

Sheaffer, R. (1995, November). Truth abducted [Review of the book *Close encounters of the fourth kind: Alien abduction, UFOs, and the conference at MIT*]. *Scientific American, 273*(5), 102–103.

11 LATER EDITION OF A BOOK Include 2nd ed. for second edition, for instance, or rev. ed. for revised edition:

White, J. B. & Wilson, W. T. (2001). *From Adam to Armageddon: A survey of the Bible* (4th ed.). Belmont, CA: Wadsworth.

Rosenthal, R. (1987). *Meta-analytic procedures for social research* (Rev. ed.). Newbury Park, CA: Sage.

12 TRANSLATED BOOK Put the translator's name (or translators' names) followed by Trans. after the title.

Freire, P. (1970). *Pedagogy of the oppressed* (M. B. Ramos, Trans.). New York: Seabury Press.

13 SAME AUTHOR Repeat the author's name with each title. Put works in chronological order.

Bruch, H. (1973). *Eating disorders: Obesity, anorexia nervosa, and the person within.* New York: Basic Books.

Bruch, H. (1978). *The golden cage: The enigma of anorexia nervosa.* Cambridge, MA: Harvard University Press.

14 EDITED BOOK For a book with an editor's name, put the abbreviation for "editor" (Ed. or Eds.) in parentheses.

Hartman, F. (Ed.). (1973). *World in crisis: Readings in international relations* (4th ed.). New York: Macmillan.

Popkewitz, T. S. & Tabachnick, B. R. (Eds.). (1981). *The study of schooling: Field based methodologies in educational research and evaluation.* New York: Praeger.

15 ONE OF SEVERAL VOLUMES Include volume number for one of several volumes:

Gianini, F. P. (2001). *History of the Missions.* Vol 2. Las Vegas: Nevada Publications.

16 PART OF A BOOK   For a part of a book, use the appropriate label—such as preface, introduction, or afterword.

Aufderheide, P. (1992). Preface. In P. Aufderheide (Ed.), *Beyond PC: Toward a politics of understanding* (pp. 1–4). Saint Paul, MN: Graywolf Press.

17 PART OF A COLLECTION   For part of a collection or anthology, identify both the article or other short item and the collection of which it is a part. If you cite several articles from the same collection, give full publishing information each time.

Borges, J. L. (1972). A new refutation of time. In S. Sears & G. W. Lord (Eds.), *The discontinuous universe: Selected writings in contemporary consciousness* (pp. 208–223). New York: Basic Books.

18 INSTITUTIONAL AUTHORSHIP   For institutional authorship, list the organization as the author.

American Psychological Association. (1982). *Ethical principles in the conduct of research with human participants.* Washington, DC: Author.

19 ENCYCLOPEDIA ENTRY   List an unsigned entry in an encyclopedia or other reference work under first word of entry. If the author of an entry is identified, include the name.

Russia. (1994). In *The new encyclopedia Britannica* (15th ed.) (Vol. 10, pp. 253–255). Chicago: Encyclopedia Britannica.

20 MONOGRAPH IN A SERIES   A monograph is a research study focused on a single topic. If it is published as part of a series of related studies, identify the series and include serial number if applicable. Monographs may be published as supplements or special editions of a professional journal. Use [Monograph] in square brackets to show that a study is bound with an issue of the journal.

Harris, P.L., & Kavanaugh, R.D. (1993) Young children's understanding of pretense. *Monographs of the Society for Research in Child Development, 58*(1, Serial No. 231).

LaRue, S. (1999). Stress disorders and the ergonomics of the workplace [Monograph]. *Journal of Applied Psychology, 84,* 152–171.

21 UNPUBLISHED RESEARCH   Identify locations of unpublished doctoral studies and the like. Identify locations of abstracts—short pointed summaries.

Steinfield. J. (2004). The language of war propaganda. Unpublished doctoral dissertation, University of Michigan, Ann Arbor.

Javorsky. L. (1999). Icons and the Russian tradition (Doctoral Dissertation, Stanford University, 1999). *Dissertation Abstracts International, 60,* 232.

B   Electronic Sources

Like other documentation styles, the APA style has evolved in response to developments in electronic communication. In research guides and Internet guidelines, you may encounter earlier variations and adaptations of the APA format. The following model entries are based on the 2001 APA *Publication Manual* (5th edition, 2001).

22 STANDARD INTERNET SOURCE   Include as much standard publishing information as is available. Specify the retrieval date and give the full URL—the retrieval path leading to the specific document. Make sure to copy exactly colons, slashes, and double slashes without adding spaces and with no final period.

Holmes, K. (1999). Use all Your Smarts: Multiple intelligences for diverse library learners. Retrieved August 22, 2002, from http://www.lesley.edu/faculty/kholmes/presentations/Ml.html

23 INSTITUTIONAL SOURCE   Start by identifying the organization or institution.

New City School. (2000). Multiple intelligences table. Retrieved 19 August 2002, from http://www.newcityschool.org/table.html

24 NEWSPAPER OR NEWSMAGAZINE SOURCE   For material from a newspaper or newsmagazine online, you may need only the host name. The host name www.nytimes.com will take readers to *The New York Times* online. Date and title will then take them to the specific item.

Brennan, C. (2001, March 11). Our obsolete voting system. *New York Times.* Retrieved August 18, 2002 from http://www.nytimes.com

25 ARTICLE FROM INTERNET JOURNAL   Include both publication date and retrieval date. Include volume number if applicable. Material published directly on the Internet will often not have conventional page numbers—if available give number of article, chapter, or section instead.

Frederickson, B.L. (2000, March 7). Cultivating positive emotions to optimize health and well-being. *Prevention & Treatment, 3,* Article 0001a. Retrieved November 20, 2002, from http://journals.apa.org/prevention/volume 3/pre003000a.html

26 ELECTRONIC COPY FROM DATABASE   If you have retrieved a copy of a print publication from an electronic database, direct
your readers to the database.

Berman, Z. (1997). New challenges to personality profiles. *Journal of Applied
   Psychology, 82,* 328–338. Retrieved January 4, 2001, from PsycARTI-
   CLES database.

27 REPORT FROM GOVERNMENT DATABASE   You may be
drawing on government reports or agency statistics traceable through the
GPO [Government Printing Office] database.

U.S. General Accounting Office. (1997, February). Telemedicine: Federal strategy is needed to guide investments (Publication No. GAO/NSAID/
   HEHS-96-97. Retrieved September 15, 2002, from General Accounting
   Office Reports Online via GPO Access: http://www.access.gpo.gov/su_docs/
   aces/aces160.shtml?/gao/index.html

28 MESSAGE TO NEWSGROUP OR DISCUSSION GROUP   In-
clude author's name if available. Give the date the message was posted. Give
the subject (the subject line or "thread") of the message. Add the number
of the message [in square brackets] if applicable.

Simones, R. (2001, February 6). Mapping the memory centers [Msg 3]. Message posted to news://sci.psychology.consciousness

29 INFORMATION SERVICE   If a document is available from an
information service like the National Technical Information Service
(NTIS) or the Educational Resources Information Center (ERIC), identify
the service and give the item number.

Kurth, R. J. & Stromberg, L. J. (1984). *Using word processing in composition
   instruction.* (ERIC Document Reproduction Service No. ED251850)

30 CD-ROM   Label the medium in square brackets [CD-ROM].
Include source and retrieval number or similar information.

Bernanos, S. (2001). *The World of Business Writing* [CD-ROM]. VocEd File:
   Item 432122.

C   Nonprint Media

31 AUDIO SPEECH OR PROGRAM   Indicate role of speakers or
performers. Label the medium in square brackets.

Sirven, K. (Speaker). (1999). *Sharing Our Planet* [Cassette Recording No. 34-09]. Portland, OR: Western Wildlife Association.

32 TELEVISION PROGRAM Identify the producer or important contributor. Label the medium in square brackets.

Siemaszko, C. (Narrator). (1998). *The Polish-Amearicans* [Television broadcast]. New York and Schenectady, WLIW/HMHT Public Television.

33 RADIO PROGRAM Identify director or important participants.

Vitale, K. (Interviewer). (1996, May 6). Interview with C. Lobos. *Behind the news.* [Radio Broadcast]. Washington, DC: Public Broadcasting Service.

34 MOTION PICTURE Start with the name of the producer or director. Include name of scriptwriter if important and available.

Fellini, F. (Writer/Director), & Zapponi, B. (Writer). (1972). *Roma* [Motion Picture]. Italy: Italo-Francese-Ultra Film. (Available from MGM-UA Home Video)

35 MUSIC RECORDING Start with the composer or songwriter if available. The note (n.d.) shows that date of composition or copyright was not available. Name the recording artists in square brackets. Name both the individual piece and the album or CD if applicable. Specify the medium: [CD], [DVD], [Record], [Cassette].

Dorsey, T.A. (n.d.). Walk over God's heaven [Recorded by Mahalia Jackson]. On *Mahalia Jackson: Gospels, Spirituals & Hymns* [CD]. New York: Columbia. (1991)

36 ART WORK Include title and location.

Martinez, F. (2001). *The Serpent God* [Art Work]. San Jose, CA: Institute of Mexican American Art.

37 PERSONAL COMMUNICATION Personal communications include personal letters, telephone interviews, and e-mail messages. Identify source and date in your parenthetical citation in your text, for instance (M. Mario, personal communication, May 2, 2003). However, omit personal communications from your list of References. They are not a matter of public record and cannot be accessed and checked by your reader.

FORMATTING THE RESEARCH PAPER

APA Style

- Follow any special instructions from your instructor or editor concerning use of a **title page** or inclusion of a **formal outline.**

- Use the title (or usually a shortened title) instead of your name as **running heads:** *Slave Revolts* instead of *Slave Revolts in the Carribean.*

- **Double-space** all materials, including block quotations.

- Use normal **5-space** indentation for the whole block quotation (40 words or more).

- Start a new page for your **References**—your final complete source list.

- Your instructor may require you to include an **abstract** on a separate page at the beginning (with the heading *Abstract*). An abstract is a brief summary of the paper (perhaps 150–250 words), showing its focus and major findings.

SAMPLE RESEARCH PAPER PAGES: APA

The following pages are the opening pages of a research paper formatted in the APA style. The sample pages are followed by the complete list of References. The **running heads** use a shortened title—not the student writer's name. Note the use of the **author-date style** both in the brief parenthetic references in the text and in the detailed list of References at the end. Note the use of specific page references for direct quotations.

running head
using shortened
title

James Perry

Professor Guth

English 176

21 November 2004

Child Criminals in Adult Courts—A Crime In Itself?

In August 1993, at a day camp in Savona, New York, Eric

Smith, a 13-year-old, brutally murdered a 4-year-old. Eric grabbed

the younger boy in a headlock, smashed his head three times with

a rock, stuffed a napkin and a plastic bag in his mouth, and pum-

meled his body with a rock. Eric's trial began on August 1 in Bath,

New York. Despite his young age, he was tried as an adult because

of the severity of his crime and also because of a law allowing chil-

dren as young as thirteen to be tried as adults when accused of

murder (Nordheimer, 1994, p. B5).

author and date
with page
number

Eric's case was an early indication of frightening trends in

America—an increase in the severity of juvenile crime, and a de-

crease in the age at which children commit crimes. His trial also

heralded a continuing trend in American juvenile justice—children

are being tried in adult courts in more cases and at younger ages.

Experts, elected representatives, and the general public have been

grappling with the issue of how to deal with juvenile crime, and

treating youths as adults became a popular solution. Many issues

are relevant in the debate over whether to try children as adults—

how major a problem is juvenile crime; is being harsh with juve-

nile criminals in the best interest of the defendants and in soci-

ety's best interest, in terms of rehabilitating criminals, deterring

Child Criminals 2

and reducing crime, and justice; is treating child criminals as adults the most effective and most cost-efficient way of dealing with them; and so on.

The alternative to treating juveniles as adults is a more rehabilitative approach—some experts advocate more preventive efforts, as opposed to more punishment-oriented programs such as trying youths in adult courtrooms. In this paper, I intend to show the causes for the growing sentiment toward trying youths as adults. Then I intend to argue that while juvenile crime is a problem, it may not be the epidemic that it has been made out to be, and that although it is necessary to be firm in dealing with juvenile criminals, the best way to deal with them may not necessarily be through adult courts and strictly "getting tough." A summary of recent research available online from the American Civil Liberties Union is titled "Defusing the Myth: Prosecuting Children as Adults Doesn't Work to Decrease Crime." The authors claim that transferring children from juvenile courts to adult criminal courts does not decrease the number of repeat offenses and may in fact be counterproductive (ACLU, 2000).

In a way, the American justice system seems to be coming full circle. The nation's first juvenile court was established in 1899 in Cook County, Illinois, as a way to deal with young offenders in a more rehabilitative style, as opposed to the harsher justice found in adult courts (Andrews, 1994.) However, by the 1960's, the public had become more concerned about juvenile crime, as the youth population was growing and becoming more violent. Americans began to question the principles and effectiveness of the current

preview of the argument

author and date in parentheses

juvenile justice system and argued in favor of harsher, firmer alternatives. The 1966 U. S. Supreme Court case *Kent* v. *United States* established guidelines for the transfer of young offenders to adult courts. The youths' threat to the safety of the public and amenability to treatments within the juvenile justice system were to be considered (Houghtalin & Mays, 1991). Since this time, more and more laws have been proposed and implemented to make it easier, and in some cases mandatory, for youths to be sent to adult courts for certain crimes, both violent and nonviolent. The public seems to want young criminals to be held responsible for their crimes and to be punished, and they believe that this can best be done in adult courts, where child criminals presumably will face harsher sentencing, often including time in adult prisons.

Measures of treating juvenile offenders as adults have been proposed and supported for several reasons. While some experts advocate and have implemented more preventive measures, these are difficult to implement and would have more of a long-term effect, leaving Americans wondering "what we are supposed to do in the meantime" (Methvin, 1994, p. 95). Bob Herbert argued that attempts to rehabilitate young offenders and treat them lightly are "well-intentioned" but "out of touch with the increasingly violent reality of juvenile crime" (1994, p. E15). Other measures had failed to reduce juvenile crime; for instance, gun control laws were not believed to have a significant effect on violent crime by youths, since they tend to obtain the guns through illegal means anyway (Witkin, 1991, p. 28). Although experts disagreed as to the extent and seriousness of current juvenile crime, the public felt that juve-

quoted phrases

Child Criminals 4

nile crime is a major problem, and they supported measures to
deal with it. In the words of a Maryland assistant public defender,
the public's focus on juvenile crime created the "political climate"
that supported antijuvenile crime measures (Stepp, 1994, p. A12).

Many officials within the justice system believed that some
young criminals should be treated as adults and tried in adult
courts. A study published in August 1994 showed that many
judges in the juvenile justice system thought that "the criminal
justice system should deal with young criminals more in the way
it deals with adults." For instance, two out of five judges surveyed
thought child offenders should be eligible to receive the death
penalty in some situations, and a majority felt that the minimum
age for facing murder charges should be lowered ("Tougher Treatment," 1994, p. A16). Former administrator of the Office of Juvenile Justice and Delinquency Prevention Ira Schwartz found that
"juvenile court judges and youth probation workers are among the
staunchest supporters of jailing for juveniles" (1989, p. 18).

Many legislators, and a large portion of the general public,
shared the sentiments of these justice authorities. Maryland delegate Joseph F. Vallario Jr. said that "if [youths] want to do adult-
type crimes, we're going to treat them like adults" (Stepp, 1994,
p. A12). Another Maryland delegate, Ulysses Curie, wrote that because of the increasing violence and youth of juvenile offenders,
"the juvenile system must be changed to respond to this reality"
by treating youths more like adults (1994, p. C8).

Both Democrats and Republicans supported measures to treat
young criminals more like adults; both of the Maryland delegates

*short title for
unsigned article*

*bracketed
addition*

Child Criminals 5

quoted above were Democrats, and a major part of the Republi-

cans' "Contract with America" was the "Taking Back Our Streets

Act," which supported harsher punishment of crime ("Youth and

Crime," 1995, p. 18). In recent years, many states have added leg-

islation that lowered the ages at which youths can be tried as

adults for certain crimes, added new crimes to those for which a

juvenile may or must be tried as an adult, implemented mandatory

sentencing for children convicted of certain crimes, and so on. For

instance, Louisiana added attempted murder and aggravated bat-

tery to the list of offenses for which a juvenile may be tried as an

adult.

A rare dissenting opinion was registered by Supreme Court

Justice Brennan in *Stanford* v. *Kentucky* (1992). Citing an earlier

court opinion, he said:

normal indent for
block quotation

> The reason why juveniles are not trusted with the privileges
>
> and responsibilities of an adult also explains why their irre-
>
> sponsible conduct is not as morally reprehensible as that of
>
> an adult. Adolescents are more vulnerable, more impulsive,
>
> and less self-disciplined than adults.

[End of sample pages.]

References

American Civil Liberties Union (2000, August 11). Defusing
the myth: Prosecuting children as adults doesn't work to
decrease crime. Retrieved September 12, 2004, from
http://www.aclu.org/congress/kids.htm

Andrews, J. H. (1994, March 7). Criminals, but still children.
Christian Science Monitor, p.17.

Armstrong, S. (1994, March 7). Colorado tries more carrot and
less stick in punishing juvenile crime. *Christian Science Monitor,* pp. 1, 4.

Bayh, B. (1989). [Foreword.] In I. M. Schwartz, *(In) justice
for juveniles: Rethinking the best interests of the child*
(pp. xi–xiii). Lexington: Health-Lexington.

Burns, K. S. (2004, Fall). Juvenile punishment. Retrieved September 12, 2004, from http://www.karisable.com/crpunyouth.
htm

Curie, U. (1994, February 6). Reality requires tougher responses
to juvenile crime. *The Washington Post,* p. C8.

Early, D. E. & Corcoran, K. (2004, January 11). Lifestyle attracting more young members. *San Jose Mercury News.*
pp. 2B–3B.

Fiagone, C. (1995, February 13). Jacksonville's tough answer
to problem of youth crimes. *Christian Science Monitor,*
pp. 1, 14.

Houghtalin, M. & Mays, G. L. (1991). Criminal dispositions of New
Mexico juveniles transferred to adult court. *Crime and Delinquency 37,* 393–407.

Howell, J. C. (2003). *Preventing and reducing juvenile delinquency: A comprehensive framework.* Newbury Park, CA:
Sage.

National Center for Policy Analysis (1997, May 16). The federal
government and juvenile crime. Retrieved September 12,
2004, from http://www.public-policy.org./~ncpa/ba/
ba229.html

Nordheimer, J. (1994, August 2). Murder trial begins for teenager.
The New York Times, late ed., p. B5.

Renner, M. (1999). Ending violent conflict. In World Watch Institute, *State of the World.* New York: W.W. Norton.

Stanford vs. Kentucky. 106 U.S. 339 (1992).

Stepp, L. S. (1994, October 15). The crackdown on juvenile
crime—Do stricter laws deter youths? *The Washington Post,*
pp. A1, A12.

Tougher treatment urged for juveniles. (1994, August 2). *The New
York Times,* late ed., p. A16.

Youth and crime. (1995, January 10). [Editorial.] *Christian Science Monitor,* p. 18.

GLOSSARY OF TERMS

abstraction A general idea (often *very* general) that "draws us away" from the level of specific data or observations; large abstractions are concepts like justice, dignity, and freedom

ad hominem Getting personal in an argument; distracting from the merit of ideas by attacking the person, character, or private life of an opponent (Latin for "directed at the person")

allusion A brief mention that brings a whole story or set of associations to the reader's mind

analogy A close comparison, traced into several related details, often used to explain the new in terms of the familiar

analysis Explaining a complex phenomenon by identifying its major parts, stages, or causes

bandwagon Trying to sway people by claiming that the great majority is on the speaker's or writer's side (and that he or she must therefore be right)

brainstorming Freely calling up memories, data, or associations relevant to a topic, without at first editing or sorting them out

cause and effect The logical connection between actions and their consequences, making us focus on reasons and results

claim What we assert in an argument and then need to support with evidence or examples

classification The setting up of categories that help us sort out a mass of data

cliché A tired, overused expression that may have been clever or colorful at one time but has long since lost its edge

cluster A network or web of ideas centered in a key term or stimulus word, from which various strands of ideas and associations branch out

comparison Tracing connections to demonstrate similarities and contrast differences

connotation The attitudes, emotions, or associations a word carries beyond its basic factual meaning (or denotation)

context What comes before and after a word or a statement and helps give it its full meaning; the setting or situation that helps explain what something means

data Facts, observations, or statistics that provide the input for reasoning or interpretation

deduction The kind of reasoning that applies general principles to specific situations

definition Staking out the exact meaning of a possibly vague, ambiguous, or abused term

dialectic The kind of reasoning that makes ideas emerge from the play of pro and con; ideally, dialectic proceeds from thesis (statement) to antithesis (counterstatement) and from there to synthesis (a balanced conclusion)

discovery frames Sets of questions that help a writer explore a topic

doublespeak A verbal smokescreen designed to cover up unpleasant facts (such as calling an airplane crash "unscheduled contact with the ground")

draft A possibly unfinished or tentative version of a piece of writing, subject to revision

fallacy A common pattern of faulty logic, leading to wrong conclusions

figurative language Language using imaginative comparisons, such as calling someone a gadfly (metaphor) or punctual as a clock (simile)

hasty generalization Generalizing from a limited sample, such as labeling a brand of cars defective because two that you know about were defective

image Something we can vividly visualize; something that appeals vividly to our senses

induction The generalizing kind of reasoning that finds the connecting thread or common pattern in a set of data

inference The logical jump from facts or observations to what we interpret them to mean

innuendo A damaging hint stopping short of an outright charge that could be challenged and refuted

jargon Pretentious, overblown pseudoscientific or unnecessarily technical language

metaphor An imaginative comparison that treats one thing as if it were another, without using a signal such as *like* or *as* ("he *surfed* to the speaker's table on a *wave* of applause")

narrator In fiction, the person—real or imaginary—telling the story

paraphrase Putting a statement or passage into one's own words

peer review Feedback given to a writer by classmates or fellow writers

persona The identity assumed or the public role played by a writer in a piece of writing (the persona may be different from the writer's private personality)

post hoc fallacy Short for *post hoc ergo propter hoc,* Latin for "it happened after this; therefore it's because of this"; blaming something on a highly visible recent event rather than on true long-range causes (there was an earthquake after a nuclear test; therefore the test triggered the earthquake)

premise A basic shared assumption on which an argument is built

rationalization A creditable, reasonable-sounding explanation that clears us of blame

redundancy Unintentional duplication that makes for dense, lumpy prose: "The problem will *eventually* resolve itself *in due time*"

rhetoric The practice or the study of effective strategies for speech and writing (sometimes used negatively to mean empty or deceptive use of language)

simile An imaginative comparison signaled by such words as *like* or *as* ("the library had bare solid walls *like* a *prison*")

slanting Presenting only evidence or testimony that favors your own side

syllogism A formal deductive argument that moves from the major premise ("mammals need air to breathe") through the minor premise ("whales are mammals") to a logical conclusion ("whales need air to breathe")

thesis The central idea or unifying assertion that a paper as a whole supports; the claim a paper stakes out and defends

transition A link showing the logical connection between one sentence or paragraph and the next

valid Logically correct (but logically correct reasoning may lead to untrue conclusions if based on faulty premises)

CREDITS

PHOTO

Page 000 (top) © NYT Circulation Department/The New York Times, (bottom) © AP/Wide World Photos; Page 34, © Ed Young/Corbis; Page 36, © Michael Newman/PhotoEdit; Page 38, © Bruce Davidson/Magnum Photos; Page 44, © Corey A. Morris; Page 156 (left), Nuri Vallbona, Americanos: Olmos Productions, (right) Antonio Perez, Americanos: Olmos Productions; Page 216 (left and right), © Gordon Parks; Page 288, © AFP/Corbis; Page 348, © David Bacon; Page 348, Courtesy of Scientific American; Figure 7.2, Jessie Scanlon/Wired, Condé Nast Publications, Inc.; Page 468, © Jim Zuckerman/Corbis; Page 578, © AP/Wide World Photos; Page 628, Noel Snyder/US Fish and Wildlife Service; Page 670, © Steve Dunning/Getty Images.

TEXT

Roger Angell, "Return of the Cliché Expert." © 1996 Roger Angell. Originally published in *The New Yorker*. All rights reserved. Reprinted by permission.

Arthur Ashe, "A Black Athlete Looks at Education," *The New York Times*, February 6, 1977. Copyright © 1977 by the New York Times Co. Reprinted with permission.

Annette Asimov, "Ebonics: Opening Pandora's Box (interview with Toni Cook)," from *Sunday Examiner and Chronicle*, January 19, 1997. Copyright © 1997 San Francisco Chronicle. Reprinted by permission.

Margaret Atwood, "Dreams of the Animals," from *Selected Poems, 1965–1975* by Margaret Atwood. Copyright © 1976 by Margaret Atwood. Reprinted by permission of Houghton Mifflin Company. All Rights reserved; From *Selected Poems, 1966–1984*, by Margaret Atwood. Copyright 1990 by Margaret Atwood. Reprinted by permission of Oxford University Press.

T. A. Badger, "Workers Whose Jobs Go Overseas Look for Help," *San Francisco Chronicle*, August 5, 2004. All rights reserved. Distributed by ValeoIP. Reprinted with permission.

Fred Barbasch, "Beyond the Finger Pointing," *The Washington Post*, Sunday, April 25, 1999. Copyright © 1999 The Washington Post. Reprinted with permission.

Adriana Barton, "Growing Up Hippie," *Elm Street* (April 2003). © 2003 Adriana Barton. First North American Anthology Rights. This article was originally published in *Elm Street* magazine in April 2003. Revisions of article subject to author approval.

William J. Bennett, "Love, Marriage, and the Law." Copyright © 1996 William Bennett. Originally appeared in the *Wall Street Journal*. Used with permission.

Paul Berman, "Under the Bridge" from *A Tale of Two Utopias: The Political Journey*

INDEX OF AUTHORS AND TITLES